A HISTORY
OF SURNAMES

A HISTORY OF SURNAMES
OF THE BRITISH ISLES

A CONCISE ACCOUNT OF THEIR
ORIGIN, EVOLUTION, ETYMOLOGY,
AND LEGAL STATUS

BY

C. L'ESTRANGE EWEN

Author of "Ewen of East Anglia and the Fenland,"
"Witch Hunting and Witch Trials," etc.

"If any doe vaunt of their names, let them
looke to it, lest they have *inania nomina*."
W. CAMDEN (*Remaines*, 1603, p. 134).

Baltimore
GENEALOGICAL PUBLISHING COMPANY
1968

Originally Published
London, 1931

Reprinted
Genealogical Publishing Company
Baltimore, 1968

Library of Congress Catalog Card Number 68-54687

Made in the United States of America

CONTENTS

Origin of life — Slowness of evolution—Animal language—Development of vocal organs—Articulate speech—Production of language—Primitive speech—The first personal names—Prehistoric art—Invention of written language—The earliest records of names—Various methods of bestowing names—Signification of names—Ancient races of Britain—Arrival of Celtic nations—Disputed origin of the Picts—The Roman occupation—Teutonic conquest—Survival of the Britons—their languages and names—Early history of Ireland—Invasion of the Northmen—Languages spoken in Britain—Personal names in Britain.

Possible existence of non-Aryan names. Sanskrit names and their classification—Names of the ancient Greeks—and of the Gauls—Early Gaelic names of the Irish and their classification—Cóir Anmann—Irish epithets or secondary descriptions —Ogmic inscriptions—Doubtful antiquity of Irish surnames—Clan names—Early Cymric names in Britain—Old Welsh grammatical notes—Classification of Welsh descriptions—Roman names in Britain—Conclusions.

Early alien influence—Anglo-Saxon personal names —their grammatical classification—their personal epithets or secondary descriptions—their classification according to origin—The suffix -ing—Saxons erroneously supposed to have surnames—Domesday Book—Names of the burgesses of Colchester—their names the forerunners of English surnames —Names of the Northmen—Scandinavian personal names as components of place-names—The runic alphabet and descriptions — Norse epithets and classification of secondary descriptions—Conclusions.

PREFACE

EVERY known person, place, or thing has been labelled with one or more distinctive appellatives. Natives of the British Islands were originally given a single name, afterwards two were thought necessary, gift-name and surname, now it is not uncommon to find an individual labouring under a plurality of such indicia, the complete designation comprising one, two, or more personal names and one, two, or more family names. There are now over 100,000 different British surnames, a large proportion of which exist with their origin veiled in doubt, if not completely obscured, providing a vast field for the exercise of the skill of both genealogist and philologist. All surnames, like place-names, were originally words with common-sense significations, and it is astonishing to find that, subjected to various corrupting influences, many have become so meaningless as to baffle elucidation by the present-day student.

Much has been written on the romance of names, but I see in the interesting study of onomatology no more than a series of elusive problems, calling for prosaic inquiry, logical deduction, and rational solution. The superficial appearance of romance has arisen through an under-valuation and lack of appreciation of the polyglot speech of the native races and the varied alien settlers in the British Isles, coupled with a disregard of the very prevalent tendency of speakers of all tongues to twist a word which conveys no meaning to them into one with a sound which strikes the ear familiarly, however grotesque and far removed in signification from the original it may be. The language and place-names of Britain, derived as they are from a number of tongues no longer understood by the people, have undergone similar changes, and many curious examples may be found, as, for instance, Blackmonster which was obtained from Blanchminster, Godliman from Godalming, Blackall from Blackhall, and Abraham from Adburham. A good Cornish example is Penny-come-quick, the modern variant of *pen y cum gwic* " the head of the creek coomb " ; and possibly with more humour than truth, tavern signs are said to have been changed from Bachanals to Bag o' Nails, and " God encompasses us " to " Goat and Compasses ". Recent corruptions by soldiers have made " Japan " from *du pain*, and given us the word " napoo " from *il n'y a pas de plus*. Sailors also are responsible for some remarkable metamorphoses : a well-known yacht the *Halcyon* was better

known as " All sane ", the French ship *Bellerophon* became the
" Billy Ruffian ", and *O mihi Beate Martine* is believed to
have given us the expression " All my eye and Betty Martin ".
Names of persons have suffered in similar manner, and very
often at the hands of the bearers themselves: thus a woman
baptised by the unusual name of Delariviere was married as
Dillamoretta.; another named Sigismunda, according to an
entry of her marriage, had become Sydgistermondayer ; and
Irene was buried in Geldeston Churchyard as Iearenery.
Processes which enable such changes to take place are bound
also to produce extraordinary surnames, which to the shallow
inquirer may lead to inferences pointing to romantic origin,
but which are, in fact, peculiarities arising from nothing more
than vulgar corruption, such as the surnames Argument from
Egremont, Bramble from Broomhill, Tallboys from Taillebois,
Mimpress and Mainprice from *mean praz*, " stony meadow ",
and so on. The daring adventurer who embarks upon a voyage
of discovery of the sources of our more curious appellatives
must constantly bear in mind the probability of such surnames
having originally been very ordinary words or names in one
or other of a dozen languages, otherwise he will find himself
wandering aimlessly in the mist of grotesque conjecture or
wallowing in the storm-troubled waters of unwarranted
deduction.

The existing literature of personal nomenclature is a library
in itself : in addition to numerous articles in periodicals,
I have seen over 200 books, and my list includes as many
more ! Eliminating those which appeared to me to have no
practical value to the serious student of the subject, I have
catalogued the remainder under the caption " A Short
Bibliography ", and include this, hoping that it may be of
some service to the inquirer who may wish to carry
investigation beyond the scope of this present volume.

Five dictionaries of surnames have been published, namely
by Arthur (1857), Lower (1860), Barber (1894), Bardsley (1901),
and Harrison (1912). Of these works I prefer the method of
Bardsley, who gives dated and documented examples of each
surname taken from authentic records of various periods,
which arrangement enables the reader to exercise his own
judgment in accepting the origins and significations offered ;
but unfortunately the value of the work is greatly minimized,
because the compiler made little note of records of earlier
date than A.D. 1275, and consequently overlooked many Old
English survivals, and, moreover, he did not deal with Scottish
and Irish surnames at all. The result may be likened to a
ship built without a keel. Harrison covers a more extensive
field, and makes the most scientific attempt of the five, giving

etymological notes, but providing little evidence of actual employment of the surnames. Barber, on a smaller scale, is purely etymological, as is Arthur, the American pioneer of this class of dictionary ; and Lower provides varied information collected haphazardly from many sources, and as these three compilers rely largely upon conjecture, the resulting derivations are often little short of astounding. Of the two most recent works I have availed myself freely, but I hope with the circumspection and verification necessary to an inquiry where mistaken identity is so frequent.

The earliest English essay dealing with fore and family names is that contained in *Remaines concerning Britain*, 1603, by the eminent antiquary William Camden, Clarenceux, which without going deeply into the subject, gives many sound facts relating to English surnames, and has been largely drawn upon by later writers. Of the more modern English books, the most impressive are Robt. Ferguson's *English Surnames*, 1858 ; *The Teutonic Name-System*, 1864 ; *Surnames as a Science*, 1883 ; M. A. Lower's *English Surnames*, 1842, 1843, 1849, 1875 ; H. B. Guppy's *Homes of Family Names*, 1890 ; C. W. Bardsley's *English Surnames*, 1873–97 (5 editions) ; S. Baring-Gould's *Family Names*, 1910 ; and E. Weekley's *Romance of Names*, 1913, 1914, 1922, and *Surnames*, 1916. For personal names the most ambitious account has been Miss Yonge's *History of Christian Names*, 1884.

These books arouse the latent interest, they educate and amuse, but they do not satisfy. Each volume presents useful features, which, however valuable they may be, do not comprise a thorough exposition of the subject, since each writer overlooks one or other salient factor in the history and structure of our surnames, and even taking them all together, a thorough account and comprehensive view cannot be obtained. Knowing the impossibility of determining with certainty the origin of many surnames from inspection, I will not harp on the errors which abound in these works : no one can possess a full knowledge of ancient local names, trades, personal names and obsolete words in the numerous languages of Britain, many of which are lost to the lexicographer, and only live quite unsuspectedly in our family names. A large amount of the information contained in these books, and I do not except that which I now present, must be accepted with caution. One name may be derived from a plurality of sources, and several distinct appellatives may have similar origin. Appearances are most misleading ; what look like Chinese, as Ching, Tangye, Yuan, etc., are of nothing more than native Cornish and Welsh derivation, and such English-looking names as Lamb and Hare are sometimes corrupt

Irish. The laws of philology are often of little avail, and a wide
analysis is essential to success. As topography and philology
go hand-in-hand in the elucidation of place-names, so must
genealogy and philology be allied in a determination of the
origin of surnames, and information should be subjected to
scientific investigation.

Of the works of specialists I have derived most aid from
Searle, Kemble, Björkman, Forssner, and Redin (Old English) ;
Woulfe (Irish) ; Moore (Manx) ; Charnock and Dexter
(Cornish). German and Scandinavian inquirers have made a
much more scientific study of names than has been attempted
in this country. Of further Continental writers on Indo-
European names whose investigations have been the greatest
use to me I may mention : Fick (General), Förstemann (Old
German), Kalbow (Old French), Leite de Vasconcellos
(Portuguese), Lind (Norwegian), Michaëlsson (French), Nielsen
(Danish), Schönfeld (Old German), Socin (Mid. High German),
Stark (German), Winkler (Dutch, Flemish, and Friesic).
In addition to works relating to christian and surnames I
have also found invaluable for identifying local surnames the
excellent volumes published by the English Place-Name
Society, under the joint editorship of A. Mawer and F. M.
Stenton. In all cases I have acknowledged in foot-notes the
sources of my information.

The vast extent of the onomastic library is so impressive
that one is impelled to inquire : what object is achieved by
the production of such voluminous essays ? A cursory
investigation is sufficient to show that a number of writers like
Bowditch, Batchelor, and Howell, or versifiers like Clark,
attempt nothing more than humorous medleys ; others, again,
are content to rely solely upon brilliant guess-work to satisfy
the curious, who crave to know the significations or origin
of their names. A few students, mainly continental linguistic
experts, have concentrated on some particular phase of name-
building, subjecting the data to critical analysis, and producing
scientific monographs. Of what value are these labours ?
It has to be answered that if the study of history, ethnology,
philology, biography, and genealogy is of any importance
in the advancement of mundane matters, then the investigation
of surnames has likewise a value, if only subsidiary, and will
repay investigation. It is manifest that to the historian
collecting material from original records, a study of the names
of his period is essential, otherwise confusion and omission
of salient facts must occur. Anthropologists will find that
sometimes an analysis of surnames is a most useful check on
figures obtained from stature, hair, pigmentation, or cranium
measurements, which details determine the nature of the blood,

but cannot tell, as comparative lists of surnames may, how long that blood has been in any particular district. In a number of places where the ancient Britons are supposed to have survived, a chronological inquiry into the nature of their names discovers the fact that such presence was due to a modern immigration of Cymry. (See pp. 152–3.)

The philologist will recognize in our names numbers of archaic words, some of which greatly antedate any examples which can be culled from literature; thus " gribble ", which is not known to dictionarians before the year 1478, occurs as a personal description two centuries earlier; " Burgullian," a word supposed to have been invented in 1467, being in similar use in the thirteenth century, and " friese " traceable back to 1280, and so on. The linguistic experts would be interested in the pure Cornish words which appear in the descriptions of fourteenth-century men of Devon, a few examples of which are noted on pp. 178–9. To some extent surnames have interested the professors : Skeat utilized them to illustrate the effects of the Norman language upon the pronunciation of English, and the profound German grammarian Maetzner cited the surnames Boys, Children, and Woods, etc., as plural examples ; but had he fully studied such names would not have fallen into the error. It is, of course, well known to grammarians that a number of nouns, adjectives, and verbs in common use in the English language were, in fact, nothing but surnames, as boycott, lynch, burke, blanket, derrick, dahlia, galvani(sm), guillotine, hansom, macadam, martinet, quixot(ic), mesmer(ize), brougham, chesterfield, pasteur(ize), gladstone, nordenfelt, wesley(an), sandwich, morse, plimsoll, vandyke, watt, and zeppelin, to specify a few. The biographer and genealogist of medieval families can make little headway in their researches without a knowledge of the multiplicity of possible variants in orthography, the linguistic equivalents which were current, and a realization of the polyonymous system of " surnaming " which prevailed in the middle ages.

Even to those who are not interested in the scientific aspect, the study of surnominal descriptions will be found as pleasant a way of imbibing general knowledge as the solution of a cross-word puzzle ; for instance, the morning list of " hatches, matches, and despatches " will prove material for half an hour's interesting conjecture, and even a telephone directory may serve as a light holiday reader.

I hope that my present essay, constructed on entirely new lines, provides a concise but comprehensive view of the subject, treating it chronologically, racially, etymologically and legally, maintaining throughout a true perspective and sense of proportion, free from preconceived notions, or the ethnic

biases which, in some cases, have overweighted the judgment
of previous writers, such as, for instance, the anonymous
author of the *Norman People*,who based his whole argument on
the suppositious equation—Norman blood = Norman names ;
or Ferguson, who derived a typical Welsh name like Owen
from the Teutonic or Scandinavian, and Barber, equally
guilty, who affirmed that Bevan is of Flemish origin.

The present volume is designed more particularly to attain
certain objects which may be summarized :—

History of Surnames.

1. To provide a chronological history of surnames of Great Britain
and Ireland. (See pp. 29–220.)

2. To establish a distinction between personal descriptions and
surnames. (See pp. 72–5.)

3. To date the evolution of descriptions into surnames by means of
statistical tables compiled from original records. (See in the index
under " Statistics " for a list of the Tables.)

4. To correct various errors and misapprehensions regarding the
antiquity of hereditary family names. (See pp. 59–62, 75–7, etc.)

Language of Surnames.

5. To stress the polyglot origin of British surnames, and the great
influence of immigration. (See pp. 21–3, 134–59, 189–93, 200–205,
and *passim.*)

6. To emphasize that race, language, and names are not interdependent. (See pp. 23, 189–92.)

Sobriquets as Surnames.

7. To define " nickname ", and appraise the relative value of
alternative epithets in the formation of surnames. (See p. 326.)

Official Surnames.

8. To show that names in official records are not necessarily the
actual names. (See pp. 106, 166, 169, 189, 202, 203, etc.)

Localization of Surnames.

9. To illustrate the necessity for knowing the original habitat before
determining the signification of a name. (See the examples given
above, p. xiii and *passim.*)

Value of Surnames.

10. To exemplify the value of chronological collections of surnames
as an aid to the study of history, philology, and anthropology. (See
pp. 134–47, 236 and *passim*, and note the special example, p. 206.)

Classification of Surnames.

11. To introduce a complete system of surnames. (See pp. 221–3.)

Etymology of Surnames.

12. To evidence the great possibilities of orthographic variation
and corruption. (See pp. 299–301, 322.)

13. To list the principal components of surnames and to provide a key by which the origin of many names may be readily discovered. (See pp. 365-80.)

Law of Surnames.

14. To summarize the medieval law, giving for the first time early instances of royal licences to change name. (Chapters XV and XVI.)

With regard to head No. 3, I will meet the critic half-way by admitting that the analyses are neither complete nor correct, but, nevertheless, I believe the errors will not affect the general conclusions, and that taken as a whole, they give a very fair indication of the lines on which the description developed into the surname. The reason why so many names are entered as unclassified is partly because there are some which I cannot determine, and partly because there are others which fall into two or more classes. These might be counted as one-half or one-third as the case might be, but the result would still be an inaccurate total, since even though one name may be derived from two sources, yet the name of one individual can only come from one source, which is unknown. However, I shall hope with fuller knowledge of the subject, and further extended survey, to obtain more exact figures at some future time, yet I fear it to be a case where the greater the knowledge the less is the exactitude of classification possible.

. Referring to head No. 4, I may observe that unfounded claims of great antiquity for British surnames are common ; thus the Prynnes claim descent from an Anglo-Saxon king who was nicknamed Præn ; Bardsley has mentioned a lady named Mason, who seriously believed that she was descended from Mnason, who figures in the New Testament (Acts xxi, 16) ; and a writer in *Notes and Queries* (27th July, 1901) had a servant-girl named Balaam, who was firmly convinced that her great-grandfather owned an ass which had powers of articulate speech, such fact being proved by a verse in the Bible (Num. xvi, 30). I have myself pointed out (*Ewen of East Anglia*, p. 444) that if the pedigree in the Anglo-Saxon Chronicle were reliable I could trace my descent from Adam ! But I should not, of course, claim any distinction on that score. I have endeavoured to investigate the antiquity of hereditary surnames *de novo*, because even in better informed quarters it is manifest that some blunders have occurred, and are yet being repeated ; for instance, Turner in 1799 mistranslated an Anglo-Saxon document, and consequently relegated the introduction of hereditary surnames to a date before the Conquest, the error being repeated in six further editions, the last being in 1852 ; and in the game of follow-my-leader, accepted without question by Ferguson (1858), Lower

(1860), Folkard (1886), Barber (1894), Blagg (1900), and Baring-Gould (1910), affording a striking instance of the danger of basing an important argument on second-hand information.

Regarding sobriquets (No. 7), I hope that the instances which I give will modify the common belief that many surnames are derived from nicknames. The dictionary of Bardsley possesses such great merits that it is yet in most frequent demand as a reference work, and I must therefore emphasize the fact that in a large number of cases the compiler in deriving a name from a nickname was labouring under a misapprehension. For instance, regarding Shakespeare, the Canon, after making reference to " silly guessing " of others, observes : " Never a name in English nomenclature so simple or so certain in its origin. It is exactly what it looks—Shakespear." With this opinion I entirely disagree, and suggest that the evidence now brought together will show that if there has been any foolish conjecturing Bardsley himself was equally responsible.

My summary of the law contains new and important matter which may be of interest. Several writers have attempted to assert the ancient prerogative of the Crown to license assumption and change of surnames, and I have critically examined the evidence adduced by Finlayson (1863), and more recently Fox-Davies (1906), and adopted without question by Baring-Gould (1910), and show how weak it is, if not entirely non-existent. In lieu I am able to cite three licences of undoubted authenticity for the years 1273, 1314, and 1367, being several centuries earlier than anything of the kind hitherto reproduced, but which in my opinion show no more than that the royal right extended to the control of tenants in chief, Anglo-Irishmen, and Jews. The modern law is so clearly summarized in the existing legal handbooks, that in outlining present procedure, I have nothing further to do than to quote Halsbury and Green.

I hope that I have succeeded in producing a succinct and clear statement on the fourteen main points laid down ; and if undue emphasis is given to what is obvious to the practised genealogist or nomenclaturist, my excuse must be that I write for all classes of readers in the hope of popularizing a subject which has an educative value, and can be of great interest, breathing as it does the very life of the middle ages.

My object having been nothing more than to compile a general history of surnames, such a work not having been attempted before, I fear that some disappointment may be felt with the few derivations given ; but histories of individual names are the work of the genealogist and the dictionarian rather than the chronicler, and, therefore, I have not over-loaded my instances with conjectural etymologies which have little or no practical value. The subject will not be exhausted until we get a dictionary constructed by philologists on chronological principles identical with those which have been adopted in the compilation of that monumental work, the *New English Dictionary*, but perhaps with additional notes on the distribution of the rarer names. The present volume is not more than a first introduction to such an enterprise, and a second step would be a more exhaustive list of elements than that presented in the following pages. In the meantime, I have arranged systems of members and variants which provide keys to the origin of a great many thousands more than the sources indicated, which will enable the reader himself to have the pleasure of discovering possible origins of many of our peculiar surnames. If, therefore, the desired name be not found in the index, it should be divided into what appear to be its elements, and each component searched for separately ; clues will then be obtained pointing to the more normal forms of the members, which may be combined, providing what should be at least a possible original form for the name in question. The reader may test the system by applying it to a number of our names of more curious appearance taken, for instance, from the London Directory, such as Bidgood, Brandewine, Everwin, Goodheart, Lemon, Loveday, Monday, Rainbow, Raindeer, Snowball, Turbot, Vinegar, Whisker, Whiteleg, etc.

Those who may employ this system should always bear in mind that most surnames are derived from more than one source, and that certainty was never more elusive than in this branch of inquiry. There is only one royal road to the determination of the origin of a surname, and that is to compile an authentic biographical and historical pedigree which dates back to the first assumption of the name.

C. L'ESTRANGE EWEN.

ROYAL AUTOMOBILE CLUB,
PALL MALL,
LONDON, S.W. 1.

ABBREVIATIONS

Add. Additional.
adj. adjective.
A.N. Anglo-Norman.
Anc. Ancient.
a.q.d. ad quod damnum.
art. article.
A.-S. Anglo-Saxon.
Ass. R. Assize Rolls, P.R.O.
BCS. Cartularium Saxonicum (W. de G. Birch).
Bret. Breton.
Brit. Mus. British Museum.
c. circa, about.
Cal. Calendar.
Cam. Camden.
Cart. Cartulary.
cf. compare.
Cl. R. Close Rolls.
Comm. Commissary.
Cott. Cottonian.
C.P. Common Pleas.
C.R. Chancellor's Roll.
Ct. Court.
Cur. Reg. Curia Regis.
D., Du. Dutch.
Dan. Danish.
dat. Dative.
Dict. Dictionary.
dim. diminutive.
Dir. Directory.
D.L. P.R.O. Duchy of Lancaster.
Dom. Bk. Domesday Book.
E. English.
E. Ch. Proc. Early Chancery Proceedings.
E.E. Early English.
e.g. for instance.
Eng. English.
f., fem. feminine.
Flem. Flemish.
Fr. French.
Fris. Frisian.
G. German.
Gael. Gaelic.
gen. genitive.
Gr. Greek.
Hd. Hundred.
Hebr. Hebrew.
Hund. R. Hundred Rolls.
Ibid. In the same place.
Icel. Icelandic.
i.e. that is.
Ind. Indictment.
Inq. Inquisition.
Ir. Irish.
K.B. King's Bench.
KCD. Codex Diplomaticus (Kemble).
Lansd. Lansdowne.
Lat. Latin.
L.G. Low German.

Lib. Nig. Liber Niger.
m. membrane.
m., masc. masculine.
M.E. Middle English.
M.H.G. Middle High German.
Misc. Miscellaneous.
Mn. E. Modern English.
mod. modern.
Mon. Monument.
MSS. Manuscript.
M.W. Middle Welsh.
n. neuter, note.
n.d. undated.
NED. A New English Dictionary on historical principles (Murray's).
NF. Norman-French.
nom. nominative.
Non. Inq. Nonarum Inquisitiones.
N.P. The Norman People.
N. & Q. Note and Queries.
Obs. Obsolete.
occ. occurs.
O.E. Old English.
O.Fr. Old French.
O.H.G. Old High German.
O.Ir. Old Irish.
O.N. Old Norse.
O.W. Old Welsh.
Par. R. Parish Register.
Pat. R. Patent Rolls.
P.C.C. Prerogative Court of Canterbury.
pers. personal.
pl. plural.
p.m. post mortem.
P.R.O. Public Record Office.
q.v. which see.
R. Roll, Rolls.
Ran. Randulph, Rannulph.
Rec. Record.
Rob. Robert.
Rot. Canc. Rotulus Cancelarii.
Rot. de Obl. Rotuli de Oblatis.
Roum. Roumanian.
Sanskr., Skr. Sanskrit.
sc. scil. scilicet, namely.
S.C. 2. P.R.O. Court Roll.
Scot. Scottish.
sec. section.
sing. singular.
Soc. Society.
Sp. Spanish.
Subs. Subsidy Roll, P.R.O., E. 179 is the class number.
Surt. Surtees.
Swed. Swedish.
Teut. Teutonic.
W. Welsh.
W. William or Willelmus.
Wap. Wapentake.

A HISTORY OF SURNAMES OF THE BRITISH ISLES

CHAPTER I

ORIGIN OF LANGUAGE AND NAMES

The Origin of Speech. Geologists tell us that many millions of years ago this earth, in common with other planets, was an incandescent mass, having a temperature of thousands of degrees, and that throughout untold ages a gradual cooling process has been in progress. Upon the surface temperature falling below boiling point the enveloping steam condensed, and fluid water formed in large quantities, ultimately covering the greater part of the globe, until which liquid condition prevailed organic life was impossible. According to Haeckel, the history of living matter on our planet opened in these waters with the formation, by spontaneous generation, of simple organisms called monera, and from this plasm sprang the unicellar amœba from which, in turn, were evolved the spineless ancestors of the human race. After millions of years encouraging the development of backbone these invertebrates were finally rewarded with the possession of serviceable spinal columns, whereupon, the lengthy residence in water having proved distasteful to some of the more progressive of our fishy predecessors, and realizing the importance of means of support (even if not visible), their adventurous spirits were excited, moving them to see something of the world. With commendable perseverance, extending throughout the ages, these enterprising adventurers so developed a dual existence that they ultimately merited the title of amphibia. Making remarkable progress, if somewhat tardily, the double-living vertebrates, having tasted the pleasures of the outer world, in the course of further eons, transformed themselves, by easy stages, into many wonderful reptiles, birds, and mammals including that uncouth featherless and furless biped, man.

The one fact which emerges most clearly from the study of cosmic marvels is that evolution by natural processes is extremely leisurely. Sir Arthur Keith has concluded that

I   B

" since the human stem became differentiated from that which led on to the great anthropoid apes a period of about one million years has elapsed ",[1] possibly half of which time homo has been possessed of a brain of average capacity. Even that lengthy period is but a small fraction of the time he took to develop from the original globule of structureless plasm through many known and unknown vermalian, ichthyoid, reptilian, and mammalian forms, to attain his present rank as a primate.

Realizing the gradual fashion in which the modification and improvement in the outward forms of our progenitors took place, we are prepared to accept, without argument, the statement of biologists that the evolution of our internal organs was likewise slow. The development of vocal apparatus can have been no exception.

Many ages prior to reaching their dizzy eminence in the highest order of mammalia, the ancestors of man, in common with many of their collaterals, must have acquired the power of emitting sound. Possibly they developed a capacity for making noises before taking to terrestrial meandering, and like the frog croaked under water, or a much later stage may have been reached before they became able to emphasize their existence in some such crude manner. Doubtless, with each metamorphosis, the voice was likewise changed and its range increased, and we may rest assured that each variation and development was well tried out by a few thousand years' practice.

Like the evolution of species, the sounds of the various genera proceeded on different lines : as the species varied so did its vocal capabilities. To-day among our cousins (many times removed) we have a variety of apparently unreasoned sounds, the baa of sheep, the moo of the herd, the hee-haw of the ass, and among some of our feathered kindred, more complex and harmonious examples are familiar. Such bleating, lowing, braying, or warbling, possibly coupled with some form of " wireless ", may be a means of communication. Can these ejaculations be classed as primitive language ? Does the chiffchaff with his " till tell true jink junk " convey any news to his congeners, or is the " cherry do, cherry do, pretty joey, pretty joey, pretty joey, white hat, white hat, pretty joey " of the skylark mere idle vapouring ? And what of the song of turdus musicus, our familiar throstle, " qui, qui, qui : kweeu, quip : tiurru, tiurru, chipiwi : tootee, tootee : chiu, choo : chirri, chirri,

---

[1] *The Antiquity of Man*, 1929, vol. ii, pp. 733–4. Prof. H. F. Osborn, the eminent American palæontologist, who rejects the Darwinian theory and the common ancestry of ape and man, considers that the "dawn man" first appeared on the great plateaux of Asia 50,000,000 years ago.

chooee : quiu, qui, qui ", or the more elaborate expression of the nightingale, which has been syllabized—" Le bon Dieu m'a donné une femme, qui j'ai tant, tant, tant, tant battue : que s'il m'en donne une autre, je ne la batterais plus, plus, plus, plus, qu'un petit, qu'un petit, qu'un petit " ? [1] Do these songsters convey any message by their warbling ? Do they call each other names ? We do not know. Beyond the attempt of Garner to analyse the speech of monkeys little has been done to understand communication of the lower orders, and the existence of a language, however primitive, is not generally admitted.

According to the professorial opinions cited above, it was anything from one to fifty million years ago, not to be too exact, before the man-apes or ape-men had developed sufficient brain capacity to realize that vocal sound might be of more use than merely to express vulgar emotions. The endeavour to make additional noises developed the vocal organs, which advancement in turn made it possible to increase the variety of sounds. The speechless ape-man ultimately blossomed into the articulate speaking genus homo.

During the gradual development and improvement of the vocal apparatus, it may be inferred that the larynx passed through many stages of inefficiency, before it became a practical musical box capable of producing and emitting desired sounds at the will of the possessor. As to the nature of the sounds and the reasons for making them there has been much speculation, and opinions of eminent authorities are at variance.

Realizing the gradual evolution of the human frame, and accepting as a strong probability the tardy development of the vocal organs, it is but a logical inference that the production of articulate language and the perfecting of vocal utterance was equally slow, and that man did not suddenly emerge from a state of mutism fully endowed with the faculty of speech. No less an authority than Professor Whitney, writing fifty years ago, asserted that " language is an instrumentality ; and that the law of simplicity of beginnings applied to it not less naturally and necessarily than to other instrumentalities ".[2] This view appeals to reason, since it is difficult to believe that pre-historic man waited until his cerebrum and laryngeal organs were perfected to a high degree and functioning with maximum capacity, or reserved his first attempt at expressing the conceptions of his mind, until he could deliver a polished maiden speech. Finding that grunts, howls and bellowings indicated but

---

[1] *History of British Birds*, by Wm. Macgillivray, 1837.
[2] *Life and Growth of Language*, 1875, p. 226.

few of his sentiments with exactitude, it may be imagined
that the desire to indicate his various needs more definitely
urged the primeval savage, at the earliest possible moment,
to improve the oral means of intercourse. The necessity
for communication by sound would increase with the growth
of the roaming and hunting habits, for which pursuits an
inaudible sign language would be most inefficient. May we
not reasonably suppose that some of the earliest attempts at
vocal utterance were descriptions of animals conveyed by
imitations of the sounds emitted by them ? We have such
echoic words or onomatopes, as they are sometimes called,
in " buzz ", " hiss ", " cuckoo ", " bow-wow ", and so on,
and such vocables are in general use among all savage
races.

Professor O. Jespersen has pronounced the interesting
and pleasing dictum : " The genesis of language is not to
be sought in the prosaic, but in the poetic side of life ; the
source of speech is not gloomy seriousness, but merry play
and youthful hilarity. And among the emotions which were
most powerful in eliciting outbursts of music and of song,
love must be placed in the first rank." [1] For the grunting,
growling, croaking, shrieking, or whistling, as the case may
be, of our remote ancestry to mature into something which
might be described as song was commonplace evolution
compared with the extraordinary metamorphoses which
were occurring. We know that such a change has taken
place with some of our feathered songsters which, since their
silent crawling lacertian days, have developed into capable
if somewhat limited warblers. Assuming that pristine homo
far outstripped his collaterals in voice culture, and became
an energetic if not very harmonious chorister, it follows that
language (in more senses than one) would very soon be
created : and the primeval anthem may even have been the
occasion for the first calling of names.

Those who, like the writer, incline to the view expressed
by Professor Whitney, and believe in simplicity of the early
vocal communications, will possibly receive a shock on
turning further to Professor Jespersen, who affirms that we
are drawn to the conclusion that " primitive language had a
superabundance of irregularities and anomalies, in syntax
and word—formation no less than in accidence. It was
capricious and fanciful, and displayed a luxuriant growth of
forms, entangled one with another like the trees in a primeval
forest. Primitive speech cannot have been distinguished
for logical consistency ; nor so far as we can judge was it
simple and facile ; it is much more likely to have been

[1] *Language, its Nature, Development and Origin*, 1922, p. 433.

extremely clumsy and unwieldy." [1] Perhaps, however, the Professor does not refer to the very first practice of articulate utterance.

It is not possible to reconcile the diverse and contradictory opinions held on the origin of the spoken language, but it will hardly be disputed that the most ancient vernaculars were never given to the World suddenly like Volapuk, Esperanto, Novial, or the hundred and one other universal tongues.

Analysis of languages spoken at the present day shows that some primitive races, like the Bantu, speak a simple tongue, others of equally low culture, like the Andaman Islanders, a most complicated language, but the speech of to-day is no guarantee of the character of the linguistics current a hundred thousand years ago. Until proof is produced to the contrary, the writer will lean to the opinion that language must have arrived gradually, perhaps syllable by syllable, during the warbling or carolling age, the rudimentary speech consisting of a few monosyllabic and uninflected words. Short and simple sounds gradually becoming associated with hills, rivers, animals, forests, and so forth, would ultimately be perpetuated as generic names. There seems to be no point in asking why any particular thing should be called so-and-so, one vocable so long as distinct and recognizable would serve equally with another, and a number of words becoming, by chance, associated with one object, it would be a case of the survival of the fittest.

The Origin of Names. It is improbable that additional sounds were specially invented for the description of places and individuals, but that they were distinguished by compound names consisting of two or more simple words,[2] thus a mountain might be characterized by the title of Hima-laya (Sanskr. *hima* " frost ", *alaya* " house ", i.e. " the abode of snow "), or a person be named as the Sumerian E-an-i-mud " begotten in the house of heaven ".[3] The prodigal use of words in the composition of personal appellatives is a curious cause of extensive changes in the vocabularies of many savage races, for instance, if a Comanche called " Eagle " or " Bison " dies, a new designation is invented for the bird or beast, because it is forbidden to mention the name of anyone who is dead.[4]

The custom of giving an individual name to each human

---

[1] Jespersen, p. 428.
[2] In Lithuania, where civilization is yet primitive, *wărdas*, cognate with Eng. *word*, is used for name. L. H. Gray (*Encycl. of Religion and Ethics*).
[3] S. Langdon. Ibid.
[4] For a long account of names and words tabooed, see *The Golden Bough*, by J. G. Frazer, pt. ii, *Taboo*, pp. 318–418 (3rd edit., 1911).

being probably originated in different parts of the world, but since there were no means of permanently recording such appellatives, their purpose and nature for hundreds of thousands of years is unknown. The earliest records of names are of necessity no earlier than the most ancient extant examples of written language, an invention of comparatively recent date.

As primitive man amused himself by voice culture so did he likewise by pictorial decoration of his cave residences, and as speech resulted from early attempts at singing so has the art of writing developed from the practice of drawing. Thus the amusements of the primeval savage led to two methods of expressing the conceptions of the mind, namely, speech and writing, two factors of inestimable value in the progress of mankind.

The antiquity of the pre-historic art gallery is proved by the fact that many of the animals delineated with such remarkable skill and accuracy are antediluvian, in fact, one of the most recent investigators, Professor Cipriani, of the Florence University, holds the opinion that the decorations of the primitive South African bushmen point to a civilization existing seven to eight thousand years ago, and therefore ante-dating the Egyptians of the first dynasties and the earliest Asiatic civilizations. Having achieved skill in the decorative art, homo was on the high road to developing written language, one of the most important steps in his intellectual advancement.

Long before any alphabet had been designed, uncivilized tribes had used various mnemonic devices such as tallies of knotted cords, notched sticks, strings of shells, as memory aids ; probably also a man may have marked his own property with a private or secret sign for identification, even as he does at the present day. Some such systems of record making would suffice for many of the small segregated communities, and there are yet, in fact, primitive races which have adopted no system of writing ; other more inventive nations having developed from their ideographs (or hieroglyphs) characters and symbols more nearly corresponding to a modern alphabet.

Sumerian, the most ancient writing now known, has been traced back over 5,000 years, for which period only is there any possibility of studying names ; the nomenclaturist of to-day having, in fact, to thank the ancient scribe for his material. The oldest writings which have been preserved are on stone, clay or papyrus, the use of skins as recording material, being a later invention, the earliest examples in the British Museum dating back about 3,000 years. Paper was a development of papyrus and has continued with parchment to be employed for written records until the present day.

Systems of Naming Persons. As the races of the world acquired distinctive habits and customs, so did they adopt diverse methods of naming individuals. The essential purpose, however, of name-giving was seldom identification or recognition, for with many races appellatives are supposed to possess as marvellous properties as the soul of the bearer, and all mention or writing of them are taboo, their protection from magic and injury being as important as that of the body or of life itself. Some races are said to bestow no names —Pliny has noticed that the savages of the Atlas range were *anonymi*—and later travellers among the wild bushmen have personally observed similar conditions. Certain tribes of tropical Africa are said to call the newly born boy " a gun " and the girl " a hoe ",[1] but, of course, the prevalence of such a custom does not debar names being given later in life. The view that savages have no names is due to a failure to grasp the widespread custom of concealment which prevails among Australian blacks, ancient Egyptians, Assamese hill tribes, American Indians, and other barbarous and uncultured races.

At the present day among uncivilized tribes names may be conferred at birth, or at later times held to be more favourable to the welfare of the recipient, and to the success of such an important rite. The Manjas delay the ceremony until about the seventh year ; Australian aborigines receive their true name at the age of puberty, but with the natives of British Columbia the bestowal of the appellative is deferred until adult age.[2] Names are variously chosen, in some cases by the parents, in others by the chief of the race, as with the Bambaras.[3] The most general custom among the savage tribes was to give a child the name of a deceased ancestor, but any descriptive word which might indicate sex, order of birth, race, office, physical feature, god, historical fact, or a more fanciful concept, served the purpose of a distinguishing label.

Resulting from superstitious beliefs it was common practice among uncivilized tribes to have a working designation or nickname for practical use and a real name which might be known only to the giver, but perhaps revealed later to the bearer, who would guard it as a close secret.[4]

---

[1] *Wild Bush Tribes of Tropical Africa*, G. C. Claridge, p. 100.
[2] Geo. Foucart in *Encycl. of Religion and Ethics* : Art. Names, p. 130*b*.
[3] *L'Ame d'un peuple africain les Bambara*, 1910, p. 170.
[4] Foucart, p. 133*b*.

Among many savages there is the greatest repugnance to mention their own names : the Ojebway Indian, for instance, never even mentions his wife's name and vice versa.[1]

Designations were changeable, and also cumulative. The Waiyau boys took new names at puberty,[2] but with the Wangatas (East Africa) the father replaces his own name at the birth of the first child, forming the new name by prefixing Is (o-a-i-e) to the second element of the son's name, thus the father of Bontulu becomes Isen'tolu, the father of Bombandu calls himself Isambandu.[3] Some uncivilized tribes look upon names as omens or mascots, believing that they are responsible for good and bad luck, and so change them after sickness. Another curious custom is that prevalent with the nobles of the Kwakiutl Indians of British Columbia, who have alternate names for winter and summer.[4] The Esquimaux of Bering Strait " take new names when they are old, hoping thereby to get a new lease of life ".[5] Death among various North American Indians results in another member of the family taking the deceased's name [6] : and change of designation is common with many races after any notable event in the bearer's life : or an additional name might be adopted in like circumstances. A plurality of appellatives is not uncommonly found, and such might be bestowed at one time, or upon successive occasions, or used concurrently as one title or as alternatives employed at appropriate periods, for instance, the Dahomeyans have personal names, secret names, names of god and protecting spirit.[7]

Consideration of facts relating to widely distributed tribes leads to the deduction that in prehistoric days names were held to be of more value than mere identification labels ; that there were in force many systems of naming : that various occasions were considered appropriate for the ceremony and that different methods were employed in choosing a designation : and the number of names borne at one time likewise varied.[8] The practice of concealing the name for fear of possible evil wrought by sorcerers led to

[1] Frazer, p. 338.
[2] *Last Journals of David Livingstone in Central Africa*, 1874, vol. i, p. 81.
[3] T. Engels in *Revue Congolaise*, vol. ii (1911), p. 29.
[4] *Taboo*, p. 386.
[5] Ibid., p. 319.
[6] *Folklore of the Musquakie Indians*, by M. A. Owen, 1904, p. 83. See also *Taboo*, p. 365.
[7] *L'Ancien royaume du Dahomey*, par A. Le Herissé, 1911, p. 235.
[8] At the present day the Chinese receive a number of names at various periods of life : the " milk-name " when a month old, the " book-name " on entering school, the " marriage-name ", the " ancestral-name " for business purposes, perhaps also a nickname or other epithet, and a posthumous name is awarded the deceased. See J. D. Ball (*Encycl. of Religion and Ethics*).

the bestowal of alternative appellatives, a custom perpetuated unwittingly to-day by civilized races in the giving of nicknames. The most ancient personal names which can be traced are frequently of great length. Babylonian appellatives are commonly compounded of five or more elements forming a complete sentence, as, for instance, Ašur-etil-šamê-u-irṣiti-bulliṭ-su, " O Ashur, the lord of heaven and earth, give him life." [1] For brevity's sake one or more elements might be cut out, or perhaps the initial member only might be used.

Originally all personal names conveyed a meaning as, Hebrew, Benoni, " son of my sorrow " : Japanese, Tokutaro, " virtue first male " : and Sumerian, Ninziddamkiag, " the queen loves the faithful husband " : representative of the non-Aryan group ; and Sanskrit, Padmasundara, " lotus-lovely " : Greek, Demosthenes, " the strength of the people " : Teutonic, Winibald, " bold friend " : Celtic, Vercingetorix, " great king of warriors " : exemplifying the Indo-European group. The science of semantics now receives considerable attention, but owing to the gradual corruption which has taken place throughout the centuries, the signification of many ancient names cannot be determined, and this loss applies to names of the British Isles as well as to those of earlier civilizations.

The present volume is concerned only with the history of surnames of Great Britain and Ireland, a large proportion of which originated in descriptions now wanting or quite meaningless.[2] The successful determination of the first form and its signification often presents an insuperable difficulty, owing to the doubt caused by the number of languages known to have been spoken by our ancestors, as well as to others of which we have no knowledge. So thorough has been the mixture of the blood of our forbears that

---

[1] From examples cited by A. T. Clay in *Encycl. of Religion and Ethics*. According to T. Harada (Ibid.) Japanese names are also notable for length, e.g. " Amenigishi - kuninigishi - amatsuhidaka - hikohononin - iginomikoto ", which even puts a well-known Welsh place-name into second place. Agglutination, that is the compounding of several words into one name, is exemplified by the Basque, Azpilcuelagaraycosaroyarenberecollarea, " the lower field of the high hill of Azpicuelha " (Ripley, p. 184). Other primitive languages as Cherokee and Esquimaux likewise have very long words. Similarly compounds of great length may be found in some of the Indo-European languages, e.g. the Sanskrit, Rogaçokaparītāpabandhanavy-asanāni, " disease, pain, grief, captivity, and misfortune " (W. D. Whitney, *Sanskrit Grammar*, p. 486). Nearer home, " Mark Twain," some years ago now, introduced us to the humorous side of Germanic sesquipedalianism (*A Tramp Abroad*, 1880, p. 546).

[2] An early investigator of Irish names was Cormac mac Cullennain, king of Munster, who lived over a thousand years ago, when already the origin of some Irish names had been lost.

Britain has been aptly described as a " racial melting pot ". Before pursuing an investigation into the names of this " amphibious ill-born mob " it is necessary to have a working knowledge of the nations which have bred the Britisher, and their languages. Let us recall history.

Early Races of Britain. Albion of Pliny (first century) and Aristotle (fourth century) : the Britannia of Cæsar : and Cymru of the Britons, was once connected with the Continent, as Spain was with Africa. Mighty primeval beasts could roam at will from the plateaux of Asia or the swamps of Africa to the shores of the North Atlantic. Doubtless between glacial periods and when climatic conditions were favourable came wandering homo, engaged mainly in the chase, his choice of quarry ranging from the mammoth, rhinoceros and hippopotamus, down to lion, bear, wolf and smaller game. This earliest type of man has left few bones, pointing partly to the practice of cremation and partly to the larger carnivora having had the best of the hunt, but he can be traced by his implements like that excellent example dug up with bones of the mammoth in Gray's Inn Lane, London, nearly a century ago.

The earliest tribes were displaced or replaced by the neolithic or stone-age men, who flourished about the period when Britain was finally becoming separated by the sea from the Continent. These people constructed habitations, cultivated wheat, manufactured linen and pottery, built canoes, and practised the arts of warfare, and were more able to cope with the larger fauna of the island, which in time became extinct, a sure index of civilization. Neolithic man had workable axes, said to be made from jade brought from Asia, as well as other practical weapons, and their arts indicate influence of the great eastern races. The erection of Avebury circle, Silbury Hill, and Stonehenge point to the existence of civilized and organized communities,[1] and it is a logical deduction that an established system of personal names was in use, although since few examples of their writing, if practised by them at all, have survived, their designations are practically unknown to the modern student.[2] It is the general belief that immediately prior to the commencement of the christian era a neolithic people of non-Aryan stock was widespread throughout Western Europe, to whom

---

[1] *Civilization in Britain* 2,000 *B.C.*, by T. F. G. Dexter, p. 20. The author further cites a case of trepanning as evidencing their advancement.

[2] There are a few lapidary inscriptions said to be Phœnician, and to be over two thousand years of age, from one of which (Newton Stone, Aberdeenshire) has been obtained the name Ikar, the earliest extant example of a written name in Britain. (*Phœnician Origin of Britons, Scots and Anglo-Saxons*, by L. A. Waddell, 1924, p. 32.)

has been given the name Iberians. This ancient race, represented to-day by the Basques, has been identified by anthropologists in Wales, Ireland, and Scotland, and is supposed formerly to have occupied the entire British Isles. The Iberians were followed by the Phœnicians and Celts, known as men of the bronze age, from their introduction of the art of manufacturing that alloy. Some writers hold that the adventurous sea-faring Phœnicians were the strong force in Britain, being the civilizers of the aborigines, and that their influence is permanently recorded in our place-names,[1] megalith monument and stone circles. So diverse are the views held regarding the racial origin of the Britons, and so much confusion and disagreement exists in the terminology of the subject that it is difficult to compile a concise account of the early occupation. The neolithic men were still in noticeable strength in Britain at the beginning of christian chronology, for it is recorded by Tacitus (first century) that in addition to the Celts there were inhabiting these islands, the Silures, a race of dark complexioned and curly-haired men, descended from the Iberians of Spain.[2]

Celtic Races of Britain. The " Celtic " people who succeeded the Iberians are variously supposed to have originated in Europe, Asia or Africa, modern opinion having a considerable leaning towards the latter hypothesis. The order of the immigration has given rise to much discussion and leading writers are at variance at their tenets. In whatever region or regions the Celts first found existence, a very general view is that they came into Britain and Ireland from south or east, in several waves, and at different periods. Numerous authorities have concluded that there were two main streams of emigrants, the one flowing through Northern Africa, Spain, and Southern France, and the other into Greece, Italy, Germany, and Northern France (Gaul).

Ancient chroniclers relate that from the settlers in Spain came those Gaedhils or Gaels who crossed the sea and took possession of Ireland.[3] The northern tribes must be looked to for the ancestors of the Cymry, commonly called " ancient Britons ", who succeeded the Iberians and populated England both before and after the Roman occupation.

By some investigators it has been inferred that the Gaels or Scoti, who colonized Ireland (Scotia) also sailed

---

[1] A writer in *Notes and Queries* (17th March, 1928, p. 189) suggests that the Cornish name Bolitho is an example of a Phœnician personal name, from Baal-Iathon (the gift of the Lord): Baliatho occurring on an Algerian tombstone : but another etymologist considers Bolitho to be nothing nearer the heavenly than " big belly ".

[2] *The Life of Agricola*, chap. 11.

[3] Nennius, ed. by J. A. Giles, 1908, p. 389.

eastwards and occupied Wales, Cornwall and Devon at a remote pre-historic period. Other writers hold the reverse opinion—that the Gaels arriving in England from Gaul "drove out the aborigines", and then proceeded into Ireland. It is, however, quite unlikely that a clean sweep of the inhabitants of the British Isles was made at any time ; a realization of the few ships [1] and roads existing will show that, without adequate means of sea and land transport, the numbers of fighting men available at any one time would be quite inadequate to scour the country, and the natives being acquainted with the hills, woods and marshes could readily escape from a comparatively small military force.[2] Doubtless the Celtic influx, like the later Saxon occupation, was spread over hundreds of years, during which time by intermingling of race a Celtiberian nation was formed, as admittedly was the case on the Continent.

No matter in which order colonization by the two Celtic races may have taken place, it is clear that ultimately and at the time of the Roman invasion (B.C. 55), the Cymry were predominant in England and Wales, the Gaels in Ireland and the Isle of Man : both races being intermingled with the Iberians, and to some extent with each other. As the Cymric element gathered strength it pushed its way north, driving out or subjecting the natives. Considerably later, a number of the Gaels or Scoti, who had established themselves in Ireland (Scotia), crossed over to what is now Argyllshire and founded the Scottish kingdom of Dalriades. According to Pinkerton the first emigration occurred about A.D. 258, but it was not until 503 that a permanent settlement was effected.[3] The Irish Cruithne similarly crossed over to Galloway.[4] There were then four different nations races settled in Scotland : the Iberians, the Gaels, the Cymry, and the Romans.

The Picts. There has been much speculation, and even heated argument, as to the origin of the natives of Scotland who, notwithstanding the coming of the Celts, retained their independence and monarchy. John Pinkerton (1787), prejudiced against everything Celtic, was very strongly of

[1] The Romans with 800 ships and complete organization could do no more than conquer part of Britain at a time. The Norsemen had smaller fleets : 350 ships sailed up the Thames in A.D. 851, and 490 came up the same river in 994. In 892 they had 700 vessels and 30,000 men in France (A. Mawer, *Vikings*, pp. 15, 37, and 51). Canute is said to have had a ship with 60 pairs of oars, and a fleet of 1,400 vessels, but sometimes these "ships" carried no more than 25 men.

[2] Tacitus, at a much later date, refers to the Britons, who knew the ground, seeking safety in the shelter of distant and pathless wilds (ch. 37).

[3] *Enquiry into the History of Scotland*, by J. Pinkerton, vol. ii, chs. 2 and 3.

[4] *The Races of Britain*, by John Beddoe, 1885, p. 52.

opinion that the Picts were of Gothic origin. He wrote, " It is granted by all, and indeed beyond a doubt, that the Piks must either have proceeded from Scandinavia, Germany or the south of Britain : and that they must have been either Goths or Celts. If Goths, they spoke the Gothic tongue, the parent of the present German, Danish, English, etc. If Celts, their speech was either Cumraig, that of the German Celts ; or Gaelic, that of the Gaulic Celts. That they were Goths shall be shewn from the consent of all the ancient writers and from other arguments." [1] The Celtic (language) is so full of old Gothic words, that no man of sound sense will take upon him to say if the term be really old Gothic or Celtic." [2] " If the Piks were Welch or Irish, who can account for Pikland being unknown in the Christian records, while all Wales and Ireland were swarming with saints ? " [3]

G. Chalmers (1807) was equally convinced to the contrary that the Picts were Cymry from England [4] : " Pictish kings' names are undoubtedly Cambro-British." [5] From a consideration and extensive analysis of etymological peculiarities in place-names of Scotland, Chalmers concluded that the Celtic influence had been the more pronounced, [6] but Pinkerton had explained this fact by his belief that the Cymry were not expelled by the Picts until about B.C. 200. [7]

Professor Rhys (1852), [8] from his transliteration of ogmic inscriptions and grammatical study of the words, inferred that the Picts were of similar race to the Basques, that is non-Aryan. [9]

R. G. Latham (1857) believed that the northern elements in Great Britain were Scandinavian, Pomeranian and Prussian. Another writer suggests that they were Finns, [10] and yet another, Lapps. [11]

W. F. Skene (1876), following a statement by Bede, declared that the Northern Picts (i.e. those north of a line from Ben Nevis to a point between Aberdeen and Stonehaven) " appear to have been purely Gaelic in race and language. . . . The main body of the Southern Picts also belonged no doubt to the Gaelic race though they may have possessed some difference in the idiom of their language ". This

---

[1] *Enquiry*, vol. i, p. 121.   [2] *Ibid.*, vol. i, p. 146.
[3] *Ibid.*, vol. i, p. 150.   [4] *Caledonia*, vol. i, p. 199 *et seq.*
[5] *Ibid.*, vol. i, p. 207.   [6] *Ibid.*, vol. 215 *et seq.*
[7] *Enquiry*, vol. i, p. 132.
[8] *Inscriptions and Language of the Northern Picts* (Soc. of Antiq. of Scot.), 1892.
[9] The origin of the Basques is a lively source of argument.
[10] Dr. McRitchie (*Testimony of Tradition*, 1890).
[11] *Ibid.*, p. 96.

eminent authority also refers to tribes of British and Frisian settlers being incorporated with these Southern Picts.[1]

L. A. Waddell (1924) sums up :—

" It transpires by the new evidence that the Picts were the primitive small-statured prehistoric aborigines of Albion or Britain, with the ' River-bed ' type of skulls. They were presumably a branch of the primitive small-statured, narrow-browed and long-headed dark race of matriarchist Serpent-worshipping cave-dwellers of the Van Lake region, [Asia Minor], the Van, Biani, Fen, or Khal-dis or primitive ' Chaldees ', Caleds or Caledons, who in the early prehistoric times in the Old Stone Age, sent off from the central hive swarm after swarm of ' hunger marchers ' under matriarchs westward across Asia Minor to Europe, as far as Iberia and the Biscay region, after the retreating ice. The hordes, which ultimately reached Albion overland, formed there the ' aborigines of Albion '. They appear to have entered Southern Albion by the old land-bridge at Kent, after the latter end of the last glacial period, when the reindeer, mammoth, and woolly rhinoceros still roamed over what is now called England. And then, long ages afterwards, in the late Stone Age, presumably before 2000 B.C., they gave off a branch to Erin under a Van, Ban, or Fian matriarch, forming the aborigines of Ireland." [2]

The vexed question remains unsettled, and it is only possible to express the probability that the north was peopled by various races at different times, each new arrival inter-mingling to some extent with the previous one. The Picts may therefore have been to a certain extent of the native Iberian blood, with a partial mixture of Gael, Cymry, and perhaps Goth, the proportion of ingredients varying in different parts of the country. The language may well have been Iberian or Celtic modified by the intrusion of other tongues, but as the extracts have demonstrated, the opinions of those best qualified to judge are completely at variance on this point also.

The Roman Occupation. The " Romans " who governed Britain were of many races, being drawn from various tribes of Europe, Asia, and Africa, already subdued and romanized. In like manner numbers of Britons were utilized in carrying on military enterprises abroad, most of those that remained, it may be expected, being reduced to slavery. The laws and institutions controlling this mixture of nations would be Roman, and the language Latin for the patricians and Celtic for the plebeians. In England the Cymry were under the sway of the Romans until about the beginning of the fifth century when the legions were withdrawn, but it is to be supposed that evacuation was not complete, since there must have been some intermingling of the native

---

[1] *Celtic Scotland*, vol. i, p. 231.   [2] *Phœnician Origin*, p. 125.

Celt and the foreigners, and many of the latter would find it distasteful to leave what had become, in four centuries, the country of their ancestors. The stream of Roman immigration ceasing, the Latin language and names would decline, to be ultimately superseded by the Cymric tongue and appellatives, and Britannia, Caledonia and Hibernia become again almost peopled by Celtic speakers. In the North there were the mysterious Picts, it is true, and possibly various Scandinavian settlements, and in England the remnant of Roman alien auxiliaries, but generally speaking throughout the whole of the British Isles Gaelic and Cymric languages were spoken, Celtic names were in use, and, with the exception of such as had been bestowed by the Romans and are yet current, Celtic place-names likewise.

Teutonic Races of Britain. Gothonic visitors were probably not unknown in Roman times, the first arrivals being predatory bands, but by the middle of the fifth century, the expeditions, becoming larger and more frequent, ultimately assumed the nature of conquest and colonization. At the end of the sixth century, after 150 years of intermittent fighting, the Briton still retained as much of his native land on the western side of Britain as did the Angles, Saxons, and Jutes, on the eastern side. The territory under native rule was West Wales, i.e. Cornwall, Devon, and Somerset : North Wales, i.e. all territory west of the River Severn, and the great kingdom of Strathclyde stretching from Buckinghamshire to the Clyde. The Jutes held Kent and Hampshire : the Angles dominating all country south of the River Forth down to the north of Essex : and the Saxons, the remainder of England. Various colonies in the more inaccessible or untillable parts of England may also have continued native : elsewhere the " ancient Briton " became the under-dog, although it is unlikely that he was outnumbered by the Saxon.

The lowlands of Scotland, that is that part south of the Rivers Clyde and Forth, were thus about equally divided between two races : Strathclyde, the western part, being ruled by the native Briton, and Bernicia, the eastern part, being dominated by the Angles. The Picts occupied the extensive territory north of the Clyde and Forth, with the exception of what is now Argyllshire, which region had been seized by the Scots from Ireland.

Rivalry for the dominion of Britain led to varying changes in rulership until Ecgbert, king of the West Saxons, in the early ninth century, reduced the other kingdoms of Mercia and Northumbria (formerly Bernicia and Deira) to subjection. This enterprising and successful warrior also carried on active hostilities against the Celts, reducing all the Britons south of the River Dee to a state of vassalage : the Picts, Scots, and Strathclyde Welsh alone retaining their independence.[1]

Fostered by the writings of a few historians the extraordinary delusion still prevails in some quarters that the Cymry were completely annihilated by the Saxons.

An. cccc.xc.   Her Ælle & Cissa ymbsæton Andredes ceastere & ofslogon ealle þa þar innan wæran. na belaf ðar an Brytt to laue.[2]

" In this year (490) Ælla and Cissa besieged Andredes-ceaster, and slew all that dwelt therein ; not even one Briton was there left."

So runs the Anglo-Saxon Chronicle, which record influenced Gibbon (1776) to write, " the last of the Britons, without distinction of age, or sex, were massacred in the ruins of Anderida." [3] Hume (1778) was as misleading, " Those few natives, who were not either massacred or expelled their habitations, were reduced to the most abject slavery. . . . A total extermination of the Britons became the sole expedient for providing a settlement and subsistence to the new planters." [4]

The writings of Beda and Gildas refer to great mortality from sword, famine, and pestilence, but also point to survivors having become slaves. Notwithstanding that several historians of later date than Gibbon and Hume had expressed greatly modified views regarding the supposed extirpation of the Britons, the anonymous author of *The Norman People* (1874), entirely ignoring the surviving Celtic element, but referring to a later date, wrote, " the Norman, Danish, and Saxon races formed the three great constituents of the English nation." [5]   Green (1877) perpetuated the fiction, " Not a Briton remained as subject or slave, on English ground. . . . All was now (A.D. 577) purely English," [6] and in a further work, " The Britons had been wholly driven off the eastern half of the island." [7]

Since the days of Gibbon, many historians, philologists, and anthropologists have inquired into this important phase of English history, concluding very differently as the following extracts demonstrate.

[1] My notes on the Saxon conquest are culled from *History of the Norman Conquest*, by E. A. Freeman.
[2] One of six versions given by B. Thorpe (Rolls Ser. 23), p. 25.
[3] *The Decline and Fall of the Roman Empire*, by Edw. Gibbon (ed. J. B. Bury), vol. iv, p. 152.
[4] *History of England*, 1778, vol. i, p. 27.
[5] p. ix.
[6] *History of the English People*, by J. R. Green, 1877, vol. i, p. 28.
[7] *Conquest of England*, by J. R. Green, 1883, p. 2.

Turner, S. (1799).[1]—" The Anglo-Saxons, as they advanced, did not, as some have fancied, exterminate the Britons . . . the fierce warriors of Germany wanted husbandmen, artisans, and menials for domestic purposes. There can be no doubt that the *majority* of the British population was preserved to be useful to their conquerors."

Palgrave, F. (1832).[2]—" In the latter periods, the Loegrian[3] Britons appear to have existed, either as distinct people in larger territories, divided from the tracts inhabited by their Saxon lords; and in all cases, they were probably much more numerous than is usually supposed."

Pike, L. O. (1866).[4]—" History does not afford us any evidence that this portion of the island England ever became really Saxonized otherwise than in speech; and we may reasonably suppose that in the west of Northumberland, in Cumberland, notwithstanding a few Scandinavian raids upon the coast, in the west of Yorkshire, in Lancashire, perhaps even in Cheshire, and Shropshire, in Herefordshire, in Monmouthshire, in the west of Somersetshire, and in Devonshire, a population exists only less purely Celtic than that of Cornwall or of Wales itself. It seems, then, that all the direct or indirect historical evidence which can be drawn from analogous cases, lead us to the conclusion that, in the part of the island which is now called England, the population was, before the arrival of the Danes, probably more British than Teutonic."

Stubbs, W. (1866).[5]—" The new race found the convenience of ready-built houses and accumulated stores of material: and wherever the cities were spared, a portion at least of the city population must have continued also. In the country, too, especially towards the West and the debateable border, great numbers of Britons may have survived in servile or half-servile condition; some few of the greater men may have made, and probably did make, terms for themselves, especially in the districts appropriated by the smaller detachments of adventurers; and the public lands of the new kingdoms must have required native cultivators. But all these probabilities only bring out strongly the improbability of any general commixture or amalgamation of the races."

Nicholas, T. (1868).[6]—" No signs appear of an ' exterminating ' warfare being carried on by either Romans or Germans. The natives, if submissive, are everywhere allowed to remain in their native districts—their title to property and liberty being changed—by the Romans they are invited to the privileges of citizens of maternal Rome, and by the Germans they are pressed to ' become Saxons '. Whole tribes pass over accordingly, and hosts of the common people of other tribes follow. Those who wish to retain their language and customs are allowed to live in towns of their own, or to possess parts of towns, even within the bounds of the Anglo-Saxon kingdoms, and to live also under laws and magistrates of their own. Some 500 years

---

[1] *The History of the Anglo-Saxons*, 7th edit., vol. i, p. 277.
[2] *The Rise and Progress of the English Commonwealth*, pt. i, p. 462.
[3] The Loegrian Britons were the Cymry remaining in England.
[4] *The English and their Origin*, p. 57 et seq.
[5] *The Constitutional History of England*, 1880, p. 70.
[6] *The Pedigree of the English People*, 1868, *p.* 542.

after the first Saxon invasion, a great part of the South and West of England is called *Wealh-cynne*—the dominion of the Welsh, and the whole of Devon and Cornwall is still decidedly Celtic. In the North the kingdom of Strathclyde survives till a few years of the Norman Conquest. At this time the inhabitants of Britain are mainly composed of the Ancient Britons."

Allen, G. (1881).[1]—" There are good reasons which may lead us to believe that a large proportion of the Celts were spared as tillers of the soil, and that Celtic blood may yet be found abundantly even in the most Teutonic portions of England . . . The facts seem to indicate that while the modern English nation is largely Welsh in blood, it is wholly Teutonic in form and language . . . To sum up in a single sentence, the Anglo-Saxons have contributed about one-half the blood of Britain, or rather less ; but they have contributed the whole framework of the language, and the whole social and political organization ; while, on the other hand, they have contributed hardly any of the civilization, and none of the religion. We are now a mixed race, almost equally Celtic and Teutonic by descent, we speak a purely Teutonic language, with a large admixture of Latin roots in its vocabulary ; we live under Teutonic institutions ; we enjoy the fruits of a Græco-Roman civilization ; and we possess a Christian Church handed down to us directly through Roman sources from a Hebrew original. To the extent so indicated, and to that extent only, we may still be justly styled an Anglo-Saxon people."

Knowing from the Chronicles that the Saxon occupation was spread over several hundred years, any supposition that the native Britons were exterminated is *prima facie* unfounded. The invaders' ships were few and small and dependent largely upon favourable wind and weather, with the landing places consequently doubtful : the native population was large, but without defensive organization, and a militant minority arriving unheralded, even though in small bodies, was enabled to seize land and settlements and consolidate its position. In course of time the two races bartered, fraternized, and intermarried, and the Saxon adventurers of one century had become intermixed and part and parcel of Britain long before the Teutons of the succeeding century arrived.

In view of the consensus of the opinion of the leading inquirers it is unnecessary to labour the point of survival of the Briton, and it may be concluded that Hume and Green made hasty and illogical deductions, and that there were at least as many natives in the Teutonic part of Britain as Saxons, but that the language of the invaders ultimately prevailed, and the popularity of native names declined with the use of the British tongue.

Although the Anglo-Saxon language gradually ousted the British, large numbers of the native words remained, and

[1] *Anglo-Saxon Britain*, pp. 55, 70, 233.

are in use in England to the present day. Whitaker (1771) discovered 3,000 British terms forming part of the English language [1] : and Chalmers (1803) noted that the Saxons adopted many of the Celtic names of hills and rivers, and a number of terms from " the more copious and expressive speech of the Britons ". [2] Garnett (1843) has pointed out " how necessary it is for the etymologist to take the Celtic element into consideration in the investigation of the languages of Western Europe ".[3] Kemble (1846) wrote, " A strict application of Celtic philology to the names which occur in our earliest history, would probably supply unlooked for evidence of a much closer and more friendly intercourse than we at present anticipate between some classes of the Britons and their Saxon invaders. . . . Names unintelligible to the Teutonic scholar suggest a far more general mixture of blood among early conquerors than has been generally admitted." [4]

The currency of so many Celtic words points to considerable survival of the native races and the investigations of anthropologists and archæologists lead to the same deduction.[5] Of the two branches of research the writer prefers that of the archæologists—the discovery of Celtic domestic remains in the same strata, and side by side with coeval Saxon household articles evidences intermingling of the races, but the statistics of nature of hair, colour of skin, stature, shape of head, or details of face, eye, and nose of living persons fail in historical value for want of proof that the ancestors of such persons lived in the same spot in Saxon days. In fact it will be demonstrated, by means of lists of surnames, that large numbers of Celts came into England long after the Norman conquest, and their descendants are now leading anthropologists to over-estimate the survival of Celtic blood.

Celtic personal names in England may have survived the Saxon conquest to some extent, but in common with the Gothonic appellatives, lost popularity after the Norman occupation. Subsequent immigration has again brought into England a large number of Celtic names, but it must not be rashly assumed that they point in any way to survival of the ancient race of England. The blood descendants of the early Britons of England are the most unlikely people now to have Cymric names ; even in parts of Wales, Scotland,

[1] *The History of Manchester*, by Rev. J. Whitaker, 1771–5, vol. ii, p. 238 *et seq.*   [2] *Caledonia*, by G. Chalmers, 1887, vol. i, p. 221.
[3] Proc. Philological Soc., 1843, vol. i, p. 176.   See also *Gælic Etymology of the English Language*, by C. Mackay.
[4] *The Names, Surnames, and Nicnames of the Anglo-Saxons*.   Proc. Arch. Inst., 1846, pp. 102 and 85.
[5] Reference may be made to the notes by Grant Allen in *Anglo-Saxon Britain*, p. 56 et seq.

and Ireland, where native blood and language has been continuous, many ancient names have died out.

Ireland. The aboriginal inhabitants of Ireland are believed by ethnologists to have been likewise of that mysterious non-Aryan race which still survives in Spain and elsewhere. According to legends, which form the most ancient history of Erin, the island was invaded by successions of warriors from North, East, and South, who, by various ancient authorities, are termed Celts, Greeks, or Iberians. The southern colonists, from their name of Scoti, gave to the island the name of Scotia, which their emigrants, in turn, carried to Caledonia, now Scotland.

Ireland or Erin, the Ierne of Aristotle : Hibernia of Julius Cæsar : and Juvernia of Juvenal, was partitioned by the Scoti into five divisions, now reduced to four. The dawn of the christian era found the various kingdoms engaged in constant struggles for supremacy and the over-lordship, which conditions prevailing for many centuries, the annals record a succession of sanguinary fights resulting in much slaughter and spoliation of the country. Neither Romans nor Saxons attempted the conquest of Ireland.

Invasion by Northmen. By the end of the eighth century ravaging bodies of Scandinavians, or Vikings, as they are called, had already visited both Britain and Ireland, and these incursions becoming more ambitious and successful led to permanent settlements being effected in both islands. Ultimately the sporadic raids became organized invasion culminating in victory and large territory of Northumbria and East Anglia being ceded to the enterprising colonists. Scotland and Strathclyde likewise suffered from the acquisitive Northmen, and to obtain protection voluntarily submitted to Eadward (922-4), whose over-lordship then extended throughout the whole island. The kingdom of Britain thus founded was, sixty years later, subjected to Danish invasions, and in 1017 Cnut was formally acknowledged King of all England, Emperor of all Britain.[1] In Ireland the Danes were also firmly established in the eastern part, with Dublin as principal town. The Northmen, towards the end of the ninth century, wrested Normandy, the ancient Neustria, from the Franks, under whose domination it had been after the decay of the Roman power. The adventurous Scandinavians, not content with these exploits, made much more ambitious voyages, and in the ninth century went south to Morocco, east to Turkey, and during the tenth and eleventh centuries not only discovered Greenland but also, it is believed, a considerable extent of the eastern coasts of North America, which lands were repeatedly

[1] *History of the Norman Conquest*, by E. A. Freeman.

visited by the Vikings in subsequent centuries before the
" discovery " of Columbus.[1]

In ancient chronicles a good deal of confusion exists
between the terms Danes and Norwegians, both called
" Nordmanni ", and it is not thought necessary in this work
to endeavour to disentangle them, even if it were possible to
do so.[2] The point of importance is that the Northmen were
adventurous, capable, and organized colonists, who exercised
a great influence on the building up of the British nation,
and likewise in the making of our names.

The Languages of Britain. The unknown languages of the
aborigines of Britain were superseded by Celtic tongues,
which spread throughout the whole islands. As the Celtic
speech had become obliterated in Southern Europe by Latin,
so in turn did it give way in England to the Ænglisc, although
it possibly held out longer than generally supposed and
lingers yet, as we have seen from the philologists' views
quoted above, although cloaked in the obscurity of Saxon
word-forms. The Rev. John Evans considered that the
language of the Cymry was probably spoken in the north
(i.e. Strathclyde) until the fourteenth century.[3] In Cornwall
(West Wales) as late as the reign of Charles I, were living
people who had no knowledge of the English language, and
even a century later the Cornish dialect was not entirely
extinct in that county.[4] In Brittany many descendants of
refugees from England yet speak forms of the ancient
language, and in considerable parts of Wales, Man, Scotland,
and Ireland the native tongues have been preserved to the
present day.[5] One result of the successes of Julius Cæsar
was to change the language of Gaul, the Franks adopting
the speech of the Latin people, but the Romans were unable
to impose their tongue upon the Cymry of Britain.

The known Celtic languages were seven, namely, of the
Goidelic group—Irish, Gaelic (Scotland), and Manx ; of the
Brythonic group—Welsh, Cornish and Breton, and possibly
Gaulish, of which little of either words or names is preserved.
Probably all seven tongues have been current in the British
Isles at one time or another, but they are now reduced to
the first four named, each of which is represented by several
dialects.

The Norse language has been freely used in the Viking
settlements throughout the British Isles, and from survival
of Scandinavian phrases it has been suggested that the tongue

[1] *The Flatey Book*, Norrœna Soc., 1906.
[2] Particulars of the respective activities of the two races may be found
in *The Vikings*, by Allen Mawer, 1913.   [3] *Ancient Britain*, p. 103.
[4] *A Handbook of the Cornish Language*, by H. Jenner, p. 16 et seq.
[5] The 1891 census recorded over 500,000 persons speaking Welsh, and
nearly as many with a knowledge of it.

may have been spoken in certain districts in England as late as the reign of Henry II (1154–89),[1] and still later in the Isle of Man, which was held by the Scandinavians until 1219.

The language which is variously called Ænglisc, Anglo-Saxon, or Old English, is largely the Low German of the tribes, who in the fifth and sixth centuries conquered Britain. It belongs, according to one commonly accepted classification, to the Teutonic subdivision of the Gothic branch : according to other philologists, to the Germanic subdivision of the Teutonic branch, of the Indo-European or Aryan tongues : its relationship to the Celtic, which it has so largely superseded, may be conveniently illustrated in a table.[2]

INDO-EUROPEAN LANGUAGES

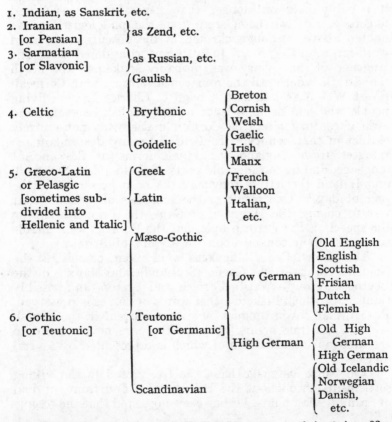

1. Indian, as Sanskrit, etc.
2. Iranian [or Persian] } as Zend, etc.
3. Sarmatian [or Slavonic] } as Russian, etc.
4. Celtic
   - Gaulish
   - Brythonic
     - Breton
     - Cornish
     - Welsh
   - Goidelic
     - Gaelic
     - Irish
     - Manx
5. Græco-Latin or Pelasgic [sometimes subdivided into Hellenic and Italic]
   - Greek
   - Latin
     - French
     - Walloon
     - Italian, etc.
6. Gothic [or Teutonic]
   - Mæso-Gothic
   - Teutonic [or Germanic]
     - Low German
       - Old English
       - English
       - Scottish
       - Frisian
       - Dutch
       - Flemish
     - High German
       - Old High German
       - High German
   - Scandinavian
     - Old Icelandic
     - Norwegian
     - Danish, etc.

[1] E. Ekwall in *Introduction to English Place-names*, vol. i, pt. i, p. 92.

[2] Authorities are not in perfect agreement as to the affinities of the languages, but the table has been arranged to give an average view. Further information may be obtained from H. Sweet (*New English Grammar*, 1892). E. Adams (*Elements of English Language*, 1892) : T. G. Tucker (*Introduction to the Natural History of Language*, 1908).

The first three branches have had little effect upon the English tongue, or upon the names of Great Britain and Ireland, but the languages of the Celtic, Græco-Latin, and Gothic branches can all be traced in our surnames. It must be emphasized that race, language, and personal names are not interdependent, and may and do differ in one nation, and the proved presence of one of the three elements is no argument for the existence of either of the other two. Failure to grasp this axiomatic principle has led to some most illogical dicta.[1]

Personal Names of Britain. An entire change of blood of a nation would, under any conceivable conditions, be spread over a very long period : the ousting of one language in favour of another is likewise a slow process in lesser degree ; but the change of the names of a nation might be accomplished in a generation. Consequently, it may be concluded that in England the proportion of Celtic blood exceeds the proportion of Celtic words absorbed, and that ratio in turn exceeds the proportion of Celtic names preserved. In Wales, Scotland, and Ireland native names have been preserved to a greater extent, although many of the most ancient died a natural death.

Roman names failed to attain any permanent popularity with the natives of these islands. The Northmen brought personal names and secondary descriptions, but they remained less with us than those they bestowed on towns and villages. Saxon names had a long innings, partly interrupted by the Northmen, finally giving way to Norman and Breton appellatives, and again being introduced by incomers from the Low Countries. In later years of English speech, various aliens—Flemings, Frisians, Lombards, Dutchmen, Spaniards, and Hebrews—to name a few, brought their native names, most of which were abandoned on landing, others being translated into English, others again corrupted to pass as native, providing the inquirer into origins of British names with a series of absorbing problems which may well defy elucidation by the most practised and assiduous investigator, as will be more particularly gathered from the data presented in following pages.

[1] As an example of unsound deduction I may cite the views of the anonymous author of *The Norman People*, who pointed to the great numbers of names of Norman-French appearance as evidencing the prevalence of Norman blood regardless of the fact that a form of Norman-French was the language of the officials of England and of their records, and personal descriptions or additions were entered in French (Anglo-Norman as sometimes called), and being repeated, in many cases became surnames of men of Saxon origin.

CHAPTER II

EARLY PERSONAL NAMES AND DESCRIPTIONS IN THE BRITISH ISLES

Non-Aryan Names. For thousands of years before family names became customary in Britain, men were identified by personal appellatives, sometimes being further distinguished by additions or supplementary epithets. Since many personal names became in time secondary descriptions, and the descriptions in turn ultimately blossomed into surnames, a brief consideration of ancient gift-names, their construction and types, is a wise and helpful preliminary to a thorough understanding of the origin, nature, and classification of surnames.

It will have become transparent from the foregoing dissertation that the earliest personal names used in the British Isles of which it is possible to know anything, must be of the debatable neolithic or bronze age races, variously believed to be akin to the Iberians or equally mysterious Etruscans, or, perhaps, of more remote Asiatic or African origin. These conjecturally non-Aryan names should, by virtue of the greater antiquity, receive first attention, but those which can be identified, and then only doubtfully, are few and of no early date. Professor Rhys (1852), who concluded that the Pictish language was allied to the Basque, alludes to the following example (among others), taken from a " carefully written and punctuated ogam from Lunasting ", Shetland, as non-Aryan.

✠ Ttocuhetts : ahehhttmnnn : hccvvevv : Nehhtonn : i.e. " Rests here below priest Nechtonn." [1]

On the other hand, E. W. B. Nicholson (1896) considered that the inscription was Gaelic, and should read :—

Ait Ui Cuthaidh : a-h-àit mun Chuaibh Nehton : i.e. Hearthside of O'Cuhetts : his hearthside about *Warlikes* of Nehton.[2]

The latest investigator, Dr. L. A. Waddell (1924), who deciphered the inscription on the famous Newton Stone, reads it without difficulty in a dialect of the Gothic of the Eddas.

✠ XaTTUI CUH XaTTS : +H XaHHTT MaNaNN : HaCC FFEFF : NEDT. ON Na. " (This) Cross at *Xattui*-Cuh (city) of the *Xatt* (or *Khatt*). (This) Cross (is erected by) *Xahht* Manann (son of) Hacc Ffeff (who) rests aneath, weening in hope nigh."

[1] " Northern Picts," by J. Rhys (*Proc. Soc. Antiq. of Scot.*, ser. III, vol. ii).
[2] *Vernacular Inscriptions of Alban*, by E. W. B. Nicholson, p. 4.

It is a reasonable supposition that some of the ancient names of Ireland and Wales which do not readily yield up their secrets to the philologists may be of an earlier language corrupted out of recognition, but in view of the great uncertainty which exists and the widely different opinions held in well-informed circles, it will be small service to labour the point, and we may pass on to a consideration of the names of the Indo-European group, which provide the substance of British nomenclature.

Sanskrit Names. With a few possible exceptions, British names were of the Indo-European group of languages, of which Sanskrit, the ancient literary language of India, is representative of the earliest known. A profusion of the ancient names have been preserved in such records as the *Sacred Books of the East*, and in view of the relationship of Sanskrit to early European appellatives, their grammatical composition provides an interesting preliminary study.

The system of naming persons by the Aryans of ancient India was not uniform, but a very general practice was to give three names, one being secret and one astrological.[1] In the absence of any recognized system of classification, Sanskrit personal names may be divided tentatively, according to form and construction, into three main classes.

1 *Dithematic or Compounded.* A prominent feature in the Sanskrit language is the combination of vocables to form compounds, and this characteristic is at once apparent in personal names, not only in Sanskrit, but in those of nearly all the ancient Indo-European nations. The largest class is, in fact, formed by those appellatives compounded of two themes or components, which members or elements have been called appropriately the prototheme and deuterotheme respectively [2] : in Jayadeva (*jaya* " victory ", *deva* " god ") *jaya-* is the prototheme or first element, and -*deva* the deuterotheme or second element. The components may be two nouns as Vrkâjina (*vrka* " wolf ", *jina* " skin ") ; two adjectives as Mahâpûrna (*mahâ* " great ", *pûrna* " full ") ; or adjective and noun as Mahâçva (*açva* " horse ") ; or the compound may have other parts of speech in its composition.[3] Certain vocables may be used as either first or second part of the name ; others, again, are reserved exclusively for either the initial or final component.

Examples of exclusive prothemes are : *Su-* " good ", as

---

[1] For further particulars on this point reference may be made to the article on Indo-European names by L. H. Gray, in *Encycl. of Religion and Ethics*.

[2] *Onomasticon Anglo-Saxonicum*, by W. G. Searle, p. xii.

[3] On the formation of Sanskrit compounds see *A Sanskrit Grammar*, by W. D. Whitney, 1889, p. 480 et seq.

Su-mitra (*mitra* " friend ") ; *Dhûma-* " smoke ", as Dhûma-varna (*varna* " colour "). Examples of exclusive deutero-themes are : *-gupta* " protected ", as Deva-gupta (*deva* " god ") ; *-varman* " weapon ", as Canda-varman (*canda* " furious "). An example of a component usable either as first or second element is *simha* " lion ", e.g. Simha-râja (" lion-king " or " great king ") : Vira-simha (*vira* " hero ", " man ", etc.).

Fick gives a small list illustrating the reversibility of the members in dithematic names, as Yajña-krt, Krta-yajña ; Ketu-dharman, Dharma-ketu ; Vrddha-kshatra, Kshatra-vrddha.[1] Repetition of the same element to form a compound occurs rarely, as Râja-râja.

2 *Monothematic or Uncompounded.* Single element names as Vrsan " bull " and Sakuna " bird " occur, but without certainty that they have not been originally part of a compound. Fick considers that they were constituted independently, but calls them leaning (*angelehnte*) names, dependent on full-names (*Vollnamen*).[2] The majority of appellatives falling into this class are, however, diminished forms of dithematic names ; the deuterotheme may have been entirely dropped, e.g. Yaçaç-candra becomes Yaças (" glory ", " splendour ") : or it may be the first element which has been omitted, e.g. Yaças from Câru-yaças.

3 *Derivatives.* Into this category fall names which are derived from classes (1) and (2) by various processes, such as addition or subtraction of letters and syllables, or changes in form. Such changes might be classified according to grammatical structure in various ways, but for the present purpose it is convenient to note only two distinct types of derivatives. Of the first kind are names of classes (1) and (2) (mutilated or otherwise), with additional prefix : as the preposition *vi* in Vi-kata, Vikrama-nidhi, Tri-vikrama : or suffixes as *vant* in Hiranya-vant. Of the second subclass are names with diminutive terminations which lengthen it as Devadatta-ka or shorten it as Deva-ka.[3] Among the Indo-European races generally, there is a great tendency to shorten compound names before suffixing, a feature which it will be shown had a great influence in the multiplication of genealogical surnames of the British Isles. Derivatives might alternatively be subclassed as hypocorisms (pet-names), diminutives, and

---

[1] *Die griechischen Personnahmen*, von August Fick (1874), p. cxci. I have taken most of my examples from this work. The hyphens are inserted to distinguish the elements.

[2] Ibid., cxliii.

[3] Fick's view is that diminutive endings which lengthen names should be separated from the shortening forms, although the Greeks group them together.

augmentatives, but determination of the exact nature of these names is most uncertain. Taking an English example, for instance, who is to say whether " Little Willie " is a pet-name, an opprobious epithet, or merely a diminutival distinction from " Big Willie " ? The same difficulty in classification is present in the derived names of Sanskrit as well as in those of other Indo-European languages.

Hypocoristic names are undoubtedly common, as Musika " mousie " : Sakuntala " birdie ", or an unadorned element, as Câru from Câru-deva, etc. ; the general principles of their formation were recorded by Panini, a grammarian teaching 2,000 years ago, and is fully recognized. To illustrate how live (*lebendig*) the hypocoristic names were in later times, Fick refers to a market called Kamalâ-haṭṭa, after Kamalâ, the pet-name of Queen Kamalavati.

The words adopted for the construction of names were chosen for their capacity of succinctly describing the appearance, qualities, or acts of the bearer, but often prophetically and figuratively. Most prevalent of the descriptions are those relating to battle, victory, animals, plants, offices, possessions, race, and deities. It is to be surmised that at first the two vocables were chosen to form a name expressing a sensible concept, although later on they appear to have been combined regardless of the resulting significance. This seeming lack of fitness is true of some compound names of other Indo-European races, but doubtless the explanation to some extent lies in our own want of a full understanding of the diverse significations of the elements, even a thousand years ago the meanings of some names having been lost. It will be shown, at a later stage, that with regard to O.E. names other considerations than sensible signification prevailed in composition.

Occasionally a theme was repeated in one family forming a kind of identification label, such as Kumbha, " pillar," son of Kumbhukarna, " maker of pillars " ; Madri, daughter of Madraraja ; Kusambuja, son of Kusambha. Some components were very much used owing to being adopted as class indexes distinguishing sect, cult, or caste. This repetition of themes in one family, as a quaint conceit, was likewise practised by Greeks, and as we shall see by Teutons and Celts also.[1]

[1] See the Anglo-Saxon example on p. 51. This system was also in use by non-Aryan races. In Japan the *toriji* or character-in-common was employed in a family for several generations, e.g. members of the Tokugawa family were called Iyeyasu, Iyemitsu, Iyetsuna, Iyenobu, and Iyetsugu (T. Harada). A somewhat similar system has been noted in China, but the repetitive theme does not always take the same position (J. Dyer Ball). In Arabia also, e.g. three sons were named Hasan, Husain, Muhassan. For a Hebrew example see p. 147.

In addition to personal names, further identification was obtained by secondary descriptions; and sometimes a multiplicity of such augmentations were bestowed, particularly in the case of deities. Indra was " many-named ", Ahura Mazda had twenty different epithets, and in the Mahâbhârata sixty-two descriptions are given to the epic Indian Arjuna.[1] These descriptions fall into two classes, characteristic as Dhanamjaya, " booty-conqueror " : Kapipravara, " having the excellent monkey "; or genealogical as Paurava, " descendant of Puru " ; Kuntiputra, " son of Kunti ".

Indians bearing more than one name are sometimes said to be surnamed, such as " Bhavabhuti surnamed Sri-kantha " and " Bhatta Narayana surnamed Mrigaraja ", but these additional epithets are not family names as the term is understood at the present day.[2]

These few selected details of the method of Sanskrit name-composition are in general equally applicable to the forming of appellatives by other Indo-European races, as will be more fully particularized with regard to Irish, Welsh, and Anglo-Saxon designations in following chapters.

Personal Names of Greeks and Gauls. Before passing on to the names of the Celtic races of Britain, it may be noticed that the Greeks, whose origin is still a subject for discussion, in common with other European races, found personal names alone insufficient for distinction, and used secondary descriptions for more particular discrimination. Sometimes the addition was a characteristic epithet, sometimes a place-name, but more often a patronymic which might be formed in various ways.

Uios (υἱός) or other word for son might be used, but more often it was suppressed : the article ὁ might or might not remain as Φάλιος Ἐρατοκλείδου (Phalios Eratokleidou, i.e. Phalius [the son] of Eratoclides) : Ἀλεξανδρος ὁ Φιλίππου (Alexandros o Philippou, i.e. Alexander the [son] of Philip). Jannaris gives, as performing a similar service, suffixes : -ades as Λαερτιάδης (Laertiades, i.e. son of Laertios) : -ides as Πριαμίδης (Priamides, i.e. son of Priamos) : -ion as Κρονίων (Kronion, i.e. son of Kronos) : -is as Ταντᾰλίς (Tantalis, i.e. daughter of Tantalos).[3]

The precise relationship between the numerous tribes of ancient Greeks with the many other races of Europe will probably never be determined. No nation is of pure race, and customs of an early people, including systems of nomenclature,

---

[1] See *Encycl. of Rel. and Ethics*, art. by L. H. Gray.
[2] See the definition, p. 73.
[3] *An Historical Greek Grammar*, 1897, p. 290 et seq., where also information regarding the formation of pet-names and nicknames by violently shortening proper names may be found.

may survive long after their independence, language, and religion have perished. It would serve no purpose of the present essay to discuss whether Greeks were Celts, or Celts were Greeks, or what peculiarities, as distinct races, they obtained from a common source, but in a later chapter on the etymon it will be shown that one of the most popular names of the Celts was also prevalent with the Greeks.

The principal sources of the most ancient Celtic names are the inscriptions found on coins, and Gaulish and British monumental stones.[1] In numbers the survivals are not vast, but the same double-element names are to be found, which compounds of two words are clearly the original form, as in Sanskrit, Greek, and other languages. Some vocables, nouns and adjectives, are used solely as protothemes as *avi-* " good ", " well ", e.g. Avi-cantus ; others as deuterothemes as *-tigernus* " lord ", e.g. Eu-tigern. Other words are used equally for either first or second element as *catu* " battle " (W., Bret. *cad*, *kad* : Ir. *cath*), as in Catwallon (Catu-vellaunus) and Vello-catus. Uncompounded names as Vepus may be found (probably, however, a diminished form of Vepo-talos), and the significa-tion of which has not been determined.[2] A quasi-compound is Camulo-genos, " offspring of Camulos."

The Gauls had a suffix *cnos*, *cnon*, genitive *cni*, equivalent to Gr. *-ides* and Lat. *filius* ; on a bilingual stone the two forms Druticnos and Druti filius being noticed.[3]

The structure and signification of Gaelic and Cymric names will now be more particularly investigated.

Early Gaelic Names of the Irish. The early history of Ireland so far as handed down by bards and annalists is a romantic story largely compounded of myth and legend : by the time the christian chroniclers were enabled to collect and record the verbal narratives the ancient traditions having become embellished with much imaginary glory and exaggerated importance. Notwithstanding their fabulous nature and historical imperfections these records provide a happy hunting ground for the nomenclaturist, and a good collection of the picturesque early names can be extracted, but it must be remembered that they are not coeval, and should only be considered as typical of the age in which the chronicle was written.

The ancient names of Ireland in their structure are often reminiscent of the fanciful names of the East, and it is not improbable that two systems were in current use, one of which

---

[1] *Alt-Celtischer Sprachschatz*, von A. Holder, 1896, comprises a com-prehensive list.

[2] *The Welsh People*, by J. Rhys, 1923, p. 63.

[3] *Lectures on Welsh Philology*, by J. Rhys, 1879, p. 31. *Studies in Irish Epigraphy*, by R. A. S. Macalister, 1897, pt. i, p. 8.

being due to survival of aboriginal non-Aryan customs, the other of more regular type corresponding to the Sanskrit examples given above.[1]

Irish personal names, like the Sanskrit appellatives, may be conveniently divided according to form and construction into three main classes.[2]

1 *Dithematic or Compounded.* The elements or themes forming compound names may be (i) two nouns, as Faol-chadh[3] " wolf-warrior ", Mur-ghal " sea-valour ", Tuath-al " people-ruler " ; (ii) two nouns, the first of which governs the second in the genitive case, as Cú-chatha " hound of battle ", Maol-anraith " chief of the storm ". The second name sometimes takes the article, as Cú-an-aonaigh " hound of the fair " ; or is preceded by a numeral, as Dubh-dá-inbhear " black of the two river mouths " ; (iii) two nouns connected by a conjunctive particle, as Cú-gan-mathair " motherless hound " ; (iv) a noun preceded by a qualifying adjective, as Ciar-mhac " black son ", Fionn-bharr " fair head " ; or followed by the adjective, as Bairr-fhionn " fair head " ; Giolla-dubh " black lad ".

2 *Monothematic or Uncompounded.* Names with a single original element, that is, not being reduced forms of com-pounded names, as Breac " speckled ", " spotted " ; Guaire " noble ", " generous " ; Teimhean " dark ", " grey ". Such names are indistinguishable from diminished forms of dithematic names where a second element is dropped, as Aodh, which may be derived from Aodh-ghal or Aodh-lugh ; a first element elided, as Bran, a shortened form of Art-bhran or Faol-bhran ; or the element retained may undergo slight changes, as Bairre, Báire, or Barra from Bairr-fhionn, or Fionna, Fionnu, or Finnia from Fionn-bharr.

3 *Derivatives.* One subclass of derivatives consists of names formed from nouns, adjectives, and other names by the addition of prefixes and suffixes, as Ain-mhire, Comh-ghall, Su-ibhne, Cath-ach, Dubh-dha, Colp-tha, etc. Another subclass consists of names to which are added diminutive suffixes, *-án* (*-eán*), which termination originally had the force of a patronymic like Gr. *-ides*, and signified " son of " : *-agán* (*-eagán*), a double diminutive from *-óg* and *-án* ; *-éin*, *-ín*, and *-óg* (*-eóg*), as Artán, Muireagán, Finnéin, Cairín, Mocholmeóg. Some names have three forms of diminutives,

---

[1] *The Welsh People*, p. 66 et seq.
[2] My examples are taken from *Sloinnte Gaedheal is Gall*, by Rev. P. Woulfe. This authority makes eight classes in all, which number I have reduced by combining four dithematic classes, two monothematic classes, and putting together derivatives and diminutives. For fuller information on Irish names reference may be usefully made to that work.
[3] Hyphens are introduced to divide the elements.

as Dubh, Dubhán, Duibhín, Dubhagán. Corresponding to -*án*, in the names of males, is a feminine termination -*nat*, as Damhnat, Rónnat.

All names in use in Ireland were native until the coming of Christianity, when ecclesiastics introduced Hebrew, Greek, and Latin appellatives, upon adopting new names at ordination, but these foreign appellatives do not appear to have attained any great popularity among laymen. In the Annals occur Adam, Abel, Noe, Joseph, Aaron, David, Daniel, John, etc., the last-named (formerly Eóin, now Seán) being the only one which exhibited any great staying power. Patrick and Michael, now so popular, were not used by Irishmen until after the Norman conquest. Saintly names are rare, and when adopted usually formed one element of a compound, such as Maolmhuire " servant of Mary ", Giollapheadair " servant of Peter ". *Maol* (O. Celt. *maglos*) also signifies " chief ", as in Maolcaoin " gentle chief ". Giolla (probably Norse *gisl* " a pledge " or " hostage ") was largely used by the Northmen to form baptismal names, on their conversion to Christianity. Woulfe states that many Danish and Norse names passed into Irish families during the ninth, tenth, and eleventh centuries, and gives the following examples : Amhlaoíbh, Aralt, Bruadar, Caplur, Dubhghall, Eanrac, Gothraidh, Íomhar, Lochlainn, Maghnur, Oirtín, Oitir, Raghnall, Ruaidhrí, Ruadhrac, Siocphraidh, Sitreac, Somhairle.

The signification was recognized as being more important than the actual name itself, which might be changed, providing an identical meaning was retained, and in like manner diminutive suffixes might be varied.

Irish names are declined like other nouns : in compound nouns both elements may be inflected, or the second member only.[1]

Additional Descriptions of the Irish. Persons mentioned in the Annals have either single or double appellatives. In the latter case the cognomina, epithets or augmentations were fanciful additions given from time to time (probably invented and bestowed long after the death of the bearer) rather than the product of necessity permanently retained in practical use during lifetime.

All Irish names, at one time, had a common-sense meaning, and the derivation and signification of the additional descriptions have received some attention from antiquaries, but as early as the twelfth century origins were becoming obscure and translations doubtful, possibly due to some so-called Irish names being aboriginal and non-Aryan.

The following selection of names and descriptions of kings

[1] For further particulars reference may be made to Woulfe, p. 14.

who, according to the ancient chroniclers, ruled over Ireland from the year of the Deluge, A.M. 2242 (2958 B.C.), to the commencement of the christian era is collected from the *Annals of the Four Masters* (1632–6), and the derivations of the epithets are from the *Cóir Anmann* (Fitness of Names), which onomasticon is thought by its learned editor to have been compiled not earlier than the twelfth century.[1]

Nuadhat Airgetlamh : Nuadhat of the silver hand (an artificial hand with complete motion).

Enna Airgthech (silvery), because silver shields were made for him. O'Donovan renders this name " the plunderer ".

Fiacha Finscothach, because there were flowers (*scotha*) of wine (*fina*) in his reign.   Mageoghegan (*Annals of Clonmacnoise*) says : " abundance of white flowers."

Gedhe Ollghothach, of the mighty voice.

Sedna Innarraighe, because he first gave wages (*indarrad*) to soldiers in Erin.

Eochaidh Uaircheas, because in his fleets, when he attacked Greece, were *uara* " fresh ", *cesa* " skiffs ", in the prows and poops of which he kept all that he had seized.

Conaing Begeaglach, " little fear " ; if not *becc-fiacla*, of the little tooth.

Duath Ladgrach, i.e. *luath* " swift " : *agra* " pleading ".

Reachtaidh Righdeargh, of the red forearm : *derg* " red " : *rig* " forearm ". Alternatively, *rigdai* " royal " : *derc* " eye ".

Iaranngleo Fathach, " prophetic," but Keating has " Iron-fight the cautious ".

Eochaidh Ailtleathan, the broad-jointed.

Fearghus Fortamhail, " prevailing." Lynch says " the powerful " or " brave ".

Enna Aighneach, that is, complete (*óg*) was his hospitality (*enech*).

Crimhthann Cosgrach, " triumphant."

Eochaidh Aireamh, that is, *ar-dam* " on one ox ", being the first to put a yoke upon the necks of oxen. Alternatively *ar-úam*, ploughing of graves, being the first to dig the ground to make a grave.

Nuadha Neacht, i.e. *nicht* from *nix* " snow ", or from *nox* " night ".

Classification of Additional Descriptions. Such distinctive descriptions are classifiable under four heads, which may be termed : Characteristic, Local, Genealogical, and Occupational.

Characteristic descriptions form the largest class, and may relate to the bearer's appearance, such as : Enna Derg (the red), Simon Brecc (the freckled), Cessair Chruthach (the comely) ; or to character, as : Cormac Cas (the cruel, or *cass* " swift "), Loegaire Lorc (the fierce or rapacious or the parricidal), Cernach Sotal (the proud) ; or to physical attributes, as : Conall Guthbind (sweet-voiced). A considerable number of second names described acts of the bearer,

[1] *Irische Texte*, von Wh. Stokes und E. Windisch. Dritte serie, 2 heft.

or events which occurred during his life, as: Aed Gusdan (*gus* " deed ", *dana* " bold "), Conn Cét-chathach (*cét* " hundred ", *cath* " battles "), Eochu Apthach (" the deadly ", from the pestilence prevalent in his time). The condition of the bearer may also be recorded in a second name, such as Sírna Saeglach " long-lived " ; or his principal possessions are noted, as Oengus Ollmuccaid (*ollmucca* " great swine "), or his nationality, as Cairbre Cruithnechán (the Pictling).

Local descriptions may also be found : Esomain Emna (the fearless one of Emain Macha, where he was reared) ; Manannán mac Lir (the name of Oirbsen, a chapman, who dwelt in the Isle of Man : *manannan*, from his place of origin ; mac lir " son of the sea ", because of his skill as a pilot) ; Cairbre Luachra (of Luachair) ; Mac Brocc " son of badgers ", the description bestowed upon one who was born in the warren of the badgers.

Genealogical descriptions, that is, those which name a relative (in which term may be included a foster parent), were also in use, such as : Mog Néit, given to one Oengus, from the name of the foster father who reared him (Mog Néit, Net's slave).

> " Oengus was Mog Néit's first name
> At his life's beginning without a lie,
> And Mog Néit was his name afterwards,
> Until active Goll, son of Morna, killed him."

The commonest description of this class was the patronymical, such as : Conmael mac Emir (*mac* " son "), but Corbmac ua Cuind, i.e. grandson of Conn. Corc was called after his mother Duibfind ; and Lugna Fer Tri was named after his wife (*fer Tri* " Tri's husband ").

Occupational descriptions were likewise referred to : Eochu Fiadmuine (*máine feda* " treasures of the forest ", meaning that he was a hunter) ; Irél Faith " the prophet " ; Conall err Breg (champion of Bregia).[1]

Certain descriptions or secondary names as *gelta gaeth*, *rúamann duach*, or *birnn buadach* could not be explained by the medieval nomenclaturist, although he did not readily admit defeat, as the following examples from the *Cóir Anmann* will illustrate.

"Eochaid Cupa, son of Catháir, why was it said of him ? Not hard. In the same battle of Mag Ága a combat took place between him and Assal Échtach son of the champion. Assal wounded Eochaid seriously in the combat, and a wave of foam of the blood of his body came through his battle-garb. Wherefore he is called Eochaid Cupa, ' foam.'

"Ethne Uathach, horrible, why so called ? Easy to say. When the Déissi took the girl to rear her they used to give her the flesh of

[1] This selection of names has been made from *Cóir Anmann* (Irische Texte).

children to eat so that she might the more rapidly grow up (and be married). For it had been determined that they would get land and a settlement as her bride-price. Or, again, she used to cut off the ends of the little-fingers of her own children so that they might be the longer-lived : for at first no children were left to her, (but all died prematurely). For that cause the children felt a great horror for her. Wherefore she is called Ethne the horrible.

"Aed Ordnide, that is, Aed Dorndine, ' suckfist.' He used to suck his fist after he had been weaned. Hence he is called Aed Suckfist.

"Laignech Faelad, that is, he was the man that used to shift into *fáelad*, i.e. wolf-shapes. He and his offspring after him used to go whenever they pleased, into the shapes of the wolves, and after the custom of the wolves, kill the herds. Wherefore he was called Laignech Fáelad, for he was the first of them to go into a wolf-shape.

"Mac Con, whence is it ? Easy to say. There lived a hound named Eloir the red in the house of Ailill bare-ear, when Mac Con was a babe in Ailill's house. Now the babe crept on his hands and knees to seek the hound, and the hound would squeeze the little boy against its belly, and it was impossible to keep him from going to visit the hound. Hence Mac Con, son of the hound, is said.

"Nuada Fullon. Fullon was the name of the druid who reared him, and Fullon was the first druid who cast a spell on a wisp so as to send [thereby] a human being a-flying. Hence *dlui fulla*, madman's wisp, is said by the Irish from that time to this. Or *fullon* is the name for ' beauty '. Hence Nuada Fullon, that is Nuada the beautiful.

"Fiacha Sraibtine, that is, a stream (*sráib*) of fire (*tened*), which was cast into his ships when he was at sea in the eastern world. Or in Dún Sraibtine in Connaught he was reared. Or, again, showers of fire used to come in his reign. Or Fiacha Roibtine, that is rough was he. Fiacha Roibtine then, i.e. Fiacha the Rough. Or Fiacha Srabtine, that is streams (?) of fire used to break out of the red arrows which they had when they burnt the fortress on the Continent in the east. Or

    ' A *sraftine* (helmet) which was anyone's protection
    Mider wore around his face :
    From this is called the king
    Whose name is Fiacha *sraftine* '."

If it is accepted that the ancient inhabitants of Ireland bestowed epithets upon each other in any such manner as our anonymous authority would lead us to believe, it will occasion no surprise to hear that some persons collected a plurality of second names.

"Eogan, son of Mog Néit, had four names, to wit, Eogan Mor, ' great,' Eogan Fidfeccach, ' wood-bending,' Eogan Taidlech, ' splendid,' and Mog Nuadat, ' Nuada's slave ' : whereof the Poet said in the Elucidation."

    ' Four names without grief
    Were on Eogan Mór
    Eogan Fidfeccach, the generous-hospitable,
    Eogan Táidlech, (and) Mog Nuadat.'

" Eogan was his name from parental origin . . . Mór, ' great,' because he was great above every one, and (so were) his children and his kindred after him.

" Eogan Taidlech, ' splendid,' was (also) said of him. Once upon a time Eogan Mór went into Spain on a visit. He who was then king of Spain was Éber the Great, son of Midna. Now Eogan on that journey met with great affection in Spain. The king had then a stately unmarried daughter, named Bera daughter of Éber, and because of the great reports of Eogan she had given him ' love in absence ' before he went into Spain. So then Eogan wedded the maiden, and she bore him noble offspring, even a wondrous son, Aillill Ólumm, and a brace of daughters named Scothnian and Caimell.

" At that time there used to come in every year a lovely vancoloured salmon from the River of the Elements in Paradise to the river Tiber, and from Tiber to the river Ebro in Spain. Thus was that salmon, with a covering of most beautiful wool, and a kind of every colour through it. Now while Eogan was in Spain that salmon was caught by Éber and that woollen covering was stript from it, and that wool was given to Éber's daughter. Now of the covering which had been on the salmon the damsel made for Eogan a splendid shining mantle : and 'tis that mantle which Eogan wore when he came (back) to Ireland. Conn of the Hundred Battles was then in the kingship of Erin. Splendid and shining was the brightness abiding on Eogan from that mantle. Wherefore the name Eogan Táidlech, ' splendid,' clave to him.

" Eogan Fidfeccach, he was (also) called, why was this ? Easy to say. Eogan had three fortresses, and the name of each was Fidfecc. Now Eogan was setting and bending and weaving the wood at each : wherefore he is called Eogan Fidfeccach, from bending (feccad) the wood (fid) in setting it : or Figfecc, from weaving (fige) the same wood.

" Mog Nuadat, whence is it ? Easy to say. Dáire Barrach, son of Catháir Mór, 'tis he that reared Mog Nuadat, that is, Eogan son of Mog Néit. Once upon a time the fortification of Dún Aillinne was undertaken by Dáire Barrach. Now there was then in Erin a famous rath-builder, Nuada Long-heel, son of Oengus, son of Fer dá chrích in the district of Cualnge. In him was the strength of a hundred, and he would eat the fill of fifty. This slave was brought to Dáire to fortify Dún Aillinn. When they were in the trench a-digging it, they came upon a huge stone in the trench, and the slave was unable to raise it. . . . Then Eogan entered the trench, and he alone lifted it up, and hurled it into the southern angle of the fort. . . . Then said the druid to the slave : ' Noble is thy slave to-day, O Nuada ! ' . . . Wherefore Mog Nuadat, ' Nuada's Slave,' clave to Eogan, and from Nuada he was named according to this version." [1]

Now this account was written in the twelfth century ; and while it is evident that the compiler was concerned with ancient epithets or nicknames, yet one cannot help feeling that if hereditary surnames had been in use at the time of writing, as some writers would have us believe, mention would have been

---

[1] *Cóir Anmann.*

made of that fact, and notice taken of the genealogical description " son of Mog Neit ".

Ogams. The earliest contemporary Celtic writings are those in the rectilinear characters known as ogams. The oldest of such records are found sculptured on the edges of the faces of squared stones, and a few are supposed by some authorities to be over 2,000 years old, although other writers consider that the earliest examples do not date back further than the beginning of the christian era, and that they were not erected by pagans. These monumental records have been found in Scotland, Ireland, Wales, and Cornwall, that is, those parts in which the Gaels and Cymry settled, and form a permanent record of Celtic names of great antiquity.

The inscriptions have been carefully examined, deciphered, and translated, but authorities being often in disagreement, the transliterations suffer, like the annals, in being open to suspicion.[1] A few stones are biliteral; such a one is that found in the Killeen Cormac cemetery at Colbinstown, co. Kildare, the inscription, transliteration, and translation, according to Macalister,[2] being as follows :—

Ogam :   ··· III · IIIII ·· IIII · III ····· ····· III ·   IIII . III III ..   IIII

Transliteration : **U V A N O S A V I I V A C A T T O S**

Roman :   **I V V E   E D R V V I D E S**

Translation : Ogam : [Stone] of Uvan, grandson of Ivacatt. Roman : Ivve[n]e, son of Drui.

With regard to the Roman inscription it may be noted that the capital R has no special signification. Brash's illustration shows that the letters gradually increase up to the R, and the remainder are gradually reduced, the final S being about equal to the initial I.[3] Macalister considers that DRVVIDES signifies " son of Drui ", where -*ides* is equivalent to -*gnos*, a suffix used as a method of expressing filiation in some Gaulish inscriptions (see above, p. 29).

As an example of the difference of opinion which prevails among Celtic scholars it may be mentioned that Shearman, followed by Stokes, from a different reading of the ogmic inscription transliterated it DUFTANO SAFEI SAHATTOS,

[1] J. F. Shearman, in *Proc. of the Royal Irish Academy*, vol. ix, p. 253 ; and *Journal of the Royal Hist. and Arch. Assoc. of Ireland*, 1873, 4th ser., vol. ii, p. 544 et seq. *Christian Inscriptions in the Irish Language*, 1878, ed. by M. Stokes, vol. ii, p. 2, and illustrated, pl. i ; *The Ogam inscribed Monuments of the Gaedhil*, by R. R. Brash, 1879, p. 308, and illustrated, pl. xl ; *Ogham Inscriptions in Ireland, Wales, and Scotland*, by Sir S. Ferguson, 1887, p. 70 ; *Studies in Irish Epigraphy*, by R. A. S. Macalister, 1897, pt. i, p. 78.
[2] *Studies*, etc., vol. i, pp. 9 and 78.
[3] *The Ogam inscribed Monuments*, p. 310.

i.e. the stone of Dustan the wise sage. Brash made the inscription to be :—

··· ⫶⫶⫶ ˙ ⫶⫶⫶⫶⫶ ˙˙ ⫶⫶⫶⫶ ˙ ⫶⫶⫶ ···· ····· ⫶⫶⫶⫶ ˙   **I . III III ..**   ⫶⫶⫶⫶

UFANOSAF E I SAHATTOS
IV VE[R]E DRVVIDES

"Ufano, Safei, Sah and Attos, four just druids," which seems to be a not improbable interpretation. Dr. S. Ferguson also considered that the Latin inscription should be read in this manner.[1] J. Rhys supplies the transliteration UWANOS AWI EWACATTOS and gives the Latin version as IVVENE DRVVIDES for IVVENES DRVVIDES, to be construed in the genitive as meaning Lapis Sepulcralis Juvenis Druidis (*es* is an occasional form of the gen. ending *is*).[2]

The following selection of names consists of examples of readings given by Macalister :—

In the genitive[3] : Broinionas, Isini, Denaveq, Vitalin, Marin, Brocc, Feqreq, Toicaci, Vuruddrann.

In the dative : Vedacu, Manu, Amadu.

A nominative form from the Isle of Man is Maqleog.

A striking difference between Irish names as obtained from the Chronicles and from the stones is that the latter are free from the fanciful epithets or nicknames, and the only form of additional description is the genealogical. Examples : Eracobi maqi Eragetai, Maile-Inbri maci Brocanuni, Doveti maqqi Cattini, all words being in the genitive case.

Maqvas "son", later *maq*, became in the genitive *maqi*, *maic*, *mic* ; descent from a grandfather being indicated by *avi*, as Maqi-Decceddas avi Toranias (all gen.). *Avi*, in O.Ir. *aue*, became *ua* and *o*, and has had a great influence in the formation of Irish surnames, of which so many commence with O'. Macalister states that " it may be taken as invariable that when two *maqi's* are found consecutively in one inscription that the second is the initial member of the following name : compare Trenagusu maqi Maqi Treni at Pembroke with the associated Latin Trenegussi fili Macu-Treni ".[4] Have we here the origin of the Irish surnames in Mac. ?

Irish Surnames. The native historians consider that family names came into use, in obedience to an ordinance of Brian Boru, early in the eleventh century, but the sole evidence is a fragment of a manuscript supposed to be part of the life

---

[1] *Proc. of the Royal Irish Academy*, vol. i, ser. 2, No. 4, p. 32.
[2] *Lectures on Welsh Philology*, 1877, p. 214.
[3] For forms of genitives see Macalister, pt. i, p. 13 et seq.
[4] p. 10. For the important word *muco* and its meaning also see Macalister.

of Brian. " It was during his time surnames were first given (*is ri a linn tucad sloinnte ar tus*)." [1]
Woulfe (1923), the most recent writer, assigns an even earlier date to the first adoption of hereditary surnames :—

" Ó Cléirigh was probably a fixed surname as early as the beginning of the 10th century, for we find the death of Tighearnach Ua Cléirigh, lord of Aidhne, recorded in the *Annals of the Four Masters* at the year 916, and that of his brother Flann Ua Cléirigh, lord of South Connacht, who was slain by the men of Munster, at the year 950. I doubt if we have any older surname in Europe." [2]

Instances of surnames which became fixed before Brian Boru began his reign are given as Mac Egan, O'Cahill of Ui Fiachrach, O'Doherty, O'Donnell of Tirconaill, O'Gallagher, O'Heyne, O'Keeffe, O'Scanlan of Ui Fiachrach, O'Sullivan, and O'Toole, but, on the other hand, Woulfe says that " many others as MacCarthy of Desmond, MacMurrough of Leinster, MacNamara of Thomond, O'Byrne, O'Callaghan, O'Dea, O'Donoghue of Desmond, O'Dugan of Fermoy, O'Melaghlen of Meath, O'Molloy of Feara Ceall, and O'Shaughnessy, cannot have become fixed until long after Brian had been laid to rest at Armagh ".

The proof of the antiquity of any surname cannot be deemed absolute without a confirmatory pedigree, and in view of the great interest on this point it is unfortunate that Woulfe provides no genealogical support of his claim, nor does he, in fact, cite any source where such might be found. The twelfth-century Cóir Anmann would surely have given some indication of the prevalence of surnames had they been recognized. O'Hart (1887) in his hundreds of Irish pedigrees has no suggestion that the early Irish had surnames or even perpetuated a second name ; and it is difficult to believe that Tighearnach and Flann, both described as descendants of Cléirigh, could be said to have possessed a surname any more than " James and John the sons of Zebedee ".[3]

A system of second names, borne in common with other persons, was in use in Ireland at an early date, and are known as clan names, but they have no connection with family names, although some of them have become such. O'Donovan says that these tribal names were formed from those of ancestors, by prefixing a word as *cinel* " kindred ", " race ",

---

[1] *Topographical Poems of John O'Dubhagain*, by John O'Donovan, 1862, p. 9.

[2] It may be mentioned that great antiquity is claimed for family names in China, where they are traced back 2,000 to 3,000 years. *China Review*, xiii (1884–5), p. 124. The Japanese have family names of two kinds *kabane* and *uji*, which are placed first. As early as A.D. 815 a record of surnames was published (T. Harada).

[3] Mark, x, 35 ; Luke, v, 10.

" descendants " ; *clann* "children ", " race ", " descendants " ;
corc, corca " race ", " progeny " ; *dal* " tribe ", " progeny " ;
muintir " family ", " people " ; *siol* " seed ", " progeny " ;
sliocht " progeny " ; *tealach* " family " ; *ua* " grandson ",
" descendant " (plural *ui* ; dat. or abl. *uibh*). Regarding the
latter O'Donovan says : " this word, which is evidently cognate
with the Greek *viós, filius*, appears in the names of Irish
tribes more frequently than any of the preceding terms, as
Ui-Neill ' the descendants of Niall '. Some have supposed
Ui to signify ' land ' or ' territory ', but erroneously, as
appears from the *Vita Columbæ*, where *ua, ui, uibh* is rendered
nepos, nepotes, nepotibus." [1]

Early Cymric Names in Britain. It has been mentioned
that some historians hold that the Gaels occupied Britain
before the coming of the Celts,[2] but it is generally admitted
that by the time Roman interest in these islands was actively
aroused, the main spoken language was Cymric. The population
is unknown, but may be put at less than a million, and after
the Norman Conquest the free Cymry in Wales alone would
be not more than one-tenth to one-fifth of that number.

The principal sources available for the collection of early
Cymric names, apart from monumental inscriptions, are the
Mabinogion, twelfth century, the Triads of Arthur,[3] Iolo MSS.,
Brut y Tywysogion (Rolls Ser. 17), the Book of Llan dâv,[4]
Myvyrian Archaiology,[5] and ancient pedigrees.

The names on ogmic stones in Wales are said to be Gaelic,
in fact, Brash claims " that the entire list of pre-historic
names recorded by the Welsh bards are purely Goedelic ".[6]
Rhys (1879) was equally certain to the contrary : " The
reasoning which seems to have led to the conclusion that our
early inscriptions are Irish will not for one moment bear
examination." [7] At one time, of course, the most ancient
names of Welsh and Irish were identical, as was the language ;
and as words have survived, common to both tongues, so
did some personal names, as will be more particularly
illustrated later.[8] Very ancient names, therefore, may have
the appearance of being of either language, but whether
Irish or Welsh they are latinized in inscriptions, and not
always correctly : e.g. Catacus . . . filius Tegernacus
(Llanfihangel, Brecknock). In some names no inflection is

---

[1] See also " Early Irish Population Groups," by J. MacNeill : *Proc. of the Royal Irish Academy*, vol. xxix, sec. C.
[2] See p. 12. Brash cites the evidence of chroniclers (*Ogam inscribed Monuments*, ch. xvii).
[3] *Four Ancient Books of Wales*, by W. F. Skene, 1868, vol. ii, p. 457.
[4] From the Gwysaney MS., ed. by J. G. Evans and J. Rhys, 1893.
[5] Owen Jones, 1870.   [6] *Ogam inscribed Monuments*, p. 382.
[7] *Lectures on Welsh Philology*, pp. 154 et seq.
[8] p. 358.

apparent : Catgug f(il)ius Gideo (Wareham, Dors.), Margeteud f(ilius) Ecettey (Carew, Pembrokeshire).[1]

Classification of Cymric Personal Names. Like the Irish, Cymric personal names may be divided, according to form and construction, into three main classes :—

1. *Dithematic or Compounded.* The elements or themes forming compound names may be (i) two nouns, as Cadwaladyr " war-chief " (*cad* " battle " : *gwaladr*) ; (ii) a noun preceded by a qualifying adjective, as Gryffyd (*cref* " strong " : *fydd* " faith "), Gwen-llian (*gwyn* " white " : *llian* " linen ") ; or followed by the adjective, as Pen-wyn " fair-headed " (*pen* " head " : *gwyn* " fair "), Bran-wen (*bron* " bosom ").

2. *Monothematic or Uncompounded.* Names with a single original element, that is, not being reduced forms of compounded names : (i) adjectives, as Eniawn " upright " (*uniawn*), Uthyr (*uthr* " awful "), Meredydd (occurs formerly as Margeteud, now Meredith : *mawreddog* " magnificent ") ; (ii) nouns, as Enaid " soul ", " life ", Gwynach (*gwynaeth*, f. " felicity ", " bliss "), Budic (*buddug*, f. " the victorious one "). The single element names are indistinguishable from diminished forms of compounds, and may, of course, be nothing more than abbreviations.

3. *Derivatives.* One subclass of derivatives consists of names formed from nouns, adjectives, or other names, or single elements, by the addition of affixes, such as *ec* or *oc* (Mod. W. *awg, og*), e.g. Caradoc (*Caradawg* " abounding in love "). Other affixes noted on inscriptions are -*agn*-, -*egn*-, -*on*-, -*ic*-, -*iv*-, etc.[2] Another subclass consists of names to which are added diminutive suffixes : Bleddyn " a wolf's cub " (*blaidd* " a wolf "), Gwendol-en (*gwendal* " fair fronted "), Cad-og, from Cadwallaon.

Many of the ancient British names are now entirely disused, such as Gwyndeg, Saithenyn, Gwrtherin (a prince of Rome), Tybiawn, Arwystl, Ceredig, Dunawd, Edeyrn, Mael, Dogvael, Rhufawn, etc.

Examples of tenth or eleventh-century Celtic names of Cornwall from the manumissions in the Bodmin Gospels are : Arganteilin " silver-elbow ", Budic " victorious ", Catgustel " battle hostage ", Catuutic " battle victorious ", and others of which the signification is obscure : Dengel, Ewsannec, Gaudreit, Grantcant, Guenguiu (f.), Guentanet, Gurient, Iarnwallon, Leumarch, Moruiw, Oncenedl, Tancwuestel, Wuenumon, etc.[3] These names are very similar to Breton

---

[1] *Inscriptiones Britanniae Christianae*, ed. A. Hubner, 1876, Nos. 35, 32, 96.
[2] *Lectures on Welsh Philology*, by J. Rhys, 1879, p. 359.
[3] B.M. Add. MS. 9067 : Printed in *Codex Diplomaticus Ævi Saxonici*, vol. iv, pp. 308–17, and W. Stokes in *Revue Celtique*, vol. i, p. 338.

appellatives of the same period, some examples of which are given below on page 78.

With the spread of biblical knowledge alien names were introduced, David and John (Jevan or Evan), in particular, gaining an immense and lasting popularity.

Originally names were compounded of words to give a common-sense signification, but reversal of themes similar to that noticed in Sanskrit and Greek appellatives may, nevertheless, be found. A Carmarthenshire inscription, for instance, commemorates Barrivendi son of Vendubari.[1]

The meaning of some names is very uncertain, e.g. Gwladys is said variously to signify " princess " or " lame ".

Like the Romance languages Welsh has lost the distinctive endings of the cases. An interesting grammatical feature which has left its mark on Welsh and Cornish surnames is the sound-change known as mutation, being an assimilation with the object of economizing effort in pronunciation. By this process the noun or adjective following a proper noun undergoes soft mutation of the initial consonant, thus in Welsh *p* becomes *b*, *t* becomes *d*, *c* becomes *g*, *b* becomes *f*, *d* becomes *dd*, *ll* becomes *l*, *m* becomes *f*, and *rh* becomes *r*. Some notes on Cornish mutation will be found on p. 379.

It is to be gathered from the Mabinogion that a change of name was not looked upon as unusual ; thus, in the tale of Pwyll, prince of Dyved, a lost boy was called by his guardian Gwri *wallt euryn*, because his hair was as yellow as gold, but on being returned to his parents, and his mother, who was doing penance for his loss, thankfully saying that it was an end to her trouble (*pryderi*). " Pryderi," said Pendaran (the Bard), " shall his name be." " It were more proper," said Pwyll, " that the boy should take his name from the word his mother spoke when she received the joyful tidings of him." [2]

It seems to have been a common proceeding on the part of the Bards and Druids to change a person's name on the spur of the moment : but in this case it is not clear whether it was the first or second name, or the whole double appellative which was altered. Cadwaladr Uendigeit (*bendigaid* " the blessed ") is said to have had his second distinction changed to the somewhat discreditable title Catguommedd " the man who would not fight ".[3]

In a few instances persons named in lapidary inscriptions have additional descriptions, as in the Llandyssilio (Pemb.) stone : Clutorigi fili Paulini Marinilatio, which in modern Welsh would be *Clodri fab Peulin Merynllyd*.[4]

[1] *Celtic Britain*, by J. Rhys, 1904, p. 319.
[2] *The Mabinogion* (Guest, 1849), vol. iii, p. 69.
[3] *History of Wales*, by B. B. Woodward, p. 140.
[4] *Inscribed Stones of Wales*, by J. Rhys, p. 7.

Additional Descriptions of the Cymry. Old British names do not provide us with the wealth of vivid imagery which has been noticed among the fanciful appellatives of the Irish, nevertheless the Cymry found the advantage of secondary descriptions, which like those of the Irish may be classified under four main heads: Characteristic, Local, Genealogical, and Occupational.

Characteristic: By far the greatest class consists of personal epithets, which may refer to the bearer's appearance, as Meruyn Urych (*brych* " the freckled "), d. 844, *Brut*; Maelawc Cam, i.e. Maelog " the crooked ", d. 904, *Brut*; Rys Voel " the bald " (*Myv. Arch.*, p. 263); or to the character of a person, such as: Rhodri Mawr (the great), d. 917, *Brut*; Rhodri Molwynog (*moelwynoc* " passionate "), d. 754, *Brut*; Howel Da (the good), d. 948, *Brut*; Madawg Ddrud (*drud* " the bold "), *Myv. Arch.*, p. 59; Rhys Gryg (*cryg* " harsh "), *Myv. Arch.*, p. 257; Aedan Uradawc (*vradog* " the treacherous ") [1]; Ryderch Hael " the generous " [2]; Gweir Gwrhyt Uawr (Gweir of great manliness), Triads.[3] Physical attributes might be perpetuated, such as: Benlli Gawr (*cawr* " giant "), Skene, i, 318; Charadawc Ureichuras (Caradoc " thick arm "), Triads [4]; or possessions might be noted: Eliffer Gosgorduawr (of the great retinue), Skene, ii, 454; Gwgawn Cledyfrud (*cleddyf* " sword ", *rhudd* " ruddy "), Triads [5]; cf. Etlym gleddyf coch, *Mab.* i, 382; Osla Gyllelvawr (the great knife), *Mab.* iii, 433; Angharad Law-eurawc (golden hand), *Mab.* i, 378; Pudarn Pesrut (" with the crimson coat ": *pais* " coat ", *rhudd* " crimson "). The condition or quality of a person also gave rise to epithets, as Sawyl Penuchel " pre-eminent " (*uchel*), Skene, ii, 454; Rys Ieuangc (the younger), *Myv. Arch.*, p. 257; Helen Luiedauc " the prosperous " (*llwydd* " prosperity "), *Triads*.[6] Strangers were dubbed with their nationality, as: Rein Yscot (the Scot), *Brut*; Serigi Wyddel (the Irishman), *Iolo MSS.*; and metaphorical and fanciful names were common: Idwal Iwrch " the roe-buck ", d. 773, *Brut*; Lles Lleuvermawr (the great light), Woodward; Chynan Genhir (*gên* " life ", *hir* " long "), Skene, ii, 454; Pabo Post Prydein (the pillar of Prydein), Skene, ii, 454; Dinwaed Uaglawc (*ffaglog* " blazing "), *Triads*.[7]

Local: Descriptions from place-names occur rarely as: Pendaran Dyved (a principality in South Wales), *Triads* [8]; Tutuwlch Cornue (of Cornwall), Skene, ii, 454; Clydno Eidin (of Eidin), Skene, ii, 454. It may be mentioned that one of the legendary genealogies endeavours to convey the impression

---

[1] Skene (cited), vol. ii, pp. 455–65.   [2] Ibid.   [3] Ibid.   [4] Ibid.
[5] Ibid.   [6] Ibid.   [7] Ibid.   [8] Ibid.

that princes gave their personal names to their lands, and then retook them as additions, e.g. Meirion called his territory Meirionydd, and became known as Meirion of Meirionydd ; Mael named his lands Maelienydd, and was himself called Mael of Maelienydd, and so on ; but the story is not to be relied upon. That there was a precedent for the adoption of local names appears from C. Julius Cæsar, who noted that the maritime portion of Britain was inhabited by those who had passed over from the country of the Belgae, " almost all of whom are called by the names of those states from which being sprung they went thither." [1]

Genealogical : The commonest form of description in this class is that specifying the filial relationship, as Geraint *mab* Erbin (Triads).[2] *Map* is equivalent to the Irish *mac*, both formerly being *maqv-i*, and is found as *vap*, *mab*, *fab*, etc., and later still as *ap* and *ab*. The word was very often latinized, as Concenn *filius* Catteli, Catteli *filius* Brohcmail, etc. (from the pillar of Eliseg). The word *eil* or *ail* " second " was also used in a similar sense to *map*, as Cadwallawn eil Cadfan " Cadwallon second in succession to Cadvan ", i.e. Cadvan was his father ; Morvran eil Tegid " Mirvran the son of Tegid ".

Occupational : Descriptions of this category have not been noticed, unless perhaps some of the kings' titles may be so classified : e.g. Maxen Wledic (*gulad* " ruler ") ; others were variously dubbed Arglwydd " lord ", Feiniard " judge ", Teirnoe " sovereign ", and Ynad " judge ".

In some cases these secondary descriptions were probably the inventions of the bards and bestowed posthumously. There was nothing of the nature of family names in use among the Britons, and the necessity even for additional descriptions was small, owing to the native method of reciting genealogy backwards for half a dozen generations or so, which pedigree system of description was doubtless occasioned by the ancient tribal customs and laws of family relationship wherein the exact blood tie was a factor of such importance that, in some cases, it was necessary that the grade of kinship should be known for nine generations.[3] The following extract, which has been selected to illustrate the two methods of secondary description, is taken from a thirteenth-century transcript of the Bonhed Gwyr y Gogledd (genealogies of the Men of the North, i.e. Cumbrian and Strathclyde Britons).

" Clydno Eidin a (*and*) Chynan Genhir a Chynuelyn Drwsgyl a Chatrawt Calchuynyd meibon (*sons*) Kynnwyt Kynnwydyon mab (*son*) Kynuelyn mab Arthwys mab Mar mab Keneu mab Coel." [4]

---

[1] *Commentaries*, bk. v, c. 12.   [2] Skene (cited), vol. ii, pp. 455–65.
[3] See the *Tribal System in Wales*, by F. Seebohm, 1904, ch. iii.
[4] Hengwrt MS. 536 : *Four Ancient Books of Wales*, by W. F. Skene, 1868, vol. ii, p. 454.

In Rome the British are known to have adopted the
" surname ",[1] and no doubt in some cases under Roman
influence in this country, but with the departure of the legions,
they must have reverted to the native system of nomenclature.

Roman Names in Britain.   Roman towns, forts, walls,
and roads remained in Britain, but their laws, arts, language,
religion, together with their system of nomenclature, completely vanished with their legions, but this introductory
account of early names of the British Isles would be
incomplete without a brief reference to the comparatively
elaborate method which must have been prevalent among the
ruling classes of England during the first four centuries of
the christian era.

The Romans at first had but one name, such as Romulus,
Remus, Curtius, Tacita, etc., but later they followed the
system of their more advanced neighbours,[2] and adopted
second names, as Numa Pompilius, Hostus Hostilius, Ancus
Marcius, etc.   Afterwards, with division into clans and families,
and the desire for further distinction and possibly greater
importance in the eyes of the public, they used three classes
of names, called the prænomen (the forename), the nomen
(name), and the cognomen (surname).   The prænomen or
forename, like our christian name, marked the individual,
as Marcus, Gaius ; the nomen or nomen gentilium the gens,
clan, or tribe, as Tullius, Julius ; and the cognomen, the
family, as Cicero, Cæsar.   A plurality of names became common,
and we find such multipartite examples as Marcus Tullius
Cicero, or Gaius Julius Cæsar.   Sometimes a fourth name
called the agnomen was added, and such an appellative might
be derived from some illustrious deed, thus Publius Cornelius
Scipio received the additional distinction of Africanus, from
his conquest of Africa,[3] or the final addition might be a name
retained for identification when assuming the names of another
family, thus Octavius, when adopted by Cæsar, received the
names of Caius Julius Cæsar Octavianus.[4]

The prænomen was given eight or nine days after birth, and
one only was used, being chosen for its appropriate significance,
as Salverte observes, " to indicate whether a child had been
born in its parents' old age, or while he was far away on a
voyage (Proculus), or after the father's death, but during the
grandfather's life (Opiter), or at a stranger's house and far
from home (Hostus)." [5]   Repetition of prænomina in one family

---

[1] *History of the Names of Men*, by A. J. E. Baconniere-Salverte, translated
by L. H. Mordacque, 1862, vol. i, p. 134.
[2] The Etruscans had three names.   (J. B. Passeri, *Dissertation*, 1767.)
[3] According to A. Gilman (Rome, 1887, p. 15), " Lucius, of the Cornelian
family and of the particular branch of the Scipios who won fame in Africa."
[4] Baconniere-Salverte, vol. i, p. 138.   [5] Ibid., p. 120.

was common among the Romans, as it became with our
christian names down till the nineteenth century, the eldest
son perpetuating the name of the father, the second son that
of a near relative. Sometimes, even, two or more brothers
were given the same prænomen, as, for instance, the two
brothers Metellus, the contemporaries of Cicero, or the three
sons of Caius Julius, who all bore the forename of their
father.[1]

The nomen, the second name in order, was an adjective
signifying the clan to which a person belonged, sometimes,
writes Freese, a kind of patronymic, as Julius from Julus, or
a local name as Norbanus, Acceranus. Nearly all ended in
-ius (-æus, -eius, -eus) ; -acus (Divitiacus) is peculiar to Gallic :
-na (Cæcina, Pomperna) to Etruscan ; -enus (Arulenus) to
Umbrian names. Verres as a gentile name stands by itself ;
perhaps it was originally a cognomen.[2]

Nomen and prænomen, jointly being found insufficient
to express the distinction required, the next step was the
introduction of the cognomen, an epithet distinguishing one
branch of the gens from another, which often became the
family name of the direct descendants of the first bearer.[3] These
descriptions or cognomina fall into four classes : (i)
Characteristic, describing peculiarity, as Cato (from catus
" wary " or " subtle ", also " sagacious "), Sapiens " wise ",
Scævolo " left-handed ", Crassus " fat " ; Funarius, a cognomen
of Gratianus, is equivalent to funalis equus " a trace-horse ",
so called because of his great strength ; Nigrinus " swarthy ",
Pætus " blink-eyed ", Parra " owl ", perhaps ; Mucco, from
mucus, " dirty-nose " ; Marcellus, a family name in the
plebeian gens Claudia, is a diminutive derived from the
prænomen Marcus, signifying " a large hammer ". (ii) Local,
as Tarquinius, the fifth king of Rome, who came from
Tarquinia in Etruria ; Coriolanus, the cognomen of Caius
Marcius, because he destroyed Corioli. (iii) Genealogical :
Agrippa, being both prænomen and cognomen, seems to provide
an example of this class. (iv) Occupational, as Metellus, a
cognomen in the gens Cæcilia, meaning " a hired servant " ;
Missor, a cognomen occurring on an inscription, signifying
" an archer ".

If Camden is to be believed, names were given by the
Romans to commemorate the most trivial and ridiculous
events. " Tremelius was called Scropha or Sow, because when
he hid his neighbour's sow under a pad, and commanded his
wife to lie down thereon, he swore when the owner came in

---

[1] Baconniere-Salverte, p. 127. Similar cases will be noted in English
families.
[2] J. F. Freese, in Encycl. Brit. (1910), art. " Names ".
[3] Baconniere-Salverte, vol. i, p. 131.

to seek the sow that he had no sow but the great sow that lay there, pointing to the pad, and the sow, his wife. So one Cornelius was surnamed Asina, for that when he was put in assurance for payment of certain sums in a purchase, he brought his ass laden with money, and made ready payment." [1] Perhaps it is as well that the Roman system of nomenclature did not become an established feature in our social life.

The hereditary cognomen was followed by the *cognomen secundum* or agnomen (fourth century), an individual name, and there being no law regulating the adoption of names, the custom of taking these additional appellatives ran to a ridiculous extreme, as it has during the last century among the upper classes in this country. Freese states that as many as thirty-six names occur on one inscription. Names were frequently indicated on monuments by initial letters,[2] as M. Tullius M. f. M.n. M.pr. Cor. Cicero, that is Marcus Tullius, Marci filius, Marci nepos, Marci pronepos, Cornelia [tribu] Cicero.[3] *Cognomentum* is an equivalent for *cognomen*, and a nickname or sobriquet was sometimes termed *nomen contumeliosum* or *ignominosium* (reproachful and ignominious).

Foreigners, upon obtaining Roman citizenship, were given the prænomen and nomen of the person by whose means they were granted the privilege, and they often added their native proper name as cognomen, thus Archias, the poet, who received citizenship from Lucullus (Licinius), became A. Licinius Archias.[4] A Gaul was named M. Antonius Gniphon (*gnif*, W. " toil ", " trouble ", *onn* " ash " : metaphorically " fighting lance or ash ").[5]

With the commencement of the christian era the wave of extravagant personal nomenclature had passed, and by the time the occupation of Britain was completed, persons vaunting an excessive number of names were few. Although the native Briton, with his cumbersome method of genealogical identification, could scarcely have considered the Roman system by comparison unwieldy, yet it took no permanent hold nor apparently had any influence, and died out with the last of the legions in A.D. 409 (Zosimus). Some of the Romans, such as Maximus Wledic, were satisfied apparently even with British names.

Conclusions. In the brief analysis of the personal names of the Indo-European group, which has been attempted in the above pages, two features stand out prominently, and are most deserving of notice and emphasis. It has been shown in the

---

[1] *Remaines*, 1870, p. 145.
[2] *Œuvres de Mons. Boindon*, 1753, vol. ii, pp. 103 et seq.
[3] J. F. Freese, in *Encycl. Brit.* (1910).
[4] Baconniere-Salverte, vol. i, p. 133.
[5] Ibid.

first place, that the general system of forming personal names was by compounding words, there being, however, an increasing tendency to shorten the resulting dithematic appellative by dropping a component and turning the remaining first or second element into a diminutive or pet-name. In later chapters it will be demonstrated that this practice, followed by all the races contributing to the nomenclature of the British Isles, has had a great influence in multiplying the variants of our genealogical surnames.

A second point of importance is the growing custom of identifying the individual by a description or address additional to his personal name ; and such secondary distinctions fall according to derivation into four classes : (i) Characteristic, answering the question—What is his personal peculiarity ? (ii) Local, answering—Where is or was he located ? (iii) Genealogical, answering—Who is his most important kinsman ? (iv) Occupational, answering—What is his vocation ? This system of classification serves adequately for the secondary names of all the races of the British Isles, but the most popular class of epithet among the later Celtic group was the genealogical, as will be made apparent in further chapters. These descriptive epithets are of great importance to the subject under consideration in this essay, as they are the forerunners of the modern surname or family name.

The extravagant system of naming prevalent with the Romans was decaying at the time of the subjugation of Britain, and even the more moderate method which remained, attained no permanence in this country, and may be dismissed from further consideration.

In the next chapter a further stage will be reached in this historical account of British family names, by consideration of the early Teutonic and Scandinavian names of Britain.

CHAPTER III

Early Gothonic Personal Names and Descriptions in Britain

Early Alien Influence. As briefly recalled in the opening chapter, the Teutons ultimately overcame the Celts in the greater part of England, resulting in the various dialects of the Ænglisc tongue superseding the Cymric, and the perishing of the native names in England.

The population of England, during the Roman period, has been estimated at about 750,000,[1] and by the time of the Norman conquest it had doubled.[2] The increase, slow as it was, must not be put down entirely to the propagation of Cymry and Saxon, the inflow of other races had already commenced, adding to the population, and to the variety of our languages and our names.

Asser mentions that " Franci autem multi Frisones, Galli, Pagani, Britones et Scoti, Armorici ", both nobles and persons of low degree, submitted to the rule of Alfred (ninth century).[3] The Franks and Frisians were the principal merchants of Western Europe, and considerable commerce was carried on by them with the Anglo-Saxons, who required manufactured articles and technical workmanship, which could not be obtained in England. Another great factor in the introduction of alien names into Britain was the considerable religious intercourse, which commenced with the arrival of Augustine and his companions in A.D. 596, and was maintained largely by the activity of foreign monks. It is manifest, therefore, that in any extensive list of English names, even at this early date, some may be alien. The great influence of the Norsemen, who themselves brought Frisians to the country, will be mentioned towards the end of this chapter.

Anglo-Saxon Personal Names. The researches of Turner (1799–1852),[4] Kemble (1846), Birch (1885),[5] and Searle (1897) have provided foundation for an inquiry into the nature of Anglo-Saxon (Old English) personal names.[6]

---

[1] *British History*, by John Wade, 3rd ed., p. 6.
[2] *Rise and Progress of the English Constitution*, by Sir E. Creasy, 1907, p. 57. The author refers to various estimates of from a million to two millions.
[3] *De Rebus gestis Ælfredi.*
[4] *History of the Anglo-Saxons*, by Sharon Turner, 1852, 7th ed., vol. iii.
[5] *Cartularium Saxonicum*, by W. de G. Birch, 1885–93.
[6] In compiling these notes I have availed myself freely of the valuable observations on O.E. nomenclature made by Kemble, Turner, Searle, and Redin.

That the Anglo-Saxon parents gave names to their infants at birth or baptism is evidenced by several tenth-century charters, which record that the persons named had been so called by will of " their parents " from the cradle and " not from accident ".[1] Every one of these designations, like those of other Indo-European races, originally had a signification, sometimes personally descriptive, as Mucel " large " ; often metaphorical, as Æðelwulf " noble wolf " ; prophetic, as Eadwig " prosperity in war " ; or entirely fanciful, as Heahstan " lofty rock ". These names are not always translatable, owing to corruption, apocopation, or scribal error, and possibly, in some cases, to the language not being identifiable. A few examples, representative of many others, will illustrate the main characteristics of Old English names.

BOYS

Ælfred : *ælf*, m.f. " elf " ; *ráed*, m. " counsel ".

Beorhtwulf : *beorht*, adj. " noble " ; *wulf*, m. " wolf ".

Dunstan : *dunn*, adj. " brown " ; *stán*, m. " rock ".

Ceolmund : *céol*, m. " ship " ; *mund*, f. " protection ".

Eadric : *éad*, n. " prosperity " ; *ríce*, adj. " rich ".

Hereberht : *here*, m. " army " ; *beorht*, adj. " bright ".

Leofsige : *léof*, adj. " beloved " ; *sige*, m. " victory ".

Osbeald : *ós*, m. " a god " ; *beald*, adj. " strong ".

Rædwine : *ráed*, m. " counsel " ; *wine*, m. " friend ".

GIRLS

Ælfgiva : *ælf*, m.f. " elf " ; *giefu*, f. " favour ".

Æðelswið : *æðel* " noble " ; *swið*, adj. " strong ".

Deorwynn : *deor*, adj. " dear " ; *wynn*, f. " delight ".

Gislðryð : *gisl*, m. " hostage " ; *ðryð*, f. " strength ".

Heahburh : *heah*, adj. " high " or " haughty " ; *burh*, f. " castle ".

Wulfðryð : *wulf*, m. " wolf " ; *ðryð*, f. " strength ".

There is no certainty about the translations; each element of a compound has often many meanings, so that a considerable range of significations may be found. Sometimes a sensible interpretation is not readily discovered, as Wulfstan " wolf-rock " or " wolf-stone ", and it is to be inferred that the idea conveyed by these compound names was of small importance.[2]

Even slaves appear to have had figurative and flowery names, as, for instance, Sæðryð, which may be rendered " sea-power " or " glory " ; in fact, the bondmen appear to have retained fanciful appellations longer than their overlords.

---

[1] Brit. Mus., Cott. MS., Claud. B. vi, pp. 34, 62, etc. *KCD.*, vol. v, Nos. 1164, 1215, " qui ab incunabulis suæ infantilitatis, non fortuitu sed uoluntate parentum, nomen accepit Wulfric."

[2] *English Place Name Society.*, vol. i, pt. i, p. 168. A. S. Ellis thought that a name like Bern-ulf was so constructed as to indicate a descent from the Bernings and the Ulfings (*Yorks. Arch. Journal*, 1879, vol. v, p. 291).

A certain number of the names found in the O.E. records
which are not translatable may be corrupt forms, possibly
of Cymric or Pictish designations ; in which connection Kemble
has mentioned Puch, Pechthelm, Padda, Oiddi, Maban,
Uelhisc, Pehthat, Pehthætius, Cynyath, Theabul [1] ; and
Searle gives a longer list.[2] Numerous foreign names—Norse,
Frankish, Frisian, Flemish, and so on—also add to difficulty
of recognition,[3] and identification is so uncertain that it is
improbable even the philologists would come to any
agreement on the point.

Classification of Personal Names. Fick concluded that
the German name-system exceeded in splendour and completeness others of the Aryan group, although superseded by
the Sanskrit in brilliant transparency, and by the Greek in
proportionate beauty.[4] Old English names, however, like
Sanskrit, Gaelic, and Welsh, may be conveniently placed
according to form and construction into three classes.[5]

1. *Dithematic or Compounded.* The majority of O.E. personal
names consist of two themes or members, mostly monosyllabic,
which components may be (i) two nouns, as Wulf-helm ;
(ii) two adjectives, as Æðel-heah ; or (iii) an adjective and
noun, as Æðel-stan.[6] As has been noticed with Sanskrit
names, certain of the vocables may be employed as either
first or second member of the compound, others are found only
as the initial element, and others, again, are reserved for the
final member. Examples of exclusive protothemes are :
Æðel-, Cúð-, Cyne-, Éad-, Ós- ; and exclusive deuterothemes :
-lác, -láf, -gifu, -waru, the second member being usually of
the same gender as that of the person, but there are occasional
exceptions, as Eadmund (*mund*, f.). A neuter noun cannot
supply the final element. Components usable either as first
or second elements are common, as Daeg, Héah, Sige, Wulf,
and as with Sanskrit names inversion of themes is not rare,
thus we may find Bealdric and Ricbeald, Beorhtwulf and
Wulfbeorht, etc. Repetition of the same element to form a

---

[1] " The Names, Surnames, and Nicnames of the Anglo-Saxons " (*Proc.
Arch. Inst.*, 1846), p. 85 n.

[2] *Onomasticon Anglo-Saxonicum*, p. xxix.

[3] The Celtic element in early English personal names has received notice
in *Keltisches Wortgut im Englischen*, by Max Förster (*Festschrift Liebermann*) :
the Old German influence has been investigated by T. Forssner (*Continental-
Germanic Personal Names in England*) : and our Scandinavian names have
been inquired into by E. Björkman (*Nordische Personennahmen in England*).

[4] " Das indische Namensystem welches uns noch zu betrachten übrig
bleibt, übertrifft alle seine Verwandten an glänzender Durchsichtigkeit, wenn
es sich auch in massvoller Schönheit nicht mit der griechischen, an Pracht und
Fülle nicht mit der germanischen Namengebung messen kann."

[5] Authorities differ in their classification of O.E. names. Searle has six
classes, four of which I call monothematic ; and Redin formally divides
these uncompounded names into five groups.

[6] Kemble, p. 86.

compound occurs rarely, as Wulfwulf, which has been noticed on a coin of Eadweard the Confessor, and possibly Godgod, a moneyer of the time of Cnut.

2. *Monothematic or Uncompounded*. Single-element names are common, but they are probably elliptical or diminished forms of compounds ; the fact that a corresponding dithematic name is now unknown is no proof of non-existence. If any single-element names were formed independently, it is probable that they were few.[1] Uncompounded names may be divided into (i) Strong names, as masc. Beorn, Wine, God, Lull ; fem. Badu, Hild, Hwatu, Eafu. (ii) Weak names, as masc. Æsca, Beorna, Tun(n)a, Dudda ; fem. Beage, Gode, Hune, Crawe. (iii) Names in -*i*(-*e*), masc. Ecgi, Godi, Ini, Lulle.[2]

3. *Derivatives*. The principal formations are with an *l*- suffix, as -*il*, -*el*, -*ul*, -*ol*, -(*i*)*la*, -*ula*, -*ella*, -*ele*, e.g. Duddel, Hiddila ; with a *k*-suffix, as -*ic*, -*uc*, -*oc*, -(*i*)*ca*, -*uca*, -*eca*, e.g. Baduca, Honoc ; with suffixes -*ig*, -*i*(*g*)*a*, -*n*-, -*ede*, e.g. Dudig, Lullede.[3] Suffix -*cin* is of L.G. origin, and will be discussed in a later chapter.[4] Some of these suffixes have a diminutive force only, others form pet-names, but it is not now possible to distinguish them.

O.E. names are declined like other nouns, thus Ælfred becomes Ælfredes in the genitive, and Ælfrede in the dative. Many feminine names follow the weak declension, such as Marie, gen. Marian ; Eve, gen. Evan. Foreign names often follow their native system of declension, but sometimes they are latinized, and not too strictly, the accusative ending being also used in the other oblique cases, as Cýrum for the dative of Cýrus.

The themes of the parents' names were sometimes perpetuated in those of the children, for instance, we find that the nonsensical name Wulfstan, already mentioned, was the result of compounding elements from both the father's name, Æðelstan, and the mother's, Wulfgifu [5]; and quite possibly, following out the same principle, another child may have been christened Æðelgifu. Sometimes one element was repeated throughout several appellatives of the family, e.g. the names of six children of Eormenræd of Kent were : Eormenbeorh, Eormenburh, and Eormengyð : Æðelðryð, Æðelræð, Æðelbeorht ; and the sons of Ordheah were Wulfheah and

---

[1] For a summing up on this point and further information on uncompounded English names, see *Studies*, etc., by Mats Redin.

[2] Ibid., p. xxxix. Redin includes in this class diminutives and names in -ing, for which latter see below, p. 57.

[3] Ibid., p. 172.

[4] It may be of interest to compare the German suffixes as given by F. Solmsen (*Indogermanische Eigennamen*, 1922, p. 174) : -*chen*, -*gen*, -*ken*, -*i*, -*ig*, -*igo*, -*k*, -*ke*, -*la*, -*le*, -*li*, -*lo*, -*z*, -*za*, -*ze*, -*zo*.

[5] *Vita Wulfstani*, ed. by H. Wharton ; *Anglia Sacra*, vol. ii, p. 244.

Ælfheah.[1] Saxon pedigrees show that adoption of one initial was also practised ; for instance, of thirty descendants of Ecgbryht, twenty-nine had names commencing with Æ, E, or Ea ; and of Sledda's posterity nineteen out of twenty had the initial S.[2]

As an example of name-building the vocable Léof, which may be either an adjective denoting " dear ", " beloved ", and " agreeable " or a noun meaning " beloved one " and " friend ", may be mentioned, it being found in English records compounded with -flǽd, -gǽr, -gár, -géat, -gifu, -god, -gýth, -héah, -heard, -helm, -hild, -mǽr, -man, -nóth, rǽd, -réd, ríc, -sige, -stán, -swíð, -thegn, -ðrýð, -waru, -weald, weard, -wen, -wíg, -wíne. In like manner numerous names may have the same second element, as, for instance, -sige, m. " victory ", " success ", which is found compounded with Ælf-, Æðel-, Beorht-, Beorn-, Burg-, Céol-, Cōēn-, Cyne-, Éad-, Eald-, Ealh-, Éan-, Earn-, Gód-, Here-, Hilde-, Hún-, Léof-, Wiht-, Wil-, Wulf-. Many of these names have become perpetuated in English surnames, often in very corrupt form, as will appear in later pages.

Additional Descriptions of the Anglo-Saxons. The number of Gothonic and Celtic names (eliminating variants) preserved in records of England of date prior to the Norman conquest is perhaps about 10,000,[3] and since the number of protothemes given by Searle is 293 and the number of deuterothemes is 120, it is possible that this number was exceeded.[4] It cannot be said, therefore, that the ratio of the number of different names to total population was small[5] ; it may have been as much as one for every 100 persons ; nevertheless, it was found that single names were insufficient distinction (in more senses than one), probably due to the fact that some, such as Ælfwin (Alwin), Leofric, and Godwin were greatly overworked, and secondary appellatives were bestowed or assumed to minimize the confusion. These additional names were called in O.E. *fréonama*, literally " free-name ", *cuðnama* " familiar " or " friendly name ", and *tónama* " other name ", from which latter word came E.E. " to-name " or " twa-name ". Such secondary names were either alternatives like the present day nicknames, or they were personal descriptions or addresses added to the original appellations.

---

[1] Kemble, p. 88. Searle, p. xiv. Similar customs prevalent among other races have been mentioned, p. 27 n.
[2] See the pedigrees, *Chron. Flor. Wig.*, ed. B. Thorpe, vol. i, pp. 250, 257.
[3] A rough estimate from Searle's list, which is, however, not exhaustive.
[4] Names continue to be discovered, sometimes by etymologists studying place-names, sometimes by the investigator of E. and M.E. surnames.
[5] The ratio of baptismal names to population at the present day is much smaller.

Early chroniclers give occasional examples of both classes of second name. Beda records . . . Adilbergæ filia Adilbercti regis, quæ alio nomine Tatæ vocabatur [1] (who by another name is called Tata). Simeon of Durham under year 737 entered Aldwine qui et Wor,[2] and under year 801 Edwine qui et Eda dictus est [3]; and the *Saxon Chronicle* under date 984 has Ælfheah, "seðe oðran naman wæs geciged Godwine," i.e. Ælfheah, who by another name was called Godwine.[4] The fair sex also boasted " to-names " : by Ælflæd's will (*c.* 960) a lady named Crawe " crow " received a legacy,[5] and elsewhere another is doubtfully complimented by being called Enede " the duck." Kemble, from a comparison of two charters, points out that " another lady, whose real name was Hroðwaru, was better known by the familiar, though not very graceful, name of Bucge, *cimex*; perhaps upon the principle of that insect being also ' a familiar beast and a friend to man ' ".[6] As this name has received a good deal of notice by various writers, who have accepted it at face value, it may be said, definitely, that it can have had no reference whatever to the unceremonious and offensive insect, since, although that undesirable companion was sufficiently enterprising to call for attention from Aristophanes (fifth century), it was quite unknown in Britain in Saxon days, and for centuries later. A suggestion has been made that this name has been derived from W. *bwg* " a goblin ", as without doubt has M.E. *bug*.[7]

" Thou shalt not nede to be afraid of any bugs by night."

Matthew's Bible, Psalm xci, 5.

The most probable solution, however, is that the name, as it appears, Buga (m.), Buge (f.), Bugga (m.), Bugo (m.), is nothing more than a hypocoristic derivative from a compound, such as Buge-red, Burg-red, or Hea-burga.[8] On the introduction of the obnoxious pest to England, in later years, it had bestowed upon it, unfortunately, a name which conflicted with one already in wide and distinguished use among its new hosts. The derivatives of this ancient appellative are numerous : one writer gives thirty orthographic forms,[9] but now that the

---

[1] *Ecclesiastical History* (Bohn), vol. ii, p. 9.
[2] *Historia Ecclesiæ Dunhelmensis* (Rolls Ser. 75), vol. ii, p. 34.
[3] Ibid., vol. ii, p. 65.
[4] Ed. by C. Plummer, p. 124.
[5] *Codex Diplomaticus Aevi Saxonici*, ed. by J. M. Kemble, vol. iii, p. 274. See also Chiapelli, *I Nomi di Donna*, p. 18.
[6] *Names*, etc., p. 96, referring to charters in the Codex, Nos. 82 and 124.
[7] Bugge was also a N.F. equivalent for " a badger ", according to Kelham.
[8] Heaburg cognomento Buggae. See Redin, p. 115.
[9] *Surnames and Sirenames*, by J. Finlayson, p. 56.

original signification is unknown, the surname has ceased to be popular in this country.[1]

The additional epithets often received greater recognition than the name given at baptism, and sometimes were used in preference to the font-name in confirming charters and other legal instruments. The Norman lady Emma, first the wife of Æðelræd and afterwards of Cnut, was given a Saxon name Ælfgyfu, each appellative being used in documents respectively of the years 1018 and 1019[2]; and on occasion she was designated by both names Ælfgifu Imma.[3] A grant of Cnut is to "ministro qui Leofwine nomine et Bondan sunu appellatur cognomine".[4] The ancient historian also found the additional description a useful index of identity; the Chronicle of Winchcombe, under year 801, mentions . . . regem Cantuariorum Eadbrihtum cognomento Pren.[5] The eleventh-century chronicler, Florence of Worcester, also provides examples of second names, mentioning under year 1066 a certain Shrewsbury butcher, Godwinus Porthund, id est oppidi canis (Town-dog)[6]; also, A.D. 1042, Danico et præpotenti viro Tovio, Prudan cognomento[7]; and again Benedictus cognomento Biscop, a minister of king Oswiu (A.D. 653),[8] and Anfridus cognomento Ceocesfot (A.D. 1052).[9] Also the lady known as "the Duck" had the further name Candida (the white).[10] The significations of these secondary appellatives are not always traceable, e.g. Mol, Ucca, Pilia, Bycga, Roda, Fila, etc., have not been identified.[11]

It does not appear that second names were commonly used, at any rate, the large collection of extant charters, enrolled judgments and wills, provide few examples until the tenth century; it is to be noticed, however, that the deeds preserved are mainly royal grants, and the witnesses—the comites, companions, and councillors of the king, whose rank, after the seventh century, in recognition of precedency is always specified, usually in Latin, sometimes Anglo-Saxon, and occasionally merely by an initial letter. The few names of laymen, other than milites or ministri, which can be derived from these early sources, have no additional description of

---

[1] A Mr. Bugg, who was supposed to have changed his name to Howard, caused some dissension. Thoroton (*Hist. of Notts*) records that a son of Sir Ralph Bugge took the name of Bingham; but " the other sons remained Bugges and produced more Bugges " (Finlayson). In 1857 a Mr. Bedbug changed his name (Bowditch).

[2] *KCD.*, vol. iv, pp. 1 and 2.   [3] Ibid., vol. vi, p. 190.

[4] Ibid., vol. iv, p. 26.

[5] Kemble (*Proc. Arch. Inst.*, 1846), p. 93.

[6] *Flor. Wig.*, ed. by B. Thorpe, vol. i, p. 158.   [7] Ibid., vol. i, 196.

[8] Ibid., vol. i, p. 21.   [9] Ibid., vol. i, p. 210.

[10] Ibid., vol. i, p. 140. " Ægelfleda Candida, cognomento Eneda."

[11] Kemble (*Proc. Arch. Inst.*, 1846), p. 93.

any kind. Continental records yield the same barren results in this respect.[1]

The following notes on witnesses' names are gathered from charters in the *Cartularium Saxonicum* and *Codex Diplomaticus Aevi Saxonici*.

A.D. 674. Grant by Wulfhere, king of the Mercians, to Berhferð, his kinsman. Witnesses' names :—

✠ Wita episcopus   ✠ Totta episcopus   ✠ Ofa princeps
✠ Eadbriht princeps ✠ Tepra princeps   ✠ Cynred princeps
✠ Eadbald minister   ✠ Hearnbriht minister ✠ Eada ✠ Eoppa
✠ Offa.

In the attestation to a grant by Suæbhard, king of Kent, A.D. 676, twelve out of the sixteen names are without additional descriptions, and to a charter of Lotharius, king of Kent, A.D. 679, all the eleven witnesses were given single names. During the eighth and ninth centuries very similar practice prevailed : in a grant by Wiglaf, king of the Mercians, to Hanbury monastery, A.D. 836, of thirty-eight appellatives (excluding the grantor), twenty-six have descriptions, such as regina, archiepiscopus, episcopus, abbas, and dux ; twelve witnesses having nothing additional to their personal names. The tendency was to increase the number of named witnesses ; a grant made by king Æðelstan at the Witenagemot at Luton, A.D. 931, has no less than 100, all of whom have an official description. The witnesses to a grant of king Eadred, A.D. 955, were provided with the following descriptions : archabiscop, episcopus, pontifex, didasculus, antistes, presul, biscop, ætheling, monachus, euax, cliton, dux, princeps, miles, minister. It is not until we get away from the royal grants that evidence is found pointing to the use of characteristic epithets or local descriptions.

In the Record of Medehamstede (Peterborough Abbey), towards the end of the tenth century, are given the names of a number of " festerman " or " land-sureties ".[2] Ekwall, who has analysed these names, states that of some seventy names, "twenty-eight are certainly Scandinavian, the rest being English or possibly English ".[3] This proportion of aliens need occasion no surprise, since the Norse immigration had been proceeding for 200 years. The personal names have in a number of cases additionally an address, as Sumerlyda æt Stoce, or Styrcyr on Uptone : a genealogical description,

[1] Reference to the cartulary of the Abbey of Fulda (Prussia) shows that, up to the eleventh century, laymen attesting charters were not given secondary descriptions. *Codex Diplomaticus Fuldensis*, herausgegeben von E. F. J. Dronke, 1850.
[2] *Cartularium Saxonicum*, vol. iii, p. 369.
[3] *Intr. to the Survey of English Place-Names*, p. 73.

as Brenting, or Ulf Doddes suna; others, again, are
distinguished by their vocation, as Oswi preost, or Æðelwine
ealdorman, and others by some characteristic, as Ælfric cyld
or Eadric litle.

A grant by Cnut, A.D. 1033, differs from the charters of
the English kings in having many witnesses with single names,
but here also the tendency towards secondary descriptions is
noticeable.

✠ Ego Ælugiua regina consensi ✠ Ego Æðelnoð archiepiscopus
confirmaui ✠ Ego Ælfric archiepiscopus corroboraui ✠ Ego
Ælfwine episcopus ✠ Ego Æðelric Brihtmer episcopus ✠ Æðelstan
episcopus ✠ Ego Godewine dux ✠ Ego Leofric dux ✠ Siward dux
✠ Ælfwine dux ✠ Osgod Clapa ✠ Toui Pruda ✠ Ðurcyl ✠ Harald
✠ Ðord ✠ Halfden ✠ Godric ✠ Ælfric ✠ Rold ✠ Swane
✠ Orm ✠ Ulfkitel ✠ Forna ✠ Godwin ✠ Faryem ✠ Ketel
✠ Merseat ✠ Gamal ✠ Basins ✠ Orm.[1]

Osgod and Tovi are elsewhere described as ministers.
The witnesses' names to an Anglo-Saxon grant of Bishop
Ealdred, A.D. 1049–58, appear as follow :—

And ðisses is tó gewitnysse eall se hired (retinue) on Wigeracestre
and se hired on Eofeshamme and se hired on Persceoran ; and
Leófríc eorl ; and Odda eorl, and Ælfric his bróðor, and Berhtríc
Ælfgáres sunu, and Owine, and Wagan, and Ægelríc ðaes bisceopes
bróðor, and Ceólmær, and Atsur, and Ecebearn, and Ordwig, and
Æðestán fætta, Ælfward æt Langadúne, and ealla ða yldestan þegnas
(chief thegns) on Wigeraceastrescíre Denisce and Englisce.[2]

Here at least one (and probably two) of the persons named
are Welsh.

The expanding employment and increasing variety of the
descriptions corresponds to the movement which was taking
place in France, as extracts in the following chapter will
establish. On the Continent the French or Latin preposition
de was more in use than *aet* and *on*, or Latin *apud* and *de* in
England. On the other hand, the English *-ing*, if not already
obsolete, was soon superseded by Scandinavian *-sune*, which
was to have such a great influence in the moulding of English
surnames. In Flanders and Germany neither territorial
preposition nor filial desinence had yet become customary.[3]

[1] *KCD.*, vol. iv, p. 44.   [2] Ibid., vol. iv, p. 137.
[3] In a " liste des tributaires de l'avouerie ", A.D. 1070, an original document
of L'Abbaye de S. Pierre au Mont Blandin a Gand (A. van Lokeren, p. 99),
several of the tributaries have second names, as Helia de Hosthus, Yda de
Asbroch, Margareta Badwagens, Greta Stopens, Lisa dicta Honrecrop, etc.
To a confirmation by Robert le Frison, A.D. 1072, most of the witnesses have
" addresses ". An original grant, A.D. 1125, by Siger de Munte to the Abbey,
names 31 serfs of whom 26 are identified by addresses, nine of which are
" de Munte ", surely evidence that it was not a surname. An exception is
" Otbertus vocatus de Bacerothen ", indicating that persons were assuming
place-names as secondary descriptions.

While one could hardly rely on the ancient Welsh genealogy cited above, which shows that nine sons of Cunedda Wledig took territorial descriptions,[1] nevertheless, it seems probable that, even if there had been no Norman invasion, the English would have adopted local descriptions equally with other nominal distinctions.

Classification of Additional Descriptions. The Anglo-Saxon descriptive epithets and addresses, like those of the Gaels and Cymry, answer the questions—What is his personal peculiarity? Where is or was he located? Who is or was his most important kinsman? What is his vocation? A few typical examples of these four classes of personal distinctions, in O.E., O.N., and Latin, will now be given, exactly as they appear in the records.

Characteristic : c. 962, Wulfric sé Blaca (the black) ; c. 970, Brihtric Grim (the savage) ; c. 1006, Æðelric Ealda (the old) ; c. 1006, Brihtric Reada (the red) ; 1020, Ælfsige Cild (the child) ; Durcyl Hoga (the wise) ; 1024, Tovi Hwíta (the white) ; 1032, Brihtric Geonga (the young) ; *temp*. Cnut, Ælfword Kæntisce ; Mantat Ancer (the hermit). The definite article may be either *sé* or *ðe*.

Local : Five different types of local descriptions were in use : (i) c. 962, Wulfstan æt Sealtwuda ; (ii) c. 962, Ælfgar on Meapaham ; (iii) c. 975, Oswulf de Grettune [2] ; (iv) c. 1050, Osgod apud Heailea ; (v) c. 1060, Ælfwin Gortune.

Genealogical : Four systems of genealogical description were noticed : (i) 547, Gódulf [wæs] Geating ; 804, Æðelheah Esning ; (ii) c. 962, Sired Ælfredes sunu ; 1032, Dorð Đurcylles nefa ; 1046, Hunewine Heca sunu ; (iii) c. 1055, Ulf filius Tofi ; 1060, Godricus filius Eadgyfe (f.) ; (iv) 1033, Godwine Brytæl ; 1077, Wulfwine Sired (i.e. Sigered, now the common surname Sired, e.g. John Syred, Suff. Poll, 1790, p. 80).

Occupational : c. 962, Wine Préost ; c. 970, Ælfheáh Ealdorman ; c. 981, Wulgar Clericus ; 1012, Wada Miles ; c. 1016, Æðelwine Scírman (the shire-man) ; 1023, Briteh Munuc (the monk) ; c. 1031, Æðelric Bigenga (the cultivator) ; *temp*. Cnut, Đored Steallare (the marshal).

Double descriptions may be found as : Wulfhun ðes blaca æt Sumortune (Norf. tenth cent.), *KCD.*, ii, 133.

The various methods of forming genealogical descriptions lead to some detailed notice of the important suffix *-ing*.

The Suffix -ing. (O.N. *-ingr*, O.H.G. *-ing*) This substantival suffix, the precise signification of which is uncertain, occurs in Old English and German names, and has several applications. Formerly it functioned in lieu of a filial desinence,

---

[1] Iolo MSS., p. 521 : *Vestiges of the Gael in Gwynedd*, by W. B. T. Jones, p. 31.
[2] Not contemporary.

as is clearly evidenced by the entry in the *Anglo-Saxon Chronicle*, under date A.D. 547.

Ida wæs Eopping. Eoppa Esing. Esa wæs Inguing. Ingui Angenwitting. Angenwit Alocing. Aloc Benocing. Benoc Branding. Brand Bældæging. Bældæg Wodening. Woden Freoþolafing. Freoþelaf Freoþulfing. Friþulf Finning. Finn Gódulfing. Gódulf Geating.[1]

The suffix here seems to have had merely a prepositional force equal to " of ", and implying " son of ", as in the sentence, " of English parents Swift was born in London " [2] ; or in the colloquial expression " Dick o' Jenny's ".

" Son of " continued to be so indicated until the arrival of the Northmen when, following Scandinavian practice, the filial relationship gradually came to be much more definitely and satisfactorily expressed by *sunu*. To-day, surnames with affix *-son* are common in England, as are those with *-sen* in Denmark and Norway. In Germany the corresponding *-sohn* is little used, and in France there is no equivalent suffix.

The suffix *-ing* had also the broader sense parallel to Gaul. *-cnos*, Grk. - ιδης, Ir. *ua*, and to have implied " descendant of " (see p. 39). It may also have converted a place-name, or a personal appellative, into a clan-name, as Bromleagingas, " the people of Bromleah " (Kent),[3] or Basing, " the followers of Basa ".[4]

These illustrations evidently do not exhaust the varied applications of the suffix, for Kemble has contended that *-ing* sometimes has a purely genitival function, equivalent to *es*, so that " Æðelwulfing land " has the same value as " Æðelwulfes land ", which partly confirms the view expressed above. Elsewhere it is maintained that the *-ing*-form names are inflexible adjectives analogous to G. Pariser, " Parisian " " from Paris ", Londoner " from London ",[5] etc., but rather *-ing* seems to be equivalent to " one ", an individual (cf. *earming* " poor one " or " wretch ").

Redin, who devotes a chapter to names in *-ing*, expresses the possibility that such may be by-names and not patronymics, citing such cases as Ealdulf Bosing and Ailword Pudding.[6]

Since so many English surnames are those of localities, it

---

[1] *The Anglo-Saxon Chronicle*, ed. by B. Thorpe (Rolls Ser. 23), vol. i, p. 28, col. 2.

[2] Thackeray (*English Humourists*).

[3] J. M. Kemble (*Proc. Phil. Soc.*, 1848, vol. iv, p. 1).

[4] A Mawer (*Enc. Brit.*, Art. " Place-Names ").

[5] T. Watts (*Proc. Phil. Soc.*, vol. iv, p. 83). See also Nils Bergsten, *A Study in Compound Substantives*, pp. 41, 49.

[6] *Studies on Uncompounded Personal Names*, pp. 163 et seq. Valuable monographs on place-names in *-ing* are by E. Ekwall, 1923, and S. Karlstrom, 1927.

is well to note that -*ing* occurs in a great number of place-
names, which it is difficult to class definitely either as geonymics
or patronymics. If the former, then -*ing* signifies " meadow "
in N. and E. dialects (Ice. *eng*, Dan. *eng*, Swed. *äng*).[1]
Ing- likewise occurs as a first element in numerous compound personal names, as Ingweald, Ingwulf,[2] etc., and the
diminished form also became a personal name (now the
surname Inge).

It will be manifest that considerable difficulty exists in
determining at sight the exact function of -*ing*, and when the
suffix is met with in surnames caution must be exercised in
deciding the class to which such an appellative is to be assigned.

From -*ing* is obtained the diminutive suffix -*l-ing*, as in
deorling " favourite ", now the well-known surname Darling.

Anglo-Saxon " Surnames ". Such additional descriptions
as the above were intended merely for individual distinction,
but being still in use at the time when it became customary
to repeat a description in one family, some of them, as Young,
Anker, Gretton, Keating from Geating (if not a local name),
Alderman, etc., became established as surnames, but it is
most improbable that any one of these names has been borne
in the same family from Saxon times. H. Harrison (1918) writes
of " surnames " from the early sixth century, instancing the
name of Hengist's son, who was named Eric Æsc (i.e. " lance
or spear, from the ash-wood shaft ").[3] Æsc would, by some
persons, be called a " nickname ", but in the present essay
it ranks as a " description ". The individual application of
the word stamps it as being of entirely different nature to the
modern surname, and it is unlikely that the Anglo-Saxons
ever had hereditary family names. Turner, a century ago, had
arrived at the same conclusion, but it is amazing to find that
the eminent Anglo-Saxon scholar made a single possible
exception, stating that " one Saxon MS. seems to express an
actual surname Hatte ".

" Hwita Hatte was a keeper of bees in Hæthfelda ; and Tate
Hatte, his daughter, was the mother of Wulfsige, the shooter ; and
Lulle Hatte, the sister of Wulfsige, Hehstan had for his wife in
Wealadene. Wifus and Dunne and Seoloce, were born in Hæthfelda.
Duding Hatte, the son of Wifus, is settled at Wealadene ; and
Ceolmond Hatte, the son of Dunne, is also settled there ; and Ætheleah
Hatte, the son of Seoloce, is also there ; and Tate Hatte, the sister of
Cenwald, Mæg hath for his wife at Weligan ; and Ealdhelm, the son

---

[1] Bosworth's *A.-S. Dictionary*, 1898.
[2] *Zur Englischen Namenkunde*, von Erik Björkman, p. 48. Numerous
references Schönfeld, p. 147 ; Förstemann, col. 956, etc. *Saxons in England*,
by J. M. Kemble, 1876, vol. i, p. 60 n. *Proc. Phil. Soc.*, vol. iv, p. 1.
[3] *Surnames of the United Kingdom*, vol. ii, p. 1.

of Herethrythe, married the daughter of Tate. Werlaf Hatte, the father of Werstan, was the rightful possessor of Haethfelda." [1]

Turner held the erroneous opinion that this was a literal translation of part of a document, which, as it provides an excellent example of the names of bondmen, and illustrates the care with which their pedigrees were preserved, may be printed *in extenso*.

Dudda wæs gebúr intó Hǽðfelda and he hæfde þreó dóhtor, an hátte Deórwyn óðer Deórswyð þridde Golde. And Wulláf on Hæðfelda hæfð Deórwynne tó wífe and Ælfstán æt Tæccingawyrðe hæfð Deórswyðe tó wife, and Ealhstán Ælfstánes bróðar hæfð Goldan to wífe. Hwíta hátte ðæs beócere intó Hǽðfelda and Táte hátte his dóhtor ðæs Wulfsiges módor scyttan, and Lulle hátte Wulfsiges sweostar Héhstán hæfð tó wífe on Wealadene. Wifús and Dunne and Seoloce syndan inbyrde tó Hǽðfelda, Duding hátte Wifúse sunu sit on Wealadene, and Ceólmund hátte Dunnan sunu sit eác on Wealadene, and Æðeleáh hátte Seolecan sunu sit eác on Wealadene, and Táte hátte Cénwaldes sweostor mæg hǽfð tó wífe on Welugun, and Ealdelm Hereðryðe sunu hæfð Tátan dóhtor tó wífe. Wærláf hátte Wærstánes fæder wæs riht ǽht tó Hǽðfelda heóld ða grǽgan swýn. ✠ Bráda hátte wæs gebúr to Hǽðfelda and Hwíte hátte ðæs Brádan wíf wæs gebúres dóhtor tó Hǽðfelda, seó Hwíte wæs Wærstánes and Wærðryðe and Wynburge þridde módor and se Wærstán sit æt Wádtúne hæfð Winnes sweostor to wífe, and Wine hæfð Wærðryðe tó wífe. And Dunne sæt on Wádtúne wæs inbyrde to Hǽðfelda, and Deórwyn hátte hire dóhtor hæfð Cynewald on Munddene tó wífe, and Deórnáð hátte hire bróðar bið mid Cynewalde, and Dudde hátte Wifúse dóhtor sit æt Wilmundesleá. Cynelm hátte Cénwaldes fæder wæs gebúr intó Hǽðfelda, and Manna hátte Cénwaldes sunu sit æt Wádtúne under Eádwolde ; ✠ Buhi hátte wæs Drýhtláfes móddrige wæs áfaren út of Hǽðfelda intó Eslingadene, and Æðelwyn and Eádugu and Æðelgýð heó wǽran þreo gesweostra, and Tilewine and Dudda wǽron ealle ðǽre buge bearn, and Ealhstán Tiliwine sunu, and Wulfsige Eáduge sunu, and Ceólem Æðelgyðe sunu, and Ceólstán and Manwine. Ðis cýn com of Felda Deórulf Cyneburghe sunu and his twá sweostar, and Cynríc æt Clæfring is heora eám ðás men synd Tátan magas æt Hǽðfelda ðæs gebúres.[2]

Robert Ferguson (1858), who so thoroughly investigated Teutonic names, followed Turner without challenge, saying : " We find this Anglo-Saxon family with unquestionably a regular surname." He further observes that the name Hatt " corresponds with the Old German names Hatto, Haddo, Heddo, and Chado, different forms of the same word, signifying ' war '—and consequently with our Haddo, Head, and Chad. Many of the baptismal names mentioned in this document have also become English surnames, as White,

[1] *History of the Anglo-Saxons*, by Sharon Turner, 1852, vol. iii, p. 11 n.
[2] MS. Cott. Tib. B. v., f. 76b. Printed in *KCD.*, vol. vi, p. 211.

Tate, Wolsey, Hastings, Dunn, Sellick, Dudin, and Maggs ".[1]

A third nomenclaturist (M. A. Lower, 1860) "assumed that although the use of surnames may, on the whole, be regarded as one of the importations of the Norman Conquest, yet they were occasionally hereditary among the Anglo-Saxons at a date anterior to that event, and many generations before the general adoption of family designations. This is pretty satisfactorily proved," he concludes, citing the above Cottonian MS.[2]

A fourth authority (A. Folkard, 1886) accepted Lower unquestioned, concluding "that at dates long anterior to the Conquest, surnames were in use among the Anglo-Saxons ".[3]

The erroneous translation of Turner does not at any time appear to have been disputed, and the unsound deductions arising therefrom received a new lease of life, appearing in the more modern works of Barber (1894), Blagg (1900), and even Baring-Gould (1910) blotted a most readable book by repeating the absurdity, as showing " that before the Conquest the tendency to assume surnames had already spasmodically manifested itself ".[4] This eminent author even went a step further and derived the surname Hatte " from Heathfield which is Hattes-field, being owned by Werlaff Hatte ".[5] Etymology on the rampage with a vengeance !

The document, which is no doubt of greater antiquity than the Conquest (1066), is a record of serfs and their families, and there is no reason whatever to suppose that *hátte* is a name, description, or addition of any kind. There is no difference in meaning between " hátte Deórwyn " (is called Deorwyn) and " Deórwyn hátte " which occurs lower down. Hatte is the third person, singular number, present or preterite tense, indicative mood of the irregular passive verb *hatan* " to be called " or " named ". The word occurs similarly elsewhere : Ðes ys ðæs manes nama ðe Byrhsie gefreáde et Petrocys stowe Byhstán háte Bluntan sunu [6] . . . (This is the man's name whom Byrhsie freed at St. Petroc's, Byhstan he is called, son of Blunta.) Æilsig bohte ánne wífman Ongyneðel hátte and hire sunu [7] . . . (Æilsig bought a woman called Ongyneðel and her son). The first part of the document, which was

[1] *English Surnames*, by Robt. Ferguson, 1858, p. 16. Also *The Teutonic Name-System*, 1864, p. 14.
[2] *Patronymica Britannica*, by M. A. Lower, p. xiii.
[3] *The Antiquary*, vol. xiii, p. 64.
[4] Even the legal mind accepts the evidence unchallenged (as Lionel Cresswell in *Stemmata Alstoniana*, 1905).
[5] *Family Names and their Story*, by S. Baring-Gould, 1910, p. 23.
[6] *KCD.*, vol. iv, p. 309.
[7] *KCD.*, vol. iv, p. 313.

erroneously translated by Turner, may, therefore, be rendered as follows :—

Dudda was a boor in Hæthfeld, and he had three daughters, one was called Deorwyn, another Deorswyth, the third Golde. And Wullaf in Hæthfeld hath Deorwyn to wife, Ælfstan at Tæccingawyrth hath Deorswyth to wife, and Ealhstan, brother of Ælfstan, hath Golde to wife. There is one called Hwita, the bee-keeper, in Hæthfeld, and his daughter called Tate, mother of Wulfsige, the archer, and the sister of Wulfsige, called Lulle, Hehstan hath to wife in Wealeden. Wifus and Dunne and Seoloce were born (on the estate) at Hæthfeld. A son of Wifus, called Duding, dwells in Wealeden, and a son of Dunne, called Ceolmund, also dwells in Wealeden, and a son of Seoloce, called Ætheleah, also dwells in Wealeden, and a sister of Cenwald, called Tate, Mæg hath to wife in Welugun, and Ealdelm, son of Herethryth, hath a daughter of Tate to wife. The father of Wærstan, called Wærlaf, was a lawful serf at Hæthfeld, he held the grey swine.

Domesday Book. A valuable book of reference for Saxon names is that important territorial register, now commonly known as Domesday Book. Sometime after 1083, possibly in the year 1085, this great survey of the possessions conquered by William was commenced, and the various county inquisitions being carried out simultaneously, the work was rapidly carried out, the returns of the commissioners being finally methodized and transcribed in 1086.[1] Among the valuable antiquarian and historical information preserved in this manuscript is the name of every place then existing in England, with the exception of those in the four northern counties.[2] Regarding persons, Ellis has computed that 283,242 of all classes are mentioned, of whom 111 were specified as Waleis or Walenses, and 296 as Francigenæ,[3] but of this quarter of a million inhabitants not more than about 5 per cent are named, and among the names there is very great repetition. Eliminating duplicates and variants, the different appellatives amount to less than 3,000, of which the greater proportion are Teutonic. An example of the names preserved in this monument of English history will now be given in the exact form in which they appear, Latin terminations, however, being omitted. The letter *w* is represented by *uu*, as *v* is by *u*.

[1] Printed by the Record Commission, 1783–1816, 4 vols.

[2] " Northumberland, Cumberland, Westmoreland, and Durham are not described in the survey, nor Lancashire under its proper name ; but Furness, and the northern part of the county, as well as the south of Westmoreland, with part of Cumberland, are included within the West Riding of Yorkshire. That part of Lancashire which lies between the rivers Ribble and Mersey, and which at the time of the survey comprehended 6 hundreds and 188 manors, is subjoined to Cheshire ; and part of Rutlandshire is described in the counties of Northampton and Lincoln, etc." *A Manual for the Genealogist*, by Richard Sims, 1888, p. 2.

[3] There are separate enumerations for Francigenæ servientes and Servientes francigenæ, but the distinction is not stated.

Isti sunt burgenses Regis qui reddunt consuetudinem : Coleman,
Leuuin, Uluric, Eduin, Turchill, Ulftan eudlac, Leuuin Crist, Manuuin,
Aluric, Herdedun, Alfeihc pr', Leuot, Uluric, Suertlinc, Aluuart,
Eduin, Goda, Sprot, Edric, Goduuin, Goduuin uuachefes, Blanc,
Aluric, Stanart, Goduin, Uluric, Alsi, Aluuard, Manuuin, Leffesse,
Leuuin, Uluuin, Godinc, Goda, Uluuin monitor (i.e. the crier), Alfgar,
Uluart, Aluuin, Alfgar pr', Frent, Osgot, Uluric, Artur, Eduin, Saluare,
Leflet, Aluric, Goduuin, Sprot, Grimolf, Sagar, Aluric, Aluuin, Uluric,
Sprot, Uluuart, Leuuin, Goduin, Golstan, Uluuin, Uluuart, Uluuin,
Goduuin, Alfsi, Lefstan, Godric, Alric, Not, Brictuuin, Lefflet, Alric,
Eduuin, Scadebutre, Manuuin, Golduuin, Uluric, Osiet, Eduuin,
Uluric, Aluuin, Eduuin, Uluuin, Blactan, Manstan, Aluric, Leuuin,
Aluuin, Leuuin, Edric, Leuuin, Uued, Ulsi, Goldric, Goda, Calebot,
Manstan, Ulfeih, Manuuin, Winemer, Sacrim, Leuric, Uluuart, Uluuin,
Lefflet, Godric, Dereman, Turstan, Dullel, Goddæ, Got cill', Stan,
Oriet', Alfstan, Toui, Goldinc, Leuiet, Blacstan, Manuuin, Aluuin,
Lefsun, Aluric, Brummam, Aluuin, Saulf, Leuuin, Uluric, Alfstan,
Goduuin, Golduin, Goduuin, Wicga, Ledmar, Ulfstan, Godesun, Elebolt,
Goduuin, Godeua, Lefstan, Eduard pr', Hacon, Ailbriest, Tate,
Sauuart, Berda, Uluuart pr', Cullinc, Aluuolt, Filieman, Godeua,
Siuuard pr', Pic, Uluuin, Leueua, Aluric, Aluuen, Uluric, Will' peccatu
(i.e. sin), Best, Rosell', Leuuin, Goda, Uluuin, Leuesun, Golman, Pote,
Godric, Siric, Alric, Liuidi, Brictric, Lefstan, Uudebil, Blacstan,
Alflet, Ulueua, Goda, Ascere, Godric, Brunloc, Alnod, Goduuin, Leuuin,
Aluric pr', Roger, Godric, Aluric, Suertinc, Godid, Brunuin, Uluuin,
Brungar, Sunegot, Siuuard, Ulstan, Leffiuf, Sagrim, Uluuin, Leuuin,
Leuric, Godinc, Westan, Ainolf, Tunric, Alstan, Alfsi, Goldere, Godsune,
Uluuin, Aluric, Goduuin, Pecoc, Aluuin, Brictric, Manuuin, Uluric,
Godsune, Brunuin, Manuuin, Edric, Leueua, Ouuin, Alstan, Aluolt,
Manuin, Aluuart, Lemer, Stanhert, Uluuin, Sæuuele, Leuret, Alueua,
Ulstan, Leuuin, Leueua, Aluric, Godric, Ulric, Uluuin, Aluuen, Tescho,
Uluric, Stotinc, Herstan, Leuric, Edric, Dela, Hunec, Manuuin, Aluric,
Got hugo, Leuuin, "Dimidius Blancus," Lefsune, Alueua, Leueua,
Sueno, Ulsi, Alflet, Rad' Pinel, Orlaf, Galt (i.e. Walter), Horrap,
Aluuin, Stamburc, Ulftan, Chentinc, Sprot, Eduuin, Got flet, Mansune,
Godinc, Ulueua, Uluric, Lorchebret, Goldere.[1]

This list of names of men and women is of particular interest,
because the names of burgesses in general are omitted in
Domesday Book, the recording clerk resting with certification
of the numbers ; and also because some of the most interesting
names have not been included in Searle's list or Ellis's index.
Of the 275 householders nearly all bear Saxon names : Owin
may be Welsh ; Roger, Galt, Pinel (who was a tenant in chief),
Lorchebret, Scadebutre, Dullel, Rossell', look like Norman.
These foreign names need occasion no surprise, as even before
William's peaceful visit to England in 1051, numbers of Norman
and French officials, merchants, and craftsmen, had already
settled in this country.[2]

[1] *Domesday Book*, Essex, 103b–105b.
[2] *Anglo-Norman Language and Literature*, by J. Vising.

This selection of eleventh-century names emphasizes three facts : (i) that monothemes were rare, being not more than 9 per cent, and still fewer among the Saxons. (ii) The great repetition in the O.E. names, no less than sixty-eight having the deuterotheme *-uuin* or *-win* (*wine* " friend "), of which thirteen are Ulwin, ten Alwin, thirteen Lewin, and eleven Godwin. The second element *-ric* is found in forty-three cases, Uluric occurring twelve, and Aluric eleven times. (iii) The decay of the ancient orthography, e.g. Leoflæd has become Leflet, Ulfweard is written Uluuard, and Leofmær is corrupted into Ledmar. These spellings compared with those of the Hatfield boors of not much greater antiquity, convey the impression that the O.E. names suffered considerably at the hands of the Norman scriveners (see below, p. 85).

In view of the great repetition in the personal appellatives of the burgesses, it is remarkable that only 6 per cent display secondary descriptions, of which small proportion half were priests ; but too much reliance must not be placed on the completeness of the scribe's work in this respect, as it is known that second names were largely omitted in the final copy of the book.

Some of these personal names became English surnames in later years : from Lewin, a shortened form of Leofwin, we get Lewin, Lewinson, Levin, Levinson, and other variants ; Sprot (possibly Scandinavian) has given us Sproat, Spratt, and Sprout ; Stanart and Stanhert originated some of the present Stannards and Stonards, others being derived from place-names. Goodwin and Goodwyn are modern representatives of Goduin ; Osgot has become Osgood ; Turchill may easily be our Turtille and Turtle ; and Not, otherwise Noth or Knut, has propagated Nott, Notts, Nutson, and Nutts, to name a few. Blacstan may well have survived in the name Blackstone, which is also derived from Blaxton, Yorks. ; Brictwin, in its modern dress, is Brightwin ; Dereman, as Dearman, is yet represented in the *London Directory* ; Hacon (perhaps Norse) still exists, as do Coleman and Blank ; and Wicga has its descendants in Wigg, Wiggs, and Wigson. Tate is now not uncommon in the same orthographical form, and may be a survival of Norse Teit, from which the Orcadians have obtained their surname Tait ; Siward is now more generally Seward and Seaward ; Best indicates a possible source of the modern Best, which also occurs Beast ; Levesun is yet with us, but whether Jewish (Levi), Welsh (Lewis) or Saxon, is not always apparent. Ascere is the modern Asser and Asher, and Brunwin and Brungar, now Brunker, are in the *London Directory* ; Mansune, a useful early example of Manson, may be Scandinavian, occurring in Norfolk Fines; Alnod has the modern derivative Allnutt, and Ulsi is an early form of twentieth-century Wolsey.

The frequent occurrence of Old Norse or Icelandic names leads to some detailed consideration of the names of the Norsemen.

Names of the Northmen. Brief reference has been made above to the extensive nature of the voyages of discovery and widespread schemes of conquest and colonization carried out by the Vikings; and the very great permanent Scandinavian influence which pervaded the British Isles will be readily realized, even if it were not in daily evidence in our place-names.

Stephens (1866–7), the eminent authority on runic monuments, expressed the view, in no uncertain terms, that the Teutonic element in Britain, in early days, was not nearly so overwhelming as supposed by our historians, and that on the contrary a large proportion of British blood is Scandinavian.

" There is no longer a doubt as to that great historical fact (of which we have so many other independent evidences (archæological and historical and linguistical and geographical and topographical, and ethnographical), as well as an endless flow of ancient tradition on either side of the North Sea), that the old populations of Danish South and North Jutland, the old outflowing Anglic and Jutish and Frisic settlers, mixt with Norse and Swensk adventurers and emigrants, who flockt to England in the 3rd and 4th and 5th and following centuries, were chiefly Scandinavians, Northmen, not Saxons, still less Germans." [1]

Later archæologists have proved the authority of the Scandinavian settlers from their introduction of new territorial divisions, land measurements, social systems, judicial customs, and coinage. As may be expected from their geographical position, the Orkney and Shetland Islands, the Hebrides, and the Isle of Man, provide the most important Viking remains, such as the rune-inscribed crosses. In England, abiding Scandinavian control was greatest in the northern counties, the situation of the settlements of the Northmen being indicated in many cases by Norse-Icelandic elements in the composition of place-names, as, for instance, *thorpe* " a hamlet ", *by* " a homestead ", and so on. Numbers of our surnames, such as Booth, Wray, Thwaite, Beck, are derived from these O. Norse place-words.[2] Personal names are largely used as components in the forming of local designations, e.g. nearly 200 Scandinavian appellatives have been detected in the composition of place-names in the N. Riding of Yorkshire

[1] *The Old Northern Runic Monuments*, by Geo. Stephens, 1866–7, p. xi.
[2] See p. 376.

alone, many of which have become perpetuated as English surnames. A few examples have been selected :—

Boltr, in Boltby (surname Bolter) ; Farmann, in Farmanby (surname Fearman, Firmin, etc.) ; Gamall, in Gammersgill (surname Gammell, Gamble, Gemmell, etc.) ; Griss, in Gristhorpe and Gristhwaite (O. Icel. *griss* " a young pig " : surname Grice) ; Gunni, in Gundale (surname Gunn, Gunnis) ; Hattr, in Hatterboard Hill (perhaps the origin of some of our Hatters) ; Haukr, in Hawkshill (surname Hawk, Hawkes, and possibly some Hawkers) ; Hrafn, in Ravenscar, Ravensworth, etc. (surname Raven) ; Ketill, in Kettlethorpe (surname Kettle) ; Klak (O. Dan.) in Claxton (surname Clack) ; Ormr, in Ormesby (O. Icel. *ormr* " a snake " : surname Orme) ; Russi, in Rosedale (surname Russ) ; Sveinn, in Swainby (O. Icel. *sveinn* " boy " : surname Swaine).[1]

The Viking influence, to a lesser extent, is to be noticed in the place-names of Wales.[2]

Runes. No Icelandic or Old Norse writings of earlier date than about the year 1200 now exist, and the runes are the principal source of our knowledge of the names of the earliest of the visitors from the North. Stephens points out that this modified method of writing was unknown to Saxons or Germans, so that names taken from them are assuredly Norse. The runic alphabet appeared in this country at the close of the Roman period ; a good example being that which appears on a large knife found in the bed of the River Thames, and now preserved in the British Museum.[3] This alphabet which follows, according to Stephens, is of date about A.D. 400–500.

ᚠᚢᚦᚩᚱᚳᚷᚹᚻᚾᛁᛄᛇᛈᛉᛋᛏᛒᛖᛜᛞᛚᛗᛟᚪᚫᚣᛠ

F U Þ O R C G W H N I Y YO P A S T B E NG D L M Œ Á Æ Ü EA

ᛒᛠᚷᚾᚩᚦ BEAGNOTH

As with the transliteration of the ogams, the professors are sometimes at variance, and the following selection of names taken from British stones of supposed dates from A.D. 500–1000 should be accepted with reserve :—

Emund, Cunibalth, Onswini, Onlaf, Stan, Æli, Ræhæbul, Isah or Hasi, Gudred, Ælchfrith, Hilddigüth (f.), Ædred, Sigeric, Gislheard, Tidfirth.

There are many runic inscriptions to be found in the Orkneys, and the ensuing examples of names are taken from

---

[1] *English Place-Name Society*, vol. v, p. 322.
[2] *Norse Place-Names in Gower*, by A. G. Moffat (Viking Club, 1898).
[3] Stephens, vol. i, p. 36.

stones of various unknown dates of the ninth to the twelfth centuries.

Molfr (or Tholfr) Kolbainssonr, Ghaut, Vemuntr (Wemund), Orkasonr, Nuari, Kulturmr, Sikurthr, Iru, Kiaebik, Ingibiorgh (f.), Haelghis, Oframr Sigurthersonr, Otar (or Iota) Fila, Arnfithr Matr (perhaps "the greedy", Stephens), Koukr Traenilsonr, Haemuntr Hartheksi (hard-axe), Lothbrok (f.), Okonaekn (Ogdonagn, "probably a Gaelic name, perhaps corresponding to modern O'Donovan": Rafn), Arnfithr, Staein, Ikikaethir (f.).

Personal Names of the Northmen. The Scandinavian languages are so closely allied to the Gothic, that the Old Norse names often differ little from the Saxon in spelling, and not at all in their formation, so that what has been said above regarding the classification of Anglo-Saxon appellatives applies equally to the Norse-Icelandic : dithematic names are common as Finn-biorn, or Bryn-hildr (f.) ; monothematic names, as Brúnn or Leggr ; derivatives, as Láki from Thorlákr ; Brynki from Bryn-jólfr, and Friða from Holm-friðr.

Regarding the declension of Old Norse personal names, Helfenstein has the following note :—

"Some of the masculine proper nouns follow the strong, others the weak declension ; the former commonly have the thematic -a, as Gunnar, gen. Gunnars, dat. Gunnari ; Askr, Alfr, etc. Such as Grípir, Brímir, etc., follow the declension of hirðir, that is, the themes in -ja. The declension in u is frequently followed by proper names, especially those ending in -mundr, -undr, -hiörtr, -biörn, -vindr, -viðr ; as Sæmundr, Völundr, Arn-biörn, etc. Some decline weak, as Bragi, Loki. Feminine nouns which decline strong may be attributed either to the declension in a or i, because both are identical in the singular."[1]

Additional Descriptions of the Northmen. It will be noticed from the above selection of names that both characteristic and genealogical descriptions additional to personal names were in use. The reader of the Norse annals cannot have failed to observe that by the thirteenth century these supplementary names became more common and that they were often of the most pointed and uncomplimentary nature, such as Árni spýtu-leggr "spindleshanks", Asbjorn krókauga "crook-eye", Einarr klíningr "oily tongue", Hákon galinn "the silly", Hrólfr nefja "nosy", Jón fótr "limp-leg", Lifólfr skalli "bald pate", Thórarin kyllinef "cod-nose", Thórarin breiðmagi "broad paunch", þorfinnr hausakljúfr "skull-splitter", þorir tré-skeggr "tree-beard".[2]

Some ninth-century Danish and Norse names may be obtained from the *Liber Vitæ* of Durham, and eleventh-century

[1] *A Comparative Grammar of the Teutonic Languages*, 1870, p. 330.
[2] Further reference may be made to *Norsk-Islandska Personbinamn* av E. H. Lind, where several thousands of such names are indexed.

examples are found in a codex of the Gospels in the library of York Minster. Few are provided with second names, the most notable being Hálwaerð Sæfugalasuna, which at first sight looks to be a parallel to the modern insult " son of a sea-cook ", but Safugel " sea-fowl " is a personal name, and so in this case is a genealogical description. In later years when second names became common, there is no doubt that like the Anglo-Saxon they were of four types, but although the Norsemen held Man until the thirteenth century, and their language was spoken till an even later period in the north, no lists of their names were preserved, and it is necessary to turn to the Sagas to prove the point.

From the Hakonar Saga has been taken the following selection of names of persons attending a meeting at Bergen in the early thirteenth century.[1]

Characteristic : Ivarr nef (the nosy), Amundi remba (the cockscomb), Gunnar grjónbakr (porridge-back), Kolbjorn rauði (the red), Oláfr mókr (the drowsy), Haraldr stangar-fylja (stakepole), Friðrekr slafsi (the slobberer), Eilifr keikr (back-bent), Páll vaga-skalm (barrow-pole), Ivar geslíngr (gosling).

Local : Ásólfr af Austrætt (of Eastairt), Saxi af Haugi (of Haug), Amundi af Grenland (of Greenland), Hávarðr í Sandbúi (in Sandby).

Genealogical : Gregoríus Jónsson, Gunnbjorn Jóns-bróðir.

Occupational : Eistein Logmaðr (the lawman), þorgeirr Erkidjákn (the archdeacon), þorgeirr Biskupsmaðr (the bishop's man). Possibly also are in this class : Einriði Bækill (the bookling), Hallvarðr Bratti (the climber), Eysteinn Ræðismaðr (the talker).

Of fifty-eight persons named, all except one have a secondary description, but there is nothing of the nature of family names, hereditary or otherwise. It is reasonable to infer that these appellatives fairly represent those that were current in the Isle of Man and Shetlands and parts of Ireland. Some of the Norwegians came to England from their settlements in Ireland and the Isle of Man, where they had become accustomed to the Gaelic form of genealogical description leading to such bi-lingual combinations as Niel Glundubh, a tenth-century king of Ireland, or " Thorfynn mac Thore " found in an eleventh-century charter. The Gaelic influence is yet more noticeable in some compound place-names.[2]

English surnames derived from Old Norse names and descriptions will be mentioned in a later chapter.

Conclusions. Before closing this chapter the progress which

---

[1] Rolls Ser., vol. ii, p. 75.
[2] E. Ekwall (*English Place-Name Soc.*, vol. i, pt. i, p. 35).

took place from the retiral of the Romans in the fifth century to the coming of the Normans in the eleventh century may be summarized. In the first place it has been noticed that Celtic personal names were largely abandoned in those districts which came under the domination of the Saxons, and where the Old English language was introduced : that is the larger part of England, and the district now known as the Scottish Lowlands. In the greater part of the British Isles where the Celtic languages remained, so did the native names.

The popularity and increasing use of Saxon names received a considerable check in the ninth century and onwards, by the arrival of the Northmen. The northern and eastern counties of England, the islands of the north and west of Scotland, the Isle of Man, and parts of Ireland, came under Scandinavian rule, and the Norse language and names made a bid for supremacy. Celtic and Nordic names, therefore, then formed a very considerable proportion of the appellatives of the British Isles.

Secondly, it has been noticed that both Saxons and Northmen, like the Cymry, Gaels, and other races of the Indo-European group, used for distinguishing purposes secondary appellatives or addresses in addition to their forenames. The prevalence of this custom tended to increase, and is a point of great importance, which should not be confused with the practice of giving secondary names or nicknames to be used in lieu of or alternately with the font-name. These additional descriptions, Saxon or Norse, like Gaelic and Cymric, fall, according to source, into four classes already defined. Such descriptions formed essentially marks of identity of the individual, and were not hereditary among Gaels, Cymry, Saxons, or Normans. It is certain that hereditary family surnames were unknown in Great Britain at the coming of William the Conqueror.

CHAPTER IV

NORMAN AND BRETON NAMES AND DESCRIPTIONS, A.D. 1066–1154

Norman Influence. William, duke of Normandy, as the first step in asserting his right to the English crown, landed at Pevensey on 28th September, 1066. Harold, after routing the Norsemen at Stamford Bridge, marched southward, but only to sustain defeat at the Battle of Hastings by the combined forces of Normans, Bretons, and Frenchmen, operating under the command of William. This victory was followed by the conquest of England, the last notable foreign invasion to which Great Britain has been subjected.

The population of England in 1066 is unknown, and it is only possible to estimate, approximately, the number of persons living in this country at that early date. Sir Edward Creasy puts the figure at between a million and a half and two millions, of whom, he says, at least one-third perished during the reign of William I, and he further calculated, as a set-off, that alien immigrants during the same period numbered between two and three hundred thousand.[1] The enterprise, valour, chivalry, mental capacity, and political ability of the Normans have received glowing tributes by our historians, Freeman, for instance, pointing out that " the indomitable vigour of the Scandinavian, joined to the buoyant vivacity of the Gaul, produced the conquering and ruling race of Europe ".

At the time of the Conquest the language of the Normans, commonly called Norman-French, was a debased Latin, embracing Teutonic, Celtic, and Scandinavian elements, and the names of the conquerors had similar characteristics. The formation of their appellatives, therefore, follows on similar lines to those already sketched, and need not be repeated. The diminutive suffixes (see below, p. 274) are, however, of special interest, and, as will be shown, had a great influence in multiplying variants of English names.

It will be gathered from the figures given above that a large number of foreign names were brought into England,

---

[1] *Rise and Progress of the English Constitution*, 1907, p. 60. The author of the *Norman People* concluded that the Conquest involved the migration of a nation, and that " according to all appearance, a third or more of the English population is Norman ", but his figures, based on erroneous deduction, are greatly exaggerated.

accelerating and accentuating a change of personal appellatives, which had already commenced. As the native Celtic names had given way to those of the Saxon and Norse invaders, so in turn were the Gothonic designations largely dropped, regardless of race or language, in favour of those in popular use by the Norman settlers. Owen, Howel, Einion, and Gwenllian, having been displaced, were followed by a long vogue of Ulwin, Sigefrith, Thurcytel, and Ælfgifu, which in turn yielded up their popularity in favour of the Rodbert, Hugo, Guy, and Matilda of the latest incomers. Notwithstanding the great change which rapidly took place, many O.E. names survived, often in almost unrecognizable form, and it is hoped that the analysis of their composition to be attempted in a later chapter will enable some of these lost appellatives to be rediscovered.

Resulting from the Norman Conquest are two features worthy of emphatic notice, first, that although native designations apparently fell largely into disuse, such fact is no indication of change of race.[1] Great numbers of Norman personal names formed the genealogical descriptions of both native Celts and Teutons, and ultimately became established as family names : that the Welsh people alone have been responsible for the perpetuation of some of the most popular names of the Normans is evidenced by the great repetition of Roberts, Williams, and Jones in our directories. The second point of great importance to the subject, to be firmly impressed, is that the language which had superseded the native Cymric, throughout the greater part of England, was able to preserve itself and remain the language of the people, although not of the upper classes.

The custom of bestowing secondary appellatives, noticed above as being so popular with the Norsemen, was, as may be expected, likewise prevalent among the Normans. It will be recognized that most of these medieval descriptions were liable to repetition, and becoming by repute associated with one family, in some cases gained acknowledgment, no longer as the distinction of a mere individual, but as the generic name of his family, applying equally to every member of it. *Repetition, however, does not necessarily indicate inheritance.* This point, being overlooked, has led some inquirers into the antiquity of

---

[1] The anonymous author of *NP.* considered that hereditary surnames are " memorials of race which can never be obliterated ". He ignores the possibility of English persons being given French names by the Norman clerks, and incidentally claims many good old English names to support his contention that the Norman blood preponderates. As this work is still quoted as authoritative, it is necessary to sound a warning note. As an instance may be mentioned Ordericus, the English historian, whose name appearing barbarous to the Normans, was changed by them to Vitalis. *Eccl. Hist. of England and Normandy*, ed. by T. Forester, vol. iv, p. 223.

hereditary surnames to relegate their introduction into Britain to an earlier period than is actually the case ; but before proceeding with an investigation it is advisable to realize that there is a considerable difference between the past and present conception expressed by the word " surname ", which, like some other English vocables, has now no longer its original signification. Nowadays at least ninety-nine out of every hundred persons, if asked what they understood by the word " surname ", would reply at once " a family name ".

Definitions of Description and Surname. The word surname is one of that growing class of English vocables which have greatly changed in meaning, e.g. " cunning " formerly meant " skilled ", an " idiot " was a private person, a " knave " was a male, a " miser " a wretched person, " vivacity " meant " longevity ", and " wit " " was the equivalent of " knowledge ".

Originally a surname or surnoun (Medieval Latin *supranomen, supernomen*) [1] was :—

(i) An address, descriptive epithet, name, or title, added to a person's baptismal name for distinction.

1291–2. " Et si acun eit deus surnouns cel surnoun se tiegne dount il est plus conu." (And where anyone has two surnames, that surname shall hold by which he is best known.) Britton (F. M. Nichols, vol. i, p. 321).

c. 1325. " Richard queor de lyoun. That was his sournoun." Ritson (*Metr. Rom.*, vol. ii, p. 311).

1344. " R. persone del esglise de B . . . Ceo nest en ceo cas forqe surnoun." (In this case it is only a surname.) *Year Book, Trin.* 18 *Edw. III* (Rolls Ser.), p. 247.

" Simon whose sirname is Peter." Acts, x, 5.

(ii) An alternative name given to a person.

Eleventh century. " Habuit etiam prius ex Ægelfleda Candida, cognomento Eneda." *Flor. Wig.*, ed. by B. Thorpe, vol. i, p. 140.

" Joseph called Barsabas (son of Saba), who was sirnamed Jus." Acts, i, 23.

(iii) A personal name given to an unbaptized person.

1698. " There are several persons who purchase by the name of Thomas, John, etc., who were never christened, but in such cases those are surnames only." *Ld. Raymond's Reports*, vol. i, p. 305.

---

[1] Wharton's Lexicon informs us that there are " a thousand instances in court rolls and other ancient muniments where the description of the person is written *over* the christian name, this only being inserted in the line ". Although I have handled a good many old rolls I have never seen anything of the kind. In Domesday Book quite a number of second names may be found written over the christian name, but as it is not the general practice, the impression is that such insertions were to supply clerical omissions or were the result of reconsideration by the compiler. In manorial rolls I have noticed the name of the attorney written above that of his client. From German records, however, Socin (*Mittelhochdeutsches Namenbuch*, p. 461) gives examples of secondary descriptions written over the personal names of witnesses to grants to the Zurichberg Monastery, but it seems to have been a rare practice, and is possibly not found in the original documents.

(iv) A clan name.
" O'Maolmuaidh, slaor an sloindeadh " (noble the surname).
Poem of John O'Dubhagain, v, 14.
" To resset ony rebellis and surname of Clangregour." *Reg. Privy Council Scot.*, vol. i, p. 361.

These four applications of the word " surname " are archaic, yet modern writers continue to use it in sense (i) causing much misunderstanding. To express sense (ii) the word " nickname " or an equivalent is now generally employed ; and to express sense (iii) " first name " or " personal name ", it being a " christian name " by courtesy only ; and to express sense (iv) clan or sept name. The unfortunate modern use of archaism (i) is exemplified by the following extracts :—

1846. *The Names, Surnames, and Nicnames of the Anglo-Saxons.* J. M. Kemble.

1863. " The Kings of Egypt were surnamed Pharaoh," J. Finlayson, *Surnames and Sirenames*, p. 6.

1901. " An early Danish surname Osgod Clapa . . . at the court of Canute," Bardsley's *Dictionary* : Art. Clapp.

1918. " Eric . . . d. A.D. 512, who was surnamed Æsc, i.e. Lance or Spear," H. Harrison, *Surnames*, vol. ii, p. 1.

1925. " Les surnoms apparaissent dès le ixe siècle (Charles Martel, Pépin le Bref)," *Les Noms de Personnes*, par Albert Dauzat.

1927. " Je passe à mes exemples de ˌplus de deux surnoms . . . Pierre de Compens, drapier, Le Vieil," *Etudes*, par K. Michaëlsson, p. 128.

In archaic sense (ii), that is, as an equivalent of nickname, the word " surname " is still employed.

" Besides the patronymics, the local surnames, the surnames descriptive of the bearer's person, there are others which are not as intelligible, surnames which are mere pet names or nicknames . . . In some cases the surname or nickname seems to have altogether supplanted the baptismal name." Freeman, *Norman Conquest*, 1876, vol. v, p. 564.

Notwithstanding that eminent writers continue to employ the word " surname " to signify any secondary appellative of an individual, the writer considers that such usage being misleading should either be qualified or cease entirely, and therefore such an individual indicium is termed a " description " throughout this essay, in preference to " addition ", which might refer to vocation or address. The modern idea of a surname limits it to hereditary names, yet gives it the more extended function of application to all members of the family.

Examination of early pedigrees shows that the additional epithets or descriptions concurrently developed into hereditary names of two different types. One such type is a patronymic which is inherited or perpetuated only by the eldest legitimate sons in succession ; the second type is the family name, as we have it to-day, a patronymic of a male parent, the common right of user being inherited at birth by all legitimate children of the bearer, the sons only of whom transmit it to their legitimate children, and so on, generation after generation. By the nomenclaturist, the word " inheritance " is used in the sense of a birthright, which passes at birth, and independently of the death of the parent, and is a right to joint user, but not a right to sole ownership. In English law there is no property in a surname.

Early genealogies are replete with family names of the first mentioned type : Camden, writing in 1603, noticing a number of such cases, observed that even then, in France, it was customary for the eldest son to perpetuate the father's name, but the younger sons took names of the lands allotted to them.[1] This type of surname continued in England until the fourteenth century, by which time it had been almost superseded by those of the second type, the hereditary surname or patronymic borne in common by all members of the family, main line and collaterals, as defined above.

Of the second mentioned type, a good early example is the ancient local surname d'Oilly (now Olley, Doyle, Doyley). It appears that the Sire d'Oilleia la Ribaude of Normandy had several sons, who came to England in 1066 : Robert Wido(Guy) and Ralph de Oilgi being mentioned in Domesday Book, 1086 ; and since all their known descendants were likewise named d'Oilli,[2] this family name is one which, by the year 1100, had all the characteristics of the modern surname, being a local name in use for three generations, regardless of the fact that the bearers had no interest or association with the place by which they were known. All surnames are now of this second type, yet they are liable to change at the whim of the bearer (see below, p. 410).

It will be realized that, at various times, a second name has been a description :—

(i) Additional to a personal name of an individual.

(ii) Alternative to a personal name of an individual.

(iii) Additional to the personal names of the eldest legitimate sons of a family in succession.

(iv) Additional to the personal names of all members of a family, being transmitted by males to their legitimate children, generation after generation.

Although, as has been said, the word " surname " is still currently used to express all these four concepts, yet in this

¹ 1870 edit., p. 151.
² The Topographer and Genealogist, vol. i, p. 368.

book, unless otherwise stated or qualified, it is only in the last sense that the word is employed, a sharp line of distinction being drawn between personal names : descriptions or addresses (i, iii), surnames (iv), and nicknames (ii).[1] Most of our ancient surnames will be found to have passed through two or three of these classes.

Strictly speaking, a " surname " cannot come into being until the second generation at least, and it ceases to exist as a family name if the genealogy in the male line is not continuous, but there are exceptions, and in such cases the second name may be termed a courtesy-surname. Sometimes, for instance, the " surname " passes with the property to someone not a blood kinsman, and, again, second names are acquired or adopted, but in both cases such designations are surnames only by courtesy.[2] Names of these classes will be considered further in a later chapter (pp. 264–270).

The employment of surnames is sufficiently general to be called universal, and they are now a more certain mark of identity than font-names. In Britain, by general custom, the surname is placed after the christian name, but there is no authoritative regulation on this point.

Antiquity of Surnames. Camden, the eminent sixteenth-century antiquary, was among the earliest of the investigators who devoted attention to the discovery of the antiquity of family names. He and divers whom he knew had " pored and pusled vpon many an old record and evidence " for the purpose of finding hereditary surnames before the Conquest, without success. He expressed his views as follows :—

" About the year 1000 (that we may not minute out the time) surnames beganne to be taken vp in France, and in England about the time of the Conquest or else a very little before, vnder King Edward the Confessor, who was all Frenchified. And to this time doe the Scottishmen referre the antiquitie of their surnames although Buchanan supposeth that they were not in vse in Scotland, many yeares after. But in England certaine it is, that as the better sort, even from the Conquest, by little and little, tooke surnames, so they were not setled among the common people fully vntill about the time of King Edward the second, but still varied according to the father's name as Richardson, if his father were Richard, etc. This will seeme strange to some Englishmen and Scottishmen, which, like the Arcadians, thinke their surnames as ancient as the Moone, or at the least to reach many an age beyond the Conquest. But they which thinke it most strange (I speake vnder correction), I doubt they will hardly finde any surname which descended to posteritie before that time : Neyther have they

---

[1] For definition of nickname see p. 326.

[2] Eyton (*Antiquities of Shropshire*, vol. ii, p. 305) says : " The Norman aristocracy adopted a system which, though in idea patronymic, was in practice anything else. In short, if I may coin the words, it was equally *avonymic* or *proavonymic*, or something higher still."

seene (I feare) any deede or donation before the Conquest, but sub-
signed with crosses and single names without surnames, in this manner
in England :   ✠ Ego Eadredus confirmavi.   ✠ Ego Edmundus
corroboravi ✠ Ego Sigarius conclusi.   ✠ Ego Olfstanus con-
solidavi." [1]

Little fault can be found with this opinion, and Buchanan,
evidently the historian, whom Camden mentions, had a much
sounder view than his namesake of two centuries later, who
cites as ancient surnames in Scotland : Graham (A.D. 404),
Dunbar, and Murray, no evidence whatever being offered,
reference to " historians " unnamed being considered ample
proof. The later Buchanan continues :—

" The third and most clearly documented instance of any hitherto
advanced is that of the illustrious surname of Douglas in king Solvathius'
time, in the year 770. Of which surname Sir William Douglas went
lieutenant to prince William, king Achaius' brother . . . to the service
of Charles the Great, first emperor of the West, after which the said
Sir William, having settled in Tuscany, was ancestor of the Douglasii
there, and in the low countries, who have always retained the ancient
surname, etc., and arms." [2]

Lower (1849–75), as has been shown above, was also
anxious to establish the occasional use of family names in
England " beyond the ingress of the Normans ", and in further
support he cites a single grant from Thorold de Bukenhale,
sheriff of Lincolnshire, of the manor of Spalding to Wulfgate,
abbot of Croyland (Crowland, Lincs.), dated 1051. His
documentary evidence is untrustworthy and his inferences
quite unsound, but even in this day of more scientific inquiry,

---

[1] *Remaines concerning Britain*, by W. Camden, 1603, p. 92.
[2] *An Inquiry into . . . Antient Scottish Surnames*, by Wm. Buchanan,
1820, pp. 7, 9. G. B. di Crollalanza, 1886, says : " Un Guglielmo, cugino
d'Acaio, che regnava in Scozia verso l'anno 787 è il capostipite della gente
Scotta diramatsi in varie città d'Italia," but no authority is cited. C. Poma
supposes that the Counts Douglas Scotti of Piacenza took the name of Douglas
at a much later date than the thirteenth century, " and probably without any
historical foundation " (*Trans. Phil. Soc.*, 1920, pt. i, p. 53). Ancient
assumptions of surnames are common in Scottish histories. The author of the
Genealogie of the Sainteclaires of Rosslyn declares, on the authority of one of
the Buchanans, that Malcolm Canmore in a general council at Forfar in 1061
" volens ut Primores, quod antea non fuerat, aliarum more gentium, a praediis
suis cognomina caperent ". Many new surnames were given to the families
of the Scots as Mar, Calder, Lockhart, Meldrum, Gordon, Seaton, Liberton,
Lawder, Shaw, Leirmont, Strachane, from the lands they had in possession,
some from their office as Stewart, Dorward, Bannerman, Forman, etc. Some
from the names of valiant men, as Kenneth, Gray, Kent, etc. (R. A. Hay,
1835, p. 3). A tall story is told of the Scottish surname of Coulthard, which
is still put forward as of great antiquity, notwithstanding the fictitious nature
of the family evidences commencing with an invention called a " marriage
settlement " dated 21 Kenneth III (tenth century). This " evidence " is
cited again quite recently over the name of an F.S.A. Scot. (*Weekly Scotsman*,
29th March, 1930).

like the Saxon document referred to above, are still being repeated.[1]

It will be advisable to disregard the opinions of Camden, Turner, Ferguson, Buchanan, and Lower on the point of antiquity of surnames, and to consider the subject *de novo*, using for the investigation documents which are above suspicion.

In view of the barrenness of the search for early surnames in English documents, which has been disclosed in the last chapter, the preliminary inquiry will be directed towards Continental records of pre-Conquest dates. The earliest Norman, Breton, and French documents containing names which are available to the student are mainly grants to religious houses, of which a good selection may be found in *Collection de Documents Inédits*, and in the works of Lobineau,

---

[1] I notice T. M. Blagg (1900) has accepted Lower's remarks, and even Dauzat (*Les Noms de Personnes*, 1925, p. 48) chooses Dubb and Tuck, to illustrate " surnoms . . . ont subsisté dans les noms de famille actuels ". The document, according to the printed version, is as follows :—

" Ego Thoroldus de Bukenhale . . . donavi & tradidi Deo & sancto Guthlaco Croylandiae . . . in villa de Spaldlyng, totum manerium meum . . . cum omnibus terris & tenementis, reditibus, servitiis, averiis, & utensilibus, quæ habui in dicto manerio . . . cum omnibus appendiciis suis, scilicet Colgrinum præpositum meum, & totam sequelam suam, cum omnibus bonis & catallis, quæ habet . . . Item Hardyngum fabrum, & totam sequelam suam, . . . Item Lefstanum carpentarium & totam sequelam suam . . . Item Ryngulphum primum . . . Idem (*sic*) Elfstanum piscatorem . . . Item Gunterum Liniet . . . Item Outy Grimkelson . . . Item Turstanum Dubbe . . . Item Algarum nigrum . . . Item Edricum filium Siwardi . . . Item Osmundum molendarium . . . Item Besi Tuk . . . Item Elmerum de Pyncebek . . . Item Gouse Gamelson . . . Istud meum chirographum apud Leycestriam . . . anno Dominicæ incarnationis MLI."

Regarding the names in this " early " charter, Lower observed :—
" Now while the terms reeve, smith, carpenter, the first, fisher, the black, miller, etc., applied respectively to Colgrim, Harding, Lefstan, etc., are merely personal descriptions : Liniet, Dubbe, Tuk and De Pincebeck, have the appearance of settled surnames. The same distinction is observable between Edric the son of Siward and Grimkelson and Gamelson. Indeed some of these surnames are yet remaining amongst us, as Dubbe, Tuk, Liniet and Pincebek—now spelt Dubb, Tuck, Linney and Pinchbeck, a fact which I think goes far to prove that they were hereditary at the time when the deed of gift was made."

It is not possible to follow Lower in his argument that because the second names are similar to modern surnames, it was evidence that they were hereditary from this time (1051). Like the O.E. and Norse names cited above, such names may have repeated themselves in the same family without having attained any hereditary characteristic, but there is, unfortunately, no evidence to show that these particular names did repeat themselves as second names at this early date. Tochi, Toka, Toke, etc., appears as a personal name in Domesday Book (1086) and its contemporaries, but there is nothing like Liniet, Dubbe, and Pincebeck in such records, nor in the Liber Wintoniensis ('1103–15), Lindsey Survey (1115–18), and Pipe Roll (1130–1). It is also unfortunate for Lower's argument that he did not select an original document. The Croyland charters are but modernized versions, if not the actual forgeries that numerous writers believe them to be.

Regarding the authenticity of the Ingulfine charters, see " Ingulf and the Historia Croylandensis," by W. G. Searle (*Camb. Antiq. Soc.*, xxvii, pp. 153, 206).

Marchegay, Yeatman, Round, and in the *Monasticon Anglicanum*. As an illustration of the single nature of witnesses' names in the ninth century, the following list of Celtic names from a foundation charter of the Abbey of Plélan by Salomon, " princeps " of Brittany, is representative :—

" Ratuili episcopus Aletis ; Pascuuethen ; Bran ; Nominoe filius Boduuan ; Ronuuallon filius Bescan ; Drehoiarn ; Iaruocon filius ejus ; Ratfred ; Tanetherht ; Hinuualart ; Catuuoreth ; Hetruiarn ; Sidert ; Trethian ; Kenmarhoc ; Guethenoc ; Arvidoe ; Saludem ; Hedreuuedoe ; Hidran ; Gleudalan ; Koledoc ; Balandu ; Tenior ;   Arthnou ;   Eucant ;   Uuoran ;   Gleu ;   Chourant ; Ronuuallon ; Judhoccar ; Uuadel ; Judlouuen presbyter ; Louencar presbyter ;   Anauuedoe presbyter ;   Bili clericus ;   Conuuoion clericus ; Haelican presbyter ; Egreval presbyter ; Ricarth presbyter." [1]

De Courson (1863), who gives a list of about 700 personal names collected from Breton charters, remarks that surnames became common in the first half of the eleventh century, but by " surnames " he clearly means nothing more than epithets or descriptions.[2]

By the eleventh century the Normans, like the Anglo-Saxons, had found the desirability of adding descriptions to the names of witnesses. An original grant by Richard (II), duke and prince of the Normans, to the Abbey of Mont St. Michael, *circa* 1026, is attested as follows :—

T[estes] Rotbertus archiepiscopus ; Hugo episcopus Ebroicencis ; Herbertus episcopus Luxoviensis ; Niellus vicecomes ; Tursten vicecomes ; Alveredus vicecomes ; Walterius vicecomes ; Richardus vicecomes ; Guimundus vicecomes ; Hubertus ; Osbernus [?] frater comitisse ; Hunfredus frater ejus ; Roscelinus ; Normannus Silveron ; Bernardus filius ejus ; Osbertus filius Arfast ; Ranulfus frater ejus ; Hugo clericus, et multi alii.[3]

An original charter by Rotbert, son of the above-named Duke Richard, to the same Abbey, and of a few years later date, is witnessed, among others, by the following :—

Hugo vicecomes filius Turstingi ; Ricardus de Crolei ; Rodulfus Taisson et frater ejus Ernis ; Osbertus filius Erfasti ; Nigellus vicecomes ; Fulco filius Gerardi ; Rabel ; Willelmus filius Turstingi.[4]

Secondary descriptions, as with the Saxons, were rarely given to the lower classes. Countess Hildegard (1046) named her serfs in a deed of gift :—

Goslenum (Goscelin) ; Girbuidum ; Isembardum ; Frogerium ; Obergam (Oberge) ; Seualdum ; Rohodum ; Simonem ; Constantium

[1] " Chartularium Abbatiæ Sancti Salvatoris Retonensis " (*Collection de Documents Inédits*, p. 192).
[2] Ibid., p. ccxxxiii.
[3] *Calendar of Documents preserved in France*, ed. by J. H. Round, vol. i, p. 250.
[4] Ibid., p. 251.

Rufum (i.e. Constant le Roux) ; Obrannum fratrem ejus ; Richildim ; Milisendim ; Dodam (Dode) ; [names are latinized in the accusative case.] [1]

Documentary evidence is insufficient for a comprehensive and exact comparison of the growth in use of secondary descriptions in England and Normandy respectively, but the impression gained from the witnesses' names to available charters is that progress of one country was in parallel with that of the other. In both cases ecclesiastics and crown ministers had rank specified ; but regarding untitled laymen, the practice varied considerably : one English document (c. A.D. 1018) gives fourteen persons additional descriptions [2] ; another, of later date (c. 1064), has ten personal names only [3] ; and, on the whole, excluding clerics and court officials, there are as many with as without descriptions. Eleventh-century Norman charters show that of 100 lay witnesses seventy had descriptions in addition to their personal names, no count being made of those who were described by relationship to other witnesses. [4] In the Cartulaire de l'Abbaye de Chartres, a list of forty-three witnesses to a deed (ante 1034) shows that fifteen had single names and twenty-eight some secondary description (65 per cent). [5]

The comparison, admittedly, is not wholly satisfactory, but it points to the fact that the English were not beholden to the Normans or French for an introduction to this method of identification, even if the evidence already given is not sufficient to establish the native custom of bestowing second names by Gaels and Cymry.

Norman and French Descriptions. As has been noted with the Gaels and Saxons, it is evident that four classes of descriptions were in use with Normans, Bretons, and French.

Characteristic. Examination of charters sealed prior to 1066 shows few hereditary descriptions of the characteristic class. Taisson, signifying " badger " (now the modern French surname Tesson or Teysson), cited above, is apparently an early example of a metaphorical description or nickname which ultimately became a surname, but it is quite possible that it was of some entirely different origin. In a grant of William, prince of the Normans, to the Abbot of Marmoutier, c. 1048, the name is written Taison (Radulfi Taisonis) [6] ; and in another charter of the same prince, c. 1050–60,[7] and also again in 1063,[8] it occurs as Taxonis (gen.). A modern transcript of a charter of Henry I, sealed c. 1126, gives the

---

[1] *Archives d'Anjou*, par Paul Marchegay, vol. iii, No. 33.
[2] KCD., vol. iv, p. 10.   [3] Ibid., vol. iv, p. 172.
[4] *Cal. of Documents.*   [5] Vol. i, p. 175.
[6] *Cal. of Documents*, vol. i, p. 421.   [7] Ibid., vol. i, p. 201.
[8] Ibid., vol. i, p. 424.

name as Tayson.[1] A similar name is Gernon (N.F. *guernon, grenon* " moustache "), which was a real distinction, the Normans being generally clean shaven.

> " N'ont mie barbes ne guernons
> Co dist Heraut, ' com nos avons '."
> *(Roman de Rou, 7133).*

Rotbert Grennon, Guernon, or Grenon (1056–62),[2] is possibly the same Robert Gernon who held under William I in various counties in England in 1086. Other examples of pre-Conquest Norman characteristic descriptions are : *c.* 1026, Hugo Laicus (the layman) ; *c.* 1042, Neillus Juvenis (the young) ; *c.* 1042, Hunfredus Parvus (the small) ; *c.* 1063, Hugo Britto (the Breton). Possibly of this class are : *c.* 1042, Hunfredus Namo ; *c.* 1055, Odo Instigande (elsewhere Stigandus) ; and 1066, Willelmus Trenchfoil.   Examples from early Breton charters are : 846, Cowalcar qui et Ebolbain ; 860, Maenhoiarn qui et Urvoid ; 868, Maenhoiarn qui et Cornic ; 871, Cumhael qui et Boric ; 1040, Gradlon Crosleboc ; 1052, Bernard Loba.[3] The cryptic *qui et* was the recognized formula which afterwards gave way to *alias*.

The French, like Romans, Normans, and Norsemen, were fond of bestowing pointed epithets, as appears by the following examples taken from the *Cartulaire de l'Abbaye de Saint-Père de Chartres* : 1034, Rodolfus Delicatus ; 1066, Amalricus Sine Pilo (without a hair) ; *c.* 1070, Radulfus Pinguis Lingua (fat tongue) ; 1070, Roscelinus prænomine Equulus (little horse) ; 1070, Gualterius Pungens Asinum (pricking the ass) ; 1080, Herbertus Canis Parvulus (very small dog) ; *c.* 1080, Walterius Blancus Oculus (white eye) ; 1102, Gaufridus Non bibens aquam (not drinking water). Following the Romans, the French attempted to distinguish between prænomen, cognomen, and agnomen, but the distinction is not obvious, and the terms appear to be misapplied, e.g. 1077, Vir nomine Girardus prænomine Caper ; 1061, Walterus cognomine Fugans Lupum ; twelfth century, Garinus agnomine Trussebacon.[4]

Local Descriptions. Under the organization known as the feudal system, of which one of the fundamental principles was the holding of land by vassalage in return for services, usually military, it was the most natural order of things that the tenant should become known by the name of his fief, the foundation of his value to his suzerain, and measure of his importance in the world ; and since a tenant of the Crown sat in Parliament in virtue of the barony held by him, that,

---

[1] *Calendar of Documents preserved in France,* ed. by J. H. Round, vol. i, p. 522.   [2] Ibid., pp. 395, 423.
[3] De Courson, p. ccxxxiii.   [4] M. Guérard, 1840, vol. i.

when in the thirteenth century summons was made by writ, the name of such territory should be entered. It cannot be doubted that the feudal system was responsible for a number of territorial designations being perpetuated, ultimately to become family names, but, nevertheless, the great majority of our local surnames have no origin in the holding of a lordship.

It will have been gathered that territorial descriptions, such as de Montford (Monteforti), de Braiose, de Warenne, de Vere, d'Aubigny, de Montgomeri, etc., came into common use with the Norman lords in the eleventh century, but the practice was not confined to the Normans ; for instance, in the eleventh-century deed preserved in the Chartres Abbey cartulary, which has been noticed above, of the names of forty-three witnesses, nine were local with the preposition *de* ; two others being of different local type, viz. Hubertus Dunensis and Guido Jerusalem. At first, like the Anglo-Saxon addresses with preposition *æt*, and the territorial additions to the names of Scottish lairds of the present day, such distinctions applied only to the holders of the lands for the time being, were not hereditary. In the British Isles, surnames in current use are Mountford, Bruce, Warren, Vere, Daubeney, Montgomery, etc., but it does not follow that the bearers are descendants of those who were first known by the names, or even that their ancestors ever owned any land.[1]

Other examples of pre-Conquest local descriptions are: (i) 1059, Gauffridus de Bailliol [2] ; 1059, Galterius ad barbam de Davidisvilla ; 1060, Ricardus de Drincourt ; 1066, Turgisius de Tracei (now Tracy) ; (ii) ? 1031, Rogerus Todelensis (of Tosny). The preposition *de* took the place of *æt*, and not being confined to landholders, became common in latinized descriptions of all classes down to the servile ; sometimes giving way to the Welsh *o*, but never to the English equivalent " of ", until the fourteenth century.

Genealogical descriptions. Norman distinctions of this class were of two types : the one expressing the relationship in Latin or French ; the other by the mere addition of the personal name of the progenitor. The main sources of early examples are the charters, which being written in Latin, words expressing family relationship are usually also in that language, as : (i) *c.* 1055, Turoldus filius Osberni de Freschenes ; *c.* 1060,

---

[1] W. Paley Baildon (*Baildon and the Baildons*, vol. ii, pp. 4–10) holds the contrary view, saying that he has never met with a " clearly proved instance " of *de* indicating " place of birth ", and that a name like " de Baildon " implies a descent from a person who took his name " from his being a member of the family which was seated at Baildon ". Yet on a later page he writes : " In most of such cases, de Ireland, de Craven, de Nottingam, etc., the *de* probably denotes origin and nothing else."

[2] This name came to England, occurring in Domesday Book, 1086 ; another of the name becoming king of Scotland in the thirteenth century.

Serlus filius Alveredi ; c. 1060, Ricardus Britesonis filius ;
c. 1063, Hamo de Valle filius Guidonis ; c. 1063, Gauslinus
frater Lisiardi. (ii) c. 1063, Galterius Tyrrellus (perhaps the
Walter Tirelde of Essex, 1086, founder of the family of Tyrrell
in that county, a namesake of whom accidently killed William
Rufus).

Fitz, derived from Lat. *filius*, was used in all records
written in the Norman-French language. Rarely in Breton
charters the native method of expressing genealogy was
retained, and may be illustrated by an interesting eleventh-
century example :—

Cujus rei testes sunt Houel Comes & uxor ejus Hadevis ; Kadou
mab David ; Killæ mab Gusfred ; Saliou mab Gulchuenn ; Guenn
mab Gualch ; Lancelin mab Budoere ; Derian mab Tanki ; Kadoret
mab Huelin ; Even mab Edern ; Jungomarch mab Gurgarael ;
Rudalt & Loies Huarnn filii Altfred ; Cadiou citharista (the player on
the cithara) ; Benedictus Abbas ; Jungomarus Abbas ; Justus Mon-
[achus] ; Riwallun Mon. ; Tanki ; Perenesius ; Trehanton Monachi ;
Anni Domini MLXIX.[1]

In a number of cases the word *filius* was dropped entirely,
and the baptismal names Giffard, Talbot, Bertram, Crispin,
etc., may be found as budding surnames, prior to the Conquest.
A charter of the Abbot of S. Père de Chartres (1060) mentions
among the nobles of William, count of Normandy, Walter
Gifard and Robert Bertrann [2] ; the first named occurring in
the genitive, iufardi, in a transcript of a charter of William,
prince of the Normans, to the Abbot of Marmoutier, c. 1048.[3]
In other eleventh-century deeds this genealogical description
occurs as Giphard, Gilford, Gifard, and Gisford,[4] the name
being introduced into England at or soon after the Conquest.
Bertrand or Bertram, as both personal and family name, is
found in pre-Conquest documents. An eleventh-century gift
(1061 or 1080) to the Abbey of Bernay [Eure] is witnessed
among others by Willelmo Berthramno [5] ; and to a charter
of Hugh de Montfort to St. Himer [Calvados], about the year
1067, Robert Bertramn bears witness.[6] Elsewhere the orthographical form is Bertrann, Bertran, and *de* Bertram.[7] The
name of the patron saint of shoemakers was popular as a
personal name, and occurs also as a secondary description in
early records, Gislebert Crispin being witness to a charter of
William, duke of Normandy, *circa* 1050 [8] ; occurring again in
a document of the year 1055 [9] ; and Milo Crispin held numerous
manors in England in 1086. The personal name Talbot was

¹ Cartul. Kemperley (i.e. Quimperlé), *Histoire de Bretagne*, vol. ii, col. 120.
² *Cal. of Docts.* (Round), vol. i, p. 456.   ³ Ibid., p. 421.
⁴ Ibid., pp. 137, 400, 431, 503.   ⁵ Ibid., p. 137.
⁶ Ibid., p. 120.   ⁷ Ibid., pp. 186, 253, 341.
⁸ Ibid., p. 252.   ⁹ Ibid., p. 423.

well on the way to becoming a surname before the Conquest :
Hugh Talebot, a nobleman living *c.* 1060,[1] and Geoffrey and
Richard Talebot being under-tenants in Essex and Beds
in 1086, according to the Domesday Survey. Another
embryonic surname was Pagan, a witness to a deed of 1055
being Ralph Pagan.[2]

At this early date there is little sign of the free use of
diminutives and double diminutives, which afterwards became
such a prominent feature in the names of Normandy and
France.

Occupational descriptions. To the above-mentioned deed
of 1055 a witness is Hugh Buteiller, providing one of the earliest
examples of a name of this class to become hereditary. In
Domesday Book his name is latinized Hugo Pincerna. Other
examples of pre-Conquest occupational descriptions are :
1031, Osbernus Dapifer ; 1055, Geraldus Senescal ; *c.* 1060,
Rotbertus Venator (the hunter) ; *c.* 1062, Hugo Forestarius ;
c. 1066, Ilgerius Pedagogus ; *c.* 1066, Giraldus coquus ; 1066,
Morinus Pistor (the baker).

The next survey will be of Anglo-Norman sources, commencing with an account of the inhabitants of Winchester in
or before the year 1066.

Liber Wintoniensis, A.D. 1066.[3] The first part of this
survey, made in order to ascertain what King Edward the
Confessor had held in Winchester, as of his own demesne,
was compiled between the years 1103 and 1115, according to
Round. Bishop Lyttelton (1756) thought " the great number
of sur-names amongst the Confessor's tenants as remarkable,
and considered they must have been Normans settled here
by the King ".[4] With this opinion the writer does not agree,
examination of the font-names of the tenants with double
appellatives showing that, with one or two exceptions, they
are undoubtedly old English, and are, therefore, most unlikely
to have been borne by aliens. Upon enumeration it was found
that in the first part of this " Domesday Book " there were
about 600 persons named, of whom half were tenants in the
time of Edward the Confessor, and, therefore, living in 1066,
the remainder flourishing at the making of the survey. The
document consequently provides a valuable list of early
designations, but in making deductions therefrom it has to
be remembered that the names are from a city only, where
additional descriptions would be in use before necessity had
coined them in the villages, and the proportion of double
names would be above the average ruling over the whole

[1] *Cal. of Docts.*, vol. i, p. 24.   [2] *Ibid.*, p. 422.
[3] Edited by Sir Henry Ellis (Rec. Comm.).
[4] *British Topography*, ed. by R. Gough, vol. i, p. 388.

country. It must also be borne in mind that the extant copy of the record was made perhaps thirty or forty years subsequent to the survey, which in turn was investigating tenancies of forty years previously.

At this stage reference will be made only to names of the tenants living in 1066. Of these persons 55 per cent had single names, as exemplified by the following illustrations, the more common Anglo-Saxon appellatives of which representative selections have already been made being eliminated.

Babbi (possibly Scand., and origin of some of the modern Babbs) ; Balloc (? Celt.) ; Bolle ; Brun ; Brunman ; Bullochsiega (see also below, p. 98) ; Chiping ; Climehen ; Colling (now Collins, Collings) ; Dalphin (now Dolphin) ; Dodesmere ; Euerwin ; Farman (formerly Færeman, now Fairman, Fearman, etc.) ; Fugel (now Fowle, Vowell, Voules, Fuggles, etc.) ; Fulges and Fulcard (now Fulchard) ; Godesbrand (perhaps the modern Goodbarne, Goodban, etc.) ; Got (now Good) ; Hachehasse ; Hauoc (O.E. *hafoc* " hawk ") ; Helbing ; Hizema ; Huneman ; Issiran ; Lancdelere ; Lufmancat ; Lefflet (i.e Leofflaed) ; Luteman ; Mandole ; Pilluc ; Pot (now Potts) ; Pucheshele ; Safugel (see p. 68) ; Sideloc ; Sireman ; Snuewin (elsewhere Snæwine) ; Tart'e ; Totelbied ; Tutel (now Tootle, Tuttle, etc.) ; Victric ; Wenestan (now Winston) ; Wnprice.

Characteristic descriptions, so far as they can be identified, do not account for more than 4 per cent of the total. Hwit and Ruffus are noticeable, and Francigena, i.e. Frenchman, also comes into this class; Blanchebiert (ancestor of our Blackbeard and Blackbird), Clenehand (cf. Whythand, Yorks. Poll Tax, 1379), Flathege, Fulebiert, Littleprot, Penifeder (modern Pennyfather), Penipurs, Softebred, Witegos, may likewise be nicknames, but it is unsafe to judge hastily from sound and appearance.

Local descriptions, such as de Chrichlelada (Cricklade), or de laforda (now Ford), accounted for but 5 per cent of the total.

Genealogical descriptions. About 10 per cent of the tenants were identified by the addition of names of relatives, in three different forms—

(i) Alwinus Aitardessone ; Alwinus Sidessone ; Odo Ticchemanessone ; Leflet Ecregeles docter (O.E. *dohtor* " daughter ") ; Alwinus Childebroder.

(ii) Alwinus pater Chepingus (*sic*) ; Osbertus filius Oini (Owen if not Odin) ; Sawinus frater Wnstani.

(iii) Edric Ceci ; Godwin Goce.

In four of the examples of type (i) the font-names are latinized, the fifth being purely O.E. ; all of type (ii) are latinized throughout ; the last two descriptions are O.E and Norman respectively. Rather more than half the descriptions of this class are native.

Occupational descriptions in O.E. or Latin were in the proportion of 11 per cent, e.g. Brandwirchte (brandwright), Chenicte (knight, if not the personal name), Faber (the smith), Fenarius (the hay-seller), Hosarius (the hosier), Monetarius (the moneyer), Parcherius (the parker or pindar, now Parker, Pindar, Pinner, etc.), Savonarius (the soapmaker, now Soper), Scalarius (the stile or laddermaker), Sutor (the shoemaker).

Some of the double names provide an interesting study, and many of them cannot be identified with certainty : Ellis has referred to what he calls the French affectation of murdering names, and no doubt the deviation was considerable under Norman influence. In a further selection the Latin terminations of the christian names have been omitted.

Leovric Abeaham ; Bictric Bade ; Lewin Balloc ; Brucstan Banne ; Ulueve Betteslaf ; Lippestan Bittecat ; Gilebert Bochenel ; Alestan Braders ; Aluered Caddebelloc ; Godwin Cederli ; Lewin Chane ; Ulward Cheppe ; Edric Chuet (Chute is a village in Hants) ; Godwin Clawecuncte ; Alestan Coppede ; Theodric Coq ; Burewold Crul ; God' Cunnebried ; Leuing Drache (now perhaps Drake) ; Wuinestaha' Escitteport ; Godwin Forz [1] ; Wenestan Fotebord ; Burewold Frefhewin ; Andrebode Gangeor ; Edwin Godeswale ; Godwin Gretsud ; Ediwin Gule (now perhaps Gull) ; Luwold Gustate ; Wlward Harengar ; Godman Helteprest ; Alwin Heuere ; Borewold Horloc (now Horlock) ; Alwin Jeltfange ; Welestan Opchieher ; Elmar Pictuerte ; Alwin Poplestan ; Godwin Porriz ; Godwin Sarz [1] ; Estan Scodhe (elsewhere Scodies) ; Godwin Socche ; Alnod Stud (now Studd) ; Aluric Sulebiert ; Aluric Toi (now Toye) ; Ulgar Wantar ; Lewin Waterpotes ; Alwin Watmaungre ; Lewin Wrtwos ; Edwin Wridel (perhaps the solution of some of our Riddels).

Skeat has analysed the effect of Norman influence upon the making of English genealogical surnames, and from his valuable notes the following details are extracted :—

The English *th* caused trouble and was treated in three different ways : (i) By omitting it, the prototheme Æthel- becoming Æl-, giving us Aylward and Aylwin for Æthelweard and Æthelwine. (ii) By turning *th* into *t*, thus Thurbeorht gives Turbett. (iii) By turning *th* into *d*, when the *th* occurs in the middle of a name or at the end of it, as Æthelwine becoming Adlin and Edlin.

The final *-ald* was changed into *-auld* and *-aud* : e.g. O.E. Regenbeald became in M.E. Reynebaud from which is derived the Mod. E. Rainbow. The same *-ald* also became *-all*, as in Kimball from Cynebeald.

There was a tendency to turn the letter *w* into *v* before *a, e,* or *i,* and to drop it before *o* or *u.* Examples are : Ælfwine,

[1] Terminal *z* is very often nothing more than a sign which indicates apocopation (see below, p. 297).

from which Elvin and Elwin ; Hereweard, from which Harward and Harvard. In Ayloffe from Æthelwulf and Reynold from Regenwold (i.e. Regenweald) the *w* was entirely suppressed.

Final *h* was replaced by *k*, as Elphick for Ælfheah, or *ch*, as Alfech, "which readily passed into the 'voiced' form Alfege (with Norman *ge* = English *j*)." [1]

Domesday Book, A.D. 1066-86. For investigation of the appellatives entered in the Great Survey, Ellis's *Introduction* may be advantageously examined. This most useful work furnishes fairly accurate indexes by which persons named in the record are classed under three heads : (i) Tenants of William *in capite* ; (ii) persons holding lands in the time of Edward the Confessor and through later years anterior to the formation of the Survey ; (iii) under-tenants of lands at the formation of the Survey.

A glance at the second list, which contains about 2,000 examples (eliminating duplicates and variants), as may be expected, shows that it is composed largely of Anglo-Saxon names, and it is not surprising therefore to find, on a count of one thousand entries, that 85 per cent of persons had single names. Actually the proportion might be greater, as frequently several individuals bearing the same font-name for want of distinction have been indexed as one person. Of the 15 per cent having additional descriptions, 1 per cent only have characteristic epithets, 3 per cent are local, 2 per cent genealogical, 7 per cent occupational, the remaining 2 per cent being accounted for by double names not identifiable with certainty. A few examples of single and double names will now be given. Taking in the first place a selection of the single names which are found without secondary descriptions, a number will be recognized as having become surnames ultimately, but it must not be supposed that such family names date from the eleventh century. Latin terminations are omitted.

Old English : Ældred (now Eldred) ; Ælfec (now Elphick) ; Ælgar (now Algar, Elger) ; Ælsi (now perhaps Else) ; Ailof (now Ayloffe, Ayliffe, Iliffe, etc.) ; Balduin (formerly Bealdwine, now Baldwin) ; Bot (now Bott) ; Brixi (formerly Beorhtsige, now Brixey ; also occurs as a place-name, possibly in error—Godel de Brixi, Kent, 6*b*) ; Brungar (now Brunker) ; Burchard (formerly Burgheard) ; Camp (" soldier ", now Camp, Kemp) ; Colbert (formerly Colbeorht) ; Cole (probably not genuine O.E. ; Redin, p. 46) ; Collinc (now Collins, Collings) ; Doda (now Dodd) ; Donninc (now Dunning) ; Frane (now Fraine) ; Fulcher (formerly Folcric) ; God (now Good) ; Godric (now Goodrich) ; Halden ; Hardinc (now Harding) ; Hune (now Honey) ; Lambe (from Lambert perhaps) ; Levedai (formerly Leofdæg, now Loveday) ; Leuinc (now Lewin) ; Raven (formerly Ræfen ; *hræfn* " the raven ") ; Sauuard (now Seward) ; Sparhauoc (now Sparrowhawk, Spark) ;

[1] *Trans. Phil. Soc.*, 1907, p. 60 et seq.

Suetman (now Sweatman, Sweetman) ; Tunne (now Tunney) ; Turbert (now Turbot, Turbutt) ; Wada (now Wade) ; Wlsi (now Wolsey).

Norman : Alan (now Allen) ; Austin (formerly Augustine) ; Durand ; Eudo ; Hugo ; Ivo ; Pagan ; Walter. Norman names are themselves often of Teutonic origin.

Cymric : Artur ; Euing (if not an O.E. *-ing*-name) ; Ewen ; Grifin ; Juing or Iving ; Madoch (now Maddock, Mattock) ; Morganau ; Merefin (now Marvin) ; Ouen ; Ouuin ; Rees ; Riset (an under-tenant) ; Tuder (i.e. Theodore ; an under-tenant) ; Wihomarc.

Gaelic : Donecan (an under-tenant) ; Doneuuald (an under-tenant) ; Finegal (the white foreigner) ; Ghille (O.Ir. *gilla* " servant ") ; Ghilander (Gael. Gilleandrais " servant of St. Andrew ") ; Ghilebrid (servant of St. Bridget) ; Ghilemicel (servant of St. Michael) ; Ghilepatric (servant of St. Patrick) ; Magbanec ; Malcolun (O.Ir. Maelcolumban " servant of Colman ") ; Melmidoc (? Maelmaedhog) ; Meurdoch (now Murdoch).

Scandinavian : Canud ; Chctel (now Kettle) ; Cnut (now Not) ; Eiric ; Fin (a Dane) ; Hacon ; Iric ; Osbern (Asbiörn, now Osborne) ; Phin (a Dane) ; Ram (the strong) ; Simond (a Dane) ; Strang (a Dane) ; Suain ; Thorbern ; Tol (a Dane).

Flemish : Drogo (de Bevraria, ancestor of Briwere, Brewer) ; an under-tenant was " Rainbertus Flandrensis " ; Gerbodo, Lanbert, Manbodo, Erenbald, Franco, Balduin, Albert, Alelm, Radulf, Roger, Turstin, Tedbald, Wazelin, Wazo, as vassals of Drogo, were also, doubtless, Flemings.

Hebrew : Adam ; Eli ; Joseph ; Salomon ; Isac (tenant in chief) ; Manasse (gen., tenant in chief). The bearers of these names were not necessarily Jews, e.g. " Isaacus prepositus canonicorum Sancti Andreæ " (*Exon. Dom.*, p. 71).

Many names in Domesday Book are apocopes (see p. 272), such as Asul, shortened from Asulf, Blon from Blond, Pantul from Pantulf, and Toul from Toulf. Probably apocopation is the cause of many of the apparently uncompounded names with which this record abounds, such as the following examples :

Ape (possibly alien ; Redin), Bil, Burro, Dot, Feg, Fisc, Fot, Gos, Grene, Grim, Gudda, Gunni, Har, Her, Hoch, Hoga (prudent), Lant, Ledi, Let, Lord, Ludi, Mal, Man, Manno, Mere, Mule, Novi, Oda, Olf, Orde, Orm, Padda, Pat, Roc, Rold, Sɘxa, Scula, Sol, Sort, Sota, Sport, Stam, Sten, Ster, Strik, Suet, Suga, Teit, Thol, Thure, Toc, Tof, Tone, Tope, Tor, Tord, Tou, Tumi, Unban, Unfac, Untan, Waga, Wand, Wege, Wiga, Wine (see also below, p. 252).

A selection of double names of persons holding lands in the time of Edward the Confessor, and prior to the Domesday survey, will now be given. The Latin terminations of fore-names have been omitted.

Edwin Alferd (perhaps the modern Alford) ; Goduin Alfit ; Gameltorp Bar (i.e. Scand. Barn) ; Siuuard Barn ; Turchil Batoc ;

Bricmer Belehorne (occurs also 1275, Hund. R.) ; Leuin Benne ;
Osmund Benz (now Bence) ; Aluuin Boi ; Alric Bolest ; Alsi Bolla ;
Aldred Bot (now Boot) ; Brictmar Bubba (now Bubb) ; Godric
Burnes ; Aluric Busch (now Bush) ; Aluric Camp (now Kemp) ;
Galter Canud (i.e. Cnut, now Nott, Nutt) ; Aluric Capin (now Capen) ;
Aluric Capus (Lat. " capon ") ; Uluric Cassa (now Cass, Cash, Case) ;
Uluric Cauua ; Uluric Chenp ; Wluuin Chit (now Chitt) ; Godric
Cloch ; Leuric Cobbe ; Grimbold Crac ; Leswin Croc (now Crook) ;
Aluuin Cubold ; Aluuin Deule ; Leuin Doda (now Dodd) ; Aluuard
Dore ; Aseloc Durand ; Ulf Fenisc ; Goduin Franpalt ; Raimund
Girald ; Aluuin Gotone ; Albert Greslet ; Robert Grino(n) ; Alnod
Grud ; Turkil Haco ; Ulric Hagana (now Hagan) ; Uluuin Hapra ;
Aluuin Horim ; Aluuin Horne ; Turgod Lag ; Robert " Lasciuus " ;
Wluuard Leuet (formerly Leofgeat) ; Robert Malet (now Mallet) ;
Godric Malf ; Ailmar Melc ; Aluuin Prochestan ; W. Perci ; W.
Peurel (now Peverell) ; Aluric Pic (now Pick, Pike) ; Godric Poinc ;
Tedric Pointel ; Godric Scipti ; Aluric Scoua ; Goduin Sech ; Edric
Spuda ; Edric Spur (O.N. *spörr* " sparrow ") ; Aluric Stari (now
Stare) ; Aluuin Stichehare ; Aluric Stikestac ; Aluuin Stilla (now
Still) ; Osmond Stramun ; Aldene Tope (now Toop, Toppe) ; Rold
Torif ; Algar Trec ; Aluric Wand (O.E. " mole " ; now perhaps
Want) ; Goduin Wardham ; Siuuard Welle ; Aluric Welp (now
Whelp) ; Uluric Wilde ; Aluuin Wit (i.e. the sage, now Witt).

Names of Tenants in Chief, A.D. 1086. This index gives
about 600 different names (eliminating duplicates and variants),
and many of these are repeated in the other two lists. Taking
a thousand persons holding direct from the Crown, it was
found that 33 per cent had christian names only recorded ;
actually the proportion must be greater, but some inaccuracy
is due to the fact that in the indexes, for the very want of
additional distinctions, several individuals bearing the same
appellative have been treated as one person. Of the 67 per cent
persons having distinctive epithets or addresses, in addition
to baptismal names, it was found that their descriptions were
in the following proportions : characteristic, 5 per cent ;
local, 17 per cent ; genealogical, 9 per cent ; occupational,
27 per cent ; the balance of 9 per cent being accounted for by
double names not really identifiable. In the examples which
follow, Latin terminations of forenames have been generally
omitted, and initials only given for the most common names.

Selection. Ruald Adobed ; Goisfrid Alselin ; Roger Arundel ;
Rad. Baignard ; W. Belet (now Bellett) ; W. Bonvalest (*bon valet*
" good youth ") ; Alured Brito ; W. Cailgi ; Leuuin Chaua ; W.
Chievre (the goat) ; Godvin Clec (perhaps Clegg) ; Aluuard Collinc
(now Collin, Collins) ; W. Corniole ; Godric Cratel ; Milo Crispin ;
Rob. Fafiton ; Ran. Flamme ; Ran. Flanbard ; Rob. Flavus ; Nigel
Fossard ; Ansger Fouuer ; Rad. Framen ; Ric. Fresle ; Rob. Gernon ;
Berenger Gifard ; Hugo Gosbert ; Goduin Haldein (O.N. Halfdan
" half Dane ", now Haldane) ; W. Hosed ; Ric. Inganie (Engaine) ;

" Herveus Legatus " (now Leggat) ; W. Leuric ; W. Lovet ; Gunfrid Maldoith ; Gislebert Maminot ; Turstin Mantel ; Aluuard Mert ; Leuuin Oaura ; Goisfrid Orlatele ; Rad. Pagenel ; Bernard Pancevolt ; Anschitil Parcher ; Rad. Percchaie (now Percy) ; Rad. Pinel ; W. Piperellus (i.e. Peverel) ; Ric. Pugnant ; W. Scudet ; W. Spech ; Ric. Sturmid ; Ivo Taillegebosc (Taillbois, now Talboys) ; Gislebert Tison ; Berenger Todeni ; Uluric Waula ; Alric Wintremelc.

Names of Under-Tenants, A.D. 1086. In this list are to be found about 1,400 different names (eliminating duplicates and variants), many of which are also repeated in the other two indexes. Similar investigation of the names of a thousand persons yields quite different results from those furnished on p. 86 relating to earlier tenants, pointing to the increased employment of descriptions within two decades of the Conquest ; it is found, however, that single names still preponderate, being 61 per cent of the whole, the second names being made up of : characteristic, 2 per cent ; local, 16 per cent ; genealogical, 4 per cent ; occupational, 10 per cent ; the balance in this case being 7 per cent. In the examples which follow, Latin terminations of forenames have been generally omitted, and initials only given for the most common names.

Selection. Walter Achet ; Nigel Albin' ; Estrat Aluric ; Leuuin Aluric ; Rob. Armenteres ; Hugo Asne (the ass) ; W. Baderon ; W. Balt ; Bernard Barb ; Rob. Baro ; Rad. Basset ; Walter Bec ; W. Belfou ; Rad. Bloiet ; Hugo Bolebec ; Serlo Borci ; W. Brant ; Roger Buissel ; Hugo Burdet ; W. Cardon ; Rad. Carnot' ; Uluric Cepe ; Aluric Chacepol (now Catchpoll) ; Rob. Clarenbolde ; Roger Corbet ; Rob. Cruel ; Goduin Cudhen ; Roger Daniel ; W. Denomore ; W. Denuers (now Denvers) ; Rad. Faeto ; Rad. Fatatus ; Aluuin Flint ; W. Folet ; W. Forist ; W. Froissart ; Rad. Gatelea ; Godric Goduuin ; Anchitil Grai (also de Grai) ; W. Gulaffra (now Gulliver) ; Hugo Hubald ; Hugo Maci ; W. Malbedeng ; Goisfrid Martel ; Alured Merleberg ; W. Moion ; Hugo Molebec ; W. Orenet ; Osbern Paisfor ; W. Pantulf ; Rob. Parler ; Rad. Passag' ; Roger Peteuin ; Roger Picot ; Rad. Pipin ; Ric. Poingiant ; Walter Ponther ; Girald Reimund ; Goisfrid Runeuile ; Leuin Scoua ; W. Scudet ; Edric Sigar ; Stefan Stirman ; W. Stoches ; Akile Sufreint ; Ricard Surd've ; Goisfrid Talebot ; Rad. Termit ; Goisfrid Tornai ; Rob. Veci ; Aluric Wanz ; Roger Wareng' ; Nigel Wast.

For purposes of comparison with later records, the names of the tenants in chief and under-tenants in 1086 have been added together, and the following percentages obtained : single names only, 45 per cent ; second names of the characteristic class, 4 per cent ; local, 17 per cent ; genealogical, 6 per cent ; occupational, 20 per cent ; the balance of 8 per cent being names not classifiable.

The small selections of the designations of the various classes of tenants, Saxon, Scandinavian, and Norman, are representative of the personal names, and the additions attached to them for distinction in official records of the eleventh century. The scribe, no matter what his nationality may have been, had to wrestle with appellatives in half a dozen strange tongues, and then so far as he was able to latinize the forenames and often the second names likewise, and, as may be expected, a good deal of corruption in orthography resulted, rendering discovery of the original form uncertain in these later days. Some of the corruptions which the O.E. names suffered at the hands of the Norman scribe have been mentioned above,[1] and notes on the latinization of names will be given in a later chapter.[2] An attempt to determine the etymology necessitates, in the first place, bringing together a number of representative appearances of the name, an undertaking so large as to be outside the scope of this volume, and its immensity may be readily gauged by a glance over Chapter XIV, where a method of investigation is illustrated.[3]

Classification of Additional Descriptions, A.D. 1086.

The main features of each class of second names appearing in Domesday Book may be noticed.

Characteristic descriptions. The common epithets relating to appearance : White, Black, Small, Big, Long, etc., appear in O.E., Fr., or Lat. guise, as Oslac Albus, Robertus Blundus, Robertus Niger, Aluric Blac, Siwardus Rufus, Aluric Parvus, Aluric Petit, Esba Biga, Edric Lang, Godricus Longus. An unusual Latin description is Dimidius Blancus (half-white). Other descriptions of similar type are : Grossus and Crassus, " the fat " ; and in Breton records the more expressive epithet *crassavacca* appears, but vacca may be here used in the old sense of a " beast of burden " or " carrier ". Edeua Faira (the fair) may be the same lady as Edeua Pulchra, which means the same, and she may be the still more fortunate Edeua Dives (the rich). Leuuinus Calvus (the bald) provides another example of an English forename in combination with a Latin description. Character is represented by Ædricus Grim, evidently the same as Edric Salvage (the ferocious), who is also called Sylvaticus (the forester) ; descriptions relating to condition or quality are : Ricardus Juvenis (the young), Edricus Pur (i.e. pure, but which might be *puer* " boy " or " child "), Robertus Bastard had no uncommon epithet, and one which seems to

---

[1] p. 85 above.   [2] p. 346 below.
[3] Reference may also be made to the works of Björkman and Redin, where the critical examination and systematic inquiry necessary for the solution of the onomatological problems is fully exploited.

have carried no reproach. A few persons have racial distinctions attached to their personal names, as Ewen Brito, Anunt Dacus (i.e. Danicus), Osmundus Angevinus, Ascolf Anglicus. Latin peculiarities are Fulcherus mala opa (perhaps for opera, i.e. " bad or evil works ", see below, p. 347) in Rutland ; a similar epithet in Essex, Durandus malis operibus, and another curiosity in the same county, Rogerus Deus salvæt dominas (God save the ladies). It may be worth noting that Godsalve is a modern Essex surname. True nicknames, being alternative names, are Barbatus, borne by Hugh de Montfort ; and Denasez, given to a man whose nose had been cut off in battle, but in this case the epithet is added to the second name forming a " double-barrelled surname " of very early date.

Local descriptions. The proportion of addresses found among the under-tenants is practically the same as among the overlords, pointing to the possibility that, even at this early date, Fr. *de* (of), represented in the records by Latin *de*, was not solely a territorial proposition ; in later years it came into common use by recording clerks in entering late residence or place of abode and work of all classes. The great increase in local descriptions, namely 17 per cent against 3 per cent in the case of persons holding prior to the survey, may be due to Norman influence, but since such distinctions have been already noticed among the Anglo-Saxons, is more likely to have been natural progress due to the law of necessity. In later years, in some of the remote country districts of England, the proportion of villagers *de* the various parishes in which they lived, or in which they had at some time resided, exceeds anything found in French lists. English *æt* and *on*, being no longer used, local descriptions are of three types : (i) Radulfus de Berchelai (now Berkeley), Goisfridus de Floc, Siret de Cilleham ; (ii) Albertus Lothariensis, Hugo Flandrensis or Flandriæ, Hugo Silvestris (of the wood) ; (iii) Hugo Bolebec, Hugo Maci, Robertus Veci, Goisfridus Tornai.

Genealogical descriptions. This class of distinction, in a few years, increased from 2 per cent to 6 per cent of the total ; the three indexes supplying examples which may be divided into three types : (i) Ælric Meriete sune, Leuricus Hobbesune, Goduinus Tokeson, Aluuinus Dodesone ; (ii) Agenulfi pater, Ainer et noverca ejus (and his stepmother), Aldgið (i.e. Ealdgyth) uxor Griffin (wife of Griffin, evidence of a Saxon and Welsh alliance in Warwickshire), Almarus frater Stigandi, Eddied soror Odonis, Alsi filius Brixi, Ulf pater Sortebrand, Johannes nepos Walerani (nepos usually signifies " nephew ", but sometimes " grandson " or other relative) ; (iii) Edric Sigar, Radulfus Pipin, Milo Crispin. The *-ing*-form of genealogical description had ceased to be used. In the case of

Alward Collinc, the second appellative is also found as a forename.

Occupational descriptions. This class likewise increased its proportion, 7 per cent becoming 20 per cent, and it is curious to note that office or occupation is recorded more often in the case of suzerains than under-tenants, a condition largely arising from the number of ecclesiastics, who invariably had their rank specified. Additions of vocation were generally in Latin, and consequently rarely originated surnames, although most of them became family names in their English equivalents. A few examples may be given :—

Accipitrarius (the falconer ; now Faulkner, Falconer) ; Arbalistrarius (the cross-bowman ; now Alabaster, Allblaster, etc.) ; Arcarius (the keeper of the treasure-chest) ; Archidiaconis (now Archdeacon, Arcedeckne) ; Aurifaber (now Goldsmith) ; Balastarius, Balistarius (the cross-bowman ; now Balistier, Ballister, Bannister, etc.) ; Bedellus (the bailiff ; now Beadle, Beadall, Biddle) ; Camerarius (now Chamberlain) ; Canonicus (now Cannon) ; Capellanus (now Chaplin, Caplin, Chaplain) ; Carpentarius (now Carpenter) ; Cocus (now Cook) ; Comes is equivalent to Earl, which is not the origin of that surname ; Constabularius (now Constable) ; Consul (i.e. Comes q.v.) ; Cubicularius (the bed-chamber servant) ; Dapifer (the sewer or server of dishes ; now Dapifer, Sewer) ; Diaconus (now Deacon, Deakin) ; Dispensator (the house steward ; now Spencer, Spenser) ; Episcopus (now Bishop, Bishopp) ; Forestarius (now Forester, Forster, Foster) ; Fossator (the diker) ; Granetarius (the keeper of a granary) ; Harparius (now Harper, Harpur) ; Ingeniator (the engineer, in its broadest sense ; now Jenner) ; Interpres or Latinarius (the interpreter, now Latimer) ; Joculator, Joculatrix (now Jester) ; Lorimarius (the maker of horses' bits ; now Lorimer, Larimer, etc.) ; Lardarius (the larderer ; now Lardiner, Lardner) ; Machinator (probably an engineer) ; Marescallus (the farrier ; now Marshall) ; Medicus (the healer) ; Miles (the soldier or knight ; now Knight) ; Monachus (now Monk, Munk) ; Monialis (the nun) ; Pincerna (the cup-bearer) ; Piscator (now Fisher, Fishman) ; Portarius (now Porter) ; Pistor (now Baker) ; Prebendarius (the provider of fodder for horses) ; Prefectus or Prepositus (the reeve, bailiff, or steward ; now Reeves, Bayley, Steward, etc.) ; Presbyter (the priest ; now Prest, Prester, Priest) ; Sacerdos (the priest) ; Scutularius (the scullion) ; Scriba (the scribe ; now Scriven) ; Stalrus (the staller) ; Stirman (the ship's mate or steersman ; now ? Sturman) ; Tegnus (the thegn) ; Thesaurarius (the treasurer) ; Tonsor (now Barber) ; Venator (now Hunter) ; Vinetor (now Vintner).

Domesday Book was compiled from information contained in the various county returns, at present non-existent, but there are twelfth-century transcripts of three of the commissioners' original reports, which are known respectively as the Inquisitio Comitatus Cantabrigiensis, the Inquisitio Eliensis, and the Exon. Domesday. These copies of the original returns, in comparison with Domesday Book itself, show that the compiling clerk of the latter considerably condensed the information supplied to him, with the result that many secondary descriptions of persons were omitted in the final version of the Great Survey. **Inquisitio Comitatus Cantabrigiensis, A.D. 1086.**[1] It may be of interest to know to what extent names suffered under the diligent pruning of the Domesday Book scribe. Comparison of this copy of the original returns of the commissioners for Cambridgeshire, with the survey as finally edited, shows that single names of persons living in 1086 increased in the abridgment from 25 per cent to 66 per cent, or, in other words, 75 per cent of persons, who had been distinguished with additional descriptions, now had but single names. Characteristic descriptions decreased from 3 to 1 per cent, local 39 to 18 per cent, genealogical 8 to 3 per cent, occupational 13 to 7 per cent, while unclassified double names were reduced from 12 to 5 per cent. The loss of second names and descriptions in the ultimate process is more particularly illustrated by the following extracts.

Inquisitio Comitatus Cantabrigiensis.		*Domesday Book.*
Nicholaus de Kenet . . .	p. 1	Nicol
Will' de uuarenne . . .	p. 1	Will'o (abl.)
Thobillus tegn' . . .	p. 1	Tochil teign'.
Gaufridus de mandauilla .	p. 2	Goisfrid'
Hugo de Portu . . .	p. 3	Hugo de Porth
Wihumar' dapif' . .	p. 4	Wihomarc
Ædiva bella . . .	p. 4	Edeua [pulchra]
Euerard filius brientii . .	p. 9	Eurard'
Enisam musardus . .	p. 11	Enisant
Galt'us giffard . .	p. 12	Walterius Gifard
Hugo de Bolebech . .	p. 12	Hugo
Grimbald' aurifaber ho' ædive	p. 15	Gribald' ho' Eddeue
Godric' diaconus ho' re .	p. 16	Godric ho' regis
Picot'	p. 16	Picot de Grentebrige
Horulfus, Alestanus, Wichinz	p. 18	iii soch'i
Goduuin' child . . .	p. 22	Goduin
Esgaro stalro . . .	p. 26	Asgaro stalro (p. 39)
Thursten' filius Ric' . .	p. 29	Turstin'
Godeuuin' de linacra . .	p. 30	. . . .
Anketillus de furnels . .	p. 33	Anschitil'
Rob' filius fafitoni . .	p. 35	Rotbert' Fafiton
Aluric' camp . .	p. 37	Aluric
Radulf' de scamnis : Radulf' Brito	p. 37	ii milit'
Alurici child . . .	p. 38	Alurici Cilt (p. 37)
Roger' de sumereio . .	p. 39	Rogeri'
Alsi sq'trebil . . .	p. 41	Alsi teign'

[1] Brit. Mus. Cott. MS., Tib. A, vi, ed. by N. E. S. A. Hamilton, 1876.

Inquisitio Comitatus Cantabrigiensis.		*Domesday Book.*
Wido andegauensis	. p. 42	Wido
Girard' Lotariensis	. p. 42	Girard'
Gisleb't' cū barba	. p. 42	Gisleb't'
Rob't' gernun	. p. 43	Robert' gernon (p. 45)
Godlamb	. p. 51	Gollam
Godwinus Wambestrang	. p. 54	Goduin
Hugo pincerna	. p. 60	Hugo
Alwin' hamelecoc bedellus	. p. 61	Aluuin' [coc] bedell'
Will's de Kahannes	. p. 69	Willelm' de Cahainges
Gomanus homo ediue	. p. 71	Gogan hō Eddeue
Rad' de Bans	. p. 75	Radulf'
Radulfus de bans de rembercurt	. p. 79	Radulf' de Widone (i.e. 2 persons)
Hunfrid' dansleuilla	. p. 82	Hunfrid'
Almar' de Brona	. p. 86	Almar'
Rad' Latimar'	. p. 88	Radulf'

The names of the *juratores* were entirely omitted by the economical compiler of Domesday Book, but in the original draft in nearly every case was entered not only baptismal name, but also an address or description and sometimes both. The following is a selection :—

Ulfric' de teuersham ; Silac eiusdem uille (showing that Teversham was merely an address) ; Osmund' parvulus (the tiny) ; Baldeuuinus cum barba (the bearded) ; Goduuin' nabe sone ; Ulric' hag de lintona ; Gerardus Lotaringus de salsitona ; Hugo Farsi ; Azor ; Godmar' de Grettona ; Uluric de gretona ; Firmin Lifget ; Hugo Petuuolt ; Alfuuin Odesune ; Walter' Monacus.

Some of the names of the jurors are of considerable interest. De Gretton may be an early surname ; according to the narrative of Thomas of Ely, the twelfth-century monk (*Historia Eliensis*), Oswulf de Grettune and Goding de Gretune were witnesses *c.* A.D. 975, but the descriptions, formerly merely addresses, latinized two centuries later, get the appearance of names, and *de* should be Englished. The modern surname Firmin was supposed by Bardsley to be the same as Farman, but here it appears as a distinct forename, bearing out a supposition by Skeat. Firmin may possibly explain the modern Fireman.

Inquisitio Eliensis, A.D. 1086.[1] This document contains a copy of the original returns of a survey of the possessions of St. Ethelreda's Abbey at Ely, extending into the counties of Cambridge, Norfolk, Suffolk, Hertford, Huntingdon, and Essex. Analysing 400 names from the index of the Record Commission publication, it was found that 40 per cent of persons had single names. Of the remainder, 2 per cent were characteristic, 34 per cent were local, 5 per cent genealogical,

[1] Ibid., also Trin. Coll. O. 2, 41, and O. 2, 1.

13 per cent occupational, the balance of 6 per cent being double names not readily classifiable. Some double names are :

Algar Chapa (Cloppa in Trin. Coll. MS., Cappe in Inq. Cantab., and Cabe in Dom. Bk.) ; Alriz, i.e. Aluricus mus (Trin. Coll. MS.) ; Alriz serdere ; Alriz wordepund ; Alsi Berd ; Herveus Bedruel (Bredruel in Trin. Coll. MS.) ; Hugo Pedefold or Petuuolt (Pedenfot in Trin. Coll. MS.) ; Radulfus Baiard ; Willelmus Cardon.

The differences in the orthographic rendering of these names in the various manuscripts is eloquent of the difficulties which the etymologist has to face, and clearly illustrates the danger of theorizing from one example of a name only. Further comparison provides Cavelaio and Cheleia, Quetelinge and Chertelinge (now Cheveley hundred), Huscarlo and Huscard, Mucellus and Michellus, Turbert and Turbern, Sterlig and Sterling, Sturmidus and Surmi, Syla and Silac.

The Exon. Domesday, A.D. 1086. This Exeter record, which is supposed to be an exact transcript of the original returns made by the Conqueror's commissioners, presents a description of the counties of Wilts, Somerset, Dorset, Devon, and Cornwall. Analysing 1,000 names, it is noticeable that 68 per cent of the persons have single designations, and only 32 per cent have descriptions in addition to their birth-names.

Of the secondary titles, characteristic descriptions are scarce, amounting to less than two per cent of the total, and they mainly repeat those found in Domesday Book. Of the more unusual epithets may be noticed : Bernardus sine napa (perhaps corresponding to " shortneck ", cf. Chortneke in Hund. R.), Radulfus tortemanus (crooked hand), Odo cul de lou, or latinized, Odo culus lupus (cf. Cullus de Boue, the Latin form of Oxenstern). Local names comprised 14 per cent, being mainly addresses in Latin form, as :—

Radulfus de Brueria (i.e. " of the heath ", now Brewer) ; Alueredus Ispaniensis or de Hispania (now Spain) ; Willelmus Pictavensis (of Poictiers) ; Willelmus de Capra (possibly the preposition is not required ; Fr. *le chevre* " the goat " ; now Chivers) ; Rogerus de Corcella (now Churchill) ; Radulfus de Pomaria (now Pomeroy, Orchard, Appleyard) ; Odo Wintoniensis (now Winchester) ; Odo Flandrensis (now Flanders) ; Rogerius de Molis (now Moels, Mills) ; Alueredus Merleberga (now Marleborough) ; Rotbertus de Alba Marula (now Albemarle) ; Hugo Redonensis (of Rennes).

Genealogical descriptions account for about 3 per cent only, and are of the types mentioned on p. 91 ; the 6 per cent of descriptions classed as occupational also being largely repetitive of Domesday entries.

The Shaftesbury Rental (? 11th century).[1] The register of the monastery preserved in the British Museum contains

[1] Brit. Mus. Harl. MS. 61, ff. 37-89.

a rental with the names of the tenants, lands held, and particulars of the tenures and payments, relating to various places, mainly in Dorset and Wilts. It is not contemporary, but the documents entered are those from the eighth century onwards, the first seventeen pages of the rental being copied from one which may be coeval with Domesday Book. No less than 93 per cent of the tenants have single names, some of the more uncommon being :—

Bucellus ; Daie ; Egith ; Hastewul ; Isoldus (occ. in Dom. Bk. Iseldis, Dorset) ; Kippingus (Cheping, Wint. Dom.) ; Passet ; Sacon ; Sewy (occurs in Wilts and Oxf. in Dom. Bk.) ; Scellingus (i.e. Scilling, an early Wessex name, now our Shilling) ; Smewinus (also occurs in Dom. Bk. and later) ; Spilman (Spileman in Wint. Dom.) ; Wacer (O.E. *wacor* "watchful ", "vigilant ") ; Walwanus ; Wita (i.e. Hwita, a baptismal name as well as description or sobriquet).

Of the remaining 7 per cent of the entries, local descriptions claim about 1 per cent, among them de Stafford (Robert of Stratford was a tenant in chief as recorded in Dom. Bk.) ; genealogical descriptions being almost unknown, say 1 per cent, and occupational 3 per cent ; unidentified double names accounting for 2 per cent, among which were early examples of the common name Caldecote (now Calcott, Caldercourt, Callcut, Chaldecroft, etc.) ; and Glide (O.E. *glida* "a kite "), now usually Glyde.

Summary, 11th century. The research among the extant evidences of the reigns of the two Williams brings us to the end of the eleventh century, and we may pause and digest the accumulated data. Of the 5,545 persons noticed in the above analyses, no less than 62 per cent have but a single name recorded ; the remaining 38 per cent having descriptions additional to their forenames in the proportions : characteristic 2 per cent, local 13 per cent, genealogical 4 per cent, occupational 12 per cent, and unclassifiable 7 per cent. These descriptions are O.E., Latin, and Norman-French. It is clear that in some cases the same name was borne by several persons in common, as the citations relating to Giffard, Bertram, Crispin, Talbot, and Gernon have evidenced ; but while this repetition cannot at this time have been recognized as complying with any law or custom, or fulfilling any hereditary function, such personal names repeated had, in effect, become family names. Permanence among characteristic, local, or occupational descriptions must have been much rarer.[1] In

[1] The author of the *Norman People* (1874), p. 39, after making an exhaustive collection of Norman names, concluded that " hereditary surnames were in use by all classes in Normandy in the middle of the eleventh century ". I find nothing in support of his opinion, but rather that the Normans did not themselves consider their names hereditary until long after the conquest.

France, even two centuries later, few hereditary surnames were in evidence, as may be realized by reference to the list known as *Le Rôle de la Taille de Paris* (A.D. 1292).

For the remainder of the Norman period, namely, the first half of the twelfth century, suitable material for the critical investigation is scarce ; but further reference may be made to the " Winton. Domesday ".

Liber Wintoniensis, A.D. 1103–15. Consideration may now be given to the names of householders of Winchester, flourishing in the time of Henry I. Sir Henry Ellis and Dr. Round having accepted the opinion of Bishop Lyttelton, that Normans were settled in this city by Edward the Confessor, special attention should be given to these names. It has been shown above (pp. 83–5) that in the year 1066 Norman personal appellatives were rarely borne by the inhabitants of Winchester, and now from this list, compiled less than half a century later, it appears that most of the forenames are alien, the inference from the change being that Norman influence prior to the Conquest cannot have been as strong as supposed by the Bishop.

Analysis of the names of the householders in the time of Henry I demonstrates that the number of individuals with single names had fallen from 55 per cent to 27 per cent. Among the remaining 73 per cent few characteristic descriptions (mainly French) can be noticed. Compared with the 1066 list, local distinctions, all of *de*-type, show an increase to 15 per cent (from 5 per cent).

Selection. Osbert de Auco ; Hugo de Chiuilli ; Ric. de Curci ; Ran. de Curleio ; Wigot delinc (Lincoln) ; Rad. de Felgeriis ; Hen. de Port ; W. de pothearcar' ; Baldwin de Rediver (now Redvers) ; Herebert de Sancto Quintino.

Genealogical descriptions of three types now total 20 per cent, against 10 per cent in 1066, and may be exemplified : (i) Godwin Grenessone (Grene, like Blac, Hwita, and Brun, was a personal name, the last three being characteristic descriptions also), Rad. Holinessone (Hollin or Holling must have been a personal name) ; (ii) Ruald' filius Faderlin, Osbert frater Maiesent, Robert filius Nunne (an O.E. personal name, and consequently quite a different entry to that in the Hundred Rolls under Northampton : " Alicia la Nonne et Robertus filius ejus ") ; (iii) W. Bertram, God' Pot (now Potts), Gisl' Gibart, Girard Barrat', Ascelin Goldman. About 70 per cent of the entries of this class are latinized, the English examples having become reduced from 50 to 10 per cent ; the remainder being Norman without filial expressions. These figures are not representative of the entire country ;

in some parts a much greater number of English appellatives were preserved as distinctions, as an analysis of Norfolk names referred to below will demonstrate.

Occupational descriptions have likewise more than doubled, being now the largest class, comprising 25 per cent of the total. These distinctions are yet mainly Latin, but Burgeis and Casier (now Burgess and Cassier) appear to be French. If *casier* here signifies " treasurer " it is an interesting early example. Some Latin examples are : Napparius (the keeper of napery, now Napier ; Audouen (i.e. Owen or Ouen) Napparius may have been Welshman or Frenchman), Potarius (now Potter), Palmarius (the palmer, a pilgrim to the Holy Land ; now Palmer), Parmenter (the tailor, now Parmenter, Parmiter), Scaldeator, Scrutarius (? rag-dealer), Tailator (i.e. *taleator* " a teller " or " tallier "), Taneator (now Tanner), Tornator (now Turner).

A further selection of double names of various classes follows :—

Roger Amberlang ; Alwin Barbitre ; J. Bensetoute ; Alwin Bollochessege ; Arnulf Burdin (now Burden) ; Ricard Dublet (now Doublet) ; Rad. Escouell (now Scovell) ; Rob. Fresle ; Herbert Gidi (perhaps the modern Giddy) ; Anchetill de Jorz ; Alwin Lefeller ; Rob. Marmion ; Siward Mus ; Godwin Nalad ; Hugo Oillard ; Rog. Patin' ; W. Tardif ; Godwin Withmundin.

Lindsey Survey, A.D. 1115–18.[1] The next document in point of antiquity relates to the county of Lincoln, and is a record of the more important landholders, and an expected feature is the large proportion of persons with descriptions additional to their personal names. Analysing the appellatives in the index, it was found that 18 per cent of persons had baptismal names only, about 61 per cent having local or genealogical descriptions, a feature which becomes more prominent the further north the investigation is carried. Of the remainder, characteristic epithets claimed about 1 per cent, occupational 9 per cent, and unclassified double names 11 per cent.

Of characteristic names Macherellus may have become Mackerel ; and Purcell, supposed by Lower and Bardsley to be derived from *porcellus* " a little pig ", is latinized *de Porcellis*.

Of second names which do not occur in Domesday Book were noticed Bilion, Devilla (from d'Eyvill, now Devil), Hundefot, Mischin, Olliet, Pilat', Ticio (otherwise Tison), Turmant (probably O.E. Thurmund), and the Norman territorial names, de Bussa, de Calz, de Laceles, de Laval,

[1] Brit. Mus. Cott. MS., Claud. C. 5, ed. by Jas. Greenstreet.

de Lovetot, de Renni, de Sali, de Vermis, de Vilers, most of which have become surnames.

Pipe Roll, 31 Hen. I (1130-1).[1] This most ancient record of the Exchequer does not cover England in its entirety, eight counties in the north and west being imperfectly represented. Taking the names of 1,000 persons, it was found that no less than 95 per cent had secondary descriptions or addresses, the remaining 5 per cent having baptismal names only entered. The characteristic class is again the smallest, claiming only 2 per cent of the total, the examples being very similar to those already given (p. 90), with a few appellatives indicating race, as Anglicus, Daniscus, Norriscus; some others being: W. de Ainesf' senex, le Puilleis, Hubert cum testa (*testa* as used by Pliny was a coloured spot on the face), Ursus (the bear), Bucherellus (the young buck), Nanus (the dwarf). By far the most popular form of description on this roll is the local, about 42 per cent of persons being *de*, *del*, or *de la* some place name, together with a few of the type Blehericus Wallensis; others more unusual being Ailwardus de Risembergehundred (Bucks), Robertus de terra wasta (waste land), Symon de Sais (possibly a contraction for Saisdona hundred, Staffs or Glouc.), Robertus de Quercu (ancestor of some of our Oakes), Ric. Marisc' (*mariscus* or *mariscallus*, now Marsh or Marshall).

Twenty-one per cent of the descriptions were genealogical, and occupations were given in 15 per cent of the cases, low Latin equivalents being with few exceptions in use. Of those not previously mentioned are the following :—

Bercharius (the shepherd) ; Carbonellus (the charcoal-man) ; Cementarius (the mason) ; Cortinarius (the curtain-maker) ; Corvesarius (the cordwainer or cobbler) ; Faber (the smith) ; Falconarius (now Falconer, Faulkner) ; Forbator (the furbisher) ; Hosarius (now Hosier) ; Monetarius (the moneyer ; now Monier) ; Ostiarius (the doorkeeper or porter ; now Usher) ; Soparius (now Soper) ; Scriptor vel Scriba (the writer) ; Serviens (the sergeant, servant or vassal) ; Vielator (the player on the viol) ; Villanus (the villein, a servile tenant).

It is of interest to note the scarcity of O.E. personal names, almost 90 per cent on this roll (fortunately not representative) being Norman or biblical. This feature has an important bearing on the moulding of English surnames, and will be touched upon more fully at a later stage in the investigation.

Liber Wintoniensis, A.D. 1148. Reference may now be made to the last part of this record, being a rental taken by bishop Henry of Blois. Upon analysis of the names it was found that by comparison with those of the tenants in 1066, double appellatives had increased from 48 to 69 per cent.

[1] Ed. by Joseph Hunter, 1833.

Of single names, the following is a selection of those which afterwards became surnames :—

Aldit ; Alebast (now Alabaster) ; Basset (Fr. dim. *bas* " short ") ; Bonifacius (Lat. *bonum* " good " ; *facere* " to do ") ; Coppa ; Cupping ; Duchet (now Duckett) ; Fareman ; Friday ; Golburg ; Gunter ; Herman ; Mallard ; Muriel (now Merrell, Murrell, etc.) ; Palefrei ; Patric ; Peitewin ; Porcell ; Seman ; Silvestre ; Strod.

These names are mainly O.E., with a fair number of O.F. varieties, a few Latin, and an occasional Norse appellative, as P'atrick. Some names of curious appearance are : Crabeleg, Hoppecole, Pieferret, Semetonius, and Turneteil ; and it seems possible that not only nicknames, but occasionally local and occupational descriptions were entered in lieu of personal names, e.g. Froggemore, which being a most improbable baptismal name, is, on the contrary, actually the name of several localities in Hampshire to the present day. Crabley and Semeton may also have been places, while Travetier " shop-keeper " is undoubtedly occupational, and so may be Alebast, a possible contraction for Arbalester " the cross-bowman ".

Of the 69 per cent of additional descriptions, 4 per cent were identified as characteristic, 14 per cent local, 13 per cent genealogical, 23 per cent occupational, the balance of 15 per cent being not classifiable at sight with any certainty.

Summary and Conclusions. The year 1154 saw the end of the Norman dynasty, with the death of Stephen, in whose time " all was dissention, and evil, and rapine ". Critical examination of the records for the period 1100–54 shows that during that unsettled time a great increase in the use of additional descriptions occurred ; of the 2,140 persons noticed in the table (p. 131) 83 per cent being found to have second names, which were in the proportions: characteristic 3 per cent, local 29 per cent, genealogical 19 per cent, occupational 18 per cent, and unclassified 14 per cent.

The various descriptions being entered in the records solely for identification of the individual names, therefore, were not necessarily surnames. Normally a man might have no second name, and the clerk would manufacture a label, even if it were only the word *alter* " the other ", which often appears in Domesday Book, in cases where two tenants, bearing the same name, hold land in the same vill. On the other hand, some men, known by several alternative names, might have no addition entered in the register, and such an omission could occur in the case of a great suzerain as well as in that of the under tenant. The royal family had no surname—they did not require one— although early kings were commonly distinguished by nick-names such as " The Confessor ", " The Bastard ", " Rufus ", " Beauclerk ", etc., presumably behind their backs.

Among the upper classes a secondary title was rather the boast of power or possession of lands than of ancestry, and by the early twelfth century a description had come to be recognized as the distinguishing mark of a person of consequence ; in fact, says the learned Camden, it was a disgrace to have but a single name. When King Henry I proposed to marry Mabel, daughter of Sir Robert Fitzhamon, to his natural son Robert, the lady declined the offer, on the ground that he had no second name. According to a metrical chronicle :—

" So vair eritage as ich abbe (have) it were me gret ssame (shame)
Vor to abbe an louerd (lord) bote (unless) he adde an toname."

The King replied :—

"   . . . thou seist wel in this cas
Sire Roberd le fiz haym. thi fader tuo name was
& as vair tuo name he ssal abbe."

The King proposed " le fiz rei ", but the " damoysele ", admitting that it was a fair name, looking to future probabilities, asked : " But what should his son be called then, and others that of him come ? " The King, realizing that the maid asked nothing extravagant, replied :—

"   . . . Thi louerd ssal abbe an name
Vor him & vor is eirs. vair withoute blame.
Vor Roberd erl of gloucestere. is name ssal be . . . & is eirs." [1]

So after all Sir Robert received nothing of the nature of a modern surname. From this trivial conversation we can gather little that is definite ; we obtain the impression that to-names were essential to those with fair heritages, and were apparently recognized as hereditary, yet, if so, there could have been no argument against Fitzrey, except that in the second generation it would be, literally, a misnomer. Eyton, the Shropshire antiquary, thought that *fitz* signified " descendant of " [2] (equivalent to Irish O'), but had that been so, there would have been no objection to Fitzrey as a surname. In drawing conclusions on this point, it should be remembered that the chronicle attributed to Robert of Gloucester is not contemporary, and the account of naming the illegitimate son of Henry I is doubtless based on nothing more than oral tradition, and coloured by the custom prevalent at the time of composing the chronicle, namely, the thirteenth rather than the twelfth century. A writer has endeavoured to show that both Henry I and Edward I also, on occasion, commanded names to be assumed (i.e. Moubray and Clavering respectively),[3] but satisfactory documentation is wanting. The register of Cokersand Abbey records a case of an assumption of name and title, with approval of King Henry II and his Parliament.

[1] *The Metrical Chronicle of Robert of Gloucester* (Rolls Ser. 86), vol. ii, p. 634.
[2] *Antiquities*, vol. ii, p. 305 n.   [3] J. Finlayson (1863), p. 20.

Ivo Tailbot genuit Elthredum ; Elthredus Ketellum ; Ketellus Gilbertum ; Gilbertus Will ; qui quidem Willielmus fecit se vocari Willielmum de Lancaster, et fecit se vocari coram rege in parliamento, Willielmum de Lancaster, baronem de Kendale. That is, William, the great-great-grandson of Ivo Tailbot (the Domesday tenant), caused himself to be called William of Lancaster and caused himself to be called before the King in parliament William of Lancaster, Baron of Kendal.[1]

Discussion of the value of this entry will be left to a further chapter (p. 384). By the middle of the twelfth century the most popular form of description was the address, and the suffix -*ensis* in this connection having become obsolete, these additions embodied the preposition *de*, and this form of distinction was, as will be seen, seldom an indication of territorial possession. The next class of description in numerical importance was the genealogical, the indication of kinship. The filial desinence -son was suffering a temporary eclipse, and is not to be noticed in the records, Lat. *filius* being the common expression, with *fitz* in Norman-French documents, and W. *ab* and Ir. *mac* in use among the native Celts. Characteristic epithets are rare, which fact should be specially noticed in view of the great prominence given by some writers to surnames supposed to be derived from nicknames. Many persons, however, were described by office or vocation in Latin or French, the use of English for official documents, apart from genealogical descriptions and rare exceptions, not having yet commenced.

[1] *Monasticon Anglicanum*, vol. vi (2), p. 909.

CHAPTER V

The Angevin or Plantagenet dynasty (1154–1485), commencing with the accession of Henry II, saw England engaged in perpetual struggles, resulting in the annexation of Wales, partial subjugation of Ireland, and failure of the attempts to conquer Scotland. The successive disturbances in the realm, continuing for a century and a half, shook the feudal system to its foundation, with beneficial effects resulting in the establishment, in their present form, of political institutions, laws, languages, habits and customs, including the general use of hereditary surnames.

Pipe Roll, A.D. 1159–60.[1] From 1155 onwards the great series of Exchequer accounts runs in unbroken order, and names of all classes of the people of England for any required county for any year may be conveniently examined. As with the earlier roll, the officials have been punctilious in recording " to-names ", no less than 94 per cent of persons having secondary descriptions. Recognition of personal characteristics is small, amounting to 5 per cent, of which names nearly one-half are racial, as Angevinus, Sarracenus, etc. The largest class is that of local names, supplying 35 per cent, all of *de*-type. Genealogical descriptions account for 21 per cent of the entries, a few of which, generally O.E. or N.F., have no relationship expressed, a rare Latin example, without *filius*, being Willelmus Johannis, perhaps due to clerical omission.[2] Occupational names are in the proportion of 19 per cent, the unidentified names making up the balance of 14 per cent.

The second half of the twelfth century saw the official scribes occasionally using the French article in forming descriptions, as Gaufridus le Lohareng, on this roll, in place of Gaufridus Loharengus of the previous year ; from which name has been derived the surnames Lorraine and Loring.

Liber Niger Scaccarii, A.D. 1166. The Black Book of the Exchequer is a return by each tenant in chief of those who held knights' fees under him and the names, therefore, are those of the rank of gentlemen and upwards.

---

[1] Pipe Roll Soc.

[2] *The Complete Peerage*, vol. iii, p. 611, mentions some other early examples of the dropping out of filius, the oldest being of the reign of Stephen, but this elision had commenced in pre-Conquest days. The citation of Richard Talbot, 29 Edw. I, is antedated by over two centuries by Hugh Talebot, *c.* 1060. (See above, p. 83.)

As may be expected in a record of Norman nobility the appellatives bear little trace of Anglo-Saxon origin, and are quite unrepresentative, since for every person whose name is entered, there are 999 who are not so noted, among whom were many persons with Saxon names, as may be clearly seen by examination of the Pipe Roll for the corresponding year (13 Hen. II, pp. 21–9), for instance. Families of Saxon origin were adopting Norman baptismal names wholesale, and these in turn were ultimately to become surnames, consequently Norman names are no index of Norman blood. In later years Welshmen by thousands took the commoner Norman names, but they remained Welshmen, and Williams, Roberts, Richards, etc., are now recognized as the hall-mark of a Welshman, and it is to be concluded that in these earlier days the English had in the same manner adopted the alien christian names.

Two sets of extracts, one from Yorkshire and one from Devonshire, have been analysed, and comparison of the results shows little difference in the tendencies of descriptions in North and South, and, as might be expected of landholders, single names are rare in both cases, the favourite descriptions being territorial, the proportions being much higher than in any of the sources previously examined. To the results of the enumeration and classification are added, for comparison, corresponding figures relating to servile tenants from various records, likewise of the twelfth century.

TENANTS IN CHIEF								
County	Approx. No. of names analysed	Single baptismal names	Characteristic	Local	Genealogical	Occupational	Double names unclassified	References
		%	%	%	%	%	%	
Yorkshire .	300	1	3	59	19	4	14	Liber Niger.
Devonshire	200	1	3	62	25	—	9	,, ,,

SERVILE TENANTS								
Norfolk .	160	60	4	4	17	6	9	RamseyCart. (Rolls Ser. 79), iii, pp. 261–9.
Huntingdonshire	260	50	7	6	24	9	4	Ibid., pp. 241–60.
Kent . .	120	17	7	31	16	12	17	P.R.O. Subs. E 179, 237/51.

These few figures provide a striking contrast ; on the one hand practically all the overlords boast second names, largely of local type ; on the other hand a big proportion of the servile tenants are known by font-name only, and few by place of residence. Further, it is to be noticed that while there is little difference in the names of landowners, north and south, yet those of servile tenants varied considerably in different parts of the country, and secondary appellatives were much more in use in the South than in the North. It may be worth special note that at this early date (Hen. I) no less than 37 per cent of the Kent bondmen, possessing double names, were recorded by local descriptions, that is names with preposition *de*, the English equivalents so prominent in later Kent records not having yet made an official appearance.

Pipe Roll, A.D. 1174–5. Analysis of 1,000 names on this Exchequer roll shows, in comparison with the Pipe Roll previously noticed, that local descriptions were on the increase ; figures relating to other classes not being sufficiently altered to call for comment, are given in the table on page 131, where they may be conveniently compared with the others. Latin descriptions show the first sign of giving way to French and English, which amount jointly to about 1 per cent of the total. The following examples may be of interest :—

Ailsius le Bedell' ; Simon le Bret ; Will' del Carner ; Rogerus le Cauceis (Chalceis, C.R.) ; Henr' le Cheisire (Caisere, C.R.) ; Robertus le Chenteis (Kentesius, C.R.) ; Hug' le Cordewan' ; Marsilius le Cordewan' ; Odo de la Faleisia ; Robertus Lefranceis ; Ric' le Furmentin ; Robertus le Gragier (Grangier, C.R.) ; Osbertus de la Herlotere ; David' le Larden' ; Willelmus le Latimer ; Henr' le Lotaring' ; Eustach' le Mordand' ; Rad' le Naper (Napier, C.R.) ; [Al]anus le Neucument ; Petrus Petit grant ; Henr' de la Rivere ; Sim' le Tanur (Tanator, C.R.) ; Joh' le Tort ; Walterus le Traine.

It will be noticed that the Chancellor's Roll gives, in some cases, latinized versions of the French and English names. Alanus le Neucument is a triglot example, Latin, French, and English, the description giving the surname Newcomen, yet to be found in the *London Directory*.

Boldon Book, A.D. 1183.[1] This survey of the Palatinate of Durham made by order of Hugh de Piuset (de Puteaco), nephew to Stephen, king of England, now exists only in transcripts. It contains a useful list of about 350 names of northern persons of all classes. The comparatively large number of single names, about 26 per cent, is in striking contrast to other rolls of the period, and local names are

[1] Bodl. Lib., Laud 542. Printed by Rec. Comm., also Surtees Soc., 1852, vol. xxv.

correspondingly scarce and much below the average, which peculiarity is the more surprising the North being so essentially the home of local descriptions and surnames. It was, however, the very fact of wanting bynames which led to so many people, in later years, being given addresses for family names.

Names are in general latinized, the French article being noticed only once, in the form *del*. There is a tendency to elide the preposition *de* ; Alanus de Bentofte occurs also as Alanus Brentofte and Alan Bruntofte.

Pipe Roll, A.D. 1190. Turning to another Exchequer roll, it was found that persons with single names numbered but 3 per cent, the proportion of other classes of descriptions being very similar to those in the roll of sixteen years previously. The full figures are given in the table on page 131, where they may be most conveniently examined and compared with the other assembled data.

Curia Regis Roll, A.D. 1196-1200. The records of the King's Court provide comprehensive lists of appellatives of all classes. Taking, for instance, the rolls for 7 Ric. I – 2 John, analysis of 2,800 entries shows that 3 per cent were single names. Of the persons honoured with a secondary distinction, 3 per cent are characteristic, no less than 55 per cent can be described at sight as local, 25 per cent as genealogical, and of the remainder 5 per cent were occupational, the balance of 9 per cent not being readily classifiable.

The O.E. preposition *æt*, which had been so long disused in official records, now begins to appear in its native form, e.g. Rogerus ad Fontem (Sussex) is also called Rogerus de Attewell ; Rogerus de Atteville is entered under Devon, and in the roll for 1203 occurs Ricardus Attehull (Surrey). The reason that the English *atte* has escaped the official censor in these instances is no doubt because it has coalesced with the governed word, and appeared to the entering clerk as part of the place-name, a conjecture explaining the redundant *de*. Doubtless such descriptions, common enough in conventional use, in general were converted into French or Latin equivalents by the recording scrivener.

It may be emphasized here that whenever medieval descriptions and surnames are mentioned the reference is to the names as officially registered. Actually the bearers would be known in their home villages quite differently, and were rarely called by French or Latin names, which, like the twentieth-century silk hat, were only kept for formal occasions. The majority of English families are descendants of the medieval bondmen, who at one time formed the greater part of the population, and, rising slowly through the various classes of tenants in villenage to freemen, ultimately became successful farmers or tradesmen, or perhaps country and professional gentlemen.

Scottish Descriptions, c. A.D. 1200. In 1174 (Treaty of Falaise) William did homage to the English King for the Scottish crown; but fifteen years later Scotland (excluding the Western Isles held by the Norsemen) again became independent. Under ecclesiastical influence, the country outside the Northern and Western Highlands had become largely anglicized; the inhabitants being identified by Scandinavian, Gaelic, and Teutonic descriptions, of which examples have been given. The following list of witnesses to the *divisæ* or bounds of Stobo (Peeblesshire) illustrates the nature of twelfth-century official descriptions of the Lowlands of Scotland.

D'ns Adam fil' Gilberti ; D'ns Milo corneht ; D'ns Adam fil' Edolfi ; Joh'es Ker uenator aput swhynhope ; Gillemihhel queschutbrit aput tresquer ; Patricius de hopekeliov ; Mihhyn brunberd aput corrukes ; Mihhyn fil' Edred aput Stobb' ; Cristinus heremita de kyngeldores ; Cospatricius heremita de Kylbeuhoc ; Padinus fil' kercau aput corrukes ; Gillemor fil' kercau ap' corrokes ; Cristinus gennan seruiens ap' tresquer ; Gylcolmus faber aput pebbles ; Gylmihhel fil' Bridoc aput kyngeldures ; Gylis fil' Buht ap' d'umedl ; Gillecrist' fil' Daniel' aput glenwhym ; Math'eus, Jacobus, et Joh'es, filii Cosmungho sacerdotis ap' Edolueston' ; Cospatricius romesare ; Randulfus de Maggete ; Adam de seles clericus ; Gillecrist' fil' huttyng ap' Currok' ; Gilbertus persona de Kylbevhoc ; Gylmor hund apud Dauwic ; Mihhyn senescallus de Dauwic ; Dudyn de Brouhtune ; Patricius fil' Caswale ap' stobb' ; Adam et Cosouold fil' Muryn aput castrum oliueri.[1]

The document being in Latin, the half-dozen or so macs, which might have appeared, are represented by *filius*. It will be noticed that no less than one-third of the christian names have the prefix *gos-* or *gille-*, both signifying " servant " or " disciple ".[2] The Gaelic nature of these names, coupled with the few earlier instances in Yorkshire (see p. 87), may be of interest, pointing to the Gaelic speech of the Scottish lowlanders at this time.

Twelfth-Century Comparisons and Inferences. Before proceeding to an investigation of thirteenth-century descriptions progress may be marked. For the reigns of Henry II and Richard I (1154–99) an analysis of 3,100 descriptions, mainly from Exchequer records, gives the following proportions : characteristic 4 per cent, local 48 per cent, genealogical 17 per cent, occupational 10 per cent, and

[1] *Registrum Episcopatus Glasguensis* (Bannatyne Club, 1843), vol. i, p. 89.
[2] See p. 31 above. Also *Notes and Queries*, 7th Dec., 1878, p. 443.

unclassified 10 per cent ; single personal names accounting for 5 per cent only. By tabulating the results of the various analyses, development may be seen at a glance.

Dates	No. of names	Single	Charac-teristic	Local	Genea-logical	Occupa-tional	Un-classified
A.D.		%	%	%	%	%	%
1066–1086	5545	62	2	13	4	12	7
1101–1154	2140	17	3	29	19	18	14
1159–1190	3100	5	4	48	17	10	16
1196–1200	2800	3	3	55	25	5	9

While these figures are weak in detail, they are strong in the aggregate, and show unmistakably that from the Norman conquest, over a hundred years were required to provide every person, even for purposes of official record, with a secondary description. It is also manifest that these distinctions, to the extent of more than half, were of the local class, half as many being genealogical. Latin was still the predominant language of record, French and English being sparingly used.

It may be asked, can any of these descriptions be rightly called surnames ? Persons living in the year 1200 were, perhaps, four to six generations in descent from their ancestors, who saw the Norman invasion, quite sufficient length of time for Domesday Book names or descriptions to have repeated themselves and acquired the permanency of family names ; but without having authenticated pedigrees of the families in question, it is not possible to do more than hazard a guess as to the ratio of surnames to descriptions. Considering the figures obtained from the *Rotuli Curiæ Regis*, it was noticed that of the 55 per cent local descriptions, 53 per cent had the prefix *de*, and of the 25 per cent of genealogical descriptions, 24 per cent had *filius* or other word indicating kinship prefixed. A few of these instances were, no doubt, latinizations of Norman territorial or fitz-names, but the greater proportion of the 77 per cent of second names with *de* and *filius*, together with those of the characteristic and occupational classes with *le*, are unlikely to have been hereditary surnames at this time.

In view of the fact that the second largest class of descriptions is the genealogical, that is those derived from baptismal names, it is of interest to note the effect of the Norman Conquest upon such individual names. A glance at any of the old rolls of names is sufficient to show that three or four generations had been sufficient to greatly reduce O.E. font-names, the figure for the 1130 Pipe roll, for instance, being 10 per cent, but it has to be noticed that it is not possible to obtain good lists of the names of the lower orders. Turning again to the *Rotuli Curiæ Regis*, and taking 1,000 male examples, in only 7 per cent of the instances could native forenames be discovered, and later on the proportion became much less. There are, of course, plenty of names of Teutonic origin, because many of the Norman appellatives are such : of the 93 per cent of alien names William accounted for 14 per cent, Richard 9 per cent, Robert 8 per cent, Ralph 6 per cent, Roger, Walter, John, and Thomas 5 per cent each, Henry 3 per cent, Geoffrey, Gilbert, Hugh, Reynold, and Simon 2 per cent each, the remaining 23 per cent covering sixty-nine different names. All these personal names are, of course, given in the rolls in their Latin form.

With regard to *secondary* descriptions of the genealogical class it was found that fully one-third (36 per cent) were O.E. Native personal names numbering but 7 per cent (the corresponding figure 100 years previously being 10 per cent), how can it be explained that O.E. secondary genealogical descriptions amount to 36 per cent ? If hereditary surnames had been in general use by the year 1100, it could be answered that the personal names had become family names before Saxon names had ceased to be fashionable at the font. But genealogical surnames had not been in such use ; and the figures given above show that even in the year 1200, 24 per cent of the 25 per cent genealogical descriptions could not have been surnames. The point, being of considerable interest, will be returned to at a later stage when further figures have been provided.

Exactitude in statistics relating to names must not be expected ; it will be readily understood without exemplification that such important factors in an analysis, as the social scale of the person listed, the class of record, the district, town, and county, are often unknown, and the want of permanency in the name of any one family or even individual adds to the uncertainty.

Plurality of Descriptions. The unsettled and transient nature of second names may be illustrated by a few examples. Baudrey le Teuton living at the Norman Conquest had six sons known by their different addresses, viz. Nicholas de Bascheville (now Baskeville), Fulk de Alneto (now Dawney), Rodbert de Courceio (now de Courcy), Richard de Nova Villa (now Neville), Baldric de Balgenzaio, and " Vigorius Apuliensis ".[1]

Essolf, son of Ulf fil' Gamel, the Domesday tenant of Berkin (co. Derby), had, according to the pedigree given by Yeatman, four sons, Peter de Berkin, Jordan (of Thornhill),

[1] *History of Noble English Families*, ed. by H. Drummond, 1846, p. 9. I have not verified these names.

Richard de Tong, and John de Bayldon [1]; about the beginning of the twelfth century William de Ledes being son of Thomas, son of Peter de Berkin.[2]

Possibly the most striking example of this nature is found in a pedigree, first noticed by Camden and given in the *Visitation of Cheshire* (1580).[3] William Belward of Malpas (Ches.) had two sons David (de Malpas) and Richard; David had three sons, variously distinguished in the Latin genealogy as de Malpas, Gough, and de Golborne; Richard's five sons were known as de Cotgrave, de Overton, Litell, de Hampton, and de Coddington; Gough had a son described as de Egerton, and a grandson Wigland; Golborne's second son was pedigreed as de Goodman; Little had a son Kenen le Clerk, and a son of Hampton was called Houa Bras. No dates are given, but the family evidently flourished in the thirteenth century. Here may be seen in the one family characteristic, local, and occupational descriptions resulting ultimately in fourteen different surnames; and a bearer of any one might himself be known by two or more distinctions. For instance, Richard son of Gilbert Crispin does not occur as Richard Crispin in the Domesday Survey, 1086, but as Ricardus filius Gisleberti (Kent, 14) and Ricardus de Tonebridge (ibid.); moreover, Ordericus Vitalis (1073) names him Ricardus de Benefacta (i.e. de Bienfaite), and elsewhere he is called Ricardus de Clare.[4]

One other example of this plurality of names will suffice. The name of a twelfth-century Welshman, Gruffydd ap Jorwerth, in England, Griffin or Griffith or even Jetun son of Gervase Goch, or latinized Griffinus filius Jelvord, occurs in the *Rotuli Curiæ Regis* as Griffun Walensis, in the *Rotuli Oblatis* as Griffin de Sutton, and in the Haughmond Cartulary as Griffin de Kinerton, the two last names being derived from his lordships, consequently the designations are characteristic, local, and genealogical, and Welsh, Latin, and English.

It is manifest that down to the thirteenth century there were no recognized rules for the assumption of second names, and such want of system long prevailed, although there is evidence (see below, p. 383) that, as early as 1267, it was recognized in London that a man should take the name of his father.

Probably it generally happened that the eldest son became known by the name of his principal estate, and a younger son might be designated by some manor he possessed, or by a characteristic or occupation.[1]

---

[1] Baildon (ii, 33) calls all four Fitz Essulf, giving their five descendants different names.

[2] *Feudal History of Derbyshire*, by J. P. Yeatman, vol. iii, p. 5.

[3] Harl. Soc., 18, p. 160.   [4] See Ellis, vol. i, p. 495.

[5] *Camden's Remains*, p. 151.

Not only could numerous families of different surnames derive from one progenitor, but a number of persons of the same secondary description might have progenitors of different families and names. For instance, in 1347 Edward III, by letters patent, granted licence to John of Pulteneye (four times Mayor of London) to effect a settlement of the manor of Ospreng (Kent), the remaindermen being Robert " de Pulteneye ", son of William Oweyn ; William " de Pulteneye ", son of William Erneys ; and Thomas " de Pulteneye ", son of John Spigurnel ; and in 1346 a pardon was granted to John " de Pulteneye ", son of Hugh Neel of Pulteneye. Here are four persons named de or of Pulteneye, whose respective fathers were called Oweyn, Erneys, Spigurnel, and Neel ; and no one of whom, apparently, had any interest in the manor of Pulteney (Leic.), which was held by John of Pulteneye at his death in 1349 ; but it is, of course, a reasonable assumption that they had some interest in the village of Poultney to enable them to maintain themselves in that place.

Down to the end of the fourteenth century examples of sons with different names to their fathers are not rare.[1]

1368.   John Mareschall, son of Richard " de Okelesthorpe ". Coram Rege Roll 430, East. 42 Edw. III, m. 15d, Rex.

1409. Thomas Richardson, filius Ricardi de Schagh de Waldershelf. *Yorks. Arch. Journ.*, 1879, vol. v, p. 76.

Importance of Genealogy.   So important a factor is genealogy in determining the status and permanency of a family name that great disappointment results from an attempt to compile a list of early families whose descent is fully authenticated.   Notwithstanding the work of the learned societies specializing in historical and genealogical research, the thousand or more family memoirs which have been published, the vast number of pedigrees given in county and local chronicles, and the collections of antiquaries, it is a difficulty to find many families whose pedigrees, extending back to the Conquest, are dated and documented to satisfaction. Charters, usually undated, are frequently but copies of later date, the chronicles and monastic accounts largely based on gossip, and being rarely coeval are not above suspicion, yet such uncertain data forms the foundation on which is built by hasty speculation the most unwarranted conclusions, and the whole offered without citation or authorities.   Even if the genealogy may be accepted, the names or their orthographic forms are commonly open to grave doubt, accuracy on this point not having been thought of importance, and back-naming being often indulged in ; for instance, John le Brun,

[1] See Baildon, vol. ii, p. 12 ; *Notes and Queries*, 27th March, 1852, p. 290.

son of John son of William, does not prove that William was called le Brun, although he would be so honoured in the pedigree.

Of the characteristic class, in particular, few names, if any, can be traced back in unbroken succession to the Norman Conquest. Wake, which was sometimes written Vigil (Lat.) or la Vielle (Fr.), was originally the personal name Wac, and occurs as a second name in a charter of 1027,[1] but the pedigree thereafter is not continuous. Another ancient name, Malet, is said to be a nickname, with various meanings, but on the face, looks like a diminutive from one of the names in Mal-. Even Corbet may be an old personal name, Corbus occurring in the seventh century (Förstemann). Descriptions from localities offer the greatest field for the discovery of ancient surnames, Bruce, Lacy, Montgomery, Montfort, Mortimer, etc., occurring in Domesday Book, as de Braiosa, de Laci, de Montgomeri, de Monteforti, de Mortemer, etc. English local surnames of early date are more difficult to find. The family of Brompton, for instance, with a genealogy proved to a period more remote than Domesday Book (1086), does not evidence its surname before 1176.[2] The representative of an ancient family like Meriet (Merriott of Soms.) occurs as "filius Harding" as late as 1166 (Lib. Nig.). The family of Shirley provide a typical example of the unsettled nature of surnames, they being lords of Estington (Warw.) and Shirley (Derb.) were apparently known by both names until the thirteenth century, when the former fell into disuse. Of early genealogical surnames Giffard is an excellent example, several kinsmen bearing that second name being noticed in Domesday Book, and Tyrrel (Tirelde in Domesday Book) is also one of the oldest surnames according to Round.[3] No example of an occupational surname tracing back to the eleventh century has come under notice.

Assize Rolls, A.D. 1219–31. In an investigation of thirteenth-century names particular reference will be made to lists of plebeians, such forming the backbone of British surnominal nomenclature. In the first place an examination will be made of Assize Rolls, which include appellatives of all classes of persons, but more especially landowners, the principal business of the itinerant justices being to take assizes of novel disseisin and mort d'ancestor. This class of record also furnishes lists of amercements imposed upon delinquents of every grade of society, as well as valuations of chattels of deceased criminals, and victims of accident, providing a useful and varied selection

---

[1] Yeatman (*Derbyshire*, vol. ii, p. 194).
[2] Eyton (*Shropshire*, vol. iv, p. 241).
[3] *Feudal England*, p. 473.

TABLE I

COMPARISON OF CLASSES OF DESCRIPTIONS, ADDRESSES, AND SURNAMES PREVALENT IN 11 COUNTIES OF ENGLAND

Compiled from the Assize Rolls, A.D. 1219–31

P.R.O. Reference	County and Year	Status of Persons named	Approx. No. analysed	Single Baptismal Names %	Characteristic Without article %	Characteristic With French article %	Local Without preposition %	Local With Latin or French prepositions %	Local With English prepositions %	Genealogical Without Relationship expressed %	Genealogical With Relationship expressed %	Occupational Without article %	Occupational With French article %	Second Names unclassified %
1042	Northern—Yorkshire, c. 1231	Litigants, Attorneys	250	—	1	1	—	56	—	1	27	2	2	10
271, m. 21	Western—Gloucestershire, c. 1221	Culprits, Sureties	150	—	2	—	—	65	—	2	8	4	6	13
733A, m. 13–14	Shropshire, c. 1222	,, ,,	150	—	1	3	—	62	—	—	14	3	3	14
801, m. 11–12	Staffordshire, c. 1227	,, ,,	120	—	4	1	1	33	—	2	27	9	9	14
2, m. 3	Central—Bedfordshire, [c. 1219]	Essoiners, Essoinees	100	—	1	2	2	44	—	3	32	2	—	13
36, m. 10	Berkshire, c. 1225	Culprits, Sureties	120	—	3	3	3	46	—	—	18	7	4	16
54	Buckinghamshire, c. 1228	Litigants, Attorneys	200	—	4	—	—	48	—	1	28	2	3	14
481, m. 2	Eastern—Lincolnshire, c. 1219	Litigants, Attorneys	150	—	1	1	1	46	—	2	32	4	1	12
229, m. 20–22	South-Eastern—Essex, c. 1227	Culprits, Sureties	250	—	2	1	—	57	—	1	18	6	1	14
358	Kent, c. 1227	Litigants, Attorneys	200	—	—	2	—	65	—	1	16	1	5	10
755, m. 11–12	South-Western—Somersetshire, c. 1225	Criminals, Fugitives	50	—	—	4	8	24	—	4	2	4	18	36
755, m. 10	Somersetshire, c. 1225	Essoiners, Essoinees	200	—	2	4	1	59	—	6	5	6	5	12
		Totals	1940	—	2	2	1	53	—	2	19	4	4	13

I

of names. From the information obtained a special analytical table has been prepared, evidencing that in the early thirteenth century the great majority of persons were still described by their present or recent place of abode or work. Of 1,940 persons named, rather more than one-half were identified by local descriptions of *de*-type, the next class in numerical importance being the genealogical. This is the earliest record coming under the present survey in which no single names were noticed. In strong contrast are the figures obtained from a list of criminals and fugitives given at the end of the Somerset roll : only 24 per cent of the local descriptions being of the unsettled *de*-type, few genealogical second names appearing, no less than 18 per cent of the delinquents being identified by occupations with French article *le*. Perhaps this striking peculiarity may be explained by the fact that criminals were often rovers, without a permanent place of abode or of no known or admitted parentage, and the clerk had perforce to indicate them by their supposed or apparent occupation.

Pipe Roll, A.D. 1230.[1] Analysing 2,000 entries in the index of this record it was found that the number of persons with baptismal names only was 1 per cent, characteristic distinctions being given to 6 per cent, no less than 54 per cent being identified by the addresses ; 12 per cent were genealogically distinguished, 9 per cent had occupation noted, and 18 per cent were passed as not classifiable with certainty.

The particular feature of this list is the number of French descriptions, or perhaps one should say Anglo-Norman, because they are often quite indistinguishable from English, the article *le* being used indiscriminately with words in both languages. Many of these additions ultimately became surnames. Some typical examples follow :—

Bacheler (a young esquire or knight ; now Bacheller, Bachelder) ; Barbe de Or (gold beard) ; a la Barbe ; de la Basoche [2] (a special court) ; Bataille (battle ; now Battell) ; le Batur (a beater or fuller ; now Bater, Beater) ; le Baylly (now Bailey, Bayly, Bayless) ; le Bel (the handsome ; now Bell) ; le Bon (the good ; now Bone) ; Bonvalet (good groom) ; Braz de fer (strong arm ; now Ferbrace) ; Brisehaunche (bruised or broken hip) ; de la Bruera (heath ; possible origin of some Brewers) ; le Brun (brown ; now Brown) ; le Buffle (the fool or jester) ; Calicer (the chalicer ; possibly confused with Challis from Calais) ; le Chen (the dog, if not a misreading for *le Cheu*, i.e. *keu* " the cook " ; now Kew, Chew) ; Cheval (an apocopated form of Chevalier ; now Chivell, Shovel) ; Cheure (the goat ; now Chivers) ; le Cirer (the wax chandler) ; Dent de fer (strong tooth) ; Dimichevaler (a half knight,

---

[1] Pipe Roll Soc.
[2] In Latin records the *de* is Latin and *la* French ; in the case of del Estappe, *del* is presumably French, but may be a hybrid. Further discussion on this point will be found on p. 175.

TABLE II

Comparison of Classes of Descriptions, Addresses, and Surnames Assigned to Small Tenants
Compiled from Manorial Records, etc., A.D. 1259–87

County and Year	Reference	Approx. No. analysed	Single Baptismal Names %	Characteristic Without article %	Characteristic With French article %	Local Without preposition %	Local With Latin or French prepositions %	Local With English prepositions %	Genealogical Without Relationship expressed %	Genealogical With Relationship expressed %	Occupational Without article %	Occupational With French article %	Second Names unclassified %
Northern—													
Western—													
Staffordshire, 1259 (Alrewas Manor)	Salt Arch. Soc., N.S. x, pt. 1, 2	300	—	1	1	4	11	—	18	34	16	4	11
Worcestershire, 1270 (Hales Manor)	Worc. Hist. Soc.	200	—	2	2	1	48	1	10	8	9	7	12
Central—													
Buckinghamshire (Olney Manor) [1284	Close R, 12 Edw. I, m. 7d, 8d	200	—	4	5	—	13	1	12	14	20	9	22
Derbyshire, 1284 (Yeatman, 111)	Forest Rolls	300	—	1	1	2	48	—	2	19	7	7	13
Northamptonshire, 1276.	Close R., 4 Edw. I, m. 17d	100	—	4	5	—	18	2	8	22	4	19	18
Eastern—													
Lincolnshire, 1294	Close R., 22 Edw. I, [m. 5d	150	—	3	—	—	19	—	5	29	10	5	29
Suffolk, 1268 (Rendlesham Manor, etc.)[1]	P.R.O., S.C. 2, 203/ 100	150	—	1	1	2	25	—	10	7	15	—	39
South-Eastern—													
Kent, 1263	P.R.O., S.C. 2, 181/73	100	—	—	3	2	29	—	8	12	9	9	28
South-Western—													
Wiltshire, 1262 (Ashton Manor)	P.R.O., S.C. 2, 208/1	100	—	1	1	2	14	—	9	6	18	—	49
Totals .		1600	—	2	2	2	28	—	8	19	12	6	21

[1] Part of this Roll is reproduced in *Ewen of East Anglia.*

i.e. a tenant of half a knight's fee ; cf. Nicholas Halfknyth, 1388, *Anc. Ind.*, K.B. 9, 9, m. 20) ; le Engleis (the English ; now Inglis) ; Especer (now Spicer) ; del Estappe (of the staple or mart ; now Staple, Staples) ; le Estraunge (the strange ; now le Strange, L'Estrange, Strange) ; de la Faleyse (of the cliff, sand, or rock ; now Fallows) ; Frauncchevaler (free knight) ; le Goyz (the lame ; now possibly Goose) ; le Gras (the fat ; now Grace) ; de la Hache (of the crooked piece of land ; now Hatch) ; le Marbrer (the hewer of marble) ; de la March (of the march ; now March) ; le Marchaund (the merchant ; now Marchant) ; le Moine (the monk, friar ; now Munn, but confused with Mohun) ; la Papa (the priest, father ; now Pope) ; de la Pomeraya (of the orchard ; now Pomroy) ; le Pugneur (the fighter, i.e. the champion) ; le Puleter (the poulterer ; now Poulter, Pulter) ; del Punt (of the arch ; now Punt) ; Quatermayns (four hands ; now Quartermain) ; le Sage (the wise ; now Sage) ; Vache (the cow ; but possibly a form of the Norman name Wace) ; la Veille (the vigil, cf. Hugo Vigil, otherwise Hugh Wake ; now Veal, Viel, which is also derived from *le viel* " the old ") ; Viz de lou (wolf-face).

An example of a pure English noun and " French " article is le Briggwricht, which, however, does not appear to have survived as a surname. Le Luggere (now Luggar, Lugar) is more fortunate, although the signification is uncertain. Some of the Luggers are probably corruptions of O.E. Leofgar.

The use of English prepositions has become slightly more noticeable, although they do not appear as separate words, and evidently have survived, only because the clerk did not grasp the significance of *atte-*, e.g. de Atteholm, de Atteneston, Attestrede, de Boveton, Bovewode. With one exception these names occur in southern counties. For about two centuries the native prepositions were employed, mainly in records of the South ; and thereafter they fell into desuetude, except in a few instances where preserved by coalescence.

Manorial Court Rolls, A.D. 1257–87. Records of local courts provide a source for the names of the country folk, but it is probable, however, that these rolls were often written up from the rough notes by professional scribes, who followed the practice of the higher courts in latinizing names, nevertheless a nearer approach to the native descriptions should be obtained. The earliest records of manorial courts now existing are of the thirteenth century, but rolls for the reigns of Henry III and Edward I are few. The information which has been obtained from these sources has been eked out with some extracts of rentals given on the Close Rolls, and the whole entered in a statistical table. Compared with the figures obtained from the Assize Rolls, a very great reduction in the number of persons identified by local descriptions is found, in fact, there is a near correspondence to what was noticed in the case of fugitives of the early part of the thirteenth century, but the similarity is from different causes. Most of the lower classes of tenants had been all their lives in the same place, and unless the courts were held elsewhere could not be described as of any town or village, although they could and were often distinguished by some local feature such as their place of dwelling or work.[1] Such descriptions have survived in a great number of surnames, providing, perhaps, the most interesting feature of the present subject. This phase may be illustrated in the first place by a selection of descriptions from the Halesowen (Worc.) rolls. [2]

Latin *de, ad, in* : de Aula (hall) ; de Birches ; de Bosco (wood) ; in Bosco ; de Broke ; de Brueria (heath) ; de Grene ; de Hem (boundary) ; de Holies (hollies) ; de Hulle (hill) ; de Hyll ; de Lappol ; de Liche (lich) ; de Longele ; de Longforlonge ; de Mere ; de Molendino (mill) ; de More ; de Pire (pirie) ; de Port (gate) ; ad Portam ; de Putte (pit) ; de Puttewei ; de Pyrecote ; de Watecroft.

Latin *de, in* : Fr. *le, la* : de la Broke ; de la Grene ; de la Hay ; de la Holies ; de la Het (heath) ; de la Lade ; en le Le ; de la Leye ; de la Lowe ; in le Put ; de la Zate (gate).

English prepositions : Abovethenbroc ; Attebroc (has survived as Addenbrook) ; othe Hethe ; atte Leye ; Attelicha ; atte Lone ende (lane end) ; atte Lowe ; ate Pirye ; ate Yate.

The interchangeability of the prepositions is illustrated by : de Broke, de la Broke and Attebroc ; de Brueria, de la Het, and othe Hethe ; ad Portam (gate), de la Zate, ate Yate ; and sometimes they are duplicated, as de Bovebroc. Further investigation will be in the store of names preserved in that vast record known as the *Rotuli Hundredorum*.

Hundred Rolls, A.D. 1275–6.[3] For thirteenth-century names the most extensive list is provided by the *Rotuli Hundredorum*, the rolls of the hundreds. During the turbulent reign of Henry III numerous usurpations of the rights of the Crown and exactions and oppressions of the people had taken place and remained unchecked, until Edward I, on his return from the Holy Land, at the end of the second year of his reign, proceeded to remedy the abuses. The first step taken was a survey to obtain the necessary evidence, the *index nominum* to which valuable record contains about 70,000 entries, and allowing for duplications, perhaps 15,000 to 20,000 different names and descriptions. Analysing 2,000 of the entries relating to various counties it was found that, confirming previous figures, practically no personal name was recorded without an additional description, and the number of unidentifiable

[1] The entries from the Forest Rolls (see Table II), being on a different footing, are noticeably distinct.

[2] Edited by J. Amphlett, 1912.

[3] Printed by the Rec. Comm., 1812. Various counties are wanting : Chester, Cumberland, Durham, Lancashire, Surrey, and Westmoreland. Monmouth, then being in Wales, was likewise omitted.

second names had increased to 27 per cent. Of the remaining descriptions, 50 per cent could be classed as local, nearly all being of the prepositional type ; 18 per cent occupational, 4 per cent genealogical, and 1 per cent characteristic.

In making deductions from an analysis of the names in this list it is well to note that of the 1,420 pages more than half are devoted to the five counties of Oxford, Cambridge, Huntingdon, Norfolk, and Lincoln, and the space occupied by the returns from the six northern counties is less than 3 per cent of the whole. The record must, therefore, be considered as a source for the names of the South and Midlands only, and this geographical limitation will explain the presence of so few descriptions expressing genealogy, the use of the words *filius*, *filia*, etc., having practically ceased in the South. The Hundred Rolls are especially valuable for the counties of Cambridge, Huntingdon, and Oxford, providing many names of servile tenants. The comparative table shows that even among the lowest rank of feudal tenant single names were the exception, and that occupational names were more liable to be borne by cottars, genealogical names, for some unexplainable reason, being particularly favoured by the sokemen of Hunts, the only one of the three counties possessing many of this class of tenant.[1] Local and characteristic descriptions are generally uniformly distributed among all ranks in the counties under consideration.

Taking the rolls in their entirety, characteristic and genealogical names are found to have been much more prevalent among servile tenants than among those of higher social standing, who were distinguished more often by local descriptions. The comparative figures will be found in the table on p. 131.

Considering the nature of the names, the most noticeable feature is the growth of English, and particularly the use of the prepositions first noticed under date *c.* 1200. Typical descriptions are : atte Skolehus, Binetheton, Bi Suthe, Boveton, Bysowthewimpel, Hunderewalle, Overbec, Sidernefenne, Underhill, Withoutentoun. The article *la*, *le*, *li* seems to have been adopted into the English language and is more frequently found in conjunction with English words than with French, e.g. de la Bear, de la Broke, de la Felde, de li Heys, de la Hill, de la Lane, de la More, de la Neulande, de la Stoke, de le Tuneshende.[2] Some purely English descriptions noted were : Theobaldus ye Hattere, Lucia ye Aukereswomman, Adam at þe Ock, Alice Blissewenche.

---

[1] Sokemen are tenants in ancient demesne (Blount), but there are also other definitions, and, in fact, the exact status of the various tenants is uncertain, and doubtless varied throughout the country.

[2] See p. 173 for further observations on the article.

TABLE III

COMPARISON OF CLASSES OF DESCRIPTIONS, ADDRESSES, AND SURNAMES ASSIGNED TO FREEMEN AND BONDMEN

Compiled from the Hundred Rolls, A.D. 1275

County	Class of Tenant	Approx. No. analysed	Single Baptismal Names %	Characteristic Without article %	Characteristic With French article %	Local Without preposition %	Local With Latin or French prepositions %	Local With English prepositions %	Genealogical Without Relationship expressed %	Genealogical With Relationship expressed %	Occupational Without article %	Occupational With French article %	Second Names unclassified %
Cambridge	Freemen (*Libere tenentes*)	200	—	4	4	1	21	—	17	7	21	4	21
	Customary (*Custumarii*)	100	—	3	1	3	12	2	20	10	15	3	31
	Cottars (*Cotarii*)	150	—	5	2	3	6	—	23	4	29	4	24
	Villeins (*Villani*)	200	—	4	4	—	20	—	19	7	15	4	27
	Serfs (*Servi*)	70	—	3	3	—	14	4	17	2	14	5	38
Huntingdon	Sokemen (*Socmanni*)	200	1	3	—	1	16	—	21	25	12	3	18
	Cottars	200	1	7	3	1	20	—	5	6	20	11	25
	Bondmen (*Bondi*)	150	2	2	1	—	20	—	8	9	12	12	34
Oxford	Free	200	—	5	7	1	30	4	9	8	9	12	15
	Cottars	200	—	7	2	2	15	—	20	2	20	5	30
	Villeins	200	—	5	3	—	22	10	22	9	8	5	16
	Serfs	200	—	9	2	2	24	8	16	7	4	5	23
	Natives (*Nativi*)	200	1	7	3	1	20	1	16	8	9	7	27
Totals	All classes	2270	—	5	3	1	19	2	16	9	14	6	25

Page 119

With the decline in the use of the distinctive words *filius*
and *filia*, names were sometimes written as Hugo Philiberti,
Johanna Mariote, or Willelmus Margarete, but the English
nominative form, as Henry Maynard or John Roger, was also
used, and the genitive ending (*es, is, ys,* or *s*) also begins to be
noticeable, and at first most frequently in the names of women,
thus Robertus filius Radulfi became Robertus Rolle (Raoul),
but Matilda filia Radulfi was written Matilda Rolles. In a
list of Huntingdonshire sokemen appear Hugo King, Bele
and Felicia Kinges, Elena fil' Rad' le King, Thom' le King
(p. 609), and Will's Aleyn and Beatrice Aleynes (p. 611*b*).
There was no precise rule, many surnames of women are without
the final sibilant, which is occasionally found added to the
second names of men (see below, p. 247).

To examine further the questions arising from the relative
preservation of O.E. first and second names, and to determine
whether the native appellatives were more prevalent than the
Norman among the servile classes, an analysis of 500 names
of male bondmen, cottars, etc., in the county of Huntingdon
has been made. It has been mentioned that in the year 1130
(sixty-four years from the Conquest), the general ratio had
fallen from the maximum to 10 per cent, being further reduced
by the year 1200 to 7 per cent, and now in 1275 among the
lower orders, where the native names might be expected to
have survived, to but 1 per cent. Of the most popular male
Norman names, William was found to have increased to
19 per cent, being followed by John 16 per cent, Richard
10 per cent, and Robert 7 per cent ; the remaining 47 per cent
being made up by twenty-eight different names.[1] It is evident
that a very small variety of personal names was in use, and
that few Saxon appellatives were current.

At this time (1275), among the servile tenants, O.E.
secondary descriptions outnumbered the O.E. personal names
by ten to one, the following examples being taken from the
Huntingdonshire lists :—

Adelmer and Athelmer, Albert, Albot, Aylbrich, Aylrun, Aylsy,
Berich, Bigge, Bonde, Brunig, Buc, Clubbe (cf. Cloppa : Dom. Bk.) ;
Colling, Copping, Doning, Edous, Eylmer, Fin, Goderayl, Godrich,
Govi, Grim, Gulde, Hereward, Ingelram, Leverich (Leofric), Notte
(Noth), Outi, Seled, Semar, Seward, Sweting, Syred, Thurstan, Ulf,
Widding, Wilde, Winter, Witwif.

These names not being preceded by *filius* have the
appearance of being settled surnames or well on the way of

---

[1] This conclusion is supported by statistics given in *The Complete Peerage*,
1913, vol. iii, p. 625. It may be of interest to note that in Paris, 1292, corresponding figures were : Jehan, 19 per cent ; Guillaume, 10 per cent ; Pierre,
7 per cent (Michaëlsson, p. 60).

becoming so. If they are surnames they must have become
so since 1200, when it has been shown that there were few
genealogical surnames ; and, further, the 7 per cent of O.E.
personal names in 1200 must have produced 42 per cent of
O.E. second names in 1275. Three possible reasons for this
apparent multiplication present themselves : (i) the more
characteristic nature of the O.E. names may have tended to
their preservation as distinctive additions in greater
proportion than the Norman ; names such as William and
John being of comparatively small service for the purpose,
the bearers of Norman names would be the most likely to
acquire descriptions of other classes.   (ii) Teutonic names
after losing popularity in this country may have been reintroduced by aliens ; but unfortunately no means exist of
determining to what extent. (iii) In some parts of the country
O.E. names may have been much better preserved than
generally appears : an excellent example of such survival is a
list of names of men of Lynn (Norf.) in 13 Hen. II (1166–7),
which may be found on the Pipe Rolls.[1]   In this instance, a
century after the Conquest, of about 150 persons, fully one-
half have O.E. or Norse forenames, and 44 per cent may be
recognized as O.E. ; and of the genealogical descriptions over
70 per cent are undoubtedly English.   This proportion of
O.E. names is very much in excess of what is usually found at
this period, the opposite extreme might be illustrated by
figures from the coeval *Liber Niger Scaccarii*, where analysis
shows that there were practically no O.E. names.

Scrappy as these figures are, it must be concluded that
although the great increase in the popularity of Norman
names is undoubted, yet far more O.E. names survived than
is generally admitted, and many of these are preserved to-day
in our surnames. In a later chapter a table of elements will
be provided which it is hoped will enable many O.E. personal
names to be recognized in modern family names.

Welsh Descriptions and Names.   The English kings
from William the Conqueror onwards had claimed Wales as
part of their dominions, but for two centuries the Cymry
successfully resisted all attempts to subjugate them ; nevertheless, intermingling of the two races was the first step leading to
the supersession of the ancient system of distinguishing persons
by reciting their pedigrees. In 1267 Llewellyn ap Gruffydd,
sovereign of the greater part of Wales, having severely defeated
the English, was acknowledged as Prince of Wales by
Henry III. In 1275 warfare again broke out, Llewellyn, two
years later, being forced to accept terms of peace, which
provided for his realm passing to the English crown at his

[1] p. 20.

death, but rebelling again in 1282 he was defeated and slain, and by the Statute of Rhuddlan (1284) Wales was united to England, and divided into counties.[1]

Before closing this conspectus of thirteenth-century appellatives, the descriptions and names in use in the principality must be noticed, and for this examination convenient lists are those of the taxpayers under the subsidy imposed in the twentieth year of Edward I (1292).[2] The data which has been obtained from these Exchequer records will be found in a table on the opposite page. The effect of the strong English influence, particularly in the larger towns, will be noticed at once, e.g. in Rhuddlan the descriptions are wholly Latin and French, and, except for an occasional Welsh personal name, the roll might pass for an English record. In the country districts the ancient native system of genealogical identification was still accepted by the recording clerk ; for instance, all the taxpayers of Pengwern have Welsh descriptions, of which no less than 79 per cent are genealogical. These family descriptions are occasionally miniature pedigrees giving three generations, as Eynion ap Eynion ap Bledyn ; or, in the Latin form, as Cadogan filius Madyn fil' Galfrid'. *Ap* is sometimes omitted by the scribe, as Heylin þloyt. The use of the Saxon thorn was not uncommon, and may be read as th, thloyt being an attempt to spell phonetically, as thlewelyn, etc. What are apparently three names, e.g. Jorwerth duy vyngam and Kenewrec voel duy, are likewise the result of such clerical omissions.

The Mid. W. words expressing kinship are *ap* " son ", *merch* " daughter ", and *gwraig*, formerly *gwreic*, " wife." These words, owing to mutation of initial consonant when following proper nouns of either gender, appear in the records in various forms. *Ap* and *ab* are interchangeable ; thus on consecutive lines in the Montgomery roll (m. 5) are Eneas ap Madoc and Howel ab Madoc, Madoc ab Adaf and David ap Adaf. Other forms of the filial sign which occur are *map*, *vab* (elsewhere *fab*), as Ricardus map þloyt (*llwyd* " the grey "), Eynon vap goch (*coch* " the ruddy "). At a later stage the *b* and *p* coalesced with the following appellative resulting in such surnames as Bowen and Parry (ap Harry). Mab also signifies " a man " (Laws of Howel dda), which may explain such entries as " filia map Conn ", Map Wyn, Map Maur, Map Seis, etc., all without forename. In other cases Map was omitted, as Cantor (*cantwr* " the singer "). Similar short entries are found in Latin, as Fabro (abl.), corresponding to those already noticed in the Winton. Domesday. Mape and Vape

---

[1] *Statutes of the Realm*, 12 Edw. I, c. 5.
[2] Preserved in the Public Record Office.

TABLE IV

COMPARISON OF CLASSES OF DESCRIPTIONS, ADDRESSES, AND SURNAMES PREVALENT IN 6 COUNTIES OF WALES

Compiled from the Subsidy Rolls, A.D. 1292

P.R.O. Reference	County and Place	Approx. No. analysed	Single Baptismal Names %	Characteristic — Welsh %	Characteristic — Without French article %	Characteristic — With French article %	Local — Welsh %	Local — Without preposition %	Local — With Latin or French prepositions %	Local — With English prepositions %	Genealogical — Welsh %	Genealogical — Without Relationship expressed %	Genealogical — With Relationship expressed (Latin) %	Occupational — Welsh %	Occupational — Without French article %	Occupational — With French article %	Second Names unclassified %
242/55 m. 2	Denbigh—"Glynvaur"	76	4	11	—	—	1	—	—	—	76	—	3	1	—	—	4
242/52 m. 4	Flint—Bangor	72	—	17	—	—	—	—	3	—	66	6	—	—	4	—	4
m. 1	Flint	75	—	1	1	7	—	—	44	—	1	3	3	—	15	—	8
m. 18	"Hydraduch"	75	—	21	—	—	2	—	—	—	65	—	11	—	3	17	—
m. 14	Pengwern	57	—	19	4	1	—	—	—	—	79	—	—	—	—	—	9
242/2	Rhuddlan	74	—	—	—	—	—	—	54	—	—	1	4	—	20	7	—
242/53 m. 4	Merioneth—Llanfrothen	92	9	14	—	—	—	—	1	—	51	1	12	1	4	—	7
m. 2	"Penaran"	74	12	24	—	—	—	—	3	—	35	7	5	1	4	—	10
242/56 m. 2-4	Monmouth—Abergavenny	200	2	9	—	—	—	1	2	—	68	1	5	—	3	1	8
242/54 m. 11	Montgomery—"Breter"	88	6	10	6	—	—	—	—	—	73	—	6	—	—	—	3
m. 13	"Sclantgyry"	54	7	28	2	2	—	—	22	—	46	2	7	—	2	2	2
m. 17	Welshpool	103	3	9	—	6	—	—	—	—	1	3	12	—	14	16	12
242/56 m. 9	Pembroke—Cilgerran	130	6	18	—	—	4	—	1	—	56	—	3	—	5	—	7
	Totals	1170	3	13	1	2	1	—	9	—	48	2	6	—	6	3	6

appear as descriptions in a Herefordshire Controlment Roll.[1] Map was also an O.E. baptismal name, cf. Godric Mappesone, which is noticed in Domesday Book.[2] Map undoubtedly became a surname; a twelfth-century charter of Walter Mapes (a latinized form of Map) is witnessed by " Philippo Map nepoti meo ".[3] Merch, by mutation, becomes *ferch*, *verch*, or *vergh* (verth in the Denbigh roll, as Wladuz verth Jeuan, Eua verth vadoc " daughter of Madoc "), and is generally written ver', but it is never used in the Flint roll, where daughter is invariably represented by fil'.

The father's personal name may be omitted, and that of the son, followed by a description of his parent, as Kadogan du ab y gwr byrr (Cadogan the Black, son of the short man); but *gwr* is usually omitted—Jevan ap y melyn (son of the yellow), Wenlyana ver hen (daughter of the old), Win ap was crek (son of the petty servant). A peculiarity is the fusion of Welsh and English, as Gron' ap ypalmer (son of the palmer), but hybridization in the composition of descriptions is not uncommon, cf. Owenson, Evanson.

In thirteenth-century Welsh *y* is often *e*, and the article joined to the following word in the same way, as map Ekedyn (*y cethin*) "son of the dusky", map Egof (y gof) " son of the smith ".

In some descriptions the adjective comes before the noun, e.g. David ap Gwyn Iuan, Goch Yrgon, Griffyt heuen Jolyn " easily-smiling Jolyn " (cf. *hywên Hywel*. Pryddyd y Moch, cited by Owen Pughe).

Classification of Welsh Descriptions. It has been explained that Welsh, like Saxon and Norman descriptions, fall into four classes—characteristic, local, genealogical, and occupational; and of these the genealogical distinction or recitation of pedigree was for long the principal method of identification.

Characteristic descriptions. In the first place the native laws, and secondly the great repetition of baptismal names, made the cumbersome pedigrees necessary, but these under English influence gave way to briefer auxiliary indicia, of which the characteristic description was the most popular, amounting to 13 per cent of all names, English and Welsh. No large number of these epithets appear, however, to have been perpetuated as surnames, but the possibility is shown by *vachan*, now Vaughan; *llwyd*, now Lloyd, Floyd; *coch*, now Gough; *hen*, now Henn; *gwyn*, now Gwinn, Gwynn, Wynne, etc. A selection of these with the English equivalent will now be given.

[1] P.R.O., K.B. 29, 91.
[2] Herefordshire, f. 181.
[3] *Gualteri Mapes de Nugis Curialum*, Camden Soc., 1850, p. 13.

Bach (little, small) ; Bedar (the deaf) ; Bluth (*plydd* " soft ") ;
Bongam (the crook-shanked) ; Botyn (*pwtyn* "short body ") ;
Brekiyn (pimpled or freckled) ; Bul, Bule (*bwl* " round ") ; Buncan
(*bwn* " spear " ; *can* " shining ") ; Chwyt (*chwith* " awkward ") ;
Cloff (the lame) ; Cucor (*cuchwr* " frowner ") ; Cul (the slender) ;
Druch (*trwch* " churl ") ; Dry (the foremost) ; Dou, Dw (*du* " black ") ;
Dwn (the dusky) ; Ekedyn (*y cethin* " the dusky ") ; Fest (the speedy) ;
Gadarn (*cadarn* " strong ") ; Gam (*cam* " crooked ") [1] ; Gloff (*cloff*
" lame ") ; Goch, Gohc, Gouch (*coch* " ruddy ") ; Goran (*cor*
" dwarf ") ; Grach (*crach* " puny ") ; Gwethel (the Irishman) ; Hagir
(*hagr* " deformed ") ; Hardy (*harrd* " handsome ") ; Hen (the old) ;
Hurthan (*hurth* " stupid ") ; Hyr (*hir* " long ") ; Kam (*cam*
" crooked ") ; Kedyn (*cethin* " dusky ") ; Kwta (*cwta* " short ") ;
Las (*llas* " blue ") ; Lawen (*llawen* " merry ") ; Libin (*llibyn* " a
lank one ") ; Lloid, Lhoid (*llwyd* " grey ") ; Llydan (the broad) ;
Moelwyn (*moel* " head " ; *wyn* " white ") ; Off (the frail) ; Penwyn
(*pen* " head " ; *wyn* " white ") ; Seys (*sais* " Saxon ") ; Succanuor
(*suckanwr* " a drunkard " ; Salesbury) ; Symlen (the simpleton) ;
Syw (the smart) ; Vachan, Vahhan (*bychan* " little ", " small ",
surname Vaughan) ; Vawr (*mawr* " great " ; also occurs as Fawr) ;
Velyn (*melyn* " yellow ") ; Ver (*byr* " short ") ; Voelyn (*moelyn* " bald
head ") ; Vongam (*bongam* " crook-shanked ") ; Voyl, Woyl (*moel*
" bald ") ; Voylvrych (the bald freckled one) ; Vras (*bras* " fat ") ;
Vrych (the freckled) ; Vyrr (*byr* " short ") ; Wan (*gwan* " weakling ") ;
Wamal (*gwammal* " capricious ") ; With, Wyith, Wyth (the brave) ;
Wras (*bras* " fat ") ; Wydel, Wydil (the Irishman) ; Wyneu, Wynew
(*gwineu* " brown ") ; Wyn, Wen (*gwyn* " fair ") ; Wyr (*byr* " short ").

The class of some secondary names is indeterminate, thus
the word *llwyd*, signifying " grey ", is a characteristic epithet,
but being also a font-name, it further becomes a genealogical
description. It is also difficult to distinguish between some
characteristic descriptions and place-names, e.g. *Penbras*
" large head " might fall into either category ; Voelgoch,
i.e. " red hill ", is local, but Voelyn " bald head " might be
either place-name or characteristic description, cf. *dos y fyny
moelyn* " go up thou bald head " (2 Kings, ii, 23).

Local descriptions. The documents being in Latin, the
preposition *of* is generally represented by *de*, but exceptionally,
in the list for " Estone " in the commote of Prestatyn, the
Welsh *o* was freely used as the following extract will illustrate.

De Houa ap Madauc	De Wilkyn o pase	De Gibbe Robin
Gronou ap dyagu	X'ana opase	Houa duy
Adaf ap edlyn	Madauc ap bledyn	Madauc hoyw
Eynion ap adaf	Magr' dauid	Jorwerth seys
Eynion ap Maylcwyt	Hiscot okelly	Robt' o dycse

[1] So common is *cam* as a description that one might be excused for
suggesting that it originated the modern surname Game, but etymologists
hold the opinion that the words game and gammy (lame) are not derived
from W. *cam* (*gam*).

Jevan ap g(ry)ffryd	Rob'o olisce	Robin cochil
Hise yscoder	Jeuan ap Gronou	Philip opase
Robt' oargre	Jeuan ap pyll	Matho opase
Henr' albach	Llywarth ap madauc	Robt ofenton
Henr' pote	Jeuan ap madauc	Risard o pase
Gronou queuen		Wilkin o sordeleye

Elsewhere " opase " is written de pase, de passo, and del pas ; okelly, which looks like an Irish name, but is Welsh, signifies " of the grove ".

Local descriptions without prepositions are uncommon, and were not found to number more than 1 per cent of the whole, and few, if any, became surnames. A small selection may be given :—

Blayn (blaen " a point ") ; Briwdor (bryw " brisk " ; dwr " stream ") ; Dalreyn (talrwn " head-ridge ") ; Draus (traws " a cross ") ; Ebren (y pren " the tree ") ; Ewern (y wern " the alder trees ") ; Gelyn (celyn " the holly wood ") ; Ledan (the swamp) ; Moylgoch (the name of a hill) ; Pant (a hollow) ; Penbras, Penwras (pen " head " ; bras " large ") ; Porth (a gate) ; Voelgrun (moel " head " ; grwn " ridge ") ; Vrnant (wr " over " ; nant " brook ") ; Warch (gwarch " a cave ").

The following local descriptions may possibly have originated surnames : Dorweyn, Drwry, Keli, Keri, Keyswin, Tredewyn, and Yal, the latter, at any rate, is famed. A few Welsh surnames of the local class will be found in a later chapter (see p. 242).

Genealogical descriptions. As stated above, this type of distinction sometimes recorded the personal name of father and grandfather, three generations in all. Some of the English rolls go to a greater extreme in identification, the Controlment Rolls, for instance, name the Welshman by a pedigree of six generations. In a few cases in the Subsidy Rolls, the father's name was given without *ap*, following the growing English practice of dropping *filius* or *fitz*.

Bled, Bleych, Bleyth (blaidd " wolf " ; corresponding to the Saxon name Ulf) ; Gethin ; Gwaspadric, Was patric (" servant of St. Patrick " ; the Welsh equivalent of Gillepatric ; see pp. 37, 87) ; Gwy ; Gymen ; Kethyn ; Kyw du ; Oweyn ; Patric ; Seysil ; Slemen ; Tuder ; Wagyl ; Wecheches.

Occupational descriptions. A few distinctions of this class were noticed, but it is rare to find one which has been perpetuated as a surname.

Bard (bardd " priest ") ; Barun (barwn " a chief ") ; Bugel (bugail " a shepherd ") ; Cath (kaeth O.W. " serf ", " bondman ") ; Crouther (crythwr " a fiddler " ; also occurs as le Cruethere, mod. Crowder, Crowther) ; Egof (the smith) ; Escob (the overseer) ; Eurych (the tinker or goldsmith) ; Gyn (cyn " chief ") ; Henewas (the old servant) ;

Heusawr (the herdsman) ; Hudol (the juggler) ; Meyr (the steward) ; Pen (the head) ; Pennayth (the principal) ; Saer (the craftsman) ; Seythor (*saethwr* " archer ") ; Spedor (*spadwr* " a gelder ") ; Turnaur (*turniwr* " a turner ") ; Was, Gwas (the servant ; in the Hund. Rolls Waz occurs under Wilts. and Oxf., but may be a form of the personal name Wace) ; Wr (*gwr* " a man ") ; Yswn (*yswein* " esquire ").

The Welsh Subsidy Rolls are, on the whole, well written ; the Flint record in particular being a delight to the reader, except for the want of distinction between *c* and *t*, but the scribe makes amends by " dotting " his i's, a valuable help to the transcriber of manuscripts, and most unusual in these rolls.   The orthography is thirteenth-century, the principal characteristics of which are the use of *k* for *c*, *z* for *s*, and initial *e* for *y*.   All vowels are interchangeable medially.   In addition to ordinary mutations (see above, p. 41), there are the usual palæographic variations, as, for instance, *u*, *v*, and *w* ; consequently equations may be found, as $b = f = m = u = v = w$.   There are numbers of orthographic variants, e.g. Iuan of the Flint roll occurs elsewhere as Yewan, þevan, and Zeuan.   Occasionally names are aspirated as Jarword ab Howeyn.

Irish Descriptions and Surnames.   The conquest of Ireland being completed by Henry II, in 1175 the Treaty of Windsor was concluded with Roderick O'Connor of Connaught, the head king, by which he consented to become Henry's liegeman, and to pay an annual tribute.   John, in 1210, with " the common consent of all men of Ireland, ordained that the laws and customs of the realm of England should be kept therein ", nevertheless the sanguinary disturbances continued, until by a succession of disasters extending over a century, the sphere of the influence of the English crown dwindled to ten counties and liberties, the independent Irish being treated as enemies.   It appears, however, that many Englishmen had adopted the native language, laws, and customs.

" After the murder of the Great Earl of Ulster, William de Burgo, the third Earl of that name, in 1333, and the consequent lessening of the English power in Ireland, many, if not all the distinguished Anglo-Norman families seated in Connaught and Munster became Hibernicised—*Hibernis ipsis Hiberniores*—spoke the Irish language, and assumed surnames like those of the Irish, by prefixing Mac to the christian names of their ancestors, but not O' in any instance ; for which latter fact no reason has been assigned.   Thus the De Burgos, in Connaught, assumed the name of Mac William . . . from these sprang many offsets, who took various surnames from their respective ancestors as the Mac Davids, Mac Gibbons, Mac Walters, and Mac Raymonds." [1]

J. O'Donovan in *Topographical Poems*, 1862, p. 21.

The well-known lines—" By Mac and O, You'll always know true Irishmen "—are, therefore, somewhat misleading, since many Macs must have been Englishmen, but Woulfe states that " the practice of forming surnames with Ua (or Ó) had almost certainly ceased before the coming of the English ",[1] so that the verse is partly a correct statement. By the Statute of Kilkenny (1366), in an attempt to check the growing custom, it was ordained *inter alia* that " every Englishman leave off entirely the manner of naming used by the Irish ".[2] This enactment clearly recognizes a difference existing between the English and Irish methods of " naming ", as late as the fourteenth century, so that it must be concluded that the native method of distinction was yet largely, if not entirely, the ancient genealogical description.

It has been noticed that great antiquity, comparatively speaking, is claimed for hereditary surnames in Ireland. Woulfe suggests the eleventh and twelfth centuries as " the period within which the great bulk of Irish patronymics became fixed and began to assume the hereditary character of family names ", but he admits that, although by the end of the twelfth century surnames were universal among Irish families, " they were not at all at first of a lasting character, and in some instances were laid aside after a generation or two in favour of new surnames taken from less remote ancestors." These early " surnames ", then, do not strictly comply with the modern conception of the word as defined above. In the absence of evidence to the contrary, it is to be supposed that the Irish, like the Welsh, only developed the hereditary surname habit through English influence, there being few Norse or Danish surnames in Ireland; in fact, the Scandinavians, following the early English, had largely adopted the native system of nomenclature.

Woulfe conjectures that Ó Dubhghaill (O'Doyle), Ó Harailt (O'Harold), Ó hEanraic (O'Henrick), Ó hlomhain (O'Hure or Howard), Mac Oitir (MacCotter), and some few other surnames represent Norse or Danish families.[3]

Although the Norman influence was not as strong in Ireland as in England, Wales, and Scotland, yet the native Celtic names largely gave way in popularity to the Norman appellatives, which, like the Scandinavian, tended to become hibernicized, e.g. Hoireabárd for Herbert, Réamonn for Redmond, etc.

The form in which Irish names of the thirteenth century were entered by English or French clerks may be illustrated by some extracts from the Justiciary Rolls for 1295 (Latin).

---

[1] *Sloinnte Gaedhael is Gall*, p. xviii.   [2] See p. 425 below.
[3] Work cited, p. xxv ; q.v. for further instances.

Limerick pardons. Douenild Macdecam OKynnedy ; Regin. Maccloni ; Douenald Macharthon ; Ph. OHanwan ; Royry OKynnedy ; Murihirt Ofechan ; Thomas Ofechan ; Royry OKeinnedi ; David OKeynedy ; Schiteruk Oconoc ; Comdin Ocon'e ; Merkud Ofardeny ; Douenald OKennedy ; Merkod Maccarthen ; Maurice OKeinnedy.

Cork pardons. John Omoriharthy ; Luke Omoryharthy ; Walter Omuryharthy ; David Olannan ; Bridin Olannan ; Malmory Olethan ; Eyno Odowyngort ; Maur Ocarbri ; Will. le Blund de Cnokmurne ; Englin Ocorechan ; Crachin Odowingort ; Mahyn Ohochwyth ; Malmori Ohachwyth ; David Ohachwyth ; Thomas Oconyli ; Neiuin Onyhyn.

Of the thirty-one persons the forenames of thirteen certainly are not Celtic : Schiteruck seems to be the Norse Sihtric, and the origin of the others is obvious. Among the second names perhaps may be recognized : O'Kennedy, MacLoonie, O'Fegan, O'Connor, MacCartin, O'Moriarty, O'Lannan, O'Leehan, O'Carbry, O'Corrigan, O'Conolly, and O'Nyhane. The simplicity of the descriptions in these pardons provides a striking contrast to a series of three centuries later, which will be found below. Mac and O' prefixes were not confined to the perpetuation of personal names, but sometimes referred to an ancestral tradesman, as Mac an tSaoir (son of the craftsman), Ó Gobhann (descendant of the smith),[1] being in composition similar to the Welsh example given above (p. 124).

Mac is sometimes written Mag before vowels and the consonants *c, g, l, n, r, bh, dh, fh, mh, sh, th.*[2] Mac and Ó may be dropped, their function being served by the suffix *-ach* (*-each*), added to the nominative case of the name of the ancestor, as Mac Suidhne or Suidhneach, O'Briain or Brianach, etc.[3]

The unfixed nature of second names is illustrated by the record of an action of novel disseisin brought into the English court at Clonmel in the year 1295 : William le Teynturer of Artfinan *versus* Henry le Norreys, who says that William is *hibernicus* (i.e. an Irish *nativus*), and of servile condition, etc. The jurors being " asked, of what name of the Irish and of what condition, they say that he is of the Omoleyns and that his father was called Thomas Omolyn, born at Iniseheenan, William himself says he is not *Hibernicus* but *Houstmannus* (an Ostman), viz. Macmackus of the city of Limerick ".[4]

Scottish Descriptions and Names. Towards the close of the thirteenth century Scotland was under independent sovereignty, the Western Isles having been recovered from the Norsemen ; and after a long period of peaceful relationship

---

[1] Woulfe, p. 15.
[2] Ibid.
[3] Ibid., p. 21.
[4] *Cal. of Justiciary Rolls*, vol. i, p. 59.

with England was soon to commence hostilities which lasted for centuries. The long continuance of friendly intercourse had, however, accelerated the spread of English speech, customs, and names, particularly in the districts south of Forth and Clyde.

The Gaelic names of Scotland do not differ materially from those of Ireland, but the people of the Lowlands, although largely bearing Gaelic names, had accepted a system of secondary descriptions parallel to that in force in England, as amply illustrated by the extract given above under year 1200.

Summary and Conclusions. A comparison of the names of burgesses, 1086 (see p. 63), with later lists, English, Welsh, and Irish, has clearly shown that the popularity of O.E., as well as native personal names, received a severe check with the incoming of the Normans, and this feature of British nomenclature will receive further confirmation by extracts from Subsidy Rolls of the early fourteenth century, to be given in a later chapter. Nevertheless, large numbers of O.E. names, reinforced by others of Teutonic origin, brought in by aliens, did survive, ultimately to become our surnames, although often in corrupt form, as will be evidenced in later sections.[1]

It is manifest that the ancient custom of bestowing secondary descriptions, both alternative and additional to the personal name, became more general among all classes of the people, until by the end of the twelfth century it was unusual to find a person without an official identification label. It will have been gathered that these marks of distinction under Anglo-Saxon, Danish, and Norman rule were latinized by government clerks or the legal scribes, that from the middle of the twelfth century they often became frenchified, and towards the end of the century, English, the language of the people, commenced to assert itself. In Wales, Scotland, and Ireland the native languages and systems of naming remained, except in those parts under strong English influence.

To facilitate the drawing of definite conclusions from the evidence outlined in chapters four and five, touching the increased employment of descriptions additional to personal names, their distribution geographically and socially, and growth of their hereditary nature, a table has been prepared giving the relative proportions of the four classes of descriptions, addresses, and possible surnames appearing in various classes of records at different times during the period 1066–1275.

---

[1] H. J. Ellis (MS. Dept. Brit. Mus.) wrote that "the supersession of the English or Saxon names by the Norman-French was practically complete by the end of the thirteenth century". (*The Complete Peerage*, vol. iii, p. 600.)

TABLE V
The Relative Use of Descriptions in England
Illustrated by Comparative Figures

	Date and Authority	Status of Persons enumerated	Approx. No. analysed	Single Baptismal Names	Descriptions				
					Characteristic	Local	Genealogical	Occupational	Unclassified
				%	%	%	%	%	%
1.	1066. Liber Winton. (1103–15)	Householders of Winchester.	320	55	4	5	10	11	15
2.	1066–86. Domesday Bk.	All classes of tenants.	1000	85	1	3	2	7	2
3.	1086. Domesday Bk.	Tenants in chief	1000	33	5	17	9	27	9
4.	1086. Domesday Bk.	Under tenants.	1000	61	2	16	4	10	7
5.	1086. Domesday Bk.	Burgesses of Colchester.	275	94	—	—	—	3	3
6.	1086. Inq. Com. Cantab. (12th cent.)	Tenants in Cambs, all classes.	200	25	3	39	8	13	12
7.	1086. Inq. Eliensis (12th cent.)	Tenants of Ely Monastery, all classes.	400	40	2	34	5	13	6
8.	1086. Exon. Domesday.	Tenants in S.W. counties, all classes.	1000	68	2	14	3	6	7
9.	? Shaftesbury Rental	Tenants in Dorset and Wilts, all classes.	350	93	—	1	1	3	2
10.	1103–15. Liber Winton.	Householders of Winchester.	240	27	3	15	20	25	10
11.	1115–18. Lindsey Survey.	Tenants in Lincs.	200	18	1	30	31	9	11
12.	1130–1. Pipe Roll .	General . .	1000	5	2	42	21	15	15
13.	1148. Liber Winton.	Tenants in Winchester, all classes.	700	31	4	14	13	23	15
14.	1159–60. Pipe Roll .	General . .	400	6	5	35	21	19	14
15.	1166. Lib. Nig. Scaccarii	Knights of Yorkshire.	300	1	3	59	19	4	14
16.	Do.	Knights of Devonshire.	200	1	3	62	25	—	9
17.	1174–5. Pipe Roll .	General . .	1000	6	4	49	15	12	14
18.	1183. Boldon Book .	Tenants in Palatinate of Durham, all classes.	200	26	2	28	15	15	14
19.	1190. Pipe Roll .	General . .	1000	3	5	50	18	6	18
20.	1196–1200. Curia Regis Roll.	General . .	2800	3	3	55	25	5	9
21.	1219–31. Assize Rolls	General . .	1940	—	4	54	21	8	13
22.	1230. Pipe Roll .	General . .	2000	1	6	54	12	9	18
23.	1259–87. Manorial Rolls.	Small Tenants .	1600	—	4	30	27	18	21
24.	1275. Hundred Rolls	General . .	2000	—	1	50	4	18	27
25.	Do. . . .	Servile Tenants	2270	—	8	22	25	20	25
			23395						

By comparing enumerations 3 and 15 it will be gathered that in eighty years (1086–1166), among the upper classes, secondary descriptions increased from 67 to 99 per cent, while in similar manner, from 1 and 10, it may be deduced that in about forty-three years (1066–c. 1109) the numbers of double names of small householders rose from 45 to 73 per cent, no very clear later indication being obtained until 1275, by which time all the lowest classes in the social scale received distinguishing appellatives.   Information is not sufficiently detailed to enable any sound deduction to be made as to the relative prevalence of additional descriptions in North and South, or city and village, but the point is of minor importance, as in a few years time the custom of double-naming was spread throughout the English-speaking parts of the British Isles. These identification descriptions, like those of Gaels, Cymry, and Anglo-Saxons, have been conveniently divided according to their nature into four classes—characteristic, local, genealogical, and occupational, but it is frankly admitted that no very great degree of exactitude in classification can be obtained.   Inaccuracy and doubt are the consequences of a combination of adverse conditions militating against definite and entirely satisfying results.   The ever-present difficulties which already have been indicated may be recapitulated under seven heads, the insurmountable nature of which will be readily understood by the discerning student without further elaboration or excuse.

1.   The class is not always determinable by inspection, e.g. Wolf may be a baptismal name and genealogical class, or it may be given as a sobriquet and fall into the characteristic class, but possibly it might be local from the name of a hostelry or shop.

2.   Two persons of the same name may be indexed under one head.

3.   Double-named persons are often indexed under two heads, whereas a single name occurs but once.

4.   Persons may have more than one description. See p. 110.

5.   The descriptions registered are often official inventions, and not those by which the person is commonly known.

6.   Popularity of type of description varied between North and South, city and village, upper and lower classes, and the records are rarely proportionate or uniform in range, e.g. Domesday Book does not cover the whole country, nor does it name the serf class.

7.   Documents are seldom original or coeval, and suffer not only from scribal errors of omission and commission, but the tendency for the copyist to modify a name in accordance with the custom prevailing at the time of writing.

Notwithstanding the great possibility of error through insufficiency or uncertainty of detailed information on the points specified, it is thought that this analysis of 23,395 early descriptions of the eleventh, twelfth, and thirteenth centuries should indicate the general tendencies during the embryonic stages of surname-making and have more practical value than a host of chance opinions and wild imaginings. Speaking generally of conditions prevalent all over England, the following deductions can be submitted with confidence :—

1. Characteristic descriptions, sometimes called nicknames or sobriquets, were rare among both upper and lower orders, and form a very small class at all times and places. In the extreme North the article was not used in the composition of descriptions.

2. Local descriptions were used by all classes equally. The preposition *de*, in the records, is generally Latin and is equivalent in value to " of ", " at ", or " in ", and coupled with a place-name did not indicate territorial suzerainty, but was part of an address used for distinguishing purposes by servile tenant as well as overlord. The introduction of such descriptions was not entirely due to Norman custom, but *ad*, *apud*, *de*, etc., in Latin and French documents took the place of O.E. *æt* or E.E. *atte*. Local descriptions greatly increased from 1066 up to the first quarter of the thirteenth century, when a decline commenced. In the North the Latin preposition was predominant ; in the South English was freely used.

3. Genealogical descriptions were employed more by tenants in chief than under-tenants in 1086 ; in later years the tendency was opposite. In the twelfth century descriptions of this class expressed in Latin were much commoner in the North than the South.

4. Occupational descriptions were fairly uniformly distributed, but the article was much less used in the North than the South.

From an analysis of entries on the Curiæ Regis Rolls (1200) it was estimated that secondary descriptions, having *de*, *le*, or *filius*, etc., amounting to 77 per cent, could not be surnames ; and now by calculation on a similar basis, using the Hundred Rolls (1275), it is found that 54 per cent of the additions were unlikely to have reached the hereditary stage, although in London and perhaps other large cities it had become the recognized custom that a man should have the same second name as his father.

CHAPTER VI

INFLUENCE OF MIGRATION ON BRITISH NAMES

Introduction of Alien Names. The previous chapters have clearly illustrated the complete change of personal names and descriptions which followed upon the successive Saxon and Norman occupations of England. For many subsequent years the greater parts of Wales, Scotland, and Ireland were unaffected and remained true to their native Celtic names, and their genealogical method of distinguishing one man from another.

Following upon the success of William the Conqueror, political and commercial relations with the Continental powers expanded, and cross-Channel traffic greatly increased, all available shipping being fully employed. "Frenchmen of all classes came over in thousands, and occupied important posts, whether in the court, in noble households, or as teachers and skilled workmen in the service of the Church." [1] For five centuries the English crown had possessions of varying importance in France, the last territory to be lost being Calais in 1558. In the medieval chronicles there are repeated notices of the influx of Bretons, Normans, Angevins, Burgundians, Poitevins, etc., from various parts of France, Brabanters and Flemings from the Low Countries, Florentines and Lombards from Italy, Spaniards and Germans, with a plentiful quota of Jews. All brought their native names, but a comparatively few, if resident any length of time, retained them in their purity, or even at all. As the British linguistic ability depreciated, the insular prejudices of everything foreign increased, until the purely English scribe looked with disdain upon foreign names, annihilating them rather than defile his register.

Alien appellatives might be treated in three different ways :

(i) Dropped entirely, being replaced by country of origin or race, as Champagne, Norman, etc.

(ii) Dropped entirely, being replaced by a new English descriptive name, as Newman, Small, Weaver, etc.

(iii) Translated into English: thus Blanche became White, Schwartz Black, and so on, a method of procedure much in evidence at the present day.

Nevertheless, where colonies became established, the native names were in many cases preserved, often, however, finally

---

[1] *Anglo-Norman Language and Literature*, by J. Vising, p. 9.

DISTRIBUTION OF ALIEN INFLUENCE

to be corrupted. As the English language gained in popularity, the knowledge of other tongues lessened, and the tendency among English clerks was to give a foreign name the nearest English sound, and ultimately a large number of new and curious names were created, the etymology of which is now a tax to the united skill of philologists and genealogists.[1]

---

[1] In the same way that we twist names so do the French. Baring Gould (p. 315) notes a case, which came under his own observation, of Pengelly being converted into Pain-au-lait. This is an important point for consideration, because curious French or German names are often cited to support strange English nicknames, whereas in all probability both are corruptions.

The notes which follow have been collected with a view to illustrating, by means of names, the immigrations of aliens, and also the distribution and movements of the native races, an important step in grasping the full etymological possibilities of an English surname.

Flemings in England.   In addition to the large numbers of Normans, Bretons, and Frenchmen, immigrants from the Netherlands freely arrived in Britain from the time of the Norman invasion onwards.   Walter Bec of Flanders, together with a contingent of his countrymen, was at Hastings with the Conqueror in 1066 ; and De Lisle lists, Baudouin, Eude, Gerbaud, Guinemar, Hugue, Josce, and Renouf, describing each as le Flamand.   The various Domesday Books of 1086 evidence the permanent stay of the Flemings, the vassals of Drogo have been mentioned above, and Hugo Flandrensis, Beds, Odo Flandrensis (Flandrigena in Exon. Dom.), Winemarus Flandrensis, Bucks, and Walterus Flandrensis (possibly the above-named Bec), in various counties, are noticed.   According to the *Anglo-Saxon Chronicle*, 100 men, Frenchmen and Flemings, were killed by the Northumbrians in 1080,[1] and in 1102 thieves from Auvergne, France, and Flanders broke into Peterborough Monastery.   A coeval writer records that about the year 1107 part of Flanders was overwhelmed by the sea, a disaster causing many of the inhabitants to emigrate.[2]   A settlement was effected by some of the refugees in Northumbria, on territory east of the Tweed, but this colony was transferred to Pembrokeshire four years later, as Florence records, and augmented by further immigrants at later dates.[3]

Henry II, soon after his succession in 1154, banished Flemings and other foreigners, according to Gervase of Canterbury, a contemporary chronicler, who was referring to the mercenaries under the command of William of Ypres, engaged by Stephen,[4] but in 1173 it appears that 140 Flemings were drowned in England,[5] and in 1184 they wasted Norwich ; nevertheless, King John, according to the *Scala Chronica*, sent for so many " Pikardes, Normannes, and Fleminges " that to quote the words of Leland " wen they cam the Cuntery had much a do to fede them ".[6]   The Flemings were again expelled from England by the terms of Magna Charta, 1215, and in 1270

---

[1] *The Anglo-Saxon Chronicle*, ed. by B. Thorpe, vol. i, p. 351.

[2] *Caradoc of Llancarvan*, translated by H. Lloyd, and re-edited by Powel : Orderic Vitalis, *Eccl. Hist.*, ed. Le Prevost, v, p. 42.

[3] *Chronicon Florentii Wigorniensis*, vol. ii, p. 64.

[4] *Opera Historica*, Rolls Ser., 1879, ed. by Wm. Stubbs, vol. i, p. 161. Gwillelmus de Ypre et omnes fere Flandrensis qui in Angliam confluxerunt . . . ab Anglia recesserunt.

[5] Florence, vol. ii, p. 153.

[6] *Collectanea*, ed. T. Hearne, 1770, vol. i, pt. 2, p. 535.

they, with the exception of denizens, were further ordered to leave the country, and again in 1305, upon a request from the King of France,[1] but the various prohibitions do not appear to have been very thoroughly enforced. At various times during the thirteenth and fourteenth centuries royal protection was given to Flemings to visit England to purchase wool, and so many must have remained that Higden (fourteenth century) observed that Picts and Danes having been destroyed there were left five races in Britain, namely Scots, Britons (i.e. Welsh), Flemings, Normans, and Englishmen [2]; and although he was writing of an earlier date, his opinions may have been coloured to a certain extent by what he actually saw around him. There is no doubt that considerable numbers of Flemings did establish themselves, developing the industry of England and Scotland, and introducing a great number of new names to Britain. Several villages such as Flemingston in county Glamorgan and Flemington in Lanarkshire indicate possible sites of the settlements of immigrants from Flanders, but their names are found to be widespread.[3]

The description Fleming, commencing with Flandrensis of Domesday Book, abounds in the records in various forms, such as :—

Walin Flandr', Pembr. 1130. (Pipe R.)
Adelulf Flandr', Norf. 1130. (Pipe R.)
Hugo Flameng', Yorks. 1200. (Rot. de Obl.)
Alard le Flamanc', Suss. 1203. (Cur. Reg.)
Rog. le Flemeng, Somers. 1208. (Rot. de Obl.)
J. Flaumbard, Yorks. 1230. (Pipe R.)
Walt. le Fleming, Lincs. 1275. (Hund. R.)
Pet. a flemyng, Kent, 1523. (Subs. 124/96, m. 38.)

In Welsh records the Flemings may also be traced. The Flint Subsidy Roll for 21 Edw. I has Lloywarth ap y Flemis; another undoubted Fleming being Wilkyn Flemis of Iscoyd, Flint; and in the same place other aliens were: Etbroc, Knokel, Hiscoe, Delloc, Dagmer; and in Ewloe: Atkyn Olspe and Hots Char.

The Flemings were industrious and clever workmen, and accordingly suffered much from local jealousies and insular prejudice : Jack Straw's men in 1379 " slew manny Flemynges and other men " [4]; and two years later, resulting

---

[1] Thomæ Walsingham, *Historia Anglicana*, Rolls Ser., 1863, ed. by H. T. Riley, vol. i, p. 108.

[2] *Polychronicon* Ranulphi Higden, Rolls Ser., 1869, ed. by C. Babington, vol. ii, p. 153.

[3] See the concise account by H. Owen, in *Archæologia Cambrensis*, 1895, 5th ser., vol. xii, p. 96.

[4] *Grey Friars Chronicle*, in Monumenta Franciscana, Rolls Ser., ed. by R. Howlett, 1882, vol. ii, p. 157.

from the peasants' revolt engineered by Wat Tyler, many Flemings were beheaded in London.[1] All who failed to say " bread and cheese " without a foreign accent are said to have been sent promptly to the block, and possibly some such linguistic test may be the explanation of the curious epithet which may be found gracing even the official rolls.

Geof. Cheseandbrede, 1303, Yorks. (Knights' Fees, Surt. Soc.)
Rob. Chesandbred, 1346, Yorks. (Pat. R.)

Descriptions of the same type are : " Bread or Ale," Adam Bred aut Ale occurring in a Shrewsbury Subsidy Roll of 1327 ; and Henry " Drink all up ", which may be seen in the Essex Fines, 1281–2, but such titles are probably corruptions of place-names.

In Scottish annals the natives of Flanders are frequently mentioned. The *Scala Chronica* records that in 15 Hen. II " William King of Scottes enterid yn to England, having many Fleminges with hym ".[2] Jordan Flandrensis appears as witness to a grant of David I to the monks of Kelso in 1144, and Mainard, a Fleming, burgess of Berwick, was made provost of St. Andrews in the same reign[3] ; under date 1227, Richard Flandrensis is named in a perambulation at Forfar,[4] and Stephen Flandrensis was justice of Lothian in 1259.[5] Some Flemish names in early Scottish records are Tankard, Cruter, Freskin, Swartbrand, Bald, and Baldwin.[6]

A Scotsman having been expelled from Flanders, in 1347 it was enacted that all Flemings in Scotland were to be arrested and their goods confiscated[7] ; and in 1466 trading with Flanders was prohibited, but by the opening of the sixteenth century reciprocal commerce was again extensive.

Some of the eminent Scottish families who derived from the Flemings are : Sutherland, Moray, Douglas, Leslie, Fleming, and Innes. The Percys, according to Camden, came from Brabant.[8]

The Flemings evidently ventured into Ireland also at an early date, for the name Fleming had ramified strongly by the end of the thirteenth century.[9] John le Flemeng is mentioned in a plea at Limerick in 1295, and Adam le Fleming

[1] *National Review*, March, 1890, p. 55.
[2] Work cited above, vol. i, p. 532.
[3] *Acts of the Parliament of Scotland*, vol. i, p. 85 ; also Jordan Fantosme's *Chronicle*, where there are repeated references to the daring and courage of the Flemings (Rolls. Ser. 82, vol. iii.)
[4] *Acts*, etc., vol. i, p. 91.
[5] Ibid., vol. i, p. 98.
[6] For an account of these and many more Flemings in Scotland, see *Caledonia*, new ed., vol. ii, pp. 604 et seq.
[7] *Acts of the Parliament of Scotland*, David II, 1347, c. 9.
[8] *Caledonia*, vol. ii, p. 609.
[9] From the registrations of births it may be estimated that in Ireland in 1890 there were upwards of 7,000 persons bearing the name Fleming.

was pledge at Ardart in the same year : Eva Flandrensis and Amerosus le Fleming and others are also noticed in the same roll, and numerous other instances could be cited.[1]

Classification of Flemish Descriptions. The Flemish language is a low German dialect akin to Dutch and was not unlike Old and Middle English. The nature of the names of fourteenth-century Flemings will be illustrated by a portion of the list of those killed at the Battle of Cassel, 1328.

Che sunt ceaus qui morurent en le bataille de Cassel, de le castelrie de Berghes, de le paroche de Ghivelde. Inventore faite par Jehan kief et Thieri le brabandere.

Pieter donker ; Jakemard worckyn ; Heinri heinem ; Gilles bigghe ; Boudene cobboud ; Baudewyn ghueraerd ; Willaume oubrecht ; Pieter de le Planke ; Jehan Colin ; Obrecht li boeter ; Robyn waghenbeen ; Jehan michiel ; Ghys waedscoe ; Guillaume de le waghenbrugge ; Jehan li chevalier ; Masyn boyd ; Jehan de winkere ; Jehan donkerlin ; Jehan le raed ; Gilles de le bussche ; Michel le vinckere ; Michel castelein ; Mœnin seulin ; Lauwers moys ; Coppyn slubber ; Gilles louwer ; Jehan ; Coppin et Ghys herman ; Collin willart ; Sentkyn pankouke ; Michel de raet ; Jehan moen de leke ; Jehan capond ; Boidyn mael ; Coppyn le visch ; Pieter riquaerd ; Jehan fiex laureins ; Wautier wilzin ; Lippin jakemyn ; Jehan Lam ; Gilles le beeste ; Hannin heine ; Heine li wlf ; Mikiel fiex wlf ; Herdoc ; Jehan gabard ; Coppyn warisont ; Jehan lammin ; Pieter maelgar ; Pieter aremoud ; Mathys staes ; Coppyn moen ; Colyn bladelyn ; Coppyn capout ; Pieter ghys ; Christiaen sniekebant ; Pierres dofwerpere ; Philippe le maunier ; Michel weytin ; Pieter tien *ou* tieu ; Hannin baldekyn ; Andrieu de le linde ; Gilles le tolnare.[2]

These second names, like those of other Indo-European races, fall into four classes :—

Characteristic.—le Beeste (?) ; li Boeter (? the mocker) ; Donker (dark) ; Pankouke (Flem. *pannekoek* " a fritter ") ; le Vinckere (the conqueror) ; Slubber ; Waghenbeen (*waeghe been* " unsteady leg ") ; li Wlf (probably genealogical).

Local.—de le Bussche ; de le Linde ; de le Planke ; de la Waghenbrugge.

Genealogical.—(i) fiex Wlf ; fiex Laureins. (ii) Wilzin. (iii) Aremoud ; Baldekyn ; Bigghe ; Bladelyn ; Boyd (i.e. Bodo) ; Capout ; Cobboud (cf. Dom. Bk. Cubold) ; Colin ; Coppin ; Gabard (i.e. Waldbert) ; Ghuerard (i.e. Gerard) ; Heine ; Herman ; Jakemyn ; Lammin ; Louwer ; Maelgar (i.e. Madalger) ; Michiel ; Moys (Moses) ; Oubrecht ; Riquaerd ; Waedscoe (i.e. Vasco) ; Warisont ; Weytin ; Willart ; Worckyn.

Aphæretic forms are common, as Moen (i.e. Symon) ;

[1] *Cal. of Justiciary Rolls of Ireland*, vol. i, p. 2.
[2] *Les Flamands a la Bataille de Cassel*, par E. Mannier, p. 41.

Seulin (i.e. ? Marcelle) ; Staes (i.e. Eustace) ; Tieu (i.e. Matthew). Examples of apocopes are : Ghys (i.e. Gisbert) ; Lam (i.e. Lambert).

Occupational.—Castelein (chatelain) ; li Chevalier ; le Mauniere (the miller) ; le Raed (the counsellor) ; le Tolnare (tax collector) ; le Visch (the fisher) ; de Winkere (also le Vinkere : *de* is here the Flemish definite article, *le* the French). The signification of a few of the names, such as Capond, Dofwerpere, and Sniekebant, is not clear. The most pronounced feature of fourteenth-century Flemish appellatives is the large proportion of genealogical second names, many of which are abbreviated by aphæresis, apocopation, and syncope.[1] They are Semitic, Teutonic, and French, but mainly Teutonic, and a large number of compounds contain the familiar elements : *adel, beald, bert, brand, god, her, regen, ric, sig, wil, win,* and *wit,* which being brought to England could hardly fail to be confused with the O.E. survivals.

Frisians in England.   Although as favourably placed geographically, and it cannot be doubted that many Frisians came to England, few are noticed. It has already been stated that the Frisians carried on considerable trade with the Anglo-Saxons, and they are specifically mentioned as resident in England in the ninth century by Asser [2] ; a colony of Frisian merchants in York is noticed in the life of S. Liudgeri, and Bede refers to a London Frisian. Before the Norman Conquest the Frisians had lost their independence, but there is no reason to suppose that their intercourse with Britain was stayed, although their race might be obscured, and doubtless many good old English names are of Frisian origin, as well as such place-names as Friezland (Yorks), Frieston and Freston (Lincs.), Frisby (Leic.), Friston and Freston (Suff.), and Friston (Suss.).

Frisians, like other aliens, were often given the name of their country or race, and it may be noted that Friese is the older form of Frisian.

> Ricardus Fresle, Notts. 1086.   (Dom. Bk.)
> Alicia de Fresa, Rutl. 1205.   (Rot. de Obl.)
> Willelmus de Frisa, Worc. 1230.   (Pipe R.)
> Fresburn de Frise, a merchant of Alemannia, 1242.   (Cl. R.)
> Ricardus le Frese, Suff. 1280.   (Pat. R.)
> Galfridus Freys (Frois), Lond. 1275.   (Hund. R.)

These extracts show that the Frisians were coming into Britain, and the nature of their fifteenth-century names will be illustrated by a selection taken from an Oldenburg bailiff's *lagerbuch* (stock-book) dated 1428 :—

[1] For definitions of these terms see p. 272.
[2] See above, p. 48.

Alerd Strom ; Robeke van Westerloye ; Olteke Sising ; Gherke Swanke ; Bories de heckler ; Johan van Emeden ; Lubbeke bi der beke ; Hinrik de trippen maker ; Johan Poppehoves ; Hermen de grever ; Johan Pothusen ; Stoleken wiff ; Wilke koherde ; Hilke Stalen ; olde Johan de scroder ; Johan Logheman ; Stamer Hermen ; Tide Louwe ; ` de junge Hinrik Kok ; Oltman bi der muren ; Johan Houwerke ; Johan Twistreng ; Beke Gherdelmans ; Hinrik Meyerken swager ; Johan Bowering ; de lange Oltmann Storm ; Aleff ; Wendel Brudinges ; Kord de herde ; Hinrik Wilde ; Brun tor molen ; Lubbert de scherer ; Beyer ; de olde Hinrik Kok ; Roleff bi den kerkhoue ; Johan Volquens ; Robeke de sluter ; Kord Sire ; Heineke de sagher ; Hermen Brun ; Wigger ; Hanneke Haseking ; Gherke Boneken swager ; Willem Kok ; Tideke Vese ; Hinrik van der hude ; Klawes Emeken ; Krumme Goldsmit ; Gherlich Swarte ; Johan Poppehoff ; Johan Billo ; Otte Kernemelk.[1]

It will be noticed that the Frisians were not far advanced with surnames, several even had no secondary appellatives. The descriptions fall into the usual four classes, and it may be observed that *van* is equivalent to " of ", *de*, as with Flemish, being the article " the ". There can be no doubt that Friesic names have in many cases become British ; in fact, several of the above may be recognized as familiar. The great prevalence of *k*-suffixes, and their influence on English names, will be discussed in a later section (p. 275 et seq.).

Winkler states that feminine names are made from the masculine by affixing *je, tse* or *tsen, tsje* and *ke* ; as Douwtsen from Douwe, Mintsje from Minne, and Ofke from Offe.[2] Many male names already have the *-ke* ending, in which case, for instance, Oepke might become Oepkje.

A collection of Helmond (N. Brabant, Holland) names shows that by the fifteenth century, descriptions in the Netherlands had become rather complicated, as the following examples illustrate :—

Art Peter Meeuessoen (1418), i.e. Art (son of) Peter son of Meeus (Bartholomeus) ; Art van den Loe Henrics Metten soens soen (1403), i.e. Art or Arnold of the Loo son of Henry son of Mette ; Hoegard wilen Jans Godartssoens van Bruheze (1423), i.e. Hoegard son of the late Jan (son of) Godart of Bruheze ; Willem Ghevarts Luten Medemanssoen soen (1401), i.e. William son of Gebhard, son of Lute, son of Medeman ; Heynken Heynen Diddekens Tsweertssoens soen (1431), i.e. Heynken (dim. of Hendrik) son of Heyn, son of Diddeken (dim. of Diederik), the Innkeeper.[3] The composition of names of " vrouwen " is not so clear : Aelbert Lemken Ruelkensdochter (1418), according to Winkler, is Aelbertje or Aelbertken daughter of Lemke,

---

[1] *Friesisches Archiv*, von H. G. Ehrentraut, vol. i, p. 466.
[2] *Studiën in Nederlandsche Namenkunde* door Johan Winkler, p. 203.
[3] Tsweerts = des weerds.

son of Ruelken ; and Peter Corstken Lemmens dochter (1496), is Peterken daughter of Corst son of Lemmen.[1]

Some considerably longer descriptions may be found cited by Winkler, but it is unlikely that any such were accepted in England, and it may be imagined with what contumely a Dutchman, who offered one of these polyonymous designations to an English clerk, would be received.

Various Immigrants. In addition to the Normans, Bretons, Flemings, and Frisians, numerous other immigrants from various nations arrived to swell the numbers of aliens in Britain. The following brief notes will serve, not only to illustrate the origin of some modern surnames, but also to show in small measure the people trading with Britain, many of whom becoming denizens, introduced their own names.

Alman (i.e. German). The Patent Roll, A.D. 1217, refers to Helmewy, Markeward, and Folbrict, "mercatores Theutonicos." German miners were also brought to work in the Cornish mines, in the thirteenth century.

Walt. le Aleman, Yorks. 1200.   (Cur. Reg.)
Ric. de Alemannia, 1220.   (Pat. R.)
"Terricus Teutonicus," Soms. 1230.   (Pipe R.)
Terric le Alemaund, Bucks. 1275.   (Hund. R., i, 42.)
Hen. de Alemayne, 1311.   (Pat. R.)

It is to be noted that other districts than German may be called Allemannia (see Freeman, *Hist. of Norm. Conq.*, ii, 254). Also, in some cases, Aleman may be the occupational description ; or genealogical, as Alemannus de Florencia, 1242 (Pat. R.) : German, Jarman, etc., are also genealogical, Germanus and Jarminus being common in O.E. records; also cf. Germanus de Hode, thirteenth century (Testa de Neville) : "Thomas Germain, mercator de Chastelvile," 1224 (Pat. R.), and Dionisius Germayne, Cornw. 1439 (probably from St. Germaine).

Angwin (the Angevin from Anjou).

"Osmundus Angevinus," Essex, 1086.   (Dom. Bk., 2b.)
Baldric and Peter Andevagensis, Lincs. 1199.   (Cur. Reg.)
W. Angeuin, Beds. c. 1219.   (Ass. R. 2, m. 3.)
W. Aungeuin, Bucks. c. 1228.   (Ass. R. 54, m. 5.)
Maurice le Angevine, Oxf. 1275.   (Hund. R., ii, 758.)
Tho. Angewyn, 1462.   (Pat. R.)

Braben, Brabazon (the Brabançon or Brabanter from

---

[1] " Aelbert Lemken Ruelkensdochter (1418), dat is Aelbertje of Aelbertken of Adelbertha (Albertina in wanvorm), de dochter van Lemke die een zoon was van Ruelken. En Peter Corstken Lemmens dochter (1496), met andere woorden Peterken of Pietertje, Pietje (Petronella), de dochter van Corst (Corstiaen, Christiann) die een zoon was van Lem of Lemmen (Willem)."

Brabant). Traders from Brabant were known in London in the reign of Æthelstan.

Walt. Brabesun, Oxf. 1275. (Hund. R., ii, 853.)
Heliscus de Brabayn, Lincs. 1275. (Hund. R., i, 294.)
Tho. Brabezon, Yorks. 1275. (Hund. R., i, 105.)
J. de Brabancia, 1292. (Fine R.)
Roger le Brabazoun, Lond. Edw. II. (Plac. de Q.W.)
W. Brabancon, Staff. 1380-1. (Poll Tax.)

Burdell, Burdeleys (the Bordelais or Burdegalian).

Hugo le Burdeleis, Norf. 1180-1. (Pipe R.)
Reimund Vidan de Burdegala, Kent, 1229. (Cl. R.)
Bertram de Burdegala, citizen of Bordeaux, 1235. (Pat. R.)
Remunihac de Bordeaus, Dev. 1275. (Hund. R., i, 96.)

Burgon, Burgoyne (the Burgullian of Burgundy).

Robt. Burguignon, Lincs. 1158-9. (Pipe R.)
J. le Burguinun, Lond. 1172-3. (Pipe R.)
W. de Burgelay, Northants, 1180-1. (Pipe R.)
Rohesia de Burgeleia, Ess. 1195. (Pipe R.)
Pet. de Burgundia, 1224. (Pat. R.)
Hugo Burgundiensis, 1243. (Cl. R.)
Hugo le Burguynon, Hants. 1257. (Fines, 1836 ed.)
Bertram le Burgelun, French merchant, 1271. (Pat. R.)
J. de Burgoyne, Soms. 1275. (Hund. R., ii, 134.)
W. de Burguilun, Norf. 1277. (Cl. R.)
Pet. le Burguillon, Ess. 1285. (Cl. R.)
Edm. Burgulliun, Heref. 1287. (Cl. R.)
Rob. le Burgulion, Lincs. 1314. (Cl. R.)
W. Burgoigne, Lancs. 1377. (Pat. R.)

The *NED.* says that Burgullian was supposed to be a term of contempt invented of the Bastard of Burgundy at a tournament, 1467, but these extracts show the term to have been in use two centuries earlier.

Champagne (between Lorraine and Burgundy).

Rob. de Champaine, Kent, 1200. (Cur. Reg.)
Rob. de Campania, Kent, 1203. (Cur. Reg.)
Hugo de Champaign, Wilts. 1228. (Cl. R.)
J. de Chaumpagne, Oxf. 1311. (Pat. R.)

Champion and Champayn became confused, e.g. Walter Champion alias Champayn, Hants, 1426 (Pat. R.).

Dane, Dennis (the Danish).

Turchillus Danus, Hunts. 1086. (Dom. Bk. f. 203*b*.)
W. Danies, Northants, 1196. (Cur. Reg.)
J. le Daneys, Soms. 1230. (Pipe R.)
Rann. le Deneys, Suff. 1249. (Fines, 1836 ed.)
Nich. Skone de Denmark at Flete, Lincs. 1380-1. (Coroners' Roll 82, m. 11.)
J. Denys, Notts. 1392. (Pat. R.)

There was a Danish colony in Longdon, Worc., 1275 (Eld, p. xiii).

It is to be noted also that Dennis is a form of Dionysius, and Dane is a variant of Dene.

Dutchman (from Holland). The title Dutchman does not appear to have been in use before the fourteenth century.

Giles Duchman, Cambs. 1343. (Gaol D. 17 Edw. III, m. 39.)
Hen. Ducheman, Yorks. 1355. (Roll of Freeman, Surt. Soc., xcvi.)
J. Duche, cook, 1383. (Pat. R.)
Hans Ducheman, Mdx. 1384. (Pat. R.)

Examples of Dutch names will be found on pp. 203–4.

England, English, Inglis (Scot.). A possible explanation of this description is that Englishmen going abroad, acquired the name (see under Channel Islands), and afterwards returning to their native land, retained it. Anglois and Anglais are common in France and N. Italy ; Inghilesi in Tuscany, Inglese being the general form in Italy. (See C. Poma in *Trans. Phil. Soc.*, 1920, pt. i, p. 51.)

Ascolf Anglicus, Norf. 1086. (Dom. Bk. 117.)
David Anglicus, Lincs. 1200. (Cur. Reg.)
Walt. Ingeleys, Oxf. 1275. (Hund. R., ii, 869.)
Ralph de Englysman, Norf. 1281. (Ass. R. 823, m. 4.)
Rob. le Engleys, Westm. 1310. (Plac. Abbr.)
Pet. Engelond, Norf. 1322–3. (Gaol D. 49, m. 69.)
Rob. Inglys, Yorks. 1345. (Pat. R.)
Thom. Englysch, Norf. 1357. (Coroners' R. 102, m. 24.)
Ric. Englisshe, Oxf. 1370. (Pat. R.)

Engelond may possibly be "the meadow land". (See p. 59.)

Florence (Italy). In the thirteenth-century Patent Rolls there are repeated references to the merchants of Bologna, Siena, Florence, Venice, Genoa, Piacenza, Lucca, etc., some of whom settled in this country.

J. de Florentin, Ess. 1229. (Cl. R.)
W. Florentyn, Surr. 1268. (Pat. R.)
Clerekyn de Florencia, a tenant in Dorking, Surr., c. 1275. (Pat. R.)
Gerard de Florencia, a merchant of London, 1287. (Cl. R.)

The surname Florence was also derived from the baptismal name.

Francis, Frank, French.

Godwinus Francigena, Wilts. 1066. (Lib. Wint. 534*a*.)
Rob. Lefranceis, Warw. 1174–5. (Pipe R.)
Ric. Franc', Ess. 1201. (Cur. Reg.)
Rog. le Franceis, Notts. 1201. (Cur. Reg.)
W. Gallicus, Wilts. 1202. (Cur. Reg.)

Rob. Francigena, Oxf. 1203. (Cur. Reg.)
W. le Fraunke, Wilts. 1293. (Pat. R.)
Ric. le Freynsh, Soms. 1327. (Subs.)
Ric. le Frensh, Suss. 1327. (Suss. Rec. Soc. x, 154.)
W. Fraunceys, Cambs. 1343. (Gaol D. 17 Edw. III, m. 32d.)
J. Frensshe, Ess. 1378-9. (Indictments, file 23, m. 6.)
Ric. Frankissheman, Yorks. 1379. (Poll Tax, p. 243.)
Eliona de France, 1394. (Pat. R.)
Rob. Frenssheman, Norf. 1430-1. (C.P. 40, 680.)

Gascoigne, Gaskin. A large wine trade was carried on with Gascon merchants, and in 1291, Edw. I ordered the merchants of Gascony and Guienne, who were subjects of the English crown, to be treated as denizens. On the Patent Rolls, 1300, forty merchants of Gascony are named.

Ric. de Kageworthe de Gascon', Soms. 1225. (Ass. R. 755, m. 10.)
Ph. le Gascoyn, Salop. 1266. (Fines, 1836 ed.)
Ph. de Gascon', Salop. 1275. (Hund. R., ii, 80.)
J. Gaskwyn, Kent. 1375. (Pat. R.)
W. Gascon. 1398. (Pat. R.)
Nich. Gascoigne, 1398. (Pat. R.)

Holland.

Suein de Hoilanda, Notts. 1165-6. (Pipe R.)
Adam de Holand, Kent. 1272. (Fines, 1836 ed.)
Albertus de Hoylland of the land of the earl of Holland, a merchant, 1295. (Pat. R.)

This surname is probably more often derived from place-names in Lancashire, Essex, or from the division in Lincolnshire.

Lombard (Italy). *The Annals of the Four Masters* records that 1410 B.C. Aenghus Olmucadha fought twelve battles against the Longobardi, but it is highly improbable that Lombards were known in Ireland so early.

J. Lumbard, Oxf. 1275. (Hund. R., ii, 695.)
Lovericus Lambard, Kent, 1299. (Pat. R.)
Maninus Lumbard, merchant of Lucca, 1309. (Pat. R.)
Pet. de Lumbardye, Lincs. 1310. (Pat. R.)
W. Lombard, Salop, 1327. (Subs.)
J. Conyard Lombard, 1432. (K.B. 27, 683, m. 23d.)

Possible confusion exists with Lambert, Lambard, etc.

Lorraine, Loring (France).

Albertus Lothariensis, Heref. 1086. (Dom. Bk.)
Josc' le Lohareng, Glouc. 1163. (Pipe R.)
Geof. Loharengus, c. 1200. (Cur. Reg.)
W. le Loereng', Berks. 1200. (Cur. Reg.)
J. le Loreng, Oxf. 1275. (Hund. R., ii, p. 783.)
Eustace de Loryng, Scotland, 1343. (Pat. R.)
Rog. Loryng, Herts. 1425. (Pat. R.)

Petwin (from Poitou, France).

Rog. Pictaviensis or Peteuinus, Norf.   (Dom. Bk. *passim*.)
Walterus de Barkeston frat' Hug' Peiteuin, Lincs. *c.* 1227 (Ass.
R. 229, m. 3.)
Walt. de Peytevin, Heref. 1230.   (Cl. R.)
Pet. le Peytevin, Soms. 1250.   (Fines, 1836 ed.)
Geof. Peytevyn, Norf. 1272.   (Fines, 1836 ed.)

This surname is also from the O.E. name Peohtwine (eighth
century) and possibly from the Jewish also ;   Peytevinus de
London' Judaeus, 1249 (Fines, 1836 ed.).

Spain. It is commonly supposed that there are, in various
parts of the country, descendants of survivors of shipwrecked
mariners of the Armada.   In the absence of proof it will be
more reasonable to assume that the Spanish blood arrived in
a more comfortable way, and of which there is plenty of
evidence.

Alueredus Ispaniensis, 1086.   (Exon. Dom. Bk.)
Aluredus de Hispania, Wilts., etc., 1086.   (Dom. Bk.)
Herueus de Ispania, Ess. 1086.   (Dom. Bk.)

Morant, the historian, says that these early names refer to
Ispania or Hispaine in Essex (ii, 301, 363, 480), but De Lisle's
list gives Auvrai d'Espagne among the companions of the
Conqueror, 1066.

Jocelin de Hispania, 1217.   (Pat. R.)
J. de Ispania, Glouc. *c.* 1221.   (Ass. R. 271, m. 22.)
Ric. de Hispania, Salop, *c.* 1222.   (Ass. R. 733*a*, m. 14.)
Geof. de Spaygne, Leic. 1327.   (Subs.)
Geof. de Spayne, Yorks. 1327.   (Subs. E 179, 211/6, m. 3.)
Hankin Spaniard esterling, Lincs. 1378-9.   (Coroners' R. 82, m. 6.)
W. Spanalld, Yorks. 1379.   (Poll Tax, p. 166.)
J. de Spanye de Lenn Epi. cordewan', 1381-2 (Anc. Indictments,
K.B. 9, file 166, m. 66.)
J. Spayne, Notts, 1392.   (Pat. R.)

Veness, Venus (Venice, Italy).

Rob. de Venuiz, Hants. Wilts. 1130.   (Pipe R.)
W. de Venuz, Hants. 1164-5.   (Pipe R.)
Leonard de Veneiz, Midx. 1200.   (Rot. de Obl.)
Leonard de Venetia, Suff. 1205.   (Rot. de Obl.)
Rob. de Venuz, 1207.   (Rot. de Obl.)
J. de Venuz, Wilts. 1275.   (Hund. R., ii, 272.)
Ric. de Wenise, Oxf. 1315.   (Pat. R.)
J. Venuz, 1322.   (Pat. R.)

Some foreigners, not specifically defined, are dubbed
Frenne, " an alien " or " stranger ", as Rob. le Freyne, Bucks,
1275 (Hund. R.) ;   from which are derived the surnames

Frayne and Frean, which also have other origins. Extraneus is sometimes held to be an equivalent of "the foreigner", the modern surname being Le Strange, never Stranger. Peregrinus "the foreigner" may also be found, and Finegal has been noticed above. A Cornish name is Euren from *voren* "strange", "foreign".

Jews in England. An investigation into the origin of British names would be incomplete without some notice of the designations borne by Israelites who established themselves in this country. Under Antonius Pius (A.D. 86–161) the Jews had been permitted to become citizens of the Roman Empire, and to form communities in the different Roman provinces, but, although mentioned in our Saxon laws, Hebrew immigrants to Britain have left no identifiable mark on the records of date prior to the Norman conquest. During the reigns of William the Conqueror and his successor, our representatives of the Semitic race acquired considerable influence in England, but their increasing wealth and power led to hostility, accompanied by cruelty and oppression, which, after 200 years, culminated in expulsion ; nevertheless, the enforced exodus of the Hebrews may not have been absolute, and it seems unlikely that Jewish names ceased to exist in these islands, wherefore it is advisable to give some consideration to the onomatology of this persecuted and oppressed race.

The greater proportion of the several thousand names which occur in the Old Testament have identifiable significations, such as Benjamin (son of the right hand), Caleb (dog), Eli (a foster son), Jabez (he will cause pain), Magog (expansion), Tobiah (distinguished of the Lord), and Zeeb (wolf). Other designations, in some cases, have become so corrupted that their meanings cannot now be determined with certainty. It is of interest to note that like the Anglo-Saxon custom of repeating a theme of the father's name in that of the sons, so it was an occasional practice among the Jews to perpetuate one of the elements, thus Ahijah and Ahimelech were sons of Ahitub (*ahh* "brother").

As the Jews spread over the earth in search of sanctuary, there was a growing tendency to adopt the names of the countries in which they found refuge : Babylonian, Persian, Aramaic, Arabic, Greek, and Roman designations being drawn upon,[1] further alien appellatives being added by converts to Judaism. By the time the Jews arrived in England many of their names were no longer Hebrew, but some well-known examples, such as Isaac (laughter), Solomon (peaceable), Levi (adhesion), have preserved their purity throughout the vicissitudes of thousands of years.

[1] Jos. Jacobs (*Jewish Encyclopædia*).

Jacobs has calculated that in 1194 the number of Jews in England was about 2,000, that is about one-seventh or one-eighth of one per cent of the population, and they were practically all settled east of a line drawn from York to Exeter.[1] Some common personal names of the thirteenth century were :—

Men : Acir, Benedict, Bonami, Bonevie, Cok, Cress, Deudoné, Deulegard, Deulesalt, Dyey, Genta, Hakelin, Hakin, Jornin, Licorice, Mandaint, Peter, Pictavin, Sadekin, Salle, Saunte, Serfdeu, Sweteman, Tony, Ursell, Vives.

Women : Antera, Avegaye, Belaset, Biket, Bonfet, Bonne, Ernina, Fluria, Giva, Henna, Iveta, Milkana, Muriel, Prude, Reyna, Slema.

In this short list several languages are represented : Fr. Deudoné (Theodore), which occurs latinized as Deusdedit (Sanskrit *Devadatta*, Ital. *Diodati*, etc.), in the original Hebrew was Elhanan, Elnathan, or Jonathan, i.e. God gave ; Bonfet was perhaps Jafet (beautiful) ; Cress, a shortened form of Deulecresse, was anciently Gedaliah, "the Lord increase him," as an old writer says, or "magnified of the Lord". Benedict was a latinized form of Berachyah (whom Jehovah bless) ; Deulesalt was otherwise Isaiah (the salvation of Jehovah) ; Vives, equivalent to Chaim (life), and latinized Vitalis, might be Jehiel (God lives) ; and Serfdeu is clearly another form of Obadiah (servant of the Lord). Biket is said to be a diminutive of Rebecca (a rope with a noose), and Hakelin or Hakin are diminutives of Isaac (laughing).

Additional Descriptions of the Jews.   Thousands of years ago the Jews had found a single personal name insufficient for individuality. An example of the distinctive additions is provided by the names of the twelve apostles which illustrate two of the four classes of description into which names have been divided : characteristic, as Simon the Zealot or Judas Iscariot (man of Kerioth) ; and genealogical, as James the son of Zebedee. Simon Peter exemplifies a double name.

In England before the expulsion Jewish descriptions and surnames fell into the same four classes into which Celtic, Saxon, and Norman designations have been placed.

Characteristic.—Isaac l'Aveugle (the blind), Leo Blund, Manasser le Enveyse (the jolly), Peitivin le Fort (the strong), Judah le Franceys, Manasser le Gros, Abraham le Jovene (the young), Manser le Petit, Josce Quatrebuches, Vives le Remangor (the romancer), Aaron le Riche, Isaac Senex (the old).

---

[1] *The Jews of Angevin England*, p. 381.   Jacobs erroneously states that the Jews comprised one per cent of the population of England. The proportion, on his own figures, was much less.

Local.—Biket de domo Isaac, Jurnet de Norwicz, Ysaac de Russie.

Genealogical.—In Hebrew : Moses ben Isaac (son of Isaac), Miriam bath Jacob (daughter of Jacob), Abraham Levi. In Latin : Peitevin fil' Jacob, Abraham filius Avigay (i.e. Abigail, sons were commonly called after their mothers), Muriel uxor Juda, Jacob sororius Joscei fil' Morelli, Abraham gener Elie (son-in-law of Elias), Samuel socer Benedicti (father-in-law of Benedict), Jose Salvage (a personal name).

Occupational.—Leo Aurifaber, Jacob le Clerk, Sampson le Cyrurgien, Benedict Gabbay (treasurer of a synagogue), Ysaac Medicus, Deulecresse le Prestre, Vives Scriptor.

In the characteristic class were sometimes vulgar descriptions, which may be termed nicknames or sobriquets, such as Moses sine braciis (without arms), Deudone cum pedibus tortis (with crooked feet), Moses cum naso (with the nose). Animal names, Latin, French, and English, were common: le Chat, Leo, Mutuns, Pigge, Reynard, and Ursell.[1]

Some difficulty in identification is caused by the custom prevalent among the Jews of having two names for alternative use, a sacred name for domestic and religious purposes and a secular name to be used in worldly intercourse, e.g. Benedict otherwise Elias son of Ursell otherwise Isaac was variously called Benedict le Riche, Benedict the son of Isaac, Elias ben Isaac, and Elias the son of Ursell,[2] and might have been as appropriately described, Benedict the son of Ursell.

The secondary descriptions of the Jews were used equally in one language as another, thus in a Hebrew starr may be found trace of our ubiquitous friend Cohen, who in a Latin document might appear as Episcopus, being discovered in a Norman-French record as L'Eveske, or called in English, Bishop. All four variants became hereditary surnames.[3]

It is evident that in certain circumstances now unknown a Jew was not permitted to change his surname without royal licence, for which authority a bezant was payable to the treasury.[4]

Such Jewish descriptions which became hereditary surnames were doomed to a short existence in Britain, for in the year 1290 Edward I banished the Jews from the country, and it is said that 15,000 departed. Some names may have been preserved by apostates, or others finding means of evading the regulation, living perhaps in the guise of Lombards or other alien merchants suffered to enter the country (see " Jerusalem ", p. 190 ; Abraham and Isaac, p. 193 ; Licorice,

---

[1] *Studies in Anglo-Jewish History*, by Rev. H. P. Stokes, 1913, p. 65.
[2] Ibid., pp. 68–9.   [3] Ibid., pp. 18–22.   [4] See p. 407.

p. 339), but not until the Commonwealth could the unconverted Jew freely enter England. The financial operations which the Jews had made so specially their own were thenceforth carried on by the Lombards, the Templars also doing most profitable banking business, until their order was dispersed.

Celtic Invasion of England. Having demonstrated the great possibilities of alien influence in the formation of British surnames, attention will now be given more particularly to local racial movements and their effect on the nomenclature. It has been mentioned that one result of the Saxon invasion of Britain was the almost complete elimination of Cymric names throughout the greater part of England, and although much native blood remained, the English language and names became predominant. This condition underwent considerable modification in later years as the country became more settled, and it is to be surmised that during the intervals when conditions were more favourable some of the exiled Cymry gradually worked their way back from Brittany, Cornwall, Wales, and the North into Saxon England, the land of their ancestors.

The success of William, duke of Normandy, undoubtedly resulted in a considerable influx of Cymry, and increase of Celtic blood in England, with a corresponding improvement in the status of the native Briton. One-third of William's army at Hastings was composed of adventurers from Brittany, many of them descendants of the Celtic exiles from Britain, hundreds of years before. As a result of William's success, grants of lordships were made to his supporters, and a good share fell to the Breton leaders, who must have established retainers on their estates, but in less than a decade many of them had been expelled from the country, upon the failure of the conspiracy to overthrow King William, which was organized by Ralph de Guader, a powerful Celt of the half-blood.

Unnoticed by historians, the next Celtic invasion of England was more gradual and peaceful, extending over many centuries, and still continues; the Cymry, being the first to lead the way, were followed by Gaels from both Scotland and Ireland, a great stimulus to migratory movement being one of the results of the ravages of the plague.

Influence of Epidemics. Pestilence is one of the major historical events which have to be considered in tracing out the history of surnames. Notable plagues which desolated this country were those which overwhelmed us in the years 1348–9 and 1361, that of the earlier date being the more severe of the two principal catastrophes. The contagion, originating in China, journeyed westward through Turkey, Italy, Germany, and France to England, making its appearance in Melcombe

Regis (Weymouth) in the latter half of the year 1348.[1] Propagating death and terrible suffering throughout the kingdom, the virulent disease caused the wildest terror among the helpless people, completely disorganizing social life, the administration of the government, and the development of the country. The population at this time may well have been three or four times what it was in 1066, yet it has been estimated from Poll Tax assessments of 1377 to have been then less than twice (2 to 2½ millions). It cannot be doubted that half the population perished, many families becoming extinct, and embryonic surnames lost.

Parliament was prorogued, law courts carried on with difficulty, and it is probable that many manor courts ceased to function entirely during the height of the epidemic, it being grimly significant that there are few rolls for the twenty-third year of Edward III, and what might have been a valuable mine of information on the question of extinction of names is not available.[2] The " Black Death ", as the scourge was called, did not respect rank, but the rich, living in less unhealthy conditions, were possibly not overwhelmed in the same proportion as the lower classes. One result of the sweeping disaster was that many of the village communities were so seriously depleted, if not entirely destroyed, that manual workers were able to demand and obtain much higher wages than formerly, notwithstanding the attempts of Parliament to restrain them. The Statute of Labourers, 23 Edw. III, records that " a great part of the people having died from the pestilence, and considering the grievous incommodation caused by scarcity of servants, ploughmen and labourers should take only the wages which had been customary in 20 Edw. III ". Any person refusing to do so could be committed to gaol till he found surety to serve in the manner prescribed, and both master and man were liable to punishment. By a second Act, 34 Edw. III, labourers absenting themselves out of their services could be outlawed, imprisoned, and burnt on the forehead with an iron formed to make the letter F in token of falsity.[3] This threatened punishment did not greatly deter the working men, and many thousands were presented, as appears from indictments which are yet extant.[4] The improved payments and conditions of labour became more attractive

[1] *Chronicon Galfridi le Baker*, ed. by E. M. Thompson, p. 98 ; *Eulogium Historiarum* (Rolls Ser.), iii, p. 213.

[2] Some good rolls which might receive attention of the historians of the Plague are the Brancaster (Norf.) roll, S.C. 2, 192/36, and Ruthin (Flint) rolls, S.C. 2, 217/14 and 218/1. Further information regarding the pestilence may be obtained from *The Black Death in East Anglia*, by Rev. A. Jessopp, and *The Great Pestilence*, by Cardinal F. A. Gasquet.

[3] *Statutes of the Realm*, vol. i, pp. 307, 336.

[4] I give a few examples of the indictments in *Ewen of East Anglia*.

to outsiders, and particularly to Welshmen. Geoffrey le Baker, a contemporary chronicler, records that the plague devastated Wales,[1] but perhaps the mortality was not so great as he supposed ; at any rate, scarcity of labour in the Principality did not deter great numbers of Welshmen from seeking work in England. The public records of dates both before and after 1349 supply abundant evidence of the migration of Cymry and also Gaels ; and from thousands of examples the following names of aliens have been taken as an illustration of this peaceful invasion. Welsh, Irish, and Scots, having no hereditary surnames at this period, were, upon arrival here, often called after their nationality or the name of their country of origin, but countless others were given English descriptions and have so lost their identity. The following selection of names derived from country and race, taken as they are from the eastern counties only, will show how the Cornishmen, Welshmen, and Bretons spread from west to east over the larger part of England.[2]

Brittany : Roger le Bretun, Suff. temp. John (Fines) ; Hugh Briton, Norf. 1208–9 (Ass. R. 558, m. 8*d*) ; Ric. de Britan', Hunts. temp. John (Cur. Reg.) ; W. Breton de Weston, Lincs. (Harl. 742, f. 119) ; Simon le Bretun, Cambs. (Cott. MS. Claud. C. ix, f. 39) ; Hugh le Breton, Hunts. 1259–60 (Fines) ; W. le Breton, Norf. 1275 (Hund. R.) ; Alice Bretun, Norf. 1275 (Hund. R.) ; J. Britone, Ess. 1275 (Hund. R.) ; Andrew Briton, Suff. (Eye Cart. Add. 8177, f. 167) ; Alice le Bretun, Suff. 1291–2 (Ass. R. 839, m. 2) ; John de Bretagne, Shrops. 1292 (De Banco R. Hil., 20 Edw. I).

Cornwall, Devon, etc. : Ric. Cornubiensis, Yorks. *c.* 1231 (Ass. R. 1042) ; Pet. de Cornewaleys, Hunts. 1267 (Fines) ; Thom. le Cornewaleys, Norf. 1275 (Hund. R.) ; Beatrice Cornewaleys, Norf. 1275 (Hund. R.) ; Ric. de Cornubia, Lincs. Edw. II (Abbr. Rot. Orig.) ; David Walsshman de West Wales, Norf. 1362–3 (Coroners' R. 102, m. 6).

Wales : In Domesday Book 111 Waleis and Walensis are mentioned, according to the enumeration of Ellis. Waliscus, Lincs. 1162 (Pipe R.) ; Rob. Waliscus, Suff. temp. John (Pipe R.) ; W. Walensis, Ess. temp. John (Pipe R.) ; Matilda la Waleyse, Cambs. (Cott. MS. Claud. C. ix, f. 55) ; Ric. le Waleis, Norf. (ibid., f. 260) ; David Waleis, Cambs. (ibid., f. 32*b*) ; W. Walens', Ess. *c.* 1227 (Ass. R. 229, m. 21) ; Hen. le Waleis, Yorks. *c.* 1231 (Ass. R. 1042, m. 2) ; Ralph Walensis, Suff. temp. Hen. III (Fines) ; Rog. le Waleis, Suff. temp. Hen. III (Fines) ; W. de Walenz, Norf. 1275 (Hund. R.) ; W. Walse, Hunts. 1275 (Hund. R.) ; Thom. le Walys, Bedf. 1275 (Hund. R.) ; Hyllaria la Waleyse, Hunts. 1275 (Hund. R.) ; W. de Wallenc', Norf. 1275 (Hund. R.) ; W. Wallicus, Cambs. 1275 (Hund. R.) ; Walt. Walseman, Cambs. 1275 (Hund. R.) ; Agnes de Walensis, Cambs. 1275 (Hund. R.) ;

[1] Work cited above.
[2] See *Ewen of East Anglia* for numerous other examples.

Reg. le Walays, Lincs. 1275 (Hund. R.) ; Ric. de Walys, Hunts. 1275 (Hund. R.) ; Cecilia le Walche, Suff. 1293–4 (Gaol D. 63, m. 10) ; W. le Waleys, Suff. 1293–4 (ibid., m. 10d) ; Howel le Galeys, Suff. 1304–5 (Ass. R. 843, m. 19) ; J. le Walshe, Norf. 1312–3 (Gaol D. 48, m. 15) ; Rob. le Waylsman, Lond. 1326 (Coroners' R.) ; Walt. Waleys, Suff. 1327 (Subs.) ; W. Walsse, Leic. 1327 (Subs.) ; Rog. Walscheman, Leic. 1327 (Subs.) ; J. le Walsshe, Cambs. 1337–8 (Gaol D. 7a, m. 23) ; J. Waillshman, Lond. 1339 (Coroners' R.) ; Ric. Walshman, Suff. 1356–7 (Coroners' R. 176, m. 1) ; Alice de Wallia, found dead by John Walssheman, Cambs. 1359–60 (Coroners' R. 18, m. 50) ; Thom. de Wales, Norf. 1362–3 (Coroners' R. 104, m. 8) ; Rog. Walysman, Lincs. 1372–3 (Coroners' R. 74, m. 6) ; J. Walch, Lincs. 1376–7 (Coroners' R. 82, m. 1) ; J. Walle, Lincs. 1377 (Coroners' R. 82, m. 2) ; J. Welssche, Ess. 1378–9 (Indictments, K.B. 9, 23, m. 6d) ; J. Walsh, Ess. 1378–9 (Indictments, K.B. 9, 23, m. 6) ; Ric. Waleson, Lincs. 1380–1 (Coroners' R. 82, m. 11d) ; Ad. Willscheman, Norf. c. 1380 (Subs. E 179, 149/45, m. 1d) ; J. Walschomo, Leic. c. 1380 (Subs. E 179, 133/26) ; J. Vallisschomo, Leic. c. 1380 (ibid.) ; Allan Gibbon alias Welchman, Suff. 1608–9 (Coram Rege R., 6 Jas. m. 459).

It has to be noted that Wales is a parish in Yorks, which may have been the source of some of the names, but it cannot be doubted that in the majority of cases, appellatives of the types exemplified were borne by Welshmen, and that this small selection of country and racial descriptions, taken from records of the eastern counties only, demonstrates clearly that Bretons, Cornishmen, and Welshmen distributed themselves throughout the larger part of England during the eleventh, twelfth, thirteenth, and fourteenth centuries. It is a fair inference that many of the immigrants lost their identity by taking English names of locality or occupation ; others, bearing names of unmistakable Welsh origin, may be readily recognized, as for instance :—

W. Beivin, Dev. 1166 (Lib. Nig. 1771, p. 120) ; Thom. Griffin, Wilts. 1205 (Rot. de Obl.) ; Ric. Oein, Hants. 1207 (Rot. de Obl.) ; Rad. Beivin, Leic. 1207 (Rot. de Obl.) ; Owen (Audoenus), Norf. 1206 (Cur. Reg. R. 43a, m. 5d) ; J. Owayn, Wilts. 1271 (Fines) ; Rob. Bevin, Lincs. 1275 (Hund. R.) ; Rog. Beyvin, Dev. 1275 (Hund. R.) ; J. Bovin, Yorks. 1275 (Hund. R.) ; Hen. Howen, Oxf. 1275 (Hund. R.) ; W. Howel, Beds. 1275 (Hund. R.) ; Mariota Powell, Hunts. 1315–6 (Ramsey Court R.) ; Amabilia Bewen, Lincs. 1318 (Add. MS. 5845, f. 110) ; W. Beuyn, Suss. 1332 (Subs.) ; Rog. Beuyn, Suss. 1332 (Subs.) ; J. Powel, Norf. 1370–1 (Coroners' R. 104, m. 32d) ; Amicia Yevan de Galys, Suff. 1371–2 (Gaol D. 152, m. 43) ; W. Beuyn, Bucks. 1391–2 (Gaol D. 181, m. 9).

In later years the numbers of Welsh names greatly increase and probably few towns could now be found without an example of Evans or Owen. It may be noted that Bevan may also be a local name, e.g. W. de Bevin or Bevan, Dors. 1204 (Rot. de Obl.).

Scotsmen in England. Owing to the constant warfare between Scotland and England, few Scotsmen came over the border on peaceful missions; nevertheless, their local and ethnic descriptions may be traced in most counties of England. The following examples have been taken from southern counties as being the more remote; in the northern records large numbers of persons were dubbed Scot.

Humfrey le Scot, Wilts. temp. Ric. I (Cur. Reg.) ; Edm. and Thom. Scottus, Hunts. temp. Hen. II (Cart. Mon. de Rameseia) ; Walt. de Scotia, Hants. 1207 (Rot. de Obl.) ; Rob. Scoticus, 1224 (Pat. R.) ; W. Scot, 1224 (Pat. R.) ; Margareta Scot, Norf. 1230 (Pipe R.) ; J. Scot, Oxf. 1232 (Cl. R.) ; Reg. le Scot, Oxf. 1232 (Cl. R.) ; Walt. le Escot, Glouc. 1232 (Cl. R.) ; Lucas le Escot, Suff. 1240 (Ass. R. 818, m. 45) ; Alex. Sckot, Suff. temp. Hen. III (Fines) ; J. le Scot, Norf. 1255–6 (Fines) ; Ad. le Escot, Suff. 1257–8 (Ass. R. 820, m. 29) ; Rob. Scot, Kent, 1255 (Ass. R. 361, m. 63) ; Agnes Scotica, Hunts. 1275 (Hund. R.) ; Walt. Scot, Norf. 1275 (Hund. R.) ; J. le Scot, Cambs. 1275 (Hund. R.) ; Rog. Skot, Hunts. 1275 (Hund. R.) ; Rog. Scoticus, Lond. 1275 (Hund. R.) ; Stephen filius Ivonis le Scot, Suff. 1286–7 (Ass. R. 827, m. 51) ; Thom. le Escot, Suff. 1286–7 (Ass. R. 827, m. 1b) ; Ad. Scot, Kent, 1300–1 (Subs. E 179, 123/4) ; J. de Scotia, Norf. 1292–3 (Fines) ; Andrew Scot de Scotia, Norf. 1359–60 (Coroners' R. 102, m. 24).

Scotland is a surname which may be derived from a hamlet in Lincolnshire, or from the personal name (if not an error for Scolland), e.g. Thom. fil' Scotlandi, Kent, 1164–5 (Pipe R.).

Irishmen in England. At early date considerable numbers of Irishmen found their way to England as their names on the rolls testify :—

W. de Hibernia, 1224 (Pat. R.) ; Walt. Hibernensis, Wilts. 1230 (Cl. R.) ; J. de Hibernia, Salop, 1231 (Cl. R.) ; Geof. de Hibernia, Hants. 1233 (Cl. R.) ; J. Irland, 1255, Kent (Ass. R. 361, m. 63) ; Ralph de Hibernia, Cambs. 1260–1 (Ass. R. 82, m. 33) ; J. le Yreys, Oxf. 1275 (Hund. R.) ; Step. de Yrlond, Bucks. 1275 (Hund. R.) ; J. de Irelond, Suff. 1327 (Subs.) ; Reg. de Irlond, Suff. 1327 (Subs.) ; J. de Hibernia, Suff. 1328–9 (De Banco R. 275, m. 66d) ; J. le Irisshe, Cambs. 1330–1(Gaol D. 7a, m. 5) ; J. le Irych, Suff. 1335–6 (Gaol D. 64, m. 12) ; J. de Irlond, Suff. 1343–4 (Gaol. D. 64, m. 28d) ; J. Iryssh, Suff. 1349–50 (Indictments, K.B. 9, 114, m. 26) ; Rob. de Yrlaunde, Suff. 1351–2 (Harl. MS. 27, f. 104) ; J. Irlond, Ess. 1358–9 (Gaol D. 18c, m. 56) ; Ad. Savage de Irland, Lincs. 1365–6 (Gaol D. 48, m. 30) ; Nich. Irissche, Herts. 1378–9 (Coroners' R. 24, m. 8) ; Walt. Chapman de Hibernia, Cambs. 1390–1 (Gaol D. 181, m. 9) ; Nich. Iryssh, Cambs. 1406–7 (Gaol D. 8 Hen. IV, m. 64) ; Mat. Irishman, Northants, 1449 (K.B. 27, 753, m. 42) ; J. Iryssh de Hibernia, Devon, 1480 (K.B. 27, 875, m. 115).

Irishmen in Wales. Further examination of the Welsh
Subsidy Rolls, to which reference has been made, evidences that
the taxpayers were not confined to Welshmen and Englishmen ;
among the residents being Irishmen as well as the Flemings
mentioned above. The Gaels at various times occupied parts
of Wales, if not the whole of that country, as they did the Isle
of Man ; but long before the Norman conquest they had been
completely driven out or subdued.

Forty-four localities in Wales are said to have the word
Gwyddel in the composition of their names, such as Porth y
Gwyddel, Cefn Gwyddel, etc., which fact no doubt points to the
Gwyddelians or Irishmen having been associated with
such port or ridge. Some writers argue that the presence of
the label Gwyddel proves that the Irishmen dominated the
country ; but, if so, what would be the object of specifically
defining a place as Irish so-and-so ? Is it not more probable
that these place-names were merely Irish residences or
colonies ? Unless, of course, *gwyddel* means " brake " or
" bush " as suggested by Rhys.[1] Apart from this latter
signification, and the possibility of yet some other equivalent,
the presence of the word *gwyddel* in place-names can indicate
nothing more than that there were once Irishmen in Wales,
and it may have been after the Norman conquest that they
arrived ; in fact, historians record that a branch of the noble
sept of the Geraldines or Fitzgeralds settled in Merionethshire
in the thirteenth century.

If there be no other meaning for *gwyddel*, entries on these
Subsidy Rolls indicate the presence of Irishmen in the thirteenth
century, who were given the name " Gwyddel ", as Englishmen were dubbed " Sais " by the natives.

Madoc Wydel, Comot de Keveyloc, Montg. (242/54).
Zevan Wythel, Brunmeyr, Montg. (242/54).
Ithel Gwethel, Keyswin, Mer. (242/53).
Jorwerth Wydel, Pendeley, Flint. (242/52).
Gryffryd Wydel, Merton, Flint. (242/52).
Jeuan Wydel, Talaard, Flint. (242/52).

It is curious that these " Irishmen ", without exception,
all bear Welsh baptismal names, and possibly they had mothers
of native extraction.

Welshmen in Scotland and Ireland. Not only England, but
Scotland also proved attractive to Welshmen, 15,000 of whom
were under the command of the King of Scotland in 1296.[2]
Bodies of Welshmen also found their way to Ireland, where they
settled, observing a separate existence to the native Gaels

---

[1] Lecture on Welsh Philology, p. 177.
[2] *Annals of Ireland* (Rolls Ser. 80), vol. ii, p. 326.

and maintaining their own language, names, and habits. One such colony was formed in the Baronies of Forth and Bargy, co. Wexford, and is supposed to have been a Welsh and English settlement made in the twelfth century.[1] According to a series of returns supplied to Sir William Petty, written about 1680, they then "preserved their first language [? English] and observed the same form of apparel their predecessors first used", which is "according to the English mode, of very fine exquisitively dressed frieze, comlie, but not costlie; that they invioblie profess and maintain the same faith and form of religion", and that "they seldom dispose of their children in marriage but unto natives or such as will determine to reside in the Barony". Examples of surnames of the old colonists are said to be Hore, Cod, Stafford, Whitty, Rossiter (i.e. Wroxeter, Salop), Sinnot, Murphy, Stephen, Quiney, etc.,[2] if appearance counts for anything, English and Irish, rather than Welsh.

A more exclusively Welsh settlement may have been in co. Kildare or Kilkenny, the following being the names of a body of men who are alleged to have robbed and beheaded a man in the street of Carrymagriffin in 1305 :—

Translation.—John Madoc ; Madoc Iewan ; Rys Madoc ; Will. Not ; Meiler Madoc ; Will. Iygnon ; Will. son of Gilsosonach Obroder ; John de Leye ; Thomas son of Dauy of Lystouth ; Iygnon brother of the same David ; Ph. Iewan ; Meiler son of Roger ; Gronou le Waleys ; Will. Bafok ; and Madoc son of Walter Gronou ; together with Henry Madoc ; Henry Not ; Ph. Ithel ; Ithel Birlosk ; Madoc Robyn ; Iewan Robyn ; John Boscher le Waleys ; David Fyn ; Iewan son of Mewrich Cuach ; John son of Walter Cuach ; Lewelin Fadde ; Adam Tuddyn of Cassilgossyn ; David son of Gwen le Waleys ; and Madoc le Waleys.[3]

In the cartulary of St. Mary's Abbey, Dublin, there is a fifteenth-century reference to one Harry Walshe, capytayne of the Walsche men. The name Waleys occurs about eighty times on the Justiciary Rolls for the years 1305–7 ; and has greatly ramified, it being estimated from the statistics of the Registrar-General of Births in Ireland that in 1890 there were then about 50,000 persons in that country bearing the names Wallace, Walsh, and Welsh. Welsh personal names which are also familiar as surnames in Ireland are Madock, Davey, Griffith, Howell, Evans, etc.

[1] *Trans. Royal Irish Academy*, 1788, vol. ii, "Antiquities," pp. 19–41, art. by C. Vallancey, who calls the colonists both Britons and English. The language in 1836 was an English dialect (see example in Latham's *English Language*, p. 395).
[2] *Surnames in Ireland*, by Sir R. E. Matheson, 1909, p. 26.
[3] *Cal. of Justiciary Rolls of Ireland*, Edw. I, pt. ii, p. 104.

Norsemen in Scotland. For over four centuries (say, A.D. 800–1250) the Norsemen had dominated the whole of the western part of Scotland, which lengthy period was punctuated with many fierce disputes, shedding of blood, and much devastation of the country. Following upon the defeat of the Scandinavians at the Battle of Largs, warfare terminated, and in 1266 a treaty was signed by the two kingdoms, whereby, for a money payment, the Western Isles and Man were ceded to the Scottish Crown. In "some notes on the Norsemen in Argyllshire and on the Clyde", a writer sums up as follows :—

" It is not to be supposed that this political event, albeit of the highest importance, made any appreciable change in the racial situation. For four long centuries the population had been steadily assimilating Norse blood, Norse laws and customs, Norse speech and lore. These things are not much affected by the signature of a treaty, and as a matter of fact our West Coast (Scotland) to-day, six and a half centuries after this particular treaty was signed, is still saturated with the traditions and characteristics of the northern Fjord-land it so much resembles." [1]

The Orkney and Shetland Islands remained under Scandinavian rule until the fifteenth century, and it is to be supposed that the Norse language was spoken in the islands for several centuries afterwards. The following West Highland surnames are said to have a Norse derivation [2] :—

Norse Original	Derivative
Asketill	McAskill.
Eystein or Oistin	('Uisdean), Hutcheon, McCutcheon, MacHuiston, Macquisten, [Hutcheson, Houston].
[Guthröð	(Goddard), Godfrey, Guthrie].
Guthorm	McCodrum.
Harald	(Arailt, MacArailt), McRaild.
Ivar	McIver.
Kol or Kali	McColl, McCall, Coulson.
Hjalmund	McCalman, McCalmont.
Hromundr	McCrimmon.
Lagmundr	Lamond, Lamont, McClymont (?).
Ljotr, Ljot	McLeod.
Magnus	(Manus), McManus.
Nikolas	Nicol, Nicolson (a Skye family for centuries), Macnicol.
Olaf, Qla	Aulay, McAulay.
Rögnvald	Ranald, Clanranald, Ronald.
Svein, Sven	MacSwan (a Skye name), Swanson, possibly Macqueen (but probably = MacCuinn = son of Conn).

[1] R. L. Bremner (*Saga-Book of the Viking Club*, 1903, vol. iii, p. 369).
[2] Ibid.

[Thorbjörn   .   Thorburn, Thurburn.]
Thorkell   .   .   Torquil, McCorkle.
Thorketil .   .   McCorquodale, McCorkindale.
[Thorstein   .   Thurston, possibly Hourston.]
    [Names enclosed in square brackets are not distinctively West
Highland.] [1]

Norse Names in England.

To show the prevalence of Scandinavian names in England in the fourteenth century the following list of names has been compiled from a roll of the freemen of York in 1378 [2] :—

Joh. Mawer, magr, magri, " lean."

Wm. ffelagh', félagi.

Adam Lepper, leppr.

Joh. Laafe, Láfi, lági.

J. Cele, sæli.

J. Strowg, strúgr, strjúgr.

R. Syre, Sýr.

Th. Crokebayn, krákubein.

Simon Scaif, skeifr.

J. Mawbarn, meybarn.

J. Barker, börkr.

J. Strenger, strengr.

J. Sturmyn, stórmunnr.

Joh. Catelyn, ketlingr.

Thom. Bolle, Bolli.

Rob. Mansblode, mannsblóð.

Ric. Mundeson, Munda (i.e.
    Asmundar) son.

Joh. Rout, rauðr.

Thom. Trout, trauðr(i).

Wm. Seper, seppr(i).

— Thecar, þekkr.

Joh. Hayfy, háfi.

Agnes Sprote, sproti.

Rob. Couper, kaupr.

— Tote, tota.

Thom. Storre, stórr.

Hen. Sterre, starri.

Joh. Lyster, leistr.

Rob. Grisse, gríss.

Joh. Bone, bón.

Matilda Snere, snæri, snara.

J. Balne, baldni.

— Boller, böllr.

Wm. Skyftlyng, skiftingr.

Symon Vendilok, Wendelok,
    vendiloka.

Ric. Bulmer, bólmr.

Joh. Snawe, snáfr.

Wm. Od, Oddr.

Many of these descriptions, if not already established as hereditary surnames, ultimately became so.

Summary and Conclusions.

The reader who glances over this chapter cannot fail to realize the great influence which aliens, additional to the Norman and French element, have had in the making of our surnames; and but for the fact that thousands of the foreigners were dubbed with the country of origin or the corresponding ethnic adjective, the number of extraneous appellatives would have been much greater. In a further investigation of the effect of alien immigration, it will also be demonstrated that a large proportion of foreigners were given English names on arrival in this country, and their descendants are now surnominally indistinguishable from British. In England the greatest early increase of alien

[1] Another list is given by E. McClure in Saga-Book, vol. i, pt. iii, p. 271.
[2] Compiled by J. Stefansson (Saga-Book, vol. iv, p. 309) from Surtees Soc. publication. See also E. Björkman (Nordische Personennahmen in England).

population, apart from Danes and Normans, appears to have been due to the Flemings, many of whom bore names which may well be mistaken for O.E. Owing to the banishment of the Jews before surnames became general, their influence is little noticed in surnames which can be traced as having originated in Britain. It has to be concluded, so far as England is concerned, that modern descendants of the majority of the foreigners who became denizens cannot have surnames which are distinguishable as of foreign origin. In Scotland many of the great historical families are of alien origin, like Bruce and Wallace, and in this chapter it has been shown that numbers of Scottish and clan names derive from Flemish and Norse sources. In Ireland the foreign element is equally pronounced, and Norman, Norse, English, and Welsh influence in the nomenclature is widespread.

A point of importance to ethnologists, which has been strongly presented, is the eastward movement of the native Celts, which gained in strength after the Norman conquest, with the increasing freedom and security, the better wages and the more comfortable living, and culminated in a migration extending throughout all the counties of England, as can be traced in thousands of the descriptions and surnames of the middle ages.

CHAPTER VII

FOURTEENTH-CENTURY NAMES AND DESCRIPTIONS

England again becoming English. The opening of the century found England in a state of poverty, the result of the continuous contests which had been waged against Wales, Scotland, and Ireland, the sufferings of the people accentuated by civil war, and trade reduced through the expulsion of the Jews. Adding to misfortune, the country was visited, during the first twenty-five years, with an unparalleled succession of disastrous famines : wheat rose to ten times its normal price, cattle were destroyed, and the people starved to death or were killed by troops of robbers, who infested the country. Notwithstanding the prevalent afflictions and the attendant misery, the constitutional and social life of the people advanced on progressive lines, the most important development bearing on the making of surnames being the growing popularity of the English language.

At the commencement of the fourteenth century the English, French, Gaelic, Irish, and Welsh tongues were living in the British Isles, and in certain districts or settlements Cornish, Manx, Norse, and Flemish were also freely spoken, Latin being largely used for legal records. Hebrew had been banished *sine die*. It is said by Robert Holcot (fourteenth century) that the Conqueror had ordained that no person should plead in the King's Court unless in French, but the laws were not drafted in Anglo-Norman until 1275.[1] The nobility and gentry conversed in French, and instruction in schools and preaching in churches were given in the same language. About the year 1348 Edward III ordered an English motto to be embroidered on his tunic [2]; Richard II delighted the Commons at Smithfield by a spirited address in English [3]; and by the end of the century English was again becoming the common language of conversation, although French was still retained in the highest circles and the law courts. In 1362 it was enacted that in " any courts whatsoever " all pleas should be " pleaded, shewed, defended, answered, debated, and judged in the English tongue, and that they be entered and inrolled in Latin ".[4] The transition from French to

---

[1] *Statutes of the Realm*, vol. i, p. 26.
[2] *The Complete Peerage*, vol. iii, p. 598.
[3] *The National Review*, March, 1890, p. 47 (art. by H. Evershed).
[4] *Statutes of the Realm*, vol. i, p. 376.

English statutes is said to have occurred suddenly in 1377,[1] and soon afterwards Parliamentary petitions began to be written in English.[2] Chancery bills and answers continued in French until the early fifteenth century. In Scotland progress of the vernacular was parallel, but in Ireland the statutes were continued in French until 1508. Latin maintained its utility as the chief written language of the law, and, except for the brief Commonwealth period, it was not until 1731 that it was superseded in legal records.

The language of the documents has had some influence on the moulding of surnames, since, for instance, it is not to be supposed that names like Faber and Rufus would have come into existence had it not been customary to write in Latin, and, moreover, to latinize English names. Fortunately the latter practice had ceased before second names had become fixed as family appellatives, and few Latin surnames have survived. The most powerful linguistic influence bearing on the making of family names was the spoken tongue, and so the bulk of British names are English, French, Gaelic (Ir. and Scot.), and Cornish, the survival of Welsh names being very small and quite out of proportion to the patriotism of the medieval Welshman, and the popularity of the old British speech.

Fourteenth-Century Descriptions. Previous chapters have illustrated the gradually increasing use of second names, addresses, or descriptions, until a stage was reached, towards the end of the thirteenth century, when single names were almost unknown in official records. It has been demonstrated that the added descriptions were of four different classes, which have been termed characteristic, local, genealogical, and occupational, and that the local descriptions or addresses, from very small beginnings prior to the Conquest, rose to be the greatest class including fully half of all additional distinctions. We shall be prepared, therefore, to find that upon descriptions germinating surnames, by far the greatest class of the latter fall likewise under the heading of local.

The relative popularity of the four classes of descriptions was not uniform throughout the country and investigation will now be directed towards determining the respective lines of progress in the various counties and among the different classes of society.

For the fourteenth-century names of England no more convenient source can be found than the lists of taxpayers,

[1] *The History of English Law*, by F. Pollock and F. W. Maitland, vol. i, p. 86 n.

[2] A petition in Parliament in English occurs under date 1386 (Rot. Parl., vol. iii, p. 225). In the same rolls for 1 Hen. IV there are Latin, French, and English entries (iii, pp. 423–4).

M

which are comprehensive, allowing comparison of names of citizens with villagers, and the appellatives of one county with another. The principal extant records of this class are the returns of the assessments under the general twentieth granted in 1327, and the returns of the monies levied by the collectors of the tallage of groats in 1377.[1] These records originally contained about two million names, of which a large proportion are yet in excellent preservation.[2] Another useful source for obtaining names of any desired county is the great series of manorial court rolls preserved mainly in the Public Record Office and the British Museum. A selection of names for the representative counties of Lancashire, Shropshire, Huntingdon, Norfolk, Essex, Cornwall, York, Cumberland, and Dorset, taken from these original sources, will now be given.

Lancashire Names, A.D. 1324. List of persons fined at the hallmote of Ightenhill, 17 Edw. II (Hilary). (P.R.O., S.C. 2, 183/11, m. 4.)

De Will'o de Whitacre	De Ellot' que fuit vx' Will' Hare
Rob'to de Peure	Andr' fil' Will'i
Rob'to del Holyns	Joh'e fil' Will' de Grimlay
Auicia fil' Dobbe	Joh'e de Griddestwesil
Salbe fil' Dobyn	Rog'o le Mazoun
Elia de Scolefeld	Adam de Ang^m
Th. de Wolpitgrenis	Ric'o de Griddestwesill
Joh'ne le Gronne	Joh'ne de Wolwro
Nich'o del Fernyside	Will'o le Fissher

Selection of Descriptions. Bitheyate, Bythewell, Busshell, de le Byron, del Clough, Coldecol, Cragge, Cropholing, del Ediholes, le Forsterknave, Gilmyn, de Grenacre, Halmark, le Harperson, del Heghgate, Kay, Kaynok, Kippax, Kirwyn, de Knoll, Kynght, le Lewod, le Madde, fil' Malkin, del Moels, le Mon, de Pariz, Plokett, Pope, Qwerderay, de Rolegh, le Roo, Senker, dil Shagh, le Specker, del Stok, le Stubber, Sutor, Swetemilk, fil' Teddy, Tempest, Tydy, le Vesty, le Walsh, del Well, dil Wode, del Wodehouse, de Worston, del Wyndibonck.

Notes.—Holyns, i.e. " of the Hollies " : still a common form in Scotland. Griddestwesil (O.E. *twisla* " a fork ") : the -twisle names are numerous in the North, such as Entwistle, Birtwistle, etc., and suffer curious modern corruptions and misunderstandings as Bird-whistle. Mazoun is an obsolete form of mason. Wolwro (*wro, wra, wray* " a sheltered spot ").

---

[1] These records, known as Subsidy Rolls, are preserved in the P.R.O., the class reference being E 179. Some of the counties have been printed and indexed.

[2] The later roll is of persons of the age of 14 and upwards, who number 1,376,442 (excluding those of the counties palatine of Chester and Durham). *Archæologia*, vol. vii, p. 337.

Byron appears to be O.F. *buron* " a poor cottage " (Cotgrave).
Kay is equivalent to " quay ". Qwerderay is an old form of
cordery or ropery. A specker is a cobbler, and a stubber is
one who clears land. Gilmin or Guillemin was the name
given to hermits of an order founded in the twelfth century
by disciples of St. William. Regarding Senker, the *Promptorium
Parvulorum*, *c.* 1440, notes : " bryllare of drynke, or schenkare
(propinator)." Cf. Shynekere, Suff. 1275 (Hund. R.).

Shropshire Names, A.D. 1327. List of taxpayers under
the twentieth of 1 Edw. III. (P.R.O., E 179, 166/1, m. 5*d*.)

Wylaston	*Longgedone*
De Pet' Page	De Edmundo de Longgedon
Dauid ap yaref	Rog' Mascot'
Robt'o de Wylaston	Ric'o Mauncel
Joh'e de Neunham	Rog' fil' Will'i
Ric'o Wylcok	Will'o fil' Ric'i
Griffino ap Reryth	Rog' Harald
Gorgonnow	Will'o fil' Joh'is
Youan Gogh	Regin' fil' Rad'i
Dauid Kenwrek	Rog' fil' Ric'i
Dauid ap Youan	Will'o le Skynner'
Dauid ap Eddeneuet'	Ric'o Chasegrey
Dauid ap Kenwrek	Ric'o Fabro
Griffin ap Youan	

These extracts relating to two places in the same hundred
provide an interesting contrast in methods of expressing
" son ". Probably the descriptions with *ap* are those of native
Welshmen (cf. Madoc ap Ad' and Ph'o fil' Ade), but there may
be exceptions, as Dauid fil' Gorgonnow. It has been noticed
above that in Welsh Subsidy Rolls fil' was reserved for
daughter, e.g. Tangwistil fil' Jago, but Madauc ap Jago.

Huntingdonshire Names, A.D. 1327. List of taxpayers
under the twentieth of 1 Edw. III. (P.R.O., E 179, 122/4.)

Offord Cluni (m. 8*d*)	*Offord Daneis* (m. 4*d*)
De Beatr' Cassaundre	De Joh'n de Broughton
Th'm de Hemyngford	Rob'to Faukes
Joh'n Garden'	Ad' Neulond
Will'o Durant	Steph'o Bered
Siluestr' Fisshere	Agn' Taillour
Will'o Custance	Joh'n Widewyl
Joh'n de fel'usham	Th'm Gouy
Joh'n Bollo	Matill' Kyneman
Ad' Duk'	Joh'n Liteman
Joh'n Brian	Ad' Gurnay
Joh'n Pannewic	Th'm Faukes
Will'o Baroun	Alicia Pariz
Will'o Bolle	Rob'to Ared
Gilb'to Alloit	Joh'n Brid

Offord Cluni (m. 8d)

De Gilb'to Polle
  Mabill Fekere
  Will'o Palmer
  Joh'n Baroun
  Isab' Elys
  Audr' Moubray
  Henr' Hildegar
  Joh'n Ballard
  Rog'us fil' Gilb'ti
  Galfr' Chapma'
  Petro de Chikewell
  Th'm de la Granre
  Felicia Cristemasse

Offord Daneis (m. 4d)

De Matill Wyndout
  Joh'n Perewyne
  Osb'to le Garden'
  Joh'n Boykyn
  Rob'to le Rous
  Rob'to Ferbrace
  Will'o Mariot
  Robt'o Golde
  Ric'o de souche
  Audr' le moigne
  Thoma Elf
  Will'o Segge
  Nich'o Letice
  Simon' le Roo
  Isabell Plesaunt
  Robt'o Daniel
  Matill Hoke
  Simon Tredelef
  Joh'n le Man

A few of the duplicated names have been omitted. A further selection of names of the county follows :—

Albyn, Bacheler, Barnelby, Baroun, Basse, Berenger, Bibecok, Bonefey, Botte, Boutcourd, Brembil, Bully, Burgeis, Buxton, Cartewright, Catel, Chateryz, Child, Conquest, Crane, ad Crucem, Drewe, Dykyn, Gery, Godwyf, Golding, Gosselyn, ad Grenam, Grimbaud, Haroun, Hereward, Holy, Hosebond, Husee, Irenmonger, Jardin, Julian, Ladde, Lambsheued, Lomb, Louerich, Maynstrong, le Noble, le Nunne, Pilgrym, Rande, Raven, Rodecok, Rydeman, Sabyn, Scurlebek, Sharpenho, Souereyn, Sparke, Spyx, Tebbe, Texde, Thurston, Vaus, Vesey, in Venell, Wage, Waldeschef, Walenz, Walkelyn, Wardeboys, Wenge, West, Wyne, la Zouch.

Norfolk Names, A.D. 1327. List of taxpayers under the twentieth of 1 Edw. III. (P.R.O., E 179, 149/7, m. 23.)

Villata de Northcreyk

De Rob'to de Thorp
  Edm'o de Pakenham
  Editha Porter
  Ric'o Calye
  Rog'o de Apetone
  Hug' Hardi
  Will'o filio Presb'ri
  Ric'o de Burgh
  Joh'ne Veltre
  Barth'o Fabro
  Rob'to Lenald
  Will'mo Crane
  Math'o Bakon
  Joh'ne de Aylsham
  Petro Ponnok

De Reg' Bene
  Godefr' Schirreue
  Rob'to Juet'
  Henr' Palle
  Robt'o Cup'e
  Eluiua Scryuen
  Ameday
  Claric' Pek
  Will'mo Toly
  Will'mo Poye
  Sewale Hereward
  Simone Jordon
  Galfr'o de Sculthorp
  Cetill Talman
  Seloua Bernard

De Rad'o filio eius
    Adam filio Pet'
    Walt'o Gueppard
    Ranulpho Pellipar'
    Martino Capell'o
    Rob'to Cokerel
    Rob'to Clere
    Petro Dauy
    Barth'o Bene
    Simone de Creyk
    Will'o Em
    Cater' Hochon
    Emma Howes
    Rob'to Heruy
    Joh'nna Burgeys
    Adam Grys
    Isabell' Ameday
    Reg' Freman
    Will'mo filio Steph'
    Crist' Swyft
    Ketell' Reymond

De Richemay de Burgh
    Thoma Ameday
    Emma Fairweder
    Joh'ne de Derh'm
    Joh'ne Fresschebred
    Emma Bettes
    Abelotha Mannyng
    Rad'o Girre
    Will'o s'uiente Rector'
    Nich'o Meire
    Rog'o Schek
    Rog'o Bobyn
    Rad'o Algwyth
    Joh'ne Tholy
    Cater de Estgate
    Godmanno capell'o
    Simone de Waltone
    Joh'ne Punnok
    Edm'o Toly
    Will'o de Wymondh'm
    Andr' Clynt

A few of the duplicated names have been omitted.

Essex Names, A.D. 1327. List of taxpayers under the twentieth of 1 Edw. III. (P.R.O., E 179, 107/13, m. 4*d*.)

Colchester Borough

De Math'o Wenlok
    Joseph Alianore
    Rad'o le Bakere
    Ric'o le Barber
    Martin Cissore
    Will'o de la Marche
    Thom. le Mareschal
    Joh'ne Hotfot
    Thom' Fraunceys
    Ric'o de Cofford
    Joh'ne Wygg'
    Ric'o de Colne
    Warino fil' Will'i
    Edm'o Grymbaud
    Joh'ne Parles
    Joh'ne le Wolf
    Cristina la verrere
    Rob'to atte Wade
    Joh'ne de Dyham
    Joh'ne de Colec'
    Ric'o le Taillour
    Wimark Rodbryth
    Simo'e atte Cherch
    Nich'o Wastel

De Rob'to fil' Walt'i
    Will'mo Molendinar'
    Will'mo le Kyng
    Joh'ne atte Dych
    Joh'ne fil' Will'i molendinar'
    Elia fil' Joh'nis
    Joh'ne Jurdon
    Matild' Pfale
    Nich'o le Gros
    Joh'ne Rauen
    Edm'o le Chaloner
    Mich' Naples
    Alano le Hirde
    Joh'ne Somer
    Joh'ne de Bergholte
    Adam de Castello
    Alex. atte Watere
    Al' Prentiz
    Willo Gylemyn
    Joh'ne Olyue
    Saer' de Domland
    Joh'ne Edward
    Rad'o Knyht
    Hugon' le Pottere

De Simo'e Saleman	De Simo'e Martyn
Rog'o Leuegor	Will'o atte Hacch'
Gonnora atte Brok	Joh'ne Alwyne
Joh'ne Fabro	Joh'ne Sweyn
Thom' de la Mote	Wil'mo le Tiller
Will'o Aylmar	Rad'o Ode
Joh'ne le Parker	Juliana Pach'
Simon' le Kynge	Will'o atte Park
Simo'e Pope	Joh'ne de Salyngg'
Simo'e atte Bregg'	Marger' Sarcok
Galfr'o le melnere	Joh'ne Vyel
Ph'o Rokele	Joh'ne le Draper
Joh'e Dauy	Will'o de la Fermarye
Joh'ne de Ratlesden	Joh'ne de Bottyngham
Joh'ne le Deighe	Adam le Sowehalere
Joh'ne Gyloun	Petro de Aston
Joh'ne de Tendringg'	Walt'o le Tauerner
Joh'ne Rogg'	Henr' Welch
Joh'ne Monde	Will'o Basset
Ric'o Norreys	Galfr'o Dounyng'
Thom' Curteys	Joh'ne Swarthar
Will'o Pyking'	Thom' atte Hath'
Joh'ne Hakeney	Joh'ne de Sutton
Adam de Leycestr'	Joh'ne Cosyn
Will'o de Grome	Alic' Willes
Joh'ne Andreu	Joh'ne Pagon
Joh'ne Persoun	Matill' Sayer
Will'o List	Petro de Harlyng'
Joh'ne le Cok	Rob'to Scot
Galfr'o Tinctore	Joh'ne Lotoun
Joh'ne Maydegod	Will'o de Sartere
Will'o atte Tye	Joh'ne Fynch
Joh'ne atte Halle	Ric'o Dollard
Joh'ne Caperoun	Simo'e Smelt

A few uncertain readings and some duplicates have been omitted. This list affords an interesting comparison with that of Colchester burgesses given on p. 63; the almost complete extinction of O.E. personal names and their better preservation as second names is clearly illustrated. It is not to be supposed that persons were known in their home life by the names which appear in these official lists, e.g. Willelmus Molendinarius would be known by his friends as " the milner " ; John of Colchester could hardly have been so called by his acquaintances in Colchester. It may perhaps also be noted that all the latinized names have the terminations of oblique cases, ablative or genitive. (Cf. Cumberland, p. 168.)

Notes.—Verrer is a worker in glass ; Wade is possibly a boundary line ; Wastel, which is bread of finest flour, in this case is probably a contraction for Wasteland ; Chaloner, i.e.

a maker of chalons, a sort of woollen stuff ; Salyngg, probably salt-pits ; Deigh, i.e. a dairy-keeper ; Tye, an enclosure or common ; Fermarye is the infirmary of a monastery.

Cornish Names, A.D. 1327. List of taxpayers under the twentieth of 1 Edw. III. (P.R.O., E 179, 87/7, m. 7.)

Parish of St. Peran

De David Penhal	De Ric'o Bosneys
Rog'o Colla	Joh'ne Shywarton
Th'ma Trenans	Joh'ne Fentengempes
Simone Roke	Laur' de eadem
Joh'ne Present	Ric'o Hawys
Walt'o Treworyn	Ric'o Collock
Ric'o Ankensi	Rad'o Penwore
Joh'ne Russel	Will'o Trefelene
Rob'to Taranbol	Joh'ne Hendredewel
Joh'ne Bondy	Rog'o de eadem
Joh'ne de Hendr'	Joh'e Nanspara
Regin' Treuithik	Henr' de eadm
Martino de eadm	Joh'ne Kerkyby
Will'o de Kaer	Joh'na Tywarnayl
Elena de eadm	Marco Nansmelyn
Ric'o Chypians	Alex' Breydan
Thm' Tresek	Joh'ne Westa
Walt'o Cissore	Nic'lo Peng'non
Nich' Hendresek	Nich'o Renn
Thm' Rees	Henr' Schauen
Rad'o de eadm	Joh'ne Jacony
Laur Wanchelok	Joh'ne Fabr'
Nich'o de eadm	Joh'ne Tyrel
Math' Eglestornel	Nich' Stochay

Some notes on Cornish names will be found on p. 235, and a list of elements of local names, which will enable the significations of some of the above examples to be determined, on p. 377. Chypians appears to be *chypons* " bridge house ".

Yorkshire Names, A.D. 1327. List of taxpayers under the twentieth of 1 Edw. III. (P.R.O., E 179, 211/6, m. 5.)

Pikering

De Joh'e Bencol	De Rob' de Holden
Jacob Fullo	Will'o fil' Hug'
Agn' Haget	Ric' del Clee
Will'o Astin	Joh' Lang'
Galfr' Benne	Isabell de Hospital
Joh' Fab'	Joh' Widde
Joh' del Marrays	Will'o Knit
Will'o ate Bogh	Ad' Dressur
Elen Lighfot	Ad' Trusseluf

De Rob' Bellard
  Joh' fil' Ad'
  Galfr' atte Mar'
  Alic' de Wandesd'
  Thom' fil' Will'i

De Rob' del Wode
  Ric' de Kirkeby
  Thom' Rede
  Joh' Hog

Notes.—Bogh is an old spelling of Bog ; Bellard is the bell herd or bull herd ; Hog may be a form of Hugh or Hodge, but it is to be noted that in some parts of the country it means a " young lad " ; cf. Gael. *og* ; it is also local, e.g. del Hog (Parl. Writs, 1313).

Cumberland Names, A.D. 1333.   List of taxpayers under the fifteenth and tenth of 6 Edw. III.   (P.R.O., E 179, 90/2, m. 21*d*.)

Braythwaite

Joh'nes Bercar'
Joh'nes de Moreland
Joh'nes Serotson
Elyas de Ponte
Thom's del Meles
Norman de Embleton
Joh'nes Walleson
Will's Wyetson
Ric'us Whit Wilkinson
Robt'us de Stangre
Thom's Trane
Adam Tyssone
Joh'nes fil' p'poiti
Adam Crassedalman
Joh'nes Sutor
Eda Smalle
Joh'nes Stort
Joh'nes Neucomen
Nich'us de Brakanthuayt
Adam Parissow

Rad'us de Birkthwayt
Thom's Collemanson
Thom's de Mosergh
Hug' Moserghson
Thom's del Scales
Laurentius Burell
Thom's Prestson
Rob'tus de Berwyk
Adam Collan
Joh'nes Foughel
Alanus del Thwayt
Ric'us Belle
Galfr' Pacok
Joh'nes Medicus
Joh'nes del Wodde
Joh'nes Wys
Rob'tus Candelane
Joh'nes Bride
Will's del Bek
Will's del Wadhall

The above list contains a selection of the entries only ; some other Cumberland descriptions or surnames are :—

Antecriste, Armstrang, Barondale, Basbroun, Bodenbrig, Bolthorn, le Boys, Bricesone, Bullok, Bursy, Campioun, Charboc'le, Chully, Clouenheued, Crogelyng, Fairban, Gamel, Gibriche, Griffin, Grubson, Homelblod, Joppeson, Kay, Kirkebride, Licokson, Lolly, del Lymkilne, Lyster, Maw, Moyses, de Neubigging, Pape, Pebils, Pikspal, le Procuratour, Rayncok (also fil' Raincok), Raisemyst, Redeheued, Schale, Scharpe, Schepman, Scherwynd, Sparow, Stracour, Swaynson, Tankard, Thorald, Todde, Todhunter, Trumper, de Unthank, le Wadder, Worschep, del Wraa, Ysmaisone.

Notes.—Thwaite, i.e. " a clearing ", is a typical element of a North English place-name ; Scale is a hut (or a steep hill : Halliwell).

Dorset Names, A.D. 1334. List of taxpayers under the fifteenth and tenth of 7 Edw. III. (P.R.O., E 179, 103/5, 23*d*.)

Bridport

De Adam Kene	De Joh' Duke
Petr' Goldsmyth	Hug' Sendelon
Ad' Lankestok	Joh' Hatter
Thom' Daunz	Will' Lankespath
Ric'o Baker	Ric'o Alayn
Joh' Kaymesworth	Ric'o Hayward
Joh' Goulde	Rad'o Deyeson
Rob' Bounde	Will' Deygher'
Joh' Cole	Will' Cuff'
Nich'o Hanne	Joh' Wyme
Laur' Couk'	Will' Tracy
Joh' Cake	Joh' Barbur
Will' Barry	Will' Beymu'ster
Joh' de P'ret	Joh' Bottestoke
Edward Robe	Will' Cissor
Joh' Oure	Will' Bu'ne
Will' Croukern	Will' Maurey
Will' Colt	Ric'o Hykecok'
Will' Marleford	Joh' atte zerde
Will' Cokridel	Petro Prest'
Joh' atte Butte	Willo Quarel (i.e. quarry)
Joh' Bounde	

Comparative Features. It is manifest at first sight that progress was not uniform throughout the country; comparison of the examples, say, for Cumberland and Huntingdonshire, Lancashire and Cornwall, or Shropshire and Essex, will show at a glance the particular characteristics of the identification labels appertaining to each county. The varying peculiarities of the descriptions afterwards largely influenced the formation of the surnames of the respective counties.

The result of analysis of a much more extended list has been tabulated and will be found on p. 170. This table is most helpful in determining the progress made in the evolution of the surname from the description, and from the data several definite conclusions may be made. In these lists single names are practically unknown, amounting to not one per thousand, but it would be an unwarranted inference that every person at this time had a supplementary description permanently tacked on to his baptismal name; it being evident that the recording clerks considered it a duty to give every taxpayer a mark of identification, the great use of *filius* and *de* demonstrating the fact that few of the people, especially in the North, had "to-names", the scribe being constrained to inquire the name of the father or the address.

TABLE VI

COMPARISON OF CLASSES OF DESCRIPTIONS, ADDRESSES, AND SURNAMES PREVALENT IN 18 COUNTIES OF ENGLAND

Compiled from the Subsidy Rolls, A.D. 1327–34

P.R.O. Reference	Counties	Divisions	Approx. No. analysed	Single Baptismal Names %	Characteristic Without article %	Characteristic With French article %	Local Without preposition %	Local With Latin or French prepositions %	Local With English prepositions %	Genealogical Without Relationship expressed %	Genealogical With Relationship expressed %	Occupational Without article %	Occupational With French article %	Second Names unclassified %
	Northern—													
E 179 90/2	Cumberland	Leath Ward	260	—	3	—	—	30	—	3	30	14	1	19
195/1A	Westmorland	Kendal Ward	250	—	1	—	1	35	—	4	30	18	—	11
211/6*	Yorkshire N.R.	Pickering Liberty	350	—	2	—	2	36	1	3	17	13	1	25
	Western—													
116/1*	Shropshire	Bradford Hd.	400	—	4	1	4	28	1	7	19	6	11	19
177/1*	Staffordshire	Totmonslow Hd.	570	—	2	3	2	37	5	10	12	4	9	18
200/1*	Worcestershire	Blackenhurst Hd.	270	—	3	5	1	20	4	23	—	8	8	28
	Central—													
122/4	Huntingdonshire	Toseland Hd.	350	—	4	1	4	9	5	26	2	13	13	23
133/1*	Leicestershire	Goscote Hd.	400	—	4	1	5	17	2	24	4	12	7	24
192/4	Warwickshire	Knightlow Hd.	300	—	2	2	3	20	5	20	5	7	16	20
	Eastern—													
135/14	Lincolnshire	Elloe Wapentake	300	—	3	—	3	13	3	21	18	12	—	27
149/7	Norfolk	Flegg and Holt Hds.	250	—	4	3	3	6	1	39	2	10	—	32
180/6*	Suffolk	Wilford Hd.	300	—	3	2	—	27	—	27	—	9	8	24
	South-Eastern—													
107/13	Essex	Tendring Hd.	300	—	1	1	3	12	18	19	—	11	12	23
123/10	Kent	Bleangate and Wingham Hds.	400	—	4	—	4	25	15	14	1	12	—	25
189/3*	Sussex	Steyning Hd.	220	—	2	7	2	19	18	11	—	8	14	19
	South-Western—													
87/7	Cornwall	Penwith Hd.	300	—	3	1	30	11	—	9	2	9	3	32
103/5	Dorsetshire	Puddletown Hd.	150	—	3	1	7	14	11	18	—	6	4	36
169/5	Somersetshire	Winterstoke Hd.	300	—	2	5	4	4	12	20	—	12	8	33
		Totals	5670	—	3	2	4	21	5	16	8	10	7	24

* These rolls have been printed.

Adding together local names with prepositions, genealogical names with *filius*, etc., and occupational and personal with the article *le*, the percentage of the whole examples analysed is 43 per cent, which is to say, that respecting 43 per cent of the families named, there is a clear indication that they had not yet obtained surnames. In this calculation the very few surnames which may have incorporated permanently the French preposition *de* have been ignored as, on the other hand, have of necessity those descriptions without the preposition, but which had not yet become hereditary.[1]

Second names, the immediate forerunners of surnames, were becoming increasingly common, but much more so in the South than in the North. The Cumberland analysis shows 39 per cent of descriptions without preposition, filial expression, or article; the Midland counties 52 to 70 per cent; and Cornwall 83 per cent. Further reference will be made to the exceptional figures obtained from the last-named county.[2]

Names not readily classifiable are noticed to be increasing, particularly in the South, due in a considerable extent to the influx of foreigners, but the banishment of the Jews had cleared the country of their distinctive appellatives, although not of biblical names.

The slow adoption of surnames in the North, as evidenced by the Lancashire extracts given above, is typical of the descriptions of Northern England in the early fourteenth century. Analysing a few hundred entries, no less than 51 per cent were found to have the preposition *de*, or the preposition + article, *del* or *dil*; 29 per cent had words expressing kinship, as *filius*, *uxor*, *relicta*; 14 per cent were distinguished by occupations; and only 6 per cent had descriptions which could possibly rank as surnames. Even at the present day the northern villagers make little use of their official second names, in evidence of which an unnamed writer relates :—

" A few years ago I sought an heir-at-law in a town on the borders. I was referred to a man called ' Dick o' Jenny's ' ; he being the son of a second marriage, the mother's name was used to distinguish him, rather than his father's. Pursuing the inquiry, I found the first wife had been a ' sister of ould Tommy at top of th' huttock ' ; her daughter had married ' John o' Bobby ', and ' John o' Bobby's lad ' was the man I wanted. When I had made him out, it was with some difficulty that I ascertained (though amongst his kindred) that he bore the family name of ' Shepherd '." [3]

---

[1] I see that Mr. Eld, comparing the names of the Worcester rolls of the years 1275 and 1327, found that of 4,644 " surnames " in the later record, 1,971 had occurred in the same villages fifty-two years before (p. xii). That is to say, that 42 per cent of the persons apparently had hereditary family names.

[2] See p. 181.   [3] *Notes and Queries*, 1st May, 1852, p. 424.

In striking contrast to the Lancashire names are those of Shropshire. In Wolverley and Horton, of fifteen descriptions, no less than eleven had *filius* incorporated, a peculiarity probably arising from Welsh influence, although in some entries *ap* was preferred to the Latin equivalent. The extracts given above for Willaston and Longden provide an interesting contrariety, as already has been noticed. Considerable use of the genealogical description is, however, also said to be common in parts of Lancashire, possibly due to the retention of the old native custom. Referring to Strathclyde, which after the Norman Conquest became part of Scottish territory, and " so remained until Edward I abolished the Cymric laws and usages, bringing the natives under the jurisdiction of the English crown ", Woodward (1853) says :—

> " The language lingered a little longer ; and some traditions of the old times still exist ; while in Lancashire we yet meet with a vulgar provincialism, which seems to be one of the last remnants of the kingdom of Rheged,—instead of surnames, the names of the progenitors are used, as with the Welsh, as, John son of Thomas son of Richard son of Edward, etc., the pedigree being traced back for many generations in some cases." [1]

A feature of great interest is the growth in the use of the desinence " son " in the North, as is clearly evidenced by the Cumberland names. In the South the filial suffix made no official appearance for two centuries ; and since its notice in Winchester in the early twelfth century does not again figure in the records until the fourteenth, and then generally in the names of foreign merchants, e.g. an entry on the Close Rolls, 1311 (p. 303), cites nineteen aliens, of whom fifteen had " son " affixed to their second names. Of possible English origin, the following examples are representative :—

Rog. Dodesune, Shrops. 1283 (Cl. R.) ; Rob. Chonesone, Norf. 1283 (Cl. R.) ; W. Paskessone, Cambs. *c.* 1292 (Fines) ; Hen. le Lakesone, Lincs. 1308 (Cl. R.) ; Hugh Brunessone, Chesh. 1310 (Cl. R.) ; Joan relict of Pennesone, Ess. 1311 (Colchester, Court R. Jeayes) ; Nigel Maggesone, Yorks. 1314 (Cl. R.) ; W. Mayesone, Shrops. 1314 (Cl. R.) ; W. Belesone, Yorks. 1319 (Cl. R.) ; J. Gibbessone, Herts. 1320 (Pat . R.) ; W. Sibbessone, Herts. 1320 (Pat. R.) ; Hugh de Grenessone, Northumb. 1321 (Cl. R.), local or error (?) ; Adam Kingessone, Yorks. 1321 (Cl. R.) ; Hugh le Smythessone, Northumb. 1321 (Cl. R.) ; Jordan Tibbesone, Warw. 1327 (Subs.) ; J. Belesone, Suss. 1327 (Subs.) ; Ric. Emmesone, Suss. 1327 (Subs.).

The scarcity of the affix -*son* in the South is evidenced by the Subsidy Roll of Sussex, 1296, the only examples being le Smythessone, Godesone (which may be a personal name),

[1] *History of Wales*, 1853, p. 134.

and Dyson, which is probably a form of Tyson, also a Sussex name. A name ending in -*son* must not be recklessly assumed to be of this type, and in view of the fact that *d* and *t* are a common interchange the following examples are worthy of consideration :—

Ralph Taisson, Teissun, Tessun, temp. John (Cl. R.) ; Adam Tison or Tysun, Lincs. 1204–5 (Cl. R.) ; Ric. Dysun, London, 1275 (Hund. R.) ; Hen. Tysun, Suss. 1275 (Hund. R.) ; Ralph Dyson, Suss. 1296 (Subs.) ; Adam Tyssone, Cumb. 1333 (Subs.) ; Ralph Deyeson, Dorset, 1334 (Subs.).

Local Descriptions. It will be noticed that local descriptions are nothing more than addresses—in the form " of the Hostel ", " of Hillestrete ", or " of Pakenham " ; the documents being in Latin, " of " and sometimes " at " and " in " occur as *de*, and because there is no Latin article, " the ", when required, appears as *la* (Fr.), the rest of the distinction being commonly in English.

Subject to possible errors, referred to later, it may be accepted that if a surname can be traced back to a *de* or *de la* form, it is of local origin, but if to *le* or *la* only, then it is of either the characteristic or occupational class. The following examples are of local descriptions, derived more particularly from topographical features of various counties, north and south.

Cumberland.—del Garthus (the garth house), del Garth (of the yard or enclosure ; now Garth, Gath, Garside, Gartside, Garthside, etc.), del Milnhus, de Neubigging (the new building ; now Newbiggin, Newbegin), de Unthank, del Weld, del Wraa (the corner, nook ; now Wray, Ray).

Kent.—de Hellestrete, de la Hethe (now Heath).

Staffordshire.—del Felthouses, de la Hay (hedge or enclosure), de le Herdinges, del Hostel, de la Schawe (a small wood ; now Shaw), de la Spoune (*spong*, a narrow projecting part of a field ; now Spon, Spong), del Stones, del Syde.

Devonshire.—de la Combe (a valley), de la Doune (a down), de la Knolle (a hillock), de la Slade (a dell or boggy land), de Swanecote, de la Vise (? *veise*, a fissure), de la Weye, de la Ya (? *yeo*, a stream bringing water to the miners), de la Yaldelonde (also Yolleland, now Yelland).

Some detailed consideration will now be given to *le* and *de*.

The Article. The Latin demonstrative pronoun *ille* " that ", reduced to two cases, became in O.F. *li* (subjective case) and *le* (objective case) ; also in the feminine *la*, but ultimately the subjective case became obsolete, leaving the modern French *le*, *la*, *les*.[1] There is no article in Latin.

[1] Brachet's *Historical Grammar*, ed. by R. Toynbee, 1896, pp. 182.

Although the records were in Latin, and names, in general, latinized, occasional appearances of the article *le*, in the composition of descriptions, begin to be noticeable in rolls of the first half of the twelfth century (e.g. 1130, le Puilleis).[1] The use of the article became increasingly common up to the end of the thirteenth century, but by the end of the fourteenth, in descriptions of persons, had completely fallen into disuse, being exceptionally noticed in 1439 (pp. 191, 192) ; remaining, however, in place-names.

The article is employed equally with English or French (which includes Anglo-Norman) words, and it was the common practice to use *la* with natural objects, as la Feld, la Hole, la Combe, la Water, la Stone, la Lane, la Orchard, etc., when following the preposition *de*, but exceptionally, in about 5 per cent of cases, *le* may be found, as Petronilla de le Le (Oxf., Hund. R., ii, 709).

Le is more often found in conjunction with prepositions other than *de*, cf. in le Fenne, de la Fenne ; en le Dene, de la Dene, but there was no precise practice on this point (e.g. en la Hale, de la Hale). Some of the examples give the impression that *le* had been adopted as an English word (e.g. in le Trees, 1287 ; Inq. p.m., ii, 393).[2]

In characteristic and occupational names of males it was usual to use *le*, and in similar names of females *la*, but there are exceptions : Le Wydewe, Alicia le Palmer ; and *la* may be used in masculine names, interesting examples for comparison being Stephanus la Wayte (Herts, 1253, Fines, p. 176) and Willelmus le Wayte (Wilts, 1262, Fines, p. 382). Robert Ward was also called le Ward, la Warde, and de la Warde (1317, Inq. p.m.). In some cases *le*, in the description of a female, is the result of the father or husband having been distinguished in such manner.[3]

Combined with the prepositions *de*, *à*, *en*, the masculine article became *del* (de le), *al* (à le), *enl* (en le) ; from *del* came Fr. *du*, which is common in personal descriptions of France and the Channel Islands, and, although used in law reports of the thirteenth-century English courts, is rarely found in English descriptions in Latin records, as Johannes du Boys (Oxf., Hund. R., ii, 702), more commonly de Bosco " of the wood ".

The want of any generally recognized system may be illustrated by the following examples taken from the Hundred

[1] See p. 99.
[2] The article *le* seems to have become confused with the preposition *lez* (derived from Low Latin *latus* " near ", as lez à lez " side by side ") ; cf. the place-names Walton le Dale, Aix-les-Bains, Plessis-lez-Tours, Aix-la-Chapelle, but, of course, Walton le Dale may be Walton (in) le Dale (cf. Sutton in *la* Dale).
[3] The article was sometimes used unnecessarily, cf. le Gidye, p. 339.

Rolls, 1275 : ad Grenam, ad le Grene, de Grena, del Grene, dil Grene, de le Grene, de la Grene, atte Grene, super le Grene, and other forms are to be found elsewhere, e.g. Rog. othe Grene (1327, Shrops. Subs.).

The form *li* is not common : Hugo li Baylgy and Johannes li Walteys were noticed in the Hundred Rolls, 1275 ; *a la* being also rare, as " Roberto a la Feld ", which, in a consecutive paragraph, occurs as Robertus de le Felde (Oxf., Hund. R., ii, 780).

Le has occasionally coalesced with the following word, giving such surnames as Labby, Labbett, Lefevre, Leper, Lestrange, Levesque, Lyle, etc., a modern tendency being to add an apostrophe as L'Estrange.

The English article, banished by the Norman scribes, began to make surreptitious reappearances by the end of the thirteenth century, but it was an irregularity. A few examples may be seen on the Hundred Rolls, as " at þe Ock " (ii, 111). With the increased desire for brevity, and the consequent dropping of all forms of the article and prepositions, any chance that the English article had of becoming established in this connection was destroyed, and it is little to be noticed.

The Preposition *de*. The Latin preposition *de* " of ", " at ", " in ", " from " was preserved in French without change.

As noticed above, the Anglo-Saxons had used *æt* and *on* in the composition of local descriptions, and *apud* and *de* in Latin forms of the same ; and in the thirteenth and fourteenth centuries, the latter, the more frequently employed, is often followed by *le* and *la*, with which it coalesces, giving the impression that it is French. In an entry in the Subsidies, for instance, like " de Willelmo de la Feld ", both first and second *de* are Latin words, and so it must be assumed in cases like del Feld, dil Hill, etc. In exceptional cases, such as where a family is known as de la Riviere, *de* might be French, but generally speaking in the rolls it is not. *Des* (*de les*) occurs rarely, as Adam des Loinz, 1213 (Rot. de Obl.).

De was often used in error, as Helyas de Kokerel (a personal name), 1166 (Lib. Nig.), which is also written in the same record Helyas Kokerel, but it must be noted that in French *de* is sometimes found preceding a personal name, due to ellipsis of *le fils*, in parallel to the loss of " son " in our northern " John o' Bobby ". Examples of interchange noted in the Hundred Rolls are de Tilere and le Tilere (Hunts.), and on consecutive lines de Vilour and le Vilour (Hunts.). *Le* was also used, so far as appearances go, for *de*, as " le Fen ", but there is, of course, a possibility in this case that the peculiarity was caused by clerical omission of *in*. *De* was interchangeable with *in*, e.g. on consecutive lines in the

Hundred Rolls (Oxf.) are " de Angulo " and " in Angulo " ;
or with *ad*, as de Cruce, ad Crucem, etc., consequently the
exact English equivalent of the preposition is not always
apparent : de Sonninge is " of Sonning " ; but de Angulo
is " in the Nook ", and de Cruce is " at Cross ". On the same
membrane of a fifteenth-century roll occur [1] :—

Will's fil' Petri de Welle de Pilleslegh.
Will's at ye Well de Pyllesley fil' Petri at ye Well de Pyllesley.

It may .be noticed that W. *o* and Ir. *de* (in some cases)
are equivalent to Lat. *de*, but that Friesic and Dutch *de* is
the definite article, and possibly some of the apparent errors
may have been due to Low Country influence, e.g. a Nether-
lander might give his name as " de Herde ", an occupational
description, which in this country would pass for something
quite different ; cf. Ralph de Englysman, which occurs in a
Norfolk plea roll of 1281 (Ass. R. 823, m. 4).

In the fourteenth century, English prepositions came to be
used more freely, a common equivalent for *de la* being *atte*,
as de la Wode, atte Wode ; the literal translation " of the "
occurring rarely, as " othe Wode ", a form which was most
favoured in Shropshire.

In translating records it is usual to leave the *de*, owing to
uncertainty as to its appropriate equivalent, but, strictly
speaking, such a name as Thomas de Bradschagh de Knottisford
(1400, Pat. R.) should be rendered Thomas of Bradschagh of
Knottisford, as he would be referred to by his friends in ordinary
conversation, or in any English writing.

" There was slayne with the lord Perse
Sir John of Agerstone." (*Chevy Chase.*)

At a later period the first " of " was dropped giving the
more concise form, Thomas Bradshaw. In translating from
French records *de* should also be englished.

In some cases *de* and *de la* coalesced with the following
noun, resulting in preservation, and the permanence of such
surnames as Darcy, Deville, Delafeld ; and in the same way
were formed names with English prepositions, as Atwood,
Underhill, etc. A modern tendency is to add an apostrophe
as D'Arcy, etc.

Prepositional Descriptions. Some examples of the use of *de*,
de la, etc., have been given (p. 173), and now it may be noticed
that the Latin prepositions *ad*, *in*, *super*, *juxta*, were more
frequently employed in records of the central counties, as :—

Leicestershire.—ad Grava (now Grave, Graves) ; super la Grene ;
super le Hutt ; ad Pontem (at the bridge).

[1] P.R.O., K.B. 29, 91 (East. 12 Hen. VI).

Huntingdonshire.—super Collem (upon the hill) ; in Crofto (now Croft) ; ad Fontem (at the spring) ; juxta Hayle (near the hall ; now Hale, Haile, etc.) ; in Via (on the highway).

The lists for the southern counties present a striking contrast, local descriptions with Latin prepositions being much less in evidence ; English phrases, such as bi the Water, in ye Lane, over the Brok, of the chircheyard, Abouenyekyrke, atte Sole (the pond), othe Wode, Underwalle, Upethehulle, beyonde the Town, Byntheweye, Wythouthetown, become increasingly prominent. Curiosities may be found, such as : Ricardus de atte Bourland (Devon, m. 22), Johannes atte Nitheretochene and Gilbertus de Nitheretochene, being consecutive entries showing alternative use of *de* and *atte* (Devon, m. 11).

The growing ascendancy of English addresses is one of the most interesting features of these fourteenth-century rolls : since English words may be found considerably antedating the examples in the NED., e.g. the Devon roll provides *atte gribbele* " at the crab-tree," the earliest instance in the dictionary being of date 1578. Here, too, is an origin of the surname Gribble, another being from the personal name which occurs in Domesday Book as Gribol (Lincs. 371). This important phase in the history of British surnames will be more particularly illustrated by a selection of descriptions.

Leicestershire.—atte beck (a brook) ; ouerthebrok ; atte hashe ; atte hegge ; inthehyde ; atte kirkestile ; atte kirke ; atte lyng (heather) ; onyemyre (bog) ; atte Persones ; atteplawe ; atte spyneye ; inyewro (nook) ; bithe water ; aboueyeweye.

Some derivative surnames : Beck, Brook, Ashe, Hedge, Hyde, Kirk, Ling, Mire, Myres, Parsons, Spinney, Roe, Water, Waye.

Huntingdonshire.—in the breres (briars) ; benethebrok ; atte brigge ; atte chastel ; attechirch ; atte clou gres (*clowre* " turf ") ; atte croys (cross) ; iffeld ; atte fortei (ford island) ; atte heyweye ; atte mor ; atte pertre (pear-tree) ; atte ree (stream or enclosure) ; atte snap (in Devonshire, a spring in arable ground ; Halliwell) ; atte stok (tree stump) ; attetour ; in the wallis (probably willows) ; in the wilewes ; atte yate (gate).

Some derivative surnames : Brooke, Brigg, Castle, Church, Clougher, Cross, Field, Forty, More, Ree, Snape, Stock, Tower, Willows, Yate.

Essex.—atte felde ; atte grove ; atte hale (a nook) ; atte hathe ; atte hoo (a height) ; in the lane ; atte park ; atte pyrie ; in the vanne.

Some derivative surnames : Field, Grove, Hale, Heath, Hoo, Lane, Park, Pirrie, Vanne.

Kent.—ate boor ; ate crouch (crutch) ; ate cumbe ; ate forstalle (space in front of a farm house or paddock) ; ate fysshpole (pool) ; ate gate ; ate gore (a triangular piece of land) ; ate groue ; ate hawe (an enclosure) ; atter lake ; ate lese ; ate lynche ; attemarke (a boundary) ; ate meed ; ate mollonde (land held under a special rent) ; ate nesshe (ash) ; atte pende (an arch) ; ate pette ; ate saucereye ; ate shede ; atte snode ; ate steghele (stile) ; ate strethende ; ate sweche ; atte try (possibly tree ; a corn screen according to Halliwell ; cf. atte ree) ; underdonne ; underwalle ; atte watershippe (? trough).

Some derivative surnames : Bower, Crouch, Combe, Agate (if not from Aggot, dim. of Agnes), Gore, Grove, Hawe, Lake, Lees, Lynch, Mark, Meade, Nash, Pitt, Shead, Snead, Style, Tree, Underdown.

Sussex.—atte breche (breach) ; atte claie ; atte doune ; atter oak ; atte stanstrete (stony or paved street).

Some derivative surnames : Breach, Clay, Downe, Oake, Stanistreet.

Gloucestershire.—atte brewarne (brewhouse) ; atte dogher (rabbit burrow) ; atte fisshewere ; atte gotere (gutter) ; atte home ; atte lauende (laundy, laundry) ; atte lepeyate ; atte lude ; atte oclone (oak lane) ; atte pile (a small tower) ; atte plaunche (plank) ; atte pleystude (*pley* " bank " ; *stude* " stead ") ; atte plodde (turf) ; atte snede (clearing) ; atte steorte (a tongue of land) ; atte trouwe (tree) ; atte vloddre.

Some derivative surnames : Dower, Home, Laundy, Lippett, Lode, Pile, Plank, Playsted, Snead, Stort, Tree.

Devonshire.—atte apildore ; atte apse (O.E. *æsp* " the aspen ") ; atte ayshe ; atte bear (grove) ; atte berne ; atte birch ; atte biry (hill) ; atte burghe ; atte bydene ; atte cloude (a mass of rock, hill) ; atte clyve (steep side of a hill) ; atte combe (a hollow or valley) ; atte cove ; atter doune ; atte fenne ; atte forlang (furlong) ; atte forsen ; atte grove ; atte hamme (a plot or close) ; atte heghen (hedge) ; atte hokhole ; atte hole ; atte hoo ; atte knappe (summit of a hill) ; atte knolle (top of a hill) ; atter lake ; atte lane ; atte lantshar ; atter leghe, leye (lea) ; atte lymdrie (O.E. *lind* " lime-tree ") ; atte menede ; atte mershe ; atte more ; atte muse (possibly a peat bog) ; atter ok ; atte orchard ; atte ouese (ooze, marsh) ; atte pole (pool) ; atte porte ; atte priorie ; atte putt ; atte rocke ; atte rugge (ridge) ; atte see ; atte shute ; atte slade (a dell) ; atte slo (soft ground) ; atte stout ; atte thorne ; atte torre (a high rock or hill) ; atte trewen ; atte velye ; atte wallen ; atte watershute ; atte wayte ; atte wille ; atte willeway ; atte wurthen (*worth*, an enclosed space) ; atte ya ; atte yo ; atte yete ; atte yurd.

The distinguishing descriptions given to these men of Devon, in particular, present a pen-picture of the topographical features of their charming county ; an interesting point being the survival of Cornish words : menede (*menedh* " a mount "), bydene (*bidhen* " meadow "), shute (watering-place), velye (possibly " a working ", cf. wheal), de Kelly (of the grove), atte Boscall (house of the grove) ; trewen and lantshar may also be Cornish.

Some derivative surnames : Apps, Ashe, Beer, Burne, Birch, Berry, Burge, Clive, Combe, Cove, Downe, Fenn, Furlong, Grove, Ham, Haye, Hook, Holl, Hoole, Hoo, Knapp, Knoll, Lake, Lane, Lee, Limbury, Marsh, Moore, Moss, Oake, Orchard, Poole, Port, Prior, Pitt, Rook, Ridge, Shute, Slade, Slow, Start (Stert, Stort, and Stout), Thorne, Torre, Trewen, Waite (Wayte), Willey, Worth, Yea, Yeo, Yate, Yarde.

English Prepositions. The preposition *at* (O.E. *æt*) coalescing with various cases of the definite article varies from *atter* and *atte* in Devonshire to *aten* and *ate* in Kent, where two hundred years later it had become *at* and *a*, finally being dropped altogether. It may be of interest to notice the comparative prevalence of the word in this connection. Devonshire (5,000 names), 9 per cent ; Kent (6,000 names), 9 per cent ; Gloucestershire (5,000 names), 8 per cent ; Huntingdonshire (3,500 names), 3 per cent ; and Leicestershire (3,500 names), 2 per cent.

The preposition *of* coalescing with the definite article became *othe*, and is found principally in the lists of the western counties, as Staffordshire, Othehaye and Othemarsh [1] ; and Shropshire, othe forde, othe heth, othe hull, othe stables, othe wode,[2] all which examples are of date *c.* 1380.

The growth and decline of English prepositions is best illustrated by taking the names of one county at various periods. Such figures for Kent have been tabulated on the following page, and show at a glance the comparative rise and decline of the foreign and native prepositions and the increased use of local descriptions without any preposition whatsoever.

Cornish Names. The Cornish language, as mentioned above, is of the Brythonic group, akin to Welsh and Breton, and was in use to a certain extent down to the seventeenth century, consequently until long after the formation and adoption of hereditary family names [3] ; moreover, as has been illustrated above, certain Cornish words were in use in Devonshire at the making of surnames, so it will occasion no surprise to find some of our surnames derived from descriptions in the native tongue of " West Wales ".

Jenner (1904) observes that " the modern English speech

---

[1] P.R.O., E. 179, 177/22.
[2] P.R.O., E. 179, 242/34.
[3] Andrew Borde (1542), in his *Boke of the Introduction of Knowledge*, says : " In Cornwall is two speeches, the one is naughty [i.e. inferior] Englysshe, and the other is Cornysshe speche, and there be many men and women the which cannot speake one worde of Englysshe, but all Cornyshe."

TABLE VII

COMPARISON OF CLASSES OF DESCRIPTIONS, ADDRESSES, AND SURNAMES PREVALENT IN KENT

Compiled from various Sources, Twelfth to Sixteenth Century

Year	P.R.O. Reference	Place or Division	Approx. No. analysed	Single Baptismal Names %	Characteristic — Without article %	Characteristic — With French article %	Local — Without preposition %	Local — With Latin or French prepositions %	Local — With English prepositions %	Genealogical — Without Relationship expressed %	Genealogical — With Relationship expressed %	Occupational — Without article %	Occupational — With French article %	Second Names unclassified %
Hen. II	E 179, 237/51	Preston Hd.	120	17	7			31		3	13	12		17
1227	Assize R. 358	General	200	—		2	2	65		1	16	1	5	10
1255	Assize R. 361	General	400	—	3	3	2	50	1	6	11	5	7	12
1263	S.C. 2, 181/73	Middleton Hd.	100	—		3	1	29		8	12	9	9	8
1301	E 179, 123/4	Dartford	200	—	2		4	26	4	23	3	22		19
1327	E 179, 123/10	Bleangate and Wingham Hds.	400	—	4		7	25	15	14	1	12		25
1341	E 179, 123/18	Dover	300	—	6			3	10	26		21	1	26
1352	E 179, 123/24	Toltingtrough Hd.	300	—	2		12	17	10	22		25		24
1373	E 179, 123/29	Cornilo Hd.	300	—	4			4	7	26		17		30
1384	E 179, 123/52	Folkestone and Ringslow Hds.	100	—	2		16		4	22		24		32
1401	E 179, 123/62	Cornilo Hd.	300	—	3		12		3	27		20		35
1432	E 179, 124/97	Ringslow Hd.	300	—	4		11	3	9	25		21		30
1451	E 179, 124/114	Cornilo Hd.	100	—	7		20			25		18		27
1523	E 179, 124/196	Westgate Hd.	300	—	2		20		4	33		13		29
		Total	**3420**											

Note.—E 179 are Subsidy Rolls. S.C. 2 is a Manorial Court Roll.

of West Cornwall is full of Celtic words, and nine-tenths of the places and people from the Tamar to the Land's End bear Cornish names ".[1] Some examples of old personal names from the manumissions of St. Petroc (Bodmin) have been given,[2] and other ancient Cornish names may be found in Domesday Book, and in calendars of saints' names,[3] but the most prolific sources of the early names are the Exchequer and manorial rolls at present in unindexed manuscript form.[4] The example presented on p. 167 shows that quite three-fourths of the names are Cymric.

Fourteenth-century lists of Cornish names are very distinctive ; at first sight there appear to be a considerable number of surnames derived from localities, but actually at this early date they are but addresses, the clerk, ahead of his time, having largely elided the customary preposition *de*, for instance, David Tresruf followed by Humfr' *de eadem* illustrates the common form for consecutive entries, showing that Tresruf was an address, not a family name. The extensive use of this class of description, however, did lead ultimately to many Cornubians having local surnames. In this respect the names of Cornwall may be likened to those of Lancashire, and it is worthy of note that these two counties are those in which the British language remained longest in England, but, on the other hand, in Wales itself, where the native language has been retained to the present day, this class of surname is very unusual, a possible explanation of the unexpected anomaly being that English-speaking clerks of Cornwall and Lancashire had little sympathy for the native genealogical system of description, and so entered addresses instead. The extracts from the Welsh Subsidy Rolls given above have shown that in the Principality both native and English systems were used, as they were also in the English counties bordering on Wales, but it is remarkable how few of the Welsh addresses survived as surnames, whereas in Cornwall and Lancashire family names of this class predominate.

The Cornish descriptions follow the same classification as that arranged for the Welsh, from which they are often indistinguishable. Examples will be given later : characteristic, p. 224 ; local, pp. 233–5 ; genealogical, p. 254 ; and occupational, p. 262.

Names of the Channel Islanders. After the Norman Conquest of England the allegiance of the islands was

---

[1] *A Handbook of the Cornish Language*, by H. Jenner, p. 22.
[2] See p. 40.
[3] Brit. Mus., Cott. MS. Vesp. A, xiv.
[4] Bannister (1869–71), Charnock (1870), and Dexter (1926) do not seem to have tapped this supply. The Devon and Cornwall Record Soc. has in its volume for 1910 published the names for one parish.

uncertain until the reign of John, when they were attached to the English crown, although for many subsequent years the inhabitants seem to have been treated as foreigners. In 1390 the natives of Jersey and Guernsey were exempted from tolls and customs in England, in like manner to denizens, for eight years,[1] but the Aliens' Subsidy of 1439, although it specifically excepted men and women born in Wales, omitted to mention the Channel Islanders, who paid tax as foreigners, and consequently there may be found in the records the names of a number of Guernseymen, although, in common with those of other nationalities, they were given English names on settling down in this country. For the ensuing impositions, granted in 1442 and 1449, " Gersey and Garnesey" men were excepted,[2] and nothing more is heard of them in England.

The language of the Islanders was Norman-French, of which several dialects are yet spoken. As examples of fourteenth-century descriptions and surnames the following extracts have been made from the Assize Rolls, 1309 [3] :—

Characteristic.—le Blancq ; Blaunche ; Blondel (from Blond) ; Bonamy (good friend) ; Brasdefer (iron arm) ; le Breton ; le Caufre (the bald) ; Choffyn (bald) ; la Cornaille (vulgar name for *corbeau* " crow ") ; le Crochon (the crooked) ; la Disme ; le Esturnel ; le Fillastre (the step-son) ; le Gay ; le Gros ; le Hardy (the brave) ; le Huby (the gloomy) ; le Jeune ; le Lumbard ; le Moigne (the monk) ; Lengleis ; le Noble ; le Petevin ; le Petit ; Poingdestre (literally " right fist ", but perhaps the heraldic pointdexter) ; le Rous ; le Sauvage ; le Serf ; le Utlagh (the outlaw) ; Wydecok (i.e. Videcoq ; Larchey says : " visage de coq—visage empourpre "—that is " purple-face ").

Local.—de Anneville ; du Bois ; de Bruery ; de la Court ; de la Croix ; de Kelly (see p. 179) ; des Mareys ; de la Rivere ; du Vivier (fish-pond).

Genealogical.—Amelot, Anquetil, Baudonette, Cokerel, David, Denis, Fitz-Hamon, Gervaise, Goscelin, Hamelin, Juliene, Ode, Vautier.

Occupational.—Bolanger (baker) ; le Cacher ; la Hocheresse ; la Miresse (wise woman) ; Larbelestier ; le Fevre (the smith) ; le Maceon (the mason) ; le Pelletier (the furrier) ; le Pestour (the baker) ; le Sueur (the cordwainer : Larchey) ; le Vechere.

Manx Names. The Isle of Man, the Mona of Cæsar, was intimately connected with Ireland ; the inhabitants in A.D. 416, according to Orosius, being of similar race, and it may be gathered from a story given by Cormac, in his glossary, that the language spoken was practically identical with Irish Gaelic.[4] In the ninth century the raiding Vikings commenced

---

[1] Parliament Rolls, 14 Ric. II, vol. iii, p. 281*b*.
[2] Ibid., vol. v, pp. 38*b*, 144*b*.
[3] *Société Jersiaise*, 1903, No. 18.
[4] p. 36.

their visits to the island, and in the tenth they effected settlements, Man becoming subject to the Scandinavian kings of Dublin.[1] That the people became to some extent bilingual is evident from an examination of the place-names. Moore states that analysis shows that of local names in use on the island at the present day, 9 per cent are purely Scandinavian, and 7 per cent partly so ; 68 per cent purely Gaelic, the balance being mixed, of English and Celtic and doubtful origin.[2]

In 1266 the island was ceded by Norway to Scotland, but was frequently in the hands of the English, and by the end of the fourteenth century the Scots ceased to claim Man. The names of the Northmen have become proportionately considerably less, and those that remain in use have suffered much corruption, and both Celtic and Scandinavian place-names are now giving way to English. In view of these historical facts it will occasion no surprise to find a considerable Scandinavian element in Manx personal names also. Considering surnames, Moore found that the largest number were of Irish derivation, and that in nearly every case those inherited from the Vikings " are celticized in form—that is to say, they have received the Irish prefix *mac*, and have undergone the kind of phonetic corruption which was inevitable when they had to pass through Celtic-speaking lips ".[3]

A few early Manx names, Gaelic and Norse, having been obtained from ogmic and runic inscriptions, some examples of the latter are noticed above (p. 66), but until the fifteenth century few of the appellatives have been preserved. A declaration by the Bishop of Sodor and his clergy touching a claim by Sir Stephen Lestrop, A.D. 1408, provides the following illustrations :—

Fyntt Mc Kee ; Joh'es Mc Crystyn ; Will'us Skerffe ; Will'us Mc Cowyn ; Will'us de Innow ; Pat'cius Mc Thoryngt ; Mich'us Mc Skerffe ; Andr' Mc Gray ; Joh'es Andr' ; Gybbon Mc Kane ; Pat'k Mc Kane ; Gilc'st Mc Dowytt ; Pat'k Thomlyngson ; Gybbon Mc Essas ; Gybbon Mc Kane ; Will'us Mc C'styn ; Martyn Mc Oct' ; Gilc'st Mc Nelle ; Moldonny Mc Brow ; Moldonny Mc Croyn ; Joh'es Mc Kyg ; Joh'es Markeson ; Dilnow Mc Corkyll ; Gybbon Mc Falle ; Jankyn Mc Scaly ; et Scymynd Mc Kee ; Donnald Clerc'.[4]

Notes.—Mc Kee, Mc Key, Mc Kay, Mc Kie, also occur without the *mac*, and are derived from *mac Aedha*, son of Aedh, signifying " fire ", according to Cormac. Mc Quay and Quay are probably from the same source.[5]

[1] *A History of the Isle of Man*, by A. W. Moore, vol. i, p. 82.
[2] *Manx Names*, by A. W. Moore, 1903, p. 8.   [3] Ibid., p. 4.
[4] Printed in *Monumenta de Insula Manniæ*, ed. by J. R. Oliver, vol. ii, p. 247 et seq.
[5] The derivations which I give are taken mainly from *Manx Names*, where additional particulars may be found.

Mc Crystyn, Mac Christene, Mac Crislyn, now Christian, are from Icelandic Kristín, which occurs in the *Flateyjarbóc*.

Mc Skerffe, now Scarff, possibly also Scandinavian.

Mc Cowyn, M'Owen, Mc Cowne, Cown, Cowen, from mac Eoghain " son of Owen ".

de Innow appears to be exceptionally a place-name, but Moore suggests that it is connected with Ywain, Owen, Eoghan.

Mc Thoryngt, one of the numerous Scandinavian names having the element Thor, the god of thunder.

Mc Gray, possibly a corruption of Mac Cray (*mac craith* " son of the weaver ").

Mc Kane, Mc Cann, Mc Cane, Caine, Cayne (*mac Cathain* " son of Cathan ").

Mc Dowytt, Mc Essas, are of uncertain origin.

Mc Oct, Mc Ott, Oats, Oates, the common Norman name Ote or Odo.

McBrow, Mc Brewe, Brew (either *mac Vriw* " son of the Judge ", or *mac Brugaidh* " son of the farmer ").

Mc Croyn, Mc Craine, Mc Carrane, Crayne, Crane (*mac Ciarain* " son of Ciaran ").

Mc Kyg, Mc Keg, Mc Coag, Keage, Kegg (*mac Taidhg* " son of Tadg ").

Mc Corkyll, Mc Crokell, Corkhill, Curkell, a corruption of mac Torkill (son of Thor-ketill), a Scandinavian name in the *Landnámabóc* and the *Flateyjarbóc*.

Mc Falle, Mc Faile, Mc Felis, Fayle, originally *mac Giolla Phoil* " the son of Paul's servant ".

Mc Scaly, Skellie, Skealley, contracted from *O'Scolaidhe* " the descendant of the Story-teller ".

Further sources of Manx names are the Statutes [1] and the manorial rolls. [2] What has been said already regarding Irish and Norse personal names applies equally to the appellatives of Man, but it is to be noticed that the prefix " O ", signifying " descendant of ", was never used in the Isle of Man. Mac, which in the above list occurs in twenty-one of the twenty-six names, had three centuries later almost disappeared. It may be traced yet in many names by its final consonant, in the form C, K, or Q, which now supplies the initial letter of so many Manx names, as e.g. Knickell from Mac Nichol, Costeane from Mac Austin, Kaighan from Mac Eachain, Corrin from Mac Odhrain, Quin from Mac Coinn, Kewin from Mac Eoin, Krickart from Mac Richard ; and similarly the descendants of Giolla-Eoin are known by the corrupted name Lewin, pronounced Leóne. [3] *Inneen* (Ir. *ingean*) " daughter "

---

[1] Edited by M. A. Mills, 1821, and J. F. Gill, 1883.
[2] A translation for the years 1511–15, by Rev. T. Talbot, has been printed.
[3] Moore, pp. 13–15.

generally appears as *ine*, as the early sixteenth-century examples : Agnes ine Skylycorn, Margaret ine Corkell.[1]

Genuine Manx names are of the genealogical class, with few exceptions, such as the characteristic appellatives : Cretney from mac Bretnagh " son of the Welshman ", and Gale, probably from *gall*, " a foreigner ", a name given by the natives to strangers who settled in the island.[2] As an instance of the uncertainty of classification by inspection may be mentioned the surname Crow, classed by Bardsley and Lower with other bird-names as a nickname. *Fiachan*, the Irish equivalent for " crow ", was originally bestowed as a fanciful personal name ; it afterwards became a genealogical description, *mac fiachain*, then in English form Crow was adopted as a surname. Kraka, the Icelandic equivalent for " crow ", is found in the *Landnamabók* as a nickname : it has also been noticed in use with the Anglo-Saxons (p. 53) and the Channel Islanders (p. 182), and among the Normans *corbeau* has given us the name Corbet.

Summary and Conclusions (fourteenth century). To facilitate an understanding of the changes which took place in the fourteenth century, an analytical table based on the returns of the collectors of the poll taxes of 2–4 Ric. II (1377–81) has been prepared. The extant records of this series are not nearly so useful as the excellent lists for the 1327 Subsidy, but are, nevertheless, most valuable. The two groups of names have very similar characteristics and the figures may be compared.

Dates A.D.	Approx. No. analysed	Characteristic		Local			Genealogical		Occupational		Second Names unclassified
		Without article	With French article	Without preposition	With Latin or French prepositions	With English prepositions	Without Relationship expressed	With Relationship expressed	Without article	With French article	
		%	%	%	%	%	%	%	%	%	%
1327–34	5670	3	2	4	21	5	16	8	10	7	24
1377–81	2300	4	1	11	12	5	20	2	21	4	20

The most noticeable change in the half century (1327–1377) is the fall in the use of the preposition in local names from 21 per cent to 12 per cent, the loss being almost balanced by the increase of names without preposition ; but the movement as yet was restricted to the southern counties. The use of the English preposition was maintained on the whole, but was

[1] *The Manorial Roll*, p. 10. A list of surnames found with *ine* is given on p. 86.   [2] Moore, pp. 13–15.

TABLE VIII

COMPARISON OF CLASSES OF DESCRIPTIONS, ADDRESSES, AND SURNAMES PREVALENT IN TWELVE COUNTIES OF ENGLAND

Compiled from the Poll Tax Rolls, A.D. 1377–81

P.R.O. Reference	County	Division	Approx. No. analysed	Single Baptismal Names %	Characteristic Without article %	Characteristic With French article %	Local Without preposition %	Local With Latin or French prepositions %	Local With English prepositions %	Genealogical Without Relationship expressed %	Genealogical With Relationship expressed %	Occupational Without article %	Occupational With French article %	Second Names unclassified %
E 179 130/24	Northern— Lancashire	West Derby Hd.	250	—	1	3	1	42	—	12	3	5	25	8
202/69[1]	Yorkshire E.R.	Howdenshire Wap.	250	—	3	—	10	15	4	27	4	19	—	18
242/34	Western— Shropshire	South Bradford Hd.	200	—	1	3	6	30	6	14	1	8	14	7
177/22[2]	Staffordshire	Offlow Hd.	180	—	2	1	4	11	13	27	5	20	1	16
133/26	Central— Leicestershire	Goscote Hd.	250	—	7	—	19	5	4	17	1	27	—	20
192/23	Warwickshire	Knightlow Hd.	250	—	4	—	22	1	4	22	3	28	—	16
149/45	Eastern— Norfolk	Brothercross Hd.	200	—	3	—	6	11	3	15	—	25	5	32
180/84	Suffolk	Mutford Hd.	80	—	3	—	7	9	—	19	—	22	1	38
107/60	South-Eastern— Essex	Ongar Hd.	180	—	4	—	12	1	5	23	—	35	—	20
189/40	Sussex	Chichester Rape	200	—	5	—	10	—	10	18	—	30	—	27
95/31	South-Western— Devonshire[3]	Exminster Hd.	180	—	6	—	26	2	7	17	—	12	—	30
103/48	Dorsetshire	Blandford Div.	80	—	7	—	3	—	—	33	—	21	—	36
		Totals	2300	—	4	1	11	12	5	20	2	21	4	20

[1] Printed, ed. by J. C. Cox (East Riding Antiq. Soc.). [2] Printed by Wm. Salt Arch. Soc. [3] Tinners of the Stannary.

tending to fall, also in the South, where new developments
are always first noticeable.

Occupational names by the end of the fourteenth century
were much more prevalent without the article, the change
again being largely due to southern influence, as is fully
illustrated by the analysis of Kent names (Table VII).   In
Lancashire the late use of the article *le* far exceeded anything
noticed in the other eleven representative counties.

In genealogical names the decline in the employment of
words denoting kinship is very apparent, comparison of
Tables VI and VII showing clearly that the use of *filius* having
died out in the South, was almost abandoned in the central
counties by 1377, and much reduced in the North.

In the half century (1327–1377) names with *filius, de, le,
atte*, etc., had fallen from 43 per cent to 24 per cent, and it is
to be concluded that at least 24 per cent of the people had not
yet fixed surnames, and of these by far the greater part were
in the North ; in Lancashire, in particular, 73 per cent of
persons do not seem to have had hereditary family names,
and the proportion may have been much greater.

Descriptions which do not have *filius, de, le, atte*, etc., are
well on the way to becoming surnames, but have not
necessarily reached that stage.   It may be asked—How can
it be known when a description has become a surname ?
Provided a pedigree is available, the determination of the stage
of permanence which a name has reached presents no difficulty,
but without the genealogy for reference any opinion can be
nothing more than surmise.

Characteristic Descriptions.—If a person, who by custom has
been dubbed with a name denoting his appearance, character,
relationship, nationality, or other attribute, has one or more
children not possessing such attribute, but who are likewise
designated, the second name has become an inherited surname.

Local Descriptions.—In the case where a tenant who has
been distinguished by the name of his land is succeeded by
son or grandson similarly named, it does not follow that the
name has become a perpetual inheritance of that family.
Loss or disposal of those lands might quite easily result in
a new name being adopted.   If, on the other hand, the name
were taken by members of the family born after such loss or
disposal, then it might reasonably be looked upon as an
hereditary surname.

Genealogical Descriptions.—If Robert had a son called
William who was described as William Robert's son, and if
William's son became likewise distinguished as Robertson
instead of Williamson, it is clear that Robertson had acquired
all the characteristics of the modern surname.

Occupational Descriptions.—In similar manner, if William son of John the cook became known as William Cook, although he followed a different vocation to that of his father, it is a fair inference that Cook had become the hereditary surname of that family.

In the case of a personal name followed by two descriptions, it may be taken that the first of the two descriptions, if English, is looked upon as a family name, thus in Johannes Carpenter de Caxton, Carpenter is a fixed surname. In the case where the first of the two descriptions is latinized, as in Willelmus de Cornubia de Sancto Neoto (1316), its value is uncertain, and it can only be said that Cornwall was probably a surname. (For the legal view see below, p. 394.)

The contingency, however, must not be overlooked that after the second, third, or a much later generation, it was quite possible for the surname to be again changed. It may be concluded that no definite time can be assigned for the first acknowledgment of the hereditary nature of surnames, such recognition being a gradual process which was not uniform in all classes of society, and one which, moreover, made greater strides in one part of the country than another; and it is doubtful whether the custom is yet thoroughly established throughout the British Isles. Even when the people were prepared to regard surnames as an inheritance the law said that they were nothing of the kind.

Following upon the observations on christian names of the thirteenth century, which have been presented on p. 120, it may be of interest to note the relative prevalence of the principal christian names as they appear in the West Riding of Yorkshire in the fourteenth century. In a list of 19,600 male and female names John occurs 3,400 times (17 per cent), William 9 per cent, Thomas and Robert 5 per cent each. Of female names Alice was the most popular, about 5 per cent, being followed by Joan (*Johanna*), 4 per cent.[1] While these figures cannot be compared with those given above (being male names only), yet it is evident that John had ousted William from its great popularity; but no explanation can be suggested for the change. Adam appears in no less than 2 per cent of the examples, and one result of the general use of the biblical name was a great crop of derivatives perpetuated as surnames, as will be more particularly mentioned on p. 291. Regarding variety it appears that there were eighty-six different male and eighty female appellatives in use, but O.E. names were very scarce. It is rather surprising to find that Edward did not get a new lease of life during the reigns of the three kings of that name, 1272–1377.

[1] G. T. Clark, in *Yorkshire Arch. and Top. Journal*, 1882, vol. vii, p. 189.

CHAPTER VIII

Surnames of the Fifteenth, Sixteenth, and Seventeenth Centuries

Alien Descriptions. In view of the great stream of foreigners into Britain, the ultimate goal of refugees and adventurers, the determination of the class into which a description falls, the country of its origin, and its signification become increasingly uncertain. Teutonic, Scandinavian, Gaelic, and Cymric names were preserved, but often in very corrupt form ; the foreign names were sometimes translated into English, and at other times imitated and speedily converted into something English, the more humorous the more pleasing to the entering clerk [1] ; but, as will be shown, the scribes in general refused to have anything to do with foreign names, and bestowed in lieu thereof common English appellatives, as White, Hill, Webber, etc., upon the meek and submissive stranger. [2]

Having regard to the sweeping destruction of the Subsidy Rolls of the fifteenth century, the preservation of a series of documents relating to impositions on aliens is fortunate, because a new line of investigation is opened up, and certain doubts, which, but for these records, would have remained in obscurity, are clarified. In 1439 Parliament had granted to Henry VI a subsidy *de alienigenis*, by which Act every person (excepting Welsh) not born in England, dwelling within that realm, householders or not, paid a tax, and special rolls of account were kept. [3] The records of the levies and lists of persons liable are valuable in showing the numbers and nationalities of the foreigners in the various counties, but more particularly for the purpose of this essay in evidencing that aliens in considerable numbers did not retain their native names, but, for official purposes at any rate, were given English descriptions, illustrating further the unsettled nature of surnames in the fifteenth century. And if the foreigners were given new names officially, it is even more certain that in everyday life they were also dubbed with designations understandable by the natives.

These rolls should record names, vocations, and nationality of the taxpayers, and it is with disappointment one finds that with few exceptions they are most incomplete in one or more

---

[1] For examples of scribal humour, see below, p. 349.
[2] Something similar occurs at the present day. See p. 267.
[3] *Rolls of Parliament*, vol. v, p. 6.

of these details. The documents for twenty-nine counties comprise about 9,000 items, of which 5,800 give no indication of country of birth ; but in the remainder of the entries the nationalities are either specifically cited as the fourth part of the description or they are entered in the form of a cognomen. The following remarks must be read with due consideration for the fact that the information is but 35 per cent complete.

Frenchmen and Normans account for rather more than half the specified nationalities, their forces being greatest in Devonshire, Wiltshire, and Kent, the numbers being strengthened in the first-named county by a number of Guernseymen.[1] Irishmen were prominent in Cornwall, Wiltshire, and Northamptonshire, being over 40 per cent of the specified foreigners in these three counties. It is evident that Scotsmen in the fifteenth century did not venture far afield, since they are rarely noticed south of Cumberland and Westmorland, but it must be observed that the Yorkshire rolls offered no facility for examination, and were passed over unscrutinized.[2] Dutchmen or Hollanders (42 per cent) lead the way in Cambridgeshire, Suffolk, Norfolk, and Kent (the Essex rolls not being available), but few from the Low Countries travelled further north than Northamptonshire. The Flemings also are strongest in southern counties, as Devonshire, Wiltshire, and Kent ; and, as might be expected, Bretons are found principally in Cornwall and Devonshire (the Dorset-shire roll not being available). Occasional Alemans or Germans, " Bemener," Brabans, Burdegalians, Florentines, Gascons, Gilderlanders, Lombards, Manxmen, " Norshers," Picards, Poictevins, " Portingalers," Saxons, " Selanders," Spaniards, with several *de regno* de Sweth' (i.e. Sweden) in Cambridgeshire, an " Islander " in Southwold (Suff.), together with a gentleman " surnamed " Jerusalem, taxed in Surrey, complete the list of our visitors of the fifteenth century.[3]

[1] " Gersey and Garnesey " were excepted from the later alien subsidies of 1442 and 1449. See p. 182.

[2] In the Kingston-on-Hull roll (202/114) there are a few Scotsmen entered as " Alexander Scottisshman ", " Andrew Orknayman ", and perhaps also " Donkan Shipman ". Of this style of description are " Iver Irelandman ", " Johanna F'nsshewoman ", and " Claus Ducheman ", of which sufficient examples have been given in Chapter VI.

[3] The Subsidy Rolls at the Public Record Office examined for these particulars were : Beds and Bucks, 235/18 ; Berks, 73/91 ; Bucks, 77/59 ; Cambs and Hunts, 235/4 ; Cornwall, 87/78 ; Cumberland, 90/27 ; Devon, 95/100 ; Glouc., 113/99 ; Hants, 176/585 ; Heref., 117/51 ; Herts, 120/83 ; Kent, 124/107 ; Leic. and Warw., 235/8 ; Lincs, 269/28 ; Midx., 141/69 ; Norf., 149/130 ; Northants, 155/80 ; Northumb., 158/115 ; Rutl., 165/66 ; Salop, 166/84 ; Staffs, 177/55 ; Suff., 180/92 ; Surr. and Suss., 184/212 ; Warw., 192/65 ; Westm., 195/33 ; Wilts, 196/100 ; Worc., 200/75. The class reference for all the rolls is E 179. The rolls are for various dates from 18 to 21 Hen. VI. A further subsidy was granted in 1449.

Regarding surnames it is manifest that foreign appellatives were largely ignored, and the aliens identified by second names bestowed upon them after arrival in this country, since such labels consist mainly of nationality or English localities. The most informative of the rolls are those for Devonshire, Cambridgeshire, Northamptonshire, and Wiltshire. Very few entries comprise all four of the descriptive elements, and these may be exemplified by the following extracts :—

> (de) Will'o de le kechene de Teffont serviente Normanno. (Wilts.
> (de) Bernardo Reem de ludgershale taillo' Duytissman. (Wilts.)
> Johannes Goter de Kenterber, tynker, Norman. (Dev.)

In commoner forms the trade or nationality takes the place of surname.

> Hankyn Duchesman de Tappelowe, serviens. (Bucks.)
> Hanys Dyker de Stonhous holander. (Dev.)
> Martinus Baker de Plymouth selander. (Dev.)
> Joh'nes Hoper de Northpole frenshman. (Dev.)
> (de) Nich'o Frenssh de Lavington gallico. (Wilts.)

The surname may be given, and occupation omitted :—

> de Johanne Hondewe normaunder de Ivechirch. (Kent.)
> Petrus Peryn de Bradford gallicus. (Dev.)
> de Gerardo Vampas de Nove Sar' flandrico. (Wilts.)

Surname and nationality are sometimes contradictory :—

> Johannes Breton de Litelham norman. (Dev.)
> (de) Roberto Cornish Irishman. (Cornw.)
> (de) Philippo Flemyng de Bradeford hibernico. (Wilts.)
> Mabill Walsh Irisshewoman. (Cornw.)

Walsh and Flemyng were established surnames in Ireland by this time. Sometimes the country of birth is specifically stated :—

> (de) Ric'o Deryk, nato in holand. (Kent.)
> (de) Joh'e Boye, nato in holand. (Kent.)

Both address and vocation may be omitted :—

> Martinus Florence. (Bedf.)
> (de) Rogero Champayn. (Kent.)
> Hankyn Fleming. (Kent.)
> Robinet Florantyn. (Kent.)
> Matheus Almaund. (Hertf.)

The address given may be the country of birth :—

> Henry Pikard de Pykardy. (Hants.)
> Rad'us Shepehurd de Spanieney. (Glouc.)
> Michael frensheman de franc'. (Dev.)
> (de) Ricardo Scot de Scottelande. (Northants.)
> D'n's Bened'cus Nicoll de regno de Sweth'. (Cambs.)

An unusual case of double nationality is :—

> Robertus Iryssh alias dictus Englissh de Sutton. (Cambs.)

The surname may be omitted without a compensating description.

> Gonsales de Plymmouth portyngale. (Dev.)
> Brionis de Britannia. (Dev.)
> Janyn de Parys. (Kent.)

Forename and surname are rarely both omitted.

> Norman apud Ilfardcomb. (Dev.)

Many foreigners were described as servant of so-and-so, as (de) Johanne de Hay serviente Thome atte heth (Hants), and sometimes the alien was given his master's name, as Gillam Styler serviens Johannis Styler de Haggeley (Worc.). By some clerks the utilization of the nationality for a second name was carried to such an extreme that it defeated its object of distinction; for instance, in the Cumberland roll, 127 out of 322 persons had the " surname " Scot ; and in the Westmorland list sixty-five aliens, being no less than 62 per cent of the whole, were in like manner " identified ". A small selection of second-names will now be given, those of the first list being English in appearance, and those of the second being probably of foreign origin.

Aliens with English-Sounding Names.

Bedfordshire.—Nationalities not given : Drinkwater, Gobyon, Goldyng, Graunt, Gullyng, Hoggeherd (Hoggeberd in Hunts. Roll), Lawelesse, Pancok (see p. 139), Prendregast, Quynteyn, Wheler.

Devonshire.—*Flemings* : Nythecleff. *Frenchmen* : Cardemaker, Sadeler. *Hollanders* : Bowyer, Clokmaker, Glasier, Strete, White. *Irishmen* : Irissheman, Iryssh. *Normans* : atte Broke, Broun, Carpenter, Colyer, Goldsmith, Grene, atte Oke, Stoke, Stolemaker, Sutton, Webber. *Saxon* : Glasier.

Herefordshire.—Nationalities not given : Bygge, Hawthorne, Lacy, Sadelier, Valet.

Hertfordshire.—de la gate, atte toure, of the stable, of the kechyn.

Aliens retaining Native Names.

Devonshire.—*Bretons* : Brywer, Ewen, Galowe, Jeet, Wynnowe. *Flemings* : Gele (now Gill, Geale), Hankyn (from Johankin). *Frenchmen* : Anger (Anjou), Cadok, Fort (the strong), Greser, Mayowe (now Mayo), Meter, Parys, Peaufrere (*beau frere*, i.e. Fairbrother), Pechere (fisher, now Peacher), Premat (now Primate), la voby. *Hollanders* : Deryk, Dirykkyssone, Flyght, Gy, Perwardyne. *Irishmen* : Core, Kensale, Kymmok, Overy (? Oxf.), Patrykke. *Normans* : Base (*le bas* " the short "), Bertelot, Blanchard (O.F. " whitish "), Chasse (now Chase), Chevale (perhaps *chevaler* " horseman "), Coret, Floket, Folet (frolicsome, now Follet and perhaps Foley), Gorget, Granet, Hare (le eyr), Hughlot (now Hewlett, Howlett), Huset, Jakelyne (now Jackling), Lokke, Lotyn, Malet, Mayowe (now Mayo), Nolard, Pedde (perhaps Pedder), Petyt (the small), Senteney. Also two Welsh or Breton names : Grenowe and Howel.

Kent.—Flemings : Braban, Burghgrand, Foglyn, Pipertyn. *Frenchmen* : Achard, Bernevale, Boche (cf. Michael od la Buche—" with the mouth "—a merchant of Dieppe, 1225, Pat. R.), Bry, Eldmard. *Hollander* : van Gibse. Nationality not mentioned : Abraham and Isaac.

Surrey.—Nationalities not stated : Belbake, Blet, Cokkyll (perhaps the origin of some Cockles), Dankard, Dederyk, van Doubell (perhaps now Double, Dobell), Drye, " Drynkewater nesawde " Egmond (also van Egmond), Fek, Frandyk, Frowekyn, Henyvere (cf. Enever, Gwenever, Jenifer), Heryng, Meux, Pankake, Peek, Peterkyn, Pollewike, " Henricus Pykelheryng " a joiner), Skyppe (now Skipp), Slave, Smolle, " Alicia Spekylheryng " (a servant), Spryk (now Sprigg), Vanbroke, van Wesyll.

Sussex.—Nationalities not stated : Bendebowe, Dumberell, Ganderer, Hoogar, Lukbyns, Lorette, Merlot, van Noy, van Quabeken, Petyjon, Tankard, Trosborde, Vanolotyng, van Warrs, van Wonde, Wy, Yve.

Most of the Surrey and Sussex names appear to be from the Low Countries. In the Cambridgeshire roll were noticed the names Arbogh, Daghr, Droda, and Guthe from " de regno de Sweth " (i.e. Sweden). Several thousand of the descriptions borne by persons *non natarum Anglicanarum* correspond to common English surnames, and in many cases, no doubt, were perpetuated. Little do countless bearers of such surnames as Brown, Brooke, Bigg, Sutton, etc., realize that their progenitors in this country were foreigners, and that their surnames are of no greater antiquity than the fifteenth century.

Outlawry Rolls, 1422-83. For investigation of English names of the latter part of the Plantagenet period, namely the reigns of the Houses of Lancaster and York (1399–1485), the Outlawry Rolls provide suitable material. The exigents, ranging in rank from labourer to gentleman, are distinguished not only by forename and surname, but by their vocation as well ; and examination of the additional factor leads to the inference that surnames were not yet general in the time of Henry VI (1422–61). On a count of 1,000 entries the surnames were found in 6 per cent of cases to duplicate the trades, and, as occupational names are about 25 per cent of the whole, this figure was equivalent to about 24 per cent of the occupational names being similar to the vocation carried on by their bearers. It is suggested that this proportion is rather greater than can be explained by coincidental occurrence, and points to the probability that a number of persons were yet unsupplied with surnames, at any rate, officially, and that the want was

TABLE IX

COMPARISON OF CLASSES OF DESCRIPTIONS, ADDRESSES, AND SURNAMES PREVALENT IN TEN COUNTIES OF ENGLAND

Compiled from the Outlawry Rolls, temp. Hen. VI (1422–61)

County	Approx. No. analysed	Single Baptismal Names %	Characteristic		Local			Genealogical		Occupational		Second Names unclassified %
			Without article %	With French article %	Without preposition %	With Latin or French prepositions %	With English prepositions %	Without Relationship expressed %	With Relationship expressed %	Without article %	With French article %	
Northern— Yorkshire	100	—	5	—	34	1	—	12	—	17	—	31
Western— Staffordshire	100	—	2	—	31	—	—	17	—	21	—	29
Central— Derbyshire	120	—	8	—	37	11	1	11	—	18	—	14
Eastern— Lincolnshire	100	—	5	—	28	3	—	20	—	24	—	20
Norfolk	100	—	3	—	23	2	—	12	—	33	—	27
Suffolk	100	—	6	—	21	1	1	18	—	32	—	21
South-Eastern— Kent	100	—	8	—	23	—	—	15	—	22	—	32
Sussex	80	—	1	—	20	—	3	7	—	31	—	38
South-Western— Devonshire	100	—	12	—	15	—	1	24	—	17	—	31
Wiltshire	100	—	6	—	17	—	—	22	—	38	—	17
Totals	1000	—	6	—	25	2	—	17	—	25	—	25

P.R.O. Reference K.B. 29, 91.

made up by trade-names with almost the same prodigality as has been noticed with the ethnic adjective Scot. In some cases the similarity of second names and trade was even more pronounced, for instance, of sixty Wiltshire insurgents who were exacted in 32 Henry VI, no less than thirteen had surname corresponding to trade. Some typical examples from the roll of Henry VI are :—

> Richard Corveser, corveser.
> Laurence Laborer, laborer.
> Robert Lokyer, locksmith.
> Richard Goldsmith, goldsmith.
> Richard Dykere, " pondere and dykere."

In cases where considerable bodies of men followed the same calling, and this method of distinction would have failed in its object, it was not adopted ; for instance, lists of fishers or mariners provided no one with the surname Fisher or Mariner, although all had second names. Sometimes name and trade did not exactly correspond, although having the same sense, as Robert Doubeletmaker, taillour. Certain entries (22 Hen. VI) show what is perhaps a transition stage, persons having a surname as well as a trade-name :—

Johannes Baker alias Brasyeter of Barnalstapyll (Barnstaple, Dev.), brasyeter (probably *braciator* " brewer ").

Ricardus Lok de Minty alias dictus Ricardus Crokker de Mynty Glouc.), crokker.

Lodewicus William de Taunton (Soms.), toker al' d'cus lodowicus Toker nup' de Tyuerton (Dev.), yoman.

Too much stress must not be laid on the similarity of second name and vocation, such likeness being not more than an indicator pointing to the possibility of surnames still wanting among some of the tradesmen. Even at the present day men with well known surnames are commonly addressed by their profession or trade, as Doctor, Skipper, Padre, Farmer, etc., and four centuries ago the practice may have been more prevalent, when the real surnames, not being strongly established, may have been set aside easily. There must have been also many instances where a man succeeded to a trade as well as to a corresponding surname :—

Johannes Taillour filius Roberti Taillour, taillour.

Quite possibly the family name and business had descended together for several generations, and that Taillour in this example was an established surname.

Alternative surnames might be words with the same signification :—

Thomas Schawer de villa de Halesworth alias dictus Thomas Barber, husbandman. (Schawer is an obsolete form of shaver.)

The official view regarding hereditary surnames in the second half of the fifteenth century may be gathered from an Act of Parliament, 1465 (see p. 426), designed to force Irishmen to take English appellatives which were to be of town, colour, art, or office, that is of the three classes, local, characteristic, and occupational, and the designation so adopted was *to be retained as a family name*. Genealogical surnames are not mentioned, being impermissible because they would have perpetuated Irish personal names, thereby defeating the intention of stamping out everything Irish within the Pale.

The particular features of the descriptions and surnames of the reign of Edw. IV, and their relative distribution throughout the country, will be gathered from table X.

Subsidy Roll, A.D. 1523. For English names of the early fifteenth century excellent lists are provided by the assessments of taxpayers for the fifteenth of 15 Hen. VIII. A selection of twelve representative counties has been made, and an analysis of the names tabulated (p. 199), making comparison with previous lists convenient. It is evident at first sight that the employment of the article *le* in characteristic and occupational descriptions had been at last completely abandoned, as had the use of the preposition *de* in local names. It is noticeable that Kent, always a stronghold for the *atte*-names, is responsible mainly for their preservation.

Even in the sixteenth century surnames were not always known to the clerk, and are, therefore, by no means general in the rolls, as the following extracts illustrate :—

Barnard an Esterlingborne ; Robert the bocher ; Dunkyn a Skot ; Thomas his Shepard ; John his thresher ; Lowes thresher.

The names, generally speaking, except for archaic orthography, are like those of the twentieth century, but there are to be found a few local names with English prepositions, amounting to less than 1 per cent of the total, and in the counties bordering on Wales the use of *ap* to express relationship in the genealogical descriptions was still prevalent. It is thought to be unnecessary to give examples of the names found on these rolls.

Influence of the Reformation. The great and widespread movement in the Western Church, by which the religion was changed from Roman Catholicism to Protestantism, commenced in the fifteenth century, gathering strength in the early sixteenth, too late to have any direct effect in moulding surnames, although it greatly influenced the nature of our christian names. Indirectly, however, religious persecution, by driving foreigners to seek sanctuary in this country, was the cause of the introduction of a number of new surnames, a

TABLE X

COMPARISON OF CLASSES OF DESCRIPTIONS, ADDRESSES, AND SURNAMES PREVALENT IN ELEVEN COUNTIES OF ENGLAND

Compiled from the Outlawry Rolls, temp. Edw. IV (1461–83)

County	Approx. No. analysed	Single Baptismal Names %	Characteristic		Local			Genealogical		Occupational		Second Names unclassified %
			Without article %	With French article %	Without preposition %	With Latin or French prepositions %	With English prepositions %	Without Relationship expressed %	With Relationship expressed %	Without article %	With French article %	
Northern— Yorkshire	100	—	2	—	32	6	1	14	—	18	—	27
Western— Staffordshire	100	—	5	—	32	—	—	10	1*	26	—	26
Central— Middlesex	100	—	5	—	30	2	—	25	—	18	—	20
Derbyshire	100	—	1	—	36	6	—	10	—	21	—	26
Eastern— Lincolnshire	70	—	2	—	40	—	—	12	—	21	—	25
Norfolk	100	—	2	—	35	—	—	8	—	21	—	34
Suffolk	100	—	4	—	31	—	—	12	—	29	—	24
South-Eastern— Kent	70	—	7	—	26	—	2	19	—	22	—	24
South-Western— Cornwall	100	—	—	—	36	—	—	20	—	13	—	31
Devonshire	100	—	3	—	21	—	3	26	—	22	—	25
Somersetshire	100	—	6	—	14	—	2	24	2*	18	—	34
Totals	1040	—	4	—	30	—	1	16	—	21	—	28

* With Welsh *ap*.

P.R.O. Reference K.B. 29, 113.

good proportion of which were preserved, although often corrupted into anglicized versions.

By the Act of Richard III (1483–4) aliens had been debarred from employing any but native assistants in their occupations, which disability led to the foreign tradesmen establishing themselves in various liberties, as St. Martin's le Grand, Blackfriars, the Savoy, Southwark, St. Katherine's, Westminster, and other privileged places, where the officers of the crown and of the Mayor and Corporation could not disturb them.[1] Due to the encouragement given by Henry VII (1485–1509), and an appreciation of art and learning displayed by the Tudor Court, great numbers of foreigners, distinguished persons as well as tradesmen, settled not only in London, but also, as has been evidenced above, in the eastern and southern counties.   By the time Henry VIII commenced his reign (1509), a numerous foreign population had become resident in England : Low Countrymen, Frenchmen, Germans, Spaniards, and Italians, to name a few, and foreign immigration continued to be encouraged by the Crown. In considerable measure due to the beneficial example set by the enterprising and industrious foreigner, the natural wealth of the country was exploited, and England became the leading manufacturing country of the world.

Throughout the sixteenth century further increase in our alien population was the result of the growing religious persecution on the Continent. In 1510 discontent with papal authority, and " the oppressive burdens imposed by the ecclesiastics ", led to popular disturbances, culminating in the launching by Luther of the Reformation, an event generally dated 1518. During 1512–14 England was at war against the allied forces of France and Scotland, which misunderstanding considerably accentuated the already existing ill-feeling against foreigners, although it did not entirely stop the immigration.[2] Notwithstanding that the Act, De Heretico cumburendo, was still in force, and Lutheranism opposed by the country, religious refugees continued to find their way into the eastern counties, among them being numbers of Scots who had accepted the doctrine of the reformed religion.[3] Aliens, whether denizens or not, paid double the impositions levied from natives, and in the rolls their names are generally set out separately. In 1534 the Church of England was entirely severed from papal authority, the establishment of the reformed religion being followed by a great increase in letters of denization to

---

[1] Letters of Denization, ed. by W. Page (Huguenot Soc.), vol. viii, vi; from which useful volume I have derived much information.
[2] Letters and Papers, Hen. VIII, vol. ii, Preface.
[3] History of England, by J. A. Froude, 1873, vol. iv, p. 63.

TABLE XI

COMPARISON OF CLASSES OF DESCRIPTIONS, ADDRESSES, AND SURNAMES PREVALENT IN TWELVE COUNTIES OF ENGLAND

Compiled from the Subsidy Rolls, A.D. 1523

Descriptions, Addresses, and Surnames

P.R.O. Reference	County	Division	Approx. No. analysed	Single Baptismal Names %	Characteristic Without article %	Characteristic With French article %	Local Without preposition %	Local With Latin or French prepositions %	Local With English prepositions %	Genealogical Without Relationship expressed %	Genealogical With Relationship expressed %	Occupational Without article %	Occupational With French article %	Second Names unclassified %
E 179	Northern—													
130/96	Lancashire	West Derby Hd.	100	—	3	—	56	—	—	8	—	10	—	23
212/108	Yorkshire	Pickering Lythe	150	—	3	—	17	—	—	29	—	20	—	31
	Western—													
117/93	Herefordshire	Hereford City	200	—	5	—	21	—	—	18	19*	15	—	22
166/123	Shropshire	S. Bradford Hd.	100	—	5	—	34	—	—	26	—	10	—	25
	Central—													
71/110	Bedfordshire	Flitt Hd.	100	—	13	—	22	—	1	24	—	16	—	24
165/112	Rutlandshire	East Hd.	200	—	13	—	29	—	—	25	—	17	—	16
	Eastern—													
136/313	Lincolnshire	Skirbeck Wap	100	—	4	—	36	—	—	17	—	21	—	22
180/154	Suffolk	Loes Hd.	200	—	1	—	18	—	—	20	—	26	—	35
	South-Eastern—													
124/196	Kent	Westgate Hd.	300	—	2	—	20	—	4	33	—	13	—	29
189/157	Sussex	Chichester Rape	200	—	3	—	21	—	—	23	—	32	—	21
	South-Western—													
87/128	Cornwall	Powder Hd.	100	—	2	—	24	—	—	46	—	2	—	26
96/153	Devonshire	Plympton and Roborough Hds.	200	—	3	—	33	—	—	24	—	17	—	23
		Totals	1950	—	5	—	25	—	1	25	2	17	—	25

* With Welsh *ap*.

Frenchmen as well as Germans. According to the Subsidy
Rolls of 1540, no less than one-third of the population of
London was then alien ; in some parts of the city there being
practically no Englishmen at all !

With the accession of Edward VI (1547) greater freedom
of religious tenets was tolerated, while in France and the
Netherlands the ecclesiastics carried on their unmerciful
persecution with increased vigour. Fugitives continued to
inundate this country, causing bitter complaints and threats
from the native artizans, whose trade suffered severely under
the growth of competition. During Mary's brief reign the
persecutions brought about by the re-establishment of the
Roman Catholic religion acted as a deterrent to incoming
foreigners, although few were driven out of the country, and
in 1558, with the accession of Elizabeth, the hopes of the
reformers again revived.

Huguenots. Adherents to the movement of the Reformation,
called Huguenots, had grown in such numbers in France
that they formed a strong political party. Attempts to
exterminate them failed, but continued persecution by the
Roman Catholics led to civil war and laws of great severity,
leading to unbridled slaughter, resulting in wholesale flight
of the Protestants. The fearful tortures and butchery which
took place in Flanders led to thousands of Netherlanders
seeking refuge in England, and following upon the perpetration
of the terrible massacre of St. Bartholomew (1572), hordes of
Frenchmen came over the Channel. Enumeration in 1577
showed that in that year there were in London alone, among
the unnaturalized foreigners, 2,302 Dutchmen, 1,838 Frenchmen, and 116 Italians, presumably the heads of households,
and it has to be remembered that countless thousands of others,
in the past, had become denizens and their children native-
born Britishers.[1]

The successors of Elizabeth continued to be benevolent
to the exiles, and the passing of the Edict of Nantes (1598)
permitting religious liberty to the Protestants did not induce
the foreigners to leave England, although it stayed the flow
of refugees. After the annulment of the edict (1685), accompanied by a revival of the terror, harassed people in large
numbers again sought asylum in England, Weiss estimating
that in ten years " prior or subsequent to the revocation
80,000 Frenchmen established themselves in England." [2]
Numerous churches were built to accommodate the increasing

[1] The Bishop of London's certificate, 1567, gives within the city 3,760
strangers, and in out-parishes, 1,091. The names and nationalities are in
Lansd. MSS. x, No. 5.

[2] *History of the French Protestant Refugees*, by M. C. Weiss (transl. by H. W.
Herbert, 1854), vol. i, p. 249.

body of religionists, and, with their own registers kept by their own countrymen, many of their native names have been preserved.

The immigrants were not only Frenchmen; for instance, in the *Diary of Abraham de la Pryme* it is recorded that in the year 1689 " there landed at Hull about six or seven thousand Dains, all stout fine men . . . they liked England very well . . . and many swore that they would be hanged before they would leave it." That two of the party named Straker and Bellow did not leave, the burial register of St. Mary's, Beverley is witness.[1] Possibly other Danish names were introduced, adding to the variety of English nomenclature.

Numbers of the French refugees passed into Scotland, the French tongue being spoken in a colony in Edinburgh ; and several thousands went to Ireland, and others, again, sought peace and freedom in America.[2]

The names of the Dutchmen, Walloons, and Frenchmen abound throughout Britain, although now often corrupted past recognition. An interesting study of the alien appellatives is provided by the records of the persons who obtained *ex donatione regis* letters patent making them English subjects, and admitting them to citizenship. Letters of denization and Acts of Naturalization were frequently not applied for until many years after arrival in this country, by which time the alien had often acquired an English name, so that it must not be concluded that the names in these documents are those brought from their native lands. A selection of sixteenth-century names follows :—

Belgium.—Birde, Pilgrome.

Brabant.—Brunell, Nolans.

Brittany.—Androwe, Creeke, Fillpot (i.e. Philipot), Haye, Jurden, Kirgriste, Lovewell, Mee, Parchement, Parre, Peat, Pedreneck, Pelygryne, Person (probably Piers-son), Pevenger, Plynner, Popyn, Rawe, Sanker, Stookey, Swerneck.

Burgundy.—Ashen.

Denmark.—Peterson.

Flanders.—Boome, Fysche, Hornebolte, Lotyn, Mace, Pavyllion, Pope, Raven.

France.—Almande, Asshe, Averell, Barre, Bashley, Basse, Belhatch, Bendebowe, Blancke, Bocok, Bouchier, Bryant, Burges, Bylett, Campe, Cann, Carioun, Carowe, Casher, Codde, Cotton, Crewell, Fever, Folet, Galiard, Gavell, Gotter, Grace, Groundesell, Herault, Holwigge, Hotlofte, Isle, Lashe, Lovly, Lyster, Mallard, Mallet, Martell, Maunsell, Melly, Motton, Myer, Osanne, Paymente, Peers, Perago, Peryn, Philpot, Pigyon, Pitwell, Pomerell, Potte, Quesnell, Servile, Shale, Shell, Shower, Shynyng, Sorrell, Turkey, Vergyn, Vowtier.

[1] Surtees Soc., vol. liv, pp. 16–17.

[2] *History of Protestant Refugees in England*, by J. S. Burn, 1846, pp. 19, 247.

Germany.—Austyne, Bakeman, Bakeoven, Berkemayer, Blounte, Boick, Bone, Booste, Brande, Bucke, Budde, Bullock, Busshe, Campe, Casee, Cave, Cayle, Cherrye, Conrad, Coppe, Coster, Flude, Flowre, Fortune, Fulwater, Geale, Gerle, Gobby, Gravy, Grysell, Harte, Hewyngson, Heyns, Hiolibusche, Huskyn, Kersken, Madman, Maye, Mosse, Mynter, Nayle, Neale, Otten, Peters, Prinsell, Puck, Quene, Randyke, Ratteler, Resling, Rippe, Rooke, Saltpeter, Schutt, Skelliwick, Skinke, Spilman, Starkey, Stepkin, Strickman, Talman, Tappy, Tenwalle, Vallance, Wolff, Wyman.

Holland.—Heather, Kester, Kors, Kyshaven, Leven, Mors, Noster, Pelsor, Petyrs, Roo, Sumpes, Vandelveld.

Italy.—Balby, Capone, Cavalari, Lomelino, Marruffo, Mercandini, Palavicino, Penny, Penison, Portynary, Ristico, Rizzo, Runcone, Salvaigo, Zenzano.

Normandy.—Alder, Alexander, Baron, Belhome, Blendmore, Blunder, Bonett, Boyle, Brace, Braye, Brayne, Cannell, Cant, Ferret, Fey, Flame, Foole, Goose, Goslyn, Guffey, Gunner, Hull, Jacquett, Kayne, Larcher, Large, Lever, Lovet, Meryk, Mettell, Mouse, Over, Pavier, Phesaunt, Pillorye, Pinchard, Planke, Poldon, Pullen, Pullett, Pyppen, Shapell, Sparrowe, Stowell, Tryvet, Veale, Violet.

Portugal.—Fermandres, Gunsalves, Pierreas, Rodriges.

Scotland.—Armstrong, Beake, Birde, Blare, Bolden, Fender, Fyndelason (Findlayson), Garden, Gryme, Higge, Lawdar, Little, Logye, Maxwell, Meldrum, Morris, Norrey, Paterson, Penven, Purves, Ramsey, Rosse, Rufforth, Saunders, Sutherland, Tate, Twynam, Twythy.

Spain.—Arnold, Barker, Barrett, Baykeman, Bond, Boquett, Bowerman, Boyes, Brickeman, Brickette, Brickstone, Brussel, Byen, Canon, Capell, Cilly, Cordier, Corne, Crabbey, Crane, Drake, Fosse, Frolicke, Garret, Hake, Hayette, Helden, Holewater, Hua, Huicke, Jurnett, Keye, Kiele, Knockarde, Knotte, Lambright, Late, Lopes, Lowe, Molyn, Morte, Mutton, Noblett, Nowell, Orman, Papen, Pau, Peters, Piser, Place, Pokel, Poole, Potelberghe, Profett, Quickelbergh, Rabelo, Raperlye, Riche, Rutter, Salynes, Samyn, Satler, Shillinge, Skant, Somers, Stirpe, Sublar, Swallowe, Trumper, Vigereux, Zeghers.

Turkey.—Bye.

This list of names is only a 5 per cent selection, but is sufficient to illustrate the English appearance of many names of the foreigners, confirming conclusions arrived at above (p. 193), that large numbers of apparently good old English names are of foreign origin, and have no antiquity in this country. Names with English sounds, like Blunder, Cherrye, Crewell, Fever, Gravy, Groundsell, Lovly, Mutton, Penny, Shynyng, Trumper, etc., are typical of those which are commonly classed as sobriquets, being seldom suspected of a seventeenth-century alien introduction or manufacture.

Parish Registers. Prior to the dissolution of religious houses in 1536, it had been customary to enter in various books of the monasteries, notes of births, marriages, and deaths of benefactors and their families ; and this partial system of registration seems to have satisfied all requirements, but the dispersal and destruction of the monastic libraries, and the necessity arising for the provision of other means of recording the domestic happenings led to one of the most important events in the history of British surnames, namely the establishment of permanent parish registers.[1] Although these books seem to have been kept very irregularly, they must have had a great influence in fixing the surnames, which otherwise would rarely have been recorded, officially, or in a manner available for ready reference. It was not always possible to enter surnames, even at a comparative late date, but the parson did his best to provide identifying designations :—

" Bacchus *alias* Hogtub *alias* Fat Jack *alias* John from Ld. Clive at Claremont, buried 1772." Esher Par. Reg.

It is not proposed to give examples of names from the English registers, but the following selections, from the lists of members of the foreign churches, will be found of interest :—

Members of the Dutch Church, 1550–67.—Aels, Appel, Asse, Backerheel, Backers, Beetz, Beile, Bellyns, Bitter, Bommers, Boucket, Brand, Buckeleere, Clefs, Cleyne, Cram, Cramer, Doffany, Doulcet, Drake, Dregge, Drubbele, Ente, Fogge, Fyte, Garbes, Hacke, Hauwe, Heckles, Kiets, Kinge, Lamant, Languor, Lint, Lubbers, Makereel, Matte, Mesmaker, Moon, Myrman, Noots, Paasch, Pape, Patmore, Peregryn, Pieckeman, Pinkman, Potfliet, Pottes, Prophietts, Pryns, Putman, Questy, Rabbat, Rae, Roeter, Rouke, Rudders, Sauarie, Scheck, Schellynck, Slyper, Smolders, Stamp, Stell, Streeck, Stryper, Sturm, Sun, Swer, Swerds, Swingdau, Sylt, Taalman, Tack, de Turck, Veel, Vernun, Visch, Vlesch, Warneck, Wauters, Welter.[2]

Members of the French Church, 1568.—Bison, Boulle, Buding, Bultel, Caille, Cambier, Caron, Carton, le Cat, Chabot, Chappel, Chaudron, le Chien, Clinquart, Clote, Cruel, Dary, le Febure, Flock, Fontaine, le Gay, Gruel, Hayette, Honnore, Houinne, Journet, Masse, Mondon, Mouton, Panmart, Plucquet, Quentin, Regiment, Rocquet, de la Rue, Sellen, Siret, Tacquet, Toupet, Vallin, Verret.[3]

Again, there are to be noticed numerous names which would not be suspected of foreign origin, and so also in the following list of Dutchmen and Flemings :—

Return of Strangers in London, 1571.—Backhouse, Barkeman, Battale, Berry, Blackberd, Boden, Bowman, Box, Breakpott, Brinck, le Buck, Buffe, Bulltayle, Carman, Collye, Corne, Cradell, Cure, Curtain, Dayfelowe, Denman, Firkin, Frolick, Fulwater, Garetson, Garrett, Gisling, Goseman, Grenechese, Haley, Hensbane, Hewen, Hilloke, Hurte, Hye, Jagars, Key, de Kinge, Lambright, Lamott, Lin, Lyon,

---

[1] *The History of Parish Registers*, by J. S. Burn, 1829.
[2] Huguenot Soc., vol. x, pt. 1.
[3] Ibid.

Lyst, Lytten, Money, Mosse, Paddie, Phenix, Pipler, Pluckett, Pynner, Restinge, Rutter, Serfe, Shorneback, Skarre, Skipper, Smartes, Snowke, Spekehard, Squire, Stackey, Starke, Stilman, Stonehart, Stout, Stuffott, Tape, Tressell, Tressey, Trewe, Tuller, Turpintyne, Walscott, Welder, Wente, Whitley, Wier.[1]

Dutchmen in Essex.

The south-eastern counties received large numbers of foreigners, and the following selection of names of denizens of Brabant and Flanders, who settled in Essex in the sixteenth and seventeenth centuries, will show that many of their names, if not already English, were so near to English words, names, and places that in a generation or so they were almost bound to become to all appearances English, and, in the twentieth century, the occasion of many conjectures and futile guesses at their probable origin.

Ache, Acker, Balde, Balke, Baske, Bastian, Beake, Bell, Bellecher, Bibber, Biscop, Block, Boone, Boule, Boys, Breame, Breyne, Briell or Brill, Broecke or Brooker, Buke, Bul, Bulke, Burkijn, de Burt, Bussche, Calven, Candle, Cavell, Clack, Clarebout, Clocker, Cnockart, Coel, Colman, Cool, Corte, Courtman, Covell, Crane, Cricket, Crocket, Dal, Decker, Deewe, Dover, Dributter, Dros, le Duc, Engels, Everaert, Fenney, Ferryman, Fever, Fitch, Fitse, Foller, Fox, Freburn, Frost, Gaarner, Gage, Geselle, Godschalk, Gomme, Gonner, Graaf or Grave, Gravestein, Grenerice, Griekson, Gurney, Haene, Hakke, Hartley, Havens, Hawes, de Haze, Herring, Hoorne, Housick, Hovaer, Hovell, Hull, Hure, Ingram, January, Jenner, Jude, Julaer, Kandle, Keere, Kibble, Kingsmill, Kinley, Kirck, Klerck, Knapwood, Kock, Koning, Kool, Krecket, Langelee, Loftus, Marygold, Meijnaer, Merils, Milbancke, Millecan, Morteer, Mott, Neece, Nutman, Ovaer, Painter, Pekker, Pille, Pollard, Popular, Prime, Provost, de Queecker, Rebow, Regar, Rijckewaert or Rickward, Roe, Rolfe, Roode, Ruse, Ruyting, Sallarde, Salter, Sanders, Schaft, Seaton, Sise, Sitters, Snees, Soone, Stope, Tibald, Torre, Trezel, Trooster, Usher, Vereken, Vergeins, Vool, Wade, Waele, Watzon, Weale, Weller, Wevels, Whale, Wick, Wicken, de Wilde, de Wine, Zelous, Zenner.[2]

Walloons in the Fenland.

Colonies of French or Walloon Protestant refugees became established in the Fen Country, where from their experience of drainage, gained in the Low Countries, they proved of assistance to the great Dutch engineer, Vermuyden, in carrying out his enterprise of reclaiming the inundated land. The names of some of these industrious and courageous people have been preserved in the baptismal register of the Abbey Church at Thorney (Cambs.), from which the following selection is taken :—

Alis, Amory, de Barge, Born, Brassar, Brimbell, Cage, Caillet, Cas, Clays, Coclar, Copland, Cornut, Doby, Domsen, Doré, Dornelle, Egar,

---

[1] Huguenot Soc.. vol. x, pt. i.
[2] *Register of Baptisms in the Dutch Church at Colchester*, ed. by W. J. C. Moens (Huguenot Soc., vol. xii).

le Fevre, Fleurbaye, Flour, Fontaine, Frouchar, Gante, le Grain, Guibson, le Haire, Hanot, Harle, Hecklin, Hennin, Hennoc, Lansel, Latté, Lermit, Lisy, Manié or Money, Masengarbe, Milvil, Minet, Notteau, Otter, Paren or Parent, Pierson, Pinchon, le Pla, Plancq, Potier, du Quesne, Quince, Ramery, Ris, de Riviere, le Roy, de la Rue, Salmon, Sauvage, Scribau, Six, Smacq, le Talle, Tery, Ugil, Venins, Wantier, Wattier, Zombre.[1]

Influence of Religion. The first printed version of the Bible to attain popularity among the masses was the Geneva or " Breeches Bible ", which appeared in 1560 ; the effect of the production being that the personal names of the people underwent a complete change, and parish registers so far as the personal names were concerned, in some cases, read like a muster of the natives of Palestine. The new fashion was, however, too late to affect the making of our surnames, otherwise we should labour under a great number of Hebrew names : instead of our plain Roberts, Jones, or Williams, our directories would be enlivened with such sparkling labels as Kerenhappuch, Melchisedek, or Shadrach. The extreme to which the craze for biblical names was carried led ignorant people into foolish errors, which is well illustrated by the story of the puritan who, believing that it was meet and proper to call his dog by a biblical appellative, named it " Moreover ", after the canine in the Gospel : " Moreover the dog came and licked his sores." [2]

According to Fuller, about 1564 the name " Puritans " was first given to such clergymen of the Church of England who declined to subscribe to the liturgy, ceremonies, and discipline as arranged by the bishops under the direction of Archbishop Parker, and later on the name was applied to laity as well as ecclesiastics. The sect gave most odd names to their children, as Much-Mercye, Increased, Sin-denie, Fear-not, borne by the offspring of the minister of Warbleton, in whose registers from 1585 to 1600, according to Bardsley, there are more than a hundred examples of eccentric puritanism.[3] This writer, who has fully exploited the singularities and humour of puritan nomenclature, cites such outrageous appellatives as Acts-Apostles Pegden, and Pontius Pilate Pegden, both of the same family ; Lamentation Chapman, and Safe-on-high Hopkinson ; a particularly unlucky infant, born out of wedlock, being labelled Flie-fornication, and a foundling, who did not live long to be burdened with the

---

[1] *Register of Baptisms of the French Church at Thorney*, ed. by H. Peet (Huguenot Soc., vol. xvii).
[2] *Curiosities of Puritan Nomenclature*, by C. W. Bardsley, p. 55. It adds to the humour of the worthy Canon's story to know that the correct reading is " dogs " (Luke xvi, 21).
[3] Ibid., p. 122.

distinction, Job-rakt-out-of-the-ashes. Fortunate, indeed, it is that family names had become settled prior to this phase of absurdity, and there was no chance of such atrocities becoming surnominal.

Welsh Descriptions and Surnames. In Wales the native and English systems of naming, as illustrated above, continued side by side, and there was no wholesale adoption of the English method ; but the thousands of Welshmen coming into England readily assumed or accepted surnames, as has been demonstrated by numerous examples in Chapter VI. It is to be noted that the Welshmen were sometimes known by two descriptions concurrently, Welsh and English respectively, as may be exemplified by extracts from pardons for the first year of Hen. VIII :—

David ap Jeuan *alias* David Parker.
Maurice Flood or Lloid *alias* Walshman *alias* Apowell.
Owen Holand *alias* Owen ap John ap Howell Holant.
Maurice Glyne or Glynne *alias* Maurice ap Robert ap Meredyth ap Hulkyn Lloyt.
Hugh Apholwall, Awell, Aput Halwell or Aphalwell.
Richard Lawrence, Laurence, or Larrance *alias* Richard filz Laurencii ap Howelles *alias* Richard Howellys *alias* Richard ap Laurence ap Howellys ap Griffyth ap David.[1]

An illustration of the later immigration and settlement (sixteenth to eighteenth century) is afforded by the parish registers of Ongar (Essex), where the following surnames may be found :—

Binion, Davies, Evans, Ewin, Fuellin, Gowers, Gryffin, Gualter, Gwin, Jankin, Jones, Lewis, Lloyd, Meredith, Morice, Onion, Owen, Powel, Price, Reese, Rice, Roberts, Traherne, Wallis, Williams.

Although all these people have surnames after the English custom, it cannot be doubted that most of them were of Welsh extraction, and the entries evidence the way in which Welshmen had spread over England, until now there is hardly a town of any size without its Evans or Owen.

The ancient Welsh system of genealogical naming was misunderstood by Englishmen and Scotsmen, being looked upon by them as a laughable topic, worthy of the construction of humorous tales or grotesque verse. Cheese, for instance, has been ludicrously defined as :—

" Adam's own cousin-german by its birth
Ap curds ap milk ap cow ap grass ap earth."

Even Sir Walter Scott, in *Wamba's Song*, makes the Widow of Wycombe bid " Sir David ap Morgan ap Griffith

[1] *Letters and Papers, F. and D.*, Hen. VIII, vol. i, pp. 206 et seq.

ap Hugh ap Tudor ap Rhice " wend his way as " one widow for so many was too few ".[1] In the historical play of Sir John Old-castle (1600) a Welshman offered as surety " Her coozen ap Ries ap Euan ap Morrice ap Morgan ap Lluellyn ap Madoc ap Meredith ap Griffen ap Dauy ap Owen ap Shinken Shones ". The judge replied : " Two of the most sufficient are ynow." Whereupon the Sheriff explained : " And't please your lord-ship these are al but one." [2] According to a humorous versifier another judge (evidently the Bishop of Lichfield, c. 1540 ; see below, p. 387), said he would no longer stand the Welsh method of genealogical naming :—

> " Take ten," he said, " and call them Rice ;
> Take other ten, and call them Price ;
> Take fifty others, call them Pughes ;
> A hundred more, I'll dub them Hughes ;
> Now Roberts name some hundred score ;
> And Williams name a legion more ;
> And call," he moaned in languid tones,
> " Call all the other thousands—Jones." [3]

Referring to parish registers it appears that, in the sixteenth century, one-third of the people still adhered to the native system of naming. Taking the Conway registers, for instance, of the first 260 marriages and burials (1541–58), 37 per cent of the persons were named after the Welsh style. This enumeration is supported by a deposition of Erasmus Powell, vicar of Clun, in 1629, who affirmed :—

" that in some partes of Wales the christen names of the Fathers are the surnames of the children, but are not generally soe ; but more are named by their fathers' surnames then by their christen names." [4]

A nineteenth-century observer, " during repeated and lengthy tarryings in Merionethshire, that Wales of Wales, was more than once assured, with examples of the practice, that

---

[1] *Ivanhoe*, 1820, vol. iii, 245.
[2] *Tudor Facsimile Texts*, ed. by J. S. Farmer (1911).
[3] *Bye-gones*, 11th October, 1893, p. 198.
[4] In the earliest Book of Depositions left in the Diocesan Registry at Hereford. *Notes and Queries*, 1st Sept., 1894, p. 166. A later investigator, the editor of the *Llantilio Crossenny and Penrhos* (*Monm.*), J. A. Bradney (1916) is possibly not so correct when he observes that " in the early seventeenth century the use of surnames was only just beginning to come into vogue in Wales ". Another writer (A. N. Palmer, in the *Antiquary*, vol. xv, p. 144) is perhaps not too exact either, summing up as follows : " Few Welsh surnames are of earlier date than the sixteenth century, but they were adopted during that century, and the first quarter of the century following, by the greater part of the gentry, by nearly all the members of the learned professions, by most of the richer tradesfolk, and by many others. The mass of the people, however, long clung to the older Welsh system of personal nomenclature, or to a modification of that system ; and surnames as we understand them were not, in some parts of Wales, definitely established until the beginning of the present century " (nineteenth).

it was still far from a rare thing for a son to take a christian name of his father as a surname for himself ; thus an offspring of Robert Williams (his neighbours of the same tribe being very numerous) would be styled William Roberts, and the son of Hugh Evans might become Evan Hughes." [1]   Another writer gives the following example, also illustrating the unfixed system of surnames : " Evan Thomas married Gwen Jones, and had by her three sons, Howel, Hugh, and Owen.   The eldest definitely adopted his father's patronymic as a true surname, and called himself Howel Thomas ; the second made a patronymic for himself out of his father's christian name, and called himself Hugh Evans ; while the third took, as a true surname, the patronymic of his mother, and called himself Owen Jones." [2]

In Wales there is little variety among native surnames, since they are nearly all of the genealogical class, and, in order to aid distinction, a custom has grown of bestowing the mother's maiden name as a christian name ; and for the subsequent generation to couple the two by hyphen.   There are a great number of these " double-barrelled " names among Welshmen, but, of course, they may likewise be found elsewhere.   Regarding additional names for distinction, the following note by a Welsh barrister (1893) is of interest :—

" A new and bright future appears to be dawning with regard to our Welsh surnames ; preparations for its advent have been going on for the last fifteen or twenty years, and any reader of the vernacular press must admit that they are continually pressing. We refer to the double names which some three or four hundred Welsh preachers and ministers of the Gospel have taken up. They add to their parents' surname an old Welsh personal name or a place-name, such as the name of their house or of their native parish, or of some hill or river in the neighbourhood where they passed their boyhood, or where they then happened to be residing. The following are a few well-known illustrations : Cynddylan Jones, Rhondda Williams, Elvet Lewis, Cadvan Davies, Herber Evans, Ffrwdwen Lewis, etc." [3]

The practice is found as early as 1753, and is not confined to preachers, but has been adopted by members of parliament, lawyers, doctors, musicians, etc., and still continues.

As having a possible bearing on the popularity of the native system of naming it may be of interest to note that in 1911, the population of Wales being 2,420,921, there were returned as Welsh speakers 977,366 persons over the age of three years, of whom 190,292 could speak no other language.

Scottish Names and Descriptions, A.D. 1541.   A list of

---

[1] *Notes and Queries*, 13th October, 1894, p. 293.
[2] A. N. Palmer (*Antiquary*, vol. xv, p. 147).
[3] T. E. Morris, in *Bye-gones*, 11th October, 1893, p. 197.

parishioners of Kilmacronack in Muckarne, obtained from a notarial instrument, illustrates the names of the West Highlands in the sixteenth century. As befits a formal document the names are partly latinized :—

Nigellus Joannis Mc Kennich ; Dugallus Nigelli ; Nigellus Donaldi vic Dunlewe ; Dugallus Donaldi Nigelli vic Awlai ; Anna dominici Cristini ; Gillespik Mac Gillespik vic Achem pych ; Karistina nein a doura ; Gillespik Mac Gillemore ; Gillefeilan Donaldi Macgillebane ; Cristinus Maelmore vic gillelan ; Nicolaus Johannis Sartoris ; Gillemichel Martini ; Joannes Glass Mac Gillemore vic indowra ; Dugallus Mac Gillechallum vic Philippi ; Efrica dominici vic Calman ; Katerina Vicarii Joannis Patricii vic Achromone ; Finlaus Martini vic Gillindach ; Joannes Mc Gillespic vic choan ; Gillecrist duf Mac Philip ; Joannes niger Collini vic Philip ; Finlaus fullo ; Joannes Duncani nigri fabri Katerina Columbi vic Gillebride ; Donaldus Sartoris ; Duncanus Joannis Duncani Sartoris ; Joannes Joannis Duncani vic Torcatall ; Duncanus bane mac Rowane ; Gillebride mac lucas ; Joannes Glass pectoris Mariota fabri ; Mora nein a doura ; Effririca fullonis ; Cristina fullonis ; Finlaus Macheath ; Archibaldus Jonis Sartoris ; Katerina fabri, etc.[1]

The friendly intercourse with England increasing, the tendency was to adopt the simpler system of naming which had become general among the English, although the Gaelic names have remained, having become fixed as family names, before the decline of the native language. From 1603 onwards, various proposals were made for the incorporation of the two kingdoms under one government, but not until 1707 was the Treaty of Union confirmed by the Scottish Parliament. A very small proportion of the people of Scotland are now purely Gaelic speakers, the decline being illustrated by the census figures for 1911, when the population of Scotland was 4,760,904, of whom 183,998 were returned as Gaelic speakers, 18,400 speaking no English.

In 1863, when the population of Scotland was estimated at 3,101,345 persons, the numbers bearing the twelve principal surnames were respectively as follow :—

Smith	44,200	Robertson	31,200	Anderson	26,500
McDonald	36,600	Stewart	30,600	Scott	22,400
Brown	33,800	Campbell	30,200	Miller	21,400
Thomson	31,200	Wilson	29,300	McKenzie [2]	21,300

The number of Scotts are perhaps most worthy of comment. (See p. 192.)

Irish Names and Descriptions, A.D. 1603. Irish surnames, spread throughout the world as they are, form an important section of the study of British names, and although it has only

[1] Hist. MSS. Comm., App. 2nd Rept., p. 193.
[2] *Twelfth Annual Report of the Registrar-General for Scotland.*

been possible to give a brief outline of their formation and signification, it is hoped that the main principles have been clearly stated.[1] In 1465 an attempt had been made by Act of Parliament to force the Irish living within the Pale to live like Englishmen, and to take English names (see pp. 196 and 426), and numbers of natives did anglicize their native appellatives, such changes occurring, for instance, as Mac Intire to Carpenter ; Mac Spallane to Spenser ; O'Conor to Conyers ; O'Brien to Brine ; O'Reilly to Ridley ; O'Donnell to Daniel ; O'Sullivan to Silvan, and Silvers ; O'Murchoe to Morpie ; Mac Carthy to Carter, etc.[2] Probably the desired effect was not attained, because in 1596 the " Irish had become as Irish as ever ", and Spenser for the " better breaking the heads and septs " recommended a renewal of the Statute. " And herewithall would I also wish all the O's and Mac's, which the heads of septs have taken to their names, to bee utterly forbidden and extinguished." [3] The Patent Rolls for 1 Jas. I (1603–4) preserve lists of pardons granted to Irishmen concerned in recent disturbances, and contain hundreds of names, the descriptions being very complete, including both patronymic and clan name as well as " nickname " in some cases.[4]

Owen Brady of Termonagh ; Anne Ferrall of Tenelick, spinster ; Owen McGilleklin, gent ; Dermod O'Gelleghan, yeoman ; Evelin ne Morishe, spinster ; Marie ny Dowda, widow ; Donnell McO'Clerie of Fahy ; Rorie more Offin of Castletoune ; Shane oge. McNe-Gawan, priest ; Connoghor glass O'Davine of Killala, labourer ; Teige oge ny Foorty of Dromore, yeoman ; Donnogh McDermod oge of the Clare ; Phellim O'Relly Dean in Monaghan Co. ; Manus Oge McManus boye of Mileck ; Lysagh McBrian Dariston, yeoman ; Moyler McShane McUllick of the Ovill ; Connor O'Moyle O'Fahie of Lickmolashe, clerk ; Shane O'Neile McArte of Kilultagh ; Garrat McArt O'Connor, yeoman ; Honor nyn Donnell McSwiny of Mossanglassy ; Donnell Evyalle McArt ne Kelly of the Marrowes, gent ; Donnell oge McRiccard McDumy of Culagh ; Owen McRorie McOwen roe ; Breanie McHugh oge McMahone of Rouske ; Onore nyn Dermot O'Rian More Voy of Tolleraght, spinster ; Melaghlin Duffe McDonill McTumultagh oge of Coralarie, gent ; McLaghny Mortogh O'Loghlin of Ballenenem ; Thadeus oge McTeige O'Harte of Grainge-Moyneterhart ; Brien McOwen Mautagh O'Heyne of the Lidegan ; Teige oge McTeige Daile O'Higgin, rymer ; Dermot oge McDermot grany McDermot roe, kerne [i.e. foot soldier] ; Dermot McTeige McOwen de Carty of Glanliehen ; McCragh McTeige McCahier of Kilpader, gent ; Moylmorie McOyn McColla McSwyny of Raglasse ; Donnell O'Kellie McColla McDonogh ; Teige McTirlagh McGerralt O'Connor, gent ; Philip O'Maher of Dyrina McCave.

[1] Full information can be obtained from the works cited in the Bibliography, post., also see O'Donovan, O'Hart, etc.
[2] O'Donovan, pp. 26, 29.
[3] View of the State of Ireland, A.D. 1596, p. 108 (Dublin, 1633).
[4] Cal. of Irish Patent Rolls, vol. ii, p. 17 et seq.

Walter Fitz-Redmond Rackett ; Patrick Fitz-Laghlin McDonill ; Patrick Fitz-Tirlagh O'Kellie ; Thomas Linch Fitz-Nicholas of Galway, gent ; Edmund Burke Fitz-Ullick of Derry ; Patrick French Fitz-George og of Galway, merchant ; Robert Blake Fitz-Walter Fitz-Thomas of Galway, merchant ; Arthur O'Criane Fitz-Edmond of Sligo ; Hubert oge Fitz-Hubert Fitz-William O'Birne, yeoman.

It will be noticed that in some cases both patronymic and clan name are given, and either may have the priority of position. The personal epithet follows the name which it qualifies, often appearing in curious orthographic forms such as boy (*buidhe* " yellow "), dall (blind), donn (brown), duff (*dubh* " black "), glas (green, grey), granni (long hair), mór (great), oge (*óg, óig* " young "), roe (*ruadh* " red ") ; *Inghean* " daughter ", is always abbreviated and takes various forms, forerunners of the modern *ni* (ni, I, or Ui, gen. of O or Ua), nic (Ni Mic), and Nig.

Some of the names are very appropriate, thus " Teige oge McTeige Daile O'Higgin, rymer ", may be rendered, the young poet son of the blind poet descendant of Uigin (knowledge), rhymer.

The plurality of surnames is presumably due to alternatives, these being commonly derived from different ancestors, not necessarily in direct line. Woulfe observes that " some Irish families of alien origin have two Irish surnames, one an hibernicized form of the foreign name, and the other a patronymic formed from the name or a designation of the ancestor." [1] It is popularly supposed that O'-names are more distinguished than Mac-names, but both were common in all ranks of Irish society, as these extracts from the Patent Rolls evidence.

As English names become hibernicized, so did Irish names become anglicized, a change accentuated by the Statute of 1465.[2] The phonetic process sometimes resulted in a number of variants, e.g. Ó Cobhthaigh became Coffie, Cowie, Cowhey, Cowhig, etc., and, on the other hand, one surname might come from a number of different appellatives, e.g. Coffey from Ó Cobhthaigh, Ó Cathbhadha, Ó Cathbhuadhaigh, Ó Cathmhogha. Another method of name-formation was by attempting a translation, e.g. Ó Bruic became Badger ; Mac Seáin, Johnson ; Ó Cadhain, Barnacle, etc. Other changes were by attraction, e.g. Ó Blathmhaic, anglicized Blawick, attracted to Blake ; or assimilation to an alien name, as Ó Bruadair to Broderick ; or substitution, as Clifford for Ó Clumháin.[3]

O'Donovan (1862) remarks that the " change of Irish into English names continued to increase after the Revolution of

[1] Woulfe, p. 33.   [2] See p. 426.   [3] Woulfe, p. 36.

1688, when the natives who remained in Ireland were completely subjected. About this period, numbers of the oppressed native Irish reduced their names as much as possible to the level of English pronunciation ; rejecting in almost every instance the O' and Mac, and making various other changes in their names, so as to give them an English appearance ".[1] Not only did this process work a striking change in the surnames of Ireland, but because of the large numbers of Irishmen, who settled in England and Scotland, it has created a very real difficulty for the etymologist and genealogist of English families ; for instance, Kingsley may have been O'Kinsellagh, Merryman traces back to MacGillymire, Palmer was once O'Mulfaver, Sandys came from O'Shaughnessy, and some Kings were formerly McConry (*righ* " a king ").[2] The extent of this invasion may be gauged from the census returns for the year 1851, when there were found to be three-quarters of a million Irishmen in England, about 4 per cent of the population, and the migration still continues, being no less pronounced in Scotland.

In 1890 the population of Ireland was estimated at 4,717,959 persons, and the numbers bearing the twelve principal surnames respectively were as follow :—

Murphy	.	62,600	Smith	.	33,700	Connor	.	31,200
Kelly	.	55,900	O'Brien	.	33,400	O'Neill	.	29,100
Sullivan	.	43,600	Byrne	.	33,300	Reilly	.	29,000
Walsh	.	41,700	Ryan	.	32,000	Doyle	.	23,000

A particular feature was the number of fitz-names : Fitzgeralds numbering 14,700 and Fitzpatricks 11,100, far ahead of the proportions found in England, Scotland, and France. The most prevalent mac-name was McCarthy, with 22,300 representatives.[3] There were found to be 135 different names with the prefix mac, and 440 with the prefix O'.[4]

It is of interest to note that in 1911 the population of Ireland being 4,390,219, of whom about 87 per cent were not acquainted with the native language, 16,873 persons spoke Irish only, and no less than 331,317, or 9 per cent of the inhabitants, were illiterate, and could neither read nor write. The difficulty of preserving names can be imagined.

The " Anglo-Irish War " of 1919–21 terminated with Ireland (excluding Ulster) obtaining the political status of a dominion, under the title Saorstát Éireann (Irish Free State). No regulations have been issued regarding the adoption or use

[1] *Topographical Poems of John O'Dubhagain*, 1862, p. 9.
[2] Ibid., p. 44.
[3] Special Report by Sir Robt. E. Matheson, 1909, p. 7.
[4] Ibid., p. 16. Lower (*Patr. Brit.*) gives a list of over 1,000 Irish and Scottish Mac-names.

of Irish names, or of the Irish forms of existing names,[1] but a tendency is to write personal, family, and place-names in a language which is unintelligible and unpronounceable to all but a very small proportion of the people of the world.   As the Irish seldom understand the origin of English names, some very curious results from the metamorphoses are to be noted, thus English Reade, which is derived from " red ", the characteristic description of the " auburn haired ", is given a supposed equivalent in Giolgcach, the Irish term for the common reed !

The Return of the Jews.   As has been noticed in Chapter VI, nearly four centuries after their expulsion, it was announced that there was no law preventing immigration of Jews into England : a change of opinion due in large measure to the enthusiastic labours of the great scholar Manasseh ben Israel.   Under Cromwell the Jews mixed undisguised with their fellow merchants, were free from molestation, and allowed to have their synagogues.

A list of Jews drawn up in 1660 contains very different names to those of the thirteenth century, being mainly Spanish, such as Rodrigues, Gonzales, Gomes, Lindo, etc., which may still be recognized in our directories.   At the restoration of the monarchy the London Jewish community consisted of about 35 families ; there being, a hundred years later, 8,000 Jews in London alone, and by the opening of the nineteenth century 20,000, with a further five or six thousand in the provinces.[2]

In Great Britain the Jew now enjoys full equality with the Christian, and the Semitic race is estimated to form about 1 per cent of the population, but there are said to be more Jews in London than in Palestine.   It follows that considerable numbers of the names which grace our directories are of Jewish origin, although not necessarily Hebrew, since they are drawn from numerous foreign sources, and, moreover, various Continental enactments led to the Jews acquiring artificial names very different to those they would have created for themselves.   In Austria (1788) the commissioners appointed to select the designations looked upon the occasion as a harvest, and, when insufficient financial consideration was forthcoming, bestowed most unpleasant appellatives, the following examples being among those noted by Franzos : Bettelarm (destitute), Durst (thirst), Eselskopf (ass's head), Elephant, Fresser (glutton), Galgenvogel (gallows-bird), Geldschrank (money-chest), Hunger, Karfunkel (carbuncle), Küssemich (kiss-me),

---

[1] Communicated by the Asst. Reg. General, Oct., 1930.
[2] *A History of the Jews in England*, by A. M. Hyamson, 2nd ed., pp. 168, 195, 243.

Rindkopf (cow-head), Saumagen (hog's paunch), Schmetterling (butterfly), Stinker, Veilchenduft (scent of violets), and many others equally undesirable.

In connection with this enactment Kleinpaul relates that two Jews coming from the police office where they had been given names, upon comparing notes, found that one had received a pleasing name, Weisheit (wisdom), the other the most objectional appellative Schweiszhund (bloodhound). "Why Schweiszhund?" inquired his friend. "Did you not pay enough?" "Gott und die Welt!" replied the second, "I have given half my wealth to buy that 'w' alone." [1] So it may be gathered that the worthy Israelite had to pay handsomely to avoid being called an equivalent of "Filthy Dog."

Jews in England often discard the foreign names or alter them into something which will pass as English, such as Rosenberg into Montrose, Gibowiez into Gibbs, etc. Jacobs, in analysing 5,000 names of patrons connected with Anglo-Jewish charitable institutions in 1878, found the commonest names to be Cohen, 1 in 26 ; Davis, 1 in 32 ; Levy, 1 in 35 ; Joseph, 1 in 47. [2]

Hyamson (1903) states that a not inconsiderable number of Jewish surnames consist of acrostics in accordance with the precedent set by earlier Jewish worthies. Schön or Schen is an acrostic for Schhach Neemon, "the faithful messenger"; Katz, in English "cat", for Kohn Tzedek, "the true priest"; Schatz and Kinez, the Magyar term for "treasure", for Schliach Tzibur, "the messenger of the congregation." Some of the name-forms so obtained may well have given rise to surnames : Bram means Ben Rabbi Moses ; Bran, Ben Rabbi Nachman ; Bard, Ben Rabbi David ; Bril, Ben Rabbi Judah the Levite, and so on. [3]

In 1911 the population of England and Wales was 36,075,269 (8,018,857 families or separate occupiers), of which number less than 1 per cent were unnaturalized aliens, amongst them being 95,541 Russians and Poles, 53,324 Germans, 28,827 French, and 20,389 Italians. The greatest proportion of foreigners was located in London, namely 4 per cent, but the number of Jews is not stated. These figures are eloquent of our polyglot nomenclature.

Manifold Names and Descriptions. It has been shown that by the end of the thirteenth century practically every person of both high and low degree had an official description or addition to his baptismal name. The desire for greater

[1] p. 118.
[2] *Jewish Encyclopædia*, Art. "Names", p. 157.
[3] 2nd. ed., p. 22.

distinction led to the two appellatives becoming three, and later on to a multiplicity. In the case of two designations the first was always the baptismal name and the second, at first an additional distinction, afterwards became a family name. In the case of three names one and two might be baptismal names, or two and three, surnames, and it is not always possible to define exactly the function of the middle name, but it is improbable that there were double baptismal names until the fifteenth century, and their introduction may have been even later.

Long before hereditary family names came into general use the double description was current in the records.

Characteristic + local.—Tenth century, Wulfhun ðes blaca æt Sumortune, Norf. (*KCD.*, vol. ii, p. 133) ; A.D. 1086, Gerardus Lotaringus de Salsitona (Inq. Com. Cant.) ; A.D. 1190, Robertus Brito de Baskecota, i.e. Robert the Breton of Bascote (Warw. Pipe R.).

Genealogical + characteristic.—A.D. 1086, Reynaldus Stanceberd Denasez, i.e. without nose (Dom. Bk.).

Occupational + genealogical.—A.D. 1103, Radulfus taneator cattessone, i.e. Ralph Catteson, the tanner (Lib. Wint.).

Occupational + local.—A.D. 1230, Odo Potarius de Estiggeleye, i.e. Odo the Potter of Estiggeley (Oxf. Pipe R.).

Genealogical + local.—A.D. 1301–2, Thomas Henry de Hope [of Sandhurst, Kent] (Brit. Mus. Add. Ch. 29550).

With regard to double christian names an anonymous correspondent has noted the moneyer's name ANDRVE RICAR ADAM on a coin of Alexander II of Scotland (1214–49).[1] The Close Roll of 1288 names Roger Paye Levedey, Yorks ; a deed poll, dated 36 Edw. III (1363), is executed by Stephen son of John Fylip Curpet of Fincham (Norf.) [2] ; Will. Mich. Stonhard occurs in 1421,[3] and Thomas Arnold Williamson in 1471.[4] The last six examples have probably resulted from dropping the words " son of ", it being unlikely that they are illustrations of double baptismal names.

Some cases which may have arisen in the same way give the appearance of double surnames.

A.D. 1284.   Philip Crese Erl (occurs several times in Bridgewater accounts).[5]

A.D. 1333.   Ricardus Whit(e) Wilkinson, Cumb. (See p. 168.)

The northern custom of combining the word " son " with

[1] *Notes and Queries*, 23rd Jan., 1875, p. 77.
[2] Ibid., 6th Sept., 1856, p. 197.
[3] Brit. Mus. Add. Ch., 23,538–9. *Complete Peerage*, 1913, vol. iii, p. 621.
[4] Brit. Mus., Harl. Ch., 50, D. 22.
[5] *Notes and Queries*, 23rd Jan., 1875, p. 77, per H. T. Riley. Hist. MSS. Comm., 3rd Rept., p. 311.

the patronymic also produces double surnames ; thus in 1381–2
William Johnson Wilkinson, who was a witness to two deeds
(Yorks),[1] might have been called William son of John
Wilkinson, or even William son of John son of Wilkin. In
1396 pardons were granted to Robert Johanson Dobson and
John Dicson Robynson, also two North of England examples.[2]
John Hudson Stevenson of Tatham (Lancs), 1411, was an
outlaw,[3] as likewise was Thomas Jonson Webster of Etall
(Northumb.), yeoman, temp. Hen. VI (1422–61).[4] Ricardus
Jonessone Wattesone de Worstede occurs in a Norfolk fine,
1368–9 : and a pardon was granted to (Thomas son of) Robert
" Dicunson Hulleson del More " of Derby, 1384.[5] This
particular type of combination has not been noted in records
of the South ; but in 1418 John Severelle Love was a London
surgeon.[6] Arnold Belrynger Webbe was the name given to an
alien in Kent Subsidy Roll of 18 Hen. VI (1439–40), who,
presumably formerly a bellman, had become, in his new life,
a webber ; his name being followed by that of Margareta
Belrynger.[7] In 1475 John Harry Richowe of Helstonburgh,
Cornw., husbandman, was an outlaw,[8] doubtless as in the other
cases cited above, Harry Richowe was father of John.

In Wales the omission of *ap* or the addition of a nickname
has in some cases given the appearance of treble names, and
in Scotland and Ireland, nicknames, father's name, as well as
the clan name were coupled together at an early date, as the
examples given above have illustrated (pp. 209–10). In
the Low Countries most involved descriptions became
customary, some typical fifteenth-century examples of which
have been given on p. 141. Verstegan (1605) recorded that his
grandfather, Theodore Rowland Verstegan, was born in the
Duchy of Geldres and came to England about the end of the
reign of Henry VII (*c.* 1508), and thereupon observed :—

" It is often seen in Germany that either godfather at christning
giveth his name to his godson, and therefore it cometh that many hath
two proper names beside their surnames."

No undoubted English example of a double baptismal name
has been noticed before the sixteenth century ; in 1603 Camden,
who had a comprehensive knowledge of the subject, knew
of only four cases in England, but he said that it was then

[1] *Yorkshire Arch. Journal*, 1879, vol. v, p. 76.
[2] *Cal. of Patent Rolls*, p. 686.
[3] Deputy Keeper's 37th Rept.
[4] P.R.O., Controlment Roll, K.B. 29, No. 91.
[5] *Cal. of Patent Rolls*, p. 486.
[6] H. T. Riley (*Memorials*, p. 651).
[7] P.R.O., E 179, 124/107, m. 1.
[8] P.R.O., Controlment Roll, K.B. 29, No. 113.

common in Italy and Spain to add the name of a saint to a christian name.   Examples from parish registers are :—

Arthurus Rous Russhe filius Johannis Russhe, bapt. 30th Dec. 1564. Badingham (Suff.) Par. Reg.

Anne Agnes Parnell was m. 9th July, 1571.   Saffron Walden (Ess.) Par. Reg.

Robert Browne, son of John Lillie, bapt. 18th Jan. 1592. Mexborough (Yorks) Par. Reg. [Browne was the mother's patronymic.]

Some other sixteenth-century instances may provide examples of double surnames, but opinion could only be formed after consideration of the pedigrees.   In 1547 John Dudley, Viscount Lisle, had licence to alienate the house of the dissolved hospital of St. Giles in the Fields to John Wymonde Carewe.[1] Richard Clement Fisher, of Packington, Warw., also flourished in the sixteenth century.[2]   Mark Alexander Boyd, the poet, was born in 1563, and Thomas Posthumous Hoby in 1566,[3] and on 11th October, 1588, Henry Donne Lee subscribed the Thirty-nine Articles.[4]   The possibility must not be overlooked that some of these combinations have resulted from dropping an *alias*, of the usage of which word more will be said in a later chapter ; but again, only examination of the pedigree will determine the point.

Few double names can have been bestowed at the font until the eighteenth century; for instance, in the registers of Westminster Abbey there is only one double christian name before 1705, and in the registers of Wiston, which are perfect from 1538, there is not a single instance of more than one name being given in baptism until 1781.[5]   In a Lincolnshire Poll Book for 1723, of the names of 4,990 freeholders, only five had more than one christian name.[6]   Nevertheless, by the seventeenth century triple baptismal names began to make an appearance, and also what may be fittingly described as freaks.

Dancell Dallphebo Marke Anthony Dallery Gallery Cesar Williams, sonn of Dancall (*sic*) Dallphebo Marke Anthony Dallery Gallery Cesar Williams, bapt. Jan. xviii, 1676. Old Swinford (Worc.) Par. Reg.[7]

Charles Caractacus Ostorius Maximilian Gustavus Adolphus, son of Charles Stone, tailor, bapt. 29th Apr., 1781. Burbage (Wilts.) Par. Reg.[8]

Even in recent years a child in a noble family had eighteen names, the initials of the first fifteen reading " Lyonel the second ".   A modern young lady suffered under the infliction

[1] *History of St. Giles and Bloomsbury,* by R. Dobie, p. 24.
[2] *Notes and Queries,* 3rd Oct., 1874, p. 271.
[3] *The Complete Peerage,* 1913, vol. iii, p. 622.
[4] *Notes and Queries,* 10th May, 1856, p. 384.
[5] Ibid., 18th Apr., 1857, p. 312.   [6] Ibid., 7th Nov., 1857, p. 376.
[7] Ibid., 2nd May, 1874, p. 271.   [8] Ibid., 3rd Oct., 1874, p. 271.

of twenty-six names, each letter of the alphabet being represented by an initial.[1]

In the twentieth century a welcome tendency to more
rational naming is noticeable in the highest circles : a royal
child having recently been baptized with two names only, and
will be known as H.R.H. the Princess Margaret Rose of York.
It is to be hoped that this sensible lead will be followed by
those lower in the social scale.

What are sometimes termed " double-barrelled " surnames
are now usually joined by hyphen, and are also tending to run
to seed, such unwieldy compositions occurring as :—

Nineteenth century : Hovell-Thurlow-Cumming-Bruce.　Killed
Boer War.

Twentieth century : Hobart-Hampden-Mercer-Henderson.　Living,
1930.

Historical Retrospect.　Having completed a survey of
all matters bearing upon the origin and evolution of the
surname system in the British Isles, the main characteristics
of this class of social distinction may be recapitulated.　In the
eleventh century the majority of people had but a single name,
but during the following hundred years there was a great
increase in the use of additional distinctions, and by the end
of the twelfth century it was exceptional for a person to be
without an official description or surname in England, although
in country districts, among the lesser educated classes, such
additions were and yet are in little use.　The descriptive
name (apart from nicknames) was placed after the font-name,[2]
it being a distinction of secondary importance, and it was not
uncommon for a person to have several of such additions,
derived from appearance, residence, parentage, or occupation.
Secondary appellatives, first officially noticed as hereditary
in 1267, gradually becoming recognized as family names, the
plurality of distinctions ceased to be employed, and ultimately
the additional name obtained a greater importance than the
forename.　Down to the seventeenth century books and records
may still be found indexed according to forenames,[3] but the

---

[1] In later years this class of polyonomy became common, even with the
lowest in the social scale.　In 1855 a labourer's child in Cardiff was named
James Louis Napoleon Malakhoff Broom (Her. and Gen., i, 356 n.).　The
same type of madness was prevalent at the time of the Boer War, giving rise
to a song, which if my memory serves me, had as a chorus : " The baby's
name is Kitchener Carrington Methuen Kekewich White Cronje Plumer
Powell Majuba Gatacre Warren Colenso Kruger Cape Town Mafeking French
Lyddite Pretoria Blobbs ! "

[2] The usual practice throughout Europe, but not, I understand, in eastern
countries, as Japan.

[3] See under Dedham in the Essex Ship Money Roll (P.R.O., S.P. Dom.,
Chas. I, No. 358).　*The Herald and Genealogist*, vol. i, p. 346 n., mentions
some instances, and I have noticed others in some registers of the French
and Dutch churches.

second name, the surname, had become the prior distinction, as it is at the present day. It may be roughly estimated that by the end of the thirteenth century half the people had family names, and by the end of the fourteenth perhaps three-quarters were so distinguished. The adoption of permanent second names was more rapid in the South of England than in the North, and is more noticeable among the upper than the lower classes.

The second names, at first latinized, began to appear in French and English during the twelfth century, and continued in three languages until the fourteenth century, when the use of Latin being abandoned, combined with the decline in the employment of the French and English article and prepositions, the descriptions by the end of the fifteenth became single-worded and uniform in appearance, approximating closely to the modern family name.

The secondary descriptions and surnames fall into four classes: characteristic, local, genealogical, and occupational. Referring to England, characteristic names form the smallest class, and have been of a fairly uniform popularity at all material periods, in all districts, and among all classes. Local descriptions or addresses constituting the largest class reached their greatest proportionate representation in the beginning of the thirteenth century, when a decline set in, but the resulting surnames yet number 40 to 50 per cent of the total. Distinctions of this class were in use by all classes, but were much more predominant in the North of England and Cornwall than elsewhere. Genealogical descriptions, now the second most important class of surnames, were rather more popular in North than South, and at first employed chiefly by the upper classes, afterwards became general. Occupational descriptions, formerly, in the main, official additions to the names of people of social rank, latterly became the distinctions of the manual workers, uniformly distributed.

Referring to the Celtic parts of the British Islands, it appears that in those parts of Wales, Scotland, and Ireland where English influence was strong, the English system was followed; in other parts of those countries the native genealogical method of distinction being current. Ultimately these descriptions became surnames, and now, in Wales and Ireland particularly, the majority of family names perpetuate those of ancestors.

From the Norman Conquest onwards, with the political situation becoming more settled, there were considerable movements of the native races, resulting in English, Welsh, Irish, and Scottish blood and names being intermixed and spread throughout the British Isles, and to the ethnic medley were added large bodies of foreigners of Scandinavian, Teutonic, and Latin races, who introduced new surnames, although a good proportion of the incoming strangers were given English appellatives. In addition to European aliens there are now in the British Isles considerable numbers of Asiatic, African, and American residents, some of whom have to adopt an English system of naming, if not new names altogether.

At the present day Smith is unquestionably the greatest surname, numerically, in England and Scotland, as Jones is in Wales ; Murphy holding pride of place in Ireland. It has been estimated that in England and Wales every thirty-sixth person is either a Smith or a Jones. Even in Scotland one in seventy is named Smith, and in Ireland there are half as many in proportion. In 1853 the population of England and Wales was estimated at 18,404,421 persons, and the numbers bearing the twelve principal surnames were respectively as follow :—

Smith	.	253,600	Davies	.	113,600	Roberts	.	78,400
Jones	.	242,100	Brown	.	105,600	Johnson	.	69,500
Williams	.	159,900	Thomas	.	94,000	Wilson	.	66,800
Taylor	.	124,400	Evans	.	93,000	Robinson	.	66,700 [1]

The great prevalence of genealogical surnames is due to Welsh influence.

[1] 16th *Annual Report of the Registrar-General of Births, Deaths, and Marriages in England*, 1856, p. xxiii.

CHAPTER IX

CLASSIFICATION OF BRITISH SURNAMES

A Complete System of Surnames. Modern British surnames may be divided, in the first place, according to method of acquisition, into two groups :—

> Group I. Surnames inherited at birth.
> Group II. Surnames acquired after birth.

The first of these groups includes all those secondary appellatives which identify the family of the bearer, that is, those that are repetitions of the names of the fathers. In the first instance, all such names have been descriptions or addresses assumed by the original bearer or conferred upon him by recording officials for the purpose of denoting and expressing identity. Of the two groups this is by far the most important, both numerically and for its value to the student of philology, history, ethnology, and genealogy.

The second group includes all the secondary appellatives which identify an individual, that is those names differing (with rare exceptions) from the names of the fathers. Such names have been assumed by or conferred upon the bearer, either on commencing a new career, or from dislike of an inherited name, or to preserve one from distinction, or for the purpose of disguise.

Names in the first group may be said, briefly, to record genealogy, and those in the second and smaller group to conceal it. The latter are termed surnames only by courtesy, but in some cases, being perpetuated by descendants to the second and third generation, ultimately become fully qualified names of Group I.

The investigation, which has formed the basis for the previous chapters, has been devoted entirely to the evolution of surnames of Group I from the secondary descriptions of the Celtic, Teutonic, Scandinavian, and Latin nations. The epithets, addresses, font-names, vocations, etc., forming the descriptions of all these races, having been divided, according to their respective natures, into characteristic, local, genealogical, and occupational classes, it follows, conformably, that their direct successors, the surnames, must fall into the same categories, since they answer to the same questions— what is his personal peculiarity ?—where is, or was, he located ?—who is, or was, his most important kinsman ?—

what is his vocation ?—in all cases referring to the progenitor rather than to the individual.

The appellatives now termed " characteristic " have formerly been called " nicknames " by Phillimore, Bardsley, and others. The term " local " agrees with Bardsley, and takes the place of " topographical " of Phillimore. Genealogical names have been called " personal " by some writers, and " patronymics " by Phillimore, terms which seem to be inadequate, and are therefore superseded by a more comprehensive expression. For the fourth class the title " occupational " (or " occupative ") has been generally accepted, and is retained.[1] After examination of many thousands of British surnames, and giving full consideration to their original significations, it has been found convenient to subdivide the four classes as follows :—

Group I.—Inherited Surnames

Class I. *Characteristic Surnames*

(a) From Appearance.
(b) From Character, i.e. mental and moral attribute or peculiarity.
(c) From Physical Attribute.
(d) From Possession.
(e) From Action or Habit.
(f) From Condition or Quality.
(g) From Relationship, i.e. consanguinity, kinship.
(h) From Race or Sept.

Class II. *Local Surnames*

(a) From Place of Residence or Work.
(b) From Late Place of Residence.

Class III. *Genealogical Surnames*

(a) From Personal Name of Male Parent.
(b) From Personal Name of Female Parent.
(c) From Personal Name of other Relative.
(d) From Description or Surname.

Class IV. *Occupational Surnames*

(a) From Office or Profession.
(b) From Mock Office.
(c) From Military Rank.
(d) From Trade or Vocation.

---

[1] Bardsley (1896) made five classes by dividing the occupational class into (a) Official, and (b) Occupative, but at the same time observed that " practically there are only four classes, for it is often hard to distinguish between occupation and office ".

Group II.—Acquired Surnames

Class I. *Self-assumed Surnames*

(a) Of Ecclesiastics.
(b) Of Theatrical Artistes.
(c) Of Authors.
(d) Of Business Men.
(e) Of Private Persons.
(f) Of Slaves.
(g) Of Refugees.
(h) Of Aliens.

Class II. *Reputed Surnames*

(a) Of Bastards.
(b) Of Foundlings.

It is believed that every British surname, its original nature being determined, would fall into one or other of these twenty-eight subclasses. In practice, however, in a number of cases, it is found impossible to suggest the first orthographic form or its signification with accuracy, and quite commonly an inherited name may be assigned to any three if not four main classes, e.g. Bell, which may be characteristic, derived from *le bel* " the handsome " ; local, from occupation or residence at a tavern called " The Bell ", and from Bailleul, a Flemish form of which is Belle ; or genealogical from Bell (Isabel), and O.E. Bel- (as in Belweard). A still more remarkable surname, which may be derived from a dozen different origins, and falls into four classes, is Cock, for an account of which see below (p. 282). Some further details of the peculiarities of each class will be given in the following pages.

Group I.—Inherited Surnames

Class I. Characteristic Surnames. Pride of place is given to the class of surnames, which although the smallest,[1] comprising not more than from 6 to 10 per cent of English family names, is perhaps of the most interesting and varied nature. The bearer of a name of this class is actually able to know the most prominent characteristic of a remote ancestor living at the time surnames were becoming fixed. What was his peculiarity ? The answer may be in one of several languages, and it may be a noun, as Fleming ; an adjective, as Short ; or a verb + noun, as Turnbull. Some of the characteristic names perpetuate dialectical, archaic, and obsolete words, and a considerable proportion of the appellatives which appear to belong to the class are found, upon investigation, to have origins which cause them to be placed in other categories. Of the eight subclasses provided,

[1] In the old days of individual descriptions it was the largest (see pp. 32, 42).

(*a*) appearance, (*e*) actions, and (*h*) race or sept, have given rise to the majority of the surnames.

For various notes on the origin and evolution of characteristic description the reader may turn back to p. 28, Sanskrit ; p. 32, Irish ; pp. 42, 124, Welsh ; p. 57, Anglo-Saxon ; p. 67, Norse ; pp. 79, 84, 90, 98, Norman ; p. 139, Flemish ; p. 148, Jewish.

(*a*) *Surnames from Appearance.* The most natural way of describing a man, to distinguish him from his fellows, was to give a pen-picture of his personal appearance, and particularly so if he possessed any outstanding physical peculiarity. Numerous examples of descriptions of this subclass, in a dozen languages, have been noticed in previous sections, and a selection of modern surnames will now be presented.

English : Ballard (bald-headed) ; Blackbeard ; Blunt (blonde) ; Fairfax (fair hair) ; Reade (red) ; Little ; White. *French* : Base, Bass (*le bas* " the low ", i.e. small) ; Chaff (*le chauvre* " the bald ") ; Pettit (*le petit* " the small ") ; Grose (*le gros* " the fat ") ; Rouse (*le rous* " the red ") ; Viel (sometimes from *le viel* " the old ") ; Diminutives :— Basset (dwarf) ; Blundell (blonde) ; Russell (red). *Latin* : Rufus (red). *Welsh* (see p. 124). *Cornish* : Angwin (white) ; Coath, Coad (old) ; Couch (red) ; Floyd (*luit* " grey ") ; Glass, Glaze (blue, green) ; Croom (crooked, now Crump) ; Vian, Veen (little). *Gaelic* : Boyd, Buie (*buidhe* " yellow ")[1] ; Dunn (brown) ; Campbell (*cam beul* " wry mouthed ", often pronounced Caumal) ; Muir (*mor* " great ", " big ") ; Reid (*ruadh* " red ") ; Kennedy (*ceann* " head ", *eitigh* " ugly "). *Scottish* : Cruikshanks, Lang, Laing. *Irish* : (see also p. 32). Bawn *bán* " white ") ; Begg (*beag* " little ") ; Crone (*crón* " brown ") ; Duff (*dubh* " black ") ; Fodha (*fada* " tall ") ; Geare (*géar* " bitter ") ; Glass (*glas* " grey ") ; Leagh (*liath* " grey ") ; Reagh (*riadhach* " grey ") ; Rowe (*ruadh* " red ") ; Woney (*uaitne* " green "). *Scandinavian* : Routh (*hrutr* " red "). *Aliens* : Schwartz (black) ; Weiss (white).

Peculiarities of limbs have been greatly noticed ; a king was dubbed Longshanks, the same title from another source becoming perpetuated as a surname, together with Short-shanks, Smallshanks, Sheepshanks, Foljambe, etc. Some Flemish examples have been given above, p. 139.

Names comprising epithet + personal name as Meiklejohn (Big John), or epithet + trade, as Micklewright, also appear.

W. Langgesmyht, Yorks, 1297. (Subs. : W. Brown).

W. le Longechapman, Kent, 1333. (Subs. 123/11, m. 9*d*.)

A number of surnames apparently of this subclass are of a different origin, as Fairbairn, Fairbeard, Tallboy, etc.

(*b*) *Surnames from Character.* Qualities impressed upon a person by nature or habit have become perpetuated in names

---

[1] Woulfe thinks that Boyd may be derived from Bute (p. 250), but the source given above is more probable. Boyd (occ. 1328) is also Flemish, a form of Bodo.

of his descendants, but, in the majority of cases, descriptions of this subclass failed to survive. In a York inquisition, 1337, three jurors were called Fairandgode (Chanc. Inq. No. 1487), and Hugh Proud of Noght, Yorks, was hanged for felony, 1348 (Chanc. Inq. No. 2067), and doubtless his curious distinction died with him. Of modern surnames there are Noble and Savage, and possibly Proud, which, however, is more probably from Prud, the Saxon personal name. Irish examples are: Brody (*bródach* "proud"), Dempsey (*diomasach* "arrogant"), Casey (*cathaiseach* "valiant").

(c) *Surnames from Physical Attribute.* Physical distinctions as Strong-in-the-arm naturally came to be used as descriptions, and some have survived as surnames, a well-known example being Armstrong. Firebrace and Fairbrass are of Norman origin, occurring as Ferebrache in 1190 (Pipe R.), and signifying "iron-arm". Strongman seems to be an undoubted example, yet it may be an O.E. personal name (cf. Smallman, see p. 341). The Scottish synonym, Strangman, is also to be found. Of Irish origin is Lauder (*laidir* "strong"), and a Norman equivalent is Fort. The surname Vigorous belongs to the genealogical class.

(d) *Surnames from Possession.* In the absence of second names some persons were conveniently described by their property or want of it.

Roland sine Averio (Fr. *sans avoir*, without property), Suss. 1201 (Cur. Reg. R.). Surname Sanzaver.

Ric. cum Equo (with the horse), Hunts, 1327 (Subs.).

Thom. Grenekyrtel, Leic., 1308 (Borough Rec. i, 373). But cf. Grim-kettle.

Epithets of this type were Lackland and its equivalent, Sansterre. Surnames are scarce, Shorthose is a possible example, as is Poingdestre, from the heraldic charge.

(e) *Surnames from Action or Habit.* Any outstanding act or distinctive trait in a man's method of living provided an excellent distinction, but it is questionable whether sobriquets derived therefrom survived as surnames, although there are numerous modern family names appearing superficially to have been nicknames of such a nature, as :—

Hen. Cullebulloc, Beds, 1275.   (Hund. R.)

Rob. Briselaunce, Lincs, 1275.   (Hund. R.)

W. Brekespere of Stukeley, Hunts, *c.* 1300.   (Ramsey Cart. i, 42.)

"Willelmo dicto Turnebul," Selkirk, *c.* 1315.   (Reg. Mag. Sigilla, p. 6.)

Rich. Turnehare, London, 1323.   (Coroner's R.)

Sim. Saklok, Suff., 1324.   (Pat. R.)

Gilb. Killebole, Leic., 1327.   (Subs., Fletcher, p. 69.)

Alicia Turnebuk, Yorks, 1379.   (Poll Tax, p. 66.)

A curiosity is Spurneturtoys, which is to be found in the Selby Coucher Book (i, 207), but cf. Spornecurteys, Derb., 1287 (Cl. R.). Surnames like Benbow, Breakspeare, Hotspur, Hurlbat, Shakelance, Shotbolte, Telfer (taillefer " cut iron "), Tipstaff, Wagspear, etc., are seldom what they seem, and notwithstanding that hundreds of parallel French and German examples are to be found, such surnames should not be derived from supposed nicknames without ample proof. Wagstaff, for instance, might well be a personal name (O.E. *wag, stæf*), and it has also the appearance of being local (cf. Bickerstaff, Eavestaff, etc.). Waghorn, likewise, is compounded of two O.E. elements, as is Bighorn (Testa de Nev.). Many " horn "-names are local, as Tomenhorn and Dilhorn (Staffs Subs., 1332–3), and probably also Welkeshorn, Beleshorn, Blouhorn, etc., in the Hundred Rolls, a " horn " being a " winding stream ". A " shakelock ", according to Halliwell, was a turnkey, and such a name might therefore be an occupational description. Cullebulloc and Cullehog, i.e. Killbullock and Killhog may be nicknames; they have not survived, and an even more improbable sobriquet is Killeman (Dev., 1327, Subs.), whilst Cullehar, also in the Hundred Rolls, and Cullefinche (Ramsey. Cart., i, 303) seem to be incidents unworthy of being commemorated. It is unlikely therefore that anyone of these names falls into this section.

The Turnbulls, so largely represented in the North, according to Buchanan (1820), and others, obtained the surname in the fourteenth century upon one of their ancestors turning an unruly bull which threatened to be disrespectful to King Robert I. Doubtless, like many other similar tales, the story is made to fit the name rather than the reverse. If the surname was acquired through any achievement, it is much more probable to have resulted from a daring act in the brutal sport of bull-running, which was popular from time immemorial up to the last century, being particularly associated with Tutbury (Staffs) and Stamford (Lincs). This very descriptive name was not only bestowed upon a human being, but also upon a quadruped, as is evidenced by the will of Thomas de la Mare, Yorks, 1358, wherein testator bequeaths " equum meum vocatum Turnebull ".[1] The surname ramified strongly in the northern counties and Scotland, variants being Trumball, Trumble, and possibly Trumble, Tremble, etc., but these two may be of local origin.

Ralph de Tremble, 1295–6. (Cal. of Docts. Scot., p. 169.)

The further possibility must not be overlooked of origin from Tournebu (Calvados) or Tourneville (Eure).

---

[1] Surtees Soc., vol. iv, p. 69.

Almaric de Turnebu, Hants, 1202.   (Rot. Canc.)
Rob. Turnebuel, Dover, 1240.   (Pat. R.) [1]
Adam Turneboll, Dover, 1252.   (Pat. R.)

The name of Shakespeare, popularly supposed to belong to this class, will be discussed at a later stage (p. 312 et seq.).

(*f*) *Surnames from Condition or Quality.* Into this small subclass fall such names as Senior, Elder, Younger, Newman, Bastard, Outlaw ; possibly Palmer (a pilgrim from the Holy Land) and Hanker (the anchorite), if the two latter are not occupational. Scottish examples are Auld and Ogg.

(*g*) *Surnames from Relationship.* Quite a number of terms denoting consanguinity or affinity have become fixed as surnames, such as Cousin (Couzens, Cossins, Cussen, etc.), Eam, Eames (O.E. *éam* " uncle "), Muff (*maugh* " the brother-in-law "), Neames (a dialectical variant of Eam), Uncle, etc. Godson is probably from a personal name, as may be Brother :—

De Willelmo f. Brother, Lincs, 1202.   (Ass. R. : Stenton.)   Cf. W. le Brother, Oxf. 1275 (Hund. R.).

A Norman example is Beaufitz or Beavis (*beau-fils* " son-in-law ").

(*h*) *Surnames from Race or Sept.* Many foreigners settling down in a new country, speaking figuratively, were labelled with their nationality ; thus an Englishman venturing into Cambria was called Sais, the Irishman Gwyddel, and so on, and such descriptions, in some cases, have become fixed, as is evidenced by the great number of persons bearing the surnames Welsh, Scott, etc. A series of examples of descriptions from nationalities has been given on pp. 142–6, 152–5, some other surnames of this type derived from counties being : Cornish, Devenish, and Kentish ; and from places Blythman, Chesterman, and Penkethman.

Ph. Lundenisshe, Kent, 1292. (Subs. 123/20, m. 19.)

The Irish have Brathnagh (Breatnach " the Welshman "), Lynagh (Laighneach " the Leinsterman "), Levenach (Leamhnach " the Lennoxman "), Pléamonn (the Fleming), Spainagh (the Spaniard), and Gall (the foreigner).

Clan names of the Gaels have provided a large number of surnames, as Buchanan, Campbell, Chisholm, Colquhoun, Forbes, Fraser, Fullerton, Gordon, Grant, Lamont, Lindsay, Matheson, Menzies, Morison, Munro, Murray, Ogilvie, Ross, Stewart, Sutherland, Urquhart, to name a few.

[1] Torneboel, 1255 (Pat. R.).

Class II. Local Surnames. This class comprises perhaps from 40 to 50 per cent of English surnames formed from a very large list of place-names and topographical features. These family names originated from distinguishing a man by his residence, property, place of work, or any locality having a name with which he was or had been associated, such indicia ranging from his country, province, county, town, or village, through house, forest, or field, down to a well, tree-stump, or ditch, providing answers to the question, where is or was he located ?   Names from towns and villages are particularly common in Cornwall, the North of England, and Scotland, the lesser important features being more freely represented in the southern half of England. Surnames of this class are rare from Welsh and Irish sources, but often originate in localities in Manche, Calvados, Eure, and Seine Inférieure, the more northern departments of France, with which England had continuous intercourse. The principal languages of the elements of local surnames are English, French, Scandinavian, Gaelic, and Cornish, and many ancient dialectical and obsolete words, uncompounded or compounded may be found, the principal grammatical formations being a single-element noun, as Kirk ; noun + noun, as Moorcroft ; noun + adjective, as Rosevere (Corn. *ros* "moor", *mor* "great ") ; adjective + noun, as Whitehouse ; Melrose (Gael. *maol* "bald ", *ros* "promontory ") ; preposition + noun, as Attwell ; and more complicated compounds, as Tregonwell, i.e. *tre-gun-uhal* "the dwelling on the high down ". Further reference may be made to the key given below (pp. 372–80). Subclasses are provided for surnames derived from (*a*) place of residence or work, (*b*) late place of residence ; although, without knowing the full history of a name, it is sometimes difficult to assign it to either class, some, in fact, being equally at home in both divisions.

The principal notes on descriptions and surnames of this class in preceding chapters will be found on p. 33, Irish ; pp. 42, 124, Welsh ; p. 57, Anglo-Saxon ; p. 68, Norse ; pp. 80, 91, Norman ; p. 139, Flemish ; p. 149, Jewish.

(*a*) **Surnames from Place of Residence or Work.** This very important subclass comprises surnames derived from descriptions of residences, tenures, or places of work, ranging from the great seigniories down to plots of land or household offices. The nature of the original descriptions, the ellipsis of the prepositions, and the ultimate formation and fixation of the surname have been fully traced in previous chapters (see Index).   In a few instances the preposition has been retained, e.g. de Vesci ; in others it has blended with the following word, as Devereux, Delamotte, Atthill, Underwood, Arwennack (Corn. *ar* " upon ", *winick* " a marsh ").

Norman Surnames. Many of the great tenants holding of the Crown under William the Conqueror permanently adopted the names of their estates, English and French, as family names : de Arundel, de Beauchamp, de Belesme, de Ferrers, de Gand (Ghent), de Lacy, de Mandeville, de Montgomery, de Mortimer, de Oilgi, de Perci, de Stadford, de Warenne, etc. Doubtless many other persons who had no interest in the estates, except to labour on them, were dubbed with the same names likewise when they settled in some other place. *De* like the corresponding Dutch *van*, German *von* or Italian *di, da,* is popularly supposed to be a sign of aristocratic descent, but in records of the middle ages, as has been clearly shown, it was extremely common, and had no other function than that of the English prepositions, " of," " from," or " at." Taking names from *Les Rôles de Taille Parisiens,* 1292–1313, it is to be noticed that, even at that early date, important territorial distinctions were borne by tradesmen, e.g. :—

Auberi de Paris, couturier ; Jehan d'Yvri, le boursier ; Guillaume de Saint-Lorenz, orfevre ; Pierre de Montpellier, l'orfevre ; Estienne de Valeri, orfevre ; Guillaume de Corbie, cousturier ; Jehan de Chartres, fournier ; Pierre de Mailly, maçon.

Doubtless some descendants of these Paris workmen crossed the Channel, and have founded some of the English families of Ivory, Valery, Corbey, Charters, Maile, etc., whose descendants fondly imagine that they are descended from great lords of these names.

Surnames from Buildings. A man was frequently known by the name of the place where he worked, or with which he was associated, as the following surnames evidence :—

Abbey, Cage (a prison), Capel (a chapel), Castle, Chappell, Domesday (i.e. *domus dei,* God's house), Ewery, Farmery (i.e. Infirmary), Forge, Gale (gaol), Galilee (church porch), Grange, Hall, House, Jury (Jewry), Kay (quay), Keep, Kernel (a battlement), Kirke, Kitchen, Laundry, Loft, Malthouse, Mill, Millhouse, Minster, Monkhouse, Nale (i.e. atten ale), Oriel (an entrance hall), Parlour, Parsonage, Peel, Pill (fortified house), Porch, Slot (a castle), Spence (store-room), Stable, Stannus (stone-house), Staple, Stead, Temple, Tower, Vickridge, Whitehouse, Windus (Windhouse), Woodhouse.

Five Windmills were convicted of burglary at Western Circuit assizes, 5 William & Mary, 1693.

Shop and Tavern Signs. In ancient Rome painted sign-boards were commonly fixed outside shops, taverns, and other establishments to indicate to the illiterate passer-by the nature of the services which were to be had within. The custom was widely adopted in Britain, and throughout the middle ages, when houses were yet unnumbered and reading was still an accomplishment of few of the people, the hanging signs were the most prominent feature of a business street.[1]   In the fourteenth century the law compelled publicans to exhibit signs, and in the seventeenth it was made lawful for citizens to hang out sign-boards for the better finding out their dwellings and shops.

> " And maister Frank, the goldsmith, at the Rose ;
> And maister Philip, with the fiery nose ;
> And maister Miles, the mercer, at the Harrow ;
> And maister Nick, the salter, at the Sparrow."
>
> Pasquin's *Nightcap*, 1612.

The practice at the present day is mainly confined to the publicans and publishers; other traders attempt to gain distinction and attract business by posting pictorial representations of their goods on hoardings standing often far apart from their own premises.   When one recalls the great part eating and drinking took in the lives of our ancestors, and the gargantuan feasts necessary for their existence, it is not surprising to read of large numbers of houses devoted to the refreshing of the hungry traveller.   An observer in the time of James I noted the names of forty-eight inns and taverns between Charing Cross and the Old Tower of London, some of which, like the Bell, Angel, Swan, Bear and Harrow, Bull Head, Bull, Lyon, Horns, Talbot, Cranes, etc., correspond to modern surnames.   That a man became popularly known by the sign of the establishment where he worked or lived cannot be doubted, although evidence is somewhat scarce :—

Gilbert de le Hegle, Suss. 1275.   (Hund. R.)
W. de le Whytehors, Warw. 1285.   (Foot of Fine, 244/32, no. 6.)
W. atte Whytehorse, Glouc. 1312.   (Subs. 113/4, m. 6*d*.)
W. atte Ramme, London, 1320.   (Fines.)
Godfey atte Swan, London, 1337.   (Coroner's R.)
J. atte Pye, London, 1339.   (Coroner's R.)

Bardsley noticed " a Kok " (1281), atte Robuck (1313). Atte Cok also occurs in the Hunts Subs. R. (1327).   The innkeepers often adopted as house tokens the ordinaries, charges, or badges of their overlords or late masters, so that heraldry indirectly has been responsible for some of our modern surnames.   The following family names are all known to have been inn signs, and they also correspond to heraldic emblems.

[1] In Russia, where a large proportion of the people are illiterate, the practice is yet common. I have seen many shops with painted pictures of the goods to be supplied within.

Animals : Ape, Badger, Bear, Boar, Brock, Buck, Bull, Catt, Camel, Coney, Dear, Doe (Hind, Hart, Roebuck), Dragon, Fox, Griffin, Hedghogg, Lamb, Leopard, Lion, Oliphant (Elephant), Ram, Squirrel, Stagg, Wolfe. *Birds* : Cock, Crane, Crow, Dove, Eagle, Falcon, Heron, Peacock, Pigeon, Pye, Raven, Rook.

Tavern signs were not confined to representations of animals and birds; common devices were Anchor (now Anker), Ball, Bell, Board, Bush, Cleaver, Crab-tree, Cross, Devil, Prince, Rose, Tankard, and so on, now all represented as surnames in the modern directory. The surname Garland, in some cases, may have been derived from an inn sign. Garland formerly meant a king's crown, and there was a messuage in Huntingdon or neighbourhood called Le Garlaund (2 Eliz.), and in Eynesbury (Hunts) Garland was a name as early as 8 Edw. II, but it may, of course, have been a compound of *gær* and *land*, both common elements in O.E. nomenclature. Quite a modern instance of acquiring a surname from an inn may be cited :—

" In 1841 a person named Duke was on the list of voters for Penryn in Cornwall. His original name was Rapson, but the name being very common in his neighbourhood, people long distinguished him by the name of ' Duke ', because he kept the ' Duke of York's Arms ' ; and this last name has since become the permanent recognized family name." [1]

Tavern names such as King's Head, Druid's Head, Turk's Head, Alfred's Head, Boar's Head are common, and have quite possibly originated some surnames, but there are other probabilities for the many " head "-names. Wolveshead, *c.* 1380 (Lancs Poll Tax, 130/24) might be an equivalent of Outlaw (certainly a surname), since an outlaw was said to carry a wolf's head, and might be killed at sight. Head may also refer to the headland of a field (see below, p. 232). The following example illustrates the use of the word :—John son of Ranulph Swan of Ploumannesheved, Leic. 1275 (Cl. R.). This value of head occurs in Birkenhead, other surnames of local derivation being Sheepshead (Suff. Subs.), Swineshead,[2] as :—

Nicholaus de Swineheued pro una acra in Swyneheued, Hunts, 1230. (Pipe R.)

In yet other cases head may be a corruption of herd, which undergoes numerous changes (see p. 263). In like manner there are other possible derivations for surnames, corresponding to names of hostelries; e.g. Griffin, Raven, Peacock, and Tankard, were baptismal names ; Badger is an occupation ; Hare was the heir, and so on.

Surnames from Ships. Sea-going craft were always given

---

[1] *Notes and Queries*, 1st May, 1852, p. 425. Duke does not now appear under Penryn, in *Kelly's Directory*.
[2] Weekley calls Lambshead a " genuine nickname " (p. 128) ; I doubt it.

names, and there is a possibility that some of these were transmitted to their owners, but if surnames from such a source do exist, they are difficult to identify. Such names might be Fair Weder [1] or Spilewind found in the Suffolk Subsidy, 1327 ; a more doubtful one being West Wynd, because a wynd is a narrow passage, but an undoubted seafarer was Robert Lokeinthewynde of Peterborough, who was suspected of piracy in 1324 (Pat. R.). Among the Scottish fisherman the names of boats were often given as tee-names, but the practice has fallen into disuse, under a supposition that it brought bad luck.

Surnames from Topographical Features. Under the manorial system the territory occupied by a village community was limited by the boundary *marks*, and the arable *land* separated into *fields* to provide for the annual rotation of crops. The open fields were divided into *furlongs* (furrowlong) or *shots* with *head* lands on which the plough was turned, and the furlongs were split up into *selions*, *lands*, *strips*, *ridges*, or *rigs* of an *acre* or *half-acre* by balks of turf. *Banks* between terraces were called *lynches*, abutting strips were known as *butts* ; narrow projecting parts as *spongs* ; tongues of land as *steortes* ; and odd triangular pieces were described as *gores*. From these italicized terms, common among husbandmen, were derived such surnames as Acre, Bank, Butt, Field, Furlong, Gore, Halfacre, Head (Headley, etc.), Land, Lynch, Mark, Ridge, Rigg, Shott, Spong, Storte, and Stripp. Sylion as a second name occurs several times in the Salop Subsidy, 1327, but it has not been traced as a modern surname. It is customary to say that such surnames as these were derived from places of residence, but the fact is that the holdings being scattered strips, the husbandmen had perforce to live in the villages, and it is much more probable that the labourers were known to their fellow men and the officials of the manor by the descriptions of their land holdings, which in time became their family surnames.

Surnames corresponding to words identifying local features are of considerable interest not only topographically but philologically, often providing earlier examples of M.E. words than have been recorded hitherto by the historical lexicographer. A number of descriptions of this type have been noted already (p. 177), together with the surnames derived from them, and a further selection of family appellatives which correspond to topographical features will now be given.

---

[1] This description reminds me of a well-known Scottish gentleman who was commonly known as " Charming Weather ", from his very frequent use of that expression, and had he lived in the days of surname taking, no other epithet would have had so strong a chance of survival as a family name.

English : Beam (tree) ; Beck (brook) ; Bogg ; Booth (hut) ; Bottom (a hollow) ; Brigg (bridge) ; Broom ; Camp (enclosed field) ; Carr (rock) ; Clegg (? clough) ; Cope, Coop (summit) ; Croft (enclosed field) ; Dam ; Dean (valley) ; Drain ; Edge ; Fallows ; Flatt (level piece of ground) ; Ford ; Fountain ; Gap ; Gorse ; Gott (drain) ; Greave (thicket) ; Hanger (wood on a slope) ; Haven ; Heal (corner) ; Hide (land) ; Holins ; Holt (wood) ; Hook (spit of land) ; Hope (enclosed land) ; Hurst (thick wood) ; Hythe (landing place on river) ; Jardine ; Knagg (pointed rock) ; Laund (glade) ; Law (hill) ; Load (leaning wall) ; Lone (lane) ; Lug (a land measurement) ; Lumb (deep pool) ; Maw, Mow (stack) ; Meadows ; Meals, Meols (sandbanks) ; Mott (moat) ; Mountain ; Nangle (i.e. angle) ; Ness (headland) ; Parrock (small enclosure) ; Peck, Peak ; Penfold ; Penn (enclosure) ; Platt (level field) ; Pool ; Poplar ; Popple (poplar tree) ; Rand (strip) ; Ridding (a clearing) ; Roan, Rowan ; Royd, Rodd (a clearing) ; Rood (a cross) ; Sales (hall) ; Sands ; Sass (sluice) ; Sayles (? willows) ; Sheath (spring) ; Shore ; Syke (stream) ; Tree ; Twell (i.e. at well) ; Twitchell (alley) ; Tye (pasture) ; Upfold ; Vale ; Venn (fen) ; Vennel (passage) ; Verge ; Wade (ford) ; Wall ; Ware (weir) ; Way ; Weeks, Wykes (abode) ; Willows ; Zouch (tree stump).

French : Cowdery (grove of hazel trees) ; Boyce (wood) ; Packet meadow) ; Tallis (copse) ; Travers (cross road).

Cornish : Biscoe (*bos crou* m. " dwelling ") ; Bolland (*polan* f. " pool ") ; Bray, Breen ; Clegg (rock) ; Coode (wood) ; Coumbe (*coom* m. " valley ") ; Gilly (grove) ; Glyn (woody valley) ; Gunn ; Hale ; Keir (*carn* m. rock) ; Kelly ; Loe (pool) ; Nance ; Nooth (*noath* adj. " bare ") ; Park ; Penn ; Pill (*pil* m. " hillock ") ; Praed (*prâz* m. " meadow ") ; Quick (*gwik* f. " village ") ; Rose ; Scawen (*scauan* f. " alder tree ") ; Skewes (*skéz* f. " shade ") ; Sparnon (*spernan* m. " thorn ") ; Toll (hole) ; Tye ; Vease (*véz* m. " open field ") ; Vose (ditch) ; Warn (*guernen* f. " alder tree ") ; Woon (*wón* f. " a down ").

Gaelic : Aird (a height) ; Barr (hill-top) ; Beith (birch) ; Benn (hill) ; Benny (*beinnach* " hilly place ") ; Blair (field) ; Braid (*braigh* " the top ") ; Burn (stream) ; Cairn (heap of stone) ; Cluny (pasture) ; Clyne (slope) ; Corr (round hill) ; Corrie (dell) ; Cowan (*cobhan* " a hollow ") ; Craig (rock) ; Craigie (*creagach* " rocky ") ; Cran (tree) ; Currie (*currach* " a marsh ") ; Daly (*dealg* " thorn ") ; Darroch (*darach* " an oak ") ; Deas (south) ; Deer (oak) ; Douglas (*dubh* " black ", *glas* " water ") ; Fintray (*fionn traigh* " white strand ") ; Frew (*fraoch* " heather ") ; Glaister (*glas tir* " green land ") ; Inch (*innis* " island ") ; Kelt (*coillte* " woods ") ; Kinloch (*cinn locha* " at the lake head ") ; Law (hill) ; Leckie (*leacach* " hillside ") ; Lennie (*leana* " meadow ") ; Lennox (*leamhnach* " elm-wood ") ; Linn (deep pool) ; Loch (lake, arm of sea) ; Logan, Logie (*lag* " hollow ") ; Moy (*magh* " plain ") ; Muir (moor) ; Rait (fort) ; Reay (*reidh* " flat land ") ; Stooke (*stuc* " jutting hill ") ; Tolley (*tulach* ' hill ") ; Torrance (hillock).

Scandinavian : Beck (brook) ; Carse (low land along a river) ; Dale ; Fell (*fjeld* " mountain ") ; Fleck (*flegg* " flat ") ; Halse (a neck of land) ; Ing (meadow) ; Keld (spring) ; Lund (grove) ; Scales (*skáli* " shepherd's hut ") ; Slack (shallow valley).

A pure Norse description occurs in the Bridlington Cartulary :—

"Bartholomew Suth in by" (suðr í bý "south in the village", Ekwall).

Compound Surnames: Ackroyd (oak clearing) ; Akenside ; Bancroft (bank) ; Bargate ; Bellows (bell house) ; Birkbeck ; Cobcroft ; Crossfield ; Culverhouse ; Ellerbeck ; Fallgate ; Fernihough ; Fladgate (flood-gate) ; Fouracre ; Layland ; Learoyd ; Leathley ; Longbottom ; Marsden (marsh) ; Moorcroft ; Nethercot ; Nethersole ; Oxlade (oak-slade) ; Pybus (pike-busk) ; Ridgeway ; Stockley ; Wheatcroft ; Whinwray ; Wicksteed.

Surnames from Rents. As tenants were known by descriptions of their land, it is not unreasonable to suppose that they may have been also identified by their rents, and that this peculiarity may be the origin of such surnames as Fourpeni, Fivepeni, Ninepence, Peppercorn,[1] etc., but such names may quite well be corruptions. Baldwin Eightshillings was an alien in London, 1598-9 (Subs. 146/395), and Tenpenny is from O'Tiompain (Ir.). Twopenny is said to be from the place Tupigny.

Surnames from Trees. Places of occupation and residence were often described by reference to a near-by tree ; a few which have become surnames are : Alder, Ash, Aspen, Beech, Birch, Broom, Box, Elm, Hazel, Holly, Maple, Peartree, Plumtree, Shrubb, Sycamore, Tree, Willows, Yew. Some of these may be imitative corruptions of some word of entirely different meaning, but there can be little doubt about the aphæretic examples : Noakes (atten Oakes), Nelmes (atten Elmes), Nash, Nalder, etc. Other examples of tree names will be found on pp. 178, 233. The description "wood" in various languages has originated a number of modern surnames (see p. 346).

Surnames from Rivers. The names of rivers, lakes, and fords have in like manner become surnames : Derwentwater, Manifold (Staffs), Tame, Tees, Wye, etc. In Scotland, where there is so much water, surnames of this nature are more prevalent, as Blackadder, Calder, Clyde, Cree, Eglin (stream), Frew (perhaps Ford of Frew), Garnock, Gass (water), Gedd (loch), Liddell, Minnoch (loch), Reyburn, Rule (water). Corresponding to an Irish river is Hurley. Some names, like Cam, for instance, may have other derivations.

Cornish Local Surnames. Family names derived from localities in Cornwall possess a particular interest, and are worthy of a special section, because of their perpetuation of words in a language now dead, and for the illustration they

---

[1] Bardsley, with some reason, considers this to be the nickname of a spicer : Ricardus Pepercorne, spyser, 1379. (Yorks Poll Tax.)

afford of the common habit of changing unknown words into imitative sounds conveying an intelligible meaning, no matter how far removed from the original signification. This ancient and modern trait may be amusingly illustrated by a selection taken from the hundred examples collected by Jago [1] to demonstrate the peculiar metamorphoses which have occurred in Cornish place-names in the mouths of Englishmen; curiosities which, it is to be expected, will be found paralleled in surnames derived from similar sources.

Selection.—*Porth eglos* " the church cove " is now known as Pericles ; the great danger to navigators, the Manacles, being similarly derived from *maen eglos* " the church rock ". *Maen* " rock " has also given rise to other absurdities, as Maiden Bower, and Man of War, both from *maen veur* " the great stone " ; Camel Field, Grouse Croft, and Goose Ford are explainable by *cammen* " a path ", *crows* " a cross ", and *cus* " a wood ". Purgatory was formerly *parc a dourie* " the watery field " ; Gold Arrows originated with *gweal daras* " the field by the door " ; and Gallows Park was nothing more interesting than the lowest field (*golez* " bottom "). *Bar bre* " the top of the hill " has given rise to Barbary ; *bigal* " a shepherd " has been converted into Beagle and Bugle ; *goon* " a down ", *kein* " ridge ", *bihan* " little ", *isel* " low ", are now respectively written Gun, Cane, Bean, and Whistle. " Come to good " is derived from *cum ty coed* " the wood house valley ", Paul Pry from *pol pry* " the muddy pool ", Penny Ball being the modern English form of *pen y bal* " the head of the mine ". More appropriately perhaps *Kesan* close, " the turf field ", and *Lau hir* " the long hand " are now commonly known as Kissing Close and Lawyer respectively.

Since there are few Welsh descriptions or surnames of the local class, it may be said that the Cornish appellatives carry their own note of distinction, and may be readily recognized. Camden gave this couplet :—

" By Tre, Ros, Pol, Lan, Caer, and Pen,
You may know the most Cornish men."

A few examples of compound surnames, with the original significations as given by Charnock, follow, and a list of elements with grammatical notes forming a key to the translation of Cornish names will be found below (p. 377) :—

Arwennack, *ar winick* " upon the marsh ".
Bandry, *ban dre* " the high dwelling ".
Benaleck, *benathal ick* " a place of broom ".
Beswetherick, *bos bither ick* " the house by the meadow place ".
Biddick, Fiddick, Viddick, *vidn ick* " the meadow place ".
Body, *bod wy* " the dwelling by the water ".
Boger, *bo geare* " the green dwelling ".
Bolitho, *bol ithig* " the great belly " (i.e. hill).

[1] *An English-Cornish Dictionary,* p. 200.

Borlase, *bur glase* " the green summit ".
Boskea, *bos kea* " the enclosed dwelling ".
Bullivant, *pol y font* " the head of the spring ".
Carthew, *car dew* " the black rock ".
Carver, *car veor* " the great rock ".
Chegwin, *kè gwdyn* " the white hedge ".
Coswarth, *cos warth* " the high wood ".
Forder, *veor dour* " the great water ".
Gluyas, *glew glas* " the wet country ".
Helbren, *hál bren* " the woody hill ".
Killigrew, *kelli grew* " the crane's grove ".
Kimber, *kúm ber* " the little valley ".
Mainprice, *mean práz* " the stony meadow ".
Mulberry, *moel vre* " the bold hill ".
Mylor, *moel or* " the stone boundary ".
Nankivel, *nan kevil* " the horse valley ".
Nepean, *nan pean* " the little valley ".
Pember, *pen ber* " the short head ".
Penfern, *pen warne* " the head of the alder trees ".
Pengelly, *pen gelly* " the head of the grove ".
Penman, *pen maen*, " the head of the rock ".
Pettigrew, *bedh y grew* " the crane's grove ".
Polkinghorne, *pol gan hoarn* " a pool with iron ".
Rosewarne, *rose warne* " the valley of the alders ".
Rosvear, *rose veor* " the great valley ".
Tolmie, *toll vy* " the hole by the river ".
Tredinnick, *tre denick* " the hilly place ".
Venard, *win ard* " the high marsh ".
Vinicombe, *vian coomb* " the little valley ".
Winter, Finter, Vinter, *gwyn dour* " the white water ".

(*b*) **Surnames from late Place of Residence.** Large numbers of surnames are derived from the names of countries, counties, towns, villages, or hamlets, some of which cannot now be traced, and may have disappeared. Difficulty of identification is accentuated in cases where either place-name or surname has greatly changed in orthographic form, or possibly the spelling of both has developed on divergent lines. The original descriptions of this class were in general given to a man who, having moved from one place to another, became known to the recording clerk or to his new friends as of the country of his birth or of his late town, and so on. Such descriptions are in some cases indistinguishable from those of subclass (*a*) ; for instance, let it be supposed that John was feudal tenant of a manor of Sutton, and officially recorded as Johannes de Sutton ; his groom might be Willelmus le Ostler, or Willelmus de la Stable, until he left his master's service, and went to a neighbouring town, when he probably became known to his fellow-men as William of Sutton, and to the recording clerk Willelmus de Sutton. There would then be two families of Sutton, whose names should be entered in subclasses (*a*) and (*b*) respectively ; and not only Suttons, but more aristocratic names were multiplied in this manner. A name by itself, therefore, proves nothing ; its claim for territorial origin must be supported by documented genealogy. Willelmus de London', in Berks ; Robertus de Leicestr' in Warw. ; and David de Paris in Northants, in the year 1230, are gentlemen who are most unlikely to have owned any cities (Pipe R.).

Surnames from Countries and Counties. Family names derived from countries have been very fully exemplified in Chapter VI, and in similar manner surnames corresponding to names of counties have been obtained.

> Rog. Devoniensis, Lincs. 1234. (Fines : Massingberd.)
> Walt. de Dorsete, London, 1337. (Coroner's R.)
> W. de Salop, London, 1337. (Coroner's R.)
> Walt. Devenshyre Tyler of Wycombe, Bucks. 1388. (Anc. Ind. K.B. 9, 5, m. 15.)
> Rich. Schropschyr, Durham, 1405. (Surt. Soc. xxxi, p. 108.)
> W. Barksher, Suss. 1523. (Subs. 189/157.)
> Rog. Chesshire, Shrops. 1523. (Subs. 166/123.)

The latter name occurs in a Kent roll " a chesshire " (124/196, m. 31), and in the Shropshire Poll Tax roll " de Schesterschire " (242/34). Some modern surnames are Chesher, Cornwall, Derbyshire, Dorset, Essex, Hampshire, Kent, Lancashire, Norfolk, Surrey, Westmorland, Willsher. Montgomery is not derived from the Welsh county, but the county from the surname. A Scottish representative for this section is Fife. Of similar nature are surnames from districts, as Flegg (hundred, Norf.), Holland (division, Lincs), Kesteven (division, Lincs), Lindsey (division, Lincs), Wayland (hundred, Norf.) ; and the Scottish examples, Annandale and Tweddle (Tweeddale). Descriptions which fall into the same class are En esteward, Asteward, Bi Suthe, and Binorth, found in the Hundred Rolls, 1275, such being the ancestors of the common surnames, East, South, and North ; not to mention West, which also figures prominently among modern family names.

Surnames from Towns, Villages, and Hamlets. Names of this type are very numerous, some being sufficiently distinctive as to be identifiable at sight with the county of origin, e.g. the surname Fazakerly is undoubted proof of a Lancashire source, Pitkethly of Perthshire, Gainsborough of Lincolnshire, and so on. Some surnames are so prevalent in certain districts that they have become by-words ; for instance a Cheshire proverb is : " As many Leighs as fleas, Massies as asses, and

Davenports as dogs' tails " [1]; and in a certain town of Ayrshire it is said that there are " the rich, the poor, and the Houstons." Sir Walter Scott has mentioned the unsuccessful gaberlunyie (beggar) woman of a Scottish dale, who in the bitterness of her disappointment exclaiming : " Are there no Christians here ? " received the answer : " Christians ! nae ; we be a' Elliots and Armstrongs ! " [2]

The following lists give the counties of England and Scotland with some typical names associated with them, to which is added a smaller selection of modern surnames approximately corresponding to names of places in Wales, Ireland, and France.[3] It must not be forgotten, however, that similarity of orthography is not absolute proof of origin, some towns and places are of mushroom growth, while others, perhaps of the same name, have vanished from the modern gazetteer.

Surnames from Place-names in England.

Bedfordshire : Antill (i.e. Ampthill), Bedford, Bletsoe, Coldington, Lidlington, Limbrey, Odell, Sandy, Thurley, Turvey, Yelden.

Berkshire : Aldworth, Appleford, Ilsley, Inkpen, Pangbourne, Radley, Tidmarsh, Wadley, Wallingford.

Buckinghamshire : Bulstrode (park), Chalfont, Charsley (i.e. Chearsley), Dagnall, Hampden, Kimble, Padbury, Risbrough, Seabrook.

Cambridgeshire : Brinkley, Cambridge, Camps, Caxton, Chatteris, Coveney, Coy (i.e. Quy), Elsworth, Eversden, Helsham (i.e. Hildersham), Hinxton, Papworth, Tadloo, Teversham, Wimple (i.e. Wimpole).

Cheshire : Antrobus, Bebbington, Chidley (i.e. Chedlow), Crewe, Cumberpatch (i.e. Comberbach), Davenport, Egerton, Etchells, Frodsham, Gee, Godly, Goostry, Gresty, Harrup, Hattersley, Hockenhull, Kekewich, Leftwich, Marbury, Minshull, Moberley, Mottram, Occleston, Partington, Pownall, Ravenscroft, Sandbach, Thornycroft, Twemlow, Warburton.

Cornwall : Bolitho, Carey, Carthew, Glynn, Godolphin, Gwennap, Kennel, (? Kennal Vale), Kestle, Kevern, Leland, Newlin, Pengelly, Polkinghorne, Trefusis, Tregear.

Cumberland : Aglionby, Blencow, Blenkarn, Brandreth, Cardew (manor), Carlyle, Dockreay, Gillsland, Greystock, Hornsby, Lamplough, Mulcaster (i.e. Muncaster), Ousby, Penruddock, Ponsonby, Renwick, Salkeld, Ullock.

Derbyshire : Allsop, Ashburn, Bonsall, Brailsford, Charlesworth, Chesterfield, Dethick, Eatwell (i.e. Etwall), Ensor (i.e. Edensor), Froggatt, Glossop, Kinder, Mackworth, Measham, Ogston, Padley, Shardlow, Smalley, Somershall, Tansley, Tidswell.

---

[1] Lower, 1849, vol. ii, p. 30.
[2] *Notes and Queries*, 27th Mar., 1852.
[3] For a full investigation of distribution of surnames, see Guppy's *Homes of Family Names.*

Devonshire : Bastable (i.e. Barnstable), Bodley, Coldridge, Coneybeer (i.e. Collibear), Edgecombe, Galsworthy, Hartland, Haxton,[1] Hembury, Kennerley, Lippincott (i.e. Luffincott), Luscombe, Oxenham, Satterley, Shobrok, Sorley, Upcott, Whimple.

Dorsetshire : Ashmore, Cann, Huntingford, Mintern, Oborne, Tarrant, Weymouth.

Durham : Bolden, Bradbury, Cocking (i.e. Cocken), Durham, Lumley, Shadforth, Stanhope.

Essex : Bellsham (i.e. Belchamp), Bocking, Clavering,[1] Easter, Felstead, Hedingham, Liston,[1] Pentlow, Rumfitt (i.e. Romford), Stebbing, Tilbury, Varley (i.e. Virley), Wenden, Wetherfield, Wix, Yeldham.

Gloucestershire : Beckford, Boxell, Bristow, Bulley, Cubberley, Dowdeswell, Dumbleton, Hambrook, Kemble, Kemplay, Lasbury, Slaughter, Sulley (i.e. Sudeley).

Hampshire : Chute, Dummer, Freemantle, Harbridge, Hursley, Lasham, Odham (i.e. Odiham), Popham, Tichborne, Winchester.

Herefordshire : Byford, Connop (i.e. Conhope), Garroway (i.e. Garway), Kilpeck, Knill, Lenthall (i.e. Leinthall), Lilwall, Pembridge, Pixley, Whitbourne.

Hertfordshire : Baldock, Bovingdon, Gaddesden, Hodsden (i.e. Hoddesdon), Letchworth, Munden, Patmore, Pelham, Puckeridge, Tring, Ware.

Huntingdonshire : Blunsum (i.e. Bluntisham), Molesworth, Offord, Tilbrook, Tozeland, Upwood.

Kent : Brenchley, Chislett, Dover, Hoath, Kingsnorth, Peckham, Pottam (i.e. Petham), Smerdon, Snook (i.e. Sevenoaks, cf. se'night), Welling.

Lancashire : Ainsworth, Ashworth, Atherton, Balderstone, Baxenden, Borwick, Bretherton, Cartmell, Catterall, Cheetham, Clegg, Cowlishaw, Duxbury, Earlam (i.e. Irlam), Entwistle, Fazackerley, Fearnhead, Fearnley (i.e. Farnley), Fleetwood. Furness, Garstang, Haddock (i.e. Haydock), Halsall, Hamer, Heskin, Kenyon, Lever, Maden, Oldham, Openshaw, Orrell, Osbaldston, Parr, Pelling (i.e. Pilling), Pemberton, Penketh, Pickup, Riddington (i.e. Wrightington), Shuttleworth, Winstanley.

Leicestershire : Barwell, Bibby (i.e. Beeby), Blaby, Bosworth, Bringhurst, Frisby, Gadsby (i.e. Gaddesby), Hobby (i.e. Hoby), Hornyold (i.e. Horninghold), Isley, Kilby, Osgathorpe, Quenby, Redmile, Saddington, Shenton, Skeffington, Sketchley, Twycross.

Lincolnshire : Boothby, Bracebridge, Brackenbury, Cawkwell,[1] Coningsby, Cranwell, Crompton, Crowle, Digby, Fotherby, Gainsborough, Gedney, Gilbey, Grantham, Grimoldby, Gunby, Hanby, Holbeach, Horncastle, Ingamells (i.e. Ingoldmells), Ingoldsby, Keal, Keasbey (i.e. Keisby), Kelsey, Kesteven (division), Kidney (i.e. Gedney), Kime, Kingaby, Lusby, Manby, Markby, Mumby, Orby, Panton, Pinchback, Rigsby, Silk, Spalding, Swaby, Swinstead, Westby.

Middlesex : Cornell (i.e. Cornhill), Fulham, Hammersmith, Harfield, Hounslow, Kensal, London, Staines, Turnham.

[1] From the *Glasgow Post Office Directory*.

Monmouthshire : Kemmish (i.e. Kemeys).

Norfolk : Boyland, Bradnam, Caston, Denver, Dyce (i.e. Diss), Docking, Felthorpe, Feltwell, Filby, Fincham, Foulsham, Fransham, Gatley, Gaywood, Gimingham, Hardingham, Helsdon (i.e. Hellesdon), Istead (i.e. Irstead), Kerrison (i.e. Kerdiston), Lammas, Marsham, Massingham, Pentney, Quarles, Ringland, Sculthorpe, Scottow, Sparham, Swaffield, Tilney, Walsingham, Wignall.

Northamptonshire : Aldwinckle, Blatherwick, Bradden, Brigstock, Catesby, Cosgrove, Daintree, Desborough, Dingley, Isham, Kettering, Kilsby, Lulham, Maydwell, Maxey, Orlebar (i.e. Orlingbury), Overstone, Oxenden, Pateshall (i.e. Pattishall), Steane, Weakley.

Northumberlandshire : Bellingham, Copeland, Ditchburn,[1] Espley,[1] Harbottle, Hepburn, Ilderton, Morpeth, Roddam, Shafto, Steel, Swinburn, Swinhoe, Thirlwall, Wark, Wooler.

Nottinghamshire : Bilby, Cotgrave, Gedling, Hucknall, Kelham, Keyworth, Kneeshaw (i.e. Kneesall), Nuthall, Plumptre, Scruby, Sherwood, Sibthorpe, Strelley, Tuxford, Wilford.

Oxfordshire : Banbury, Bladon, Bodycoat (i.e. Bodicote), Cottisford, Finmere, Headington, Kennicott, Kingham, Lewknor, Spilsbury, Stonor, Tew, Witney.

Rutlandshire : Ketton (possibly also Suffolk).

Shropshire : Benthall, Billingsley, Chetwynd, Dudleston, Gatacre, Henstock (i.e. Hinstock), Hickford (i.e. Higford), Hoddinott (i.e. Hodnet), Ludlow, Onslow, Pickford (i.e. Pitchford), Plowden, Sambrook.

Somersetshire : Biddescombe (i.e. Bittiscombe), Bridgewater, Burnett, Cadbury, Chard, Chedsey, Chedzoy, Clatworthy, Dunkerton, Dunster, Holdford (i.e. Holford), Horner, Kidner (i.e. Kitnor), Merritt (i.e. Merriott), Pallett (i.e. Pawlett), Portbury, Priddy, Rodney, Standerwick, Taunton, Uphill, Widdicombe, Winscombe, Wookey.

Staffordshire : Audley, Biddulph, Bonehill, Chell, Doxey, Dugdale, Farewel, Handsacre, Knightley, Muglestone (i.e. Muckleston), Okeover, Only (i.e. Onneley), Rawnsley, Salt, Shenstone, Swinfen, Swynnerton, Trentham, Wrottesley.

Suffolk : Aspell, Bardwell, Beckles (i.e. Beccles), Brundish, Bungey, Dagworth, Dunnage (i.e. Dunwich), Freston, Gaselee (i.e. Gazeley), Gislingham, Ikin, Isworth (i.e. Ixworth), Kettleborrow, Lewington (i.e. Levington), Livermore, Mendham, Pagnam (i.e. Pakenham), Peasnall (i.e. Peasenhall), Redgrave, Stoven, Sudbury, Thurlow, Woodbridge.

Surrey : Dandridge (i.e. Tandridge), Lambeth, Mitcham, Putney, Rygate (i.e. Reigate), Tilford.

Sussex : Arundel, Bathurst, Billinghurst, Chichester, Harting, Keymer, Lickfold, Pashley, Radmall (i.e. Rodmill), Roffey, Ticehurst, Twineham, Vinall, Warbleton.

Warwickshire : Brinklow, Coventry, Ladbrook, Lapworth, Packwood, Sambourn, Warwick.

Westmorlandshire : Bousfield, Brougham, Crackenthorpe, Kendal, Lupton, Murthwaite, Roskell (Rosegill), Sedgwick, Sleddall, Stockdale, Strickland, Tebay, Troutbeck, Warcup.

---

[1] From the *Glasgow Post Office Directory*.

Wiltshire : Bedwin, Brinkworth, Cherrill (i.e. Cherhill), Dancey (i.e. Dauntsey), Durnford, Grimsteed, Keevil, Kellaway, Marlborough, Ogbourn, Pickwick, Tisbury, Trowbridge.

Worcestershire : Blockley, Throckmorton.

Yorkshire : Ackworth, Bainbridge, Battersby, Brownrigg, Cowgill, Dallah, Deighton, Dent, Dowbiggin, Drax, Ellerker, Exley, Fawcett (i.e. Forcett), Flockton, Gisborne, Gomershall, Goodale (i.e. Gowdall), Haxby, Hebden, Horberry (i.e. Horbury), Huddlestone, Idle, Illingworth, Kellington, Killingback, Kilpin, Kipling, Kippax, Leeds, Lockwood, Midgley, Oulston, Oxspring, Penistone, Pickering, Potterton, Pudsey, Quarmby, Rawdon, Rome, Scargill, Selby, Settle, Slingsby, Snaith, Tinsley, Upsall, Wakefield, Whitby, Wycliffe.

The names of many places are common to more than one county and the surnames derived therefrom cannot be assigned with certainty to any special district of England, although some of the elements point to probabilities, e.g. surnames terminating in -by are mainly from Lincolnshire and the east ; in -thwaite from the north ; in -combe from the south-west ; and those with first element Pen- from Cornwall, with rare Welsh exceptions.

Selection : Allington, Alston, Appleton, Ashby, Bentley, Box, Brough, Chesterton, Chilson, Clapperton, Clayton, Clifton, Cowley, Cresswell, Crofton, Crosbie, Crosthwaite, Crowhurst, Croxton, Cullum (i.e. Culham), Dacre, Dalby, Dalton, Danby, Darley, Denby, Denham, Denston, Denton, Derham, Dewsbury, Ditton, Docker, Doddington, Dorchester, Dore, Downham, Draycott, Drayton, Dutton, Eaton, Eckles, Ellingham, Ellington, Evington, Farley, Farnham, Fenton, Fordham, Foxley, Foxton, Frampton, Frome, Fulford, Fulbrook, Furby (i.e. Ferriby), Garford, Gatcombe, Gayton, Gidding, Gillingham, Goring, Grafton, Grindley, Grindon, Haddon, Halford, Hallam, Handforth, Hannington, Hardwick, Harpley, Harrington, Hartley, Haydon, Henley, Hinton, Holdsworth, Horley, Horsington, Huish, Huntingdon, Hutton, Huxham, Ince, Ingersoll (i.e. Inkersall), Ingham, Irton, Islip, Jump, Kedington, Keld, Kelke, Kellett, Kenn, Kimberley, Kimpton, Knighton, Lamport, Langford, Langham, Langton, Lavington, Lawford, Lazenby, Leighton, Leverton, Linford, Lobb, Loxley, Luddington, Ludford, Malpas, Marsden, Marston, Melbourne, Mellor, Morden, Morley, Moulton, Nesbitt, Newnham, Newsham, Newton, Norton, Offley, Ormsby, Otley, Palgrave, Parham, Parkhurst, Penrose, Pickworth, Pilton, Prescott, Pusey, Raby, Reading, Richmond, Ripley, Risley, Rolleston, Rowley, Sampford, Shadwell, Snead, Somerby Spittle (i.e. Spital), Stainton, Staveley, Stowell, Stratton, Sturt, Sutton, Tinsley, Twyford, Upton, Walesby, Walton, Wigmore, Worthington.

Surnames from Place-names in Wales. Early local descriptions are rare :—

Jonas de Powis, 1160. (Chester Pipe R.)
W. de Glamorgan, Lincs. 1244. (Fines : Massingberd.)
J. de Flint, 1352. (Rec. Carnarvon.)

W. de Hawardyne, 1352. (Rec. Carnarvon.)
Rhys Teganwy, 1352. (Rec. Carnarvon.)

Some modern surnames are: Bodvill, Cardiff, Carew, Cogan, Conway, Dolben, Flint, Kennifeck (from Kenfig, Glam., found in Ireland), Laugherne, Penrhyn, Penrice, Powis, Prendergast, Rawbone (Ruabon), Rumney, Sully, Tanat, Yale. Glynne and Pennant may be either Welsh or Cornish.

Surnames from Places in Scotland.[1]

Aberdeenshire : Birse, Byth, Cromar (district), Cruden, Dalgaty, Dinnett, Dyce (also from Diss, Norfolk), Forbes, Gartly, Haddow, Kininmonth, Kinnear, Lendrum, Lumsden, Mennie.

Argyleshire : Easdale, Garven, Toward.

Ayrshire : Beith, Brisbane, Cassells (? Cassilis), Daly (i.e. Dailly), Dunlop, Eglinton, Fairlie, Galston, Giffen, Girvan, Irvine, Loudon.

Banffshire : Cullen (also possibly Irish), Dallachy, Forgie.

Berwickshire : Lauder, Redpath, Spottiswood.

Clackmannanshire : Dollar.

Dumbartonshire : Gartshore.

Dumfriesshire : Annan, Carruthers, Dinwoodie, Drysdale (i.e. Dryfesdale), Glendinning, Irving, Keir, Lockerbie.

Edinburghshire (now Midlothian) : Cramond, Cranston, Currie, Dewar, Dryden, Glencross, Heriot, Pennicuick, Primrose (or Carrington).

Elginshire (now Moray) : Dallas.

Fifeshire : Abercrombie, Anstruther, Cairney, Durie, Forgan, Kirkcaldy, Kilgour, Kinghorn, Torrie, Wemyss.

Forfarshire (now Angus) : Affleck, Balfour, Brechin, Claverhouse, Dargie (also possibly Irish), Deuchar, Forfar, Fotheringham, Gallery, Guthrie, Hedderwick, Keillor (hill), Lunan, Melville.

Haddingtonshire (now East Lothian) : Belhaven, Cuthill, Dunbar, Gifford (also a personal name), Gullan, Pinkerton.

Inverness-shire : Cromarty.

Kincardineshire : Allardyce, Arbuthnott, Kinmond (i.e. Kinmouth), Strachan.

Kircudbrightshire : Bogue, Galloway.

Lanarkshire : Aitkenhead, Arbuckle, Biggar (also in Lancs), Braidwood, Brownlie, Calderwood, Carmichael, Carstairs, Cathcart, Cleghorn, Clydesdale, Dalziel, Dennistoun, Glasgow, Glassford, Govan, Henshilwood, Motherwell, Sandilands, Tinto (hill), Wardlaw.

Linlithgowshire (now West Lothian) : Bathgate, Binnie, Livingstone.

Nairnshire : Geddes, Nairn.

Orkney : Isbister.

Peeblesshire : Peebles, Stobo.

Perthshire : Balharrie, Callander, Cargill, Comrie, Dron, Methven, Ogilvie, Pitcairn, Pitkethly, Rait, Strathearn (valley).

Renfrewshire : Cathcart, Eaglesham, Erskine, Houston, Paisley, Ralston, Renfrew, Semple, Shedden, Walkinshaw.

Ross-shire : Dingwall, Docherty, Foulis, Marwick.

[1] Surnames from the *Glasgow Post Office Directory*, 1914.

Roxburghshire : Cessford, Denholm (also Yorks), Eckford, Fulton, Kelso (chalk hill), Maxton, Melrose, Roxburgh, Rutherford.
Selkirkshire : Cadden, Kirkhope, Selkirk, Yarrow.
Shetland : Fitch.
Stirlingshire : Denny, Kincaid, Kippen (also personal), Stirling, Torrance.
Sutherlandshire : Sutherland.
Wigtownshire : Clugston, Gilfillan.

Most of these Scottish surnames are of Gaelic or O. Norse derivation, some few perhaps " Pictish " ; the significations often can only be guessed, and may even entirely baffle the philologist, e.g. Brise and Dinnett. The following examples of more or less conjectural meanings illustrate the nature of the formation of these compounds.

Affleck, a variant of Auchinleck (Gael. *achadh na leac* " field of the flagstones ". Docherty (Gael. *do'ach gartaidh* " davach of the corn-enclosure "). Forbes, the thirteenth century Forbeys, perhaps from *fuar bhathais* " the cold brow "). Foulis, from Gael. *fo-ghlais* " small stream ". Gartly was in the fourteenth century Garintuly or Grantuly (Gael. *garadh an tulaich* " the enclosure of the knoll "). Haddow is a contraction of half-davach, i.e. two ploughgates of land. Lendrum is Gael. *leathan druim* " broad ridge "). A Norse example is Dingwall, i.e. *thingvöllr* " field of the thing (court of justice) ".[1]

Some of the principal Gaelic, Norse, and Welsh elements and their variants found in Scottish surnames of the local class, forming a help towards identification, will be presented at a later stage.

Surnames from Place-names in Ireland. Few Irishmen bear local surnames, but some Irish names of this class have arisen outside of Erin, e.g. :—

Dionisius Cork hibernicus, Devon, 1439.   (Subs. 95/100.)

The following surnames appear to be derived from places in Ireland :—

Adair, Ardagh, Athy, Blaney, Borris, Boyle, Breen, Cashel, Cavan, Costello, Doak (Doagh), Dromgoole, Drummond, Dunhill, Finglas, Galway, Garvey, Kells, Kilcullen, Kilkenny, Limerick, Longford, Lusk, Monaghan, Pallas, Seaton, Weatherston.

Mayo, a common name in the south of England, is of French or Norman origin, and Trim is a genealogical surname, formerly an English personal name (*see* Cur. Reg. R., 1196, Bucks).

Surnames from Place-names in France and Normandy.

Baskerville (Bacqueville), Bavent, Beaver (Beauvoir), Bloss (Blois), Bollen (Boulogne), Boswell (Bosville), Bottrell (les Bottereaux), Bovill (Bouville), Brassy (Brécy), Bullen (Boulogne), Cailly, Caines or Keynes (Cahaignes), Callis (Calais), Cane (Caen), Carvell (Carville),

---

[1] From the works of J. Macdonald, W. J. Watson, and H. Harrison.

Challen (Châlons), Challis (Calais), Charters (Chartres), Chauncy (Chancey), Claville, Colville (Colleville), Conyers (Coignières), Courtenay (Courtonne or Courtenay), Crawcour (Crèvecoeur), Creasy (Crecy), Dampier, Dangerfield (d'Angerville), Darcy (d'Arcey), Dark (d'Arques), Daubeney (d'Aubigny), Devil (Déville), Dinant, Disney (d'Isigny), Dive (Dives), Doyley (d'Ouilly), Dumville (Donville), Furneaux, Furnival (Fourneville), Glanville, Greville, Gurdon (Gourdon), Gurney (Gournay), Harcourt, Havill (Hauville), Hersee (Héricy), Lacy, Lascelles (Lacelle), La Touche, Levett (Livet), Lintott, Mandeville, Massey (Macey), Molineux (de Molinelles), Money (Monne), Montague (de Montaigu), Montgomery (de Monte Goumeril), Mortimer, Montjoie, Mounteney (Montigny), Mowbray (de Moubrai), Mummery (Moubrai), Nugent (Nogent), Olley (Ouilli), Perci, Pheysey (Vessey), Pierpont, Pinkney (Picquigny), Quatermass (Quatremare), Quency (Quincey), Revell, Semper (St. Pierre), Quaritch (de Quarroges), Scovell (Escoville), Sellinger (St. Leger), Sinclair (St. Clair), Somerville, Tilley, Tracy, Troy (Trie), Turbefield (Turberville), Turney, Umfreville (Amfreville), Venables, Verdin, Vere, Verney, Vesey.

It may be noted that in general there are several places of each name, with variant spellings.

CHAPTER X

CLASSIFICATION OF BRITISH SURNAMES (*continued*)

Class III. Genealogical Surnames. One of the most convenient ways of establishing the identity of a person was to repeat his pedigree, providing an answer to the question—who are his nearest or most important kin ? And the extensive adoption in England of a modified form of such distinction has resulted in the surnames of the second largest class, which comprises 30 to 40 per cent of the whole. From various references already made to the genealogical description, it will have been gathered that it was much more prevalent among the Celtic than the Teutonic or Scandinavian races, so that to-day nearly all surnames of Welsh and Irish origin are of this class, and owing to the mass migration which has extended over many years they are to be found all over Britain, the Dominions, and the United States of America. Names of this division are, however, not only Welsh and Gaelic; a good proportion are found to be O.E., French, and Hebrew. Most genealogical surnames have been personal names, derived from the father, mother, or other relative; but occasionally characteristic, local, or occupational descriptions, with the help of the filial desinence, or ancestral prefix, have become genealogical. Surnames of the genealogical class may be subdivided, according to their origin, (*a*) from personal name of male parent, called patronymics ; (*b*) from personal name of female parent, called metronymics ; (*c*) from personal name of other relative ; (*d*) from descriptions or surnames.

For various notes on the origin and evolution of descriptions and surnames of this class the reader may refer back to p. 28, Sanskrit ; p. 28, Greek ; p. 33, Irish ; pp. 43, 126, Welsh ; p. 57, Anglo-Saxon ; p. 68, Norse ; pp. 80, 84, 91, 97, Norman ; p. 139, Flemish ; and p. 149, Jewish.

(*a*) **Surnames from Personal Names of Male Parent.** There are four distinct formations of patronymics.

(i) *Simple formation.* The genealogy having been expressed, at first, in the descriptions, by the employment of a word signifying " son ", as Lat. *filius*, N.F. *fitz*, W. *ab*, Ir. *mac* ; or daughter, as Lat. *filia*, W. *verch*, Ir. *ingean* ; or descendant, as Ir. *o, ua*, etc., a desire for brevity led to dropping the word defining the relationship, resulting in a simple genealogical description or surname indistinguishable from the parental forename, thus " Egidius filius Bernardi " became " Giles Bernard ".

(ii) *Prefixion*. The filial expression or part of it coalesced as a prefix with the personal name, as Fitzhugh, (a)Price, (ma)Cowan, etc.

The Latin *filius* became *filz* and *fiz* in O.F., and afterwards *fitz* and *fils*, and joined, in the uninflected genitive, with the following name :—

Thom. fiz le Provost, Warw. 1273. (Cl. R.)
J. le Fuiz Bernard, Bucks. 1308. (Inq. p.m.)
Matilda Fyznicole, Glouc. 1312. (Subs. 113/4.)
Simon fiz Richard *alias* fuytz Richard, Ess. 1324. (Inq. p.m.)
Rob. le fitz Wauter *alias* le fyz Water, Norf. 1326. (Inq. p.m.)
W. fitz Jon *alias* Fietz John, Hants. 1335. (Inq. p.m.)
Thom. Filtz Herber, taillour, Yorks. 1381–2. (Surt. Soc. xcvi, p. 79.)
Rich. filz Laurencii, Wales, 1509. (Pardon Roll.)
J. Fitzherbert or Fiherbert, Derb. 1509. (Pardon Roll.)

Feeharry, i.e. Fitzharris, is an Irish form. Other examples of Irish fitz-names have been given above (p. 211). Regarding Welsh compounds of this type, see above (p. 122) and below (p. 255) for numerous illustrations. Manx examples are given above (p. 183), and Scottish below (p. 256).[1]

It may shatter a common belief to say that fitz-names do not point to ancient Norman ancestry ; in fact, they were not known in France, and are commoner in Ireland than elsewhere, the Fitzes rivalling in popularity the O's and Macs (see p. 212). There is no reason to suppose that " fitz " indicated irregularity in birth [2] ; it ranks equally with *ap*, *mac*, *son*, etc., in expressing relationship, legitimate and illegitimate. Eyton, however, thought that *fitz* had the broader signification of O', being equivalent to " descendant of ", a reasonable supposition, in some instances, since *filius* sometimes occurs in the same sense (see below, p. 250).

(iii) *Genitive case ending*. This aspect of name formation has been touched upon above (p. 120). *Filius* and *filia* having fallen into disuse, the inflected genitive was sometimes retained in the parental name :—

Willelmus Johannis, Glouc. 1159–60. (Pipe R.)
Willelmus Baldewini, Kent, 1229. (Pat. R.)
Robertus Edwini, Kent, 1229. (Pat. R.)
Willelmus Gileberti, Wilts. 1235. (Cl. R.)
Dugallus Nigelli, Scotland, 1541. (See p. 209.)

The Latin genitive forms have had little or no influence on surnames, although, since the genitive ending of the second declension was often written *y*, names in modern transcripts

---

[1] Some curious corruptions are said to be Phippen from Fitz Paine and Fidgen from Fitz John (*Cok. Peerage*, where, however, no evidence is given).
[2] Dauzat, p. 48, erroneously supposes *fitz* to refer to a " fils naturel ".

may appear as Mably, Iweny, etc. Another misapprehension arising from the dropping of *filius* (see p. 215) is that two baptismal names were known before the sixteenth century, but such a combination as "Thomam Mariam Wingfeld (Hunts. Fines) probably illustrates the pre-Reformation custom of adding Mary, in honour of the Blessed Virgin.

In the thirteenth century the English form of genitive case endings, *es*, *is*, *ys*, or *s* came into official use, at first as has been illustrated above (p. 120), noticeably in the second names of women : John, Robin's son, would be called John Robin, but Margaret, Robin's (daughter), would be known as Margaret Robines (Cambs. 1275, Hund. R.),[1] and so also :—

Petronilla Cokkes, Oxf. (now Cocks, Cox) ; Cristin Edwardis, Hunts (now Edwards) ; Matilda Felippes, Oxf. (now Phillipps) ; Juliana Folkes, Cambs. (now Foulkes) ; Juliana Gegges, Oxf. (now Gedges) ; Alicia Godefreis, Oxf. (now Godfreys) ; Agnes Hobbis, Hunts (now Hobbs) ; Constancia Huwes, Oxf. (now Hewes, Hughes) ; Angn' Jakkes, Hunts (now Jackes) ; Cristiana Jemes, Cambs (now James) ; Matilda Jones, Hunts (now Jones).

Similar names of men were rarer in the thirteenth century.

Gervase Ivans, Devon, 1230.   (Cl. R.) : now Evans.
Adam and W. Jones, Warw. 1262. (Foot of Fine, 244/26, no. 1.)
Rob. Dobes, Oxf. 1275.   (Hund. R.): now Dobbs.
J. Rolves, Oxf. 1275.   (Hund. R.) : now Rolfes.
W. Trigges, Cambs. 1275.   (Hund. R.) : now Triggs.
W. Wattes, Oxf. 1275.   (Hund. R.) : now Watts.

Possibly in the early instances the terminal *s* was due to influence of the French nominative singular ending, seen in names like Jacques, Gilles, Jules, etc. The names of men with the affixed sibilant became more plentiful in proportion in the following century. By the sixteenth century the final *s* was occasionally written *ce* and *se*.

J. Evanse, 1533.   (*Letters and Papers*, Hen. VIII, vol. vi.)
W. Pearce, or Perce, or Peirs, or Perse, or Peirce, or Peirse, or Pearse, adm. B.A. 1601.   (Reg. Univ. Oxf., ii, pt. iii, 221.)

The terminal *s* is not always the genitive ending, but may be due to metathesis, as Cripps from Crisp, an apocope of Crispin. The sibilant following the k-sound has given names terminating in *x* as Simcox, Madox, etc.

Robert Vodecox, Worc. 1271.   (Halesowen Ct. R.)

That names terminating in *s* are not more prevalent is due to the fact that the genitive case ending was by no means in general use in colloquial speech, in Robert of Gloucester

---

[1] It is perfectly clear that never at any time could the final *s* have been an ellipsis for son, as stated by D. Macinlay, p. 5 ; F. Chance (*Notes and Queries*, 23rd Nov., 1861, p. 413), etc.

(thirteenth century), for instance, the uninflected " possessive " occurs : " for marie love," " the quene fader," etc.

(iv) *The filial desinence.* A second compound method of forming genealogical surnames was by the use of the filial desinence, as O.E. *sunu* " son " or " descendant " ; O.N. *sonr* ; numerous early examples of which have been given above (p. 172). Probably belonging to this category is J. Widowson (Wido, i.e. Guy), Yorks, 1366 (Cl. R.).[1] Occasionally daughter was additionally used to form patronymical descriptions in the same way.

> Leflet Ecregeles docter, Hants. 1066. (Wint. Dom.)
> Cecilia Dansdoghter, Durham, 1371. (Surt. Soc. lxxxii, p. 105)
> Marg. Simdoghter, Durham, 1378. (Ibid., p. 144.)

In view of our great alien population, it may be of interest to mention some foreign forms of the filial desinence. The French had nothing of the kind. The Germans used -*sohn* in addition to other equivalents, such as the genitive in -*s*, as Sievers ; the -*ing*, -*ung* suffixes, as Karling, Eysink, Adelung, etc., and the -*er* suffix, as Wilhelmer.[2]

The Russian language is profuse in patronymics, grammarians stating that their original character was adjectival, thus *Petr suin Alexandrov* signified " Peter the Alexandrine son ", *Anna doch Alexandrova* " Anna the Alexandrine daughter ". Maudru states that this class of adjectives admits of an honorific amplification, and the Russians use the phrases *Petr suin Alexandrovich, Anna doch Alexandrovna.* It became customary to write *Petr Alexandrov suin*, the last word being often omitted. The character of the patronymics has now come to be substantival, numerous orthographic variations of the terminations being found as -*vich*, -*witsch*, -*wicz*, -*off*, -*eff*, etc.[3] Nowadays, everyone in Russia being equal, the correct title of address is Comrade !

Leite de Vasconcellos gives examples of Portuguese patronymics in -*aci*, -*azi*, -*az*, -*oz*, -*uz*, -*ici*, -*izi*, -*iz*, -*ez*, -*es*, which termination has the same force as English -*s*; e.g. Alvarez, i.e. " son of Alvaro ". In Spanish also -*ez* is found, as Ibánez (hijo de Juan)[4] ; such terminations, however, soon become corrupt in England, e.g. Rodriguez is commonly converted into Rogers.

---

[1] It may be noted that in some instances -son is a corruption of -*ston* and possibly -*sdon* (or -s-ton and -s-don), final elements of place-names, as Balderson for Balderston, Kelson for Kelston, Compson for Compstone, Hilson for Hilston, etc.

[2] Solmsen, p. 183.

[3] *Élémens Raisonnés de la Langue Russe*, vol. i, p. 165. See Thos. Watts, in *Proc. Phil. Soc.*, 1848, vol. iv, p. 85.

[4] See Letelier, who, incidentally, supposed curiously that Irish O' is a contracted " of ".

Some other foreign terminations which may be found in our directories are : Dan., *-sen* ; Roum., *-esco* ; Du., *-zon* ; Fris., *-ma* ; Gr., *-ides.* It may be noted that Slav. *-ski* is an adjectival termination equivalent to G. *-isch,* E. *-ish,* Swed. *-isk,* etc., signifying " of or belonging to ", " of the nature or character of ". In Hebrew and Arabic " son " is indicated by *bar* and *ben,* and such words are placed before the parental name, but the Israelites also largely use *-sohn.*

(b) **Surnames from Personal Names of Female Parent.** There are but three distinct formations of this subclass, prefixion not having been noticed.

(i) *Simple formation.*

Willelmus Alis, — 1068. (For. Docts. Round.)
Rogerus Alis, — 1245. (Cl. R.)
Matilda Miriel, Cambs. 1275. (Hund. R.)
Rob. Elyenore, Lincs. 1275. (Hund. R.)
Cecilia Beatrice, Lincs. 1327. (Subs. 135/11, n. 10.)
Ric. Dameysabele, Glouc. 1327. (Subs. R., p. 28.)

Alis may not be here the feminine name ; the possibility of appellatives being epicene, that is common to both sexes, is ever present. The two examples last given may properly belong to section ii. Modern surnames are Merrill, Elenor, Aveling, Marrian, etc.

(ii) *Genitive case ending.*

Reginaldus Mablii, Cambs. 1275. (Hund. R.). Mabille is the usual genitive form. A modern surname is Mably.
W. Sibile, Leic. 1327. (Subs. R. ; Fletcher, p. 38.)
Rich. Sibely, Oxf. 1327. (Subs. 161/9, m. 10.)

The terminal *s* is scarce in early metronymics, corresponding to the O.E. practice of rarely inflecting feminine substantives in the genitive case.[1]

J. Orable or Orables, Cambs. 1275. (Hund. R.) : now Orable, Orbell.
Ad. Emmis, Cambs. 1275. (Hund. R.) : now Emms, Emps.
W. Emms, Shrops. 1275. (Hund. R.)

It has to be noted that Emma was also a male name, and possibly Orable also. An undoubted example of a metronymic is Katheryns, which occurs in the Rutland Subsidy Roll, 1523 (165/112).

(iii) *The filial desinence.* The filial suffix may be linked with the mother's name as Tillotson (from Matilda), Beatson (from Beatrice), Sisterson (Cecilia).

Hen. Damejonesone, Glouc. 1327. (Subs. R., p. 28.)

---

[1] See Maetzner, 1874, vol. i, p. 243.

These names are no indication of base birth, as often erroneously supposed.[1] The name of the most important parent formed the genealogical description or surname, e.g. John Biset was son of John de Wotton and Ela Biset, his *wife*, Worc., 1300 (Inq. p. m.). An instance of the son of a second wife taking his mother's name is not unknown, and the Welsh custom of the third son adopting his mother's personal name has been noticed (p. 208); the taking of metronymics likewise being a common practice among the Hebrews.[2] (See Liquorish, p. 339.)

Nich. Comitassone, Staff. 1294. (De Banco, R. Trin. 22 Edw. I, m. 36.)

(c) **Surnames from Personal Names of other Relatives.** Names only of suffixal type can be detected by inspection. A Chancery inquisition (thirteenth century), however, provides an example of simple formation; a man being distinguished by the name of his grandfather. " After the death of John son of Bernard, a tenant in chief of the king, his son Ralph (called Ralph son of Bernard) became a ward of the king." [3] Rarely a father is described by the name of his son :—

Joh'es del Hay pater Will'i fil' Joh'is del Hay de Sprouton, Suff. 1335. (Ass. R. 856, f. 2.)

Descriptions in which the relationship appears as a suffix are not uncommon :—

Edith Wellenewif, Soms. 1225. (Ass. R. 755, m. 2.)
Rob. Huwechild, Cambs. 1275. (Hund. R.)
W. Gamelstepsone, Yorks. 1297. (Cl. R.)
Anota Sergauntmanwife, Cumb. 1333. (Subs. J. P. Steel.)
J. Geppedoghtersone (i.e. grandson), Yorks. 1336. (Pat. R.)
J. Nicbrothere, Yorks. 1350. (Inq. a.q.d.)
J. Elysmagh (i.e. Ellis's brother-in-law), Yorks. 1379. (Poll Tax.)

" Benettyssone yn lawe fissher " was an alien in Cornwall, 1439 (Subs. 87/78). A more complicated example is Matilda Dickwyuemalkinson (wife of Dick, son of Malkin), Yorks. W. R., 1379 (Poll Tax, p. 42). The composition of the description may be compared with that of the names of servants given below (p. 348). A few surnames of this type have survived, e.g. Watmough, Hitchmough.

(d) **Genealogical Surnames from Descriptions or Surnames.** There are three distinct formations of this sub-class, simple formations falling into the other sections.

---

[1] It is surprising to find a leading modern authority like the *Complete Peerage* (vol. iii, p. 611) saying : Gervasius Caterine, twelfth century " (presumably a bastard as being named after his mother) ".
[2] *Jews of Angevin England*, by J. Jacobs, p. 371.
[3] *Cal. of Inq. Misc.*, vol. i, p. 130. In effect Fitz-Bernard had become a surname.

(i) *Prefixional.*   (1) Prefix + characteristic description.

M'Inulty (*mac an Ultaigh* " son of the Ulsterman ").

(2) Prefix + occupational description.

M'Chlery (son of the clerk).
O'Gowan (descendant of the smith).
Macintosh (*mac an toisich* " son of the thane ").

(ii) *Genitive case ending.*   (1) Characteristic names of sub-class (*g*), from Relationship (see p. 227), as Neaves, Neeves, Cousins, etc.   Generally speaking, final *s* in characteristic surnames indicates a former plural, as Crookshanks.

(2) Local.   A final *s* is not uncommon in surnames derived from topographical features, and may be either the plural formation or genitive case ending, but it is not possible to say which, from inspection.   Maetzner (1874, i, 188) thought the final *s* "frequently denoted the plural", but actually such usage seems to be comparatively rare.   Reference to the examples given on pp. 177-8 will show that the probability of names from topographical features having originally been plural forms was not more than 3 in 100.

J. Kers, Oxf. 1275 (Hund. R.) : cf. W. de le Ker, Cambs. 1275 (ibid.).

Such names, rare in the thirteenth-century records, are now common, as Barnes, Banks, Briggs, Brookes, Cairns, Clowes, Dykes, Fields, Hargreaves, Hedges, Holmes, Ings, Knolles, Nares (O.E. *knar* "rugged rock", "tree stump "),[1] Oakes, Parks, Sands, Stones, Styles, Sykes, Woods, Yates. The terminal *s* can hardly be the genitive formation in these instances, and since, in considerable measure, the plural formation has been ruled out, probably, in a number of cases, the *s* is a meaningless excrescence, the addition of a terminal sibilant being not uncommon with uncultured people.

(3) Occupational.   Descriptions derived from trades, offices, etc., are also found with final *s*.

Alice le Driveres, Cambs ; Mabilia Kings, Cambs ; Beatrix Knictes, Hunts ; Ysabel Loverdes (i.e. Lords), Oxf. ; Hubert Masters, Hunts ; Walter Quenes, Hunts ; Julian' le Smithes, Oxf. (Hund. R.)

Possibly of this class is Pepys. Pap, Pape, Pepes, and Pope are all found in the Cambs Hund. Rolls ; but Pep may be a shortened form of Pepin. And so also from personal names may be derived Loverdes, Quenes (cf. Queneson, Yorks, 1379, Poll Tax), Kings, and Knictes, from Lord, Quen, Kin, and Cniht respectively.   Modern names of this class are Masters, Reeves, and possibly Vickress and Yeamans ; but such names

---

[1] Nar may also be a personal name ; it occurs as a prototheme in Nardred (Suff. Dom. Bk.).

may be from local descriptions ; cf. atte Persones. Driveres and Smithes may possibly exhibit the feminine agential suffix, which is sometimes written -es, as in lyonnes, duches, etc., but if Driveres and Smithes are, in fact, feminine forms of Driver and Smith, then they are thirteenth-century words which have not been noted before.

(iii) *Filial desinence*. The termination -*son* is rarely found in records after the Norman Conquest until the fourteenth century, when it began to appear freely in the northern lists. *Son* may be affixed to :—

(1) A characteristic adjective :—

Alex. Scotson, Yorks. 1379. (Poll Tax, p. 206.)

(2) A local description :—

(i) Country, as Rich. Waleson, Lincs. 1380–1. (Coroner's R. 82, m. 11*d*.)

(ii) Place. Consecutive entries are Thomas de Mosergh and Hugh Moserghson, Cumb. 1333 (see p. 168.)

(3) An occupational description :—

Rob. le Reveson, Staff. 1302. (Cl. R.)
Rich. Knyghtson, Yorks. 1379. (Poll Tax, p. 217.)
J. Parsonson, Yorks. 1379. (Poll Tax, p. 18.)
J. Shepardson, Lincs. *c.* 1523. (Subs. 136/313.)

A curious entry is Walter Prestfadre followed by Walter Prestson (Leic. 1337, Pat. R.). Does it not mean Walter Priest, the father, and Walter Priest, the son ? Modern names of this class are Herdson, Hindson, Smithson, Taylorson, Wrightson, etc.

The principal influences in the formation of genealogical surnames have been the prevalence of Anglo-Saxon, Norse, Norman, Cornish, Welsh, Scottish, Irish, and Hebrew names, and some illustrative examples will now be presented.

Anglo-Saxon (O.E.) Genealogical Influence.

(i) *Uncompounded Surnames.* Many short surnames are derived from O.E. monothematic names of one thousand years ago, a feature which will be realized upon running through the following selection of personal names which all bear some resemblance to modern surnames. It will be shown in a later section that numbers of these names have originated what are erroneously supposed once to have been " nickname; " (see below, pp. 331–7).

Abbud, Adda, Æsc, Alde, Appe, Ascha, Babba, Bacga, Bæda, Bære, Baga, Bar, Barbe, Barne, Bass, Bate, Bearn, Becca, Beoscep, Ber, Bere, Bern, Betti, Biche, Biga, Bil, Binna, Blac, Blunta, Boba, Boda, Boga, Bole, Boosa, Borda, Bossa, Bota, Brad, Brand, Breme, Brid, Briht, Brode, Brord, Brum, Brune, Brunel, Bucge, Burg, Burro,

Bynni, Cabe, Cane, Cawe, Ceoc, Ceol, Cheping, Cild, Clare, Cniht, Code, Coppa, Crowe, Cudd, Cyma, Dene, Deor, Derinc, Dode, Draca, Dudde, Dunn, Durre, Dyddel, Dyre, Earne, Else, Epa, Esme, Euing, Feg, Fin, Fisc, Fram, Frod, Frome, Frood, Fug, Fugel, Gadd, Geddi, God, Golde, Grene, Gribol, Grid, Grima, Hæring, Har, Hauoc, Heardinc, Heming, Hilla, Hoc, Hoga, Hors, Hunni, Hyne, Ing, Kyma, Kysinge, Lambe, Lane, Lang, Leppa, Lind, Lord, Luca, Man, Mali, Mawa, Menning, Nun, Nytta, Ogga, Orde, Ote, Pipe, Port, Preed, Prim, Prin, Prud, Pymma, Quen, Reedes, Rudda, Særle, Slede, Smala, Snell, Somer, Spille, Sport, Starlinc, Stear, Suel, Swan, Swet, Tella, Thynne, Tirtil, Tone, Totta, Treda, Tunne, Wade, Wædel, Walle, Ware, Welp, Wiga, Win, Wintra, Wita, Wod, Wymer. (See also p. 87.)

Some O.E. names, which would be lost otherwise, have been discovered as components of place-names, and others are to be found surviving in English compound surnames, e.g. Legge. Wihtlæg is a personal name occurring in the A.-S. Chronicle ; and may have survived in the modern surname Whitelegge, which possibly, however, is nothing more than Whiteley, in the same way that Severleg was Saverley (De Banco R. Mich., 19–20 Edw. I), and Suckeleg was Suckley (1230, Pipe R.).[1] Ravenleg (Hund. R.), on the other hand, has the appearance of being a personal name of Norse origin. The theme -læg has been preserved in the place-name Legsby (Lincs), and occurs as a first element in Thom. Leggegode, Soms., 1225 (Ass. R. 755, m. 3) ; and Leggard de Aula, Cambs. 1275 (Hund. R.), if these two examples are not forms of Leodgeard. A better illustration of the survival of this personal name is :—

Andrew fil' Legge, Cambs. 1275. (Hund. R.)

(ii) *Compounded Surnames.* The following selection is of surnames which have the appearance of being derived from O.E. personal names. By using the list of elements, pp. 366–72, the original form of a number of them may be discovered.

Adlard, Adlin, Albert, Albutt, Alden, Alder, Aldin, Aldred, Aldridge, Alfray, Alfred, Algar, Allard, Allbutt, Allcorn, Allday, Allfree, Allgood, Allnutt, Alston, Alvey, Alway, Alwin, Auden, Audrey, Awdith, Aylwin, Balder, Bawden, Brightman, Brightwin, Brownson, Burridge, Cadman, Colbert, Colbran, Colvin, Culver, Darwin, Dumphrey, Earwaker, Eastman, Edmund, Elphick, Elvey, Elvin, Folger, Forman, Frewin, Fulcher, Gamlin, Garbett, Garman, Gladwin, Goodchild, Goodlamb, Goodridge, Goulston, Grimbert, Gutlack, Hardman, Harvard, Hermon, Herrick, Hildyard, Hurlbert, Imbert, Inger, Ingold, Isard, Izard, Kennard, Kendrick, Kenward, Kinmond, Lawman,

---

[1] The modern surname Legge may also have a local derivation as an equivalent of ledge (cf. Whitehegge and atte hegge) ; or of legh (meadow), of even possibly a corruption of del Egge. Common descriptions are : de la Lee, de la Leg, de Leg, a la Legh, de Legh, giving the modern surnames Lay, Lea, Lee, Legg, Legge, Legh, Leigh, Ley, etc.

Longman, Mathwin, Maymond, Maynard, Methwin, Mildred, Ordway, Otway, Otter, Radmond, Rambart, Randall, Raymond, Readwin, Redmond, Richman, Rimbault, Seamer, Seaward, Simmond, Stannard, Sunman, Theobald, Thormond, Thurstan, Unwin, Warman, Whatman, Woolmar, Woolsey.

Surnames in -ing : Benning, Billing, Bocking, Bolding, Browning, Bunting, Canning, Cocking, Colling, Dearing, Dowding, Dunning, Gilling, Golding, Gooding, Goring, Hanning, Harding, Harling, Harting, Hasting, Hayling, Helling, Hemming, Hickling, Hocking, Living, Manning, Patching, Pilling, Reading, Riching, Stenning, Sweeting, Tilling, Walling, Waring, Watling.

Regarding the -ing names in particular, the probability of other origins should be noted ; e.g. the personal name was often given to a village which afterwards originated a surname.

Norse Genealogical Influence.   These surnames are usually indistinguishable from those of Anglo-Saxon derivation, but the following are probably of Norse origin : Ankettle, Arkcoll, Arkell, Askill, Aslac, Gemmell, Grimkil, Inger, Kettle, Magniss, Oskell, Osmund, Patrick, Rankil, Usborn, although not all are to be found in modern lists.

Norman Genealogical Influence.   The following examples are representative of the surnames derived from the Norman-French appellatives which became established in spite of the overwhelming popularity of William, John, Roger, Robert, etc. : Ansell, Arment, Bertin, Bisset, Blaze, Blease, Bowkett, Buckett, Challand (Jolland), Chamen, Elwes (Heloise), Girardot, Guerin, Guichard, Guille, Lancelin, Mayo, Minett, Pepin, Perowne (Perrin), Poyntz, Wydowe (Guy).

Cornish Genealogical Influence.   Few distinctive Cornish personal names have survived as surnames, and these are mainly appellatives formerly borne by saints : Arthur, Gluyas, Jennifer (Guinevere), Jewell (Brit. Judicael or Juhel), Keverne, Key, Tangye (i.e. Tanguy, common in Brittany), Ustick (probably adjectival from Just). Possibly also Prowse (ap Rowse) and Prawle (ap Rawle). Biblical names were given a Cornish form in which some have become surnames ; e.g. the Mayows were originally Matthew, or Mayhew, as they wrote it, and Jago was James.[1] Some orthographic forms peculiar to Cornwall are : Clemens, Clemmow, Climance, etc., from Clement ; Rawle, Rawlings, Rabling, Rowling, etc., from Ralph. Jenner considers Jago, as well as Pascoe, Varcoe, Crago, and Manuel to be of foreign derivation.[2] There are considerable doubts as to the classification of some of the Cornish names. The name of a saint, as Keverne, may be adopted as a local appellative, which in turn is given as a

---

[1] *Parochial History of Cornwall*, by C. S. Gilbert.
[2] *Handbook of the Cornish Language*, pp. 198-9.

description to an individual, ultimately to become a family name strictly of the local class, but in the absence of evidence to the contrary must perforce be entered as genealogical.

Welsh Genealogical Influence. Nearly all Welsh surnames are of the genealogical class, but they are by no means restricted to those of native origin : English, Norman, and Hebrew names being largely adopted, resulting in the production of hybrids, such as Badams (W. and Heb.), Bedward (W. and E.), Pritchard (W. and Norm.-Teut.). Great numbers of Welshmen derived their names from the Normans, as the columns in the directories devoted to Williams and Roberts testify. Some examples of surnames from Welsh personal names follow :—

Abadam (ab Adam), Ameredith (ab Meredith), Anwyl, Anyon (Einion), Barthur (ab Arthur), Batha (ab Adda), Beavan (ab Evan), Beevor (ab Ivor), Bellis (ab Ellis), Benyon (ab Einion), Bethell (ab Ithel), Bevan, Biolyn (ab Iolyn), Blevin (Blethyn), Blood (ab Lloyd), Bowen, Breeze (ab Rees), Brodrick (ab Roderick), Bunner (ab Ynyr), Bunyan (ab Einion), Caddell (warlike), Cadogan, Cadwallader, Craddock (Caradoc), Enefer (Gwenever, cf. Corn. Jenifer), Evan (John), Eynon, Flewellin (Llewelyn), Floyd (Lloyd), Gethin, Griffin, Gwillim (William), Gwyther, Heaven (Evan), Howell, Inions, Jevon (Evan), Kenwright (Kenwrec), Kyffin (? Gethin), Lewis, Llewellyn, Lloyd, Madoc, Marvin, Mervin, Meredith, Meyler, Morgan, Onion (Eynon " just "), Owen, Palin (ap Heilin), Parbert (ap Herbert), Parry (ap Harry), Peddowe (ap Eddow), Pendry (ap Henry), Pinnion (ap Einion), Plevin (Blethyn), Ployd (ap Lloyd), Powel (ap Howel), Prandle (ap Randal), Press (ap Rees), Price (ap Rhys), Prickard (ap Richard), Probert (ap Robert), Probyn (ap Robyn), Proger (ap Roger), Prosser (ap Rosser), Prothero (ap Rhydderch), Prydderch (ap Rhydderch), Prynallt (ap Reinallt), Pugh (ap Hugh), Pumphrey (ap Humphrey), Puskin (ap Hoesgyn, i.e. Hoskin), Rhydderch, Rice, Rosser, Thelen (Llewelyn), Trehern, Tudor, Upjohn (ap John), Yorath (Yorwerth).

Bardsley gives Beddow (ab Eddow) of this class, but Bedo was a forename borne by three Welsh poets. In the hands of the English scrivener curious variants such as Bunion, Flood, Onions, etc., were manufactured, and yet live to grace our directories. Evan in its most frequently occurring early Welsh form is Yevan or Jevan, but there are many variants ; in *one* list of homagers at Flint, in 1344, the name appears in no less than nine different forms : Evan, Yefan, Yevan, Yevon, Yvon, Yvan, Yveyn, Yven, and Yveny [1] ; the last being latinized with the genitival inflection. Since Bardsley thought it sufficiently notable to record that the surname Irwine might commence with three different letters, it may be worth mentioning that the name Evan may be found with nine different initials : Bevan, Evan, Fevan, Heven, Ievan, Jevan, Shevan, Yevan, Zevan, and perhaps Avan and Wevan.

Scottish Genealogical Influence. Modern Scottish surnames of this class are mainly derived from Gaelic, Norse, Anglo-Saxon, and, in comparatively recent years, Irish personal names. Some distinctive Scottish surnames are :—

Aitchison, Aitken, Beattie, Carmichael, Dickie, Donaldson, Dougall, Duncan, Ewing, Farquharson, Ferguson, Finlay, Gilchrist, Grierson, Henderson, Hutchinson, Jamieson, Macalister (Alasdair), MacAlpine, MacArthur, MacAusland, Macdonald (Domhnall), Macdougal, Macfarlane (Parlan), Mackail (Cathal), Mackinlay (Fionnlagh), McInnes (Aonghas), McMurtrie (Urardaigh), MacPhail (Paul), McQueen, Macrae (Rath), MacTavish (Thomas), Paterson, Shaw (sometimes local).

Irish Genealogical Influence. Irish surnames of true native origin are nearly all of the genealogical class, formerly distinguished by the use of Mac and O', now often in part elided or dropped altogether, the corruptions being even more remarkable than anything found in English nomenclature.

Cavanagh (caomhánach, " belonging to Caoman ") ; Connelly (Ó Conghalaigh, descendant of Conghalach, derivative of Conghal, " valorous ") ; Dolly (Ó Dathlaoich, descendant of Dathlaoch, " bright hero ") ; Kinshellagh (cinnsealach, belonging to Ui Cinnsealaigh in Wexford) ; MacKean (mac Eáin, " son of John ") ; Mac Millin (mac maoilín, " son of Maoilin ") ; MacVity (mac an bhiadhtaigh, " son of the hospitaller ") ; O'Molloy (Ó Maolmhuaidh, descendant of Maolmuadh, " noble chief ") ; Sharkey (O Searcaigh, descendant of Searcach, " loving ").

Corruption may be instanced by Ó Cartáin, formerly Mac Cartáin from mac Artáin, a diminutive of Art. An example of anglicized Irish is the surname Eason, from M'Ea, from mac Aodha, " son of Aodh ". Curious hybrids may be found, thus, Cadden (Hebr. and Gael : Adam became a diminutive, Adin, from which come MacAdin, and by aphæresis 'cAdin) ; Cauley (Norse and Gael : Olaf became Amhlaoidh and mac Amlaoidh, then Mac Auley and 'cAuley). The extent of the variations found in Irish names is so great that it is impracticable to present any serviceable scheme whereby easy and certain identification would result. Further reference should be made to the works of Woulfe and Matheson, where thousands of examples are explained.

Hebrew Genealogical Influence. A number of surnames originate in biblical personal names, but they do not necessarily point to Semitic ancestry.

Aaron, Abel, Abner, Absalom, Adam, Amos, Asplen (? Absalom), Bartholomew, Benjamin, Cain, David, Elias, Gideon, Jacob, Jeremy, Jessop (Joseph), Job, Joel, Jonas, Joseph, Kane (Cain), Matthew, Moyse (Moses), Peter, Philip, Salmon (Solomon), Simeon.

Hebrew names may be hybridized by the use of the English filial desinence, as Abrahamson and Jobson; or a N.F. diminutive ending, as Jobling and Tobin; or a Welsh prefix, as the examples given above (p. 255). Some names of Jewish origin are not Hebrew, as Leo, now a surname; on the other hand Semitic appearance may mislead, e.g. Leah, which appears in the *London Directory*, is a variant of Lea, according to Bardsley.

Class IV. Occupational Surnames. As nearly every person did something to earn his livelihood, or to fill in his time, a considerable help to the identification of the individual was a reply to the question—what is his vocation? Many of such descriptive answers were registered, and by frequent repetition ultimately became stereotyped as surnames, forming a class of from 12 to 20 per cent of the total family appellatives. Surnames of this division are mainly English, but a few Latin, French, Cornish, Welsh, and Gaelic have survived, and they may be single-element nouns, as Ward; noun + noun, as Church-man; noun + suffix, as Harp-er; or verb + suffix, as Baxter (i.e. Bake-ster); many being obsolete words, even forgotten trades, giving a striking picture of the occupations of our forefathers. In addition to official, professional, and military appointments, and the numerous manual callings, a number of surnames seem to be derived from mock or imitation offices; consequently the following sub-classes have been adopted: (*a*) from office or profession; (*b*) from mock office; (*c*) from military rank; (*d*) from trade or vocation.

The chief observations on descriptions and surnames of this class which have been made already will be found on p. 33, Irish; pp. 43, 126, Welsh; p. 57, Anglo-Saxon; p. 68, Norse; pp. 83, 85, 92, 98, Norman; p. 140, Flemish; p. 149, Jewish.

(*a*) **Surnames from Office or Profession.** Names of this subclass mainly record the vocations of ecclesiastical, legal, and manorial officials. Some modern English surnames are :—

Alderman, Alefounder, Bailey, Beadell and Biddle, Canon (also Cannon, local), Cardinal, Chamberlain, Chambers, Chancellor, Chaplin, Churchman, Churchward, Cleaver (mace-bearer), Clerk, Constable, Corner (coroner), Counsellor, Damsell (*damoisel*), Deacon, Deemer (judge), Gateward, Grieve (bailiff), Grosvenor (head huntsman), Hamper (Hanaper), Harbinger, Holliman (holy man), Justice, Kingsman, Lawman, Leech, Lord (the head of a household; also a personal name), Master, Munk, Page, Parson, Passavant (? pursuivant), Pope, Potticary, Preacher, Priest, Primmer, Prior, Proctor (an attorney in a spiritual court), Reeve, Scholar, Scrimgeour (the skirmisher),

Scriven, Sellars (the cellarer), Sergeant, Sermoner, Sewer, Shannon (canon), Sheriff, Sizer, Spicknell (spigurnel, a sealer of writs), Sumner Surgeon, Vavasseur, Waight (watchman), Warden, Wardrop.

Scottish examples are Bailie (also local), and Dempster ; Irish : Cleary (clerk), Davin (*daimh* " poet ") and Ward (*bhard* " bard ") ; and a Hebrew surname of the class is Cohen. (priest).

Some early descriptions have not survived :—

Rob. Notare, Oxf. 1275. (Hund. R.)

(de) Cristofero Wryter, Northd., alien, 1439. He was probably a Scot, the profession of writer in Scotland corresponding to that of solicitor in England. (Subs. 158/115.)

(b) **Surnames from Mock Office.** It is usual to stress the influence of the medieval drama and the lengthy miracle plays, lasting sometimes for days, which " featured " every possible character from the highest heavens down to the lowest depths, often covering a period of thousands of years from the creation, and it is supposed that the principal players acquired the names of the characters which they represented year after year : such as King, Queen, Angel, Devil, and Dragon. There were also various festivals, as the May crownings, when king and queen were elected for the year. While some such origin seems necessary to explain the great number of Kings, yet it must be noted that these names are explained in most cases quite soundly without any call on the characters of the morality plays, or public games. Weekley suggests, for instance, that Hatecrist and Shunecrist arose from dramatic rôles, but the first is nothing more than " at crest ", and the second, sometimes Sonecrist, a compound of two O.E. elements,[1] is perhaps as simply explained as Lovegod, which is an O.E. personal name. Neither is it necessary to look to church festivals for Bishop and Lord ; both are personal names in Domesday Book. An amusing list of such noble-sounding surnames will be found on p. 350, all of which have prosaic origins.

Ranulfus le King : Thoma le Kyng, Glouc. 1237. (Cl. R.)

This name has survived in both Latin and French, as Rex and Roy respectively. Nothing pointing to the origin of Prince has been noticed. Roger Prince held a third part of a knight's fee in Yorks, 1166 (Lib. Nig., 1771, p. 310), and Henry Prince was a citizen of Winchester in 1238 (Pat. R.). Prince arrived too early to be the O.E. personal name Prin-s, and so like King may be a pageant name, but equally possible a tavern name ; or the bearer may have been servant to a prince. The thirteenth-century Duke was a " leader ", evidently

---

[1] A Suffolk variant is Shonecrist. Six Misses Shonecrist are mentioned in 1271 (Exc. Fines).

in a very small way ; as early as 1224 Osbert le Duc is recorded as associating with such London tradesmen as le Barber, le Dubber, and le Burser (Coroner's R.). Marquis was a personal name, occurring in the feminine.

Marchisa filiam Warneri, Yorks. 1202. (Fines.)

Earl was an O.E. personal name, found as a first element in Eorlwine (Dom. Bk.) ; Baron has a similar value to Duke, or it may be a form of O.E. Barne (Dom. Bk.) ; and Pope has been mentioned above (p. 251). Cardinal, and, in fact, any of the other names of this type, may be those of servants known by their masters' title, cf. the groom called Whiteknight (p. 348). Bishop, Lord, and Knight have been noticed above (pp. 251, 258) ; Abbott is an O.E. name (Abbud : *KCD*.), or perhaps a diminutive of Abel, and the rest can be taken at face value.

(c) Surnames from Military Rank.

Johannes le Squier, —, 1208. (Rot. de Obl.)
Ricardus le Archer, Worc. 1238. (Cl. R.)

Some modern surnames of this sub-class are : Alabaster, Banister, Bower (in some cases), Bowman, Camp, Chevalier, Footman, Halfknight, Kemp, Knight, Pickman (pike), Scorer (spy), Slinger, Squire, Thane (thegn). A Cornish example is Marrack (soldier) ; an Irish representative is Colgan (*colg* " swordsman "), and possibly a Norse name is Skiddie (*skyti* " shooter ").

(d) Surnames from Trade or Vocation. The most important division of the Occupational class of surnames consists of 75 per cent derivatives of the noun or verb + suffix type, the remainder being compounds (noun + noun), with a few exceptions as :—

Arlett (from Harlot, " a fellow "),   Day (dey, " a dairywoman "), Faraday (chapman), Fon (fool), Fool, Groom, Ladd (serving man), Man (vassal or servant), Mason, Norris (nurse), Smith, Ward (guardian). *Cornish* : Anaer, Annear (*an eure* " the goldsmith "), Andain, Endean (the man), Angoff, Angove (the smith), Gove (smith), Tyacke (*tyac* " farmer "). *Irish* : Gow (*gobha* " smith "). *Welsh* : (see above, p. 126). *Scottish* : Caird (tinker).

Assigned to this class are surnames derived from certain degrees of feudal tenants, since by their tenures they obtained their livelihood ; some, however, might be entered in class I, as they represent condition.

Boarder (bordar), Bond, Bondman, Boor, Carle, Cotter, Cotterell, Drengher, Frank, Franklin, Freeman, Frye (the free), Hobler, Tenant, Villain, Yeoman. *French* : Francom (*le franchomme* " the freeman "), Prudhomme (freeholder).

To this class also must be placed names taken from masters :—

From persons : Addyman, Fillman, Frereman, Hardman, Harriman, Human, Jackman, Ladyman, Matthewman, Monkman, Pakeman, Philipman, ? Prettyman, Priestman, Wyllnave.

From places : Smythyman.

(i) **Agential Suffixes.**

English : -er, -ier ; fem. -ess ; m.f. -ster ; with variants.

Cornish : -ar, -as *gwiadar* " weaver "; -er, as *troccyer* " fuller " ; -or, as *stenor* " tinner " ; -yas, as *sewyas* " tailor ".[1]

Welsh : -awdur, as *llywiawdwr* " governor " ; -iar, as *rhodiar* " ranger " ; -on, as *gwyddon* " philosopher " ; -or, -awr, as *cantor* " singer " ; -ur, -adur, as *ffoadur* " fugitive " ; -wr, -iwr, as *heliwr* " huntsman " ; -ydd, as *darllenydd* " reader ".[2]

Gaelic : -air, as *piobair* " piper " ; -iche, as *marcaiche* " rider ".[3]

Irish : -aire, -ire, as *sealgaire* " huntsman " (*sealg* " a chase ") ; -ach, as *marcach* " horseman " (*marc* " a horse ").[4]

French : -and, -eur, -ier ; fem. -esse, -iste.

O. Friesic : -a, -and, -en, -er, -ere, -ing.[5]

Mod. W. Friesic : -er, -der, -ert, -ner ; fem. -ster, -inne, -ske.[6]

Examples of modern surnames follow :—

-and, -ant. Marchand, Servant.

-ar, -ard. Erroneous spellings for -er.

-er. Ambler (one who rides an ambling horse) ; Berger (adopted from Fr., shepherd) ; Berner (a master of kennels) ; Binder ; Bloomer (the bloomery was a forge in iron mills) ; Blower ; Booker and Bowker (a bowger was a cashier ; boucher is an obsolete form of butcher) ; Bowdler (buddler, a worker in iron ore) ; Bowler (one who shapes the bowl of a spoon) ; Braconer (O. F. *braconier* " a keeper of hounds ") ; Bulter (sifter of meal) ; Cadger (hawker) ; Capper (cap-maker) ; Carder (one who cards wool) ; Carver ; Catcher (huntsman) ; Caunter (glover) ; Chaloner (maker of chalons) ; Chandler, Chaucer (breeches-maker) ; Cogger (one who puts cogs in a wheel) ; Coifer (capper) ; Collier (maker of wood charcoal) ; Comber (worker in wool manufacture) ; Copper (i.e. Cooper) ; Cordiner (i.e. Cordwainer) ; Corker (magician ; or caulker, one who caulks ships) ; Cosser (dealer) ; Coucher (upholsterer) ; Cowper (i.e. Cooper) ; Cramer and Creamer (a pedlar) ; Crier (an announcer) ; Crocker (potter) ; Cropper (cloth-shearer) ; Cutler ; Cutter ; Dancer ; Dawber (plasterer) ; Dexter (winnower) ; Dicker (ditcher) ; Disher (maker or seller of dishes) ; Dorturer (one in charge of a dormitory) ; Dresser (leather-workman) ; Driver (huntsman) ; Dubber (O.F. *doubeur* " a repairer ") ; Dyer ; Ewer (a servant who supplied washing utensils) ; Faggetter (one who makes faggots) ; Falconer and Faulkner (keeper of or hunter with

---

[1] Jenner, p. 77   [2] T. Rowland, 1876, p. 129.
[3] H. C. Gillies, 1896, p. 150.   [4] O'Donovan, 1845, p. 331.
[5] A. H. Cummins, 1887, p. 72.
[6] P. Sipma, 1913, p. 79. It may be noted that *-er, -ster,* and *-mer* denote origin of persons (m. and f.), as Snitser, Grouster, Hegemer.

hawks) ; Falder (i.e. Folder) ; Fanner (one who winnows grain with a fan) ; Farrer (worker in iron) ; Felter ; Fender (defender) ; Fewterer (feltmaker) ; Fidler ; Firminger (O.F. *fromageur* " a cheese-maker ") ; Fisher ; Fitter (coal-vendor) ; Flanner (maker of flawns or cakes) ; Flesher (butcher ; the term is in common use in Scotland) ; Fletcher (dealer in arrows) ; Flutter (fluter) ; Forrester ; Foster (forrester) ; Fower (cleaner) ; Fowler ; Fuller ; Furber (burnisher) ; Furner (baker) ; Galer (collector of the gale, a duty on fish) ; Ganter (glover) ; Gater (watchman ; if not Cater) ; Gauger (measurer) ; Girdler (maker of girdles) ; Glazer ; Glover ; Graver (turf-digger) ; Groser ; Harber (a host) ; Harper ; Harrower ; Hiller (slater) ; Holder ; Hooker ; Hooper ; Horder (treasurer) ; Hornblower ; Horner (worker in horn) ; Hustler (inn-keeper) ; Jester (a reciter of romances, or buffoon) ; Joyner ; Jugler ; Keeler (bargeman) ; Keeper ; Keller (? capmaker) ; Kemper (comber of wool) ; Kidder (huckster) ; Killer (butcher) ; Kilner (furnaceman) ; Kneller (? bellman) ; Knowler (bellman) ; Larder (one who lards) ; Latimer (interpreter) ; Layer (mason) ; Leadbeater ; Leader ; Leaper and Leper (dancer) ; Limner (illuminator of MSS.) ; Lister (reader) ; Loader (carrier) ; Locker and Looker (locksmith) ; Lorimer (maker of bits) ; Mariner ; Marler (clayworker) ; Mercer ; Messenger ; Messer (mower) ; Milner (miller) ; Minter (moneyer) ; Mower ; Nodder (possibly a kneader) ; Offer (Fr. *orfevre* " a goldsmith ") ; Osler (ostler) ; Packer ; Paliser (maker of pailings) ; Panter (formerly a baker, but later the pantry official) ; Pargeter (plasterer) ; Parker ; Parmenter (tailor) ; Pedder (basket-maker) ; Pelter (dealer in skins) ; Pender (keeper of a pound) ; Pessoner (fishmonger) ; Pester (Fr. " a cook ") ; Pilcher (garment-maker) ; Pillinger (barker) ; Plaister (plasterer) ; Plater ; Plumer (dealer in feathers) ; Pointer (a maker of laces for fastening clothes) ; Ponder (keeper of a pound) ; Porcher (swineherd) ; Pottinger (a maker of pottage, but confused with Pottingar, an apothecary) ; Poucher (pouch-maker) ; Poulter (poulterer) ; Poyser (weigher) ; Purser ; Quarrier ; Ranger (a forest officer) ; Raper (i.e. Roper) ; Reader (i.e. Reeder " a thatcher " ; perhaps also a maker of reeds, i.e. weaving instruments) ; Ridler (one who uses a sieve) ; Rimmer and Rymer (poet ; possibly confused with Reamer) ; Rooker (rocker or spinner) ; Roper ; Sacker ; Salter ; Sanger (singer) ; Saucer (saucemaker) ; Scambler (? bench-maker) ; Setter (stonelayer) ; Shearer ; Sheather (sheath-maker) ; Shoveller ; Skinner ; Skipper ; Slater ; Slipper (slipper of hounds) ; Sloper (clothier) ; Smelter ; Soper ; Souter (cobbler) ; Speller (preacher) ; Spencer (steward) ; Spicer (dealer in spices) ; Spier ; Spooner (maker of spoons) ; Squiller (scullery servant) ; Stabler ; Stainer (one who colours wood, etc.) ; Stalker (a poacher, except in Scotland) ; Stamper (treader of grapes) ; Storer ; Stringer (one who makes strings for bows) ; Sumpter (driver of a pack horse) ; Swingler (flaxmaker or flail-maker) ; Sworder ; Taborer (drummer) ; Tapiser (weaver) ; Tapper (tavern keeper) ; Tasker (assessor or piece-worker) ; Taverner ; Tawyer (leather-worker) ; Teller (tallier) ; Tenter (cloth-worker) ; Tewer (one who taws leather) ; Thacker (thatcher) ; Thredder (weaver) ; Thresher (flail-worker) ; Tiller ; Tinker ; Tipper ; Toller (toll-collector) ; Tozer (teaser of wool) ; Tranter (carrier, hawker, etc.) ; Trimmer ; Trinder (wheel-maker) ;

Tripper (dancer) ; Trumper (trumpeter) ; Tucker (fuller) ; Tuer (i.e. Tewer q.v.) ; Vacher (cowherd) ; Vanner (winnower) ; Venner (huntsman) ; Verrer (glazier) ; Vinter (i.e. Vintner) ; Vowler (i.e. Fowler) ; Waferer (cake-maker) ; Wagner (wagoner) ; Walker (fuller) ; Waller (wall-builder) ; Warner (warrener) ; Weaver ; Webber ; Wheeler (spinner's assistant) ; Whiter (white-tawer) ; Wimpler (veil-maker) ; Wonter (mole catcher).

Note : In the Hundred Rolls may be found Tayl-er, -ir, -or, -our, and -ur. The earlier form, which has often been retained, was without the final *r*, as Armour, Flawn, Hawke, Hogsflesh, Hunt, Mill, Paternoster, Pewter, Poulter, Webb, etc. The transition stage may be noticed :—

> Walt. le Stalke, Oxf. 1275. (Hund. R.)
> Amabil la Stalker, Hunts. 1275. (Hund. R.)

Sometimes -*er* occurs in local names, as Docker (Westm.), Dummer (Hunts). Occasionally -*er* is a variant of hewer or herd, q.v.

-iar, -ier, -iour, -yar, -year, -yer. Collier and Cullyer (maker of wood charcoal) ; Currier (dresser of leather) ; Ferrier ; Hilliar, Hillyar (tiler) ; Lockyear ; Napier (person in charge of royal table linen) ; Pavier, Paviour ; Sivier ; Spurrier ; Tawyer (leather-worker).

-or, -ur. Cator (aphetic form of *acatour*, a buyer of provisions) ; Harpur ; Landor (for Lavender, " a launder ") ; Mellor (one who collects honey) ; Naylor (nail maker) ; Tailor ; Tylor.

-ster, -ister, -istor. Feminine agential suffix attached to verbs, as Baxter, Blaxter, Blackister, Blackistor (bleacher) ; Brewster ; Dyster (dyester) ; Fewster (maker of saddle trees) ; Maltster ; Sempster ; Sewster ; Shapster (dress-maker) ; Souster (shoe-maker) ; Thackster (thatcher) ; Webster.

Note : This suffix ultimately came to be used indiscriminately with -*er*, as an agential ending irrespective of gender. By the fourteenth century it was usually replaced by the French -eresse, which, however, has left no mark on our surnames.

> Hugelina la Prestresse, Norf. 1232. (Cl. R.)
> Yda le Teleresse, Suff. 1255. (Fines, 1836, p. 200.)
> Alicia la Tayluresce, Hunts. 1275. (Hund. R.)
> Angns Pecheresse, Cambs. 1275. (Hund. R.)
> Matilda le Barbaresse, Cambs. 1275. (Hund. R.)

Cornish surnames : Bather (coiner or banker), Cauntor (singer), Hellyar (hunter), Sayer (artisan). Welsh : (see p. 126). Irish : Gleasure (glazier), Gosnell (góiséir " hosier "). Latin : Faber (smith).

(ii) Compound Occupational Surnames. Second elements are : -herd, -hewer, -knave, -maker, -man, -mason,

-master, -monger, -smith, -ward, -wife, -woman, -wright, and variants.

-ard, -art, -er, -erd, -ert, -ett. See -herd.

-ger. See -hewer.

-herd, -ard, -art, -er, -erd, -ert, -ett, -hard, -head, -itt (the keeper or tender of a flock) : as in Calvert, Coulthard, Coward, Fowlherd, Geldart, Gelderd, Gozzard (goose-herd), Hoggett, Hoggitt, Lambert, Oxnard, Stoddart, Swinnart, Weatherhead.

-hewer, -er, -ger, -ier, -year, -yer (one who cuts or shapes) : Feavearyear (? *le fevre* " smith "), Fleshhewer, Stonehewer, Stonier, Wooder, Woodger, Woodhewer, Woodyer.

Note : In -makyere (see below) -yere is an equivalent of -er.

-knave (servant or menial : obs.). Durknave.

-maker. Slaymaker (a slay is a weaving instrument).
Rich. le Harneysmakyere, London, 1339. (Coroner's R.)

-man (vassal or servant) : Ackerman, Chapman, Charman, Chessman, Cogman (cog, a kind of ship), Couchman, Courtman, Cowman, Ferriman, Flatman (several definitions), Flaxman, Gooseman, Henchman (groom), Herdsman, Inman, Ironman, Knapman, (hammerman), Loadman, Maltman, Packman (pedlar), Parkman, Pepperman, Plowman, Runciman, Shearman, Shipman, Silkman, Templeman, Tillman, Toleman, Tubman (cooper), Wainman (wagoner), Wakeman (watchman), Waterman, Wayman (hunter), Workman, Yeatman (gatekeeper).

(i) -man is sometimes the O.E. element, as Seaman for Seman, a personal name.

(ii) A corruption of -man is -ham, as in Kitchingham, the kitchenman ; alternatively -man may be a corruption of -ham, as in the local surname Deadman for Debenham.

(iii) -man is occasionally elided, e.g. Husband, Warw. 1377 (Poll Tax).

-mason. Woodmason.

-master. Rob. Ploghmaystre, Yorks. 1297. (Subs. W. Brown.)

-monger (dealer, trader). Fishmonger, Fleshmonger (Hund. R.), Ironmonger, Isemonger (iron).
Rich. le Fethermongere, London, 1322. (Coroner's R.)
Sarra the Bredemongestere is noticed by Riley (*Memorials*, xxii).

Note : -monger is sometimes dropped, as in Stokfisshe, 1339. (Riley, xxxi.)

-smith. Arrowsmith, Goldsmith, Greensmith, Nasmith (knife-smith : Bardsley), Shoesmith.

-ward (guardian or watchman). Hayward (a manorial officer), Millward, Woodward.

Note : -ward is confusable with -weard, as in Dorward.

-wife. Cristina the Flexwyf : *Memorials of London*, Riley, xxiii.

-woman. Draywoman.

-wright (artificer). Arkwright, Cheesewright, Glasswright, Plowright, Shipwright, Sievewright, Slaywright, Tellwright (tilemaker), Wainwright (wagon-builder), Wheelwright.

-year. See -hewer.

Group II. Acquired Surnames.

Class I. Self-assumed Surnames. An assumed surname may be the first or original name borne, or one taken in lieu of a discarded name, or in addition to an existing one ; and such a name may be personally manufactured, or an existing one assumed by arrangement, or pirated. The legal aspect is treated in a later chapter.

(*a*) **Ecclesiastics.** The monastic custom of changing name on dedication to the service of the Church is of great antiquity : in England cases being recorded in Saxon times, such as those of St. Fabricius, who was baptized Succath (according to Dugdale), A.D. 361, and intermediately called Magonius ; and St. Bonifice, whose baptismal name was Winfred, *c.* A.D. 700, being referred to by Bede as " Bonifacius qui et Vinfridus ".[1] An Archbishop of Canterbury (1381) was called Simon Sudbury *alias* Tibold, Godwin explaining that Simon Tibold being born at Sudbury took that name " according to the manner of many clergyman in those days ".[2] Holinshed (1577) has noted that " among spiritual men it was the fashion to take awaie the father's surname (were it never so worshipful or ancient), and give him for it the name of the towne he was borne in ". Assuming the name of a town was not, however, the general practice, as is clearly shown by comparison of deeds of the religious fraternity of Winchcombe (Glouc.).

Bond, 17th Oct., 1537.	Surrender, 3rd Dec., 1539.
Ricardus Ancelmus, Abbas	Richard Mounslow, last Abbot
Johannes Augustinus, Prior	John Hancock, Prior
Willelmus Omersley	William Craker
Johannes Gabriel	John Whalley
Ricardus Angelus	Richard Freeman
Willelmus Maurus	William Blossom
Willelmus Overbury	William Bradley [3]
etc.	etc.

The practice of changing names was also observed in the nunneries.

[1] *Notes and Queries*, 6th November, 1886, p. 376. But see 11th December, 1886, as to the supposed equivalent of Boniface and Winfred.
[2] *Catalogue of the Bishops of England*, p. 101.
[3] Albert Way in the *Archæological Journal*, vol. lx, p. 181. I have seen something similar in Blomefield's *History of Norfolk*, but cannot now trace it. Further reference may be made to *Remains concerning Britain*, by W. Camden (1870 ed.), p. 150. *Archæologia*, vol. xviii, p. 109.

> " Before she was as now you are
> The daughter of Sir Arthur Clare.
> But since she now became a nun
> Call'd Milliscent of Edmuntun." [1]

Numerous cases, however, could be cited to prove that no general rule was followed, and that the family name was retained by many monks and nuns.[2]

(b) **Theatrical Artistes.** The custom of theatrical artistes adopting other names probably dates from the time when they were held to be among the lowest in the social scale. Now that the possibility of becoming a pet of society exists, a high-sounding aristocratic name is often assumed. Some of these names are fabricated, and others are pirated, against which action there is no legal remedy. Well-known artistes who adopted theatrical names were J. H. Brodribb, who assumed the additional surname of Irving, afterwards becoming Sir J. Henry Brodribb Irving, Kt., and Charles Culverwell, who concealed his identity for stage purposes by adopting the appellative of Wyndham, under which name he also received knighthood. The assumption of foreign-sounding stage names is not uncommon among British concert artistes, an innocent venial deception to overcome the disabilities of the well-known law of a prophet being without honour in his own country; thus the Irishman Foley became Signor Foli; and the name might be latinized, e.g. a Miss Beryl Smith figured prominently on the play-bills as Beryl Faber. The same practice of changing name, sometimes for simplicity, is current among film artistes : Ullman has become Fairbanks, Francis is better known as Kearton ; Lepinsky is cut down to Lee ; Smith has become famous as Pickford, and so on.

(c) **Authors.** The adoption of pseudonyms is widespread among writers of all descriptions, but the custom does not appear to have influenced the manufacture or change of surnames. Occasionally collaborating authors operate under one pen-name, e.g. Ivor Novello and Constance Collier are jointly known as " David L'Estrange ".[3]

(d) **Business Men.** Names are commonly manufactured for business reasons, but these likewise have had little or no effect on surnames ; an historic example being that of Almack, assumed by McCall, who founded the famous Almack's Club in Pall Mall, in 1764.[4]

---

[1] *The Merry Devill of Edmonton*, 1608, Act iii, sc. ii.
[2] *Notes and Queries*, 12th November, 1927, p. 357.
[3] *Sunday Times*, 17th January, 1924.
[4] *Memoirs of W. Smellie*, by Robt. Kerr, 1811, vol. i, p. 436.

(e) **Private Persons.** The assumption of a surname by a private person has become increasingly common, and now constitutes what is called a " change of name ". The addition, dropping, or change of name may be registered and publicly advertised, but in many cases this is not done, and the omissions will provide many a pitfall for the unwary genealogist of the future. The subject is of great importance, and Chapter XVI will be devoted to a consideration of the legal aspect of the procedure in England, Scotland, and Ireland. If we may believe that an epitaph preserved by Lower has been accurately transcribed, change of name might take place posthumously :—

> " Here lieth Jack Meadow
> Whose dayes passed away like a shadow."

N.B.—His proper name was Field, but it is changed here for the sake of the rhyme ! " [1]

(f) **Slaves.** According to Eusebe-Salverte, the Roman slave upon manumission took his master's name and prænomen, preserving his own name as cognomen [2] : Freece, however, observes that the freedman, while using his own appellative as a cognomen, took the nomen of the person giving the freedom, and any prænomen he might fancy.[3] In this country the Anglo-Saxon slaves often had double names, as the Bodmin records illustrate, but if the manumitted serf did not possess a second appellative he was as well off as multitudes in a higher social sphere. Long after the Norman conquest it was common usage for a servant to be given officially the name of his master, and some examples will be found in a later chapter. In countries where slavery had not been abolished, it continued to be the practice for the freed slave to assume his master's name, as is evidenced by the West Indian case *Du Boulay* v. *Du Boulay*. Rose, a female slave of the Du Boulays, upon manumission, took the name of her master, as did her illegitimate son, who commenced business in the name. Resulting litigation was carried to the Court of Appeal, when Lord Chelmsford summed up the law as follows :—

" The mere assumption of a name which is the patronymic of a family by a stranger who had never before been called by that name, whatever cause of annoyance it may be to that family, is a grievance for which our law affords no redress." [4]

(g) **Refugees.** That refugees of all kinds should discard their family names and adopt others is obvious and calls for

[1] *English Surnames*, 1849, p. 257.
[2] Vol. i, p. 134.
[3] *Encycl. Brit.*, 1911, Edit., Art. " Name ".
[4] Law Reports, P.C., vol. ii, p. 430.

little notice. During civil war some families found it convenient to conceal themselves by a change of name, e.g. the Blunts of Bucks became Crokes, and the Carringtons of Warwickshire changed the family name to Smith.[1] The relatives of a criminal have been known to change names to avoid publicity, such as, for instance, the family of Hare, who had turned King's evidence against his confederate Burke, in the " resurrectionist " trial of 1828.[2] A more remarkable change of this nature occurred in France after the execution of Dumollard for murdering women under very revolting circumstances, whereupon over 200 persons of the same name presented petitions to the Keeper of the Seals to be permitted to change their name, some to Dumal, others to Dulard, etc.[3]

(*h*) **Aliens.** Foreigners with very distinctive imported surnames often find it desirable to effect a change of surname, and until a recent enactment they frequently disguised their nationality as well as family origin by inventing a new name or adopting a translated form of their surname or moulding it otherwise into an unidentifiable form, and so may be found such names as Rose, formerly Rosenbaum ; Lewin or Lewis from Levinsky ; or Robbins from Rubinstein. The Great War was responsible for many such changes, e.g. the two sons of Şonnenschein took the names of Stallybrass and Somerset respectively.[4] Now by the Aliens' Restriction Act, 1919 (see p. 413), unauthorized assumption is prohibited.

In Chapter VIII it has been shown that many aliens assumed or were given, officially, English names, and the practice continued until the present century ; for instance, the numerous Lithuanian miners of Lanarkshire generally acquired simple British names for the convenience of all concerned. A curious custom was formerly prevalent among Highlanders, who, upon leaving their native homesteads, were wont to assume a new name : thus the ancestors of the explorer Livingstone were known as M'Leay, in the Isle of Ulva.[5] It does not follow, however, that all Livingstones were M'Leays ; some derive their name from the village of that name in West Lothian.

Class II. Reputed Surnames. (*a*) **Bastards.** The largest class of surnames acquired after birth consists of those of persons born out of wedlock. Littleton observes that " a bastard is *quasi nullius filius*, and can have no name of reputation as soone as he is borne ".[6] If the illegitimate child be not given two baptismal names it becomes necessary for

---

[1] Fuller's *Worthies*, p. 51.   [2] *Observer*, 25th Oct., 1829.
[3] *Times*, 26th Mar., 1862.   [4] *Evening Standard*, 25th Nov., 1929.
[5] *Glasgow Herald*, 17th Mar., 1922.
[6] *Commentary on Littleton*, ed. E. Coke, 1823. p. 3*b*.

him to adopt or acquire by repute a second name conferred upon him by neighbours. In medieval days it was not uncommon for the " love begot " to take the surname of his father, but now he is more generally known as the child of his mother, and acquires her name by repute.[1] The original idea of compounding the names of both parents of the base born infant is illustrated by an entry in the Landbeach baptismal register : " Joane, whome we may call Yorkkooppe, because she was the bastarde daughter, as yt is commonlye reported of one John York and Anne Cooper, 3rd April, 1595." [2] In the fourteenth century the canon and common laws touching legitimacy were at variance, unless it is to be concluded that the preliminary ceremony of "espousals" was an equivalent of marriage, as many people of the period, supported by the canon law, evidently considered.[3] The common law of England, however, was then and until recently (1926) that "subsequent marriage of parents does not legitimate a child born of them before the marriage".

Before birth control became generally and successfully practised the proportion of children born out of lawful wedlock formed a considerable number of the population ; fifty years ago the figures being about 6 per cent in England, 10 per cent in Scotland, and 2 per cent in Ireland, the actual ratio of persons of illegitimate birth in Scotland being very much smaller owing to the laws of the country wisely legitimating base-born children by the subsequent marriage of the parents. Nevertheless, it will be realized that from the want of lawful marriage, surnames of large numbers of families must be of the acquired type. In this connection some curious questions arise; e.g. can a bastard who has been legitimated be said to have inherited or acquired his surname ? In other words, is his second appellative a surname or a "courtesy surname" only ? If the base-born child who has acquired his mother's name by repute is afterwards legitimated, does his name change upon the marriage of his parents ?

(b) **Foundlings.** The child abandoned by its parents usually has lost all means of ever ascertaining its names, and the duty of inventing a surname falls upon the authorities into whose hands it falls. So important a factor in the origin of British surnames is the naming of foundlings that it is thought advisable to quote verbatim from the *Chronicles of the Foundling Hospital* [4] :—

---

[1] Raymond's Reports, 1792, vol. i, p. 305. See Lord Stowell's judgment (*Sullivan* v. *Sullivan*). Phillimore (*Eccles. Law*, 1895, vol. i, p. 583).

[2] *History of Parish Registers*, by J. S. Burn, p. 78.

[3] For further information on this point, see W. C. Bolland (Selden Soc., xxxiii, p. xxi). Statute of Merton, 20 Hen. III (1235–6).

[4] John Brownlow, 1847, p. 207.

" It has been the practice of the Governors, from the earliest period of the Hospital to the present time [1847], to name the children at their own will and pleasure, whether their parents should have been known or not. At the baptism of the children first taken into the Hospital, which was on the 29th March, 1741, it is recorded, that there was at the ceremony a fine appearance of persons of quality and distinction ; his Grace the Duke of Bedford, our President, their Graces the Duke and Duchess of Richmond, the Countess of Pembroke, and several others, honouring the children with their names, and being their sponsors. Thus the register of this period presents the courtly names of Abercorn, Bedford, Bentinck, Marlborough, Montague, Newcastle, Norfolk, Pembroke, Pomfret, Richmond, Vernon, etc., etc., as well as those of numerous other living individuals, great and small, who at that time took an interest in the establishment. When these names were exhausted, the authorities stole those of eminent deceased personages, their first attack being upon the Church. Hence we have a Wickliffe, Huss, Ridley, Latimer, Laud, Sancroft, Tillotson, Tennison, Sherlock, etc., etc. Then come the mighty deal of the poetical race, viz. Geoffrey Chaucer, William Shakspeare, John Milton, etc. Of the philosophers, Francis Bacon stands pre-eminently conspicuous. As they proceeded, the Governors were more warlike in their notions, and brought from their graves, Philip Sidney, Francis Drake, Oliver Cromwell, John Hampden, Admiral Benbow, and Cloudesley Shovel. A more peaceful list followed this, viz. Peter Paul Rubens, Anthony Vandyke, Michael Angelo, and Godfrey Kneller ; William Hogarth, and Jane, his wife, of course not being forgotten. Another class of names was borrowed from popular novels of the day, which accounts for Charles Allworthy, Tom Jones, Sophia Western, and Clarissa Harlowe. The gentle Isaac Walton stands alone.

" So long as the admission of children was confined within reasonable bounds, it was an easy matter to find names for them ; but during the ' parliamentary era ' of the Hospital, when its gates were thrown open to all comers, and each day brought its regiment of *infantry* to the establishment, the Governors were sometimes in difficulties : and when this was the case, they took a zoological view of the subject, and named them after the creeping things and beasts of the earth, or created a nomenclature from various handicrafts or trades.

" In 1801, the hero of the Nile and some of his friends honoured the establishment with a visit, and stood sponsors to several of the children. The names given on this occasion were Baltic Nelson, William and Emma Hamilton, Hyde Parker, etc. Up to a very late period the Governors were sometimes in the habit of naming the children after themselves or their friends ; but it was found to be an inconvenient and objectional course, inasmuch as when they grew to man and woman-hood, they were apt to lay claim to some affinity of blood with their nomenclators. The present practice [1847], therefore is, for the Treasurer to prepare a list of ordinary names, by which the children are baptized."

No doubt many notable surnames were given a new lease of life by the Foundling authorities, and to-day may be the pride of their bearers ; that there are not more of these genealogical puzzles is due to the frightful mortality which at one time (1756–9) reached 70 per cent; being, however, greatly surpassed by the records of the Dublin Foundling Hospital, when in six years (1791–6) of " 12,641 children, 9,804 had died; 2,692 were unaccounted for, and only 145 were to be traced ".

The practice of the provincial parish authorities appears to have been to manufacture a surname having some bearing on the place where the child was found; and numerous examples of their skill can be found in the parish registers. One specially peculiar effort has been noticed above (see p. 206).

8th Dec., 1639.   John Acreland fownde in a dich called acrland, was baptized.   Bottesford (Leic.).

29th June, 1696.   Peter Acons, baptized.   St. Nicholas Acons.

In similar manner the foundlings of St. Lawrence, Old Jewry, were given the name Lawrence; of St. Clement Danes, Clements; of Gray's Inn, Grays or Graysin, and so on. Between the years 1728 and 1755 no less than 104 foundlings baptized at the Temple were surnamed Temple or Templar,[1] which will explain the frequency with which the name appears in the *London Directory*. The modern press occasionally takes notice of similar events; thus we learn that a baby girl found against a milestone, nine miles from the nearest town, was named Nina Miles by the York guardians,[2] and a child found in a waiting room on the Southern Railway was called Frances Southern; and countless instances of similar manufacture of names must exist, greatly adding to the uncertainty of derivation. Names known to have so originated are: Found (also Trouvie and Inventus), Aldermary, Brooker, Coalhouse, Denial, Dunstan, Godsend, Middlesex, Monday, Nameless, Parish, Penn, Porch, Portobello, Shepherd's Bush, Simon Jude, and Still.[3]

[1] *Collectanea, Topographica et Genealogica*, vol. iv, p. 159.
[2] *Evening Standard*, 28th July, 1930.
[3] *Parish Registers*, by R. E. C. Waters, 1887, p. 38. *Notes and Queries*, 26th Apr., 1851, Oct.-Dec., 1886; Lower (*Essays*, 1875, vol. ii, p. 20).

CHAPTER XI

EVOLUTION BY DERIVATION

Derivative Surnames. Evolution is not a term employed by the professor of linguistics, but it is appropriate to the change from simplicity to perplexity, which is such a marked feature in modern nomenclature. Evolution of surnames may be defined as the process of expansion, contraction, or internal orthographic development of pre-existing forms of the original description or surname until the final and permanent form is reached. The result of any such process may be called a derivative, using the term in its broadest sense, namely " a word which is not a primitive word or root " (*NED.*).

A surname may be a simple stem, as Small ; a derivative word, as Bak-er ; a compound word, as Work-man ; a derivative name, as Hugh-lett from Hugh, Cobb from Jacob ; a corruption of a name, as Barefoot for Barford ; or it may be a slight deviation from a simple stem, compound, or derivative, when it is commonly called a variant. Specific technical terms are applied to the various formations.

(i) *Derivatives by addition* (*a*, Initial ; *b*, Medial ; *c*, Final).

(*a*) Prothesis is the addition of one or more letters or syllables at the beginning of a word or name.

Prothetic name-formation is very noticeable in the composition of diminutives or hypocorisms of forenames, which have often become surnames. The most used letters are the dentals (*t, d, n*), as in Nan from Anne ; Nell from Ellen ; Nab from Abigail ; Ned from Edward ; Noll from Oliver ; Ted from Edward ; Tibbie from Isabel ; Dandie from Andrew.

(*b*) Epenthesis is the interposition of additional letters or syllables in the middle of a word or name.

Examples of such intrusion are :—

b after *m*, as in Jambe (Hund. R. 1275), Tomblin.

d after *n*, as in Hendry (1372, Cl. R.). Grindrod (Greenroyd), Standfield.

g after *n*, as in Wyngkyn, 1523 (see p. 281) ; Jengkyne, 1545, (Chislet Par. R.).

p after *m*, as in Empson, Thompson (1306, Cl. R.). J. in le Holmp, Cambs. 1275 (Hund. R.).

n before *g*, as in Messenger, Pottinger.

Intrusive vowels also appear, as Hath(a)way and Saw(y)er.

(*c*) Epithesis or paragoge is the addition of one or more letters or syllables at the end of a word or name.

In this important division fall diminutives and augmentatives, as Dick-ie, Baud-kin, Rich-on. Such names may be called hypocorisms.

Of epithetic type are variants formed by excrescency, but such names are often indistinguishable from normal forms, e.g. :—

-d, as in Hammon-d, Simmon-d, which names may be variants of the O.E. personal names, Heahmund and Simund. An undoubted example of epithesis is provided by : " Robert son of Hamo *alias* Robert Hamund," Warw. 1274 (Inq. p.m.).

-g. Leuing Drache occurs in 1066 (Wint. Dom.) : Ewingeswode is mentioned in 1150 (Cart. Mon. de Rameseia) ; but Leuing and Ewing may be O.E. *-ing*-names. Undoubted examples of the excrescent *g*, e.g. Irving, Jenning, Aveling, etc., have not been noticed before the fourteenth century. An early exception may be Luveking, 1190–1 (see p. 278).

-s also appears to be excrescent on occasion, but its ground for existence is indistinguishable from other causations (see p. 251).

(ii) *Derivatives by subtraction* (*a*, Initial ; *b*, Medial ; *c*, Final).

(*a*) Aphæresis is the falling away or suppression of one or more letters or syllables at the beginning of a word or name.

Examples of such diminished forms are common : Eng. : Jenner for Engenour, Noakes (atten-oakes), Tooke (at-hook) ; Ir. : Ryan for O'Mulryan ; Fr. : Quinet for Jacquinet ; Heb. : Jamin for Benjamin. Most of these names also may be termed hypocorisms.

" The gradual and unintentional loss of a short unaccented vowel at the beginning of a word " is called aphesis (*NED*.), as Squire for Esquire, Potecary for Apothecary. Some etymologists make no distinction between aphæresis and aphesis.

(*b*) Syncope or syncopation is the omission of one or more letters or syllables in the middle of a word or name, as Iderton *alias* Ilderton, Northd. 1509 (Pardon R.) ; Kerby *alias* Kerkeby, Kent, 1509 (ibid.). Double syncopation occurs in Chumley for Cho(l)m(onde)ley, Hilson for Hil(der)s(t)one.

(*c*) Apocope is the cutting off or omission of the last letter(s) or syllable(s) of a word or name.

Apocopation provides a great number of derivative surnames, and is exemplified by : Husband for Husbandman, Turk for Turkington, Wulf for Wulfric.

These names, in many cases, provide third examples of hypocorisms.

(iii) *Derivatives by mutation* (*a*, Initial ; *b*, Medial ; *c*, Final).

(*a*) Initial change : as in Biddicks, Fiddicks, Viddicks.

Hypocorisms are formed in this way, Peg from Margaret ; Bob, Dob, Hob, from Robert, etc., giving such surnames as Peggs, Bobbett, Dobbie, Hobbs, etc.

(*b*) Medial change : as Ballister to Bannister.

(*c*) Final change : as Bertram to Bertrand.

Terms sometimes used are assimilation and dissimilation.

Assimilation is the action by which two unlike sounds become like, as Ben-net from Bene-dict, Der-rick from Theod-ric, Har-ry from Hen-ry, Plum-mer from Plum-ber.

Dissimilation is the action by which two identical sounds become unlike or two similar sounds diverge, as Landsworth from Nansworth Hansom from Hanson, Ransom from Ranson.

(iv) *Derivatives by transposition.*

(a) Metathesis is the interchange of position between letters or sounds in one syllable of a word or name. Examples of such transpositions are Bird for Brid, Bremyngham for Bermyngham, Tankard for Tancred, McLeroy for McElroy, Niell for Neill, Pruiseil for Puirséil (Irish form of Purcell).

(b) Hyperthesis is the transposition of a letter from one syllable of a word or name to the preceding or following syllable, or it may be the transposition of two syllables in a word or name. Examples of this form of interchange are : Gundry to Grundy, Arbalester to Alebaster.

(v) *Derivatives by composition.*

Parathesis is the juxtaposition of two words without change, as Wheel-wright. In surnames the hyphen is dropped.

Diminutives and Augmentatives. . Of all the permitted deviations from the usual forms, which have been exemplified above, by far the most important in name-building are epithesis, aphæresis, and apocope. The two latter figures have been adequately exemplified (see pp. 87, 139, 272), and some further consideration will now be given to epithetic formation, mainly represented by the correlatives (i) diminutives, (ii) augmentatives.

(i) A diminutive is usually defined as an expression of something small of the kind denoted by the primitive word.

The great linguist Grimm considered that there were three types of diminutives : (1) expressing simple diminution without any accessary notion ; (2) expressing a feeling of endearment not necessarily accompanied with any notion of smallness ; (3) expressing a sense of contempt as in the Latin *homunculus, homuncio,* and the English *lordling.*[1]

(ii) An augmentative increases the force of the idea conveyed by the primitive name.

Both diminutives and augmentatives are formed by epithesis, the addition of suffixes ; but many aphæretics and apocopes are also, if not diminutive in effect, at least hypocoristic, as Nicol—Col, William—Will.

Of the suffixal types of surnames it is difficult, if not impossible, to distinguish between hypocorisms, diminutives, and augmentatives ; and probably there are few, if any, of the latter. The suffixes employed in name-formation may now be considered.

---

[1] *Deutsche Grammatik,* von Jacob Grimm, vol. iii, chap. viii.

Suffixes in Name-formation.   The Indo-European
languages abound in suffixes added to the root with the
intention of modifying the signification, and it is not uncommon
to find suffix added to suffix.   It is often difficult to divide
a name to give the appendage its correct form or signification,
or even to recognize a suffix from a vocable forming an element
of a compound appellative, and such a process pertains only to
the province of the practised philologist.   Nevertheless, a
superficial examination is of assistance to the understanding
of our surnames, and provides a survey of considerable interest.
British surnames, being derived from words in many tongues,
exhibit an unusual variety of suffixes, some of which may be
traced to more than one source.   It is necessary to consider
the suffixes principally of the Anglo-Saxon, Norman-French,
Gaelic, and Welsh languages.

The O.E. suffixes have been noticed and exemplified on
pp. 51, 56, 57, and further consideration may now be given
to those which figure most prominently in the composition
of British surnames, namely the diminutive endings with
g-sound as *-ig*; k-sounds as *-ic, -oc, -uc*; and l-sounds, as
-el, -il, -ol, and *-ul*.   In the thirteenth century names with such
terminations were still in use; e.g. in the Hundred Rolls,
1275, are to be found : Fig—Figel, Garle—Garlec, Dun—
Dunnoc, Mul—Mulluc, etc.   Such a range of derivatives may
be noticed, as Bule—Bullek, Bullig, Bulloc, Bullog, Bullok,
Bulluc, and also Bulet and Buletel.   Under Continental
influence, which, in the thirteenth century, might be Jewish,
the diminutive endings increased in number ; thus Cok—Cokel,
Coker, Coket, Cokin, and double diminutives Cok-el-in and
Cok-er-el.   Modern suffixes with diminutival force, taking
English and Scottish together are numerous ; and of those
more particularly found in surnames are *-en, -ing* (sometimes
weakened into *y* or *ie*), and the k-suffixes dealt with below.
In names from adjectives *-le* may be found, as Little.

The French diminutive suffixes, according to Brachet,
are *-eau, -el, -elle, -et, -ette, -ot, -otte*, and *-on* (with the inter-
calation of *-er, -ich, -ill*).   Double diminutive endings are also
to be found (see below, p. 289).   Augmentatives are *-ard*
and *-on*.

Welsh diminutive syllables are : *-an* (m., f.), *-en* (f.),
-ig (f.), *-yn* (m.).   T. Rowland (1876, p. 130) gives *-og* (f.)
and *-ell* (f.), and S. J. Evans notes *-cyn* (m.).   Gaelic (Scot)
endings are : *-an* and *-ag*.[1]   Cormac under *uibhne* observes
that all Irish diminutives end in *-án* or *-ene*, but J. O'Donovan
gives additionally *-ín, -óc*, and *-óg*.[2]   The formation of Welsh

---

[1] H. C. Gillies, 1896, p. 151.
[2] 1845, p. 333.

diminutive names has been exemplified on p. 40, and of Irish on p. 30.

All these Germanic, Romance, and Celtic derivative terminations have had some share in moulding British surnames, and in addition Dutch, Flemish, Friesic, and Scandinavian have also, doubtless, had influence, but in such cases they are now rarely to be identified. The Low German suffix which has been the most largely accepted is *-kin*, which may be a double diminutive *-ik-in*, or may be *-in* which has collected a *k*-sound, as did, in some cases, *oc*, which became *c-oc*(*k*), to give it a sound intelligible to the modern ear. The *k*-suffixes are of particular interest to the student of nomenclature, and may be more fully examined.

The Suffix -ke. Suffixes with *k*-sounds were general throughout Europe. Cited above (p. 26) are examples of the Sanskrit diminutive or hypocoristic termination *-ka*, which verbal appendage among others is, in various forms, in common use by the Slavonic races, as Brani-voj, Branka ; Vladi-mir, Vladko ; Rati-slav, Ratik ; Rus-mir, Rusek. The Teutonic races also largely employed *k*-suffixes in the formation of hypocorisms or diminutives. The comparative prevalence of the various forms is illustrated by the following statistics compiled from lists of names of the fourth to eleventh centuries collected from Continental archives by Förstemann (*Altdeutches Namenbuch*).

Suffix.	Gender.	Period.	Number.	Example.
-ac, -ach, -ag . . .	masc.	6th to 9th c.	11	Sulach
-ec, -ech . . .	masc.	9th c.	2	Halec
-ic, -ich, -ig, -ih, -ik .	masc.	6th to 11th c.	58	Ubik
-oc, -oh . . .	masc.	6th to 9th c.	2	Senocus
-uc, -uch, -ug, -uh, -uk .	masc.	6th to 10th c.	10	Lethuc
-a-i-ca, -a-i-u-ka . .	masc.	4th to 11th c.	13	Godica
-eke, -ike . . .	masc.	11th c.	2	Brendeke
-uchi, -uhi, -iki . .	masc.	8th to 9th c.	5	Biniki
-co	masc.	11th c.	2	Reinco
-a-e-i-u-c(h)o, -a-i-go, -iho, -a-i-u-ko . . .	masc.	4th to 11th c.	172	Ibiko
-ca, -ka . . .	fem.	9th c.	2	Deinka
-a-e-i-o-u-c(h)a, -a-e-i-ga, -a-i-u-ka . . .	fem.	8th to 11th c.	73	Winika
-uche, -a-i-u-ke . .	fem.	10th to 11th c.	8	Tabuke
-ico	fem.	5th c.	1	Ildico
-iken	masc.	—	1	Erdiken
-e-i-c(h)in, -i-hin, -e-i-kin	masc.	8th to 11th c.	57	Mannikin
-echen	fem.	—	1	Hidechen
-echina, -ecin, -i-kin, -ekinna . . .	fem.	11th c.	10	Immikin

Dividing these suffixes roughly into *-ik*, *-ika*, and *-ikin* forms (as bracketed), it is found that they are in the proportion of 19, 65, and 16 per cent respectively. Considering now records of the Low Countries solely, all three types may be found, but the *-ikin* forms greatly predominate in early rolls, outnumbering the others by six to one. In a Gelderland rental (*inkomsten*) of Werden Abbey, A.D. 983, the proportions were 0, 15, and 85 per cent. The roll is short, there being but eighty-one names, including Alaka and Lubbiko, and eleven *-ikin*-names, which latter type will be considered in a further section. It may be of interest to note, in passing, that no less than 11 per cent of names had the suffix *-tet*.[1] There were no secondary descriptions at this early date, so that the present remarks apply entirely to personal names. The *-ik* and *-ika* suffixes ultimately fell into disuse, but *-i-kin*, and particularly *-ken*, as a feminine termination, largely multiplied.

In Friesland the commonest form became *-e-ke*, and on a count of about 200 fifteenth-century personal names, no less than 35 per cent had this form of affix.[2] Both types are found in surnames, as Arneke Gherken, Gherke Buddeke, Tideke Willekens, etc.[3] In some cases the final *n* is due to genitival inflection, as Swanken moder, Stoleken wiff, " und over Hobbeken Groninges " (elsewhere Hobbeke) : " Item henke de koster vor henken robeken kamp " ; on the other hand, where no question of an oblique case in the first name arises— " Item hanneken Kreyen ", " Item Reyneken Bakhuses " may be cited.[4]

It is manifest that *-e-ke* and *-i-kin*-suffixes were both in common use in the Low Countries, *-ke* becoming the most popular northern form, and *-kin* and *-ken* the southern. Both affixes are found at an early date in England. Before the Conquest names in *-ca* may be found occasionally, as Brynca, Hysica, Baduca, Seolca, etc., and in the thirteenth century, as is evidenced by the Hundred Rolls, both personal names (single) and second names with suffix *-ka* and *-ke* are noticeable ; probably due to Friesic introduction.

Norfolk : Avit' Lanke ; Will'o Lanke ; Rog. Hanke ; Garka. *Suffolk* : Gerald Bushanke ; W. Craske ; W. Scraske. *Cambs* : Reg.

---

[1] *Oorkondenboek der Graafschappen Gelre en Zutfen*, by Baron Sloet, vol. i, p. 105.

[2] A charter of 1423 shows that *-ka* was also prevalent, i.e. Rimka, Foppeka, etc. (Epkema).

[3] *Friesisches Archiv*, von H. G. Ehrentraut, 1849, vol. i, p. 466. See also above, p. 141.

[4] A. H. Cummins (*O. Friesic Grammar*) states that native proper names follow the strong declension (p. 47). It is evident from the examples given above that in the fifteenth century Friesic names were also inflected according to the weak declension. In Dutch, proper names are declined with the prepositions *van* " of ", and *aan* " to " (R. van der Pyl, p. 49).

Bayke; Hen. Charke; Amicia Grilke; J. Matke; Rob. Planke; J. Sanke. *Hunts* : W. Selke (cf. O.E. Seolca); Reg. Wenke. *Bucks* : Walt. Broneke; Alan Bruneke; Thom. Polenanke. *Oxf.* : Edw. Achke. *Devon* : Greg. Seonka.

It would not be possible to say that each example evidences the suffix *-ke*; e.g. Planke might not be Plan-ke, but merely the English vocable " planke ".

The Suffix -kin. According to Sweet " *-čen* is a diminutive neuter ending, being an extension of the originally diminutive ending *-en* in *maeġden*, and in M.E. and Mn.E. it appears in the form of *-kin, -ikin*, whose full vowel and *k* instead of *ch* is probably the result of the influence of the French *-quin*, itself of Low German origin. Thus *manikin* ' dwarf ' is the French *mannequin*, which is itself a Low German diminutive of *man.*" [1] With regard to personal names, it is to be noticed that *-cin* and *-cyn* are forms of an O.E. deuterotheme, *cynn* " race ", " kin ", and consequently when found as second elements of O.E. names are quite possibly not diminutive suffixes, e.g. Mannecin, tenth century, which occurs as Mannekin in the Hundred Rolls (Suff.), and as Mac Mannechin in an undated Scottish record.[2] Does such a name exemplify an O.E. survival or an alien importation ? Another possibility is suggested by Charnock, viz. that *-kin* may be Cornish *kyn* " head " or *kein* " promontory ", as Bod-kyn, Bod-kein, hence Bodkin; moreover, the Welsh diminutive ending *-cyn* must not be forgotten (see p. 274).

As dictionary words in *-kin* are few, the study of surnames with that suffix has an added importance. With reference to personal names, the suffix *-kin* (or *-k-in*) is first noticed in the Low German countries, and, as far as evidence is available, it is not of such great antiquity as *-ke*, from which it is probably derived [3]; nor was it so prevalent. Förstemann's earliest example is of the eighth century, and his masculine examples (84 per cent) have terminations *-(e)chin, -(i)cin, -hin, -(e)ken, -(e)kin*; and feminine (16 per cent), *-(e)chen, -(e)china, -kin, -(e)kinna*.[4] In ninth-century Breton charters Grokin presbyter is several times mentioned; also Wetenkain and Moenken (f.); and in Ghent archives, A.D. 962, occur Abicinus and Winecin, names of manciples; Ozekino (Lat. abl.) being witness to a grant A.D. 990; and among female manciples were noticed Bavacin, A.D. 998, Athalkin, A.D. 1001, and

---

[1] *A New English Grammar*, by H. Sweet, 1892, pt. i, p. 457.
[2] *Registrum de Dunfermelyn* (Bannatyne Club 74), p. 111.
[3] Cf. Germ. *gurken* from *gurke*; and consider the names Gherken and Gherke.
[4] See the notes given above, p. 275.

Muderkin, A.D. 1007.[1] Thirteen names of manciples, who surrendered to the Abbey of Werden, included Frenkin, Immikin, Wemeka, Wineken, and Odikin.[2] Stark records among other tenth and eleventh-century examples : Waldichin, Bunikin, Willikin, Bodekin, and Bottikin.[3]

Referring to English records it will be realized that names ending in -kin may be either native or alien ; Hæðcyn, a son of Hrethel, king of Gotland, occurs in Beowulf, and Cynicin (cf. cynecinn " royal race ") in the Liber Vitæ ecclesiæ Dunelmensis. Miscin was a Wiltshire serf, A.D. 995 [4] ; Hyeken, an Essex tenant, A.D. 1046 [5] ; Mannecin [6] and Heardcyn,[7] moneyers in the time of Eadred and Eadward III respectively. Possibly the latter name occurs as Hardechinus in the Suffolk section of Domesday Book, another entry for the same county relating to Depekin (or Tepekin), a freeman of Harold. In the following century appear the earliest examples of second names with the suffix, the most ancient being Continental, Radulfus Azzekin, a Ghent witness, A.D. 1166.[8] In English archives the Pipe Rolls for 1179 mention Richard Wilekin, Hants ; for 1187-8, W. son of Ethekin, Notts ; and for 1190-1, W. Luveking, Leic. ; and W. Litleken, Staffs, occurs in the Curia Regis Roll, A.D. 1199 ; Wilkin de Ros, Kent, is noticed in the same court, A.D. 1200 ; Brunkin and Hardekin are names in the Lincs. Assize Roll for A.D. 1202 ; " Hannechin our Jew " is mentioned in 1204 (Pat. R.) ; Pollekin, Salop, in 1206 (Cur. Reg. R.) ; Lambekin, Kent, in 1213 (Cl. R.) ; and Munekin, Oxf., in 1223 (Fine R.). In general, the south-eastern localities of these early English examples point to Continental origin, and since the suffix is not French or Scandinavian, therefore to Low Country source ; and it is further manifest that the introduction, in some instances, must have been due to the Jews.

The first occurrences in literature noted by the NED. are Janekin, Malekin, Watekin, and Wilekin, for the year 1250,[9] and the suffix was then evidently in familiar use, and probably much commoner than appears by its preservation in official records. In the thirteenth century an important source of the royal revenue was the toll of 40s. per sack of

---

[1] Chartes et Documents de l'Abbeye de Saint Pierre au Mont Blandin à Gand, par A. van Lokeren.
[2] Crecelius, pt. iiib, p. 7.
[3] Die Kosenamen der Germanen, by F. Stark, 1868, pp. 62, 64. See also p. 67, Verkürzungen der mit k gebildeten Deminutiva.
[4] KCD., 1290.
[5] Ibid., 782.
[6] British Museum Collection (Grueber).
[7] Numismatic Chronicle, 1885, p. 264.
[8] Chartes et Documents, par A. van Lokeren, p. 171
[9] Old English Miscellanies, pp. 188, 191.

wool exported. The trade was largely in the hands of merchants of the Low Countries, and their licences to deal afford an illustration of the nature of their names; thus from the Patent Roll for the year 1273, in a list of about 700 woolmongers, of whom two-thirds at least were foreigners, the following examples were noticed: Hanekyn de Lundreshel, merchant of Louvain; Lambekyn de Cnesfeld, merchant of Lubek; Godekyn Munden, merchant of Almain; Godekin de Kyureld, merchant of Almain; Nicholas Nodekyn, merchant of Brabant; Walter Aubrekyn, merchant of London; and perhaps the same Walter Hauberkyn, merchant of London; John Werdekin, burgess of Len (Lynn); and John Waydekyn, merchant of Brabant. Probably all were of alien origin. Turning again to the valuable index to the *Hundred Rolls*, it is possible to determine the distribution of the suffix throughout England, always bearing in mind that the northern counties are poorly represented, and that over half the record is devoted to the counties of Oxford, Huntingdon, Cambridge, Norfolk, and Lincoln. In the 70,000 entries -*kin* was found as an element in twenty-four christian names and fifty-eight surnames :—

Forenames: *London*: Morekin de Vautham, Adekin le Fuller, Lambkin, Osekin (cf. Ozekin and Azzekin noticed above), Godekyn de Cusad' (Coufeld), Lambekin de Lamburne. *Essex*: Batekin Lahan, Batekyn clericus, Hardekin, Saykin Bude. *Oxford*: Lovekin, Elekin, Lovekin Jordan, Edekin Gomey. *Cambridge*: Derkin (Derik), Lotekin Schelhod, Lovekin (2). *Suffolk*: Houberking Messor, Mannekin de Boyton. *Kent*: Lovekyn Stukepen, Aukyn de Dokesworth. *Norfolk*: Haukyn. *Shropshire*: Lovekinus Piscator.

Second names: *Cambridge*: Bodekin, Boykin, Budekin, Chikin (2), Derkin, Feikin (2), Hobekyn (2), Maykin, Obekyn, Potekin (8), Redeking (2), Stokin. *Oxford*: Budekin, Edekin, Lutekene (3), Muneken, Polekin (2), Robekin. *London*: Auberkyn, Juberkyn, Udekyn. *Kent*: Havekyn (if not Hanekyn), Renekyn. *Berks*: Baturking. *Devon*: Daucyn. *Norfolk*: Hardeken (2), Nevekyn, Redeking, Werdekyn, Wygcyn. *Essex*: Mundekyn, Notekyn. *Lincoln*: Ratekyn, Roulekyn. *Bucks*: Akin (possibly local). *Derby*: Baskyn. *Sussex*: Bonekin. *Bedford*: Hardekyn. *Wilts*: Hynekyng. *Hunts*: Jankin. *Suffolk*: Jokin, Manekin. *Northants*: Walkyn.

Most of the first elements of these names correspond to O.E. personal names, or to diminished forms of such, but they may be identified equally as alien names, and the fact that these names preponderate in the South and East, being those counties most convenient for trading and communication with the Low Countries, is significant. Examination of 8,000 Yorkshire names on the Subsidy Roll of 1301 yielded but five examples: Benkyn, Chiken (?), Jokyn, Lambekyn, and

Ruddekyn, evidence that the foreign merchants had not to any extent settled in the northern counties.

Regarding appearances in literature, the *NED.* further states that -*kin*-names were not prominent till the second half of the fourteenth century. The A-text of *Piers Plowman* has Malkin and Perkin, the B-text adds Haukyn, and the C-text Watkyn ; Chaucer uses Jankin, Malkin, Perkin, Simkin, and Wilkin, and in the *Tournament of Tottenham* there occur Dawkyn, Jeynkyn, Perkyn, and Tymkyn.

In official use names of this class remained scarce ; for instance, taking lists of the taxpayers for the year 1327, about 5,000 Devonshire names yielded but Vadekyn and Renekyn [1] ; 3,500 Huntingdonshire names supplied Attekin and Haukyn [2] ; 3,500 Leicestershire names Adekin, Attekyne, Janekyn, and Matekyn.[3] The -*kin*-names were more numerous in Suffolk and Kent, amounting to about one-half per cent, and somewhat surprisingly a western county, Gloucester, yielded a still larger proportion, namely 1 per cent of the names examined :—

Suffolk : (11,720 entries). Chynchen, Edekyn (2), Freikyn, Hardekyn (4), Haukin (6), Hokyn, Jokyn, Lorkyn, Notekyn, Paykyn, Perkyn (3), Potekyne (4), Reynkyn (2), Robekyn (2), Rodekyn (3), Rotekyn, Stokyn (3), Tepekyn, Thomekin, Wyken, Wylekyn (4), Wysekyn.[4]

Kent : (6,000 entries). Alkyn, Beniekyn, Edekyn, Feykin (2), Hamekyn (2), Jakyn (3), Janekyn, Jeokyn, Josekyn, Joykin, Jullekyn, Lambekyn, Lorekyn (4), Lotekyn, Maidekyn (cf. the next entry Clemens de Madekyn, m. 37), Meykin (2), Notekyn, Perkin, Poucyn, Renekyn, Robekyn (2), Rosekyn, Sandrekyn, Storekyn, Willekyn (4). The name Kyn also may be noted.[5]

Gloucestershire : (5,000 entries). Adekines, Dunskin, Haukines (8), Hicken, Hobekines (8), Jacken, Janekyn-es (4), Lovekin (7), Perkines (2), Sanekyn, Wilkins (16).[6]

The *Record of Carnarvon* shows that by 26 Edw. III (1352) various -*kin*-names had reached N. Wales—Cokkyn, Dakyn, Deikin, Hulkin, Jankin, Jokyn, Roukyn, and also forms of Janke, as Jacke, Jak, and Jock.

In France -*quin* was rare : of 2,300 occurrences of the Christian name Jehan and derivatives, in the year 1296, but four were Janequin or Jehannequin. There is a corresponding scarcity of the suffix in French surnames.[7]

By 1327 christian names with suffix -*kin* were extremely

---

[1] P.R.O., E 179, 95/6, mm. 25, 33. An equivalent number of names *in dorso* I did not examine.

[2] P.R.O., E 179, 122/4.   [3] P.R.O., E 179, 133/1.

[4] *Suffolk Green Book*, No. 9.

[5] P.R.O., E 179, 123/10. An equivalent number of names *in dorso* I did not examine.

[6] Printed copy in the P.R.O.   [7] K. Michaëlsson (*Études*, p. 62).

rare in English official records ; an examination of 35,000 entries on the Subsidy Rolls for various counties yielded no example. The *NED.*, guided by literary evidence, considers that, as christian names, diminutives formed by the suffix *-kin* went out of fashion shortly after 1400. Citing a later occurrence serves the additional purpose of illustrating that *-kin* was used like the French suffixes (see p. 291) to form a distinction with the effect of " junior " or " the younger ". John Vavasour had two sons named John, the younger of whom signed his will (1482-3) " Jenkyn Vavasour ".[1] A yet later example, from the London Subsidy Roll for 1523, provides a double example in East Smithfield, namely Wyngkyn Wyngkyns.

It may be noted that Wilkin was sometimes written Petiwill, Worc. (1294), from which the shorter form la Lutle and the double diminutives Petywykin, Petywillekin, Petytwilkin (1293-4), all relating to the same person, are derived.[2]

An analysis of 3,000 names of men of Flanders, A.D. 1328, showed that 5 per cent had *-kin*-first-names, and 2 per cent had the suffix in their surnames.[3] These proportions exceed anything found in England. In later years it is noticed that the suffixes *-kin* and *-ken* became increasingly common in feminine font-names ; e.g., sixteenth-century Low Country women in Colchester were named Joeskin, Jannekyn, Martinekyne, Betkin, and Paskyne. The use of *-ken* as a diminutive ending, in Low German countries, is well illustrated by a verse from a nursery rhyme :—

> Mee lämmken, Mee !
> Dat Lämmken leep in't Holt,
> Et stött sik an een Strückelken,
> Do deed em wee sin Bükelken,
> Do seed dat Lämmken " Mee ! "

> Me-e lambkin, Me-e !
> The lambkin ran in the wood,
> He hit against a straw-i-kin,
> And hurt his little tum-i-kin,
> And then the lambkin said " Me-e ! " [4]

A few extracts from the baptismal registers of the Dutch church at Colchester may be of interest :—

1647. Maeyken, d. van Jan Doen en Maeyken. Julij 11.
1661. Janneken, d. van Carel Rykeseis en Mary. Get . . Janneken de Grave.
1663. Janneken, d. van Jacob van Gaver en Janneken. Meert 15.

---

[1] Below, p. 404,
[2] Halesowen Court Rolls.
[3] Examples, see p. 139.
[4] *The English Language*, by R. G. Latham, p. 143, where further verses may be obtained.

1669.   Mayken, d. van Tobias Faljaert en Mayken.   Get . . en Mayken Duytsche.   Dec. I.

1670.   Mayken, d. van Jan Huywelaer en Mayken.   Get . . en Mayken Duytsche.   Aug. 8.[1]

Regarding members of the Dutch church, Austin Friars (seventeenth century), of 260 women, no less than 122 had -ken font-names registered.   Over 500 names of men, on the other hand, produced but three examples, and the diminutival addition was even rarer in surnames.[2]

It will have been gathered that the suffixes -ke and -kin might be joined to either first or second element of a compound name to form a diminutive name, as Wil-helm—Wil-ke, Wil-kin ; and Jo-han—Hanke, Han-kin.   The suffix -kin (if not -kins) was corrupted into -kiss, giving such variants as Hotchkiss, Perkiss, Watkiss, etc.

The Element or Suffix " -cock. "   Grammarians and etymologists are at variance regarding the nature of this termination ; by some it is supposed to be a hypocoristic and diminutive suffix ; by others a complete and significant word in itself, and therefore an element or theme of a compound. Actually -cock is derived in a number of different ways.   In the formation of surnames " cock " plays a most remarkable part ; as an uncompounded vocable it can be assigned to three, if not to all four classes, characteristic (doubtful), local, genealogical, and occupational ; and as an element of compound names it certainly appears in all four classes.[3]   It is at first advisable to consider Cock as an uncompounded description or surname.

I.   *Cock as an uncompounded surname.*   O.E. *cocc, coc, kok* ; O.N. *kokkr* ; Dan. *kok* ; Fr. *coq* ; M.Lat. *coccus*.   The *NED.* considers " cock " to be an echoic word, citing Chaucer on chanticleer :—

> " Nothing ne list him thanne for to crow,
>   But cried anon cok, cok, and up he sterte."

(i) *Characteristic.*

(*a*) W., Corn. *coch* " red ".   This description has usually survived as Gough and Couch.

Ath' Cogh, 1352.   (Rec. of Carnarvon, p. 53.)
Ath' Coyk, 1352.   (Ibid., p. 74.)

Cocke is given by Alex. Jones (*The Cymry of '76*, 1855, p. 100) as a name derived from *coch*.   Lower (1875) records that

---

[1] *Register of Baptisms, Dutch Church*, Huguenot Soc., vol. xii.
[2] Huguenot Soc., vol. x, pt. i, p. 278 et seq.
[3] The origin of the termination was discussed in the *Gentleman's Magazine* by various inquirers as long ago as 1837–8, when some most ridiculous views were propounded.

the Secretary of the Gaelic Soc. of London derived such surnames as Alcock, Stancock, Meacock, Bacock, Laycock, Lucock, Peacock, etc., from Gaelic and Welsh characteristic surnames.

(b) Name for male birds, etc. In Scandinavian countries *kok* was sometimes given as a *binavn*. In the *Diplomatarium norvegicum* occur several examples from 1307 onwards, as Simon coc, Sander kok, Herman kok, etc.

Cf. Roger Chauntecler, London, 1324. (Coroner's R.)

(c) An early riser. In this sense Cock has been given in England as a descriptive epithet. Stowe records that among the earliest benefactors to Christ's Hospital in London was "one Richard Castell *alias* Casteller, shoomaker, dwelling in Westminster, a man of great travaile and labour in his faculty with his owne hands, and such a one as was named, The Cocke of Westminster, because both winter and summer, hee was at his worke before foure of the clocke in the morning" (*Gentleman's Magazine*, May, 1838, p. 500).

(ii) *Local.*

(a) Sign-board. Cock is one of the most ancient of sign-names of tavern or shop, and is mentioned by Pliny (first century).

(b) A short pipe or water spout. The words boss, fountain, shute, etc., were also used for various watering places.

Rich. atte Cocke, London, 1323. (Coroner's R.)
W. atte Cokke, London, 1337. (Ibid.)
Hugh atte Kocke, London, 1340. (Ibid.)
Peter de Wendlyngburgh called "atte Cokk", London, 1351. (Will., Court of Husting : R. R. Sharpe.)

Some earlier examples are given on p. 230.

(c) A heap of farm material.

David attekokes, Norf. 1275. (Hund. R.)

In this case other origins are possible.

(d) A small boat or cog.

J. del Cogges, Chesh. (Chamber Accts.)
W. dil Cok, Suff. 1327. (Subs.)
Cf. Petrus del Barge, mariner, 1359. (Freeman of York, i, 53.)

(e) A locality in Somersetshire. (Inq. p. m., 5 Edw. II.)

(iii) *Genealogical.*

(a) O.E. personal names were Cocca, Cogga, as appears from place-names, Coccanburh, and Cogganhyl.

Koc de Fraxina, Kent, 1275. (Hund. R.)
Coc de Slepe, Shrops. 1275. (Hund. R.)
Ric. le fiz Cok, Chesh. 1309. (Pat. R.)
Cok' Carnifer (i.e. butcher), Yorks. 1379. (Poll Tax.)

(b) A Jewish personal name. (Dim. of ? Isaac.) [1]

Cok son of Jacob of Canterbury, 1244. (Exchequer of the Jews.)
Cokerel son of Licorice, 1253. (Ibid.)
Vives Cok, London, 1272. (Ibid.)

(c) An anglicization of the Irish McKilly (coileach " cock ").

(iv) *Occupational.*

(a) One who aroused slumberers, a watchman of the night ; applied to ministers of religion. (*NED.*)

1346. Amorwe whan þat day gan for to sprynge Vp roos oure hoost and was oure aller cok. (Chaucer Prol. 823.)

(b) A chief or leader, as " cock-swain " now " coxswain ". (*NED.*)

(c) A form of " cook ", both words being latinized *cocus* or *coccus*, and both are represented by the same word in Teutonic and Scandinavian languages.

J. le Koc, Norf. 1275. (Hund. R.)
Rich. le Cok, Wilts. 1275. (Ibid.)

II. *Cock as a second element.* As the second part of a compound name -*cock* is found in surnames of all classes.

(i) *Characteristic.* The possibility of -*cock* being the result of a nickname is illustrated by a story told by Jas. Lackington (*Memoirs*, 13th ed., p. 33). The old clerk at Langford, near Wellington (Somers.) "having one Sunday slept in church, and dreaming that he was at a cock-fighting, bawled out ' a shilling upon the red cock '. And behold the family are called Redcock unto this day ".

The French have Beau-coq, and in *Le Rôle de la Taille*, 1292, appears Maby Bec-de-coc (i.e. Cock's bill) ; cf. Ralph Cokkebill, Warw. 1327 (Subs.).

(ii) *Local.*

(a) Corruption of " cot ", " a small shelter or hut." Common variants are Woodcock and Woodcot. Thomas de Hancoc is, however, probably genealogical, occurring as Thomas Hancoc elsewhere.

J. de Pircock (i.e. Pircote), Worc. 1270. (Halesowen Ct. R. i, 16.)

---

[1] Jos. Jacobs (*Jews of Angevin England*), p. 369, states that Cok and Coket are probably diminutives of Isaac in its Hebrew form.

(b) Corruption of *oc*. This suffix following *k*-sound may give *cock*, as layc-ock " the small lake " (cf. *layk*, sixteenth century, *NED*.)

J. de Laccok, Yorks. 1379 (Poll Tax) ; but cf. Laykyn, 1535 (London Will).

(c) Personal name. In some place-names -cock is the personal name, forming an " inversion-compound ", due to Celtic influence, introduced by the Scandinavians, as in Salcock or Sawcock (O.N. *salr* " hall "), signifying Cock's hall (A. H. Smith, *Saga Book of the Viking Soc.*, x, pt. ii, p. 203).

(d) W. " cuckoo ". Pennicook from Penicuik (Scotl.) was originally *pen y cog* " cuckoo hill ".

(e) Element of a prepositional compound.

David Attekokes, Norf. 1275. (Hund. R.)
Ralph Atecock, London, 1282. (Will., Court of Husting. R. R. Sharpe.)
Rob. Atkoc, Staff. 1332–3. (Subs. R.), but cf. Atkin (ibid.).
Possible confusion with Adcock.

(iii) *Genealogical*.

(a) O.E. personal names (see above). Cocca and Cogga may possibly exist as second elements of compound surnames, cf. Swetcoc (Cambs, 1275) and Cokswete, Ess. 1509, Pardon R., p. 231). Bilcock, Telcock, and numbers of other surnames, have common O.E. protothemes.

(b) Corruption of -*god*. Algod becomes Algot and Alcot (Dom. Bk.), and a step further would make it Alcok.

(c) Corruption of -cot (Jewish). Swetecota, a Jewish feminine name (1288, Cl. R.) would almost certainly become Swetecock, in fact, Bardsley so prints it (Swetcoka).

(iv) *Occupational*.

(a) Watchman ; (b) Leader ; (c) Cook. It is to be expected that one or other of these vocations (see above, p. 284) has, by parathesis, become a component in surnames (cf. Arkwright, Greensmith, Hayward, etc.). Swetecok might well be the medieval pastrycook, or Hallcok " the hall cook ", but there is no evidence to offer.

Alwine hamelecoc bedellus, Cambs. 1086. (See above, p. 94.)
Rich. le Personescok, Cambs. 1312. (Pat. R.)

III. *Cock as a diminutive suffix*. In name-composition -*cock* appears to have the same diminutive force as -*ke* and -*kin*, e.g. Han-ke, Han-kin, Han-coc ; Jan-ke, Jan-kin, Jan-cock ; but unlike -*ke* and -*kin*, -*cock* is rare in Continental names, and is evidently not of Teutonic or Romance origin. Some other comparisons taken from English rolls are :—

Alcok	Alkyn	Hencok	Henekyn	Pocok	Poucyn
Batecok	Batekin	Hulcok	Hulkin	Raincoke	Renekin
Bruncok	Brunkin	Jolicok	Jullekyn	Rodecok	Rotekyn
Budecok	Budekin	Lovecok	Lovekin	Thomakoc	Thomekin
Cokcok	Cokkyn	Maycok	Maykin	Wilecoc	Wilkin
Ellcoc	Elekin	Morecoc	Morekin	Wudcocke	Udekin

It has been stated above (p. 275) that the O.E. suffix -oc may have taken an additional k-sound and become c-oc and c-ock, and the following comparisons of O.E. personal names and M.E. surnames are significant.

Ælloc	Ellcoc	Hwituc	Wytcok	Pilloc	Pylecok
Alloc	Alcoc	Jannok	Jancock	Uiduc	? Wudcocke
Balloc	Balcoc	(1392)	(1397)	Wiloc	Wilecoc
Battoc	Batecok	Lenok	Lenecok		

Cok may be found affixed to names of females.

Rich. Sibelicok, Suss. 1296. (Subs. W. Hudson.)

(c) Corruption of Fr. diminutive suffix -ot after k-sound. Pecoc in Domesday Book may be nothing more than Pecot (i.e. Picot, now Pigot and Pycock, Leeds).

(d) Corruption of Celt. diminutive suffix -og in the same manner.

Suffixed in any of the above forms -cock has not the antiquity of -ke and -kin. Uncertain eleventh-century instances are Pecoc and Hamelecoc, already cited, pp. 63, 94. Possibly the earliest example which has been traced occurs in the Liber Winton, 1148, where it is recorded that Cristescoc was a tenant of the Prior. Crist was a personal name, which has been noticed as a secondary description in the list of Essex burgesses, 1086 (p. 63), and it is also a prototheme, as in the name Crist-thegn. Doubtless -s- is here the inflectional suffix denoting genitive case, and -coc may be cook, watchman, or even a minister.[1] Cristescoc is, therefore, an occupation.

" No noyse to waken the Sybarites, unless the Cockes, the Ministers . . . Few will beleeve Christs Cocke, though hee crowes to them that the day is broken." (Devil's Banquet, by T. Adams, 1614, p. 120.)

The Pipe Rolls name Anschetil Hacchecoc, Beds. (1165) and Salecoc the Jew, Heref. (1193). In the Lincolnshire Assize Rolls for 1202 occur Ralph Hellecoc (Elcock) and Walter Morcoc (cf. Morekin).[2] Witecoc figures several times on the Exchequer

---

[1] In this connection cf. Hen. Godescok, Ess. 1344 (Gaol. Del. R. 18b, m. 28d.).

[2] P.R.O. Assize Roll 479, mm. 1, 2.

Rolls of Normandy, 1198 (vol. 16); Wedercoc is a London entry on the Pipe Rolls, 1227–8, and Luuecok appears in the Lincolnshire Fines for 1236 (Massingberd), all being second names. Sauecoc and Vodecox were noticed in the Halesowen Court Rolls (Worc.), 1270–1; and reference to the vast index of the Hundred Rolls, c. 1275, exemplified the suffix -coc(k) in six personal names and sixty-two second names.

Forenames. *Yorks*: Hicchecok (2), Hanecok Birun. *Devon*: Willecoccus Russel. *London*: Wylekoc Hervy. *Hunts*: Hikoc. Second names. *Cambs*: Alcoc (cf. de Alcock in London), Badecok, Bagecok, Holekoc, Picok, Pittcok, Pocok (3), Rogekoc, Swetcok, Symcot, Walekoc, Wodecok (2). *Oxford*: Batecok (3), Becoc, Lovecok, Poucok, Poukoc, Pychecoch, Telcok, Wodecok (3). *Hunts*: Balkok, Bylkok, Cecilia Gilcok (perhaps from Gil-bert, but cf. Chicheli Giletok, probably the same person), Pylecok. *Bucks*: Adecot, Bokecot, Palecok, Vodecok. *Wilts*: Dymecock, Francok, Wylecok, Wytcok. *Beds*: Bicok, Maykoc (also Maykot) (2), Sirecok. *Salop*: Hancoc, Vodekok. *Derby*: Truccok. *Suffolk*: Cuckuk. *Norfolk*: Budecok, Odecok, Pecok, Pocok (2), Wodecok. *Lincs*: Pocok, Wodecok. *Essex*: Hathecok, Lovecok, Wodecok. *Berks*: Polecok. *London*: Batecok, Pocok. *Glouc.*: Hellecok.

From the few personal names collected by this survey it is to be gathered that either the suffix -cock was very little in use as a diminutive, or it was not in favour with official scribes, and could be thrown off as readily as the modern *ie* or *y* from Willie or Jimmy. Among the second names considerable confusion is evident between -cot and -coc, but in the majority of examples the first elements correspond to O.E. protothemes, Baga, Bil, Heathu, Hol, Love, Pil, Pita, Swet, Tella, etc., pointing to the probability of such appellatives having formerly been personal names with diminutive endings. The suffix -cock is somewhat more widely distributed than -kin, but nevertheless is more commonly found in south and east, and as is to be expected from a home product, it is more prevalent than the alien -kin in the North, as a search of 8,000 Yorkshire names on the Subsidy Roll for 1301 evidences. Second names noticed were :—

Alkock, Balcock (3), Bulekock, Lucok, Pakock (4), Pydekock, Raincoke, Wodecok.

Taking, again, the Subsidy Rolls for the year 1327, the following examples were obtained :—

Devonshire: (5,000 entries). Batecok, Jolicok, Morcok, Pocok.
Huntingdonshire: (3,500 entries). Wodekoc.
Leicestershire: (3,500 entries). Adecokes (6), Athekoc, Badecokes, Becok, Hulcok, Rodecok.
Kent: (6,000 entries). Badecok, Batetok, Bredecok, Elcok,

Gefcok, Hamekoc, Hallcok, Morcok (3), Picok, Pitecoke, Pocok, Wilkoc, Wodecok.

Suffolk : (11,720 entries).   Alcock (3), Berecok, Bunchekok (2), Cokok (6) (Cockou is common), Lyrncok, Pecok (3), Piccok, Pykok, Whitecok, Willecok, Wodecok (13).

Gloucestershire : (5,000 entries).   Alecoke, Batecoke (3), Hanecokes, Hichecokes, Lacoke, Lovecoke (2), Morcok (also cf. de Morcote), Paicocke, Pecok, Wilkokes.

Cumberland (1333) : (3 500 entries).   Alcok, Alcokson, Durkok, Licok, Lycoksone (2), Pacok (4), Raincok (4), Wilcokson.

It may be worthy of note that of these six counties, Gloucestershire had the greatest proportion of both -*kin* and -*cock* suffixes, and, moreover, in each case was the principal one to evidence the genetival inflection ; e.g. Margery Wilkokes, i.e. Margery (daughter) of Wilkok. Later on Wilcocks became Wilcox, and Hichecokes was written Hitchcox and Hiscok.

French Suffixes.   The diminutive suffixes -*el*, -*et*, -*ot*, and variants (see above, p. 274), have had great influence in the formation of English surnames. Some examples may be noticed, but again it must be said that inspection only is insufficient to determine the origin with certainty, or the nature of the suffix.

-al, -all.   A variant of -*el*, occurring in Randal, Randall, if such name is not an apocopated form of Randol(f).

-ard.   Occurs in Nisard (Denis-ard) and the English surnames, Picard and Punchard (also place-name), but the suffix is often indistinguishable from other elements and rarely to be identified with certainty.

-at, -att.   A variant of -*et* and -*ot*, as Allatt from Elliott (dim. of Elye, Elias), occurring as Aliot, 1275 (Hund. R.), Marryatt, Marratt, Wyatt (Guy). Robat occurs several times, 1275 (Hund. R.).

-el, -ell, -le.   This suffix may be, in many instances, of O.E. origin. Domesday Book examples are : Achil, Brunel, Burgel, Fitel, Gribol, Ivichel, Louel, Morel, Tochil, Wadel. Other names from Birch and Kemble are : Bercol, Duddel, Dyddel, Mannel, Monnel, Mucel, Tirtil, Tymbel, Utel. Eowel is no doubt the Welsh Howel.

W. Painell, Lincs. 1201. (Cur. Reg. R.)
Alex. Pointell, Norf. 1201. (Cur. Reg. R.)
Caterina Lovel, Oxf. 1275. (Hund. R.)
Gilb. Tatchell, Oxf. 1275. (Hund. R.)
Herv. Drabil, Cambs. 1275. (Hund. R.)

Modern surnames are : Dobel, Drewell, Hagell, Lovel, Martel, Parnell (Peter), Paynel, Pinel, Pottle, Tatchell (Eustace). Possible also Drabble (O.E. Drabba, BCS.).

-er. This termination may have a diminutive as well as an agential force, but identity is difficult. Possible examples are Giler (cf. Gile, Gilot, Gilly, etc.) and Pecker (cf. Pec, Pechel, Peket, Pegon, Pecot, etc.).

-et, -ett. A very common suffix.

> Mich. Belet, Kent, 1203. (Cur. Reg. R.)
> Rich. Hackett, 1586. (St. Jas. Clerkenwell Par. R.)

Modern surnames are : Abbett (O.E. Abba), Ablett, Annett, Arnet, Claret, Hackett (Hake), Locket, Matchet (? Margaret), Martinet, Olivet, Pasket (Pasque), Pollett (Paul), Rickett (O.E. Ric, as in Ricbeald), Sibbett (Sybil), Simnet (Simon), Tillett (Matilda), Thomasset, Willet.

-in. Another common suffix.

> Odo f. Gamelini, Somers. 1086. (Dom. Bk.)
> Rog. Paulyn, Oxf. 1275. (Hund. R.)
> Thomasin, varlet. — 1275–6. (Cl. R.)

Modern surnames are : Abelin, Gamelin, Gilpin, Godin, Ibbin (Isabel), Lambin (Lambert), Machin (Matthew), Marrin (Mary ; but cf. Morin, Morel, Moret, i.e. Maurice), Paskin, Paulin, Perrin (Peter), Phipin, Pippin, Tobin (Tobias). With excrescent *g* : Gambling, Pauling, Perring, Tilling (Matilda). These latter are liable to be confused with O.E. *-ing*-names.

-itt. A variant of *-et*, which is not noticed before the seventeenth century. Surnames are : Abbitt, Hagitt, Pavitt, Pippitt, Porritt, Sibbitt, Tippitt (Theobald).

-on. In some instances this suffix is an augmentative, as Richardon, " le gros Richard " (Ferriere) but more often it is a derivation from the ancient accusative, as Hues—Huon, Pieres—Pieron, etc.[1] Modern surnames are : Beaton (Beatrice), Fulchon (Fulcher), Guyon, Hamon, Mabon (Mabel), Paton (? Patrick), Rickon, Wyon.

-ot, -ott. A very common suffix.

> Reg. Mullot, Cambs. 1275. (Hund. R.) Cf. Mulet, Mulkyn, Mulloc.
> W. Raulot, Cambs. 1275. (Hund. R.)
> W. Robertot, Cambs. 1275. (Hund. R.)

Modern surnames are : Abbot, Abelot, Annot, Arnott (Arnold), Bagot, Emmot, Fillpot (Philip), Gillot, Ibbot, Maggot, Marriott, Millot (Miles), Perrott, Tillott, Wilmot.

-ut. A variant of *-ot*, as in Tibbutt.

Double-Syllabled Suffixes. The number of derivative surnames is increased by the use of double suffixes or double-syllabled suffixes, in most cases with a double diminutive force.

---

[1] *Essay on Romance Languages*, by Sir G. C. Lewis, 1862, p. 81.

l + n
-al-in Saralin (Soms. 1327) : Thomalyn (Kent, Ric. II. Subs. 123/59, m. 25.)

-el-in Alice Sarpeline, Oxf. 1275. (Hund. R.) Cf. Sarp, Sarpman.
Modern surnames : Catlin(g), Hanselin, Morlin(g), Odlin (Odeline : Hund. R.), Tomlin. Probably Suckling (cf. Soki, Sokeling, Suklyng, Sucklin).

-ol-in Odolina, Wilts. 1086. (Dom. Bk.) : Steph. Catoline, Cambs. 1275. (Hund. R.) Cf. Catel.

-el-on French examples are : Bousselon, Nivelon.

-il-on French examples are Jacquillon, Bancillon (cf. Bancel).

l + t
-al-et W. Hanalet, Channel Islands, 1309. (Assizes.)

-el-et Alan Bartelet, Cambs. 1275. (Hund. R.)
Modern surnames : Giblett (Gilbert), Hamblett, Herbelet, Hewlett, Noblett (Nobelot : Hund. R.)

-ol-et French surnames are : Berdolet (cf. Berdin), Pernolet (Perrin).

-al-ot Rus. Robalot, Cambs. 1275. (Hund. R.)

-el-ot J. Hughelot, Devon, 1275. (Hund. R.)
Modern surnames : Cobelot (O.E. Cobba or aphæretic Jacob), Hobelot (Robert), Pimlott (O.E. Pymma, M.E. Pym), Richelot.

-il-ot A French example is Jacquillot.

-ol-ot Thom. Bartholot, Cambs. 1275. (Hund. R.)

n + l
-en-el Pet. Tremenel, London. (Coroner's R.)

-in-el Walt. Tropinel, Wilts. 1275. (Hund. R.) Cf. Tropin. The French have Tropè, Tropel.

-on-el Rich. Cardonel, Channel Islands, 1309. (Assizes.) Perronelle is common in French.

-en-ol Robt. Gosenol (Gosce), Cambs. 1275. (Hund. R.)

-in-ol Rich. Dodinol, Salop, 1275. (Hund. R.) Cf. Dode, Dodin, Dodon.

n + n **-en-in** The French have Huguenin from Hugues.

n + t
-en-et Rich. Pikenet or Pikenot, Lincs. 1275. (Hund. R.)

-in-et Rich. Robynet, Lincs. 1411. (Parl. R. iii, 649.)
Modern surnames : Abbinett (O.E. Abba, or from Abraham or Abel, Hignett (Richard), Robinet.

-on-et Emmelotta Baudonette, Channel Islands, 1309. (Assizes.)

-en-ot See en-et.

-in-ot Hen. Godynot.

r + l **-er-el** W. Bokerel, London, 1275. (Hund. R.) Rob. Dikerel, Oxf. 1275. (Hund. R.) Rich. Foterel, Devon, 1275. (Hund. R.)

t + n
-ot-en W. Emmoten, Warw. 1375. (Subs.) Cf. Emmot. Hen. Claroten, Warw. 1327. (Subs.)

-et-in Geoff. Anketin, Ess. 1275. (Hund. R.) Cf. Anke, Ankin. Mart. Poketin, Cambs. 1275. (Hund. R.) Cf. Pochelot.

-ot-in French examples are Jannotin, Lambotin.

It is not known if r + n, r + t, and t + l types exist, no examples having come under notice. Regarding the suffix -*er*, it appears that in English it has occasionally both diminutive and augmentative force (Maetzner, i, 442), but the value of intercalatory -*er* is uncertain.

The double diminutive suffixes, it will be noticed, are joined to single syllable names or diminished forms of compounds as a general rule, but there are exceptions, as the French example Philip-on-et. Double diminutives are very rare in official records of the twelfth century, and do not become common until the fourteenth, and most of the variants are the product of even later years, being often of purely French origin. Apparently of an hypocoristic nature, the diminutive served the additional and practical purpose of providing a necessary distinction in days when it was common to bestow the same forename on several sons of one family ; thus Guillot was brother of Guillaume de Louviers, 1298 ; Jehannot was brother of Jehan de Amiens, 1298 ; on the other hand, two sons of Jehannot (elsewhere Jehan) Hecelin (1297) were both called Jehannot, a sister being Jehannete ; and Jehannot was brother of Jehannot Chase-Rat, 1299. In other instances different forms of the same name were interchangeable officially ; e.g. in various *Rôles de Taille Parisiens* Guillaume and Gillot are the same person, as are Jaques and Jaquet, Acelot and Aceline, Hue, Hugues, and Huguet, etc. In the days when second names were being taken, it would be quite possible for brothers of the same name to assume genealogical surnames with different suffixes. Exemplifying the use to which suffixes may be put, it may be said that, in Poitou, a man might be called Rouland, his wife Roulante, his son Roulu, his daughter Rouluche, and his youngest son Rouluchet, etc.[1]

The remarkable multiplication of surnames by the use of suffixes will be illustrated by four examples, Hebraic, Teutonic, Latin, and Greek, but the origin of these apparent derivatives should not be accepted unreservedly without detailed proof.

(i) Adam (Heb. " red earth ").

Simple pet form : Aday, Ade, Adee, Adey, Adie, Ady, Atty.
Suffix -cock : Adcock, Atcock.
Suffix -kin : Adkin, Aiken, Aikin, Aitken, Aitkin, Atkin.
Double diminutives : Adnet, Adnett, Adnitt, Adnot.
Simple genitive : Adams.
Genitive of diminutives : Addis, Adds, Ades, Aikens, Aikins, Aitkens.
Filial desinence : Adamson, Addison, Atkinson, Attison.
Aspirated forms : Hadcock, Haddy, etc.
Corruptions : Adkisson, Hadkiss, Hadskis, and the Welsh forms Badams, etc.

[1] *Memoirs of the Soc. of Antiq. of France*, vol. i, p. 225.

Confusion doubtless exists with derivatives of O.E. Adda, Addi, Eada, etc.

(ii) Baldwin (Teut. " bold friend ").

Simple pet forms : Ball, Balde, Baud, Bodd, Boddy, Bode, Budd, Bude.
Suffix -cock : Bawcock, Budcock.
Suffix -kin : Bodkin, Budkin.
Suffix -en : Bawden, Bodden, Boden, Bolden, Bowden, Boyden, Budden.
Suffix -in : Bawdin, Bodin, Boldin, Bolding.
Suffix -on : Bawdon.
Suffix -et : Baudet, Baudett.

In many cases these names are indistinguishable from derivatives of O.E. Boda, Bode, Buda, etc. Further confusion is probable with Badecock (Bartholomew), and with Scottish Bolden from Bowden (Roxb.).

(iii) Margaret (Lat. " pearl ").

Simple pet forms : Madge, Margery, Margrie, Pegg.
Suffix -in : Margin.
Suffixes -et, -ot : Madgett, Maggot, Margot, Matchet, Matchett, Meggett, Meggott.
Simple genitive : Margetts, Margretts, Margritts.
Genitive of diminutives : Margries, Maggs, Meggs, Peggs.
Filial desinence : Margerison, Margeson, Margesson, Margetson, Margisson, Marjerrison, Meggeson, Megson, Maggotson.
Corruptions : Marginson, Marjason.

It must not be overlooked that Magge was a common O.E. element and personal name, and therefore has not improbably survived as a surname.

W. Maggessone, Suff. 1327. (Subs.)

Bardsley considers that Pogge, Pockson, and Poxon are also derivatives.

(iv) Nicholas (Gr. victorious army).

Simple pet form : Nichol, Nicholl, Nickoll, Nicol, Nicole, Cole, Colley, Collie, Colly, Culley, Cully.
Suffix -kin : Colkin (thirteenth cent.).
Suffix -in : Colin, Colling, Collinge, Nicklin, Nickling.
Suffix -et : Collett, Collette, Nicholet.
Suffix -in-et : Colnett, Colenutt, Colinette.
Genitive of diminutives : Nicholes, Nichols, Nickalls, Nickels, Nickolds, Nickoles, Nickols, Nicks, Nix. Coles, Colles, Collis, Colliss, Colls, Collins, Collings. Nicholetts.
Filial desinence : Nicholson, Nicolson. Collison, Collisson, Colson. Nickson, Nixon. Collinson, Nicklinson, Nickinson.
Corruptions : Nickerson, Nickisson.

Some of these derivatives are doubtless survivors of the O.E. Cola. The Continental Nicolaus was likewise the source of numerous surnames. Müller (p. 21) gives, for instance, a list of Luxembourg derivatives and variants, as :—

Claas, Clæs, Claisse, Clas, Clasen, Classen, Claus, Clause, Clauss, Clees, Cleesen, Cles, Clesse, Cloos, Clos, Closen, Closener, Closs, Clossener, Colas, Coilin, Coling, Collin, Colling, Klais, Klas, Klasen, Klassen, Klees, Klesen, Nick, Nickels, Nickers, Nickes, Nicks, Nichts, Nicla, Nicles, Niclou, Nicloux, Nicola, Nicolas, Nicolay, Nikla, Nikola, Nikolay, and Niks.

CHAPTER XII

EVOLUTION BY VARIATION AND CORRUPTION

Orthographic Changes. In the last chapter the evolution of surnames and the production of new varieties by recognized grammatical processes was considered, and some attention will now be given to the large number of orthographic variants, which may follow regular laws, but sometimes are formed irregularly, in haphazard fashion, and in most unexpected guise. The signification of surnames of the latter type, in the process of mutation, may also undergo changes of various degrees which may be classed as follow :—

(i) *Signification retained.* Variation of orthography whereby the original description or surname has received a number of different forms which are recognizable as having a common origin : thus O.E. *smiδ* has become Smith, Smyth, Smythe ; O.E. *brún* has become Broun, Brown, Browne.

(ii) *Signification lost.* Corruption of orthography whereby the original description or surname has received a form and sound conveying no apparent meaning. The possibilities may be illustrated by dictionary words, such as " kickshaws ", originally Fr. *quelque chose* " something " ; and " hussif " derived from Icel. *húse* " a case ". Surnames of this type are Dunbabin, Earp, Gallafent, Kethro, Kirty, Pagriff, Remblance, Sumption, Stallybrass, Tollemache, Wotherspoon, etc., the origins and significations of which have still to be proved.

(iii) *Signification changed.* Corruption of orthography, whereby the original description or surname has so changed as to have received a meaning entirely different to the original signification. Dictionary words illustrating the process are : " country-dance " formerly Fr. *contre-danse* ; " pickaxe," from O.F. *picois* ; and " bank " originally " bench ", a money-table. Place-names have changed by imitation in the same way, a well-known example being " Birdcage Walk " which was once more appropriately called " Bocage Walk ". Similarly disguised surnames are Barefoot, from Barford ; Anthill, from Ampthill ; Egg, from Edge ; Fairbrass, from Ferbras (iron-arm) ; Greedy, from Gredhay ; Heron, from O'Ahern (Ir.) ; Physick, from Fishwick ; Swanshead, from Swineshead, etc.

Influence of Palæography. In the days when surnames were acquiring the permanent nature which they now possess, all lists of names were written by hand, and many misreadings resulted. At first sight it may seem surprising that the form of surnames should have suffered any change because of mis-spelling or mis-reading, but if it be remembered that a very large proportion of the people could neither read nor write, and those who possessed those accomplishments had no standard of spelling, it will be realized that few could dispute the entry on a register, even if they had any inclination to do so. Comparatively few records may be strictly termed original; the actual recording scribe was sometimes a poor writer and speller, and upon the fair copy being made from his draft, often by another clerk, even further divergences in the orthography of the name resulted. One list of appellatives might be compiled from an earlier one, and it would be quite useless for an illiterate yokel to tell an officious scribe that his name was Goff if the register read Goss; even if he was confident that he had always been called Goff it was unlikely that he had any documentary proof, and he had no alternative but to tell his friends that his name was Goss.[1] Brief reference may be made to some of the peculiarities of palæography,[2] which have caused trouble to the medieval scrivener as well as to the modern transcriber, resulting in some cases in a change of name.

Fig. 1. A form of an O.E. letter, *yogh*, which expressed a sound intermediate between *g* and *y*, was still in use in the fourteenth and fifteenth centuries, and is indistinguishable from the contemporary *z*, which letter is used to represent it when printed. Misapprehension as to the value of the latter has resulted in the Scottish surnames Menzies and Dalziell, which, however, have more or less retained the ancient pronunciation in Ming-is and De-ell.

Fig. 2. This terminal abbreviation usually represents *-rum*, but in some instances it is a suspension of other *r*-terminations. By a misunderstanding transcribers have extended Sa' and Bath Fo' to Sarum and Bath Forum, instead of to Sa(risberiensis) and Bath Fo(rinseca).

Fig. 3. This final compendium stands for *es, is, ys*, or *s*, usually *es*, but being remarkably like a modern *e*, is often so transcribed, a common mistake of the inexperienced copyist of parish registers, resulting in Treve for Treves, Howe for Howes, etc.

---

[1] I have known such a case even in the late nineteenth century. Only recently also, it was recorded that one Thomas Field, of Iver, Bucks, had lived for seventy-two years without knowing his real name, having always called himself Frederick Channer, and married and brought up a family in that name. When he went to claim his old age pension he found from his birth certificate that his name was Thomas Field, and finally that name was entered in his death certificate (*Evening Standard*, 14th Oct., 1930).

[2] Some of my examples are taken from *English Court Hand*, by C. Johnson and Hilary Jenkinson, 1915, to which valuable work reference should be made for further particulars.

1		2	3
g or y	*z*	*rum*	*es*

4	5	6	
F	Blactan Blactan Vltan	*a*	*ct*

7		8	9	10
c	*t*	*S*	*et*	*e e oe*

11			
Etat	*Ouyng*	*Qui*	*Cart'e*

12		13		14
D	*0*	*E*	*g*	*t'minū iɲi*

Fig. 4. The capital F has commonly been read ff, and has now been perpetuated as a supposed sign of antiquity in some of our surnames, as ffiske, ffoulkes, etc., which should be properly Fiske and Foulkes. Official indexes, such as those of wills at Somerset House, show that every name beginning with *F* was written with the double down-stroked capital, and that no names commenced with a double *f*.

Figs. 5 *and* 6. The ligatures are a fruitful source of trouble. Referring to the three examples from Domesday Book, 1086, the correct reading is Blactan, Blacstan, and Ulstanus, although the clerk was registering the names of Blacstan twice, and Ulfstan. They were printed by the Record Commission, Blacstan twice, and Vlstan. Fig. 6 illustrates the little difference between *a* and *ct* in the thirteenth–fourteenth century, but possibly this similarity has not affected transcripts. Sources of confusion of like nature are *lk* and *w* in the seventeenth-century Coram Rege Rolls and elsewhere ; and even in splendid indexes like those of the P.C.C. at Somerset House, *rw* and *w* are sometimes indistinguishable.

Fig. 7. The letters *c* and *t* in the thirteenth–fifteenth centuries, owing to careless writing, are even more alike than the examples now given, and the resulting confusion in names with the suffixes *-cot* and *-coc* has been particularly noticed above (p. 286).

Fig. 8. This peculiar thirteenth-century capital S has on occasion caused trouble, being taken for M.

Fig. 9. This sign, originating in a semi-colon, stands for the omission of *-et, -ue*, etc. Like No. 1, it has been mistaken for *z*, a familiar example being the abbreviation " viz." for vi(delicet). And so may be found, for instance, W. de Forz (Pat. R. 1216, p. 13) for W. de Fortibus.

Fig. 10. A great pitfall for the transcribers of parish registers is the letter *e*, which may be mistaken for *o* ; in fact, in the fifteenth-century *oe*, now reproduced, there is no distinction at all. Names like Meller and Nayler are often copied Mellor and Naylor.

Fig. 11. The small distinction between E, O, Q, and C of the fourteenth century is illustrated by extracts from a Coroner's Roll, A.D. 1365. In some fourteenth-century Subsidy Rolls there is no difference at all between E and Q.

Fig. 12. In some thirteenth and fourteenth-century records D and O, as in Dyn and Oyn, do not show even the distinction of the reproduced examples, and defy identification.

Fig. 13. Equally difficult are G and E in the Final Concords, the clerks themselves being confused, as comparison with the contemporary calendar shows.[1] The illustration shows, first

[1] For an example see *Ewen of East Anglia*, p. 212.

an E which may be taken for a G, and secondly a g which may often be read as y owing to the thin horizontal stroke being omitted or faded away.

Fig. 14. Uncertain readings occur with any of the letters *i, m, n,* or *u,* which are all written with little more than vertical strokes, in conjunction, and the final flourish with abbreviation mark is additionally misleading. The difficulty which transcribers have with names like Cane and Cave, Haukin and Hankin, or Hauvil and Hanvil, will be readily understood. Anciently the letter *i* was some times distinguished by a faint oblique stroke like an acute accent, which mark, later on, deteriorated into the " dot ", now a quite unnecessary feature of the printed page. When one *i* followed another, the second was given a flourishing tail, making it look like a *j,* in which form it is usually printed. To a misunderstanding of this peculiarity is due the perpetuation of the supposed surname Smijth, which occurs in the Baronetage. Names containing *ij* may usually be identified as Dutch.

Corrupt Orthography. We are apt to be amused at the inconsistent spelling of our forefathers, but it must not be forgotten that no vocabularies approaching the authority of the modern dictionary were available until the seventeenth century, and consequently, there being no single standard, one variant of a word had as much sanction as another. For names there has never been any reference list whatsoever, and consequently every writer indulged his own fancy at the moment, and as in the middle ages the majority of the people were illiterate and unable to spell their own names, they could not possibly convey the information to a recording scribe, the result being noticeable in the large number of different orthographic renderings of a surname in ancient rolls, and to a lesser extent even yet in our directories. Some names gave more trouble than others; thus in a series of nine North of England inquisitions (A.D. 1276) relating to the same affray, a suspected malefactor was variously named, of Ennutwesille, Emmetwesille, Ennetwysel, Hennetwysel, Hennetwisele, Hennethysil, Hennetwysil, Hentwysil, Hennethwisell, and Aynetwysel, the name also occurring as Hennethuysil [1] ; its modern guise being Entwisle, Entwistle, and Entwhistle.

Not only, then, is considerable variation in the spelling of a name due to dialectal influence, but further and extensive corruption was caused by the want of a standard, and a still greater profusion of orthographic mutations results from want of uniformity in the same family and even by the same person, such irregularities being common up to the eighteenth century. To the genealogist a knowledge of the variants of a name is

[1] Cal. of Chancery Inquisitions.

of very great importance, without which much information might be overlooked by the searcher. Sometimes the numbers of variants are very considerable: 33 forms of the name Bruce are recorded by Drummond (*Noble British Families*), 34 different spellings of Bunyan have been noted according to the *Dictionary of National Biography*, and W. P. Phinnimore collected a similar number of changes of Phillimore, together with 59 orthographic forms of Finnimore. W. P. Baildon has given 57 ways in which his family name has been spelt in recent years,[1] and Professor Hewins, from documents relating to his family, obtained 88 variants of the surname,[2] which number is eclipsed by the Mannerings of Cheshire, who have 137 ways of spelling the family name, according to their archives, as Bardsley records. Chaloner Smith found 500 variants of Cushion in old records,[3] and it is also said that an inventive American discovered 4,000 variations of the name Shakespeare, many presumably suppositious, but it will be shown that even that large number fades into insignificance in comparison with the possible orthographic mutations of a name with syllables commencing with vowel sounds.

The spoken alphabet of English contains forty-three sounds: the written alphabet has only twenty-six letters (of which five, namely *c*, *q*, *x*, *w*, and *y*, are superfluous) to represent them. One sound may be written in different ways, as long *a* in *fate*, *braid*, *say*, *great*, *neigh*, *prey*, *gaol*, *gauge*; and one symbol may be given different sounds, as in *bough*, *cough*, *dough*, *hiccough* (= cup), *hough* (= hock), *tough*, *through*, *thorough*. " It is, however, in the vowel sounds that the irregularities of our alphabet are most discernible. Thirteen vowel-sounds are represented to the eye in more than one hundred different ways."[4]

The possibilities of variation in surnames are much greater and may be exemplified by taking the ancient Cymric name Ywein, which is now represented in England by Ewen, and in Wales by Owen, to mention two of the modern spellings of the popular genealogical designation. Orthographically the name has varied in length from three letters, as Eun in the Assize Rolls,[5] to nine letters, as Hewghinge, the spelling in a Norfolk will[6]; and a twelve-letter form, such as Heugheinnges, would not be impossible for the medieval scribe. It

---

[1] *Baildon and the Baildons*, vol. i, p. 79.
[2] *Register of the Parish Church, Bretforton*, by W. H. Shawcross, vol. ii, p. 54. I have given a much larger selection in *Ewen of East Anglia*.
[3] So Mr. Chaloner Smith informed me.
[4] *The English Language*, by J. M. D. Meiklejohn, 1886, p. 8.
[5] *Ewen of East Anglia*, p. 29.
[6] Ibid., p. 409.

would be well within the mark to say that there are not less than 100,000 possible mutations of this name without reckoning Gaelic or Latin forms.

The first syllable might be written : Eu-, Eue-,[1] Eugh-,[2] Eughe-, Euu-, Euue-, Euw-, Euwe-, Euwgh-, Euwghe-, Ew-, Ewe-, Ewgh-[2], Ewghe-, O-, Oe-, Oaw-, Oawe-, Ou-, Oue-, Ough-, Oughe-, Ouw-, Ouwe-, Ow-, Owe-, U-,[3] Ue-, Ugh-,[4] Ughe-, Uw-, Uwe-,[4] Uwgh-, Uwghe-, Yeow-,[5] Yeowe-, Yeu-,[6] Yeue-, Yeugh-,[7] Yeughe-, Yeuu-, Yeuue-, Yeuw-, Yeuwe-,[8] Yeuwgh-, Yeuwghe-, Yew-, Yewe-, Yewgh-, Yewghe-, Yiw-,[9] Yiwe-, Yoo-, Yooe-,[10] You-, Youe-, Yough-,[11] Youghe-, Youu-, Youue-, Youw-, Youwe-, Yow-, Yowe-,[12] Yu-, Yue-, Yugh-, Yughe-, Yuw-, Yuwe-. (70.)

Common first syllables in early records were : Iw-, Iwe-, Yw-, Ywe- ; and the u and w were often written v. Taking a few simple variants : Ev-, Eve-, Iv-, Ive-, Oav-, Oave-, Ouv-, Ouve-, Ov-, Ove-, Uv-,[13] Uve-, Yev-, Yeve-, Yov-, Yove-,[14] Yv-, Yve-. (22.)

Further variants are provided by the initial aspirate, a few of the more probable being : Heu-, Heue-, Heugh-, Heughe-, Heuu-, Heuue-, Heuw-, Heuwe-, Hew-, Hewe-, Hewgh-, Hewghe-, Ho-, Hoe-, Hoav-, Hoave-, Hoaw-, Hoawe-, Hou-, Houe-, Hough-, Houghe-, Houv-, Houve-, Houw-, Houwe-, Hov-, Hove-, How-, Howe-, Hu-, Hue-, Hugh-, Hughe-, Huw-, Huwe-, Huwgh-, Huwghe-, Hiw-, Hiwe-, Hyw-, Hywe-, Hev-, Heve-, Hiv-, Hive-, Huv-, Huve-. (48).

It has also been noticed that the second syllable of Ywein suffered considerable variation at the hands of the ancient scrivener. Taking from various rolls a few examples, such as -aignes (Yvaignes), -aine (Ewaine), -ance (Ewance, -anse (Evanse), -aunce (Evaunce), -aynes (Ivaynes), -eings (Eweings), -eins (Iweins), -ence (Ewence), -enes (Ewenes), -eyn (Eweyn), -ines (Ewines), -inges (Ewinges), -nes (Ewnes), -yne (Ewyne) : it will be seen that the list might be increased :—

-aign, -aignce, -aigne, -aignes, -aigns, -aignse, -ain, -aince, -aine, -aines, -ains, -ainse, -an, -ance, -ane, -anes, -ans, -anse, -aun, -aunce, -aune, -aunes, -auns, -aunse, -ayn, -aynce, -ayne, -aynes, -ayns, -aynse, -eign, -eignce, -eigne, -eignes, -eigns, -eignse, -ein, -eince, -eine, -eines, -eing, -einge, -einges, -eings, -eins, -einse, -en, -ence, -ene, -enes, -ens, -ense, -eyn, -eynce, -eyne, -eynes, -eyns, -eynse, -in, -ince, -ine, -ines, -ing, -inge, -inges, -ings, -ins, -inse, -n, -nce, -ne, -nes, -ns, -nse, -yn, -ynce, -yne, -ynes, -yng, -ynge, -ynges, -yngs, -yns, -ynse. (84.)

[1] The final e in this and the following forms is an ornamental embellishment, and not sounded.
[2] Early modern English variants of " yew " (Century Dict.).
[3] E.E. utree " yew-tree ".
[4] Cf. early forms of Hugh (Chaucer, Huwe, and Hwe).
[5] Occurs in Yeowins. [6] Chaucer has ieu in eschieu.
[7] Early modern English variant (Century Dict.).
[8] Cf. Nieuweman. [9] Occurs in Yiwon.
[10] Cf. Looe in Cornwall. [11] Cf. Youghal in Ireland.
[12] Occurs in Yoweinge. [13] E.E. uvtre " yew-tree " (Century Dict.).
[14] Cf. Yovele, a form of Yuille.

Eighty-four different variations for the second syllable without introducing common known forms, such as -on (Ewon) and -un (Ywun). Nearly all these variants might also be aspirated (cf. Ow-(h)en, How-(h)en, Hew-(h)en), or the first sixty-two might commence with *y* (cf. Ew-(y)en), although both forms are unusual for the second syllable. The examples given are sufficient to illustrate the remarkable possibilities of medieval orthography; combining the first and second syllables the number of different names resulting from the simple variants would be $140 \times 84 = 11,760$, which total would be reduced by 1,540 (70×22), on account of duplication which occurs (e.g. Ew-ein = Ewe-in). Since Yuille may be found written Jouel, Jowel, Jewell, etc., and Ewardby occurs as Jewardby, Evan as Jevan, etc., it is not unreasonable to suggest that Owen might be written Jowen, and that another series of syllables might have the initial J. By introducing the initial J into suitable cases, and likewise the initial A (cf. Aven, Awen, etc.); by doubling the consonant *n* (cf. Evanne, Euann, Ewenne, Owanne, Owenn, Yevannce, Ivenn, etc.); by carrying aspiration to the second syllable, and likewise an initial *y*, the number of possible variants exceeds 100,000, of which, fortunately, less than 1 per cent can actually be found on early records.

Even in these days of general education, when it comes to writing down a surname our scribes are quite as erratic as were our ancestors. As an example may be cited the case of a gentleman named Kinniburgh, who records that he has received communications with his name mis-spelled in no less then 247 ways,[1] and most people have had experiences of similar nature, if only on a smaller scale. We cannot, therefore, blame Sir Joshua Reynolds (late eighteenth century) when writing regarding the death of the son of George II, for referring to the " Prince of Whales ".[2] This unusually happy insertion of the *h* leads to some consideration of the aspirate, in particular, from certain aspects which hitherto do not appear to have received attention.

The Aspirate. Occasional variants are caused by dropping an initial *h*, as Imfrey for Humfrey, Inkley for Hinkley; or a medial *h*, as Oldum for Oldham, 1509 (Pard. R.); but a more numerous class of surnames is formed by prefixing an initial *h*, as Hosegood for Osgood, or even aspirating both elements, as Howhen for Owen.

Robt. Heohyn in Marton, Norf. 1545-6. (Subs. 151/318.)
Robt. Howhen of Martyn, Norf. 1616. (Norw. Arch. Reg. 1617, f. 172.)

[1] *Daily Mail*, 28th July, 1927.
[2] *Letters of Sir Joshua Reynolds*, ed. by F. W. Hilles, p. 12.

Misuse of the letter *h*, initial and medial, is widespread and of great antiquity, and was noticed by the ancient Romans. It appears that in early days classes were distinguished, as at present, by their treatment of the aspirate : P. Nigidius observes : *Rusticus fit sermo, si adspires perperam*.[1] In the Romance languages the same peculiarity occurs, names like Ivo, Audouin, and Eudo being found written Hivo, Haudouin, and Heudo. There is also plenty of evidence to show that the Teutons placed no very definite value on the initial *h* ; in the Anglo-Saxon charters, personal names like Ælric and Hælric, Eadda, and Headda, Illo and Hillo, Odo and Hodo, and Yric and Hyryc frequently occurring. According to Sweet "in O.E., as in other Germanic languages, *h* was weakened to a mere breath initially. This is proved by the occasional omission or addition of an initial *h*, which occurs throughout the O.E. period ".[2] Another writer on the aspirate observes that " the habit of adding an *h* properly belongs to the counties that have been settled by Jutes and Angles, and not to those inhabited by Saxons"; but supporting evidence is wanting.[3] According to the map supplied by Freeman, the Jutes and Angles settled in the Eastern counties, excluding Essex, from Kent to the River Forth [4] : the Saxon territory including Gloucestershire, Oxfordshire, Buckinghamshire, Berkshire, Hertfordshire, Dorsetshire, Wiltshire, Hampshire (part), Surrey, Sussex, and Essex.

Aspiration, meaning here the prefixing of the initial letter *h* (sometimes called a decayed guttural), so far as it has affected names of persons, appears to have been of steady growth generally throughout England. The comprehensive collection of Gothonic names given by Searle in his *Onomasticon* shows that, prior to the Norman Conquest, the initially aspirated appellatives were about 17 per cent of the total number of names commencing with A, E, I, O, U, Y, and H, which proportion is considerably less than that found in dictionaries of Anglo-Saxon words, an exceptional result pointing to the fact that many names were neither Teutonic nor Scandinavian, but rather Norman or Cymric, in both of which languages *h* is little more than a semi-vowel.

For a further investigation a useful foundation is Domesday Book (1086), particularly convenient being Ellis's *Introduction*, which provides a list of about 10,000 persons. A count of the names with initials H. A, E, I, O, U (Y being then practically unused), shows the aspirated appellatives to be but 13 per cent

[1] *Auli Gallii Noctes Atticæ*, 1824, lib. xiii, cap. vi.
[2] *History of English Sounds*, by H. Sweet, 1888, p. 134.
[3] *The Aspirate*, by G. Hill, 1902, p. 84.
[4] *History of the Norman Conquest*, 2nd ed., 1870, vol. i, p. 34.

of the total; and eliminating names duplicated, of which there are a great number, and making a second enumeration, the percentage appears to be rather more, namely 15. In the language of the Normans, as in modern French, there is little aspiration (8 and 9 per cent respectively), and it would be easy to say that the influx of Frenchmen resulted in a lessened use of the initial H. Such an assumption would, however, be incorrect, as far as evidence exists, because further examination shows, somewhat unexpectedly, a greater proportion of H-names among the tenants of William than among the tenants of Edward, his predecessor, the figures of the first count being 17 per cent and 8 per cent, and of the second 22 and 14 per cent respectively. Breton influence, doubtless, was responsible to a certain extent, the language having much more aspiration than other Celtic tongues, and greatly exceeding that in Norman-French.

There is insufficient data to form an opinion as to whether, in the eleventh century, initial aspiration of personal names was uniformly distributed throughout England, but comparing the indexes of the Exeter Domesday and the *Inquisitio Eliensis* the percentages are noticed to be, respectively, 18 per cent for Devonshire and Cornwall (anciently West Wales), and 28 per cent for the Fenland.[1] The increase of aspiration in the names of " West Wales " may be due to the spoken dialect being Cornish, which like Breton has a greater proportion of words with initial *h* than modern Welsh; but it is difficult to advance any reason for the popularity of H-names in the Isle of Ely at this early date. No Scottish and Irish archives of the eleventh century are available.

During the following two centuries there was a remarkable increase in the popularity of the letter H, as is evidenced by the comprehensive collection of names in the *Rotuli Hundredorum*. Analysing 11,000 entries commencing with the aspirate or one or other of the five vowels and Y, it is found that the H-names are in the proportion of 40 per cent, but no cause is apparent to which the increase might be attributed, and it is unexplainable by any of the languages in use in Britain. As already mentioned, the influence of Latin, Norman, or Welsh would have led to a decrease, and although Anglo-Saxon, Cornish, and Breton make use of the aspirate in a larger degree, the proportion is nothing like 40 per cent. To some extent the increase may have been due to Low Countrymen, but the strength of their influence in the thirteenth century is not to be readily determined.

From the thirteenth century the growth of aspiration of secondary descriptions and surnames in England continued

[1] Using the later edition, the proportion is somewhat more.

on the ascending scale, but more slowly. In Wales the proportion was less, namely 30 per cent, according to the *Record of Carnarvon* (1353). In the Netherlands (fourteenth century), on the same basis of calculation, the H-names amounted to 48 per cent, which proportion increased to 54 per cent in the sixteenth century. Old Norse names of the thirteenth to the sixteenth centuries show a percentage of 41. In France the proportion was less, and, in fact, at the present day is about 38 per cent, which, however, is in striking contrast to dictionary figures (about 9 per cent).

Turning to modern English directories, an examination of about 2,000 names with initial letters, A, E, I, O, U, and H, given in Bardsley's *Dictionary of English and Welsh Surnames*, shows that the names commencing with the vowels were almost exactly equalled in numbers by those having H for the first letter. This proportion is very similar to enumerations made from other lists; thus 2,620 names from *Who's Who*, which, however, include a good many foreign names, yielded a percentage for the letter H of 52. In a record of *Graduati Cantabrigiensis*, which also included a number of aliens, the H-initialled names were 51 per cent of the total. In a long list of registered teachers the percentage was 55. A grand total of about 18,000 names yielded 54 per cent of names commencing with H, and 46 per cent with A, E, I, O, and U, the first-named vowel being by far the most prevalent, nearly equalling the aggregate of the other four.

A few examples relating to the counties may be of interest, in each case the percentage giving the proportion of the H-initialled names compared with those commencing with A, E, I, O, U, and Y.

Devon and Cornwall. Wills 1540–1799, 62 per cent.

Huntingdonshire. Fines 1194–1399, 40 per cent; 1400–1603, 47 per cent; Wills, 1615–52, 49 per cent. (An earlier series of Wills, 1479–1615, gives a percentage of 53.)

Lancashire. Inquests (persons and places) 1205–1307, 48 per cent; Court Rolls, 1323–4, 55 per cent; Inquisitions (including Cheshire), Stuart Period, 55 per cent.

Lincolnshire. Assize Rolls (persons and places), 1202–9, 34 per cent; Fines, 1189–1272, 37 per cent; Wills (Consistory Court), 1506–1600, 51 per cent; 1601–52, 44 per cent.

Northumberland. Assizes and Fines, 1256–99, 50 per cent.

Somersetshire. Assize Rolls, close of twelfth century—1257, 44 per cent; 1399–1460, 47 per cent; Hearth Tax, 1664–5, 59 per cent.

Staffordshire. Various Rolls, 1307–77, 42 per cent.

Suffolk. Subsidy Rolls, 1327, 45 per cent; 1524, 47 per cent; 1568, 50 per cent; Hearth Tax, 1674, 52 per cent.

Sussex. Subsidy Rolls, 1296, 1327, 1332, 47 per cent. Wills, 1541–1659, 50 per cent.

Warwickshire. Subsidy Roll, 1332, 46 per cent.
Yorkshire. Fines, 1218–31, 42 per cent; Subsidy Rolls (names and persons), 1301, 43 per cent.

While any one of these percentages may not be minutely exact the upward trend of aspiration in our surnames, from the eleventh to the sixteenth century, is unmistakeably evidenced by this analysis of 100,000 names. The most rapid growth took place before the end of the thirteenth century, and therefore, during the Norman period when, from the linguistic point of view, it might be least expected, and as stated above language had little to do with the development. It is commonly supposed that dropping or misplacing the letter *h* is a Cockney failing, but the figures now presented demonstrate that the increased use was fairly distributed all over England, the highest proportion being found in Cornwall and Devon. In Scotland and Ireland, variants due to irregular transference of the aspirate were formerly scarce, possibly accounted for by Gaelic influence, in which language *h* initiates no word, although it appears that from O'hEoghain and O'hOgain were derived Howen and Hogan.

The prominence of the initial *h* in surnames compared with its small use in spoken English is due in considerable measure to the influence of alien prefixes commencing with vowels which now fill columns of the dictionary; but a further cause for aspirated descriptions and surnames outstripping the proportion of dictionary words with the initial *h* is to be found in the statistical tables which have been provided above.

Characteristic and occupational surnames are themselves but dictionary words, and need not be considered in an inquiry upon this point. As has been demonstrated from the Onomasticon and Domesday Book, comparatively few personal names were aspirated, and likewise cannot affect the question, leaving local names as the remaining source for solution of the problem, and since nearly half the English surnames are derived from place-names, the proportion of aspiration in the latter must be largely reflected in the former. A rough count (by columns) of the place-names in the indexes of (*a*) KCD. (Anglo-Saxon period); (*b*) Close Rolls (1204–44); (*c*) Atlas of England (twentieth century); gives the proportion of H-names to those beginning with A, E, I, O, U, and Y as 50, 38, and 45 per cent respectively, pointing to a decrease, if anything. The proportion of aspirated names (mainly forenames) of the Domesday Book period has been put at about 15 per cent, which increased by the year 1275 (Hund. R.) to 40 per cent (second names). During the same 200 years the growth of second names of the local class (see Table V,

p. 131, Nos. 2–8) varied from 3–39 per cent, (average 18 per cent), to 50 per cent. The growth in H-descriptions and surnames, therefore, clearly corresponds to the increased employment of those of the local class, and this conclusion is supported by the fact that in Cornwall and the Northern counties where local surnames were most in use, so there are the more H-names.

The modern consonantal digraph *wh* appears in the rolls towards the end of the twelfth century, but the O.E. spelling was not entirely replaced for two centuries, the four forms Hw, W, Qw, and Wh, sometimes appearing almost side by side (see also p. 310).

W. le Wyhte, Suss. 1275. (Hund. R.)
W. le Huittawiere, Lond. *c.* 1280. (Will., Court of Husting, R. R. Sharpe.)
J. Hwytyng, Kent, 1300–1. (Subs. 123/24, m. 23.)
Thom. Hwytyng, Suss. 1327. (Subs. Salzman.)
Hugo Hwateman, Kent, 1327. (Subs. 123/10, m. 54.)
Thom. Hwitecroft, Kent, 1327. (Ibid., m. 33.)
J. Hwitberd, Kent, 1327. (Ibid., m. 52.)
W. Hwitsuere, Kent, 1327. (Ibid., m. 49.)
Ric. le Hwyte, Worc. 1340. (Non. Inq. ; Amphlett.)
Pet. Hwytegrom, Kent, Ric. II. (Subs. 123/59, m. 21.)
J. Hweglar, Kent, Ric. II. (Ibid.)

It is to be expected that once all persons had become possessed of hereditary surnames, which, with few exceptions, was before the end of the fifteenth century, all increase in the proportion of H-names would cease, and that is practically what occurred, although a slight tendency to increase continued, which may have been due to the desire for emphasis or to more obscure causes. A case of the formal adoption of an initial H is instanced by the ancient family name of Ywain of Worcestershire, which name, having collected a final *s* in the fourteenth century, and at various times toyed with an initial H, became finally fixed as Hewins, the family having decided that an aspirated form was sanctioned by tradition and use.[1]

In some cases the addition or loss of an initial H has quite altered the meaning of a name, e.g. Harrowsmith became Arrowsmith, if, in fact, the latter is not also an original form ; Aslak, personal name, is now found Hasluck ; Achard, another personal name, appears in modern directories as Hatchett ; Urri, a place-name, in some cases gives Hurry ; and a description like ate Wrong, i.e. "at the crooked tree" was turned into Hatewrong.

Common Equations. The vast possibilities of variation in

[1] *Bretforton Parish Register,* by W. H. Shawcross, vol. ii, p. 54.

the orthography of surnames have been demonstrated, and some examples of the most common interchanges will now be given. All vowels appear to have been mutable, even as late as the sixteenth century, as the following illustrations from the Pardon Roll of 1 Hen. VIII evidence.[1]

Medial : a = e = o = y : John Braban, Braben, Brabon, or Brabyn, Devon, p. 220.

a = i = o = u : T. Tharland, Thirlond, Thorlond, or Thurlund, Notts, p. 210.

Final : a = e = ey = ow = y : W. Bulla, Bulle, Bulley, Bullow, or Bully, London, p. 247.

e = es = is = ys : J. Edwarde, Edwardes, Edwardis, or Edwardys, Ess., p. 261.

The modern result of these differences may be exemplified by the surnames Tibbatts, Tibbett, Tibbitt, Tibbott, and Tibbutt.

The commonest vowel interchanges are between *e*, *i*, and *y*. Little or no distinction was made between *u*, *v*, and *w*, yet the difference was recognized in the sixteenth century, as appears from the following entry : T. Mayhue *alias* Mayhve *alias* Mayve *alias* Maywe *alias* Mayhowe *alias* Mayoe, Essex. (Pard. R., p. 264.)

Consonants, except *h*, *j*, *q*, *v*, and *w*, are regularly doubled, as Ashe, Asshe ; Boles, Bolles ; Philips, Phillipps, etc. Sssole occurs in the Suffolk Subsidy, 1327, for Schole. All vowels are to be found doubled, *ee* and *oo* being common, as Coke, Cooke ; Reve, Reeve ; Grenewod, Greenwood, etc. With the exception of *uu*, which is, of course, otherwise *w*, the remaining vowels are rarely duplicated and are only to be noticed before the fifteenth century.

Geoff. Baard, Lincs. 1202. (Ass. R., Stenton.)
W. le Bat or le Baat, Suss. 1310. (Inq. p.m.)
Hen. Briitloth and Winfred Briitlod, Cambs. 1275. (Hund. R.)
Piichil occurs in Lib. Vit. Dunelmensis. See also the curious instance of Smijth above (p. 298).
W. de Fauucunberg, Derb. 1295. (Inq. p.m.)
Hayys, Vyyer, and Wyyne are to be seen in the Hundred Rolls.

In the formation of British surnames the developments were much more irregular than in the derivation of dictionary words, and it would be a large undertaking, quite beyond the scope of the present volume, to formulate complete laws of variation, covering all districts and periods ; moreover, it is doubtful if even a Grimm could establish any law and order among the diverse etymological combinations and permutations which abound, so unaccountable are many of the deviations.

[1] *Letters and Papers*, For. and Dom. (Hen. VIII), 2nd ed., vol. i, pp. 203–73.

A few of the many consonantal and diphthongal equations
may be exemplified.

a = au. W. de Gamages or Gaumages, Glouc. 1223-4.   (Pat. R.)
Hen. Chancy or Chauncy, Herts. 1509. (Pard. R.)

a = aw = ay. Edm. Ralegh, Rawley, or Rayley, Dev. 1509. (Pard. R.)

a = ie. J. Hoppar or Hoppier, Warw. 1509. (Pard. R.)

a = in, as in Pottager, Pottinger.

a = od. Thom. de Wahull or Wodhull, Northants, 1304.   (Inq. p.m.)

aa = er. Thom. Stonhewaa, Oxf. 1275.   (Hund. R.)

ai = ey. J. de Staingreve *alias* Steyngreve, 1295.   (Inq. p.m.)

al = au. Alditheleg, Audithelegh, i.e. Audley.

an = ham. Geoff. de Dynan or Dynham, 1258.   (Inq. p.m.)

au = a (q.v.). **aw = ay = a** (q.v.).

ay = o. Edw. Baynes or Bones, Ess. 1509.   (Pard. R.)

b = bb = p. Jordan de Abbetot or Apetoft, Derb. 1282-3.   (Inq. p.m.)
Sibetot de Abetot, 1316.   (Inq. p.m.)   So also Buckle, Puckle ;
Beverley, Peverley, etc.

b = v. Derick Obell or Ovyll, London, 1509. (Pard. R.)

c = ch. W. Carpe or Charpe, Norf. 1275.   (Hund. R.)   J. Scawe or
Schawe, Yorks. 1509. (Pard. R.)

c = ck. Laur. de Broc or Brock, Cambs. 1275.   (Hund. R.)

c = g = k. Hen. Carle or le Karle, Yorks. 1275.   (Hund. R.)   J. Cagge,
Gegge, or Kage, thirteenth century. (Leicester Bor. Rec.) Thom.
Pycot, Pigot, or Pykott, Bucks. 1509. (Pard. R.)

c = gh. J. Ughtred *alias* Uctrede, Yorks. 1298.   (Inq. p.m.)

c = h. Hugh Scireman, Cambs. 1275.   (Hund. R.)

c = qu = qw. J. Qwykerell (i.e. Cokerell), Lincs. 1453.   (Pat. R.)
J. Conyam or Quoniam, Devon, 1509. (Pard. R.) So also in
Ireland : Cuddihy and Quiddihy.

c = ss. Thom. Crecy or Cressy, Notts. 1509. (Pard. R.)

cc = gg = kk. J. Becce, Begge, or Bekke, Bucks. 1509. (Pard. R.)

ce = s. Hen. Daunce or Dans, Suff. 1509.

ch = c (q.v.).

ch = dg. The flattening of the final sharp palatal was common.
Aldrich became Aldridge ; Partriche, Partridge, etc. (See also
the next example.)

ch = g. J. Partryche or Partryge, Glouc. 1509. (Pard. R.) W. de
Tyngewyk or Tynchewyk, Bucks. 1316.   (Inq. p.m.)

ch = h. Hugh Schepherd, Northumb. 1275.   (Hund. R.)

ch = sh. Thom. Chelton or Sheltham, Northants. 1509. (Pard. R.)

ck = gg, as in Black, Blagg ; Flick, Fligg, etc.

ckes = x. Duckesworth and Duxworth.   (Whalley Par. R.)

d = t. Marg. Simont, Rog. Simond, Cambs. 1275.   (Hund. R.)   Nic.
Coward or Cowart, Dors. 1509.   (Pard. R.)   Rob. Doogood or
Toogood, London, 1653.   (Reg. St. Thomas the Apostle.)

d = th. Thom. Wederby or Wetherby, Lond. 1509.   (Pard. R.)

dg = g = gg. J. ate Brugeende, Oxf. 1275.   (Hund. R.)   Nic. atte
Bruggeend, Oxf. 1275.   (Hund. R.)   Modern Bridgeend.

dge = ck (q.v.),

ea = ew = ou. Humph. Feaster, Fewster, or Fouster, Leic. 1509.
(Pard. R.)

ee = eigh. W. Rowelee or Roweleigh, Shrops. 1509. (Pard. R.)

ee = owe. W. Barlee or Barlowe, Ess. 1509. (Pard. R.)

eo = u. Nich. de la Huse or de la Heose, Wilts. 1300. (Inq. p.m.)

er = ier. Rich. Roger or Rogier, Hants. 1509.

er = in. Catterson, Cattinson ; Dickerson, Dickinson, etc.

er = on. Rich. Hinder or Hindon, Wilts. 1509. (Pard. R.)

er = re. Hugh de Lowther or Louthre, Cumb. 1317. (Inq. p.m.)

es = s (initial). Pet. Spilleman or Espileman, 1292. (Inq. p.m.) Edw. Spigurnel or Espigurnel, 1296. (Inq. p.m.)

ew = ea (q.v.).

ewe = ui = u, as in Brewes, Bruis, Brus, etc.

ey = ai (q.v.).

ey = o. W. Breteyn or Breton, London, 1509 (Pard. R.).

ey = owe. J. Wensley or Wenslowe, Yorks. 1509. (Pard. R.)

f = ph. Rich. Phelip, Walt. Felip, Wilts. 1275. (Hund. R.)

f = v. J. Wolfhunte or Wolvehunte, Derby, 1308. (Inq. p.m.) Hen. Ufdale, Uffedale, or Uvedale, Dors. 1509. (Pard. R.) V is a common equivalent of F in the West Country, as Vowler, Vox, Vrench, Vry; also in Ireland, Farrelly and Varrelly, etc., so also medially, as Rafferty, Raverty, etc.

f = w. W. Wymondesfold or Wymondeswold, Notts, 1509. (Pard. R.)

Fl = Ll = Thl. Lloyd and Llewelyn in the mouths of Englishmen become Floyd and Thlewelyn. Griffith Thloyd, Carm. 1335. (Inq. p.m.)

ft = t. Thom. de Lovetoft or Lovetot, Hunts. 1319. (Inq. p.m.)

g = c (q.v.) ; **g = ch** (q.v.) ; **g = ck** (q.v.) ; **g = dg** (q.v.).

g = j = y. Thom. Folgambe, Folejambe, or Folyambe, Derb. 1509. Cf. also Goscelin, Joscelyn ; Gerard, Jarrett.

g = k = c (q.v.) ; **gg = cc** (q.v.) ; **gg = ck** (q.v.) ; **gg = dg** (q.v.).

gg = k. Hen. Briggis or Brykys, London, 1509. (Pard. R.)

gg = ng. Matilda Riggebelle and Rich. Ringebelle, Suff. 1275. (Hund. R.)

gh = c (q.v.).

gh = th. W. de Brighnothe or Brithnothe, London, 1337. (Coroner's R.)

gh = y, as in Berkelegh, Berkeley, etc.

ght = ch (q.v.).

ght = te. Rich. Schipwryte, Cambs. 1275. (Hund. R.)

gn = y. J. Reignold or Reynold, Wales, 1509. (Pard. R.)

gu = gw = w. Rich. ap Gualter or Walter (also occ. Gwalter), Wales, 1509. (Pard. R.)

gw = qu. Margaret Gwelch or Quelch, 1686–8. (St. James Clerkenwell Par. R.)

h. For notes on the aspirate, see above, p. 301.

h = c (q.v.).

h = k. Elena Wolfrich, Rob. Wolfrick, Oxf. 1275. (Hund. R.) Nic. Shelton or Skelton, London, 1509. (Pard. R.)

hay = y. Leo Perchay or Percy, Yorks. 1509. (Pard. R.)

herd = man. Nich. Oxenherd or Oxenman, Lincs. 1509. (Pard. R.)

hevede = head. In thirteenth-century rolls, as Alan Bradhevede.

hw = wh. See above, p. 306.

i = or. Steph. Berwith or Barworth, Berks. 1509. (Pard. R.)

ie = a (q.v.) ; **ier = er** (q.v.).

ig = y. Geoff. Drurig or Drury, Cambs. 1275. (Hund. R.) Nich. de Meynill or Meignyll, Yorks. 1299. (Inq. p.m.)

ille = le. Phil. Constable or Constabill, Yorks. 1509.

in = a (q.v.) ; **in = er** (q.v.) ; **ins = es** (q.v.).

is = y = ys. W. de Suberis, Subery, or Suberys, Cambs. 1275. (Hund. R.)

j = ch (q.v.) ; **j = g** (q.v.) ; **k = g = c** (q.v.) ; **k = gg** (q.v.) ; **kk = cc** (q.v.).

kk = gg (q.v.).

l = n. Nich. de Bolevil or Bonevill, 1295. (Inq. p.m.)

l = r. Rob. Turbelvill or Turbervyle, 1317. (Inq. p.m.)

l = u, as in -feld, -feud, etc.

Ll = Thl = Fl (q.v.).

m = n. W. de Faucumberge or Faucunberg, Yorks. 1303–4. (Inq. p.m.) Cf. Hemming, Henning ; Mumby, Munby, etc.

m = nd. Bertrand or Bertram de Criel, Kent, 1306. (Inq. p.m.)

man = nham, as in Parman from Parnham ; Highman from Highnam ; Downman from Downham.

n = l (q.v.) ; **n = m** (q.v.).

n = nd, as in Gorman, Wyman, etc.

n = th. Madock ap Griffin or Griffith, 1321. (Inq. p.m.)

n = u. See above, p. 298.

nd = m (q.v.) ; **nham = man** (q.v.).

o = ea (q.v.) ; **o = ey** (q.v.).

o = oo = ou = ow. Giles Coper, Cooper, Couper, or Cowper. (Dors. 1509. (Pard. R.)

o = ou = u. Boveton, Bovetoun, and Bovetun, all occur. Oxf. 1275 (Hund. R.) J. Donham, Dounham, or Dunham, Notts. 1509. (Hund. R.)

o = oy. Warin de Bovile or Boyvil, Notts. 1275. (Hund. R.)

oe = ow. J. Langtroe or Langtrowe, Soms. 1509. (Pard. R.)

oi = u. Alex. Boill or Bull, Yorks. 1509. (Pard. R.)

on = er (q.v.).

oo = ow. Foole and Fowl. (Whalley Par. R.)

oo = u. J. Pooregold or Puregold, 1509. (Pard. R.)

or = i (q.v.) ; **ou = ea** (q.v.) ; **ow = algh** (q.v.) ; **ow = oo** (q.v.) ; **owe = ee** (q.v.) ; **owe = ey** (q.v.).

owgh = u. Chr. Owghtred or Utred, Yorks. 1509. (Pard. R.)

oy = o (q.v.).

oy = y. Pet. Boyle or Byle, Hants. 1509. (Pard. R.)

p = bb = b (q.v.) ; **ph = f** (q.v.).

ph = th. W. de Phickebrom (i.e. Thickebrome), Staffs. thirteenth century. (Salt Soc. xvii, 250.)

ph = wh, as in the Irish names, Phelan, Whelan.

qu = qw = c (q.v.) ; **qu = gw** (q.v.).

qu = qw = wh. J. le Quelwryete (Wheelwright), Lincs. (1286–7). (Add. MS. 5845). W. de Whixle or de Quixeley, Yorks. 1295–6. (Inq. p.m.) W. de Whitewell or de Quitewell, Dors. 1294. (Inq. p.m.) Geoff. Qwhyte of Newton, Cambs. 1447. (Pat. R.) J. Qwhytburn, Scotland, 1463. (Pat. R.)

r = l (q.v.) ; **re = er** (q.v.) ; **s = ce** (q.v.) ; **s = es** (q.v.).

s = sc. Adam le Sclattere, Oxf. 1275. (Hund. R.)

s = sh. W. Sepherd, Oxf. 1275. (Hund. R.). And. Busby, Bushby, or Bussheby, Staffs. 1509. (Pard. R.)

s = st, as Kelson for Kelston.

s = ts. W. Lyster or Lytster, Yorks. 1509. (Pard. R.)

s = z. Edm. le Masun or Mazun, Oxf. 1275. (Hund. R.) J. Vys or Vyz, Cambs. 1275. (Hund. R.)

sch = sh. Hugo le Schipwryte, Cambs. 1275. (Hund. R.)

sh = sk. J. Freshenede or Freskenede, Notts. 1297. (Inq. p.m.)

sh = th. Dishborne and Ditchborne. (Grimsby Par. Reg.)

ss = c (q.v.) ; **st = s** (q.v.).

st = t. Alex de Oketon or Okeston, Dev. 1276. (Inq. p.m.)

t = d (q.v.) ; **t = f** (q.v.) ; **tch = sh** (q.v.) ; **te = ght** (q.v.) ; **th = d** (q.v.) ; **th = gh** (q.v.) ; **th = ph** (q.v.).

Thl = Fl = Ll = Fl (q.v.) ; **u = l** (q.v.) ; **u = n** (q.v.) ; **u = oi** (q.v.) ; **u = ui = ewe** (q.v.) ; **v = b** (q.v.) ; **v = f** (q.v.) ; **v = u** (see above) ; **w = f** (q.v.) ; **w = gu** (q.v.) ; **w = v** (see above).

w = wh. W. de Whiteclive, Phil. de Wyteclive, Wilts, 1275. (Hund. R.) Rob. Whynbergh or Wynbergh, Norf. 1509. (Hund. R.)

w = y. W. de Bruwer or Bruyere, Derb. 1275. (Hund. R.)

wh = hw (q.v.) ; **wh = ph** (q.v.) ; **wh = qu** (q.v.) ; **y = gh** (q.v.) ; **y = j = g** (q.v.) ; **y = gn** (q.v.) ; **y = w** (q.v.) ; **y = ys = is** (q.v.)

ys = z. J. Traynez or Trayneys, Yorks. 1311. (Inq. p.m.)

z = s (q.v.).

The value of this list of equivalents lies in the assistance given towards the determination of possible variants, preliminary, for instance, to making a search for any given name. Taking a modern name of uncertain origin, such as Wimperis, it will be seen from the above list that *w = u = v = wh*, which is a variant of *hw, gu, ph, qu,* but, of course, not all in similar circumstances ; period, locality, and the letters which precede or follow must all be considered. *Hw* is an early form and can only be applied up to the end of the fourteenth century ; *Gu* is a Welsh variant ; *U* before another vowel is improbable, which elimination leaves (i) *Wh*, (ii) *Qu*, (iii) *V*, giving possible variants Whimperis, Quimperis, and Vimperis. The search may be widened by the use of (iv) *n* for *m*, which sometimes occurs, as in the names Vympany and Winpenny. A common change is (v) *p* for *b* (as above) ; or (vi) the *p* might be intrusive (as examples above, p. 271) ; and the terminal *is* has been shown above to be equivalent to (vii) *e*, (viii) *es*, (ix) *y*. Consequently, possible variants might be as far from the modern form as Quinbery or Wimpory, and changes might also be rung on the vowels. Wimperis in any shape or form is a scarce name, and actually all these variations are not found, but the following have been noticed, and are sufficient to illustrate the system, and to emphasize the value of a preliminary examination of the elements of a name before commencing to make a search.

(v, ix) Rog. Wymbery, chantry priest, Soms. 1545. (Soms. Rec. Soc., v, 40.)

(ix) Mat. Wymprey, curate, Lincs. 1583. (Lincs. Rec. Soc. 23.)

(i) Rob. Whimprise, Ess. 1589. (Stapleton Tawney Par. Reg.)

(viii) W. Wimpriess, London, 1676. (Reg. of St. Vedast.)

(vii) Posthuma Wimpre, London, 1679. (St. Michael, Cornhill, Reg.)

(iv) J. Winpres, London, 1684. (Christ Church, Newgate Str. Reg.)

Possible confusion may occur with Windress, Winepress, Whimper, etc., and only the genealogy can eliminate error. Wimpress and Wimpory are to be found in both London and Manchester (twentieth century).

Shake-speare and Shakes-peare. A good illustration of the evolution of a name is provided by Shakespeare, which was so little esteemed in the fifteenth century that Hugo Shakspere assumed the surname of Sawndare, because his family name, according to Merton College Register (1487), *vile reputatum est.*[1] The entry in the Bishop of London's Register reads "Saunders *alias* Breakspear *alias* Shakspeeres (1513)".[2] The name of Shakespere, now the yet more corrupt Shakespeare, originated independently in several far distant parts of England, but all the first forms are not yet entirely proved. The following series of thirteenth and fourteenth-century groups is instructive :—

(i) *Northern.* (Group 1) :—

Hen. Shakespere, tenant in Kirkland (Penrith), Cumb. 1350-8. (*N. and Q.*, 18th Aug., 1860, p. 122.)

Alan Shakespere, tenant in Carleton (Penrith), Cumb. 1398. (*N. and Q.*, 13th Aug., 1881, p. 126.)

W. Shakespere, witness in Carleton (Penrith), Cumb. 1398. (Ibid.)

(ii) *Midlands.* (Group 1) :—

W. Shakesper', surety for trespasser, Staffs. 1318. (K.B. 27, 234, m. 29.)

Simon Shakespere, trespasser, Staffs. 1325. (K.B. 27, 260, m. 118.)

Simon Schakespere, Penkhull, Staffs. 1327. (Subs. 177/1, m. 1.)

Thom. Schakesper', debtor, Newcastle, Staffs. 1335. (D.L. 30, 228/1, m. 6.)

Thom. Sschakespere, debtor, Newcastle, Staffs. 1335. (Ibid., m. 7.)

—— Schakespere, copyholder, Staffs. 1335. (Ibid.)

Robyn Shakespere, trespasser, Macclesfield Hd., Chesh. 1348. (S.C. 2, 155/85, m. 4.)[3]

J. Schakesper', plaintiff, Newcastle, Staffs. 1349. (D.L. 30, 228/4, m. 2d.)

Alice Schakespere, trespasser, Newcastle, Staffs. 1352. (D.L. 30, 228/7, m. 2.)

---

[1] *Memorials of Merton College*, by G. C. Brodrick, 1885, p. 242.

[2] *Novum Repertorium*, by G. Hennessy, p. 457.

[3] First recorded by J. A. Swettenham (*Times Lit. Suppl.*, 27th Apr., 1916).

J. Shakespere, copyholder, Shelton, Staffs. 1354. (D.L. 30, 228/10, m. 6.)

J. Shekespere in Dungelmor, Staffs. 1356. (D.L. 30, 228/11, m. 4.)

J. Shaspere, copyholder, Penkhull, Staffs. 1362. (D.L. 30, 229/2, m. 2.)

J. Schakespere (six entries), Staffs. 1362–7. (Various D.L. 30 rolls.)

J. Shakeper, defendant, Staffs. 1369. (D.L. 30, 229/7, m. 3.)

J. Saksper, defendant, Staffs. 1371. (D.L. 30, 229/8, m. 1d.)

W. Schacocspere (nine entries), Staffs. 1373–6. (Various D.L. 30 rolls.)

Numerous other references, mainly Shakespere, 1352–1400, and later.[1]

Note.—Macclesfield is 18 miles from Newcastle-under-Lyme.

(iii) *Midlands.* (Group 2) :—

W. Sakespere of Clopton (Kiftsgate Hd.), hanged for robbery, Glouc. 1248. (Ass. R. 274, m. 4).[2] (Clopton is 7 miles from Stratford-on-Avon.)

Simon Shakespeye, king's valet, Glouc. ? 1261. (? Coram Rege R.) [3]

Thom. Shakespere, mercer of Coventry, homicide and fugitive, Warw. 1358. (Coroner's R. 180, m. 3d.) [4]

Adam Shakespere, son and heir of Adam of Oldiche, tenant in Baddesley Clinton, Warw. 1389. (*N. and Q.*, 28th Dec., 1895, p. 501.) [5]

Rich. Shakspere, wiredrawer in Coventry, murdered, 1416. (K.B. 27, 655, Rex. 16.)

Eliz. Shakspere, Wroxhall, Warw. 1417. (S.C. 2, 206/97, m. 2.)

It is highly improbable that the name signifies what it appears to do, and it is most unsafe to infer that the first bearers attracted the notice of their fellows by shaking a spear. In the fourteenth century *schak* meant " shock ", as well as " shake ", and *spere* was used to designate not only the weapon, but also the man, so that the schaksperes would be

---

[1] The entries in the Newcastle-under-Lyme rolls were first noticed by C. Swinnerton (*Athenæum*, 28th Mar., 1914, p. 449), and written up sparingly by T. Pape (*Field*, Apr., 1916). I have since made complete excerpts.

[2] This extract will correct Sir E. K. Chambers (*Encycl. Brit.*), who names the place Clapton, which is 17 miles further south ; and also Sir S. L. Lee (*Life of Shakespeare*, 1915), who not only gives the wrong place, but doubly mis-spells the name " Shakespeare or Sakspere ", citing only a partial reference.

[3] W. Floyd (*Notes and Queries*, 22nd Aug., 1874, p. 146), followed by C. C. Stopes (1901) and E. K. Chambers (1930), gives an erroneous reference, and I am unable to check the extract.

[4] This entry, being the earliest dated and documented reference to a Shakespere in Warwickshire, will interest many besides the student of nomenclature. I gave a transcript of the entry with translation in the *Miscellanea, Genealogica et Heraldica*, Dec., 1930. The Rev. J. Hunter (Add. MS., 24,494, art. 246) refers to an " undated document in the Exchequer " accounting for the forfeited goods of Thomas Shakespere of Coventry, a felon, evidently the same man. Stopes and Chambers give wrong references for the latter entry.

[5] H. Norris, who found the entry, cites no authority.

the troops who took the shock of a charge, and the surname would be of the occupational class (military rank), rather than of the characteristic. Men of this class, having nothing of worldly goods, would rarely be noticed in the public records, and such an origin would explain the absence of the name in twelfth-century archives. The synonymous description "spearman", appearing about the same time, is also exceedingly scarce in early records.

J. le Sperman, —, 1284. (Cl. R.)
J. Spereman, Waltham, Ess. 1327. (Subs. 107/13, m. 8*d*.)
J. Speremon, Penkhull, Staffs. 1327. (Subs. 177/1, m. 1.)

In this connection, a point against "shake" being a verb, is that the earliest forms of the name have "sake", which variant is rarely found in the written language. Therefore it must not be assumed too readily that the name is compounded of the elements "shake" and "spear"; in fact, there is very strong reason to suppose that, in the majority of cases, it may be Shakes-pere, and of local origin. Owing to the many place-names now corrupted out of recognition or lost entirely, far more surnames may be derived in this manner than has been suspected hitherto, and upon examination of further extracts, the three Saxbys in counties Lincoln and Leicester at once suggest themselves.

(iv) *Northern.* (Group 2.)

Jordan Sacheespee, Yorks. 1182–3. (Pipe R.)
Simon Saccespee, witness, Healaugh, Yorks. before 1199. (Cott. MS. Vesp. A. iv, f. 7*a*.)
Simon Sakespee (in ? York), Yorks. *c*. 1235 (?). (Middleton MS. Hist. MSS. Comm. 1911, vol. lxix.)

Examination of forty examples of this name from thirteenth-century Yorkshire charters, rentals, etc., yielded the following variants : Sackespey, Sakepe, Sakespay, Sakespe, Sakespee, Sakespei, Sakespeie, Sakespey, Sakespeye, Sakespy, Sakespye, Saxpe, Saxpey, Shakespeie, Shakespey, Shakespy, and Syakespeye.

Hen. Sakespeye of Whithal (Wighill), Yorks. 1280. (Add. MS. 18,276, f. 143.)
Rich. de Saxby of Tockwith, Yorks. *c*. 1285. (Chart. R. 4 Edw. II.)
Rich. Shakespey, Tockwith, Yorks. 1292. (Cott. MS. Vesp. A. iv, f. 146.)

Rob. Schaksper', couper, Pontefract, Yorks. 1378–9. (Poll Tax, *Yorks. Arch. Journal*, vi.)
J. Shakespere of Doncaster, Yorks. 1433. (Surt. Soc. xxx, 32.)

Note.—York is 9 miles and Tockwith 3 miles from Wighill, which is 16 miles north from Pontefract. Doncaster is 14 miles south-east from Pontefract, and about 30 miles from the Saxbys.

(v) *Midlands.* (Group 3.)

Rich. de Sexebi, Notts. 1187-8. (Pipe R.)
Nich. and W. de Saxebi, " Warw. and Leic." 1202. (Rot. Canc. : Rec. Comm.)
Geoff. de Saxeby, Leic. 1207. (Rot. de Fin : Hardy.)
Ralph de Saxeby, Leic. 1263. (*Borough Records.*)
W. de Saxeby, Leic. 1327. (Subs. Fletcher, p. 16.)
R. de Saxeby, Leic. 1327. (Ibid., p. 19.)
Rob. Saxeby, Leic. 1381. (Subs. 133/34.)
Emma Saxeby, Leic. 1381. (Ibid.)

J. Shakespere, plaintiff, Nottingham, 1357. (*Borough Records,* i, 167.)
J. Shakespere, assault, Nottingham, 1360. (Ibid., p. 177.)
Several other examples of Shakespere, Nottingham, 1361-70.
Rob. Shakespeyr, merchant, Nottingham, 1414-5. (*Borough Records,* ii, 102.)

Note.—Nottingham is 20 miles from Saxby, Leic., and 40 miles from Doncaster,

(vi) *Eastern Group.*

Steph. son of Rich. Sakespe in Clixby, Lincs. 1202. (Ass. R. 479; Stenton.)
Rich. Sakespee, a witness in an undated charter of about the same date, Lincs. (Harl. Ch. 50, C. 24.)
Norman de Saxebi, Lincs. 1202. (Ass. R. 478 : Stenton.)
Hugh Sakespe, Lincs. 1202. (Ass. R. 479 : Stenton.)
Rich. Sakespe, pater ejus, Lincs. 1202. (Ibid.)
Rob. Sakeespe, Lincs. 1206. (Cur. Reg. R.)
Turkall de Sexeby, Lincs. 10-16 John. (Fines : Massingberd.)
Alex. de Sakespey, Lincs. 1227. (Cl. R.)
Wymarca de Saxsebi, Lincs. 1256. (Fines : C. W. Foster.)
Aunger de Saxby, Lincs. 1327. (Subs. 135/11, m. 7.)
Hen. de Saxby, Lincs. 1327. (Subs. 135/11, m. 25.)
W. de Saxeby, Lincs. 1327. (Subs. 135/11, m. 21d.)
W. de Saxeby, priest, Lincs. 1343. (*Papal Petitions,* i, 17.)

The place-names (Leic. and Lincs.) are still evidenced in family names, Saxby and Shaxby being found in various directories. The name also suffered corruption, and regarding list (iv) there can be little doubt that de Saxby, of Lincs. perhaps, became Saxpey and Shakespeie of Wighill, the further step to Schaksper' in Pontefract being possible, but not so certain. Saxby of Tockwith may have crossed the Humber from Saxby (Lincs.), about 37 miles away. In similar manner the Leicester Saxby may have given Shakespere of Nottingham, but a connecting link has not yet come to hand. The further from home that Saxby strayed the more chance it had of becoming Sakespey and Shakespere.

(vii) *London Group.*

It is said that a Geoffrey " Shakespeare " was juryman in Brixton, Surrey, in 52–3 Hen. III (1268).[1]

Walt. Shakespye in Wandsworth, Surr. 1342–3. (Fines : F. B. Lewis.)

W. Schakesper, testator, Lond. 1413. (Comm. Ct. ii, f. 12.)

Sakebye, Surr. occurs as late as 1550. (Pat. R.)

(viii) *South-Eastern.* (Group 1.)

Sakespee, Waltham, Ess. *c.* 1235. (Cott. MS. Tib. C. ix, f. 227*b*.)

Walt. Sakespe, Waltham, Ess. *c.* 1235. (Ibid., f. 232.)

Simon Sakeespie, regarder in Waltham Half Hd., Essex, 1250. (Cott. R. xiii, 5, m. 4.) [2]

Matilda Saxpe, Waltham, Ess. 1320. (Subs. 107/10, m. 23*d*.)

Rich. Saxpe, Waltham, Ess. 1327. (Subs. 107/13, m. 8*d*.)

Walt. Shakespere of Colchester gaol, Ess. 1377–9. (Controlment R. 2 Ric. II ; *N. and Q.*, 10th Jan., 1874, p. 25.[3])

J. Shakespere, king's prover in Colchester gaol, Ess., dead in 1381. (Cl. R.)

The name continued to flourish in Essex and is found in several seventeenth and eighteenth-century wills ; occurring as Saxby in Colchester, 1523 (Subs. 108/162, m. 1.)

(ix) *South-Eastern.* (Group 2.)

J. Sakespey, surety for the vicinage at a coroner's inquest in Freinden (Somerden Hd.), Kent, 1279. (Ass. R. 369, m. 1.)

J. Shakespere in Freynden, Kent, 1279. (Ass. R. 371, m. 1.) [4] (This is a duplicate entry with variant spelling.)

Thom. Sakespey in Birchden (Hartfield Hd.), Suss. 1296. (Subs. : W. Hudson.)

J. Shakespey in Ashurst (West Grinstead Hd.), Suss. 1296. (Ibid.)

J. Saxepe in Ashurst, Suss. 1327. (Ibid.)

J. Saxpe in Ashurst, Suss. 1333. (Ibid.)

Heirs of J. Saxpey in Somerden Hd., Kent, 1346–7. (Subs. 123/20, m. 32*d*.) So also in 123/22, m. 41*d* ; and 123/23, m. 45*d*.

Thom. Shakespeys in Somerden Hd., Kent, *c.* 1357.[5] (Subs. 123/48, m. 46.)

---

[1] J. W. Rylands (*Records of Rowington*, vol. i, p. xxv), who found the entry, has the failing of other Shakespearean enthusiasts, giving a wrong reference. I should be very surprised to find that " Shakespeare " appeared in a thirteenth-century record.

[2] Correcting W. R. Fisher (*Forest of Essex*), and four errors of C. C. Stopes and two of Chambers.

[3] This roll, K.B. 29, 31, was unfit for production in 1930, and I was unable to verify the extract.

[4] W. H. Hart (*Notes and Queries*, 17th Feb., 1855, p. 122) gave a transcript of this entry, making, however, a curious error, due to misplacing part of a marginal note. Stopes (1901) and Lee (1925), with striking uniformity, make the names into Freyndon and Shakespeare ; the latter writer suggesting that Freyndon might be Frittenden, which happens to be in Cranbrook hundred, a different part of Kent.

[5] Undated, but about 1357, according to internal evidence (P.R.O. List).

. . . Sa . spey in Somerden Hd., Kent, 1372. (Subs. 123/29, m. 32.)

J. Sakspeye in Somerden Hd., Kent, 1373. (Subs. 237/53, m. 24.)

Note.—Somerden Hd. (Kent) and Hartfield Hd. (Suss.) adjoin, consequently Freynden and Birchden may have been close together. It is probable that two forms of the name survived. Shakespeare occurs in Warehorne (Newchurch Hd.), Kent, in 1596; and Saxpes and Saxby in Sussex, sixteenth century.

(x) *Ireland.*

Rich. Shakespere, surety, Dublin, 1305. (Irish Justiciary R., i, 483.)

Tho' Shakesper, comptroller of customs in the port of Youghal, occ. 49 Edw. III and 51 Edw. III (1375-7). (Irish Pat. R. Cal. pp. 95b, 99b.)

The name probably long continued in Ireland, an Irishman named Shakespeyre occurring in Cheshire, 6 Edw. VI (1552-3). (*N. and Q.*, 5th Sept., 1896, p. 192.)

(xi) *France.*

The possibility of alien introduction, particularly in the southern counties, must also receive consideration. Barber, citing Moisy, states that there were two localities in La Manche called Saquespée, and, however that may be, as a second name it was not uncommon in France. N.P. (1874) drew attention to the following early entries in the Great Rolls of the Exchequer, Normandy, deducing that the persons named were the Leicestershire Saxbys.

Rog. Sake espee fined in the bailifry of the Caux, near Lillebonne, 1195.
W. Sake espee owed 2 marks in the bailifry of Hiesmes, 1195.
W. Sake espee in the bailifry of Caux, 1198.
Rog. Sac espee fined in the bailifry of Coutances, 1203.
Godfrey Sac espee in the same place, 1203.

N.P., not recognizing the name as French, inferred that it was a corruption of another name, and an English name, and concluded that the French and Leicestershire entries related to the same family, who were otherwise known as de Perers of Saxby, Leic., and Periers, near Evreux, Normandy, and that the name ultimately became Shakspeare. This opinion cannot be dealt with here, but it is to be noted that Sake espee is approximately French (*sacquer* " to draw ", *espée* " sword "; cf. *sacquer la main à l'espée* " to lay the hand on the sword ", Cotgrave). To the Norman, Saxby conveyed nothing, but it sounded like Sake-espée, which was intelligible and most expressive, signifying " Drawsword ". In similar manner, the Frenchman arriving in England with the name of

Saque-espée, would either have that name twisted into something with an English meaning, as Shakespear, or it would be translated as Drawsword (see examples below). From charters in the *Archives du Calvados* (Léchaudé d'Anisy, 1835) the following are taken :—

> Thom. Sache-Espée in Grenteville, 1241. (ii, 314.)
> Robert dit Saquespée de Touffréville, 1250, 1257. (ii, 247, 250.)
> Philippe Saquespée, vendor, 1291. (i, 205.)

It may be noted that the Department of Calvados lies across the Channel, directly opposite Sussex, and the Sussex Sakespey, Saxepe, etc., may well be of continental origin ; and in the same way Sakespic of Exeter (if a misreading for Sakespie) may have come from France or the Channel Islands.

Shakespere as a Personal Name. The further possibility of origin from a personal name must not be overlooked. O.E. *seax* " sword ", " knife ", is a common element, occurring as the monothematic name Seaxa, Saxa, Seaxo, and Saxi, in Domesday Book, and is found in Anglo-Saxon days compounded with -beald, -beorht,[1] -burh (fem.), -fritt, -gær, -helm, -leof, -ling, -red, -ric, -weard, -wig, -wulf. Sax survived, and was a common surname by the fourteenth century. Spere occurs as a personal name in Domesday Book (Sperri), and in Spereshalt, 1159 (Pipe R.) ; and as a second name it is written Spere in the Hundred Rolls, 1275. In compound names it is found both as first or second element. It is not suggested that in every instance in the following selection the O.E. theme *spere* is evidenced, but that it was common cannot be doubted.

> (i) W. Spare, Northumb. 1297. (Parl. Writs, i, 841.)
> J. Spere, Beds. 1275. (Hund. R.)
> W. Spire, Leic. 1327. (Subs. Fletcher, p. 83.)
> Osm. Spore, Soms. 1275. (Hund. R.)
> W. Spur', Norf. 1275. (Hund. R.)
> Luke Spyre, Herts, 1279. (Pat. R.)
> Cf. J. atte Sparre, Suss. 1296. (Subs. W. Hudson.)
> Rog. le Spire, Leic. 1327. (Subs. Fletcher, p. 50.)

> (ii) W. Sparegod, Cambs. 1275. (Hund. R.)
> T. Spereman, Surr. 1327. (Fines.)

---

[1] Hen. Bradley (*The Academy*, 5th Feb., 1887, p. 94) suggested Seaxberht as a possible origin, considering it very unlikely that the great poet's name meant " spear-shaker ". Of the curious derivations offered may be noticed " Jacques Pierre ", no evidence being provided. Baring Gould (p. 366) makes the bare statement that Shakespeare is derived from Schalkesboer, " the knave's farm ", and Breakspeare from Bragi's-boer, the farm of Bragi. Equally improbable is the view advanced by *The Gael* that Shakespeare is Irish (*seabbach* " hawk ", *spar* " staff "), i.e. a hawker's staff (*New Shakespearanea*, v. 28).

Simon Spirewit, Suss. 1229. (Cl. R.)
Gocelin Spurecat, —, 1267. (Pat. R.)
Rog. Spyrecok, Hants. 1315. (Pat. R.)

(iii) Thom. Wydesparre, Suss. 1296. (Subs. W. Hudson.)
W. Longespeie, Northants. 1230. (Pipe R.)
W. Godesper, Northumb. 1255-6. (Ass. R.)
W. Sharpspere, Kent, 1278. (Cl. R.)
Rad. Brekespere, Suss. 1296. (Subs. W. Hudson.)
W. Fewterspere, Chesh. 1362. (Ches. Plea R. 67, m. 118.)
Walt. Silverspire, Kent, 1327. (Subs. 123/10, 37d.)
Cf. Welsh Buncan (*bwn can* " shining spear "), 1292. (See above, p. 125.)
Pet. Shakespur, Nottingham, 1596-7. (Borough Records, iv, 244.)

Ellirsper, a Cumberland name, 1333, has the appearance of being derived from a locality. (Subs.)

It is quite possible that the names Sax and Spere were preserved in conjunction, and so also the two O.E. elements Seax and Sceaft may have given Shakeshaft (Lincs. 1380 ; Poll Tax, 130/24). It would be strange if no one of the names in Seax- has survived, and, in addition to Shakespere and Shakeshaft, the following Seax-, Shakes-, and Shake- names may be considered :—

(i) Saxelinus, Yorks. 1206. (Fines.)
W. Saxel, Lincs. 1284. (Pat. R.)
Rog. Saxelyng, Norf. 1297. (Coram Rege R.)
Thom. Sexpenne, Dors. 1392. (Fine R.)
J. Saxffen, Dev. 1508. (Anc. Deeds, A. 6107.)
— Saxberge, Glam. 1541. (Hist. MSS. Comm. 77, p. 305.)
Thom. Saxsey, Suff. 1546. (Hist. MSS. Comm. xiv, App. viii.)
W. Sexpes, —, Eliz. (E. Ch. Proc. ii, 36.)

(ii) W. Sakespic, Dev. *c.* 1180. (Hist. MSS. Comm. 55, iv, 55.)
Rich. Shakeshethe, Staffs. 1338. (Pat. R.)
J. Schakestaff, Suff. 1381. (Cl. R.)

(iii) Rog. Schakeloc, Glouc. 1186-7. (Pipe R.)
Hen. Shakeman, Ess. 1220-1. (Ess. Fines : Kirk.)
Rog. Sakebrech', Beds. 1234. (Cl. R.)
Hen. Shakelaunce, Northants. 1275. (Hund. R.)
Rog. Shakelof, Worc. 1277. (Parl. Writs, i, 836.)
Sim. Schakerose, Bucks. 1316. (Pat. R.)
Rob. Schaketrot, Lancs. 1325. (Court R., W. Farrer.)
J. Shakeleg, Ess. 1333. (Colchester Ct., R. Jeayes.)
Thom. Shakedale, Ess. 1346. (Ibid.)
J. Shakeblu, Staffs. 1359. (Pat. R.)
W. Shaketree, Yorks. — . (North Riding Rec. Soc. : N.S. iii, 34.)
Rol. Shakelady, Lond. sixteenth century. (Fines : Hardy.)

Shakelock may be occupational, and a number of the names in the third group are local, sometimes being found with preposition *de*, as de Shakecroft.

In addition to Seax- there is the even more common prototheme Sige-, which may also have given rise to some of these names, possibilities being Sigespere, Sigesceaft (cf. Sigestef, Searle).

The description " Sake espee ", no matter what its origin may have been, was liable to be englished, and may exist in one or other of the following :—

(i) Thom. Drawespe, Oxf. 1275. (Hund. R.)
   Rich. Draespere, Wilts. 1293. (Fine R.)
   W. le Drauspere, Leic. 1300. (Pat. R.)
   W. Draghspere, Worc. 1309. (Pat. R.)
   J. Drawespere, Hunts. 1345. (Pat. R.)
   W. Drawespere, Hunts. 1346. (Pat. R.)

(ii) Hen. Draweswerd, Suff. Cambs. 1275. (Hund. R.)
   Rich. Draweswerd, Ess. 1327. (Subs. 107/13, m. 4.)
   J. Draweswerd, Cambs. 1371. (Fine R.)
   W. Drawesuerd, Suff. 1437. (Cam. Soc. 49.)
   Thom. Drawswerde, Yorks. 1528-9. (Surt. Soc. v, 267.)
   W. Drawswerd, Lincs. 1530. (Linc. Rec. Soc. v, 124.)

In most of these cases a distinct origin is indicated, and the possibility that -swerd may be -sward must not be overlooked ; cf. Brownsward, which, however, may be a form of Brownsworth, and as pointed out by Bradley (*Academy*, 12th March, 1887), Drawsword might be the Dutch Drossaard.

An Italian equivalent for Shakelaunce or Shakespeare is Crollalanza (*crollare* " to shake ", *lancia* " lance " or " spear "), and in addition to Sake espée the French have Levelance (Raise-lance). The question as to whether the Italians translated from the French, and the French from the English, or vice versa, or whether the names arrived independently cannot be answered ; but England seems to have been pre-eminently the home of the " Shake "-names, and also of the " Lance "-names, of which latter the following selection may be of interest :—

(i) J. Lanceleuee in Lissington, Lincs. 1202. (Cur. Reg. R.)
   Rog. Lanceleve, Hants. 1203. (Cur. Reg. R.)
   J. Lancelevee, Dors. 1222. (Cl. R.)
   J. son of Rog. Lanceleve, Ireland, 1229. (Cl. R.)
   Rog. and J. Launceleuee, Hants. 1230. (Pipe R.)
   J. Lancelevee, Suff. 1244. (Cl. R.)
   J. son of Ralph Launceleve, Lincs. 1254. (Exc. Fines, 196.)
   Rog. Launceleve, Dev. 1275. (Hund. R.)
   W. Lanceleve, Hants. 1292. (Cl. R.)
   Rich. and Rob. Launceleue, Notts. 1327. (Subs. 159/4, mm. 8*d*, 12*d*.)

(ii) Rog. Levelance, 1 k. fee in " Merdon " and Holt, Warw. 1232.
(Cl. R.)

Ralph Levelaunce, Hardewick, Staff. 1262. (Salt. Soc. iv, 150.)

W. Levelaunce, Dev. 1276. (Cl. R.)

Ernald Leuelaunce, Warw. 1297. (Coram Rege R ; Phillimore.)

Simon and Rich. Lyuelance, Wolford M., Warw. 1327. (Subs. Carter.)

W. Lyuelaunce, Eccleshall, Warw. 1327. (Subs. Carter.)

Thom. Leuelaunce, Lincs. 1327. (Subs. 135/11, m. 22d.)

Thom. Levelaunce, Lincs. 1346. (Pat. R.)

W. Levelance, Wolford, Warw. 1358. (Ass. R. 971, m. 2.)

Symon Levylaunce, Yorks. 1365–6. (Surt. Soc. xcvi, 61.)

Based on the present material no very conclusive opinion can be formed ; but it seems not unlikely that the name Shakespeare is derived from several distinct sources. The selection of 100 instances, varying from Saxebi to Shakespeare, will provide food for thought, and even though no definite assertion can be made, believers in the nickname genesis of Shakespeare will find their faith severely tried. It is probable that the name originated in several parts of the country, the sources which are indicated most strongly being place-names. Whatever the first form may have been, it is generally found in the thirteenth century as Sakespee, and more rarely Sakespere, becoming in the fourteenth century Shakespey and Shakespere. Most of the stages may be reached in one generation; thus a thirteenth-century Yorkshireman occurs as Saxpey, Sakespeye, and Shakespeie ; another as de Saxby and Shakespey ; and a thirteenth-century man of Kent was officially both Sakespey and Shakespere. There is also an occasional tendency for the name to revert to original type, particularly when in its native county. Shakespere has also been held to be interchangeable with Breakspear (see above, p. 312), as it was with Shakestaff [1] ; and it is possible that it was also equivalent to Levelance and Drawsword, but so far in no case has the same person been found to bear two of such names.

The possibility that Shakespere, in some cases, is nothing more than a fanciful changeling is very real. It has been mentioned above (p. 31), in connection with ancient Irish appellatives, that the actual name might be changed so long as the signification was retained ; and this belief was widely held down to comparatively modern times, e.g. on p. 195 is given the case of a husbandman who was " surnamed " both Schawer (i.e. Shaver) and Barber. It is probable that Shakespere sometimes originated, neither as characteristic, local, genealogical, nor occupational description, but from

[1] Warwick Court Rolls, P.R.O. 207/88.

another name, which although apparently of the same signification, had actually quite a different meaning, such as, for instance, Wagstaff (see p. 226).

The following list of later variants compiled by G. R. French from registers, charters, leases, and other documents, while by no means exhaustive, is illustrative of the corruption in surnames which took place during the fifteenth, sixteenth, and seventeenth centuries.

Schakespeire, 1460 ; Shakspere, 1460 ; Shakespeyre, 1464 ; Shakespere, 1464 ; Chacsper, 1476 ; Schakspere, 1486 ; Shaksper, 1523 ; Sakespere, 1537 ; Shaxespere, 1545 ; Shakyspere, 1552 ; Shakysper, 1557–8 ; Shakesspere, 1557 ; Shakspeyr, 1558 ; Shakispere, 1558–9 ; Shaxpere, 1569 ; Shaskespeare, 1574 ; Shaxper, 1579 ; Shaxpeare, 1579 ; Shakspeer, 1579 ; Shagspere, 1582 ; Shakspeyre, 1584 ; Shaxsper, 1586 ; Shaxspere, 1586 ; Shaxkspere, 1586 ; Shackspire, 1589 ; Shaxkespere, 1591 ; Saxspere, 1596 ; Shackspear, 1597 ; Shaxeper, 1598 ; Shakspeere, 1598 ; Shackespere, 1598 ; Sheakspeare, 1600 ; Sackesper, 1601 ; Shakespeere, 1602 ; Schackspeare, 1602 ; Shexpere, 1604 ; " Shaxberd, the Poet which made the plaies," 1605–12 ; Shakspear, 1605 ; Shakespear, 1605 ; Shakespeare, 1605 ; Shakesphear, 1605 ; Shakeseper, 1609–10 ; Schackespeare, 1614–5 ; Shakspeare, 1616 ; Shackspare, 1619 ; Shakspurre, 1637 ; Shakespar, 1695 ; Shakesper, 1711 ; Shackspeer, Shackspeere, and Shakaspeare (no dates). Chambers (1930) gives 83 variants, without dates, and both lists could be greatly extended.

CHAPTER XIII

CURIOUS DESCRIPTIONS AND NAMES

Deceptive Surnames. Names are often anything but what they appear to the superficial observer; for instance, " John ate chyldren " of Kent, was not a fourteenth-century cannibal, but it is not to be doubted a righteous living husbandman. " Ate chyldren " is a corruption of " at chiltern ", the origin of which word is not yet determined, but in the sixteenth century was the term used to describe a certain kind of soil, and is the origin of the surname Children.[1] Nor is there any reason to suppose that the thirteenth-century Huntingdonshire villein, Richard ate Forty,[2] was a trencherman out of the ordinary; more probably he derived his description from labouring at the ford-island.

A vowel mutation may work a wonderful change in signification. John Hell of Thaxted, Essex, 1438,[3] may be compared with Thomas at Hell, executor of the testament of W. Ewen of Marlesford, Suff. 1472. Hell is manifestly a variant of Hill, although both in some cases may be O.E. *healh* " corner ", " nook ". That there were several places called Hell is clear from the description of the Yorkshireman, Geoffrey de Avernus, temp. John,[4] and from the Dorset entry, Adam de Inferno, on the Curia Regis Roll, A.D. 1200, and the more particular definition in a pardon of 1 Hen. VIII.

Jakes or Jakys, " nuper clericus Inferni *alias* dictus Thomas Jakes nuper custos recordorum Domini Regis Henrici Septimi et aliorum ligeorum suorum de Communi Banco infra locum vocatum Hell existentium et residentium." [5]

Hell was the name given to part of the old law courts at Westminster, used at one time as a record office, and Fuller refers to a former prison for the King's debtors which was called Hell,[6] and doubtless most appropriately. But what can be the explanation of the following entry to be seen in the Croydon parish register?

" Mary Woodfield *alias* Queen of Hell, 1788."

The ardent genealogist and searcher of records cannot fail to have been amused and even mystified by numbers of names

---

[1] Subsidy Roll.
[3] P.R.O. Court Roll 173/90, m. 1.
[5] Pardon Roll, 1 Hen. VIII, p. 206, m. 7.
[6] *Worthies of England*, 1662, vol. ii, p. 236.

[2] Hundred Rolls.
[4] Assize Roll 1039, m. 1*d*.

and descriptions, which at first sight appear to be equally
curious. The following examples taken from various sources
are typical of descriptions which appear in profusion in the
medieval rolls.

W.	Barlicorn, Lincs. 1233.	(Cl. R., p. 232.)
W.	Blacberd, Lincs. 1206.	(Ass. R. 480, m. 3d.)
Hy.	Blancfrunt, Beds. 1201.	(Cur. Reg. R.)
J.	Brasskettle, Chesh. 1753.	(Admons., P.C. Chester.)
Maudlyn	Brickbatt, London, 1593.	(St. John's Hackney Par. Reg.)
J.	Brokepeny, Oxf. 1275.	(Hund. R.)
Dorothy	Bucktrout, Yorks. 1629.	(Mar. Lic.)
J.	Bullymore, Norf. 1727.	(Poll, p. 107.)
Rob.	Buttermouth, Lincs. 1327.	(Subs. 135/11, m. 11d.)
Rich.	Catskin, Yorks. 1575.	(Grimsby Par. Reg.)
Nich.	Childman, Cambs. 1275.	(Hund. R.)
W.	Cockesbrayn, Suss. 1275.	(Hund. R.)
Rob.	Coffin, Beds. 1275.	(Hund. R.)
Rich.	Cokeye, Kent, 1301.	(Subs. 123/4, m. 8.)
Thom.	Cokfyssh, Kent, 1431.	(Subs. 124/97, m. 1.)
W.	Conquest, Hunts. 1327.	(Subs. 122/4, m. 3d.)
J.	Cowmedowe, Heref. 1574.	(Ledbury Par. Reg.)
Odo	Dimpel, Wilts. 1275.	(Hund. R.)
Hugh	Doggetail, Worc. 1327.	(Subs.)
J.	Domesday, Suff. 1727.	(Poll, p. 111.)
J.	Domesoft, thirteenth century.	(Add. Ch. 7592.)
Geoff.	Drinkedregges, Lincs.	(Spalding Reg., f. 151.)
Thom.	Drinkmilk, Suff. 1727.	(Poll, p. 154.)
J.	Drunken, Yorks. 1301.	(Subs. p. 23.)
Ralph	Dunghul, Hunts. 1275.	(Hund. R.)
Mary	Eightacres, Kent, 1660.	(Womenswould Par. Reg.)
Alan	Evilchild, Cambs. 1275.	(Hund. R.)
J.	Fayrmaner, Suss. 1523.	(Subs. 189/157.)
J.	Feveryear, Suff. 1727.	(Poll.)
Hugh	Findesilver, Cambs. 1275.	(Hund. R.)
J.	Fivepeni, Oxf. 1275.	(Hund. R.)
Sam.	Fullpot, Suff. 1727.	(Poll.)
Anne	Godhelpe, Yorks. 1667.	(Grimsby Par. Reg.)
Agn.	Goldfinche, Oxf. 1275.	(Hund. R.)
Serle	Gotokirke, Cambs. 1275.	(Hund. R.)
Gilb.	Greyschanke, Cambs. 1275.	(Hund. R.)
J.	Hackewude, Suss. 1230.	(Pipe R.)
W.	Halpeny, Oxf. 1275.	(Hund. R.)
Rob.	Hanging, Norf. 1275.	(Hund. R.)
W.	Harepyn, Worc. 1327.	(Subs.)
Edw.	Havejoy, Kent, 1639.	(Chislet Par. Reg.)
Nigel	Holdekorne, Lincs. 1333.	(Subs.)
Sarra	Hopshort, Lincs. 1310.	(Pat. R.)
J.	Hornepipe, Northumb. 1439.	(Subs. 158/115.)
W.	Horsepet, Ess. 1327.	(Subs. 107/13, m. 5d.)
Rich.	Hotgo, London, 1321.	(Coroner's R.)
Rich.	Hurlbatt, Yorks. 1473.	(Surt. Soc., xcvi, p. 194.)

J.	Ingoal, Ess. 1621. (Ongar Par. Reg.)
Mary	Isbroke, Ess. 1587. (Ongar Par. Reg.)
Rob.	Killebole, Leic. 1327. (Subs. 133/1, m. 8.)
Rich.	Lateboy, Cambs. 1235. (Chart. R.)
Harvey	Leapingwell, Ess. 1768. (Poll.)
W.	Lickberd, Norf. 1299. (Pat. R.)
Geoff.	Lickefinger, Norf. 1205. (Cur. Reg. R.)
Sam.	Lightwing, Norf. 1806. (Poll.)
Simon	Likelove, Beds. 1275. (Hund. R.)
Rob.	Litelbodi, Hunts. 1327. (Subs. 122/4, m. 3d.)
J.	Litelskill, Soms. 1539. (Will, 26 Dyngeley.)
W.	Longeman, Kent, 1327. (Subs. 123/10, m. 36.)
Maud	Lusshefissh, Wilts. 1294. (Cl. R.)
J.	Manipeny, Beds. 1327. (Hund. R.)
Rob.	Midniht, Warw. 1230. (Pipe R.)
Rog.	Milksoppe, 1231. (Pat. R.)
W.	Multitude, Suff. 1727. (Poll.)
Rich.	Nettelbed, Warw. 1388. (Coroner's R. 187, m. 5.)
W.	Oldflessh, Worc. 1297. (Court R.)
J.	Onehand, Suff. 1314-15. (Inq. a. q. d.)
Alice	Peckechese, Hunts. 1275. (Hund. R.)
Sim.	Pickebarli, Suff. 1200. (Cur. Reg. R.)
Rog.	Pipercorn, Lincs. 1202. (Cur. Reg. R.)
Rich.	Pitchfork, Radnor, 1789. (Par. Reg.)
Grace	Pluckrose, Cambs. 1615. (All Saint's, Cambridge, Par. Reg.)
J.	Pokepot, Ess. 1327. (Subs. 107/13, m. 1d.)
Nunn	Prettyman, Norf. 1727. (Poll.)
Hugh	Pudding, Yorks. 1230. (Pipe R.)
J.	Quartale, Dev. 1327. (Subs. 95/6, m. 32.)
Jos.	Quickfall, Lincs. 1800. (Grimsby Par. Reg.)
J.	Ratellebagge, Ess. 1275. (Hund. R.)
Thom.	Rhubarb, Oxf. 1677. (Bicester Par. Reg.)
Rich.	Ringgebelle, Norf. 1308. (Cl. R.)
Eliz.	Robjon, Ess. 1702. (Ongar Par. Reg.)
J.	Rotenhering, Yorks. 1331. (Surt. Soc. xcvi, p. 26.)
Geo.	Sawhell, Yorks. 1555-6. (Ibid., p. 277.)
Hen.	Scrapetrough, Yorks. 1293. (Ibid., p. 5.)
J.	Shepewassh, Yorks. 1377. (Ibid., p. 75.)
Geo.	Shotbolte, Ess. 1596. (Stapleton Tawney Par. Reg.)
Rob.	Silverspon, Notts. 1230. (Pipe R.)
W.	Smalwryter, Kent, 1275. (Hund. R.)
Ch'iana	Smartknave, Oxf. 1275. (Hund. R.)
Walt.	Sparegod, Cambs. 1275. (Hund. R.)
Ann	Spearpoint, Kent, 1631. (Womenswould Par. Reg.)
J.	Spilspon, Bucks. 1284. (Cl. R.)
Aug'tine	Spurnewater, Norf. 1274. (Cl. R.)
J.	Standeven, Yorks. 1558. (Surt. Soc. xcvi, p. 279.)
W.	Stercup, Norf. 1275. (Hund. R.)
W.	Strokelady, London, 1377. (Cl. R.)
Walt.	Sturpot, Beds. 1275. (Hund. R.)
W.	Stykkefyshe, Cambs. 1298. (Pat. R.)
Thom.	Swetemouth, Kent, 1351. (Subs. 123/24, m. 23d.)

J.	Thikpeny, Yorks. 1486–7.	(Surt. Soc. xcvi, p. 211.)
Jacob	Tiplady, Yorks. 1520–1.	(Ibid., p. 242.)
W.	Treubody, Kent, 1301.	(Subs. 123/4, m. 4.)
Hen.	Tukbacon, Yorks. 1393–4.	(Surt. Soc. xcvi, p. 94.)
J.	Underdonne, Kent, 1327.	(Subs. 123/10, m. 3.)
Hen.	Vernakyll, Hunts. 1439.	(Subs. 235/4.)
Eliz.	Wagtail, Lincs. 1641.	(Grimsby Par. Reg.)
Walt.	Wakewel, Soms. 1225.	(Ass. R. 755, m. 4.)
Walt.	Wanderbug, Suff. 1275.	(Hund. R.)
J.	Waytelove, Suff. Hen. VI.	(K.B. 29/91.)
Thom.	Wedlock, Yorks. 1488–9.	(Surt. Soc. xcvi, p. 213.)
Thom.	Whalebelly, Norf. 1802.	(Poll.)
J.	Whitehors, Yorks. 1333.	(Surt. Soc. xcvi, p. 27.)
Steph.	Whytegray, Yorks. 1372.	(Surt. Soc. cxxxvii, p. 155.)
Thom.	Winterflood, Ess. 1768.	(Poll.)
Rob.	Witheskirtes, Yorks. 1272.	(Surt. Soc. xcvi, p. 1.)

No attempt will be made by the writer to determine origin, meaning, or classification of these examples, which will be left entirely to the ingenuity of the reader. Some few of the descriptions are actually as represented, others require trifling orthographic changes to make them sensible ; the majority will puzzle the most astute, and are but traps for the unwary. All four classes, characteristic, local, genealogical, and occupational, are represented. Do not hastily tick them off as nicknames, nor as surnames !

Definitions of Nickname. A great number of family names are popularly supposed to have their origin in " nicknames ". Such epithets are the mainstay of the writer on nomenclature, providing him with an opening for the introduction of touches of humour, quotations from early literary sources, and generally giving welcome relief to an otherwise serious subject. Little amusement, however, will be obtained from the views of the writer, who contends that the so-called nicknames are anything but what they appear to be, and that, notwithstanding that sobriquets have been popular throughout the world at all ages, comparatively few have been adopted as surnames. It is, of course, a first essential to have a clear understanding of past and present values of the word " nickname ". Is a nickname an additional or an alternative title ? Is it of temporary or permanent nature ? Is it dispensable or indispensable ? These are questions which call for an answer before the influence of nicknames in the making of our surnames can be discussed.

According to etymologists, the word nickname is a corruption of " an ekename " (i.e. an added name ; cf. Ice. *auknafn*, Sw. *öknamn*, Dan. *ogenavn*). A fifteenth-century vocabulary clearly shows the transition stage : " nekename or ekename, *agnomen* ".[1]   The term " ekename " cannot be traced back further than A.D. 1303, but it was probably used concurrently and interchangeably with " to-name ", " by-name ", and " surname " to express any additional or alternative designation. In later years it is evident that, so far as applied to the description of the nature of the names of persons, various values have been given to the word as well as to its synonyms.

(i) An addition to the personal name.

1567. " Ilk ane o'them has ane to-name : Will of the Lewis, Hab of the Shawis." Sir R. Maitland (*Complaynt*, vii).

1611. " Edward by-named the Black Prince." Speed (*Hist. Gt. Brit.*, ix, xii, 20).

1767. " Lion's heart is . . . the by-name of K. Richard." Weever (*Anc. Fun. Mon.*, 644).

(ii) A substitution for the personal name.

. . . " Adilbergæ . . . quæ alio nomine Tatæ vocabatur." Beda (*Hist. Eccl.*, ii, 9).

(iii) An addition to both personal name and description or surname.

1775. " Brian Kennedy, tonamed Boraimh, or Taxer." Buchanan (*Inq. Anc. Scot. Surnames*, p. 49).

See also the examples, type ii, on p. 72.

(iv) A substitution for both personal name and description or surname.

1617. " James Fitz-thomas . . . was by a nicke-name called the Suggon Earle." Moryson (*Itin.*, ii, 63).

1636. " Archibald Earl of Argyle. His too name was Gillispick Dow." Ld. A. Campbell (*Rec. Argyll*, 1885, 5).

(v) A familiar variant of a personal name.

1605. " From Nicknames or Nursenames came these . . . Bill for William ; Clem for Clement." Camden (*Rem.*, 114).

1836. " A wery good name it (*sc.* Job) is, only one, I know, that ain't got a nickname to it." Dickens (*Pickw.*, xvi).

Names of type (i) have also been called surnames, but such usage is now obsolete, and the writer has considered it preferable to term them descriptions.   Names of type (v) are clearly hypocoristica or pet-names, and would not now be called nicknames.   Of the five types illustrated, (i) and (v) had the best chance of becoming surnames.   The writer's view is that the original meaning of " eke " in this connection has been lost, and that only an alternative name can be considered to be a nickname according to the modern understanding of the term ;   and such sobriquets may be alternative to either

---

[1] *Promptorium Parvulorum*, ed. by A. Way (Camden Soc.).

forename or second name, and may be temporary or permanent. If such alternative name become permanent and indispensable for distinction it has ceased to be a nickname, and is either an additional personal name or surname, or change of personal name or surname, as the case may be.

In the modified sense in which the word is used throughout this essay, a nickname may be defined as a dispensable appellative of an individual used as an alternative to his personal name or surname or both. Such a defining of " nickname " will perhaps be likened to the process of " hairsplitting ", but it is suggested that it is more conducive to clarity to have the two words " description " and " nickname " applied to two distinct concepts than to have the word " nickname " used indiscriminately for two distinct kinds of appellatives, resulting in interminable misunderstanding. For instance, in 1863, the Solicitor-General in the House of Commons, on a discussion of the Jones-Herbert controversy, stated that " the fact was that surnames grew up mostly as nicknames ".[1] At the present day this would be a most misleading observation ; surnames of local, genealogical, and occupational classes cannot now be considered as having been nicknames, although they are eke-names, and even if the whole of the descriptions and names of class 1 are admitted, the proportion cannot have been more than 10 per cent. The true nickname, as now defined, takes an even much smaller part in the history of surnames. The distinction drawn between nicknames, descriptions or titles, and surnames should be carefully observed to avoid confusion.

Prevalence of Nicknames. It has been noticed in Chapter I that among uncivilized races it was customary to bestow working appellatives upon a person so that his true name could remain his own secret, and so secure from the machinations of sorcerers. This ancient superstitious rite, perpetuated throughout the ages, ultimately remained a popular habit long after the beliefs which originated the concealment of the real name had ceased to exist. Nicknames are in general use all over the world, and all races of the Indo-European group appear to have used alternative personal epithets as well as additional designations.

Nicknames may be found in the early English chronicles and records. Some examples of Anglo-Saxon alternative sobriquets have been given (p. 53), such as " Adilberga who by another name was called Tata ". An interesting medieval name which occurs on the rolls is Brownrobin, sometimes apparently a nickname, and sometimes in part a nickname, if it is not, in fact, an inversion of Robert Brown.

[1] *The Herald and Genealogist*, 1863, vol. i, p. 463.

Et quid qui vocatur Hoen et Brunerobin : Suff. 33 Edw. I (Ass.
R. 843, m. 2*d*).
Willelmus Queinte qui se facit aliquando vocare Brunerobin :
Suff. 33 Edw. I (Ass. R. 843, m. 4).
J. Brounrobyn, Ess. 1327. (Subs. 107/13, m. 9.)
Adam filius Brounrobyn, Denbigh, 1334. (Extent, 8 Edw. III.)

Robin names were popular; a certain Robert was called
" Litelrobyn ", London, 1324 (Coroner's Rolls), and in the
same record Katherine Robynhod is mentioned. Robert,
a tailor, otherwise Robert Tailor, frequently figures as
" Brunrobyn " and " Brown Robin the Tailor " in the records
of the Corporation of Yarmouth.[1] Ultimately Brownrobyns
or Brownerobarts occurs as a sixteenth-century surname[2];
cf. Brownjohn, which is a modern surname.

Among the ancient Irish the giving of a nickname was
often equivalent to slander, and was punishable under their
law codes (see p. 425). The practice was never suppressed,
as Sir H. Piers (1682) observed :—

" It is certain they take much liberty, and seem to do it with
delight, in giving of nick-names ; if a man have any imperfection or
evil habit, he shall be sure to hear of it in the nick-name. Thus if he
be blind, lame, squint-eyed, grey-eyed, be a stammerer in speech,
left-handed, to be sure he shall have one of these added to his name ;
so also from his colour of hair, as black, red, yellow, brown, etc., and
from his age, as young, old, or from what he addicts himself to or
much delights in, as in draining, building, fencing, or the like ; so as
no man whatever can escape a nick-name, who lives among them or
converseth with them, and sometimes, so libidinous are they in this
kind of raillery, they will give nick-names per antiphrasim, or
contrariety of speech. Thus a man of excellent parts and beloved of
all men, shall be called Grana, that is naughty or fit to be complained
of, if a man have a beautiful countenance, or lovely eyes, they will
call him Cuiegh, that is squint-eyed ; if a great house-keeper, he shall
be called Acherisagh, that is greedy." [3]

Examples of seventeenth-century practice will be found on
p. 210. At the present day, throughout Britain and Ireland
the custom of bestowing epithets persists, and such nicknames
are found in every class of life, but it is to be noticed that the
value varies from a hypocoristic pleasantry to a practical
distinction worthy of the notice of the recording clerk. Not
only do nicknames differ in utility, but also in the extent of
their application. Some epithets are bestowed upon every
person of the same name ; for instance, any John Clark who
enlists in the army is forthwith known as " Nobby " Clark,

---

[1] Norf. Arch. Soc., 1852, vol. iv, pt. 1, p. 253.
[2] Reg. Univ. Oxf., vols. ii (1), p. 300.
[3] *Collectanea de Rebus Hibernicis* (Vallancey, 1786, vol. i, p. 113).

and every James or other Miller who goes to sea is hence-
forward called " Dusty " Miller. " Nobby " and " Dusty "
are true nicknames, used as alternatives to John and James,
but they are generic, common to numerous Clarks and Millers
respectively. Regarding hereditary family " bynames " the
following note is illustrative :—

"There are villages in Sussex where almost every family has a
nickname. Its members make no objection to it, and are, in fact,
rather proud of it. The extraordinary part about these nicknames is
that they pass from parents to children for generations, and that the
possessors of these nicknames have no idea either of their origin or
meaning. I recall the fact that in a certain Sussex village ten families
had nicknames—'Hotchy' and 'Diskey'—but they had not the
remotest idea why their progenitors were so called or the meaning.
Their wives were known as 'Mrs. Hotchy' and 'Mrs. Diskey', and
their children as 'young Diskey' and 'young Hotchy'. So generally
used were these nicknames, that they rarely were addressed by their
real surnames." [1]

Official Notice of Nicknames. In some parts of England
and Scotland where there is little variety in the surnames,
nicknames attain to an added importance, and are officially
noticed. In Lancashire parish registers, for instance, entries
such as the following were formerly not uncommon :—

Blackburn Parish Registers :—

Thomas Aynsworthe *alias* Lucke. 17th Mar., 1624.
John Aspden Thicke skin. 4th Nov., 1640.
Thomas Osbaldeston ould nibb sone. 22nd Dec., 1648.
James Morress Dragon. 21st Mar., 1649.
Thomas Crooke ould Fingar. 29th Mar., 1649.

In the village districts of Scotland, where the numbers of
both forenames and surnames are very limited, the tee-name
is of considerable importance in identification, as is illustrated
by the story of a stranger who had occasion to call upon a
fisherman named Alexander White, resident in a village in
Buchan. Meeting a girl, he asked :—

" Cou'd you tell me fa'r Sanny Fite lives ? "
" *Filk* Sanny Fite ? "
" Muckle Sanny Fite."
" *Filk* muckle Sanny Fite ? "
" Muckle lang Sanny Fite."
" *Filk* muckle lang Sanny Fite ? "
" Muckle lang *gleyed* Sanny Fite," shouted the stranger.
" Oh ! It's Goup-the-lift [stare-at-the-sky] y'ere seeking," cried
the girl, " and fat the deevil for dinna ye speer for the man by his
richt name at ance ? " [2]

---

[1] J. P. Bacon-Phillips in *Daily Telegraph*, 28th Jan., 1930.
[2] *Blackwood's Magazine*, Mar., 1842, p. 301.

In the register of voters authenticated by the Sheriff for the counties of Banff, Elgin, and Nairn, the tee-names are regularly entered, e.g. William Flett "Yankie", James Murray "Costie Bird", George Mair "Shy Bobbin", and so on.[1] The surname of the wife often supplies the necessary added distinction; thus James Foster Logie, to the east coast fisherman, indicates the James Foster who married a Logie, but if there was already a James Foster (Logie) in the village he might assume the wife's christian name, and become James Foster (Katie).[2] In Ireland, also, the name of the wife or mother is tacked on as an added distinction.[3]

Nicknames as Surnames. It is possible that in some cases nicknames have become hereditary surnames, but the evidence is not very strong. The origin of the surname Redcock, in this manner, has been noticed above (p. 284), and an anonymous writer records that, at Cookham (Berks) the man who used to toll the bell in the church tower became popularly known as Bomer, "which has come down to his descendants to the loss of their true surname." [4]

A parish incumbent has recorded that in Dorsetshire the nicknames of women may become hereditary names, e.g. an old fiddler's wife is called " Polly Fiddler ", and her children, whether married or single, and their children also, inherit the sobriquet. Regarding hereditary nicknames, he says : " I knew a family named Morris, which for some unknown cause—perhaps because so many of their neighbours are named Drake—has borne the *alias* of Duck, as my registers show, for at least 120 years." Another family, a branch of the widespread family of Strickland, is always called " Thirty ", the reason popularly alleged being that a former member of it, speaking of a certain cask, said : " It will hold forty gallons, I warrant ; aye, more than that, perhaps *thirty*." [5]

Causes of Misunderstanding. Bardsley compiled some statistics from the names in the *London Directory*, from which it appears that he classed about 10 per cent of 30,000 entries as having origin in nicknames. It is to be noticed that in his analysis he included duplicated names, so that a name like Brown appeared in his enumeration several hundred times, the persevering investigator's conception of a surname of nickname origin covering those appellatives which are now described as characteristic surnames. The writer considers that 10 per cent is an over-estimate for names of this class, although in the various statistics which have been given the

[1] *Scotsman*, 9th Sept., 1889.
[2] *Chambers' Journal*, 11th Sept., 1897, p. 582.
[3] " Ulster Dialect ", by H. C. Hart (*Trans. Phil. Soc.*, 1899, p. 94).
[4] *Notes and Queries*, 11th Oct., 1886, p. 355.
[5] Ibid., 23rd Dec., 1865, p. 518.

largest figure in any one enumeration, excluding the Welsh, amounted to 8 per cent, and making the necessary allowance for unidentified names, the proportion admittedly might exceed 10 per cent, but, on the other hand, it has to be remembered that many of these medieval epithets did not survive as surnames. What on superficial examination appear to have been personal epithets are often something entirely different, misunderstanding arising through a failure to grasp various processes of corruption, modification, or mutilation.

(i) Supposed nicknames due to failure to recognize archaic and corrupt forms. Eccentricities such as Pigsflesh, Hogsflesh, etc., are not nicknames, but, if not an old form (cf. Hunt now Hunter), mutilated trade names corresponding to the modern pork butcher. Flesh stands for flesher (originally fleshhewer), a word which is still in common use in Scotland.

(ii) Supposed nicknames due to failure to recognize language or dialect. Useful examples are Henn (*hen*, W. " the old "), Hogg (*og*, Gael. " the young ").

The possibilities of Welsh survival in our surnames is further instanced by : Brydd " disabled ", Dison " silent ", Els " son-in-law ", Hog " a little lad ", Mad " good ", Mân " small ", Rat " small " (Bullet), Tew " fat " (Gwylym Tew was a fifteenth-century writer). In the Hundred Rolls for Oxford, 1275, may be seen le Bryd, le Hog, le Man, and le Rat.

(iii) Supposed nicknames due to failure to recognize the original application of the description. Duck, for instance, is from le Duc or Duke, " a leader," and sometimes from Duke, an aphæretic form of Marmaduke, or even local (see p. 231).

To illustrate the great extent to which such mis-apprehensions have coloured the work of nomenclaturists there have been collected from the directories as material for an inquiry examples of surnames which might equally well have been taken from labels at the " zoo ", aviary, or the aquarium.

Surnames approximating to names of animals :—

Ape, Badger, Beagle, Bear, Beast, Beaver, Boar, Brock, Buck, Buckerell, Bull, Bullock, Calf, Camel, Catt, Cattle, Cobb, Collie, Colt, Cony, Cowe, Curr, Deare, Doe, Dolphin, Fawn, Fitch, Foal, Fox, Frogg, Galt, Genet, Goat, Grice, Griffin, Hare, Hart, Hind, Hogg, Hound, Kennett, Kidd, Kitten, Lamb, Leopard, Leveret, Lion, Man, Marten, Mole, Mule, Neat, Neuts, Otter, Ox, Palfrey, Panther, Pigge, Prickett, Purcell, Rabbitt, Ram, Ratt, Roebuck, Runcy, Seal, Slugg, Squirrell, Stagg, Steed, Steer, Stirk, Stott, Toad, Tod, Turtle, Want, Whale, Wolf.

Surnames approximating to names of birds :—

Alpe, Bird, Blackbird, Bullfinch, Bunting, Bustard, Buzzard, Capon, Cherlew, Chicken, Clough, Cock, Cockerel, Coe, Coote, Craik,

Crane, Crowe, Cuckoo, Daw, Dove, Drake, Duck, Eagle, Falcon, Finch, Fowle, Gander, Glead, Goldfinch, Goose, Gosling, Grew, Gull, Harrier, Hawke, Henn, Heron, Howlett, Jay, Kirlew, Kite, Lark, Laverock, Linnett, Mallard, Martin, Mavis, Mew, Moorcock, Musket, Nightingale, Parrott, Partridge, Peacock, Pheasant, Pick, Pidgeon, Pink, Pinnock, Pippet, Plover, Poe, Popjay, Povey, Puttock, Pye, Quail, Rainbird, Raven, Robin, Rook, Ruddock, Seafowl, Shapster, Sheldrake, Shoveller, Snipe, Sparhawk, Sparrow, Spink, Stare, Starling, Stork, Swallow, Swan, Swift, Teal, Wildgoose, Woodcock, Woodlark, Wren.

Surnames approximating to names of " fishes " :—

Barnacle, Bass, Breame, Brill, Bullhead, Carp, Chubb, Cockle, Codde, Codling, Conger, Crabbe, Cuttell, Dabb, Dace, Dory, Fish, Grayling, Gudgeon, Haddock, Hake, Herring, Keeling, Lamprey, Ling, Loach, Mackrell, Mullett, Mussell, Parr, Perch, Pickerell, Pike, Pilchard, Place, Pollock, Pope, Powter, Ray, Roache, Salmon, Shadd, Shark, Skeate, Smelt, Sole, Spratt, Sturgeon, Tench, Thrasher, Tope, Trout, Tunney, Turbett, Weaver, Welk, Whiting, Winkle.

Surnames approximating to names of " reptiles " and " insects " :—

Ant, Asp, Bee, Beetle, Blackadder, Boa, Bugge, Chafer, Cricket, Earwig, Emett, Evett, Fly, Grubb, Hornet, Locust, Maggott, Moth, Snake, Viper, Wasp.

So-called Nicknames explained.

In this list of appellatives corresponding to designations of living creatures are 250 modern surnames, which it is customary to regard as having once been nicknames of individuals of the human race. These surnames are now firmly established as family names, as various directories evidence, but it is suggested that they have never been either nicknames or characteristic descriptions. It is not practicable to take each one of the names and give chapter and verse to prove its origin, but a good proportion may be placed in their correct category.

It is first to be noticed that the Anglo-Saxons commonly bestowed animal-names upon their children. Mawer has detected the following in place-names :—

Badger (*brocc*), Bear (*bera*), Beetle (*wibba, wifel*), Boar (*eofor*), Buck (*bucc*), Bull (*bul-l-a*), Calf (*cealf*), Cat (*catt*), Cock (*cocc, hana*), Colt (*colt*), Crow (*crawe*), Dog (*hund*), Eagle (*earn*), Finch (*finc*), Goat (*bucca*), Hawk (*heafoc*), Horse (*hors*), Mule (*múl*), Raven (*hræfn*), Rook (*hróc*), Seal (*seolh*), Stag (*heorot*), Stallion (*hengest*), Wolf (*wulf*).

Mawer concludes that " these names, for the most part, at least, form a very old stratum in English personal nomenclature, and were not in living use at the end of the old English period. They most of them probably go back definitely to heathen times, and there is no evidence that they were given as nicknames, i.e. as additional names supplemental to the names given at birth. They are real personal names, traditional with the race, given at birth with little or no thought of any application of the name to the appearance or disposition of the child." [1]

That some of these names continued in use long after the adoption of Christianity, and even after the Norman Conquest, seems probable: Bucca, Earne, Múl, Ræfen, Wibba, and Wulf being names of Saxons appearing in the records. Radulfus Cattessone, 1103, has been mentioned above (p. 215); Rob. Cateson, Lincs. occ. 1327 (Subs. 135/11, m. 5*d*.); J. Cattessone, Warw. occ. 1359 (Coroner's R. 180, m. 4); and so may be found other monothemes, forming one or other element of known compounds, such as Hund-wine, Dogge-sone, Bitte-cat (see p. 85), etc.

Of the twenty-six animal and bird-names discovered by Mawer, no less than twenty-three are similar to modern surnames, and it is a fair assumption that such names, originally personal appellatives, must have so continued in use until the surname period, when they were assumed with other christian names as family designations. In equally practical manner it may be explained that other of the animal surnames are derived from baptismal names, and are not nicknames. O.E. names are: Cydda (now Kidd), Gota (now Goat), Biga (perhaps modern Pigge), Welp (now Whelp), Palefrei (Lib. Wint.). O.N. names are Gamel, Kettle, Thorkettle, Otur, and Tolfihn, from which come Camel (also local), Cattle, Turtle, Otter, and Dolphin. Ape, Ram, and Wulf occur in Domesday Book, as does Leuret (from Leofric), which gives us Leveret. Apocopation results in Lamb from Lambert, Deer from Deorman, Whale from Wealhwine, and possibly Brock from Brocker. Hypocorisms are Cobb from Jacob (but also O.E.) and Collie from Nicholas. Mole may, in some cases, be Moll (Mary), and Lambkin, a diminutive of Lambert. Corruptions result in Beagle from Beadle, Fox from Foukes, Hare from Ir. O'Hir, Lamb from Ir. O'Luane, and Foal is surely nothing more than Fool, a jester. Signboards, as fruitful sources of animal surnames, have been mentioned above (p. 231). Genet is a variant of Jeanette, Griffin a form of Griffith, and Marten of Martin.

Some of the animal-names must have originated in local appellatives; for instance, Goat is a hamlet in Cambs, but the surname may be from gott, "a water channel"; Camel is in Somersetshire; Steed is otherwise stead, "a place"; Ox is an old form of oaks; Seal is from sele or sale, "a hall"; Brock could be derived from Brook (formerly *broc*) ; several parishes are called Kennett ; and Fox may come from Vaux, pl. of *val* " valley ". Other names representative of the animal kingdom are derived from occupations : Badger is synonymous with hawker, Boar is a boor or rustic, Hart (otherwise le Hert or Herd), Hind, and Man are farm servants, and Neats were a class of feudal vassals. Panther is a corruption of Panter, the steward of the pantry.

Certain of the " zoo "-names are actually of the characteristic class, but with significations quite different from what appears at first sight. In some instances Hare has been le Heir ; Hogg is occasionally from Gael. *og* " the young " ; Turtle might be O.F. *tourtel* " crooked " ; and Grice, which occurs as *le gris*, is " the grey ". Some further possibilities arise from the Fr. surnames Bison, Verret, Mouse ; and Dutch Asse, van Wesyll, Bul, Wevels, etc. (see pp. 201–4).

Many of the bird-names are as easy of rational explanation. O.E. names are Pecoc (see p. 63), Drache (now Drake), Fugel (now Fowl), Sperhauoc (now Sparrowhawk and Sparke), Sæfugel (now Seafowl), Sprow may have become Sparrow, and Leofric, the modern Laverock. Swift was a tenth-century landowner, and Starling is a personal name in Domesday Book. Seven other examples of bird-names are given in Mawer's list above. O.N. names are Swan, from Swain or Swegen, and Partridge, in some instances a variant of Patrick. Rinnoch was also a personal name borne by a Cornish saint. Apocopation has resulted in Gull (Gule in Lib. Wint.) from some compound such as Gulbeorht. Hypocorisms are responsible for Cockerel from Cock, Daw from David, Gosling from Goceline, Howlett (How-el-ot) from Hugh, Pippet from Pepin, Robin from Robert, Gull from Juliana, perhaps, and Parrot from Pierre. Corruption gives Goose from Goce,, Falcon, i.e. Faulcon, probably from Fulkon, Quail from MacPhail (Manx), Heron from O'Ahern (Ir.), and another origin for Partridge is Beorhtric.

Bird-names from signboards have been noticed above (p. 231), and names in -cock, as Moorcock (pp. 282, et seq.). Local names have also originated bird-surnames : Craik, Pinnock, Swallow, and Jay are parishes in Yorks, Glouc., Lincs, and Shrops., respectively, and even Nightingale is a village in Monmouthshire. Clough is a ravine between hills, Grewe may be from Crewe, and Lark from the river of that name in Suffolk. Of possible Cornish origin may be suggested Goose from *coid* " wood ", and Cherlew " the rock pool ". Some others of the aviary may be actually derived from occupations, as Gander, " the ganter " or " glover " ; Shapster, formerly a dressmaker ; Shoveller, a labourer, etc. Probable archaic forms or apocopes are Falcon, Fowle, Hawke, of or from Falconer, Fowler, and Hawker. One or two examples of the characteristic class occur : Blackbird was originally blackbeard, and Henn is the Welsh equivalent for "old". Foreigners may also be responsible for bird-names ; for instance, Frenchmen were named Turkey, Phesaunt, Pullet, Sparrowe, and a Spaniard was officially called Swallowe (see p. 202).

Examination of surnames corresponding to names of fishes, reptiles, or insects shows that they are quite as unlikely to be derived from nicknames. Originating in O.E. personal names are Codd and Codling from Codda and Godda, Herring from Hæring, Skate from Sket, Shadd from Ceadda (sometimes Chad), Whiting from Hwiting, and Smelt and Tope have undergone no change since the eleventh century. Domesday Book names, Sprot and Tunna, have become Spratt and Tunney, and Bugg has been fully noticed above (p. 53).· O.N. appellatives Hakon and Thurbeorht have resulted in Hake and Turbott. Apocopes include Trout from an O.E. compound, and Fish from Fisher. Hypocorisms or diminutives are Haddock, i.e. Adock from Adam, Dabb from Dob, i.e. Robert, Emmet from Emma, Maggot from Margaret, Hornet from Horn, Cockle from Cock, and Evett from Eve. Hebrew names, as Job and Solomon, may have given Chubb and Salmon. Dutchmen brought fish-names to England, as Breame, Brille, Hakke, and Herring.

Local names have also produced fishy and reptilian surnames : Barnacle (Warw.), Cockle (Cokewill, Worc.), Dory (Dore, Derb.), Keeling, a small cod (Kelling, Norf.), Parr (Lancs), and Blackadder, a place and river in Scotland, suggest a few possibilities. From topographical features come Crabbe (cf. atte crabbe), Ling (atte ling, "the heath"), Roache (rock), Sole (pond), Pike (a peaked hill), and Bullhead may be from Bolehead, a field name. Haddock in some instances is a variant of Haydock, and Moth another form of Mott (moat). From occupational sources are : Thrasher, "a grain thresher," and Powter, "a pewterer." An example from a characteristic epithet is Bass (le bas "short"), and possibly also Dory (doré "fair", "gold").

Bardsley gives a third of these surnames as deriving from nicknames ; Lower fully believed in such origins ; Harrison (1912) and Weekley (1916) also consider many surnames rightly placed in such a category. It is believed that the explanations now offered are sufficient to demonstrate that there is no necessity whatsoever to suppose that names of living creatures given as nicknames have originated any of the modern British surnames. No doubt there are exceptions, and the suggestions now made should not be considered final without proof, but every practical source in a dozen different languages thoroughly explored before the origin of a surname is assigned to an alternative epithet. That such by-names were common is admitted, but that they became family names is a different view, the correctness of which should not be rashly assumed. If solutions are entirely elusive, there is still the possibility of the foundling christenings to fall back upon (see p. 269). Lists of plants and articles of dress can also be made from the modern directories, and upon examination their supposed origin as nicknames equally readily refuted, if the absurdity of the supposition was not manifest.

It may be noticed that single-syllable names ending in a consonant after a single short vowel, as a rule, double the consonant, as Bass, Dabb, Codd, Parr, Gull, Oxx, Pigg, Henn, Chubb, Shadd, Bugg, Kidd, Stagg, etc., an exception being Swan. In compounds also, the final syllable with a long vowel had a single terminal consonant, and with a short vowel a double consonant. Occasionally, as in Wolff, the double consonant follows a consonant, but this may indicate foreign origin.

Refutation of further errors. Besides the animal, bird, fish, reptile, insect, and plant-surnames, so familiar in sound and appearance, there exist a number of curious names like those listed on p. 324, which are also erroneously supposed to have originated in nicknames. A few illustrations will be provided to prove that these surnames had their source in some very prosaic manner, and were never at any time vulgar epithets.

Bidgood, Bigod, Bigot. Genealogical, from one or more O.E. personal names. Elements are Bæg-, Beag-, Big-, and -god.

> Rog. Bigot, 1086. (Dom. Bk.)
> Hugo Bigotus, Norf. 1130. (Pipe R.)
> Sanson Bigod, Wilts. 1166. (Lib. Nig., 1771, p. 111.)
> Thom. le Bigot, 1199. (Cur. Reg. R.)
> Rich. le Bigod, Wilts. 1227. (Chart. R.)
> Walt. Bygood or Bygod, Ess. 1383. (Cl. R.)
> J. Begegood, Byggud, Beggwade, Soms. 1530. (Star Cham.)
> J. Bidggood, Soms. 1571. (P.C.C. 19 Holney.)
> W. S. Bidgood, London, 1930. (Dir.)

The surname Bigod is commonly supposed to have originated in an oath, but one may surmise that the story is an invention. Weekley (p. 261) considers that Bidgood signifies " pray God ".

Blythman. Genealogical. Common O.E. elements are Blith- and -man, and there can be little doubt that Blithman existed as a personal name; cf. Blithhere, a Wilts landowner, c. 945. (ii) Characteristic, " the man from Blyth," Northumb.

Jas. Blythman, Northumb. 1553. (Pat. R.)
W. Blythman, Glasgow, 1930. (Dir.)

Bardsley (Dict.) : " Nick. gladsome, happy, a sunshiny
fellow." So also Lower (Patr. Br.).
Bunting.   Genealogical.   Occurring in Buntinge-díc
(KCD.) and Buntingford, Herts ; cf. Robert Bunte, Wilts,
1375 (Cl. R.) and Richard Bunt, Lancs, 1309. (Cl. R.)

Hugo Bunting, Lincs. 1275. (Hund. R.)
Rich. Buntyng, Kent, 1549. (Pat. R.)
James Bunting, —, 1654. (Mar. Reg. St. Bene't, Paul's Wharf.)
Bunt, Bunten, and Bunting all appear in the *London Directory*,
1930.

Bardsley (Dict.) : " Nick. good little pet, a term of endear-
ment for a little child, afterwards applied more generally."
Dearlove.   Genealogical.   Common O.E. elements are
Deor- and -leof ; cf. Dereman, Oxf. 1086. (Dom. Bk.)

Deorlaf, bishop of Hereford, ninth century.
Albert Dearlove, London, 1930. (Dir.)

Bardsley says : " Nick. an expression of affection " ;
Harrison admitting the possibility.
Doublet.   Origin undetermined.   In some of the later cases
probably from Robert, i.e. Dob-el-et ; cf. Dob-in-et,
Dob-l-in, etc.

Ricardus Dublet, Hants. 1066. (Wint. Dom.)
Hamo Dubel, Norf. 1275. (Hund. R.)
Isabel Doublee, Cambs. 1275. (Hund. R.)
J. Doublet, Berks. 1385. (Cl. R.)
T. and H. Doublet, London, 1930. (Dir.)

Bardsley (Dict.) : " Nick. from the bearer's custom of
using that garment." So also Lower (Patr. Brit.). Cf. Robt.
Doubeletmaker, taillour, Hen. VI (see above, p. 195).
Drinker.   Occupational.   A drencher was a tenant by
knight's service.

Walt. le Drinkere, Worc. 1297. (Cl. R.)
J. le Drencher, Worc. 1327. (Subs. p. 45.)
Gilb. le Drencher, Worc. 1327. (Subs. p. 51.)
Greg. Drinker, London, 1553. (Pat. R.)

Bardsley says : " Nick. a tippler, a toper."

Felon.   Characteristic.   (i) In the thirteenth century
" felon " had various significations, such as " cruel ", " sullen ",
" sturdy ", " brave " ; and in the fifteenth century " huge ".

Hen. le Felun, Hunts. 1275. (Hund. R.)

(ii) W. *velyn* " yellow ".

Kadogan Velyn, 1312. (Pat. R.)

(iii) Genealogical. Faelan (*faelan* " a little wolf ", becomes O'Faelain, anglicized O'Felan, Felan, Phelan, Whelan, Whelen. (O'Hart, i, 236.)

J. and Rich. Felan, Beds. 1338. (Pat. R.)
Mrs. Lucy Felon, Manchester, 1930. (Dir.)

This name may possibly be local.

J. de Felouns, —, 1325. (Pat. R.)

Bardsley's suggestion seems to be highly improbable : " Nick. ' the felon,' a treacherous person."

Giddy. Genealogical. O.E. Geddi (see above, p. 98).

Herbert Gidi, Hunts. *c.* 1110. (Wint. Dom.)
Adam Gydi, Soms. 1225. (Ass. R. 755, m. 5.)
Godwin le Gidye, Soms. 1276. (Ass. R. 1230, m. 33d.)
Thom. Gidi, Soms. 1278. (Ass. R. 1232, m. 11.)
Clarence Giddy, London, 1930. (Dir.)

Bardsley (Dict.) : " Nick. the giddy."

Licorice, Lickorish, Liquorice. Genealogical. A metronymic derived from one of the ancient Greek wolf (*lycos*) names, possibly Lycorus, son of Apollo and Corycia. It was one of the designations in use by the Jews, who seem to have been responsible for its introduction to England, and it remained after the expulsion in 1290.

Licoricia, wife of David de Oxonia, Jew, 1251. (Pat. R.)
Cokerel son of Licoricia, Jew, 1255. (Pat. R.)
Licoricia de Claytone, Staffs. 1279. (Ass R. Divers Co.)
Ralph Licoriz, Staffs. 1324. (Coram Rege R. : Salt Coll. x, 46.)
J. Lycorice, Staffs. 1351. (D.L. 30, 228/5, m. 9.)
Anna d. of J. Licorishe, bapt. 1637. (St. James, Clerkenwell.)
Arthur Liquorice, Manchester, 1930. (Dir.)
Wilfred Lickorish, London, 1930. (Dir.)

The survival or reintroduction of the common Jewish personal name is more believable than Bardsley's and Harrison's suggestion that the modern surname Liquorish is derived from a nickname " the liquorish, also lickerish, one dainty or nice in his palate " ; cf. for instance, Boosey, which surname is of the local class, being due to nothing more than occupation at a cattle-shed (O.E. *boosa*). Barber derives from Lickerrig, a place in Galway !

Peacock, Pocock, Pycock. Genealogical. Probably two or three personal names are involved : Pic, Picot, Pook, Pye.

Pecoc, Essex, 1086. (Dom. Bk., see above, p. 63.)
Ric. Pocok, Dors. 1225. (Ass. R. 755, m. 3.)
Geoff. Pokoc, Cambs. 1275. (Hund. R.)
Edm. Pecok, Herts. 1375. (Cl. R.)
J. Pecoke, Suff. 1549. (Pat. R.)
Steph. Pecocke, Radnor, 1549. (Pat. R.)
Robt. Paycocke, Yorks. 1553. (Pat. R.)

Peacock and Pocock are both in the *London Directory*, 1930.

Bardsley (Dict.) : " Nick. ' the gaudy ', ' the proud '."
Harrison considers the surname Peacock to have originated
as a nickname, and from the sign-board,

Pick. (i) Genealogical. Possible apocope of Pichard
(cf. Picot).

Pic brother of Wulfweard, Soms. 1077. (KCD.)
Simon Pic, Suff. 1275. (Hund. R.)
Agnes Pick, Hunts. 1275. (Hund. R.)

(ii) Local.

Ralph del Pik', Herts. 1291–2. (Plac. de Q.W.)

J. Pike, Essex, 1552. (Pat. R.)
Thom. Picke, 1668. (Bapt. Reg., St. James Clerkenwell.)
Henry Pick, London, 1930. (Dir.)

Bardsley says : " Nick. ' the woodpecker '. Fr. *pic*, cf.
Goldfinch, Spark, and other bird names." Also local, " at
the pike." Harrison considers Pick to be a possible nickname
from the weapon " pike ", as well as the bird.

Puttock, Puttick Genealogical. An O.E. personal name :
Puttuc was a witness, Hants, A.D. 701, and Puttoc, a Devonshire " prefectus ", A.D. 739.

Rich. Puttak, Kent, 1275. (Hund. R.)
Leticia Puttoc, Cambs. 1275. (Hund. R.)
Andrew Pottoc, Suff. 1302. (Pat. R.)
W. Puttocke, London, 1551. (Pat. R.)
C. H. Puttick : Walt. J. Puttock, London, 1930. (Dir.)

A nickname according to Bardsley : " puttock, i.e. ' the
kite ' ; metaphorically applied to a greedy ravenous fellow,
cf. Kite, Hawk, Sparrow, Sparrowhawk." Harrison follows ;
but the surname Puttock, like the rest of the bird-names, is
most unlikely to have been originally a nickname. Lower
(i, 233) says : " A woman of stained character ! "

Quick, Quickman. Local and Characteristic. Wyke
(Yorks), formerly Qwyk (1297 Subs. ; 1377 Cl. R.). Also
from the many places called Week and Wick.

Mat. de Quike, Lancs. 1202. (Fines : Farrer.)
Adam Quikeman, Kent, 1275. (Hund. R.) The man from Quike,
   cf. Blytheman.
Rob. Quic, Cambs. 1275. (Hund. R.)
Gilb. de la Quyk, Yorks. 1297. (Subs. W. Brown.)
Rog. de Quyke, Lancs. 1311. (Cl. R.)
Thom. Qwyk, Ess. 1403. (Pat. R.)
Jos. Quick, London, 1930. (Dir.)

Bardsley (Dict.) : " Nick. ' the quick ', one of active and
lively disposition." Lower had the same opinion (i, 150).
Harrison follows, but gives the additional suggestion of " a
dweller by a quick-tree ", i.e. a rowan-tree, etc.

Rigmaiden. Local. A locality and seat in Westmorland.

Rich. Rigmayden, Lancs. 1245. (Fines : Farrer.)
Thom. de Rigmayden, Lancs. 1377. (Cl. R.)
J. Rigmeydon, courssourman, 1509. (Letters and Papers :
   Brown.)
Isabel Rigmaden, Staff. 1547. (Pat. R.)
Frauncis Rygmayden, bur. 1593. (St. Michael, Cornhill.)
A. H. Rigmaiden, Liverpool, 1930. (Dir.)

Lower curiously derives this surname from a nickname
given to " a romping girl ". Having once become obsessed
with the idea that surnames are derived from vulgar epithets,
discovery of origin becomes easy. Probably Joyemaiden
(Cambs, 1275 ; Hund. R.) has as simple an origin as Rigmaiden.
Maden is a local surname.

Seafoul. Genealogical. From an O.E. personal name, e.g.
Sæfugel was a moneyer, temp. Eadw. III (Grueber).

Sæfugul, husband of Ædiuua, c. 1050. (Leofric Missal.)
Hálwærð Sæfugalasuna, a Norseman. (See above, p. 68.)
Rob. Sefoul, Oxf. 1275. (Hund. R.)
Ralph Sefughel, 1295-6. (Cl. R.)
Alan Sefoul, Norf. 1308. (Cl. R.)
Giles Sefoule, Norf. 1549. (Pat. R.)

The surname does not now appear in the directories.
Bardsley considers it to be derived from a nickname.

Smallman. (i) Genealogical. Smaleman was an O.E.
personal name, as was Lytelman (Grueber).

Smaleman of Cobbeham, c. 1100, a benefactor to Rochester
(Searle).

(ii) Smalemanni were *homines minuti* in 1130. (Pipe R.)

Ric. Smaleman, Suff. 1275. (Hund. R.)
Edw. Smalman, Heref. 1549. (Pat. R.)
M. Smallman, London, 1930. (Dir.)

Bardsley says : " Nick. ' the small man,' ' small of stature ' ;
cf. Small, Bigg, Little, Longfellow, Longman, etc." Lower
and Harrison are in agreement. It may be noticed that Smala,
Biga, Lowman (a form of Leofman) occur as O.E. personal
names. Smallbone, Smallpage, Smallpride, etc., are doubtless
to be derived as sensibly as Smallman if the truth were known.

Smart. Genealogical. An O.E. personal name.

> Smert, Suff. 1066. (Dom. Bk. 320*b*.)
> Simon Smert, Northumb. 1275. (Hund. R.)
> Adam Smart, Oxf. 1275. (Hund. R.)
> Cristiana Smartknave, Oxf. 1275. (Hund. R.)
> Very prevalent in 1930.

Bardsley says : " Nick. ' the smart,' i.e. the brisk ; cf.
Snell " ; yet he correctly divines that Snell was a fontal name.
Harrison follows. Baring Gould derives from St. Marte or
Martha ! Smartknave is in modern English Smart's knave.

Stout. Local. Atte Stout occurs in the Devonshire
Subs. R., 1327 (see above, p. 178). It is evidently the same as
the Glouc. " atte steorte " (a tongue of land, see p. 178).
Steorte was a place in Babcary, Soms. 1345. (Cl. R.). The
possibility of genealogical origin must not be overlooked ;
Stoutus or Stutus de Stutevill, alien, Notts. 1308–9. (Inq. p.m.)

> Gamellus Stot, Yorks. 1166. (Pipe R.)
> Norman Stote, Suss. 1206. (Cur. Reg. R.)
> Rog. de Stote, Northants. 1230. (Pipe R.)
> Ralph and Hugh Stote, Rutland, 1264. (Pat. R.)
> Syward Stert, Norf. 1275. (Hund. R.)
> Thom. and Luke Stout, Hants. 1314. (Pat. R.)
> J. Stot, Derby. 1332. (Pat. R.)
> J. Stort, Cumb. 1333. (Subs. see above, p. 168.)
> J. Stout, Northumb. 1334. (Pat. R.)
> Thom. Stout, Kent, 1339. (Pat. R.)
> W. Stoute, Yorks. 1379. (Poll Tax.)
> Chas. Stout, London, 1930. (Dir.)

Bardsley says : " Nick. ' the stout ' ; cf. Big, Little, etc.,"
and he also considers Stott to be derived from a nickname.
Lower and Harrison are in agreement. As far as the evidence
goes both names originated in " steort ".

Sweatinbed. Genealogical. Swet- was an O.E. prototheme
found in Sweeting, Swetman, etc., and -bed is an occasional
element, as in Rathbed (*c.* 690), a Frisian king, and the commoner English name Sigebed. There is therefore reason to
suppose that there may have been a personal name Swetbed,
which could easily be made into Sweatinbed ; cf. Th. Swetblod,
Yorks, 1275. (Hund. R.) ; Mich. Swetebryd, Kent, 1327 (Subs.
τ23/10, m. 23*d*.)

Alan Swetinbedde, Northants. 1275. (Cl. R.)
J. Suetebed in Arnesby, Leic. 1327. (Subs. p. 104.)

This curious corruption does not grace the modern directory, Sweetinburgh being the nearest in London. Bardsley thought Sweatinbed to be derived from a nickname, but the improbability of neighbours bestowing such an epithet needs no elaboration.

Thickness. Local. Thwykeness (Staff. Ass. R., 55 Hen. III) : Thicnes (ibid., 3 Edw. I).

> Robt. de Tykenes, Staffs. 1278. (De Banco R. East. 6 Edw. I.)
> Ralph de Thyknes, Staffs. 1279. (Ass. R. Divers Co.)
> W. de Thicnes, Staffs. 1280. (De Banco R. Mich. 8–9 Edw. I.)
> J. Thyknesse or Thiknes or Thiknese, 1509. (Pardon R., p. 226.)
> Cath. Thickness, Ess. 1719. (Mar. Reg. St. Bene't, Paul's Wharf.)
> Thicknesse and Hull, solicitors, London, 1930. (Dir.)

Lower says of this name : " nese or nesse is O.E. for nose, from A.-S. *nese*, and this surname therefore probably refers to the thick nose of the original bearer ! " (Patr. Brit.)

Toogood, Thoroughgood. Genealogical. Thurgod was a minister, A.D. 970. Thurgod, Turgod, and Turgot are personal names occurring in Domesday Book, 1066–86.

> Magnus f. Torgot, Lincs. 1206. (Ass. R. : Stenton.)
> Alice Thurgod, Beds. 1275. (Hund. R.)
> Geof. Togod, Hunts. 1275. (Hunt. R.)
> W. Togod *alias* Thogod, Bucks. 1278. (Cal. Gen. : Roberts.)
> J. Thurghgod, Herts. 1320. (Pat. R.)
> J. Thorowgood, London, 1693. (Bapt. Reg., St. James Clerkenwell.)
> Edw. Toogood, London, 1930. (Dir.)

Weekley (p. 262 n.) supposes Toogood to be an adjectival nickname.

Veal. Characteristic and occupational. Two possible origins are *le viel* ' the old ', and *la vielle* ' the vigil '.

> Godfrey Viele, Suss. 1206. (Cur. Reg. R.)
> Rich. la Veille, Ess. 1230. (Pipe R.)
> Phil. le Vel, Bucks. 1275. (Hund. R.)
> Isabell Velle, Bucks. 1275. (Hund. R.)
> Agn. Viel, Ess. 1275. (Hund. R.)
> Peter le Veel, Wilts. 1343. (Cl. R.)
> Peter de Veel, Glouc. 1343. (Cl. R.)
> Rich. Veale, Heref. 1549. (Pat. R.)
> Veal, Veale, Veall, London, 1930. (Dir.)

Bardsley (Dict.) : " Nick. ' the veal ', i.e. the calf." Lower, Weekley, and Harrison also consider this derivation possible in some instances. Harrison gives additionally Vial (Vitalis), a personal name. Yet another possibility exists in the Devonshire word velye (see above, p. 178), and cf. Rog. de Velay, Devon, 1230. (Pipe R.)

Vigorous, Vigrass. Genealogical. A personal name (see above, p. 109). Vigor was a Norman saint (Lower).

> W. Vigerus, Oxf. 1275. (Hund. R.)
> W. Vigerous, Dev. 1327. (Subs. 95/6, m. 11.)
> Thom. Vigerous, Heref. 1344. (Cl. R.)
> Nich. Vygrous, London, 1349. (Will., Court of Husting. R.R. Sharpe.)
> Robt. Vigerus, Ess. 1549. (Pat. R.)
> Mrs. Anne Vigrass, Manchester, 1930. (Dir.)

Bardsley says : " Nick. ' the vigorous ', i.e. the strong, etc."

These few examples will have sufficient weight to illustrate the danger of deriving a surname from a nickname merely because, at the present day, it happens to look like one. The instances of corrupt orthography of which little or nothing is known must be very great, and could such be detected it would probably be found that few nicknames, as defined above (p. 326), ever became established as surnames.

Pronunciation of Surnames. Among curiosities of nomenclature is to be mentioned the divergence between the written and the uttered form of many English surnames. In some cases it is the orthography which has suffered, the old pronunciation being retained ; in others the spelling has undergone little change, and the spoken name has become more easy to articulate. As one surname may have several orthographic forms, so it may have more than one pronunciation, as will be noticed among the following selection.[1]

Abergavenny	Aberge'nny	Bompas	Bumpas
Arbuthnott	Arbuth'nott	Bosanquet	Boo'sanket
Ayscough	Askew	Bourchier	Bow'cher
Bagshot	Bag'got	Bourke	Burk
Banchory	Ban'kory	Breadalbane	Breadal'bane
Bartelot	Bart'lett	Brompton	Brumpton
Beauclerc	Bo'clair	Burnett	Bur'nett
Beaulieu	Bew'ly	Capel	Cap'el
Bellingham	Bellinjam	Carnegie	Carneg'ie
Belvoir	Beaver	Carwardine	Carden
Berkeley	Barkley	Chandos	Shandos
Bethune	Bee'ton	Charteris	Charters
Bicester	Bis'ter	Chisholm	Chizum
Blount	Blunt	Chives	Shee'vus
Blyth	Bly	Cholmondeley	Chumley
Boleyn	Bullen	Claverhouse	Clavers

[1] Mainly taken from Jack's *Reference Book*, 1911, where a longer list may be seen.

Clerke	Clark	Iveagh	Ivah
Cockburn	Co'burn	Kekewich	Kekwitch
Coghlan	Co'lan	Ker	Car
Cohen	Co'hen	Kirkby	Kirby
Colquhoun	Co'hoon	Lefevre	Lefee'ver
Compton	Cumpton	Le Mesurier	Lemeas'urer
Cowper	Cooper	Levy	Lev'vy
Derby	Darby	Maclean	Maclane
Desart	Des'sert	Macleod	Macloud
De Saumarez	De So'marez	Magee	(hard g)
Dillwyn	Dillon	Marjoribanks	Marshbanks
Donoghue	Dun-no-hew	Maugham	Mawin
Du Buisson	.Dew'bison	Meiklejohn	Micklejohn
Duchesne	Dukahn',	Melhuish	Mel'wish
	Dushayn'	Meux	Mews, Mewks
Dymoke	Dimmuk	Molyneux	Mul'linewks
Dynevor	Din'nevor	Monck	Munk
Dysart	Dy-sart	Montefiore	Monte-fi-o're
Elgin	(hard g)	Moray	Murray
Falconer	Fawkner	Myerscough	Maskew
Farquhar	Fark'war	Ponsonby	Punsonby
Fiennes	Fynes	Powell	Poel
Fildes	(long i)	Quibell	Quibell'
Foljambe	Fool'jum	Romanes	Roma'nes
Foulis	Fowls	Rosenthal	Ro'sental
Furneaux	Fur'no	Ruthven	Ruf'fen
Geoghegan	Gay'gan	Sartorius	Sartoris
Giffard	G soft Eng., hard Scot.	Scrimgeour	Scrim'jur
		St. Leger	Sil'linger
Gillett	(hard G)	St. Maur	Seymour
Glamis	Glahms	Thesiger	Thes-siger
Gower	Gore	Tollemache	Tol'mash
Graeme	Grame	Tredegar	Tredee'gar
Grosvenor	Gro'venor	Tyrwhitt	Territt
Halkett	Hak'kett	Urquhart	Erkwart
Hawarden	Har'den	Vaux	Voks
Hepburn	Heb'burn	Wauchope	Waukop
Hertford	Hartford	Wemyss	Weems
Hervey	Harvey	Wriothesley	Roxly
Hoey	Hoy	Yerburgh	Yarburgh
Home	Hume	Yonge	Young
Im Thurn	Im'turn	Zouche	Zowche
Innes	In'nes		

Formation of Plural of Surnames. The plural number of both personal names and surnames is denoted by affixing *s* or *es* to the unchanged name, the grammatical deviations which apply to the common nouns not being followed ; thus terminal *y* is preserved, as in " the two Henrys " ; the singular *man* is retained, as in " the three Churchmans ", etc. In double names, only the second is inflected, as " twenty Sir John

Falstaffs "; but where a title is prefixed, authorities are not uniform in their practice. "We met the two Miss Browns", or "We met the two Misses Brown"; both appear to be correct with a leaning towards the first; but it is not permissible to say "We saw the two brother Smiths"; the only possible form is "brothers Smith". In addresses it is usual to inflect the title only, as "To the Misses Thomson", or "To Messieurs White".

Names ending in *s*, *ss*, *x*, *ch*, and *sh* follow the usual grammatical rule of adding *es* to denote the plural number, as Delveses, Basses, Foxes, Churches, Bushes. Sir Walter Scott (early nineteenth century) doubled a final single *s*, as Douglas, Douglasses, but this form is now obsolete.[1]

Curiosities resulting from Transcription and Translation. Since surnames were all originally words, the transformation from one language to another was always possible, and often practised. Owing to the original words or their signification being obscure in many instances, misunderstandings have resulted in curious forms, as has been illustrated briefly on pp. 212, 214, etc. One of these strange metamorphoses happened to Cavendish, which name, sounding like "giving dish", became in Manx the equivalent "Corjeag".[2] Some of our Bacons were formerly "Mushrooms" in Ireland, in the form Beacan, afterwards O'Beacain, and anglicized Bacon.[3] In similar manner Fairfield may be Beauchamp or Bello Campo; and a simple description like Wood may appear also as De Bosco, Dubosc, De Bois, Bois, Boyce, Atwood, Coat (Corn.), Goss (Corn.), and Goose (Corn.).

With regard to latinization, it has to be noticed that in addition to the letters of the alphabet, *k*, *w*, and *y* were used, the latter being an equivalent of *i*, and therefore may be found as a termination indicating the genitive case (2nd declension) and dative case (3rd declension). This use of the letter *y* has not always been appreciated by authorities of even great experience, and may be illustrated by the ancient names Ywen and Yvo, which being englished after latinization are often confused.[4] Ywen is declined in the second declension, and Yvo in the third, as follows :—

> Yvan, Yven, Yvin, Yvon — us, um, i *or* y (*genitive*), o, = Ewen.
> Yvon — em, is, i *or* y (*dative*), e, = Ivo.

It was common practice in the eleventh and twelfth centuries, and even up to the fourteenth, to latinize personal

---

[1] Maetzner, vol. i, pp. 224, 234.
[2] Moore, p. 63.
[3] Matheson, p. 8.
[4] e.g. *The Guide to the Victoria History*, p. 124.

names, descriptions, and surnames in official records. Martin gives a list containing about a thousand Latin forms of English surnames, from which the following examples have been taken :—

Acutus	Hawkwood	Medicus	Leech
de Adurni Portu	Etherington	Mentulamanus	" Toulmaine
Ala Campi	Wingfield		*alias*
Alec	Herring		Hancocke "
Apparitor	Sumner	de Monte Dei	Mundy
de Arida Villa	Dryden	de Morisco	Moore
de Atrio	Hall	ad Murum	Walton
de Aureis	Orescuilz	Nequam	Neckham
Testiculis		Nigeroculus	Blackey
de Baudribosco	Boldrewood	de Nouiomo	Noon
de Blanco Pane	Whitbread	de Nouo Oppido	Newton
de Bloys	Bligh	Nutricius	Nurse
de Bono Fassato	Goodrick	de Paceio	Pacy
de Cahagnis	Keynes	de Palude	Puddle, Marsh
Calixtus	Killick	de Parua Turri	Torel, Tyrrel
de Caniveto	Knevitt	de Pascuo	Stanley
de Capreolo	Roebuck	Lapidoso	
de Casa Dei	Godshall	de Pede Planco	Pauncefoot
Collinus	Knollys	de Pomario	Appleyard
de Conchis	Shelley	de Pratellis	Diprose,
de Corcella	Churchill		Meadows
Cornutus	Horn	de Pratis	Praty, Pretty
de Creauso	Grandison	de Pulchro	Fairfax
de Curva Spina	Crowthorn	Capellitio	
de Doito	Dwight, Brook	de Puteo	Pitt
Easterlingus	Stradling	de Radeona	Rodney
Ferratus	Fairy	Regiosylvanus	Kingswood
de Fluctibus	Flood	Rex	King, Reeks
de Fonte Australi	Southwell	Rigidius	Rivers
de Fraxino	Ashe	Rotarius	Wheeler
de Genisteto	Brounfield	de Rupibus	Roche, Rock
Gobio	Gudgeon	de Sabaudia	Savoy
Grammaticus	Grammer	de Sacra Quercu	Holyoak
Hastifragus	Brakespere	de Salicosa Mara	Wilmore
Hieronymus	Jerome	de Salso Marisco	Saumarez
de Hirundine	Arundel	de Saltu Capellæ	Sacheverel
Hispaniolus	Aspinall	de Saltu Lacteo	Milkley
Hosatus	Hussey	de Sancta Fide	St. Faith,
de Insula Fontis	Lilburne		Fiddes
Jodocus	Joice	de Sancto	Salmon
de Læto Loco	Lettley	Alemondo	
de Lato Campo	Bradfield	de Sancto	Stacey
de Lega	Leigh, Lee	Eustacio	
de Luera	Lower	de Sancto Neoto	Sennett
de Lupellis	Lovel	de Sancto Olauo	Toly
Magnus Venator	Grosvenor	de Saxo Ferrato	Ironston
de Mala Opera	Mallop	Sine Averio	Sanzaver

de Spada	Speedy	de Turpi Vado	Fulford
de Stipite Sicio	de la Zouch	Ususmare	Hussey
Sub Nemore	Underwood	de Vado Boum	Oxford
de Sylva	Weld	de Vado Saxi	Stanford
Taxo	Tesson	Velox	Swift, Fogarty
Teutonicus	Tyes	de Veteri Aula	Oldhall
Theobaldus	Tipple	de Villa Torta	Croketon
de Tosca	Tosh	de Viridi Campo	Greenfield.

The genealogist has to bear in mind the old Latin forms of the names for which he searches, and it will be noticed that the Latin " equivalent " often has a meaning entirely different from the original signification ; consequently a very particular knowledge is required of these freaks of nomenclature to avoid serious omissions and erroneous conclusions.   The legal attitude towards latinization of names will be considered in a later chapter (p. 394).

Descriptions of Servants.   Ranking among the curiosities may be mentioned the official method of identifying domestic hirelings.

J. s'vns the Kateson, Warw. 1381. (Subs. 192/23, m. 9.)
J. s'viens the Adams, Warw. 1381. (Ibid.)

" Katrina that was Jonesseruant Parker de Clare," which occurs on a Gaol Delivery Roll, temp. Hen. VI,[1] is a common form of description applied to menials as late as the fifteenth century.   In this case Katherine's surname was either unknown or wanting altogether, and so she was distinguished by the title of Katherine, servant of John Parker of Clare.   The same form was used even when the underling's second name was known.   Agnes Sparowe Joneseruantgylson de Ouresby (Lincs), labourer, was attached under the Statute of Labourers.[2]

Richard when Williamesservant the Hunt, Northants. 1332. (Pat. R.)
John Tegeantservant *alias* John Servaunt Tegeaunt, *alias* John Tegeant of Westminster, servant. (Pardon Roll, 1 Hen. VIII, p. 218.)

These curious descriptions are the result of the small importance of the second name, which was tacked on as an addition.   The servant of John Smith was known as John's servant, and for further distinction the second name of the master was added.   Sometimes the menial was called after the description of his employer.

John Whiteknyght of Wellington (Soms.) grome. *c.* 1550 (K.B. 29, 113.)

Evidently John was the groom of the " White Knight ". The title was not unusual ; e.g. " John Fitz Gerald was called

[1] P.R.O., Gaol D.R., 190, m. 9.   [2] K.B. 27, 615, m. 21.

in his lifetime the White Knight, otherwise John Oge Fitz John Knight Fitz Gybbons, 1571 " [1]; and there was a Whiteknights manor in Sonning, Berks, 1548 (Pat. R.). Unless coincidence is the cause of similarity the servant, in some cases, was identified by the name of his master. Two examples from King's Bench rolls may be noticed :—

Johannes Walssheman Dauidseruant Walssheman, Lincs. (Trin. 10 Hen. IV, 1409.[2])

Johannes White Warynesseruant White, Cambs. (Mich. 1 Hen. VI, 1422.[3])

More rarely the description was fully extended and englished, as Johannes Cook " that was the Frerys austyns s'uant of Norwyche " (Trin. 8 Hen. IV, 1407).[4] Occasionally the servant had two or three names, as is evidenced by this Norfolk example :—

Dauid herry seruant Inglose nup' de Dylham yoman *alias* dict' Dauid kensy nup' de Dylham yoman *alias* dict' Dauid Walysshman nup' de Dylham yoman. (East. 34 Hen. VI, 1456.) [5]

Scribal Humour. Some of the official scriveners endeavoured to alleviate the monotony of their routine by the introduction of " comic relief ", and the toils of the modern searcher are occasionally lightened by the discovery of a jest. In A.D. 1190 an Exchequer clerk, after charging the Bishop of Ely " with £20 for scutage on account of the knights, whom he should have sent to the army of Wales ", wrote : " But he had those and far more in the King's service in that same army, and therefore he is quit *with Angels and Archangels*. But the last words have been cancelled in deference to a respect for precedent and for the dignity of the court." [6]

In the title to a King's Bench roll, 1403, the testy clerk makes reference to the end of this " putrefacti recordi ".[7] In like manner the humorous clerk sometimes gave a twist to the names of his helpless victims ; thus Willelmus de Sancta Fide of 1205 (Cur. Reg.) [8] became Willelmus de Sine Fide and Willelmus Sine Fide in the same court in 1206.[9] Under date 1203 an attorney's name is given as Suspirium et Fletus, " a sighing and weeping," [10] and the " Stephanus Bon christien " of 1206 on the same roll is variously entered later as " Stephanum Nequam Christianum " and " Stephanum Mal Christien ".[11] In the *Liber Niger Scaccarii* (1166) a holder of

---

[1] *Statutes at Large*, vol. i, p. 387. [2] P.R.O., K.B. 27, 593, m. 17.
[3] K.B. 27, 610, m. 24d. [4] K.B. 27, 585, m. 28.
[5] K.B. 27, 780, m. 1.
[6] Intro. Pipe Roll, 1190, p. xxiii ; C. Johnson.
[7] East, 4 Hen. IV, K.B. 27, 568.
[8] Vol. iv, p. 195. [9] Vol. iv, pp. 13, 121.
[10] Vol. iii, p. 65. [11] Vol. iv, pp. 187, 189, 242.

ten knight's fees of William, Earl of Gloucester, is described
as Elias aureis testiculis,[1] which may be an allusion to an
heraldic charge, now the sign of a pawnbroker.

Two examples occurring together on a Somerset Assize
Roll, 1225, have possibly been helped by the scribe : John
Swete by ye bone, and Robert Godesblescinge.[2] Some of the
curious Latin descriptions are the result of corrupting a name
with no apparent signification into some English words which
are translatable into Latin ; thus Tyrrel, a personal name, is
supposed to be equivalent to a small tower, and is then rendered
" de Parva Turri ". In similar manner Blackey, which is
probably a corruption of some place-name, is turned into
" black eye ", and entered as Niger Oculus, and doubtless some
such procedure is the explanation of Oculus Latronis, and
Diabolus, the latter perhaps a play on the local description
d'Eiville. The Jew in particular was the butt of the facetious
quill-driver, and many curious names are not improbably the
wilful perversion of the entering clerk for the amusement of his
fellows. The single name Hatecrist, which occurs on the Pipe
Roll, 1166, seems particularly appropriate to a Jew, but later
on it is much more likely to be a corruption of " at crest ",
in parallel with Hatewrong (cf. Antecrist, p. 168).

As a specimen of the pleasantries which sometimes intruded
upon the solemnity of the law courts, the following panel is
illustrative :—

" True Copy of a Jury taken before Judge Doddridge, at the
Assizes holden at Huntingdon, A.D. 1619. The Judge had, in the
preceding circuit censured the Sheriff for impannelling men not qualified
by rank for serving on the grand jury, and the sheriff, being a
humourist, resolved to fit the judge with sounds at least. On calling
over the following names and pausing emphatically at the end of the
christian, instead of the surname, his lordship began to think he had
indeed a jury of quality."

> " Maximilian KING of Toseland,
> Henry PRINCE of Godmanchester,
> George DUKE of Somersham,
> William MARQUIS of Stukely,
> Edmund EARL of Hartford,
> Richard BARON of Bythorn,
> Stephen POPE of Newton,
> Stephen CARDINAL of Kimbolton,
> Humphrey BISHOP of Buckden,
> Robert LORD of Waresley,
> Robert KNIGHT of Winwick,
> William ABBOTT of Stukeley,
> Robert BARON of St. Neots,
> William DEAN of Old Weston,

---

[1] 1728, vol. i, p. 161.   [2] Ass. R. 755, m. 2.

John	ARCHDEACON of Paxton,
Peter	ESQUIRE of Easton,
Edward	FRYER of Ellington,
Henry	MONK of Stukeley,
George	GENTLEMAN of Spaldwick,
George	PRIEST of Graffham,
Richard	DEACON of Catworth.
[Thomas	YEOMAN of Barham].[2]

" The judge, it is said, was highly pleased with this practical joke, and commended the Sheriff for his ingenuity. The descendants of some of these illustrious jurors still reside in the county, and bear the same names : in particular a Maximilian King, we are informed, still presides over Toseland." [1]

[1] *History of Huntingdon*, by Robt. Carruthers, 1824, p. 149.
[2] From another list.

CHAPTER XIV

THE ETYMON AND ITS SIGNIFICATION

Etymological Considerations. Having traced out step by step the evolution of the surname from the personal description or address, examined the various processes of derivation, and gained an insight into the deceptive results of orthographic corruption, a possibly rash essay will now be made to reverse the operation, and taking a modern name, to attempt the exemplification of a method of working, whereby the geographical distribution, language, etymon, and original signification is discovered. By etymon is here meant the " true " or original form, that is, the primary word. At some more or less remote period all surnames have been words : of the four classes—characteristic and occupational were adopted words ; local surnames were formerly words or place-names, themselves once either words or personal names + words ; and genealogical surnames, with few exceptions, were personal names, also originally current words, sometimes of a bygone age.

Comparative philologists are able in most cases to strip such words of their grammatical adjuncts, and to lay bare the radical portion or root as it is called. It is not proposed in this chapter to attempt to discover the ultimate element, or to do more than trace a surname back to the original word, and to determine its meaning, a sufficiently difficult problem and one in which certainty is often elusive.

Possibly the most knotty questions will be found among names of the genealogical class, because the significations of some personal names had been lost even a thousand years ago. For a demonstration, the writer will take his own patronymic, formerly a personal name in Suffolk, in which county it was of at least the antiquity of Domesday Book (1086).[1] The first step is to investigate the occurrences and distribution of the name in the ancient records of Britain and the Continent, and the second is to determine the language of the original word, and its signification.

Geographical Distribution. Owen or Ewan was one of the kings of Britain during the Celtic occupation, according to the much discredited list given by Geoffrey of Monmouth, who flourished temp. Hen. I,[2] and the equally fabulous

---

[1] Sudfolc, f. 440b.
[2] *The British History of Geoffrey of Monmouth*, ed. by J. A. Giles, 1844, bk. iii, chap. xix, p. 55.

series recorded by Walter of Coventry (thirteenth century).[1] In A.D. 642, according to various Irish annals, the Britons, under their king Owen, defeated and slew the Scottish monarch, Domnall Breac, in the Battle of Strathcarn.[2] A seventh-century royal genealogy mentions a form of the name twice— Riderch map Eugein map Dunnagual map Teudebur map Beli map Elfin map Eugein map Beli.[3] In the reign of Æthelstane the Strathclyde Britons joined with the Scots and Norsemen in an attempt to overthrow the English supremacy ; but were defeated at Brunenberg, A.D. 937, and Owin, king of the Cumbrians, and Constantin, king of Scots, put to flight.[4] Owen is also called king of Gwent (Uwen Wenta cyning),[5] and is evidently the Eugenius sub regulus who in 931 attested a grant by king Æthelstan to the thegn Ælfric, of land at Watchfield (Berks) ; also appearing as a witness to further royal deeds, in one of which, by king Eadred to the thegn Ælfsige Hunlafing, gifting land at Alwalton (Hunts), he is called Wurgeat, and in another, a Saxon charter, Owen.[6] In A.D. 1018, the second year of Knut, king Malcolm entered England accompanied by Eugenius Calvus (the bald), king of the Strathclyde Britons (rex Clutinensium), gaining an important victory over the Northumbrians.[7] Owen probably died about the same time, as the Annales Cambriæ record under year 1015—Owinus filius Dunawal occisis est ; the discrepancy in date being due, no doubt, to the Chronicler's error.

Beda, the Venerable, writing of a period four years before his own birth (673), mentions Owin of Lastingham (Yorks), who came with Queen Etheldreda from East Anglia.[8] The Rev. Dr. Stukeley suggested that he was in all probability of native extraction, "for the Isle of Ely was possessed by

[1] Memoriale Fratris Walteri de Coventria, ed. by Wm. Stubbs (Rolls Ser. 58), vol. i, p. 7.
[2] Annals of Tighernac and Annals of Ulster. His name is variously spelt Ohan, Hoan, and Haan, the h being redundant. See Celtic Scotland, by W. F. Skene, vol. i, p. 250, and Chronicles of the Picts and Scots, by the same author, p. 68. See also Four Ancient Books of Wales, vol. i, p. 178.
[3] Additions to the Historia Britonum (Chronicles of the Picts and Scots, p. 15).
[4] Under year 934 Historia Ecclesiæ Dunhelmensis (Symeon of Durham), Rolls Ser. 75, vol. i, p. 76. Under year 926 Eugenius Rex Cumbrorum submits to Æthelstan at Dacre. Willelmi Malmesbiriensis Monachi de Gestis Regum Anglorum, edited by W. Stubbs (Rolls Ser. 90), vol. ii, p. 147.
[5] Anglo-Saxon Chronicle (Rolls Ser. 23), vol. i, p. 199, col. i. Gwent was the name given to territory principally consisting of the counties of Monmouth and Glamorgan.
[6] Latin and Anglo-Saxon grants from Codex Diplomaticus Aevi Saxonici, by J. M. Kemble, vol. ii, pp. 203, 304 ; vol. v, pp. 199, 208.
[7] Symeon of Durham (cited above), vol. ii, p. 156. Professor Freeman calls him Eogan or Eugenius, and Dr. Skene (Celtic Scotland, vol. i, p. 394), Eugenius or Owen.
[8] Ecclesiastical History of England, bk. iv, chap. iii.

the old Britons long after the Saxons had taken hold of England ; as before was the case in Roman times." [1]

The names Owein and Ewen frequently occur in early Welsh poems ; the *Book of Taliessin* mentions Owein mon (of Mona) and Owen ap urien ; and the *Book of Aneurin*, Ewein vap eulat (the son of Eulad).[2] According to the Welsh Triads it appears that the Roman emperor Maximus (fifth century) left a son in Britain called Owain ab Macsen Wledig, who was elected to the chief sovereignty of the Britons, and under whom Britain was restored to a state of independence, and discontinued payment of tribute to the Romans.[3] A tenth-century manuscript states that in A.D. 811 Eugem filius Margetiud moritur [4] and the *Brut y Tywysogion* mentions Ywain ap Howel, who died in 987, and Owein uab Dyfynwal, slain in 989.[5]

Among the many Ewens of note may be noticed the alleged seducer of Thaney, the mother of St. Kentigern (St. Mungo, the patron saint of Glasgow, seventh century). In an anonymous fragment of the saint's biography, written in the twelfth century, he is called " Ewen filius Erwegende, nobilissima Brittonum prosapia ortus " (sprung from a most noble stock of the Britons) [6] ; elsewhere he figures as Ewen filius Ulien, and is evidently the Ywain ap Urien of Welsh records. Geoffrey of Monmouth calls him Eventus, and represents him as successor to his uncle Augusel, king of Albania (Scotland).[7] Numerous churches in England have been dedicated to a St. Ewen or Owen ; Bristol, Gloucester, Hereford, Chepstow (Monm.), Lelant (Cornw.), Redruth (Cornw.), Bromham (Beds.), were all represented at one time, and there was also a church of St. Owen in Dublin.

In Irish annals the name frequently appears : Eogon of Inbher, also called Eugenius de Ard-Inver, is said to have been living 1730 B.C. [8] ; Eoghan More, king of Munster, was murdered A.D. 123 ; from another Eoghan More, slain A.D. 195, were descended the Eoghanachts or Eugenians ; in A.D. 465 Eoghan, son of Niall of the Nine Hostages, died and was buried in Inis-Eoghain (island of Owen or Ewen now Inishowen), from which Eoghan descended the *Cinel Eoghain*.[9]

---

[1] *The History and Antiquities of the Conventual and Cathedral Church of Ely*, by James Bentham, 1812, p. 51 n.
[2] *Four Ancient Books of Wales*, ed. by W. F. Skene, who rejects the Welsh Triads, Hanes Taliessin, and Iolo MS. as all spurious, p. 23.
[3] *Essay on the Welsh Saints*, by Rice Rees, p. 107.
[4] *Annales Cambriæ*, p. 11. In other manuscripts, Owinus and Oweyn.
[5] Rolls Ser. 17, p. 22.
[6] Printed in *Registrum Episcopatus Glasguensis*, vol. i, p. lxxviii.
[7] *British History of Geoffrey of Monmouth*, 1842, bk. xi, chap. i.
[8] *Ogygia*, by R. O'Flaherty, pt. iii, chap. iv.
[9] *Annals of Ireland by the Four Masters*, ed. by J. O'Donovan, 1851.

Eoghan, bishop of Ardstraw, co. Tyrone, is commemorated as a saint. Cawdor, a parish in the counties of Nairn and Inverness, was dedicated to St. Ewan and anciently called Borivon, properly Bar Ewan or Ewan's height.[1] The name, carried into Scotland by the Irish, became exceedingly common, where there was anciently a clan Ewen.

Medieval pedigree makers, with more zeal than accuracy, claimed to be able to recite the genealogy of the royal house of Scotland from Noah! Master Ralph de Diceto, dean of St. Pauls (twelfth century), hands on a pedigree showing William, king of Scots, 131st in descent from the famous ship-builder,[2] No. 21 in the royal lineage being Owan, who, if the genealogy were accurate, must have flourished considerably over 1,000 years before the commencement of the christian era ; and No. 88 being Ewein, who may, perhaps, be identified as one of the early kings of Scotland, invented by over-industrious historians. A somewhat similar pedigree is given by a fourteenth-century chronicler[3]; wherein Ewan, 19th in descent from Noë, appears as grandfather of Neolos, king of Athens, whose son Gaythelos was the first king "of the Scottish nation, and married Scota, daughter of a Pharaoh, being contemporary with Moses, who lived after the year 2015 B.C. and before 1075.[4] The greater part of these pedigrees must have been based on nothing more than oral tradition, and therefore cannot be relied upon for exact names or dates ; nevertheless, for the present inquiry, they have a value in showing that in the twelfth century the personal name Owan or Ewein was recognized as being of great antiquity.

Boece, " the father of lies " (1526), mentions three Scottish monarchs named Ewen, as flourishing anterior to the christian era, and in this fiction he was followed by Guthrie (1767), Carruthers (1826), and others. These collectors of traditional and mythical narratives mention eight kings named Eugene or Eugenius, A.D. 360–763, Guthrie, with conspicuous enterprise, providing portraits of them all! Although sundry of these Ewens only existed in the imagination of their biographers, their inclusion in the list helps to show that the name was recognized as one of the most ancient in Scotland. Several of these royal Ewens did actually flourish, and are

[1] *Dictionary of Christian Biography*, Art. Eoghan. In the *Annals of Clonmacnoise*, ed. by D. Murphy, Eoghan is called Owen, bishop of Ardstrathy. The Bollandists have a memoir *De S. Eugenio vel Eogaino Episcopo Ardstrathensis in Hibernia.* Consequently Ewan = Owen = Eoghan = Ivon = Eugenius = Eogainus.

[2] *Radulphi de Diceto Opera Historica*, ed. by Rev. W. Stubbs, M.A (Rolls Ser. 68), vol. ii, p. 35.

[3] *Johannis de Fordun Chronica*, bk. v, chap. 1. *Historians of Scotland*, vols. i and iv.

[4] Ibid., bk. i, chap. viii.

mentioned as early as 1270 in the *Cronicon Elegiacum*.[1] Andrew of Wyntoun also records :—

" Oure the Scottis the Kyng Ewan." [2]

" Twa yhere regnand Schyr Ewan
As Kyng off Scottis endyt than." [3]

The name also appears in records of Pictish monarchs, but it must be noted that very considerable confusion between Scottish and Pictish kings occurs in the genealogies. In the *Annales Cambriæ*, under date A.D. 736, Ougen rex Pictorum obiit ; in the *Annals of Tighernac*, A.D. 838, Owen mac Aongus is mentioned, which king is called Eoghane filius Hungus by Fordun, and is frequently mentioned in the ancient chronicles (A.D. 971 to 1317), under such names as Uven, Unen, Eogana, Coganan, Egganus, and Doganan.[4] According to Pinkerton, this Uven is a Gothic name,[5] but Chalmers,[6] and Garnett,[7] consider it to be a form of Welsh Owain ; and that it is Celtic is very probable, since the sound value of *v* in early days was not unlike the modern *w*. The same form of the name is found in the ogmic inscription at Colbinstown, co. Kildare, if the transliteration of Macalister is correct.[8]

With regard to Anglo-Saxon records, practically nothing of the name has been seen, with the exception of the few cases of Welsh origin cited above. The *Onomasticon Anglo-Saxonicum* gives a reference to one Eowine, a moneyer in the time of Harold I, whose name is noticed on a coin in the British Museum collection [9] ; but the prototheme *eo* is rare in true O.E. names, and Eowine is probably a variant of Owine, just as Eowel is of Howel. Possible forms of this name are found in early Teutonic records : Förstemann cites : Awin, Avan, Aven, and Auin (fem.).[10]

Nordic records likewise yield barren results : Olaf Nielsen in *Olddanske Personnavne* mentions Ewen and Iwan, but has

[1] *Chronicles of the Picts and Scots*, ed. by W. F. Skene.
[2] *Oryginale Cronykil of Scotland*, bk. vi, chap. i.
[3] Bk. vi, chap. ii.
[4] W. F. Skene cited above.
[5] *Enquiry into the History of Scotland*, 1787, vol. i, p. 286.
[6] *Caledonia*, vol. i, p. 207.
[7] *Transactions of the Philological Society*, vol. i (1842), p. 120.
[8] See above, p. 36.
[9] W. G. Searle.
[10] In later years, in the Low Countries, the name approached more nearly to the English and Scottish form : A.D. 1326, Wouter Ywinssoen in Renwick (*Register op de Leenaktenboeken*, Sloet) ; 1423, Jan Ywaenssoen van den Berghe (*Studiën*, etc., Winkler) ; a seventeenth-century family spelt the name Uwens, which form may be found in London. In England, A.D. 1369, Simon Yweynson of Holbeach (Lincs.), Coroner's Roll 22, m. 2 ; 1638, Thomas Huynson or Hewinson, Herts. (Lent Assizes 35/80). I have also seen Owanson and Evanson. In Scottish records of the fourteenth and fifteenth centuries Ewinson, Hewinsoun, etc., are common.

negligently omitted to say anything regarding them. Oinus dacus (i.e. danicus) was dispossessed of his land in Essex in 1066[1]; but Oinus may stand for the common Scandinavian name Odin, these two appellatives appearing to be interchangeable.[2] Under year 1170 Eoan is the name of a " Dane ", from the Orkney Islands, occurring in the *Annals of the Four Masters.*[3] Nothing more relevant to the discussion than negative evidence is to be gathered from Runic inscriptions, according to the list supplied by Professor Stephens.[4] R. Ferguson considered Owen to be of O.N. derivation,[5] and Lower gave O.N. *ovanr* "inexperienced" as the etymon of Oven,[6] but supporting evidence is entirely wanting ; the names Owen or Oven not occurring in such lists as *Islendinga Sögur* nor in any other of the rolls of early Nordic names. If Oven is derived from any old Scandinavian word, a more likely suggestion would be *úvinr* "foe", "enemy"; it may also be noticed that the very common Icelandic name Eyvindr occurs in a great profusion of orthographic forms, such as Evindr, Ewindr, etc.,[7] which, if brought to Britain, might have become Ewin by apocopation ; but, again, there is no evidence in support.

In distinction to its rarity in northern records, Eugenius (fem. Eugenia), the Latin form of Eugene, and also, according to some authorities, the equivalent to Eoghan (Gael.), Eochaid (Gael.), Owen (W.), and Ewen (Eng.), was common throughout Southern Europe at a very early date. The correct latinization of Ewen is *Evenus*, but Owen is often rendered *Audoenus*.[8]

Homer, nearly 3,000 years ago, gave Evenus as the designation of three mythical personages[9] ; Plato referred to a poet of the name, whom Eusebius, bishop of Caesarea, in his Chronicle, places at the 30th Olympiad (460 B.C.)[10] ; and another is mentioned by Seneca (first century).[11] A Greek physician called Eugenius flourished some time in or before the first century after Christ, as one of his formulæ is quoted by Andromachus[12] ; and between A.D. 300 and 850 twenty-nine bishops, ten martyrs, and four popes bore the same name. The name in forms other than Eugenius or Evenus is also

---

[1] *Domesday Book,* vol. ii, f. 25.
[2] *Exon. Domesday,* ff. 3, 9b, and 16.
[3] Vol. ii, p. 1185.
[4] *The Old Northern Runic Monuments,* 1866, vol. ii, p. 897.
[5] *English Surnames,* p. 244.
[6] *Patronymica Britannica.*
[7] *Diplomatarium Norvegicum* and *Islandske Annaler.*
[8] On the continent Audoen is often equivalent to Teutonic Audwin (O.E. Eadwine).
[9] *Iliad,* bk. ii, 693 ; and ix, 557.
[10] *Apologia Socratis,* p. 20b.
[11] *Hercules Ætæus,* line 501. Forte per campos vagus Evenos.
[12] *Dict. of Biog. and Mythology,* Art. by W. A. Greenhill.

found on the continent at an early date ; St. Ovan (Evantius) was the seventh bishop of Autun early in the fifth century [1] ; St. Ouen or Ouein (Audoenus), archbishop of Rouen, an eminent biographer of the seventh century, who promoted the foundation of many monasteries and churches of St. Ouen, died near Paris, 683 ; the present church of St. Ouen, Rouen, was begun in 1318 ; and in France several towns and villages bear the name, the place-name St. Ouen giving the surname to one of the distinguished French families, who became settled in England.

With the Celts of Brittany the name was popular ; among others, Alan, count of Brittany, had an uncle named Even (Linzoel), who was flourishing in 1027 [2] ; and Even, archbishop of Dol, died in 1081.[3]

This cursory dip into ancient history enables one to rule out entirely the possibility of Scandinavian or Teutonic origin for the name Ewen, and to express the opinion that the name is of great antiquity among the Celts, but whether they collected it from the Greeks or Latins or left it with them is not so transparent.[4]

Views of Philologists. With regard to the Celtic group, the name Ewen, in different orthographic forms, is found in Irish, Manx, Gaelic (Scottish), Welsh (Brythonic or British), Cornish, and Breton records. In England and Wales, in the majority of cases, Ewen and Owen have been derived, at least nine centuries ago, from British *Ywein*, and in Scotland and Ireland from Gaelic *Eogan*. Philologists have not had occasion to discuss the origin and signification of Ywein, but over 1,000 years ago the derivation of Eogan had received attention.

Sanas Chormaic, an etymological glossary of difficult words in the Irish language, with derivations from Greek, Latin, and Hebrew, was compiled by Cormac Mac Cullenain, king of Munster, prior to A.D. 905. The entry relating to Eogan is translated as follows :—

" Eogan or Eogen, i.e. eugen, i.e. graece : εὐ *bonus* or *bonum* latine dicitur, *gen*, however, is from γένεσις ; γένεσις autem generatio est. *Eo-gen*, then, is bona generatio."

The twelfth-century *Cóir Anmann* (Fitness of Names) follows on similar lines :—

" Eogan [referring to Eogan, the great, second century] was his

[1] *Gallia Christiana*, by D. de Ste Marthe, 1728, vol. iv, p. 338.
[2] *Histoire de Bretagne*, by G. A. Lobineau, vol. ii, p. 116.
[3] Ibid., I give some other examples in *Ewen of East Anglia and the Fenland*, p. 14, n. 6.
[4] The name of St. Eugenius frequently occurs on the coins of the emperors of Trebizond, the Greek legends giving the name in a variety of forms. (*Catalogue of the Coins of the Vandals*, by W. Wroth, 1911.)

name from parental origin, that is *eo-genesis*, i.e. good birth, for *eo* is εὐ- bona, but *genesis* (γένεσις) is Eogan's *generatio*. Of *Eo-gan*, then, *bona generatio* is the analysis.[1]

" 'Tis from this that *Eoganacht* is said of them (scil. his descendants), in virtue of the blessings which the men of Erin bestowed upon him for his hospitality and generosity towards them, and for rescuing them from the famine in which they were. From this (comes) *Eoganacht*, i.e. *bona actio*, i.e. a good act (it was) for him (Eogan) to save the men of Erin from starvation.

" Or Eoganacht, i.e. Eogan-icht, i.e. Eogan's protection to the men of Erin. Or Eogan-necht, that is Eogan's *necht : necht* ' children ', that is the seven Eoganachts are Eogan's children.

" Thence then had he the name Eogan Mor ('Great '), because he was great above every one, and (so were) his children and his kindred after him."[2]

The divergent views of modern philologists regarding this name is illustrated by the following extract from *Etymology of Gaelic National Names* (Macbain).

" EWEN, G. Eòghann (Dial. Eòghainn), M.G. *Eogan, Eoghan*, E. Ir., O. Ir., *Eogan* : *Avi-gono-s (*Avigenos, Stokes) ' well-born, good ' from *avi, friendly, good, Skr. *ávi* (do.), Got. *avi-liud*, thanks, Lat. *aveo* desire, possibly Gr. εὐ-, good (cf. here Εὐγένης, *Eugenius*), W. has *Eu-tigern, Eu-tut*, O. Br. *Eu-cant, Eu-hocar*, Gaul. *Avi-cantus*, Rhys (Hibbert Lectures, 63) refers Ir. *Eoghan* and W. *Owen* to *Esu-gen-Gaul. *Esugenus*, sprung from the god *Esus*. Zimmer regards *Owen* as borrowed from Lat. *Eugenius*. Cf., however, the *evo*- of Ogmic *Eva-cattos*, now *Eochaidh*. Hence *Mac-ewen*."

The asterisks (*) denote hypothetical words.

Notwithstanding the opinions of the early Irish writers, one cannot help thinking that a simpler origin of the Scottish and Irish Ewen and Owen would be nearer the truth. Why should Eoghan, among all ancient Gaelic names, be singled out for derivation from the Greek ? [3] In some cases Eogan may be the Greek Eugen, but so popular and widespread a name is much more likely to have originated among the ancient Celts, who lent it to the Greeks, if, in fact, both races did not obtain it from the common source of their origin. O'Brien, an eighteenth-century lexicographer, was strongly of opinion that the Irish never borrowed any part of their language from the Greeks, but, on the contrary, that the latter race derived a great part of their speech from the Celts.[4]

In addition to the above significations, the meaning of the

---

[1] The name Eugenius was also used by the Germans, who have the modern Wohlgeborn. (*Die Personennamen*, von A. F. Pott, 1859, p. 540.)

[2] *Irische Texte*, von Wh. Stokes und E. Windisch. 3 Ser. 2 Heft.

[3] I find nothing regarding Eoghan in *Die griechischen Personennahmen*, von August Fick, 1874.

[4] Preface to *An Irish-English Dictionary*, by J. O'Brien, 1768.

name Ewen has been given as " kind-natured "[1] and " young
man or youthful warrior "[2]; and of Ewin as " law-friend ".[3]
Owen is said to signify "lamb ",[4] " young warrior ",[5] " enemy ",[6]
" unsheathed ",[7] " apt to serve or to minister ",[8] and Ouen
" rich friend "[9]; Ivon or Yvon is said to mean " bow-bearer
or archer ",[10] and Yves from which is derived Even, according
to some authorities, " active or watchful ".[11] Yet Ewen and
Owen are the same name, and Ivon is sometimes an equivalent.
The diversity of opinion shows that the determination of the
etymon of the name is difficult and uncertain, and further
investigation is necessary.

Derivation. The name under consideration is in such
widespread use that it is quite possible the primitive form existed
in more than one word-base ; that one modern name (i.e.
one orthographic or one phonetic form) may be derived from
several roots is as certain as that several names may be derived
from one root. The mother-tongue of the Indo-European
languages is unknown ; according to philologists the nearest
approach to it is Sanskrit, which has preserved its words in
the most primitive forms. The root of Skr. and Pers. *yuvan*
" young ", may well be one of the word-bases of Ewan, Owen,
and even Hugh, Young, and other appellatives. For Celtic
derivation it would be possible to suggest half a dozen words in
Welsh or Gaelic which might be the origin of the name, such
as W. *euain* "to be moving or wandering ",[12] *ewyn* " foam or
froth ",[13] ; Ir. *uan* " lamb ",[14] *iwyn* " outrageous " [15]; or
Gael. *eigh*,[16] *eubh*, or *eugh* " a cry ".[17] Yet another suggestion
may be advanced : the bow and arrow is one of the most
ancient devices of hunting or fighting known to man, its origin
being lost in the mists of antiquity ; yew being the favourite

---

[1] *History of Clan Ewen*, by R. S. T. MacEwen, 1904, p. 30.
[2] *Irish Pedigrees*, by John O'Hart, 1881, p. 36. E. O'Reilly (*Irish-English Dictionary*) derives Eoghan from *eoghunn* " youth ". See also C. M. Yonge (*History of Christian Names*, vol. ii, p 141), *og* " young " and *duine* " man ".
[3] Hy. Harrison's *Dictionary*.
[4] C. M. Yonge, vol. ii, p. 140. W. *oen*, Ir. *uan* " a lamb ", followed by T. G. Gentry, p. 46.
[5] I have mislaid this reference.
[6] *English Surnames*, by R. Ferguson, 1858, p. 244. O.N. *óvínr* = O.E. *unwine* " enemy ".
[7] *The Cymry of '79*, by Alex. Jones, p. 102.
[8] *Caledonia*, by Geo. Chalmers, 1807, vol. i, p. 207.
[9] C. M. Yonge, p. 249.
[10] Ibid.
[11] Zeuss and M. de Coston. See *Dictionnaire des Noms*, par Loredon Larchey, 1880.
[12] *Welsh and English Dictionary*, by Rev. Thos. Richards.
[13] *A Dictionary in Englyshe and Welshe*, by Wyllyam Salesbury, 1547.
[14] J. O'Brien (cited above).
[15] Richards (cited above).
[16] *A Dictionary of the Gaelic Language* (Macleod and Dewar, 1853).
[17] *A Gaelic Dictionary*, by R. A. Armstrong, 1825.

material for bow staves, the yew tree occurring wild over a large area of the northern hemisphere. It is possible, then, that the primitive word for yew, if any, is the source of some personal names. In English descriptions of later days there occur Bōwer and Bowman, from bow, and Archer, from arch (Lat. *arcus* "a bow "); in Welsh, Saethwr " archer "; the Norse has Skapti, originally a shaft maker, now Scapti and Scafti (cf. Scot. Shafto), and Ice. Bog-sveigr (bow-swayer). Is it not probable also that the Celtic races had a synonymous personal name ? In Irish, Scottish, and Welsh place-names Gaelic and Welsh equivalents of the word " yew " have been identified,[1] and it is to be expected that it also appears in personal names, if not as " bower " or " archer ", then as " yewer " or some other word of similar meaning.[2] It is not necessary that the word or resulting name should date from Aryan or Sanskrit period ; it may have originated in Celtic days, and it is suggested that a modern name derived from an early Celtic equivalent of " yew " exists in the popular English, Welsh, Scottish, and Irish appellatives, Ewen and Owen.

Of the Celtic languages, the Gaulish dialects were extinct by the sixth century, and suitable examples cannot be obtained for assistance in the derivation of the names under consideration ; in fact, no one of the written records of the Celtic tongues is of earlier date than the seventh century. The oldest languages, Irish, Welsh, Breton, and Cornish, are divided into three periods—Old, Middle, and Modern, which are approximately dated 700–1100, 1100–1500, and 1500 to the present day. Irish occurs first in glosses of the eighth century ; its dialect, Scottish Gaelic, not being found at all in the first period.[3] A few glosses provide the only examples of early Breton, and Welsh is scarce until the middle period, Cornish and Manx writings not being found until a much later date. All these languages are therefore known only in comparatively modern forms, being frequently very different from the original. Personal names also have not retained the same orthographic forms during the passage of thousands of years ; in many cases a name has lost its original signification and acquired another ; some names, perhaps, have now several meanings, and several names may have the same meaning. Giving full consideration to these peculiarities,

---

[1] Youghal, i.e. *eochaill* " yew wood " (*The Origin and History of Irish Names of Places*, by P. W. Joyce) ; Gleniur, i.e. *gleann-iuthair* " glen of yews " ; Deniur, i.e. *dun-iuthair* " mount of yews " (Armstrong) ; Orwell, i.e. *Iubhar-coille* " yew-wood " (*The Place Names of Fife and Kinross*), by W. J. N. Liddall ; Ewenny, i.e. *ywenni* " yew trees " (John Walters, 1828).

[2] That " yew " is an equivalent of bow seems to be borne out by a comparison of Lat. *taxus* " yew " and Gr. τόξον " bow ".

[3] *The Book of Deir* (ninth century) is sometimes cited as containing some early examples of Gaelic, but it is not proved that they are not Irish.

the impossibility of finally and definitely fixing an etymology will be realized.

O'Hart has observed that down to the eleventh century every Irish name had some signification,[1] so that if Eogan or Eoghan is of Gaelic derivation, then both elements originally had some meaning, and if the first is not the same word as *iogh* or *eo* " yew ", then its signification has been passed over by all the Irish glossarians. The followers of Cormac will consider this point to support the theory of a Greek etymon for the name.

Eoghan is used by the eminent Celtic scholar, Dr. Skene, and some other authorities,[2] as an equivalent of the ancient Irish name Eocha or Eochaid, which usage also does not fit in with the present suggestion that Eoghan is derived from *eo* " a yew ", because Eocha or Eochaid (gen. Eachach) is said to be from *each* or *eoch* " a steed ", and is rendered " a knight " or " horseman ".[3] But has the vocable been correctly divided into its components? Is not *eochaidh* rather *eo cathaidhe* " yew warrior " (O. Ir. *cath* " battle ", *cathidhe* " warrior " ; cf. also *eo-chrann* " yew tree "[4]; and the place-name Eochaill, " yew wood," *eo* and *coill*, not *eoch* " horse " and *all* " great ") ? Another nominative form of the name is Eochu,[5] which occurs under year 494 in the *Annals of Ulster*, and under year 882 in the *Annals of the Four Masters*, and elsewhere. While Eochu is admittedly a plural form of *each* " horse ", surely in this case it is from *eo* " yew " and *cu* " warrior " (cf. here Donchu, " brown-haired warrior ", and Muirchu " sea warrior " or " sea dog "). Both Eochu and Eochaid have the same genitive form.

Dr. Macbain states that ogmic Ivacattos is equivalent to Eochaid, but *iva* is not very suggestive of " horse ", and is much more like various equivalents of " yew " (cf. D. *ijf* = OHG. *iwa* = MHG. *iwe* = G. *eibe* = F. *if* = Sp. *iva* = O. Fr. *iv* and ML. *ivus* " yew "). Professor Rhys considers *evo* equivalent to Lat. *aevum* " everlasting ", and that Evolengi of ogam inscriptions is compounded of *evo* and *leng*, and signifies " long-lived " or " he of the long life " ; but although the common bestowal of fanciful names is not denied, is it not much more likely to be " long yew ", i.e. " he of the long

[1] *Irish Pedigrees*, by John O'Hart, 1881, p. ix.
[2] Eogan, Eocha, Eocoidh, and Eugenius are equivalents in the opinion of Rev. Jas. Gammack (*Dict. of Chr. Biog.*, ed. by Dr. Smith, Art. Ewain). Dr. Skene (*Celtic Scotland*, vol. i, pp. 230, n. 2, 264, and 289) regards Cinel Eachadh, Cinel Eochagh, and Cinel Eoghan as interchangeable. In the Felan pedigree Eochaidh is also called Eoghan Breac (*Irish Pedigrees*, p. 236). Eocho buide in *Flann Mainistreach* (1014–23) occurs as Ewyne (1280 Chronicle), and Euin (sixteenth century).
[3] *Irish Pedigrees*, pp. 36 and 229.
[4] *In cath catharda* (Irische Texte von E. Windisch, 4 (2), line 336, etc.).
[5] Nominative forms of Eochaid are sometimes Eochaig, Eocach, etc. (Cf. *caidh* " chaste " becoming *caig* in Munster : O'Reilly.)

bow "? Such an epithet could reasonably be applied to a person during his lifetime. The *cattus* of Evacattus, Ebicatus, and other names appears to be *catu* or *cat*, so common in Gaulish and Breton names, and signifying "battle" (W., Corn., and Bret. *cad*). Evacattus therefore appears to be etymologically the same as Eochaid, and to mean, as above stated, "yew warrior." It may be noted that, on the contrary, Dr. August Fick considers the Irish name Eachaidh to be equivalent to Gaulish Epidius (*ep, epo* "horse ").[1]

If, however, *eoch* is the first syllable, and does signify "a horse ", it is somewhat extraordinary that the fact is omitted by all dictionarians [2] with the exception of J. B. Bullet (1754), who gives *each, ech,* and *eoch* as equivalents for horse, his authorities being some ancient unspecified MSS., but without indicating the cases, and *eoch* may well be some other form than nominative. *Eoch,* according to O'Reilly, signifies "groaning" or "sighing ", otherwise neither *eoch* nor *eogh* is mentioned in any list of the Irish compilers. Even admitting *eoch* and not *eo* to have been the stem of Eochaid, is it not probable that it has the same signification as *eogh,* and that both are merely forms of *eo* " yew "? (Cf. O. Ir. *iogh* "a yew ", Armstrong.) Before Irish writers had any standard of orthography the letters *c* and *g* were interchangeable, as they have been in Latin [3]; and to the writer there is no more difference in the meaning of *eoch* and *eogh* [4] than there is between *loch* and *logh* [5] (Bullet, 1754, Manx *logh, loghan*) or

---

[1] That there are personal appellatives in which the word horse can be traced is shown by the numerous Sanskrit names with prefix açva, Greek with ιππ-, ιππο, and Gaulish with *ep* (e.g. Epo-pennus = Each-cenn); *Namengruppen der indogermanischen Grundsprache* in *Die griechischen Personennahmen* von August Fick, p. cxciv.

[2] I have referred to forty dictionaries and glossaries. According to O'Reilly, plural forms of *each* are *eich* and *eocho*, and accusative plural *eochu*. Yet in numerous Gaelic proverbs and quotations relating to the horse collected by A. R. Forbes (*Gaelic Names*, 1905), *eoch* is never used, not even in the plural. Forbes, however, mentions *ech* and *eoth* (perhaps a misprint), as well as *each* (pp. 9, 10), and states that *each, ech, eoch,* etc., come from the root *ak* " to hasten ". In the *Scottish Celtic Review*, pp. 106 and 198, Professor Windisch, writing on the "Laws of Auslaut in Irish ", mentions *eoch* (dative) for prehistoric *eq-o* Lat. *equo*, the nominative being *ech* (p. 198). *Ech* is also the form used in the *Brehon Law Tracts*.

[3] Cf. Macistratos for Magistratos, Leciones for Legiones, etc., on the Columna Rostrata, Rome, B.C. 230. In O. Ir. *g* occurs for *c* as early as the sixth century. See Mag for Mac, dat. sing. in the Clonmacnois inscription (*Christian Inscriptions*, ed. by M. Stokes, 1872, vol. i, p. 58).

[4] The pronunciation in Irish is not the same. The *c* aspirated by an *h* subjoined to it or a full point set over it carries the soft guttural or whistling sound of the Greek χ, but the *g* in the middle or end of words, if aspirated is suppressed (J. O'Brien, 1832). The pronunciation in Gaelic is very similar.

[5] Cf. *Loch* Cé, now *Lough* Key or Kea; also the names Ua *Loch*lainn, now O'*Lough*lin; Mac *Eoch*again, Mageoghegan; O'*Beach*ain, O'*Beagh*an; O'Ceallachain, O'Callaghan; O'Gaibhtheachain, O'Gaughan. Cases of substitution of one letter for another are very common in Irish: C and G, Cannon and Gannon; G and K, Gilfoyle and Kilfoyle, etc.

lach and *lagh* "law" [1] (W. *lacha, laha*). Compare the interchangeability of M.W. *coch, cogh, goch,* and *gogh* (all nom. masc.) as they occur, for instance, in the *Record of Carnarvon.*

Having said that Owen is an orthographic form of Ewen, it may be further mentioned that, in Irish place-names, it is generally of distinct origin, signifying "river" (e.g. Owenbeg, "little river," and Owenmore, "great river"),[2] but like the personal name, the vocable *owen* is also equivalent to Eng. *ewen*; the Worcestershire river Evenlode being called in the fourteenth century Ewenlode,[3] and written in a Latin charter (A.D. 784) Eouvengelad.[4]

It is necessary to say a word about the name Evan, which, although of entirely different origin, has often been confused and even considered to be synonymous with Ewen and Owen. Evan is the Welsh representative, as John is the English,[5] of the Hebrew, Johanan, "grace of the Lord," appearing in early form as Yevan or Jevan, and becoming a popular Welsh appellative, with the spread of biblical knowledge, being certainly of much later origin than Eoghan or Ywein, which must have been in common use long before the days of Christianity.

Nothing is more uncertain than the derivation of personal names, as the opposing views of eminent scholars testify. The writer will therefore pronounce no dogmatic opinion regarding the origin of Ewen or Owen, but will merely record the impression, formed by a consideration of the cited facts, that Gaulish Evacattus and Ebicatus are equivalent to Irish Eo-chaid (not Eoch-aid), signifying "yew-warrior"; that Eoghan has practically the same meaning, being derived from an early Irish word meaning "yew" (the letters of the alphabet were named after trees, I being called *iogh* "yew"), that Welsh Ywein is akin to *ywen* "yew", and that Breton forms of the name Ivon, Yves, Even, etc., are cognate and are derived from an early form of *iven* "yew". From Eochaid, in later days, have been derived several modern Irish names, such as Iveagh, Haughey, etc., from the Irish Eoghan or O'Eoghain came Owen, and from Scottish Eoghan, Ewan, and Ewing. Cymric Ywein is now Owen in Wales, and Ewen,

---

[1] Pinkerton (*Enquiry*, etc.) has *agh* and *ach.*
[2] Exceptions occur such as Tyrone (Tyr-eoghain).
[3] Patent Rolls, 18 Edw. III, p. 409.
[4] *KCD.*, vol. i, p. 178.
[5] Lower cites the case of the name of a Welsh witness who appeared at the Hereford assizes about the year 1825. He was called John Jones, but he admitted that he also went by the name of Evan Evans. "This apparent discrepancy was explained to the Court by Mr. Taunton, afterwards Sir William Taunton, and a Judge of the court of King's Bench), who stated that Evan is the Welsh synonym of John, and Evans that of Jones, and that John Jones might be called indifferently Evan Jones, John Evans, or Evans Evans, without any real change of name." (*Patronymica Britannica*, p. xxii.)

Ewens, and Hewins in England, Even in Brittany, Ouen and Huens elsewhere in France, Uwens in Flanders, and Euen in Germany. The cognate Breton name Ivo or Ivon has become Ivey in England, and Yves in France. In conclusion the probability may be repeated that, in many cases, names similar in orthography or phonetics, or in both, are derived from entirely different sources, and that names of widely different meaning at the present time may be derived from the same word-base.

A Key to O.E. Compound Personal Names.

Some attention may now be given to genealogical surnames of Anglo-Saxon origin, which form a considerable proportion, and provide the greatest variety in the class. Although so many of the English baptismal names have become obsolete, a number retained popularity long enough to become surnames, and others were reintroduced by alien immigration. Some of these Teutonic survivals have become so corrupt as to be almost unrecognizable in their modern form, and to facilitate their discovery a list of some of the ancient and modern variants of the commonest elements found in family names derived from Teutonic and Scandinavian compound personal names has been prepared.

The principal equations noted are $c = k = g = ch$, $b = p$, (generally in German names), $\delta = d = t$, $hr = r$, $n = m$, and $w = v$. There are numerous vowel changes: $\alpha = ea = a$, $eo = e = o = i$, $au = e = o$, $i = y$, etc. Letters may be dropped, as Godwig—Godwi, or Wulf—Ulf; h may occur for a and e, or it may be added or omitted or changed into k or ch.

It should also be noted that by a process of gemination or assimilation, doubling of consonants takes place, and where " twin medial consonants occur one or other is a changeling or a trespasser ", and has to be ignored ; and it not being possible to formulate a rule for such elimination at sight, procedure must be by trial and error : thus Merrick, Hibbert, Turrell, Gunnell, and Woollard should be divided : Me-r-rick, not Mer-r-ick ; Hi-b-bert, not Hib-b-ert ; Tur-r-ell, not Tu-r-rell ; Gun-n-ell, not Gu-n-nell ; Wool-l-ard, not Woo-l-lard.

Corruption may be considerable ; thus Beorhtsige is variously written Brehtsig, Brixge, Bricsi, Brixi, to become the modern surname Brixey ; nevertheless, by keeping the outlined possibilities in view, the original form of numbers of peculiar surnames may be discovered. If, for instance, a man has an unromantic name like Gumboil, which is not far removed from Gumbol, he can trace it, by using this table, to Gumbeald, which may be rendered " brave hero ".

A Selection of Anglo-Saxon and Norse Elements with Modern Variants

A-. *See Ælf-.*

Ad-. *See Ead-.*

-ad. *See -heard.*

Adel-. *See Æthel-.*

Ægel-. *See Æthel-.*

Ælf-, Æl-, Alf-, Al-, El-. O.E. *ælf*, m.f. " elf ". Modern variant: A-, as in Agar, for Algar. Often confused with Æthel.

Æsc-, As-, Es-. O.E. *æsc*, m. " spear ", " ash ".

Æthel-, Adel-, Agel-, Ail-, Ayl-, Edel-. O.E. *æðele* " noble ". Modern variant, Edl-, as in Edlin.

-affe. *See -wulf.*

Agel-, Ail-. *See Æthel-.*

Al-. *See Ælf-, Eald-, Ealh-.*

Alch-, Alh-, Alk-. *See Ealh-.*

Ald-. *See Eald-, Weald-.*

-ald. *See -weald.*

All-. *See Eald-.*

-all, -alt. *See -weald, -wulf.*

Amal-. Modern variants : Ame-, Eme-, as in Amery, Emery.

An-, O-, On-, Un-. Old Norse, as in Anlaf, Olaf, Onlaf, etc. *See also* Ean-.

Angel-. *See Engel.*

Ans-, Os-, as in Anscytel, Oscytel, from O.N. Asketil (Áss, a heathen god ; *ketill* m. " cauldron ". Modern variants : Horse-, Hos-, Hose-, as in Hosegood.

Ar-. *See Earn-.*

Arcen-. *See Eorcon-.*

Ard-, Eard-. O.E. *eard* m. " earth ", " country ".

-ard, -art. *See -heard, -weard.*

Arn-, Ar-. *See Earn-.*

-art. *See -weard.*

As-, Os-. *See Ans-, Æsc-.*

-att. *See -heard.*

Aud-. *See Ead-.*

Ayl-. *See Æthel-.*

Bad-, Bæd-. *See Bead-.*

Bæg-, Bag-, Beag-, Beah-. O.E. *beag* " ring ", " bracelet ".

Bald-. *See Beald-.*

-bald. *See -beald.*

-ball. *See -beald.*

-bard, -bart. *See -beorht.*

Baude-. *See Beald-.*

Bead-, Beadu-, Bed-, Bid-. O.E. *beadu* f. " war ", " strife " ; Bed-, n. " prayer ".

Beald-, Bald-, Bold-. O.E. *beald* " brave ", " strong ". M.E. Baude, as in Baudewyn.

-beald. Modern variants : -bald, -ball, -bill, -ble, -bles, -bol, -bold, -bolt, -bow, as in Grimble, Winbolt, Rumball, Cutbill, Godbold.

-bed. *See -beorht.*

Beorht-, Ber-, Bert-, Berth-, Bir-, Bric-, Briht-, Brit-, Byrht-, etc. O.E. *beorht* " bright ", " shining ". Modern variant : Bright-, as in Brighteve.

-beorht. Modern variants : -bard, -bart, -bed, -berd, -bert, -bit, -bitt, -bitts, -bord, -bourd, -bright, etc., as in Harbourd, Hibberd, Sebright.

Beorn-, Bern-, Brin-, Bur-, Byrn-. O.E. *beorn* m. " man ", " hero ", " warrior ". O.N. björn, m. " bear ", as in Asbjörn, now Osborne.

-beorn. Modern variant : -bourne, as in Seabourne.

Ber-. *See Beorht-.*

-berd. *See -beorht.*

Bern-. *See Beorn-.*

Bert-. *See Beorht-.*

-bert. *See -beorht.*

Bid-. *See Bead-.*

-bill. *See -beald.*

Bir-. *See Beorht.*

-bit, -bitt, -bitts. *See -beorht.*

Blac-, Blæc-. O.E. *blac* " black ", " dark ".

-ble, -bles. *See -beald.*

Blith-. O.E. bliðe " joyous ".

Bod-, Bot-, But-. O.E. *bod* n. " message ".

-bol. *See* -beald.

Bold-. *See* Beald-.

-bold. *See* -beald.

-bolt. *See* -beald.

-bord. *See* -beorht.

-born, -borne. *See* -brand.

Bot-. *See* Bod-.

-bott, possibly -beorht, as in Turbott.

-bourd. *See* -beorht.

-bourn. *See* -brand and -beorn.

-bow. *See* -beald.

-brain. *See* -brand.

Brand-, Brang-, Brond-. O.E. *brand* m. " fire ", " flame ".

-brand, -brant. Modern variants : -born, -borne, -bourn, -brain, -bran, -bron, -burn.

Brang-. *See* Brand-.

Breg-, Bregu-. O.E. *brego* m. " ruler ".

Bric-. *See* Beorht-.

Bright-. *See* Beorht-.

-bright. *See* -beorht.

Briht-. *See* Beorht-.

Brin-. *See* Beorn-.

Brit-. *See* Beorht-.

-bron. *See* -brand.

Brond-. *See* Brand-.

Brun-. O.E. *brún* " brown ", " dusky ".

Bryn-. *See* Beorn-.

Bur-. *See* Beorn-.

Burg-, -burh. O.E. *burg* f. " fort ", " castle ".

-burn. *See* -brand.

But-. *See* Bod-.

Byrht-. *See* Beorht-.

Byrn-. *See* Beorn-.

Cen-, Coen-, Cwen-, Cyne-, Ken-, Quen-, etc. O.E. *cynn* " rank ", " family ", " kin ". Modern variants : Kim-, Kin-, Kine- as in Kimball, Kinman.

Ce el-, Cytel-, Ketel-. O.E. *citel* m. " cauldron ".

-chel, -cil, -cytel, -kel, -kill. *See also* under Ans-.

Coen-. *See* Cen-.

Col-. O.E. *cól* " cool ", " calm ".

-cott. *See* -god.

Cud-, Cut-, Cuth-. O.E. *úð* " famous ".

Cwen-. *See* Cen-.

Cyne-. *See* Cen-.

Cytel-. *See* Cetel-.

Dæd-. O.E. *daed* f. " deed ".

Dæg-, Dag-, Deg-. O.E. *dæg* m. " day ". Modern variant : Day-, as in Dayman.

-dæg, -dai. Modern variant : -day, as in Friday. O.E. *Frigedæg*.

Dar-. *See* Deor-.

Day-. *See* Daeg-.

-day. *See* -daeg.

Deor-, Deer-, Der-, Dire-, Dor-, Dyre-. O.E. *déor* " deer ", *déore* " beloved ", " noble ". Modern variants : Dar-, Dear-, as in Darling, Dearman.

Der-. *See* Deor-.

Dire-. *See* Deor-.

Dod-, Dud-. Modern variant : Dowd-, as in Dowding.

Dol-. O.E. *dol* " foolish ", as in Dolman.

Dom-, Dum-. O.E. *dóm* " judgment ", " splendour ".

Dowd-. *See* Dod-.

-drud. *See* -thryth.

Dum-. *See* Dom-.

Dun-, Tun-. O.E. *dún* m.f. " mountain ", *dunn* " brown ". Modern variant : Down-, as in Downman. *See also* Tun-.

Dur-. *See* Thor-.

Ead-, Ad-, Aud-, Ed-, Eod-, Ot-. O.E. *éad* " riches ". Modern variant : Ed-, as in Edridge.

Eald-, Ald-, Al-, Eld-. O.E. *eald* " aged ", " honoured ". Modern variant : All-, as in Allbright.

Ealh-, Al-, Alch-, Alh-, Alk-. O.E. *ealh* " temple ".

Ean-, An-, En-. O.E. *éan* " yeaning ".

-ear. *See* -here.

Eard-. *See* Ard-.

-eard. *See* -heard.

Earn-, Ar-, Arn-, Ern-. O.E. *earn* m. " eagle ".

Earp-. *See* Eorp-.

East-, Est-. O.E. *éast.* Modern variant : Es-, as in Esmond.

Ebr-. *See* Eofor-.

Ecg-, Eg-, Ei-. O.E. *ecg* f. " sword ", " battle-axe ".

Ed-. *See* Ead-.

Edel-, Edl-. *See* Æthel-.

Eg-, Ei-. *See* Ecg-.

El-. *See* Ælf.

-el. *See* -weald.

Eld-. *See* Eald-.

-ell. *See* -hild, -weald, -wulf.

-elm, -helm. O.E. *helm* m. " protection ", " defence ".

En-. *See* Ean-.

-en. *See* -wine.

Engel-, Angel-, Ingel-. Modern variant : Ing-, as in Ingram, formerly Ingelram.

Eod-. *See* Ead-.

Eofor-, Ebr-. O.E. *eofor* " bear ". Modern variant : Ever-, as in Everard.

Eorcon-, Arcen-, Erchen-. O.E. *eorcnan* " precious ".

Eorl-, Erl-. O.E. *eorl* " nobleman ", " warrior ". Modern variant : Url-, as in Urlwin.

Eorp-, Earp-. O.E. *earp* " dark ", " dusky ".

-er. *See* -here.

Ern-. *See* Earn-.

Es-. *See* Æsc-, East-.

Est-. *See* East-.

-et, -ett. *See* -geat, -heard.

-eva. *See* -gifu.

Ever-. *See* Eofor-.

Fær-, Far-. O.E. *fær* n. " journey ", *fǽr* m. " peril ".

Fast-. O.E. *fæst* " stedfast ".

-ferth. *See* -frith.

Folc-. O.E. *folc* n. " folk ", " tribe ". Modern variant : Folk-, as in Folkard.

-fowl. *See* -fugel.

Fra-. *See* Frea-.

Fre-. *See* Freo-.

Frea-, Fra-. O.E. *fréa* m. " ruler ", " lord ".

Fred-. *See* Frithu-.

Freo-, Fre-, Frie-. O.E. *fréo* " free ". Modern variants : Free-, Fri-, as in Freeburn, Friday.

-frey, -frid. *See* -frith.

Fride-. *See* Frithu-.

-frith, -ferth, -frid. O.E. *frith* m.n. " peace ", " security ". Modern variants : -frey, -phrey, as in Godfrey, Humphrey.

Frithu-, Fred-, Fride-. O.E. *frithu* m.f. " peace ", " security ".

-fugel. O.E. *fugel* m. " bird ". Modern variant : -fowl, as in Seafowl.

Gær-, Gar-, Ger-. O.E. *gár* m. " spear ". Modern variant : Jar-, as in Jarrold.

-gær, -gar, -ker. Modern variants : -ger, -ker, as in Secker. *See also* -here.

-gar, -gard. *See* -geard.

-geard. O.E. *geard* m. " court ", " dwelling ". Modern variants : -gar, -gard, -ger, -yard, as in Leggard, Hilyard.

-geat. O.E. *Geat* " Goth ". Modern variants : -ett, -yat, as in Woollett.

-gef, -gefu. *See* -gifu.

-ger. *See* -gær, -geard.

-gett. *See* -god.

-gifu, -eva, -gef, -gefu, -gif, -giva, etc. O.E. *giefu* f. " gift ", e.g. Edeva, Odgiva, etc. Modern variants : -iff, -iffe, as in Brightiff.

Gisl-. O.E. *gísl* m. " hostage ".

-giva. *See* -gifu.

God-, Gode-. O.E. *god* m. " god ", *gód* " good ". Modern variants : Good-, Got-, Gote-, Goto-, as in Goodliffe, Gotobed.

-god, -got. Modern variants : -cott, -gett, -good, as in Hargood.

Gold-. O.E. *gold* n. " gold ". Modern variants : Gould-, as in Gouldman.

Good-. *See* God-.

-got. *See* -god.

Gould-. *See* Gold-.

Grim-, -grim. O.E. *grimm*
" fierce ", " painful ".

Gum-. O.E. *guma* m. " hero ".

Gun-. O.N. *gunnr* f. " war ".

Gut-, Guth-. O.E. *gúð* f. " battle ",
" war ".

-gyth. O.E. *guð.* Modern variant :
-ith, as in Aldith. *See also* -yth.

Had-, Heathu-, O.E. *heaðu*
" war ".

Half-. *See* Healf-.

Har-. *See* Here-.

Hard-. *See* Heard-.

Heah-, He-, -heah. O.E. *héah*
" exalted ", " proud ".

Healf-, Half-. O.E. *healf* " half ".

Heard-, Hard-, Hear-. O.E.
heard " severe ", " violent ".

-heard, -ard, -art, -heart. Modern
variants : -ad, -ard, -att, -et,
-ett, -itt, as Garrard. Possibly
-od, as in Garrod.

Heathu-. *See* Had-.

-helm. *See* -elm.

Her-, Here-. O.E. *here* m.
" army ". Modern variant :
Har-, as in Harbard.

-here, -er. Modern variants :
-ear, -ger, -ier, -year, -yer, as in
Goodier.

Herle-. Modern variant : Hurl-,
as in Hurlin.

Hib-, Hig-. *See* Hyge-.

Hil-. *See* Hilde-.

Hilde-. O.E. *hild* f. " battle ".
Modern variants : Hil-, Il-, as
in Hilbert, Ilger.

-hild. Modern variants : -ell,
-ild, as in Quennell (i.e. Cwen-
hild).

Horse-, Hos-, Hose-. *See* Os-.

Hroth-, Rod-. O.N. *hróðr* m.
" praise ". Modern variant :
Ro-, as in Robert.

Hum-. *See* Hun-.

Hun-. O.N. *húnn* m. " bear-cub ".
Modern variant : Hum-, as in
Humbert.

-hun. Modern variant : -in, as in
Swithin.

Hurl-. *See* Herle-.

Hwæt-, What-. O.E. *hwæt*
" brave ".

Hyge-. O.E. *hyge* m. " courage ".
Modern variants : Hig-, Hi-,
as in Hi(b)berd.

Hyse-. O.E. *hyse* " youth ",
" warrior ".

-ic. *See* -wig.

-ier. *See* -here.

-iff, -iffe. *See* -gifu.

Il-. *See* Hilde-.

-ild. *See* -hild.

-ill. *See* -weald.

-in. *See* -hun, -wine.

-ing. *See* -wine ; *also* above, p. 57.

Ing-, Ingel-. *See* Engel-.

-ith. *See* -gyth.

-itt. *See* -heard.

Jar-. *See* Gær-.

-kel. *See* -chel.

Ken-. *See* Cen-.

-ker. *See* -gær, ger.

Ketel-. *See* Cetel-.

-kill. *See* -chel.

Kim-, Kine-, Kin-. *See* Cen-.

-lac. O.E. *lac* " play ", " strife ".
Modern variants : -lake, -lock,
-luck, as in Goodlake.

Lam-. *See* Land-.

Land-, Lan-, Lant-. O.E. *land* n.
" earth ", " territory ". Modern
variant : Lam-, as in Lambert.

Le-. *See* Leod-, Leof-.

-le. *See* -wulf.

Leaf-, Lef-. *See* Leof-.

Led-. *See* Leod-.

Lef-, Lem-. *See* Leof.

**Leod-, Le-, Led-, Let-, Lud-,
Lute-.** O.E. *leod* m. " man ",
" prince ". Modern variants :
Le-, Led-, as in Ledger.

**Leof-, Leaf-, Lef-, Lem-, Leve-,
Low-, Lyf-.** Leom-, as in
Leommær. O.E. *leof* " be-
loved ", " dear ". Modern
variants : Le-, Leve-, Liv-,
Lu-, as in Leman, Leverick,
Living, Lugar.

-leof. Modern variant : -liffe, as in
Goodliffe.

Leom-. *See* Leof-.

Let-. *See* Leod-.

Leve-. *See* Leof-.

-liffe. *See* -leof.

Liv-. *See* Leof-.

-lock. *See* -lac.

Love-. *See* Lufu-.

Low-. *See* Leof-.

-luck. *See* -lac.

Lud-, Lute-. *See* Leod-.

Lufu. O.E. *lufu* " love ". Modern variant : Love-, as in Loveridge.

Mæg-. O.E. *mæg* m. " kinsman ". Modern variant : Mey-, as in Meyrick.

Mæegen-, Main-, Mayn-. O.E. *mægen* n. " might ".

Mær-, Mer-. O.E. *mære* " famous ".

-mær. Modern variants : -mer, -mire, -more, as in Willmer, Brightmore.

Main-. *See* Mægen-.

Man-. O.E. *mann* m. " hero ".

-man, -mon. Often confused with -mund.

Mayn-. *See* Mægen-.

Mer-. *See* Mær-.

-mer. *See* -mær.

Mey-. *See* Mæg-.

-mire. *See* -mær.

Mod-. O.E. *mód* n. " heart ", " pride ".

Mon-. O.E. *móna* m. " moon ".

-mon. *See* -man.

-mont. *See* -mund.

-more. *See* -mær.

-mund. O.E. *mund* f. " trust ", " protection ". Modern variants : -man, -ment, -mond, -mont, as in Gorman, Garment, Fremont.

-net, -nett. *See* -noth.

Noth-, Not-. O.E. *nóð* " daring ", " plunder ".

-noth. Modern variants : -net, -nett, -nitt, -not, -nott, -nough, -nutt, as in Sennett, Woolnough.

-nott. *See* -noth.

-nough. *See* -noth.

-nutt. *See* -noth.

O-. *See* An-.

Od-. *See* Ot-.

-od. *See* -heard, old.

-offe. *See* -wulf.

-old. *See* -weald. Possible modern variant : od, as in Harrod.

-olf, -olfe. *See* -wulf.

On-. *See* An-.

-on. *See* -wine.

Or-. *See* Ord-.

Ord-. O.E. *ord* m. " spear ", " chief ". Modern variant : Or-, as in Orgar.

-ord. *See* -weard.

Os-. *See* Ans-, As-.

Ot-, Od-, Oth-. *See also* Ead-.

Ought-, Out-. *See* Wiht-.

-phrey. *See* -frith.

Quen-. *See* Cen-.

Ræd-, Rad-, Read-. O.E. *ræd* m. " counsel ", " benefit ".

-ræd, -red. Modern variants : -rat, -red, -ret, -rett, as in Syratt, Sirett.

Rand-. O.E. *rand* m. " shield ".

Rain-, Rayn-, Regen-, Rein-, Ren-. O.E. *regen* " mighty ". Modern variant : Rey-, as in Reynold.

-redge. *See* -ric.

Regen-. *See* Rain-.

Rein-, Ren-, Rey-. *See* Rain-.

Read-. *See* Ræd-.

Ric-. O.E. *ríca* m. " ruler ", *ríce* n. " might ", *ríce* " mighty ".

-ric. Modern variants : -redge, -rich, -ridge, -rige, -right, -ry, -rych, as in Eldridge, Goodrick.

-rich, -ridge. *See* -ric.

-rige, -right. *See* -ric.

Ro-, Rod-. *See* Hroth-.

Rum-. O.E. *rúm* " liberal ", " august ".

-ry, -rych. *See* -ric.

Sæ-, Sa-, Se-. O.E. *sǽ* m.f. " sea ", " lake ". Modern variants : Sea-, Se-, See-, as Seaman. *See also* Sige-.

Sas-, Sax-. *See* Seax-.

Sceaft-. O.E. *sceaft* m. " spearshaft ".

Se-, Sea-. *See* Sæ-.

Seax-, Sas-, Sax-, Sex-. O.E. *seax* n. " knife ".

Sed-. *See* Side-.

Sele-. O.E. *sele* m. " dwelling ".

Sex-. *See* Seax-.

-sey. *See* -sige.

Si-. *See* Sige-.

Side-, Sed-. O.E. *síd* " vast ".

Sige-, Si-, Sieg-. O.E. *sige* m. " victory ". Modern variants : Sie-, Sy-, as in Siebert, Syer.

-sige, -xi. Modern variants : -sey, -xey, as in Brixey, Wolsey.

Snæ-, Snow-. O.E. *snáw* " snow ".

Sort-. *See* Swar-.

Stain-. *See* Stegen-.

Stan-. O.E. *stán* m. " stone ", " rock ".

-stan, -ston, as in Thurston.

Stegen-, Stain-, Stein-, Sten-. O.N. *steinn* m. " stone ", " rock ".

Stir-, Styr-. O.E. *stéor* f. " guidance ", m. " steer ". Modern variant : Stur-, as in Sturman.

-ston. *See* -stan.

Stur-. *See* Stir-.

Styr-. *See* Stir-.

Sun-. O.E. *sunu* m. " son ". (Forssner thinks this word to be from a Continental etymon.)

Swar-, Sweart-, Sort-. O.E. *sweart* " swarthy ".

Sweat-. *See* Swet.

Swet-. O.E. *swéte* " agreeable ". Modern variants : Sweat-, Sweet-, as in Sweatman, Sweeting.

Swith-, -swith. O.E. *swíð* " strong ", " violent ".

Sy-. *See* Sige-.

Te-, Ted-. *See* Theod-.

Theod-, Te-, Ted-. O.E. *ðéod* f. " nation ", " tribe ".

-thegn. O.E. *ðegn* m. " retainer ", " thegn ".

Thir-. *See* Thor-.

Thor-, Dur-, Thur-, Tor-, Tur-, Ture-. The name of a god. Modern variants : Thir-, Too-, Tow-, Thoro-, Thorough-,

Thorow-, as in Toogood, Thoroughgood.

Thryth-. O.E. *ðrýð* f. " power ", " splendour ".

-thryth, -drud.

Thur-. *See* Thor-.

Tid-. O.E. *tíd* f. " time ", " season ".

Til-. O.E. *til* " good ", " brave ".

Too-, Tor-. *See* Thor-.

Torht-, Tyrht-. O.E. *torht* n. " brightness " : adj. " bright ", " beautiful ".

Tow-. *See* Thor-.

Trum-. O.E. *trum* " secure ", " active ".

Tun-, Dun-. O.E. *tún* " garden ", " dwelling ", " mansion ". *See also* Dun-.

Tur-, Ture-. *See* Thor-.

Tyrht-. *See* Torht-.

Ul-, Ulf-. *See* Wulf-.

-ulf. *See* -wulf.

Un-. *See* An-.

Url-. *See* Eorl-.

-ven, -vene, -vin, -vine. *See* -wine.

Vict-, Vit-. *See* Wiht-.

Wær-, War-, Wer-. O.E. *wǽr* " true ".

Wald-, Walt-. *See* Weald-.

-wall. *See* -weald.

War-. *See* Wær-.

-ward. *See* -weard.

Waren-. *See* Wern-.

-way. *See* -wig.

Weald-, Wald-, Walt-. O.E. *weald* n. " power ", " dominion ".

-weald. Modern variants, -ald, -all, -alt, -el, -ell, -ill, -old, -wald, -wall, as in Ingall, Sewalt, Tur(r)ill, Thorold.

-weard, -ard, -ord. O.E. *weard* f.m. " protection ", " guardian ". Modern variants : -art, -ward.

Wen-, -wen. O.E. *wén* " hope ", " opinion ".

Wer-. *See* Wær-.

Wern-, Waren-. O.E. f. *wearn* " refusal ".

Wet-, With-. *See* Wiht-.

What-. *See* Hwæt-.

Whis-, Wis-. *See* Wis-, Wulf-.

Whit-. *See* Wiht-.

Why-. *See* Wiht-.

Wi-. *See* Wig-.

-wi. *See* -wig.

Wic-. *See* Wiht-.

-wich. *See* -wig.

Wick-. *See* Wig-.

-wick. *See* -wig.

Wid-. O.E. *wid* " vast ". *See also* Wiht-.

Wig-, Wi-. O.E. *wig* n. " battle ", " strife ". Modern variants : Wick-, Wy-, as in Wyman.

-wig, -wich, -wi, -ic. Modern variants : -way, -wick, as Ordway.

Wight-. *See* Wiht-.

Wiht-, Vict-, Vit-, Wet-, Weth-, Whit-, Wic-, Wid-, Wit-, With-. O.E. *wiht* f.n. " wight ", " person ", " creature". Modern variants : Ought-, Out-, Why-, Wight-, as Oughtred, Whybrow, Wightman.

Wil-, Willa-. O.E. *willa* m. " determination ".

Wine-, Wyn-. O.E. *wine* m. " friend ", " protector ".

-wine, -in. Modern variants : -en, -in, -ing, -on, -ven, -vin, -vine, -win, -wyn, as in Godden, Dering, Selwyn, Wolven, Unwin.

Wis-, Whis-. O.E. *wis* " wise ". *See also* Wulf-.

Wit-. O.E. *wita* m. " sage ". *See also* Wiht-.

Wulf-, Ul-, Ulf-. O.E. *wulf* m. " wolf ". Modern variants : Ul-, Whis-, Wis-, Wolf-, Woolf-, Wool-, Wul-, as Ulmer, Whiston, Woolward, Wulstan.

-wulf, -ulf. Modern variants : -affe, -offe, -olf, -olfe, -le, -all, -ell, as Randle.

Wy-. *See* Wig-.

Wyn-. *See* Wine-.

-wyn. *See* -wine.

-xey, -xi. *See* -sige.

-yard. *See* -geard.

-yat. *See* -geat.

-yth, -gyth. O.E. *yð* f. " wave ", " billow ". *See also* -gyth.

Derivation of Local Surnames. It is not proposed to outline any method of inquiry into the etymology of place-names—a very extensive and perplexing subject on which a number of excellent books have already appeared, to which the reader may refer for authoritative information.[1]   In determining the signification of a surname derived from a place-name, not only are early forms of the place-name required, but it is necessary to know the county, since the signification may vary in different districts, and, moreover, the nature of the topographical features should be recognized, otherwise bad blunders will occur. As has been illustrated (pp. 237–43), many surnames of the local class carry a note of distinction, which advertises their county of origin ; others, again, are common to all parts of the country.

Local surnames consist mainly of O.E., O.N., Corn., and Gael. words, uncompounded and compounded. For

---

[1] About twenty-five English counties have been dealt with, and there are also a dozen volumes on Welsh, Manx, Scottish, and Irish place-names. Bibliographies are to be found in English Place-name Society (1924), vol. i ; and *The Place-Names of Cumberland and Westmorland*, by W. J. Sedgefield, 1915, etc.

significations of single-element names reference may be made to pp. 233-4. A compound local surname consists of a topographical feature plus a personal name, as Nanjulian (Corn. " the valley of Julian "); plus a trade, as Trengoff (Corn. " the dwelling of the smith "); plus an adjective, as Braithwaite (O.N. *breiðr* " broad ", *thwaite* " clearing "), Stroyan (Gael. *sruth* " a stream ", *an* " little "); plus a preposition, as Surtees (on the Tees); or plus another topographical feature, as Eskdale (Gael. *uisg* " water "), Calder (Gael. *coille* " wood ", *dar* " oak "). As a partial aid to identification of local surnames of both *a* and *b* types, lists of the principal elements have been prepared.

English First-Elements of Local Surnames

Able-, Apple-, as in Applethwaite.

Ac-, Ack-, Ake-, Ec-, Oak-, Ock-, as in Ackroyd, Oakford.

Ains-, Ais-, As-, Ays-, as in Aiskew.

Aiken-, Aken-, as in Akenside.

Ampt-, Ant-, as in Ampthill.

Apple-. *See* Able-.

As-, Asse-, Ash-, Ays-, Aysh-, as in Ashford.

Balm-, Bam-, Ban-, as in Bamford.

Barc-, Berk-, as in Berkeley.

Bard-, Beard-, as in Bardesly.

Baw-, Broad-, Brod-, as in Bawdrip.

Bea-, Beau-, Bee-, as in Beauchamp.

Blank-, Blenk-, Blink-, as in Blenkharne.

Brad-, Broad-, as in Bradenstoke.

Bram-, Broom-, as in Bramhall.

Broad-. *See* Baw-.

Brock-, Brook-, Bruck-, as in Brookhouse.

Brom-, Broom-, Brum-, as in Broomhead.

Brot-, Brow-, Brude-, Bryk-, as in Brudenell.

Buck-, Bug-, as in Buckby.

Bucks-, Bux-, as in Buxton.

Cal-, Cald-, Call-, Caul-, Caw-, as in Caldecote.

Cal-, Col-, Coul-, as in Calthorpe.

Camber-, Comber-, Cumber-, as in Cumberpatch.

Cap-, Cope-, Coup-, Cowp-, as in Copeland.

Cars-, Kers-, as in Carswell.

Cholm-, Chum-, as in Cholmondeley.

Col-, Cold-, Cole-, Coul-, as in Coleridge.

Cope-. *See* Cap-.

Craigh-, Creigh-, Crich-, Crigh-, as in Creighton.

Cran-, Crank-, Cron-, Cronk-, Crown-, as in Crankshaw.

Dawd-, Dodd-, Dott-, Dudd-, Dutt-, as in Dodridge.

Dead-, Deb-, Deben-, Ded-, as in Debnam.

Dom-, Dum-, as in Dumble.

Ec-. *See* Ac-.

Gran-, Green-, Grene-, as in Greenhaugh.

Ha-, Hade-, Hard-, Hatt-, Hede-, as in Hatcliffe.

Halde-, Hol-, Hold-, Hould-, How-, as in Holdgate.

Hale-, Halli-, Hole-, Holli-, as in Holliwell.

Halgh-, Haugh-, Hough-, How-, as in Houghton.

Harra-, Harri-, Harrow-, Horo-, as in Harrowden.

Heg-, Heigh-, Hey-, Hig-, as in Higham.

Hing-, Hink-, as in Hingston.

Hoad-, Hoath-, Hode-, as in Hoathley.

Ingar-, Inger-, Inker-, as in Ingersoll.

Kel-, Kil-, as in Kelsall.

Kep-, Kip-, as in Kipling.

Ker-, Kerk-, Kir-, Kirk-, Kyr-, as in Kirby.

Kers-. See Cars-.

Knap-, Nap-, as in Knapton.

La-, Lo-, Low-, as in Lowthrop.

Lad-, Lath-, as in Lathbury.

Lan-, Lang-, Lank-, Long-, as in Langham.

Lat-, Layt-, Leat-, Leet-, Let-, as in Lathom.

Lead-, Leath-, as in Leathley.

Leche-, Lich-, Lick-, Litch-, Lych-, as in Lichfield.

Londes-, Lons-, Louns-, Lownds-, Lowns-, as in Londesborough.

Loose-, Lose-, Lux-, Luz-, as in Luxmore.

Mell-, Mill-, Milne-, Myln-, as in Milnethorpe.

Mock-, Mog-, Mugge-, as in Mockridge.

Muckle-, Mucle-, Mugle-, Mugli-, as in Mugleston.

Nap-. See Knap-.

Nor-, North-, as in Northcote.

Oak-. See Ac-.

Of-, Ox-, Oxen-, as in Oxford.

Pack-, Packing-, Pag-, Paken-, as in Pakenham.

Peck-, Penk-, Pick-, Ping-, Pink-, Pix-, as in Pinkstone.

Quen-, Quim-, Quin-, Quyn-, as in Quinby.

Raws-, Ros-, Rous-, Rows-, as in Rawsthorne.

Rook-, Rout-, Ruck-, Rut-, as in Routledge.

Ro-, Row-, as in Rowbottom.

Road-, Rood-, Royd-, as in Roadhouse.

Raw-, Ri-, Row-, Roy-, Ry-, Rye-, Wry-, as in Rycroft.

Scud-, Skid-, as in Scudamore.

Sedg-, Sidg-, Sige-, as in Sedgwick.

Sprad-, Sprot-, as in Spradbery.

Star-, Ster-, as in Steresaker.

Thore-, Thur-, as in Thursby.

Tem-, Tim-, as in Timperley.

Talk-, Tork-, Turk-, as in Talkington.

Tar-, Tire-, as in Tarbock.

Toot-, Tot-, Tout-, Tut-, as in Tootle.

Wan-, Wande-, Warne-, as in Warneford.

Wedde-, Widde-, Withi-, as in Withycomb.

Wry-. See Raw-.

English Second-elements of Local Surnames

-acre, -aker, -iker, as in Hardiker.

-age. See -wich.

-aker. See -acre.

-al, -all. See -hall, -hill.

-am. See -ham.

-ard. See -yard.

-back, -beck, as in Killingback.

-bage. See -brick.

-batham. See -bottom.

-bear. O.E. bær " pasture ".

-beck. See -back.

-bee. See -by.

-bekin. See biggin.

-bell. See -ville.

-bergh. See -borough.

-bern. See -bone.

-berry. See -borough.

-bey. See -by.

-bidge. See -bridge.

-biggin, -bekin " building ", as in Dowbekin.

-bill, -ble. See -ville.

-bly. See -ley.

-bone, -bern, -born, -borne, -bound, -bourn, -bourne, -bown, -bowne, -bun, -bunn, -burn, as in Goldborn, Labern, Lightbown, Honeybone.

-borough, -bergh, -berry, -bery, -borow, -borrow, -bro, -broe, -brough, -brow, -burgh, -bury, " fortified place " as Goldsbrough, Hambro, Harbroe, Holberry, Oxbrow, Hembergh, etc.

-bottom, -batham, -botam, -botham, as in Higgenbotam, Rubbatham.

-bound, -bourn, -bown. *See* -bone.

-brick, -bage, -bidge, -bridge, -brigg, -brook, as in Fellbrigg, Harbage, Philbrook.

-bro, -broe, -brough, -brow. *See* -borough.

-brook. *See* -brick.

-bun, -bunn, as Honeybun.

-burgh, -bury. *See* -borough.

-burn. *See* -born.

-caster, -chester.

-cliff, -leaf, -liff, as in Gatcliff, Greenleaf, Topliff.

-cloth, -clough, as in Fairclough.

-coat, -cock, -cot, -cote, as in Heathcoat.

-com, -comb, -combe, -come, as in Hanscome.

-cot, -cote. *See* -coat.

-craft, -croft, as in Horscroft.

-dale, -dal, -dall, -del, -dell, -dill, -dle, -do, -dow, as in Dugdill, Kendle, Lansdell, Tindall, Lindo.

-dan. *See* -don.

-day. *See* -gay.

-den, -dence, -dine, as in Harradence, Shelmerdine. *See also* -don.

-dick. *See* -dyke.

-dill. *See* -dale.

-dine. *See* -den.

-ditch. *See* -dyke.

-dle. *See* -dale.

-do. *See* -dale.

-don, -dan, -den, as in Haydon. *See also* -den.

-dow. *See* -dale.

-dyke, -dick, -ditch, -tick, as in Hildick, Frostick.

-eard. *See* -yard.

-el, -ell. *See* -hall, -hill.

-en, -ens, -ing, -ings, -ins, as in Giddens.

-er, as in Docker.

-ern O.E. *ǽrn* " house ", as in Brewerne.

-et, -ett. *See* -head.

-ey, -ie, as Okie, i.e. " oak island ".

-field, -fill, -fitt, -fold, -fould, -full, as Ifold, Duffill, Oakenfull.

-fold. *See* -field.

-ford, -fork, -forth, -fitt, as Rumfitt, Pitchfork, Radforth.

-fould. *See* -field.

-fract, -fret, -fritt, -phrett, as in Pomfret.

-full. *See* -field.

-gast, -gest, -ghest, -grass, -grast, as in Prendergast.

-gat, -gate, -gatt, -get, -gett, -gitt, -gott, -iate, -iatt, as in Leggatt, Lipyeatt, Hardgitt.

-gay, -day, -ger, -jay, as in Goldingay.

-gest. *See* -gast.

-gett. *See* -gate.

-ghest. *See* -gast.

-gitt. *See* -gate.

-gott. *See* -gate.

-grass, -grast. *See* -gast.

-grave, -graves, -greave, -greaves, -greves, -grove, -groves.

-halgh, -haugh, -haulgh, -hough, -how, -ock, -ough, -ow, -up, as Greenhalgh, Eatock, Hindhough.

-hall, -all, -ell, as in Foxall.

-ham, -am, -hem, -man, -nam, -num, -om, -um, i.e. " farm ", as in Todman, Haysom, Lakeman, Fortnum, Foulsom.

-haugh, -haulgh. *See* -halgh.

-head, -et, -ett, -itt, as Hazlitt, Blackett.

-hearn, -hearne, -hern, -herne, -hurn, -hurne.

-hill, -al, -all, -el, -ell, -ill, -le, as in Windel, Tootill, Hartle.

-hold, -hott, as in Sparshott.

-hope, -up, i.e. " valley ", as in Kirkup.

-hough. *See* -halgh.

-house, -us, as in Kirkus.

-hurn. *See* -hearn.

-iard. *See* -yard.

-iate, -iatt. *See* -gate.

-ie. *See* -ey.

-iker. *See* -acre.

-ing, -ings, -ins. *See* -en.

-itt. *See* -head.

-jay. *See* -gay.

-lache, -lake, -lich. *See* -leach.

-law, -ly, as in Osmotherly.

-leach, -lache, -lake, -ledge, -lich, "sluggish stream," as in Depledge, Illedge.

-leaf. *See* -cliff.

-ledge. *See* -leach.

-ley, -bly, -ly, as in Emely, Hambly.

-lich. *See* -lache.

-liff. *See* -cliff.

-ly. *See* -law, -ley.

-man, -ming, as in Godalming, Godliman. *See also* -ham.

-master. *See* -minster.

-mead, -meat, as in Hardmeat.

-mer. *See* -mire.

-mere. *See* -moor.

-ming. *See* -man.

-minster, -master, as in Kitter-master.

-mire, -mer, as in Dormer.

-moor, -mere, -more, as in Elles-mere.

-nam, -num. *See* -ham.

-ock. *See* -halgh.

-om. *See* -ham.

-ombe, -ome. *See* -holme.

-ough, -ow. *See* -halgh.

-rake. *See* -ridge.

-ridge, -rake, -reet, -rick, -rigg, -rish, -ritt, -wich, as in Escreet, Hollingdrake, Horwich, Lang-rish.

-rod, -royd, as in Murgatroyd.

-sale, -sall, -saul. *See* -sole.

-sell, -sey. *See* -shaw.

-shall. *See* -shaw, -sole.

-shaw, -sell, -sey, -shall, -shar, -sher, -shier, -shire, -show, -sow, as in Hensher, Kershaw, Orm-shire. Often confused with -shire and variants.

-sole, -sal, -sale, -sall, -saul, -sell, -shall, -soll, as in Ingersoll, Shrubshall.

-son. *See* -stone.

-sow. *See* -shaw.

-stone, -son, -ston, -ton (after x), as in Pixton, Hinkson.

-strath, -streeth, -streth, -stroth, -strothe, as in Langstroth.

-ten. *See* -ton.

-thorpe, -fripp, -thripp, -throp, -thrope, -thrupp, -trip, -trippe, -trup, as in Feltrup, Guntrip.

-tick. *See* -dyke.

-ton, -ten, as in Wooten.

-tree, -trey, -try, as in Goostree, Langtry.

-twisle, -twistle, "a fork," as in Entwistle.

-um. *See* -ham.

-up. *See* -hope, -halgh.

-us. *See* -house.

-ville, -bell, -bill, -ble, as in Dumbell.

-wall, -well, as in Etwall.

-wich, -age, "a dwelling place," as in Dunnage, Bromage.

-yard, -ard, -eard, -iard, as in Hillard.

Scandinavian Elements of Local Surnames

These components are often indistinguishable from O.E. cognates.

-am. *See* -holm.

Askr-, "ash tree," as in Askham.

-batch, -beck, as in Cumberpatch, Holbeck.

-bee. *See* -by.

Big-, "barley," as in Biggar, Bigland.

-by, -bee, -bey, -bie, "a home-stead farm," as in Ferrabee, Frisbie, Manbee.

-cliff, *kleif* "steep hill side", as in Tunnicliff.

-dale, -dal, -dall, as in Kendal, Tyndall.

Eng-, " pasture," as in Engeland.

-ey, -y, " an island," as in Forty

-fell, " a hill."

-fors, " a waterfall," as in Wilber-force.

-garth, -gate, " a yard," " en-closure," as in Applegate, Lingard.

-gill, -gal, -kell, -kill, " a ravine," as in Gaskell, Havergal, Pickers-gill, Scargill.

Haver-, *hafri* " oats ", as in Havergill.

-holm, -am, -om, -ombe, -ome, -um, " an island," as Escombe.

-keld, " a spring," as in Threlkeld.

Knip-, " a hill," as Knipe.

Mire-, Myre-, " swamp," as in Myerscough.

-ness, " a nose," " point," as in Holderness.

-om, -ombe. *See* -holm.

-patch. *See* -batch.

-ra, -rah, -ray, -ry, -wra, -wray, " a nook," as in Thackeray, Docwra.

-scough, *skógr* " wood ", as in Ayscough.

Sef-, " sedge," as in Sefton.

Sower-, *saurr* " swampy ", as in Sowerby.

-staff, *staðr*, as in Bickerstaff, Wagstaff.

-thwaite, -thart, -thert, -thett, -thirt, -white, " a clearing," as in Dowthert, Smithett, Possel-white.

-toft, " a messuage."

-um. *See* -holm.

Wick-, " a village," as in Wickham.

-wang, *vangr* " a field ", as in Wetwang.

-white. *See* -thwaite.

-wra, -wray. *See* -ra.

-y. *See* -ey.

The utility of the above three lists may be exemplified by such surnames as Rawsthorne, Tirebuck, Pitchfork, and Oxenberry, which, although they have the appearance of being of local origin, cannot be found in the gazeteer or atlas. The first-elements, Raws- and Tire-, give among other variants Ros- and Tar-, which are clues pointing to Rostherne and Tarbock. Variants of the second-elements, -fork and -berry, and of the first-elements, Pitch- and Oxen-, lead to the discovery of Pickford and Oxborough. If there be reason to suppose that the name is derived from a locality in the more Celtic districts, the following Welsh, Cornish, and Gaelic lists may be used in similar manner.

Cornish and Welsh Elements of Local Surnames [1]

There are few local surnames from Wales (see p. 241), but a number of English and Scottish surnames are derived from place-names in the native British language, such as Abernethy (*aber* " mouth of a river "), Berwick (*aber*), Carstairs (*caer* " a fortress "), Cumnock (*cam* " crooked "), Darwen (*dwr* " water "). Pennant may be either Welsh or Cornish, and the majority of Celtic local surnames in England will be found to be of Cornish origin, the following list of common elements providing a means of identification :—

[1] Compiled from the works of Bannister, Charnock, Dexter, Jago, Jenner, and Williams.

-ack. *See* -ick.

-ar. *See* -war.

-ard, -arth, -varth, -warth, -worth, "high," as in Boswartha, Penarth, Pinard, Trevarthan.

bal, m. "a mine", as in Balhatchet, Carnbal.

ban, van, vadna, m. "hill", "mountain": adj. "high", as in Bandry, Ludgvan.

Bar-, Bor-, Bur-, m. "summit", as in Borden, Burgan.

-bean. *See* -wigan.

-bedh, -beth, -veth, m. "a grave", as in Boveth, Carveth, Penbetha.

ben, pedn. *See* pen.

-ber, -ver, "short," as in Creber.

Bes-, Bis-. *See* Bo-.

bidhin, bidn. *See* vethan.

-biggan, -bighan. *See* -wigan.

bin. *See* pen.

Bo-, Bes-, Bis-, Bod-, Bos-, Bot-, Bus-, Vos-, m. "a house", as in Beswarick, Biscoe, Bodcarne, Bodily, Boggis, Bordinner, Boscastle, Buscumbe, Vosper.

Bol-. *See* Pol-.

Bor-. *See* Bar-.

Bos-, Bot-. *See* Bo-.

Bran-. *See* Bron-.

bray, f. "hill", as in Bramer, Penbery.

-briggan, -brigh. *See* -wigan.

Bron-, Bran-, Bry-, Bryn, f. "hill", as in Brandon, Breen, Brydon.

Bur-. *See* Bar-.

Bus-. *See* Bo-.

Cam-, "crooked" (precedes the noun).

Car-, Kar-, Ker-, f. "rock", as in Carbis, Carthew. Dexter gives *car* "a camp".

carn, kearne, m. "a heap of rocks", as in Carne, Carnedon, Kernick, Polkearne.

Chy-. *See* Ty-.

coit, cois, coos, côs, cosse, coys, cus, god, goed, gosse, gûs, kûs, quite, quoit, m. "a wood", as in Cause, Coad, Coote, Cuss,

Goate, Good, Goose, Goss, Pencoose, Quitman, Tregoz.

com, combe. *See* cûm.

creeg, m.f. "tumulus", as in Boscreege, Cregan.

crows, f. "a cross", as in Biscow, Croggon, Crowe, Glencross.

cûm, com, combe, m. "valley", as in Comfort, Kimber.

cus. *See* coit.

De-. *See* Ty-.

-den. f. "hill", as in Pende(e)n.

deu, sew, sue, zeu, "black," as in Dewick, Carnsew, Barsue.

Din-, Dun-, m.f. "hill-fort".

Dour-, Dor-, m. "water", as in Dowrick.

dra, dre. *See* tra.

dron. *See* trevan.

er. *See* war.

fellen. *See* melan.

fenton, venton, f. "a spring", as in Penventon.

for, ford, forth, vor, f. "a way", "ford", as in Langford.

fra, fre. *See* tre.

gelly, gilly. *See* kil.

god, goed. *See* coit.

gon. *See* gûm.

gor. *See* war.

gosse. *See* coit.

gûm, gun, gon, wôn, f. "a down", as in Boconnock, Bodgun, Boggan, Gummow.

gûs. *See* coit.

Gwy-, Gy-. *See* Vy-.

gwyn, gwen, gwydn, wen, widn, win, "white," as in Gwennap, Polwin, Tredwen, Winter, Chirgwin.

hâl, hale, m.f. "moor", "marsh", as in Chynhale, Hallimore.

Hen-, "old" (precedes the noun), as in Hendin, Henwood.

-ick, -ack, "a place," as in Killick, Bodenick.

Kar-, Ker-. *See* Car-.

kearne. *See* carn.

kil, gelly, gilly, kelli, kill, killy, f. "grove", as in Bokelly, Kellock.

kûs. *See* coit.

Ky-. *See* Ty-.

Lan-, f. " an enclosure ", " church ", as in Lambron, Landew.

Lyn, m. " pool ", " pond ".

maen, mên, min, pl. vyin, " a stone," as in Hellman, Mainprice, Meanwell.

maes, meas, mes, meys, mez, vease, vês, m. " meadow ", as in Blamey.

mat, maz, vat, vaz, " good."

meaddan. *See* vethan.

mear, meer, mêr, mor, veor, vor, " great," as in Dormer, Kevear.

melan, fellen, melen, mellan, vellan, vellen, f. " mill," as in Fellenoweth, Lamelin, Melladew, Millan, Trevellance, Vellenzer.

mor. *See* mear.

nan, nance, nans, nant, m. " valley ", as in Nanscuke, Nankivel, Pennant.

park, m. " field ".

pen, bedn, ben, bin, fedn, pedn, m. " a head ", " hill ", as in Bospidnick, Dolben, Penarth.

Pol-, Bol-, m. " pool ", as in Bolland, Pollard.

porth, m. " creek ", as in Polporth.

quite, quoit. *See* coit.

re, rem, ren. *See* tre.

res, rôs, rose, f. " valley ", " heath ", as in Rose, Rosecregg.

sew, sue. *See* deu.

tra, dra, dre, fra, fre, re, rem, ren, tre, tref, treg, trem, tren, trev, trig, trin, f. " town ",

" dwelling ", as in Dreadon, Landrey.

trevan, trewyn, dron, tron, truin, m. " promontory ", " headland ", as in Madron.

Ty-, Chy-, De-, Ky-, Te-, m. " house ", as in Chinoweth, Kyvere, Tice, Tyers.

vadna, van. *See* ban.

var. *See* war.

varth. *See* ard.

vat, vaz. *See* mat.

-vean. *See* -wigan.

vellan. *See* melan.

venton. *See* fenton.

veor, vor. *See* mear.

-ver. *See* -ber, war.

-veth. *See* -bedh.

vethan, bidhin, bidn, meaddan, vidhin, vidn, vythyn, m. " meadow ", as Biddick, Trevethan.

Vos-. *See* Bo-.

Vy-, Gwy-, Gy-, Wy-, m. " river ".

vyin. *See* maen.

-war, -ar, -er, -gor, -var, -ver, -vor, -wor, " about," " upon," as in Penver.

-warth. *See* -ard.

well, " high," " lower " (Charnock).

Wheal, Whêl, " a work," as in Weale, Wheal, Wheel.

widn, win. *See* gwyn.

-wigan, -bean, -biggan, -bighan, -briggan, -brigh, -vean, " little," as in Brabyn (bray-bighan).

won. *See* gûm.

-wor. *See* -war.

Wy-. *See* Vy-.

zeu. *See* deu.

Generally speaking, the first-element of a Cornish surname is a noun, the adjective, as in Welsh, being placed second, but the latter occasionally takes precedence of the word it qualifies, as Henty. An adjective following a feminine noun undergoes mutation of initial letter : *b* becomes *v*, *p* ; *c* (*k*) becomes *g*, *h* ; *d* becomes *th*, *j* (*dh*, *t* : Jenner) ; *f* becomes *v* ; *g* becomes *w*, *c*, *q*, *k*, or is omitted ; *m* becomes *v* ; *p* becomes *b*, *f* ; *t* becomes *d* (*j*, *th* : Jenner). Some words, marked m.f. in the above list, are of doubtful gender. The examples given include some mutated forms, together with some corruptions. Prepositions are *a* " of ", " from "; *der, dre* " by ", " through "; *ware, er* " on ", " upon "; *en, yn* " in "; *dres* " over ", " beyond "; the first three of which cause initial mutation of the following noun.

Gaelic Elements of Local Surnames

Ach-, Auch-, Auck-, *achadh* " field ", as in Affleck, Auchencloss.

Adder-, *eadar* " between ", as in Adderton.

-all, " cliff," as in Kinnoull.

Auchter-, Ochter-, *uachdar* " summit ", as in Auchterlonie.

Bal-, *baile* " craft ", " village ", as in Ballingall, Balharrie.

Cam-, " crooked," as in Cameron.

Cul-, Col-, Cow-, Kil-, *cùl* " back ", coille " wood ", as in Calder.

Dal-, Dol-, Dul-, *dail* " meadow ", as in Dalgaty, Dallachy, Dollar.

Dum-, Dun-, *dun* " hill ", " fortress ", as in Dunbar, Dunlop.

Eas-, " waterfall," as in Easdale.

Esk, *uisg* " water ", as in Eskdale.

Fin-, *fionn* " white ", as in Findlater.

Gar-, *garbh* " rough ", as in Garrioch.

Gart-, " enclosure," as in Garscadden, but not in Gartly.

Gill-. *See* Kil-.

Glas-, " grey," as in Glasgow, Glassford.

Kel-, Kil-, *coille* " wood ", as in Kelton.

Kil-, Gill-, *cill* " church ", as in Killin, Kilpatrick.

Kin-, *ceann* " head ", as in Kinloch, Kincaid, Kinnaird.

Kirk, " church," as in Kirkhope, but not in Kirkcaldy.

Knock-, *cnoc* " hill ", " knoll ".

Mal-, Meal-, Mil-, Mul-, *meall* " hill ", as in Malloch.

Men-, Mon-, " moss," as in Menteith, Montrose.

Mony-, *monadh* " moor ", " hill ", as in Moncrieff.

Mul-. *See* Mal.

Muir-, " moor," as in Muirhead.

Ochter-. *See* Auchter-.

Pit-, " field," as in Pitcairn, Pitkethly.

-ros, " a projection," as Culross, Kinross, Melrose.

Strath-, Stra-, *srath* " valley ", as in Strathearn.

Gaelic suffixes denoting " full of ", " abounding in ", are : -ach, -agh, -lach, -nach, -rach, -tach. Diminutive suffixes are : -an, -can, -een, -net, -oc, -og.

For the determination of the signification of surnames of the characteristic and occupational classes, recourse must be had to dictionaries and glossaries, after collecting and arranging chronologically with counties a good number of the earliest orthographic forms, as exemplified above for Shakespeare. It must always be remembered that the majority of surnames have several possible origins, and that local names were often derived from a number of different places, all of which may not have survived; moreover, characteristic and occupational names may now have a meaning the very antithesis of the signification of five or six centuries ago.

CHAPTER XV

LEGAL STATUS OF SURNAMES

Definitions. Law has been defined as "rules prescribed by authority for human action", and such rules are civil and ecclesiastic. Blackstone (1765) divided the civil law of England into statute (or written) law and common (or unwritten) law ; the latter rules being based on the established custom of the people, and " not set down in any written statute or ordinance, but depending on immemorial usage for their support ". To a certain extent the *lex non scripta* is a misnomer, because the judges who are responsible for expounding such law rely upon written reports and judicial decisions of previous cases, and " it is an established rule to abide by former precedents where the same points come again in litigation." The rigid adherence to the doctrine of precedent is not looked upon with entire satisfaction by the administrators of justice ; only recently a judge sitting in court has referred to " the appalling chaos of case law by which judges are governed " by decisions given in the sixteenth and seventeenth centuries ".[1] Maine (*Ancient Law*) observes that " the law is always more or less behind social necessities and social opinion, and the instrumentalities adopted for bringing it into harmony therewith are three, viz. legal fictions, equity, and legislation ".[2] The first expedient need not be discussed here ; the second, equity, is defined as " a system of law or a body of connected legal principles which have superseded or supplanted the common law on the ground of their intrinsic superiority", and by legislation is meant law by statute.

Ecclesiastical law, according to Richard Burn, is compounded of four main ingredients—civil, canon, common, and statute law ; the civil submits to the canon law, both of these to the common law, and all three to the statute law.[3]

Legal Authority. With the exception of recent enactments controlling aliens there are no statutes which regulate the gift, assumption, or change of either personal or family names in England or Wales ; and ecclesiastical canons only partially control the conferring of first names, not dealing with surnames at all. The bestowal of a " christian " name

---

[1] Mr. Justice MacCardie, *Sunday Times*, 1st June, 1930.
[2] 1906 edition, p. 29.
[3] *Ecclesiastical Law*, 1781, p. 1.

is a formal proceeding sanctioned by common usage from time out of mind ; and as has been thoroughly established in the above chapters, the adoption of a family name, on the contrary, never formal, was at first due to chance repetition of individual additions, which practice being found a social convenience, identifying not only individual, but also family, ultimately became a recognized custom common to all classes. Any right which a person may have to personal or family names must therefore be based either on common law precedents, if such written decisions exist, or on the customs of the people.

A few records of proceedings in legal courts are preserved for the end of the twelfth century; the Curia Regis Rolls date from 5 Ric. I (1194) and the Assize Rolls from the following reign ; the Court of Common Pleas sprang from the Curia Regis, 1 Edw. I (1272), from which date the records commence. Of enrolments of the Chancery may be mentioned, charters, letters patent, and letters close, all of which date from the reign of John (1199–1216). On the Close Rolls are to be found deeds poll relating to change of name. Very great research of public records would be necessary to determine when a secondary description or name became a distinction of such importance in identification of a litigant as to be first noticed by legal authority. Owing to the thorough exploitation of documentary evidences of the twelfth century, it is unlikely that any contemporary dictum on the designations and descriptions of litigants of that early period will now be discovered.

Assumption of Surnames. The earliest writer on English law (Ranulph de Glanville, 1187) [1] does not mention names or secondary descriptions or additions, but a peculiarity in his forms and precedents is, however, to be noticed ; in all cases the name of the person is represented by a single letter, with the exception that, in one form of final concord, the plaintiff is represented by " W.T., the son of Norman ". Probably this was a clerical redundancy, because in the twelfth century " W. the son of Norman " would have been sufficient particularization in the class of document exemplified. It may be inferred that second names were not considered by Norman lawyers to have had more value than an address or addition of the present day, and this view is in accord with the deductions of Chapters IV and V, to which reference may be made.

The thirteenth-century jurisprudents, Bracton and Britton, in their valuable compendiums, neither touch upon the bestowal of christian names nor the conferring of " surnames ", doubtless because the first was largely controlled by the ecclesiastical authorities, and the second, at that time, was

[1] J. Beames, 1812, p. 198.

not officially recognized as creating property, any more than taking up vocations and addresses do at the present time.

An exceptional acknowledgment of the hereditary nature of surnames is preserved in a Chancery inquisition of the year 1267. A writ had issued to the escheator in London to make inquiry concerning the house in Shrewsbury of one Roger " de Derby ", who had been executed for felony, and within four days a similar writ issued in respect of one Roger " de Cantebrig ". The jurors returned that " the said Roger called himself sometimes Roger ' de Cantebrigge ' and sometimes Roger ' de Derby ', so that he had two surnames, but in that he was the son of Nicholas ' de Cantebrigge ' his true name is Cantebrigge." [1] Generally speaking, however, the law looked on at the growing custom of using additional descriptions without attempt at regulation or legislation, such not being required ; and the public accepted the gradual innovation with as much complacency as they have the more modern and less necessary fashion of multiple christian and surnames.

The assumption of a surname varied in its degree of formality ; in general, in the first instance, it was nothing more than a passive acceptance of the neighbours' invention ; but it may have been the active selection of the bearer himself, or even compliance with the command of a higher authority. Such original assumption of a surname was sometimes followed by the assumption of a new name coupled with abandonment of the old, a process which is now commonly known as a " change of name ".

Various modern writers have endeavoured to establish the ancient existence of a royal right to control both the original assumption and also any subsequent change. The two cases have nothing in common ; the ancient assumption of a name was the result of not having a generally recognized appellative ; the modern reason for assumption, i.e. change, is to replace a name already obtained and recognized.

That these two acts take place to meet entirely different requirements needs no further elaboration, yet the arguments and evidence which have been advanced to prove the Crown prerogative make little distinction, and are accordingly somewhat involved ; but in this section, as far as possible, the points of view expressed by various writers regarding the first of these acts only will be examined, leaving to a later chapter a consideration of the procedure necessary for a change of name by the bearer of his own free will, or under compulsion.

In evidence of the supposed existence of a royal right to sanction and veto the assumption of names generally, Finlayson

---

[1] *Cal. of Inq. Misc. (Chancery)*, vol. i, p. 183.

(1863) cites the entry in the register of Cockersand Abbey,[1] calling it a " charter ", and concluding that Henry II was not the sovereign " that would sit and hearken to so much assumption from a subject ", and that " De Lancaster must first have had permission granted him to bring his request before the Chamber . . . and that the approval and confirmation by the House of Peers over 700 years ago (i.e. before 1163) is exactly in keeping with the privilege of the Crown to grant licences at the present day ". This so-called charter is but a genealogical account of the descendants of Ivo Tailbois, the Domesday tenant, one of whom was the said William de Lancaster, and it is not contemporary with the alleged event. At its best the recorded item seems to have been nothing more than a statement by the Baron of Kendal as to the name by which he wished to be summoned.[2] How far the public announcement would preserve the name solely to the use of the bearer can only be surmised ; probably his own class alone would respect his adopted choice. Finlayson failed to notice the little story preserved by Robert of Gloucester, which has been mentioned above,[3] or any one of the three licences on the original rolls, now given in this and the following chapter, but adduces in support of his contention three instances of change of name alleged to be by the wish or command of Hen. I, Edw. I, and Hen. VIII respectively, on the ground that if the Crown can command a subject to take upon him a particular name [i.e. a change of name] so it can sanction and legalize the assumption of a surname.[4] As comparatively recently a gentleman learned in the law has accepted these instances implicitly without any attempt at verification, and concluded therefrom that it is wrong to assert that the Crown has no power to confer a name,[5] a critical inquiry into the nature of the documentation has now been made. Upon investigation, the evidence is found to be no more impressive than that of the Lancaster case ; the first assumption is that of Nigel de Albini, who received a grant of the lands of his attainted relative Robert Moubray, earl of Northumberland, when " by the special command of King Henry he and his posterity were commanded to assume the surname of Moubray". The story is taken from Camden (1603),[6] but the authority

---

[1] See p. 101.
[2] William took his surname from his mother, Hawise de Lancaster, the heiress of Kendal. There is a letter of Gilbert [Fitz Roger] Fitz Reinfreid and William de Lancaster, his son, to Hubert de Burgh, and the Council. (P.R.O., Anc. Corr. 1/92.)
[3] See p. 101.
[4] *Surnames and Sirenames*, p. 20.
[5] A. C. Fox-Davies (*A Treatise on the Law concerning Names*, 1906, pp. 58–9).
[6] *Remaines . . . concerning Britain*, 1603, p. 126.

quoted is Dugdale (*Baronage*, 1675, vol. i, 122*b*), who, however, says it was Roger (son of Nigel) who " did by the special command of King Henry assume the surname of Molbray " ; but as he possessed (*inter alia*) lands of that name it is quite likely that, in any case, he would have become known as " of Moubray ". Dugdale's authority is a charter in *Monasticon Anglicanum*, which, while it mentions Roger the son of Nigel, has nothing whatever about the command to assume the name.[1] If either a De Lancaster or De Moubray charter did supply any extraneous information about the assumption of a surname, it would be an exception to the general run of such documents.

The second case of assumption by command noted by Finlayson, " occurred in the reign of Edward I, who, disliking the iteration of Fitz in the name of a famous noble John Fitz Robert (whose ancestors had continued their sires' christian names as surnames), [ordered him] to abandon that practice, and to bear the local name of the capital seat of his barony (Clavering), which command John Fitz Robert complied with, and became John de Clavering." [2] This instance, also collected from Camden,[3] is not documented at all by Finlayson ; Dugdale, however, refers to " John (called John de Clavering, by the appointment of King Edward the first) ", and he cites an ancient roll in the possession of W. le Neve, Clarenceux, in 1640. The original authority is clearly the Sibton Abbey cartulary, which, however, bears out Dugdale, but not Camden, nor Finlayson. The entry, a genealogy of the founder of the Abbey, is not contemporary, and is on a par with that of the de Lancaster change of name.[4] It is of interest to note, however, that in two quite independent cases, *de* Lancaster and *de* Clavering, the monastic scribe asserts that the assumption or change was by command of the King.

Another doubtful story of change of name by royal order, which Finlayson does not notice, is also based on the dislike of a surname. It is given on the authority of Hals (1750) by Gilbert in his *Parochial History of Cornwall* [5] :—

" John Knava of Godolphin, Esq. was struck Sheriff of Cornwal by King Henry VII, 1504, who declared his great liking of that gentleman in all circumstances for the said office, but discovered as much dislike of his name after the English, not understanding the import

---

[1] 1661, vol. ii, p. 369*b*.
[2] He was summoned to Parliament by writ directed Johanni de Clavering, in 1299. It is curious that Camden calls him John Fitz Robert de Clavering.
[3] *Remaines*, etc., p. 127.
[4] Brit. Mus. Arund. MS. 221, f. 4*a*. " Robertus [son of Roger] duxit uxorem nomine Margeriam de la Suche, de qua genuit multos filios et filias, videlicet Johannem cujus cognomen rex Edwardus filius regis Henrici fecit vocari Clavering, a principali manerio suo." (*Mon. Angl.*, 1846, vol. v, p. 560.)
[5] Vol. i, p. 122.

thereof in Cornish,[1] and so further said, that as he was pater patriæ, he would transnominate him to Godolphin, whereof he was lord ; and accordingly caused or ordered that in his letters patent under the broad seal of England, for being Sheriff of Cornwall he should be styled or named John Godolphin of Godolphin, Esq. and by that name be accounted at the year's end with that king for his office in the Exchequer, and had his acquittance from thence, as appears from the Pipe Office there. Since which time his posterity have ever since made Godolphin the hereditary name of their family."

John Godalfyn was actually sheriff, 18th Nov. 1503,[2] and is called, in 1508, John Godolghan of Godolghan [3]; his son, also sheriff (1529), was called Goddolfhan, Godolghan, Godolphan, etc. The writer has not been able to find any references under the name of Knava or Nava [4]; and the pedigree in the College of Arms shows that it was a great-great-grandfather of the name of Rencie who assumed the name of Godolphin, which was then of great antiquity, unless this is another case of back-naming.[5]

The third case advanced by Finlayson is that of the great-great-grandfather of the Protector, " Richard Williams, a gentleman of good family in Wales, who changed his name to Cromwell in compliance with a wish (which there can be little doubt was equal to a command) of Henry VIII, taking this particular name in honour of his uncle, Thomas Cromwell, earl of Essex, then a favourite minister of that king." Dugdale is again said to be the source, but reference shows that he says nothing more than that Sir Richard Williams, said to have been nephew of Lord Cromwell (beheaded 1540) " being preferred to the service of King Henry, afterwards affirmed the name of Cromwell." [6]

The writer considers these " proofs " are quite insufficient to support either Finlayson in his argument that the Crown can control the original assumption of a name, or Fox-Davies' contention that occasionally prior to the reign of Charles II

---

[1] " Knava, nava, nawe, naue, signifies the same as servus, servulus, famulus, minister, administer, ministrator, in Latin." (Gilbert, vol. i, p. 122.)

[2] Fine Rolls.

[3] Patent Rolls.

[4] Nava is a continental name, possibly of considerable antiquity. See the somewhat uncertain inscription on the stone from Lamego castle (Portugal). [P]ISIRIA NAV[A] (Corpus Inscriptionum Latinarum, vol. ii, Suppl. No. 5252). In Italy it is found in Milan, Syracuse, and Verona from the fourteenth century. The Emperor Carlo VI, in 1723, conferred the title of count upon a Nava ; and in 1811 Tomasso Nava was created a count by Napoleon I (Dizionario Storico-Blasonico, by G. B. di Crollalanza, 1886). The name Nava is or was to be found in Manchester, nineteenth century, and in Glasgow, twentieth century, but in these cases was of Italian origin. If the name did ever exist in Cornwall, it does not appear to have survived.

[5] A recent work (F. G. Marsh, 1930) gives the name back to 1050 ; but of course, without any proof.

[6] Vol. ii, p. 374.

the Crown has asserted " the matter of names to be within its prerogative ", or regarding change of name, that " a name assumed without authority is simply an *alias*, and has precisely the same weight as the grandiloquent names which are assumed for the purpose of the theatre, or the haphazard *noms des plumes* [*sic*] which are adopted by so many writers ". If regulation of the assumption of a surname, or subsequent change, had at any time been a prerogative of the Crown, and subject to its jurisdiction, would not the rolls have been replete with entries of licences, or references to them ? While the necessity for a newly created peer to notify his title for approval can be understood, it cannot be doubted that such was not the practice among commoners ; nevertheless, a regulation existed in the fourteenth century controlling the names of Englishman in Ireland, the following licence being the immediate result of passing of Statutes of Kilkenny (1366),[1] Diarmid, notwithstanding his ancient Irish forename, evidently being an Englishman.

1367, 6th July. In consideration of the good place which the ancestors of Dyermyd Makmorghyth held with the king's progenitors in their wars in Ireland, and the good service of the said Dyermyd to himself, the king wills that he have and bear the name of Makmorghyth. (*Translation*.)[2]

The effect of this permission was that, notwithstanding the provisions of the Act, Diarmid was given permission to retain his Irish genealogical patronymic.

In Wales in the fourteenth century, as will have been gathered from previous chapters, the question of surnames among the natives had not yet arisen, and according to Pennant, writing in 1778 : " Thomas ap Richard ap Howel ap Jevan Vychan, lord of Mostyn, and his brother Piers, founder of the family of Trelacre, were the first that abridged their name ; and that on the following occasion. Rowland Lee, bishop of Lichfield, and president of the marches of Wales, in the reign of Henry VIII (i.e. from 1534 to 1543), sat at one of the courts on a Welsh cause, and wearied with the quantity of *aps* in the jury, directed that the panel[3] should assume their last name, or that of their residence ; and that Thomas ap Richard ap Howel ap Jevan Vychan, should for the future be reduced to the poor disyllable Mostyn ; no doubt to the great mortification of many an ancient line."[4]

Legal Views on Plurality of Surnames. In Elizabeth's

---

[1] See p. 425.
[2] Patent Rolls : *Calendar*, p. 416.
[3] It may be noted that in England and Wales the panel is the jury but in Scotland it is the prisoner.
[4] *A Tour in Wales*, p. 12.

reign a verdict was held to be void where, in a *venire facias* a juror had been returned by the name of George Tompson and in the *distringas juratores*, named Gregory Tompson, and so sworn at the *nisi prius* [1]; but upon citation of this decision in a parallel case where the *surname* Barker had been mistaken for Carter, the Court held that " there is a great difference between a mistake in the name of baptism and in the surname ; for a man can have but one name of baptism, but may have two surnames " (*Displyn* v. *Sprat*).[2]

On the contrary, it appears that where a juror was surnamed Taverner in the *venire facias* and *distringas*, but in the return of the *distringas* one Turner was named (a Court of Exchequer precedent, where the surname Mizael in error for Michael having been returned, and judgment stayed, being cited) the Court at first " doubted if the variance in the sirname be a cause to stay judgment but for variance in the christian name, they agreed clearly the judgment shall be stayed, but one may have two sirnames ; but afterwards it was resolved that judgment should be stayed " (*Fermor* v. *Dorrington*).[3]

While the latter opinion is not very gracefully expressed, it is evident that judges at this time were by no means decided as to the importance of a surname, but Lord Chief Justice Coke (sixteenth and seventeenth century), relying mainly on these precedents, held that the surname was of little consequence compared with the christian name, for he says : It is requisite that a " purchaser be named by the name of his baptism and his surname, and that special heed be taken to the name of baptism, for that a man cannot have two names of baptism as he may have divers surnames." [4]

At some subsequent, but undetermined period, it finally ceased to be customary for a man to have alternative surnames ; and the single family name received an added importance, which steadily growing enabled it ultimately to oust the font-name from its prior position. As late as the seventeenth century, however, lists of names may be found in which the christian names only are alphabetically arranged.[5]

An eighteenth-century cause is of special interest to the subject. By the will of George Barlow, 20th May, 1727, a beneficiary was Mary Barlow " in case she shall marry with

---

[1] The *venire facias* is a writ to summon the jury to appear at a day in court and upon its return with the panel of the juror's names, the record of *nisi prius* is made up and sealed, and there goes forth the writ of *distringas* to have the jurors in court, *nisi prius justiciarii venerint*, etc. (Tomlin.)

[2] Queen's Bench, East. term, 29 Eliz. Sir Geo. Croke's Reports, Eliz., pt. i, p. 57.

[3] Queen's Bench, East. term, 33 Eliz. Sir Geo. Croke's Reports, pt. i, p. 222.

[4] *Institutes of the Laws of England*, by E. Coke, 3a.

[5] See p. 218.

any person of the name of Barlow ". After testator's death
Mary married one who had been christened Robert, and called
and known by his father's surname Bateman, but who, on the
occasion of the marriage, and not before,[1] assumed and took
upon him the name of Barlow (as he himself admitted in his
answer to a bill in Chancery). It being doubtful whether compliance with the condition expressed in the will had been made,
a decision was sought in the Court of Chancery (*Barlow* v.
Bateman and others),[2] Sir Joseph Jekyll (Master of the Rolls)
remarking : " I am satisfied the usage of passing Acts of
Parliament for the taking upon one a surname is but modern ;
and that any one may take upon him what surname, and
as many surnames as he pleases, without an Act of Parliament,"
decreed that Mary had " married a person who bore the name
of Barlow " ; and upon further proceedings in 1734 his Honour
thought proper not to vary his former decree, but the second
decree was not signed nor enrolled. Both decrees were appealed
to the House of Lords, it being submitted that " respondent
Robert could not, previous to his marriage, legally assume the
surname of Barlow, otherwise than by Act of Parliament,
so as to entitle himself to this legacy ; but if assuming the name
in the manner he had done should be sufficient to entitle him
he might, in the same manner, after receiving the legacy,
reassume his own legal name, and thereby wholly frustrate
and defeat the testator's intention ". It was ordered and
adjudged that the decree of 1730 be reversed, and that the
decree of 1734, not being signed, be dismissed.[3]

Signatures. Royal families sign by baptismal name only,
and, on the contrary, it has become customary for peers, and
peeresses in their own right, in signing, to use only surnames
or peerage designations ; but peeresses by marriage sign with
christian names or their initials, followed by the peerage
designation. Bishops sign by initials followed by the name
of their see, as Dunelm, Ebor, Sarum, and Roffen, for Durham,
York, Salisbury, and Rochester respectively.

Names of Women. In Saxon days a female sometimes had
alternative names, as fully exemplified on p. 53, a practice
which was also not unknown after the Norman conquest.
The wife of Madoc, son of Griffin, was called in 1226 Duce
(Dulcia), and in 1228 Cecilia [4] ; and a daughter of Roger
Mussun (twelfth century) was known both as Cecilia and Isolde

---

[1] About three weeks before the marriage, according to the Report of
Chancery Proceedings.
[2] W. Peere William's Reports, vol. iii, p. 65.
[3] Josiah Brown's Reports of Cases in the High Court of Parliament,
1781, vol. iv, pp. 194–8.
[4] *Antiquities of Shropshire,* by R. W. Eyton, vol. ii, 116 n.

(Iseult).[1] Possibly these were the names of baptism and confirmation respectively. In *Grunsard* v. *Rous* (Com. Bench, Hil. 5 Edw. II) Beresford, C.J., stated the law on the matter clearly and concisely. There was some dispute as to the name by which a woman should be described ; by some her name was said to be Denise, by others Alice. " It may be," says the Chief Justice, " that she was christened Denise and afterwards received the name Alice in confirmation, or vice versa, and the name which the Bishop gave her will be her right name." [2]

A woman might also change her personal name on marriage : Hawise, relict of Walter de Dunstanville, married Ingelram des Préaux (twelfth century), and thereafter she appears under the christian name of Sibil [3] ; and so also on taking the veil, e.g. Katherine de Genville, prioress of Acornbury, fourteenth century, was formerly Beatrix or Matilda.[4] Jewesses also had alternative first-names, but the practice was common to both sexes with the Hebrews.[5]

In the eleventh century the female child was generally entered in official records, as e.g. Maud the daughter of John of Stanton ; and after marriage, as Maud the wife of John of Stanton ; and in her widowhood, as Maud the relict of John of Stanton (in Latin : Matilda quondam uxor Iohannis de Stanton. In French : Maude qe fut la femme Ion de Stanton). The following extracts are illustrative of the name of women as formally written in Latin.

1086. Edeua uxor (wife) Eduuardi filii Suani, Essex. (Dom. Bk. 98*b*.)
Ælveva femina (woman) de Wateman de Lond', Midd. (Dom. Bk. 130*b*.)
Uxor Wenesii, Wilts. (Dom. Bk. 74.)
Luith monialis (the nun), Warw.   (Dom. Bk. 238.)
Judita comitissa (countess), Midd.   (Dom. Bk. 130*b*.)
Eldit quædam femina (a certain woman), Berks.   (Dom. Bk. 636.)

1185. Aliz uxor Johannis de Eincurt also occurs, Aliz de Eincurt que fuit uxor Johannis de Eincurt. (Rot. de Dominabus, p. 19.)
Matillis Gulaffre que fuit filia Rogeri Gulaffre et soror Hereberti Gulaffre. (Ibid., p. 28.)
Letitia que fuit uxor Willelmi filii Mabilie. (Ibid., p. 60.)
Filia Willelmi de Flint. (Ibid., p. 71.)

1230. Edelina et Cecilia filie Rogeri, Berks. (Pipe R., p. 166.)

It was not unusual for a great heiress to retain her paternal name after marriage, e.g. Adelina de Dunstanville was also

[1] Eyton, vol. viii, p. 156.
[2] Selden Soc., vol. xxxi, pp. xxiv, 152.
[3] Eyton, vol. ii, p. 287.
[4] Ibid., vol. v, p. 23 n.
[5] *Studies in Anglo-Jewish History*, by Rev. H. P. Stokes, 1913, p. 70.

known as Adelina de Insula, her father being Humphrey de Lisle (twelfth century).[1] A woman marrying for the second time might retain the name of her first husband.[2] In a case in the Court of Common Pleas, Dublin, 1302 (*de London* v. *Archbishop of Armagh*), Matilda, daughter of Alexander de Notingham, and Matilda la Botiller, complained that she had been wrongly named in the record by her mother's name Matilda la Botiller, and that she was called Matilda de London from the surname of her first husband. At the time Matilda was wife of John de Bonevile.[3]

The following examples of wives described by names other than those of their husbands were all taken from public muniments of the city of Norwich.[4]

1255. Rob. de Wurthestede et Basiliä le Ro' ux' ej' [his wife].
1288. Will. de Devenschyr le Wayte et Alicia de Wetinge ux' ej'.
1307. Joh'es Mengy de Besthorp et Martha de Felmingham ux' ej'.
—   Thos. Toyth et Juliana le Ropere ux' ej'.
1316. Agnes Richeman relicta Ric. Holveston def'ti.
1318. Rob. de Poswyk Taverner et Alicia Godesman ux' ej'.
1352. Isabell' de Mundham fuit ux' Will'i de Dunston et nunc uxor Simonis Spencer.

It is to be noticed that although the woman retains her own name, yet that of her husband appears also, and this was general in legal process, a writ not being maintainable against a married woman without her husband being also named.[5]

In the time of Elizabeth it was still the practice for a lady to retain the name of her first husband ; e.g. Anne, wife of George Baildon, was buried at Leeds in 1577 as Mastris Anne Standish [i.e. her first husband], doughtere to my Ladye Hussye, who in turn was buried (1597) in that name, being widow of Thomas Falkingham.[6]

The following entries were noticed in the Blackburn parish register :—

Vxor Thomas Sudell Peg Nance buried 16th Aug. 1647.
Vxor Thomas Liuesey Nan Darby buried 26th Apr. 1649.

In England (followed by the United States of America) practice has crept in, though apparently comparatively recently, for a woman upon marriage to merge her identity in that of her husband, and to substitute his name for her father's, acquiring the new surname by repute. " The change of name is in fact rather than in law, a consequence of the marriage." [7]

---

[1] Eyton, vol. ii, p. 268.   [2] Ibid, vol. i, p. 381 n.
[3] *Cal. of Justiciary Rolls of Ireland*, pp. 434–6.
[4] *Notes and Queries*, 27th Mar., 1852, p. 291.
[5] *Parliament Rolls*, vol. ii, p. 82a.
[6] *Baildon and the Baildons*, vol. iii, p. 3.
[7] *Laws of England*, by the Earl of Halsbury, vol. xxi, p. 351.

" When a marriage has been dissolved or annulled on the petition either of husband or wife, the latter is entitled to call herself by her late husband's name, or by her former name, or by any other name she may obtain by reputation, provided no one thereby suffers any injury of which the law can take notice." [1]

" On a second marriage there is nothing in point of law to prevent a woman from retaining her first husband's name, but she generally adopts the name of her new husband." [2]   In the case of a peeress remarrying a commoner it appears that she may retain her title (*Cowley* v. *Cowley*, 1901).[3]

The practice for the woman, upon marriage, to abandon her patronymic, is said to be by no means general throughout the British Isles. An anonymous writer in *Notes and Queries* (1865) noticed that in Dorsetshire a married female retains her maiden name, which also descends to her children and their descendants ; but unfortunately no examples are cited.[4] A similar custom was prevalent in Wales, the following observations being by a native legal writer (1893).

" Until recently it was not uncommon for the young wife to be known by her maiden name. For instance, should Shon Robert (John Roberts) marry Shian (Jane), the daughter of William Dafydd or William Davis, his wife would invariably be called Shian Dafydd or Shian Davis (Jane Davis). The wife does not change her name at marriage, and the son uses the paternal or maternal name, as he thinks proper. It appears to have been customary in Anglesey to apply the mother's name to the daughters, and that of the father to the sons, so that should ' Shon Robert ' have married ' Shian Davis ' the sons would be called William Robert, Morgan Robert, etc., and the daughters Mary Davis, Myfanwy Davis, etc." [5]

These are evidently only familiar names, otherwise Shian would never have obtained the name Davis.   On formal occasions the name John Roberts would be used and his wife would be called " Jane Roberts or Jane Davies ".

In Scotland, for purposes of record, the practice likewise grew up of describing the wife by the names both of father and husband. The following examples are taken from the *Acts of the Lords of Council* :—

1483.   Johne Thomsone, litster, and Dowe Gray her spous. (ii, cxxvii.)
1498.   Jonet Abircrumby, the spouse of umquhile Georg Blair. (ii, 143.)
1500.   Patrick Hume of Polwarth and Elene Schaw, his spouse. (ii, 247.)
1500.   Eleanor Cathcart, daughter of Allan, Lord Cathcart, and widow of David Stewart. (ii, 385.)

[1] Halsbury, vol. xvi, p. 594.   [2] Ibid., vol. xxi, p. 351.
[3] English Law Reports, P.D.A. Div., 118, 305.
[4] *Notes and Queries*, 23rd Dec., 1865, p. 518.
[5] Ibid., 9th June, 1888, p. 451.

Entries in modern obituary notices run as follow :—

Thomas Hunter husband of Jessie Roddan.
Mary Pitkethly widow of John Hutton.
Barbara Brown wife of John Linn.
Christina Suttie widow of George Macpherson and daughter of James Miller.
Alexandrina Greig widow of Alexander M'Michen and daughter of Alexander Grieg.[1]

The official and legal method of description is clearly illustrated by the following extract from an inventory lodged in H.M. Commissary Office, in Edinburgh, September, 1930 :—

Mrs. Alice Jane Primrose or Bellingham, a daughter of the late Hon. Bouverie Francis Primrose, C.B. . . . and widow of John Bellingham who resided at Chateau Bellingham, Aix-les-Bains.

That the law did not demand such double-naming is clear from the report of a trial in a Glasgow court (*Owens* and *Collins*, 1792), where a witness cited as Isabel Maccallum, wife of John Maccallum was objected to on the ground that her maiden name Fraser should have been given ; but it was held that she was clearly distinguished ; and that in practice this was an ordinary way of naming a married woman.[2] In every-day life the married woman is addressed as in England : Mistress Smith, Mrs. Smith, etc.

In Ireland in the seventeenth century, according to Sir James Ware, " when a woman of a superior family matches with an inferior, she retained her maiden name after marriage, without assuming that of her husband." [3]

The twentieth-century practice is similar, thus Máire ni Bhriain, bean Sheáin de Búrc, i.e. Mary O'Brien wife of John Burke, equivalent to Mrs. John Burke, *née* Mary O'Brien. Some forms of female names given by Woulfe are :—

Máire Ní Domhnaill : Mary O'Donnell.
Máire Níc an Ghoill : Mary Gill.
Máire Ní mhic an Bháird : Mary Ward.
Sorcha Níg Uidhir : Sarah Maguire.
Peig Báróid : Peg Barrett.
Inghean Uí Bhriain : Miss O'Brien.
Máire, Inghean Uí Bhriain : Miss Mary O'Brien.
Bean Uí Bhriain : Mrs. O'Brien.
Baintreach Sheáin Uí Bhriain : Mrs. John O'Brien (widow).[4]

[1] *Weekly Scotsman*, 28th June, 1930.
[2] *State Trials*, vol. xxiii, p. 248. *Commentaries on the Laws of Scotland*, by David Hume, 1819, vol. ii, p. 358.
[3] *History and Antiquities of Ireland* (Harris, 1764), p. 58.
[4] *Sloinnte Gaedhael is Gael*, 1923, p. 28.

Latinization of Surnames. This subject has been touched upon briefly in Chapter XIII (pp. 346–8). In the eleventh, twelfth, and thirteenth centuries, and even later, before hereditary family names were the rule, it was customary whenever possible to translate not only the personal name, but also the description, into the language in which the document might be written, the process often meaning nothing more than adding Latin terminations to English names, as Godwin-us; sometimes, however, the changes were very complete, as Egidius (Giles), Imania (Emma), Ganterius (Glover), de Albo Monasterio (Whitchurch), de Rupe Scissa (Cutcliff), etc. The practice was apt to lead to mistakes, and from time to time caused difficulties in the law courts.

In *Alet* v. *Nansladron* (Common Bench, Trin., 4 Edw. II) the defendant excepted to the writ on the ground that his christian name was there given as Serlo, whereas his real name was Særius. The Court held that both names corresponded in Latin to a single French name.[1] Another fourteenth-century action, brought by the Prioress of White Hall in Ilchester (Soms.) against Gilbert Passeware and Simona his wife, raised the question whether a Latin grant in which Simona's name had been wrongly given, the masculine terminations, although qualified by adjectives in the feminine gender, could be valid.[2] No decision on the point is available.

In the fourteenth century the latinization or otherwise of a second name was of considerable importance in legal process, since from the language in which it was written it was determined whether it fell into the category of description or surname; the importance of the distinction lying in the fact that a surname had to be identical in " writ, count, and in all else ", whereas a description need not be so exact.[3] Generally it seems that if the " son of Walter " was named *filius Walteri* in a Latin writ, then such title was a description which could be varied, but if he was called fitz Gualter' in such a document, then it was a surname and must be retained in the same orthographic form in all other subsequent documents.

Stonor, C.J. (Hil. 11 Edw. III), ruled that if a man were described by the words " filio Thome " in a writ, then the words " le fitz Thomas " would not be adjudged a surname.[4]

The seventeenth-century view is found in Coke on Littleton (1658) :—

" It is not safe in writs, pleadings, grants, etc., to translate surnames into Latin. As if the surname of one be Fitzwilliam, or Williamson, if

[1] Year Book (Selden Soc., vol. xlii, p. xv).
[2] " Confirmavimus prefate Simoni," " warantizabimus dicte Simoni," etc. (Somers. Arch. Soc., vol. xiii, pt. ii, pp. 51, 115–7).
[3] Year Book (Selden Soc., vol. xxxix, p. xx).
[4] Ibid., p. xxi.

he translate him *Filius Willi*, if in truth his father had any other Christian than William, the writ, etc., shall abate, for Fitzwilliam or Williamson is his surname, whatsoever christian name his father had, therefore the lawyer never translates surnames." [1]

Misnomer. From some early unknown date great accuracy in orthography and precision in setting down the description of an opponent was an essential preliminary to success in litigation. Misnomer was fatal, and as deadly in effect, even though the cause of the error might be misprision of a court scribe (see example *i* below). It was hoped that records of such mistakes might have provided a clue to the status of second names in the eyes of the medieval lawyer, but little has been found pertinent to the question.

Civil proceedings were generally commenced by " original writ " obtained from the Chancellor. If the defendant found himself described incorrectly in christian or second name, name of dignity, or name of office or addition, he could plead abatement ; e.g. in 1205 a writ of Sarra daughter of Adam was quashed because it named Nicholas son of Hamon instead of Nicholas son of Philip [2] ; the uncertainty in which case needs no elaboration. (See also examples *a*, *b*, and *h*.)

Henry de Bracton, ecclesiastic and judge, compiled before 1268, a most comprehensive and practical treatise entitled *De Legibus et Consuetudinibus Angliæ*, wherein he wrote that " an appeal [i.e. an accusation] falls to the ground if there has been an error in the name or surnames (*cognominibus*) of the parties appealed, as if he has some time back called one person William, and afterwards has called the same person Robert ".[3] Writing of an assize of novel disseisin, he says :—

" Error is fatal to a writ, but not to a judgment, nor to an assise. But an error may be manifold in the person of the plaintiff, if he has erred in suing it out against the person of him, who possesses in another's name and not in his own, as a farmer or a prior or a removable canon, and it will be explained below, nor are such persons entitled to an exception nor to a complaint. Likewise an assise ought not to proceed on account of an error in the name, as if for ' Henry ' there is inserted in the writ ' William ', and the converse. Likewise, if there has been an error in the cognomen, as if it is written Hughbertus Roberti, when it ought to be written Hughbertus Walteri. Likewise it will be the same if there be an error in the name of the vill, whence a person has his origin, as if instead of ' London ' a person is described in the writ as ' of Winchester '. Likewise if there be an error in a syllable, as if one should name another Henry de Brochetone, when he ought to be named Henry de Bracton. Likewise the same will apply to a letter, as if a

[1] Page 3*a*.
[2] Curia Regis Roll, Norf., p. 313. A case where both plaintiff and defendant were misnamed occurs in Bracton's Note Book (F. W. Maitland, vol. ii, p. 686).
[3] Ed. by Sir T. Twiss (Rolls Ser. 70), vol. ii, pp. 434–5.

person has erred in naming a person Henry de Bracthon, when he ought to name him Henry de Bracton, and all these things can be proved by examples. Likewise the same will be, if the name and surname (*nomine et cognomine*) are correct, but there is an error in the description of the dignity, as if it be said in the writ Henry de Bracton, the precentor, has made complaint, instead of Henry de Bracton, the dean, and so the writ fails. Likewise if there be an error in the person, and not in the name or in the surname, as when a father and a son are called by the same names and surnames, and the disseisin has been made against the father, if the son has sued out a writ under the same name of the father concerning the disseisin of the father, he shall not recover, because the injury has not been done to him, but to his father, and so he himself shall not have a plaint, but his father, if he be living, and although he has the same name and surname, the person, however, is different to whom the injury is done, and not the same . . ." [1]

Bracton continues, pointing out various possible errors :—

" About the person a double error is possible, sometimes from the unskilfulness or negligence of the party suing out the writ, sometimes from the deceit of an adversary. But from the unskilfulness of the person suing out, as if a person has mentioned ' Peter ' when he ought to have mentioned ' Roger ', and on account of such an error the writ fails for many reasons. Likewise if a person has two names whether in his name, or in his surname, that name is to be retained by which he is accustomed to be called : because they are imposed for that reason that they may show the intention of the speaker, and we use marks in the ministry of the voice. *Idem est si in prænomine, agnomine, & cognomine* (the same thing arises if there be an error in the christian name, the family name, or the characteristic name). [2]

" Likewise there may be error about the office or dignity, as if a person has named a precentor instead of a dean, or on the contrary ; concerning the office, as if a person has named a coroner instead of a viscount, or the converse. For the name of dignity or of office is not changed any more than the proper name of a person. There may, however, be an error concerning those things, whence if the true name be expressed and there be an error about the dignity or the office, the writ holds good. But if there be an error in the name and there be no error in the dignity or in the office, the writ holds good, but sometimes the proper name is not expressed, and then the name of dignity or of office holds good, and if there be no error in them the writ also shall hold good as far as regards their successors in a civil cause, where no penalty follows. But if the action has been a penal action from an offence, it is extended to the successors, no proper name having been expressed, but not as regards the penalty, but as regards restitution, if he can restore. But if the proper name had been expressed, it would not be so. But office and dignity have for the most part reference to the same thing, but every dignity is an office, although not every office is a dignity. But an office may well be without a dignity, as the office of viscount or of coroner. Likewise if a deacon be named instead of a

---

[1] Bracton, pp. 211–13.
[2] Ibid., p. 215.

priest no proper name having been expressed, or on the contrary since a priest comprises both dignities." [1]

Britton (1291–2), referring to exceptions to writs, confirms Bracton : "And where any one has two surnames, that surname shall hold by which he is best known." [2] It is evident that towards the end of the thirteenth century second names additional to the baptismal names were in common use, and that it was not unusual for a man to have more than one ; and that the better known had to be used in legal proceedings, and as will be shown, it had to be correctly spelled.

In 1292 one Roger de Pycheworth failed to appear on a summons of Parliament, it being certified that there was no one of that name, and though one Roger Pychard answered, he was not admitted as he came without any warrant. [3]

In 1305 (33 Edw. I, Hil.) in the Curia Regis, Thomas Bardolf praying judgment if touching his free tenements he ought to answer *sine nomine*, without certainty of name ; the Court held that he ought not to answer to the writ. [4]

In days when few persons spelled their own names in the same way, even at consecutive attempts, and the majority could neither read nor write, it is surprising to find that a defendant might successfully plead misnomer if he could prove a trifling orthographic error in his name or address. With no birth registers, gazeteers, or directories, or any recognized and uniform system of spelling, it is difficult to realize how an illiterate jury settled such a point (see examples *c, e, f, j, l,* and *m* below). Quashing of writs was also due to divergences between the writs close and patent, that is to say no matter what spelling was adopted in the original writ sued out by plaintiff, it had to be followed precisely in a subsequent writ (see examples *g* and *n* below).

There will now be given a selection of extracts from the rolls which contain the legal proceedings held before the Chief Justiciar of Ireland, whose court was the representative in Ireland of the Curia Regis, the court of the King, and where the law administered was the Common Law of England.

(i) *Error in christian name.*

(*a*) 1297. Common Pleas, at Kilkenny. 16th June.

Assize of Mort d'ancestor was taken to determine if Hugh son of Maur. Bolgulagh, father of Maur. son of Hugh Bulgulagh, was seised as of fee of certain lands. The claimant Maurice, a son of said Hugh, being unable to deny that the said Hugh was a son of Hugh and not of Maurice, it was adjudged that Maurice take nothing by his writ, but be in mercy for false claim. [5]

---

[1] Bracton, p. 217. [2] Ed. by F. M. Nichols, vol. i, p. 321.
[3] *Rolls of Parliament*, vol. i, p. 71*b*. [4] *Abbreviatio Placitorum*, p. 253*a*.
[5] *Calendar of the Justiciary Rolls of Ireland*, ed. by J. Mills, vol. i, p. 139.

(b) 1307. Plea of Plaints at Cork. 22nd May.

Walter de Hereford appears against Walter Bermeiam and Stephen le Baker, of a plea of trespass. It is testified that Walter Bermeiam is not found . . . because there is not any such person, but one Adam Bermeiam. Therefore Walter takes nothing and is in mercy.[1]

(ii) *Error of orthography in " surname ".*

(c) 1299. Common Pleas at Drogheda. 18th July.

Assise of Novel disseisin. Brother Gilbert de Hegham, prior of the Hospital of St. John of Jerusalem in Ireland, and Milo Maghenan, disseised Peter Roth, etc. For the Prior it is said that he is called Gilbert de Haghham, and not de Hegham, also that he holds under the name of a wardship, by reason of the minority of Hugh son of Thomas Moor, who is not named in the writ. Peter unable to deny this (i.e. the latter plea in bar) takes nothing.[2]

(d) 1300. Common Pleas at Kilmahallok (co. Limerick). 15th June.

Assise of Novel disseisin. If Simon Hereford and others disseised Gregory de Malmesbury and his wife of freeholds, etc. Simon says he is called Hereward not Hereford, which Gregory and his wife being unable to deny, are in mercy for false claim. The writ was renewed the same day and Gregory recovered seisin.[3]

(e) 1307. Pleas at Cork. 22nd May.

Assise of Novel disseisin. If Ph. son of Robert, Alex. Daundon, and others disseised Maurice Dunre of his freehold, etc. Alexander says that assise ought not to be, because whereas he is named in the writ, Alex. Doundoun, his cognomen is not Doundoun, but Daundoun. Afterwards Maurice does not prosecute, and no decision is given on the point.[4]

(f) 1307. Pleas at Ardert (co. Kerry). 16th–20th June.

Assise of Novel disseisin. If Adam Staundoun and another disseised Benwe Stake of her freehold, etc. Adam says that assise ought not to be taken between them, because he is called Adam de Staunton and not Adam de Staundoun. The jurors giving a verdict in his favour, Benwe is in mercy for her false claim.[5]

(iii) *Error in description or " surname ".*

(g) 1295. Pleas of Assizes at Drogheda. n.d.

Assise of Novel disseisin. If Rob. Fulshawe and Roger son of Roger Gernoun disseised John de Haddessore of certain freehold. Robert says that assise ought not to be taken, because the writ patent varies from the original writ close, in that it has Roger Gernoun simply instead of Roger son of Roger Gernoun. Notwithstanding that there were three of the name of Roger Gernoun in the county, the justices quashed the exception.[6]

(h) 1300. Common Pleas at the Naas (co. Kildare). 9th May.

Assise of Mort d'ancestor. If Walter de Malmesbury, senior, father of Walter son of Walter, was seised of lands which Eva Collan holds. She says that Walter junior is son, not of Walter, but of Adam. Walter cannot deny this, and is in mercy for false claim.[7]

---

[1] *Calendar*, vol. ii, p. 381.   [2] Ibid., vol. i, p. 275.
[3] Ibid., vol. i, p. 338.   [4] Ibid., vol. ii, p. 363.
[5] Ibid., vol. ii, p. 418.   [6] Ibid., vol. i, p. 221.
[7] Ibid., vol. i, p. 329.

(*i*) 1300. Common Pleas at Cork. 11th June.

Assise of Novel disseisin. If Ric. son of Adam, and David de Carreu disseised Math. son of Adam Petit, and Johanna his wife, of his freehold, etc. Richard says that Math. had not any father called Adam le Petit, nor was any of his family so called. Math. cannot deny this, but says that the clerk of Chancery carelessly thought the word " petit " contained in the petition was the surname of " Petit " and so named him. Matthew had to give 40*d*. to withdraw from his writs.[1]

(iv) *Error in orthography of place-name.*

(*j*) 1305. Pleas at Tristeldermot (co. Kildare). 8th July.

Assise of Novel disseisin. If Will. de Bereleye and others disseised Lucia de Bereleye of her freehold in Donnaghcombre (now Donnaghcumper co. Kildare). On behalf of William it is said that assise ought not to be taken because the land where the view was made is called Donnaghcompre and not Donnaghcombre. The Jurors say that the land where the view was made is called Donnaghcompre and not Donnaghcombre. Therefore it is adjudged that Lucia take nothing by this assise, but be in mercy for false claim.[2]

(*k*) 1307. Pleas at Cork. 22nd May.

Assise of Mort d'ancestor. If John son of Ralph was seised of land in Skothagh, and if Peter his brother is his next heir. At the beginning of the writ is said : " Summon by good summoners men of the visne of Skothagh in Ykyrkyllyth : and afterwards the writ refers to land in Skothagh. Peter cannot deny this, and takes nothing by his writ, etc.[3]

(*l*) 1307. Pleas at Ardart (co. Kerry). 27th June.

Assise of Novel disseisin. If Henry son of Robert and others unjustly disseised Agnes daughter of Thomas son of Elyas of freehold in Kellifran. Henry says that assise ought not to be between them, because the tenements where view was made are in Kyllywran, and not in Kellyffran. The jurors deciding in defendant's favour, Agnes takes nothing, and is in mercy for false claim.[4]

(*m*) 1307. Pleas at Lymerick. 3rd July.

Assise of Novel disseisin. If James de Ketyng and another disseised Adam de Goules of his freehold in Rathmackantan. James says that the assise ought not to be taken, because the tenements which are put in view are in Rathmaccandan, and not in Rathmaccantan, etc. The jurors decide in favour of the first named, therefore Adam takes nothing, and is in mercy, etc.[5]

(*n*) 1307. Pleas at Cork. 22nd May.

Assise of Novel disseisin. If David son of Alex. de Rupe and others, disseised Risus Beket of his freehold in Inchetoban and other places named. David and the others say that they ought not to answer to this writ, because the writ close varies from the patent, in this, that a certain town named in the writ close Inchetoban, is named in the patent Ichecoban. The writs being inspected, etc. Risus cannot deny this, and therefore takes nothing, and is in mercy.[6]

Not only was a correct name necessary, but it had to be

---

[1] *Calendar*, vol. i, p. 335.   [2] Ibid., vol. ii, p. 93.
[3] Ibid., vol. ii, p. 367.   [4] Ibid., vol. ii, p. 428.
[5] Ibid., vol. ii, p. 435.   [6] Ibid., vol. ii, p. 367.

distinct ; thus in a suit in the manor court at Hales (Worc.), in 1294, an essoiner who gave the name Ricardus filius Thome was called a perverter of the law, because there were many who were called by that name.[1]

A cause in the Common Bench, of Easter Term, 4 Edw. II (1311) shows that Lawrence de Reppes being in debt to Edmond de Reppes, Edmund appointed his wife and Lawrence co-executors of his will, and thereafter died, the debt remaining unpaid. The executors brought a writ, but Lawrence was named therein Lawrence, the son of Ralph. A better writ had to be bought.[2]

It is evident that in the early fourteenth century on the point of orthographical detail, Custom and Common Law were completely at variance ; on the one hand it was the custom to spell a name as one pleased, and to vary it even in the same document ; on the other hand, we find the law insisting upon the most meticulous accuracy, making most particular and unusual demands upon the intelligence of the people, in fact, practically asking for the impossible and the unknown. The laudable desire for accuracy, carried to an extreme, inflicted great hardship and unnecessary expense on litigants, and ultimately it was realized that some modification was necessary to relieve them of liability for the mistake of the Chancellor's clerk. By statute 14 Edw. III (1340), c. 6, it was enacted :—

That by the misprision of a clerk in any place wheresoever it be, no process shall be annulled, or discontinued, by mistaking in writing one syllable, or one letter too much or too little ; but as soon as the thing is perceived, by challenge of the party, or in other manner, it shall be hastily amended in due form, without giving advantage to the party that challengeth the same because of such misprision.[3]

It appears by various reports of decisions that the Judges construed this Act favourably and extended its provision to covering a whole word, e.g. in *Walden* v. *Holman* (1704) it was held not to be a good plea for defendant to say that he was baptized by another name than that by which he was sued, without showing likewise that he was always known by it.[4]

The law is now more concerned with the reputed names and additions of a person and his identity than the name which may have been given to him at birth or baptism ; thus, for instance, in an indictment, the defendant should be described

[1] Essonie. Thomas de Hulle essoniat se versus Thomam filium Willelmi in mora de placito terre per Ricardum filium Thome calupniatur (*sic*) quia plures sunt qui vocantur hoc nomine. (p. 280.)

[2] *Yelverton* v. *Reppes* (*Year Book*, Selden Soc., vol. xxvi, pp. 150–3).

[3] *Statutes of the Realm*, vol. i, p. 283.

[4] *Modern Reports*, vol. vi, p. 115.

by his christian and surname, but these need not be stated correctly, provided they are sufficient to identify him.[1] A tendency in modern Acts is to call for the "true names" of a person, an expression having different meanings in different statutes, creating an anomalous position, leading to some misunderstanding.

The Marriage Act, 4 Geo. IV, c. 76, s. 7 (as did 26 Geo. II, c. 33, s. 2) requires delivery to the parson of "true christian names and surnames", but it has been held that a true name may be an assumed name and not the original. Misnomer will not annul a marriage unless one of the parties shows that he has been imposed upon; on the other hand, if fraud is the object, a wrong name in whole or in part, the addition or dropping of a name, or even the use of an original baptismal or family name where an assumed name is the better known, would invalidate a marriage. In one case misnomer for the purpose of concealment from a parent, as where William Peter Pougett, generally known as Peter Pougett, was married in the name of William Pougett (1814), annulled the marriage. In striking contrast is the case of Joseph Price (1815), who for sixteen weeks known as Joseph Grew, in an attempt to conceal himself from the army authorities, married in that name; Lord Ellenborough holding "that he had acquired the name, and that to have had a licence in any other name would have been a fraud on the Marriage Act."[2]

The Theatrical Employers' Registration Act, 1925 (15 and 16 Geo. V, c. 50) likewise asks for the "true name" as well as every other name in which the employer has carried on business, etc., but "true name" here means original name. In 1930 Harold Price, music hall artist, who for twenty-five years, in accordance with a practice usual in his profession, had become known as Tommy Mostol, and had married, and registered births of his children in that name, was fined for registering his true name as Mostol.[3] In contrast, the Marriage and Registration Act, 1856, and the Births and Deaths Registration Act, 1874, merely ask for "surname", and whether that is the patronymic, or reputed name does not appear.

Certainty in Pardons. Certainty in name, address, and description, so essential in pronouncements of outlawry, was of equal importance in pardons. A good example of the extreme to which identification was carried is obtained from the pardon by letters patent to one John Beeston, an outlaw, who is named :—

---

[1] *Archbold on Indictments*, by H. D. Roome, 1916, p. 46.
[2] *On Surnames*, by Thomas Falconer, 1862, pp. 20 et seq.
[3] *Evening Standard*, 21st Feb., 1930.

Joh'i Beston nup' de fframelyngham ad castrum in com' Suff' yoman *alias* d'c'o Joh'i Beeston de fframelyngham ad castrum in com' Suff' yoman *alias* d'c'o Joh'i Beston nup' de fframelyngham ad castrum in com' Suff' gentilman *alias* d'c'o' Joh'i Beeston de fframelyngham ad castrum in com' Suff' gentilman *alias* d'c'o' Joh'i Beeston nup' de fframelyngham ad castrum in com' Suff' gentilman *alias* d'c'o Joh'i Beston nup' de fframelyngham ad castrum in com' Suff' gentylman *alias* d'c'o Joh'i Beeston nup' de Gippewico in com' Suff' gentilman *alias* d'c'o Joh'i Beeston de Ippeswiche in com' Suff' jentilman *alias* d'c'o Joh'i Beeston nup' de Hawnes in com' Bed' gentilman *alias* d'c'o Joh'i Beston nup' de Hawnes in com' Bed' gentilman *alias* d'c'o Joh'i Beeston nup' de Hawnes in com' Bed' parker seu quocumq' alio no'i'e, etc.[1]

This extract from the King's Bench roll for Eastern term, 7 Edw. IV (1461) gives eleven different descriptions under which the rebel had been exacted in the various courts. The clerks ultimately tired of these numerous aliases, and a formula eliminating the necessity for variants in orthography, description, or address, was introduced. The following example is from a pardon of 2nd Jan., 12 Chas. II (1661) :—

> Richardo Beke de Haddenham in comitatu nostro Bucks. armigero, seu quocunque alio nomine, vel cognomine, seu additione nominis, vel cognominis, officii, seu loci, idem Richardus Beke censeatur, vocetur, sive nuncupetur, aut nuper censebatur, vocabatur, sive nuncupabatur, omnes et omnimodas proditiones, etc.

Duplication of Names. Notwithstanding the adoption of secondary descriptions, it was already found in the fourteenth century, as appears from entries on the rolls from time to time, that grave confusion arose from duplication, resulting in miscarriage of justice ; thus if one John Smith was outlawed, every other John Smith, at least in the same county, was liable to lose liberty and goods, and to suffer not only the discomforts and dangers to health which abounded in medieval gaols, but a very real likelihood of being overtaken by death before the mistake was discovered and rectified. So real was the possible risk that in A.D. 1380 Parliament was petitioned that whereas several persons bear the same " noun and surnoun ", and are put in great danger of their bodies, loss of lands and goods by reason of outlawry pronounced in such name, to ordain that every pronouncement of outlawry without the name, town, or place where defendant dwells, in addition to his name, be null and void.[2] Nothing was done, and another petition in 1402 shows that, in default of addition, several innocent persons had suffered by outlawries pronounced on

---

[1] P.R.O., K.B. 27, 824, m. 95*d*. The pardon is dated 14th Mar., 1461. Patent Roll 7 Edw. IV, pt. i, m. 14.
[2] *Rolls of Parliament*, vol. iii, p. 94*b*.

others having similar " nounes and sournounes ".[1] It was not, however, until 1413 that the prayers had effect, and it was enacted :—

That in every original writ of actions personals, appeals and indictments, and in which the exigent shall be awarded, in the names of the defendants in such writs original, appeals and indictments, additions shall be made of their estate or degree, or mystery, and of the towns or hamlets, or places and counties, of the which they were, or be, or in which they be or were conversant. And if by process which upon the said original writs, appeals, or Indictments, in the which the said additions be omitted, any utlagaries be pronounced, that they be void, frustrate, and holden for none ; and that before the utlagaries pronounced, the said writs and indictments shall be abated by the exception of the party where in the same the said additions be omitted ; Provided always, that though the said writs of additions personals be not according to the records and deeds by the surplusage of the additions aforesaid, that for that cause they be not abated : and that the clerks of the Chancery, under whose names such writs shall go forth written, shall not leave out or make omission of the said additions as is afore said, upon pain to be punished, etc.[2]

This Act is sometimes referred to as the Statute of Additions (1 Hen. V, c. 5) ; it was repealed as to civil proceedings by 42 and 43 Vict., c. 59, and *in toto* by 46 and 47 Vict., c. 49, s. 4.

Brothers of the same name. " If you have a hundred sons call them all Muhammed " is an Arabic saying ; and some such desire to reverence a superior must have inspired the virile and perfervid Scotsman, who is said to have had fourteen sons, all of whom he named Charles Edward, in honour of the Pretender.[3] Fortunately, patriotism seldom runs riot to such an extent, or the lot of the pedigree-maker would be a most unhappy one.

In Saxon days, as shown above, the elements of compound names of parents might often be repeated in those of the children[4] ; and after the Norman conquest it became not uncommon for several sons to bear the same name, which duplication might be due to the fulfilment of various desires. From very ancient days[5] down till the nineteenth century, parents were conservative in their choice of names for their children, it being customary in this country to perpetuate those of near relatives, and three sons, for instance, might be named Robert, after father, grandfather, and uncle respectively, without calling for any critical comment. Among the Jews,

---

[1] *Rolls of Parliament*, vol. iii, p. 508a.
[2] *Statutes of the Realm*, vol. ii, p. 171. *Rolls of Parliament*, vol. iv, pp. 10a, 23a, 26b.   [3] Baconniere Salverte, vol. i, p. 172.
[4] See p. 51.   [5] See Luke, ch. i, v. 59–61.

on the contrary, the naming a child after a living relative was rare.[1]

Eyton has referred to the genealogical puzzle caused by two brothers named Fulk fitz Warin (thirteenth century) [2]; and also to two brothers of Helias de Say (thirteenth century), both named Robert.[3] Rarely brothers of the same name were given additions for distinction, as John Giffard le Hof and John Giffard le Box [4] (le Boef on the Fine Rolls, 1316).

Sometimes two or more sons of the same christian name represent the offspring of different mothers, and any suspicion of duplication, therefore, should sound a warning note to genealogists. An example which has remained undetected to the confusion of all peerage compilers from Dugdale to the present day, is that of John le Strange, 2nd lord Strange of Knockin, Salop, and his half-brother John le Strange, king's yeoman; another case being that of John Matravers (Baron, 1351), who, by different wives, had two sons named John, the younger of whom had likewise two sons named John, according to the pedigree given in *Collectanea, Topographica et Genealogica*.[5]

In early French records similar duplication may be found: Michaëlsson, in a study of the names on *Les Rôles de Taille Parisiens*, 1292–1313, has noticed half-a-dozen instances of two brothers or two sisters bearing the same name; but more often in France a distinguishing suffix was utilized, thus: Jehan and Jehannot were brothers and likewise Guillaume and Guillot,[6] in parallel to the English use of -kin (see above, p. 281).

This particular trait of repetition in one family was another motive necessitating additions and the passing of the statute of 1413.

Later English records also provide examples of repetition of christian names in the same generation; in the will of John Vavasour, 24th Apr., 1461, may be noticed: ' I leave to John Vavasour, my son and heir . . . I leave to John Vavasour my younger son " [7]; and Thomas Mallory, of Papworth, Hunts, in his will, 1469, mentions John, his son and heir, and " my son John the younger ".[8] A further illustration is taken from the English will of John Parnell, of Gyrton, 8th Mar., 1545 :—

---

[1] *Encycl. of Religion and Ethics*, Art. by I. Abrahams. The practice was common in Ancient India and Greece. Ibid., L. H. Gray, p. 165b.
[2] *Antiquities of Shropshire*, vol. vii, p. 82.
[3] Ibid., vol. viii, p. 62.
[4] *Placita de Quo Warranto*, p. 86.
[5] Vol. iii, p. 78.
[6] p. 54.
[7] *Baildon and the Baildons*, vol. i, p. 526.
[8] *Athenæum*, 11th Sept., 1897, p. 354.

" Alice my wife and Old John my son to occupy my farm together, till Old John marries . . . Young John my son shall have Brenlay's land plowed and sowed at Old John's cost." [1]

Thomas Reade, of Calcott, Hunts, in his will dated 1595, mentions " my daughter Katheryn the younger " and " my eldest daughter Katheryn ".[2] Three sons of the same name are legatees under the will of Nicholas Brent of Stowe upon the Olde, 22nd Oct., 1582 :—

" To William Brente my eldest son if he live to accomplish his age of twenty years, 30l. To William Brent, my second son, 30l. : and to William Brent, my third son, 40l., etc.[3]

According to the Conway parish register, on 18th July, 1558, there were buried John ap Jonne, Jonne ap Jonne, and Jonne ap Jonne.

In Scottish records similar cases may be found :—

24th Nov., 1551.   Isabel Scot, daughter of George Scot gave and ceded her right, etc., to her sister Isobella Scot, younger. Protocol Book of Sir Alex. Gow, notary, Strathmiglo.[4]

18th May, 1564. John Woddrop senior, son of q. Thomas Woddrop junior in Dalmarnock, renounced all right . . . in favour of John Woddrop junior, his brother german. Protocols of the Town Clerks of Glasgow. Renwick, vol. v, p. 68.[5]

Fictitious Names.   Before concluding this chapter, it may not be out of place to mention several names which will be familiar to all readers of old court records, e.g. those of the ubiquitous couple " John Doe and Richard Roe ", who figure so often as pledges for the prosecution of suits. Entering names of sureties was often a mere formality, yet if omitted it was error, because the law directed the plaintiff to find pledges, hence the invention of these two persons and names. Other fictitious gentlemen were also introduced, e.g. " Hugh Hunt ", the popular disseisor, who appears in so many of the feigned suits known as recoveries. Some of the invented names entered as essoiners in Ireland in 1299–1307 show a greater variety : Ric. Not, Thomas Dod, Adam Ta, Adam Po, Adam Fot, Adam Bon, Thomas Ken, Thomas Lop, Adam Ben, Thomas Bek, Will. Beg, Thomas Pie, Adam Daff, David Doc, Adam Cat, Ric. Fox, Adam Box. The law raised no objections to these fictions.

[1] *History of Parish Registers,* by J. S. Burn, p. 69.
[2] *Notes and Queries,* 16th July, 1898, p. 51.
[3] P.C.C. Rowe, 8.
[4] *Notes and Queries,* 1st June, 1901, p. 436.
[5] Ibid., 4th June, 1898, p. 446. Some other examples I have given in *Ewen of East Anglia,* pp. 14, n. 6 ; 104, n. 7. See also Bardsley (*Puritans,* p. 4).

CHAPTER XVI

CHANGE OF FORENAMES AND SURNAMES

Change of Name. The reader of Chapter I will have realized that at all times and all places a change of name for various reasons, and at any period of life, was commonplace practice throughout the world.

" Neither shall thy name be any more called Abram, but thy name shall be Abraham." Gen. xvii, 5.

This ancient verse describes a proceeding which doubtless often took place, even without divine authority. Under the laws of Diocletian and Maximian (third century), the Romans were permitted to change nomen, prænomen, or cognomen, provided that it was done without deceit or the purpose of fraud.[1] Among the ancient natives of Britain and Ireland change of name, upon the spur of the moment, as the fancy of a druid dictated, called for no comment ; and some instances have been related above on pages 35 and 41.

With regard to second names, their transient and unsettled nature during the eleventh, twelfth, and thirteenth centuries, having been illustrated above (Chap. V), it will have been gathered that a plurality of additions or descriptions was general among the upper classes, which fact of itself negatives any supposition that the Crown had any right or interest, or could possibly exercise any prerogative in the assumption or change of surname, which proceedings were entirely uncontrolled and left to the free will of the people. That there have been, however, notable exceptions curtailing the public rights, when, for special purposes, the Crowns of both England and Scotland did compel or forbid change of surname by Act of Parliament, is evidenced not only by the Statutes of Kilkenny (1366) mentioned above, but by the Act of 1465 (Ireland), the O'Neil Act, 11 Eliz. (1568-9), the Ruthven Act (1600), the MacGregor Act (1603), and the Alien's Restriction (Amendment) Act, 1919, c. 92, s. 7. Some control also appears

---

[1] Codex de mutatione nominis. Impp. Diocletianus et Maximianus AA. et CC. Juliano. Sicut initio nominis cognominis, prænominis recognoscendi singulos impositio privatim libera est, ita horum mutatio innocentibus periculosa non est. mutare itaque nomen sive prænomen [sive cognomen] sine aliqua fraude licito jure, si liber es, secundum ea, quæ sæpe statuta sunt minime prohiberis, nulli ex hoc præjudicio futuro. (*Corpus Juris Civilis*, P. Krueger, 1888, vol. ii, Bk. viiii, tit. 25.)

to have been exercised over tenants in chief, and in the case of Jews, of which instances will now be given.

1273. Be it had in remembrance that Abraham Motun gives the King 1 bezant that his cognomen be changed.[1]

The Jews were the property of the King (although at this time mortgaged to Richard, earl of Cornwall), and as such, it cannot be doubted, were carefully indexed ; a change of name, with the necessary alteration of the register, would be a sufficient cause, if one was necessary, for mulcting the Hebrew. What name Abraham adopted does not appear, but in 1280, when he went to Flanders, he was still using his old surname.[2] The Jews generally had alternative first and second names, in some cases perhaps the result of the synagogue custom of changing the name in case of serious sickness [3]; but only in this one instance has any payment or official cognizance been noted, and in striking contrast is the entry—Hagin the son of Isaac *qui se vocari facit* (who caused himself to be called) Ben. Bateman.[4]

By the early fourteenth century the Crown had found it desirable, in further instances, to record formally its approval of a change of surname. By the Præregitiva Regis [5] (called an apocryphal statute by Pollock), alienation of the greater part of lands holden in chief was not permitted without the King's licence, and although surnames are not mentioned, it appears that the Crown had extended its authority to the control of changes of name to be effected by the alienee. A translation from the Patent Rolls of 1314 provides evidence on this point.

Feb. 23. Licence, as well as at the request as on account of his good service to Edward I and to the king (Edw. II), to Edmund Deyncurt [Baron], who affirms that his surname and arms after his death will be lost from memory in the person of Isabella daughter of Edmund Deyncurt, his heir apparent, and who heartily desires that the same may afterwards be held in memory, to enfeoff whomsoever he will of all his lands and tenements, knights' fees and advowsons of churches, which he holds *in chief*, to hold to the feoffee and his heirs by the due and accustomed services. Further grant that *the persons whom he shall so enfeoff may bear the surname of the said Edmund Deyncurt* and his arms in memory of him.[6]

The necessity for the request for permission to change the name is not apparent since Deyncurt had kinsmen of his own

[1] *Plea Rolls of the Exchequer of the Jews*, ed. by J. M. Rigg, vol. ii, p. 19.
[2] *Patent Rolls*, 1280, p. 364.
[3] *Studies in Anglo-Jewish History*, by the Rev. H. P. Stokes, 1913, p. 71 n.
[4] Plea Rolls (cited above), 36 and 37 Hen. III, 11, m. 3*d*. (Stokes).
[5] *Statutes of the Realm*, vol. i, p. 226.
[6] *Patent Rolls*, 7 Edw. II, pt. ii, m. 21 : *Calendar*, p. 89.

name. On the very same day [1] the licence was superseded by a second, which empowered the feoffee (unnamed) to regrant the manors, etc., to the said Edmund Deyncurt for his life, with successive remainders to William son of John Deyncurt, and the heirs of his body, to John Deyncurt, brother of the said William, and the heirs of his body, and to the right heirs of the said Edmund Deyncurt.[2] In 1317, in a further licence, two of the family, Master Oliver Deyncurt and John Deyncurt, were cited as feoffees.[3] Only in the first licence is permission to change the name given. It is manifest that by the fourteenth century in the case of tenants in chief, where the King had obtained a right to restrain wholesale alienation of lands, the Crown had also assumed the privilege of licensing a change of arms and a change of name, which were so often a desired accompaniment. It has been shown that in some other special instances, e.g. in the case of Jews, prior to their banishment in 1290, and with Anglo-Irishmen of the fourteenth century, the Crown exercised a like prerogative [4] ; but there is nothing to show that the King at this early date controlled or ever attempted to control assumption or change of surnames of the general public.

Change of name to cover an irregular act was, however, apt to draw attention from the law. In 8 Edw. II (1314) diligent examination and inquiry were ordered touching Richard Sherman, who changed his name to John de Trays, and prosecuted his plea against Roger de Quenby, for rape of John's wife. Roger went *sine die*, Richard being committed to the Marshal (London).[5]

It is not possible to agree entirely with Fox-Davies (1906), who writes : " Haphazardly, from time immemorial, but consistently since, at any rate, the reign of Charles II, the Crown has asserted the matter of names and changes of name to be within its prerogative, but it has, whilst definitely asserting this attitude through such of its ministers and officers as are concerned with the subject, as persistently avoided putting its prerogative to the test of legal action." [6] The first part of this statement has been shown above to have no solid foundation ; with regard to the second part it is said that in England the first " Royal Licence and Authority " to use a specific surname was a grant to Henry Cavendish, Earl of Ogle, son of the Duke of Newcastle, in 1679, to take the name of Percy, on the marriage with the heiress of that

---

[1] The roll is dated 33rd, evidently an error for 23rd Feb., 1314.
[2] *Calendar of Patent Rolls*, p. 89.
[3] Ibid., p. 651.
[4] See p. 387.
[5] *Placitorum Abbreviatio*, p. 319a.
[6] *Treatise*, p. 2.

family, his lordship being then in his seventeenth year.[1] The actual wording of the authority is of interest :—

To assume and take the surname of Percie and to bear the arms of Percie quarterly with his own paternal arms " neither of which may regularly be done, according to the law of armes, without the special dispensacon and licence of US, as We are by Our supream power and prerogative the onely Fountain of Honour ".[2]

Here may be seen the Crown asserting its sole right in no uncertain terms : change of name or arms without royal licence is irregular procedure—yet, in the modern licence, the authority asked for by the petitioner is granted without citation of the " law of arms ".[3] Is it possible that it was discovered that no such law existed ?   In later grants of authority for a change of name it is said that the cognizance of matters of that nature properly belong to the College of Arms. At what time this corporation of heraldic officers, who themselves used no surnames in grants or public instruments,[4] were given the power to control change of name is not known, but according to a return (1800) it appears that the Earl Marshal's books, which contain, *inter alia*, entries relating to change of surnames, date from the time of Queen Elizabeth.[5] According to a statement by Mr. Roebuck in the House of Commons in 1862, a regulation was made in 1783 that all applications for permission to change names should be referred to the College of Arms.[6] Had it been the special duty for the Heralds to attend to changes of name prior to the eighteenth century, some indication of their authority would surely be found in one or other of the published visitations ; but no clue bearing on the point has been discovered.

Referring to the reversal of a decree in the Court of Chancery in *Barlow* v. *Bateman* (see above, p. 388), Fox-Davies observes that this decision " absolutely upsets the bold contention that any man may change his name as he pleases ".[7] But on the reading of the report it is manifest that all that the decree upset was the view that a man could change his name for the express purpose of obtaining a qualification essential to a beneficiary, and one which he did not possess at the execution of the will, thereby defeating the wishes of the testator. Fox-Davies' " chain of argument ", based on the law of arms, is not convincing ; he says : " A name is an inheritance ; a man could not of himself create or grant an estate of

---

[1] Cokayne's Peerage : Laws of England (Halsbury), p. 352 t.
[2] Phillimore, *Index to Changes of Name*, p. xxvi.
[3] Ibid.
[4] *History of the College of Arms*, by M. Noble, 1805, p. 50.
[5] Ibid., App. M., xlii.
[6] Phillimore, p. xxiv.
[7] *Treatise*, p. 48.

inheritance to himself, therefore no man can create a name for himself ; therefore no man can validly change his name by his own sanction and authority only." [1]

Mr. Justice Chitty (1886) had said : " The law was that a coat of arms descended as an estate of inheritance (Comyn's Digest, sub. lit. Court of Chivalry). A man could not of himself create or grant an estate of inheritance to himself. It was, therefore, plain that a mere voluntary assumption of a coat of arms was not enough ; but that a properly authorized grant, i.e. a grant by the Heralds' College, was essential to a fair compliance with the condition of an ordinary name and arms clause " (*Austen* v. *Collins*).[2]

The two cases are not analogous, and there are two reasons why Mr. Justice Chitty's opinion as to assumption of arms should not be applied to an assumption of name : (*a*) The Heralds have been empowered to grant arms and to regularize the bearing of them ; no body is known to have been authorized to control the assumption and use of names. (*b*) As to inheritance ; a man succeeds to undifferenced arms only on the death of his father ; but he inherits the right to share his father's surname at birth. As men assumed cognizances until the right to do so was taken from them, so they will assume or change names at will, until the law steps in and rules otherwise. In France and Germany the custom was similar until the passing of ordinances controlling the use of names.

In 1822 Abbot, C.J. (Lord Tenterden) in the King's Bench remarked : " A name assumed by a voluntary act of a young man at his outset in life, adopted by all who knew him, and by which he is constantly called, becomes . . . as much and effectually his name as if he had obtained an Act of Parliament to confer it upon him " (*Luscombe* v. *Yates*).[3]

In 1863, in the House of Commons, the Solicitor-General observed that " while everyone was at liberty to change his surname, no one else was obliged to recognize the change unless he pleased. When, however, by usage, a man had acquired a name by reputation, then persons in public authority were bound to acknowledge the new surname ".[4]

The modern view on the assumption of surnames is summarized by Sir H. H. Shephard, LL.D. (1912) : " A man may assume any name he pleases in addition to or substitution for his original name ; and in adopting even the name or combination of names by which another person is already

[1] *Treatise*, cited.
[2] *Times*, 6th May, 1886.
[3] Barnewell and Alderson's Reports (K.B., vol. v, p. 556).
[4] *Herald and Genealogist*, 1863, vol. i, p. 463.

known he does not commit a legal wrong against that person.[1] The law concerns itself only with the question whether he has, in fact, assumed and has come to be known by a name different from that by which he was originally known." [2] No Act of Parliament, Royal Licence, Deed Poll, or any advertising, or any formality whatsoever is required for lawful assumption of a surname.[3]

A person who in executing an instrument subscribes a surname which is not his, may be sued in such name, and is bound as he would be if he had signed his real name.[4]

Changes of names exhibit eight different characteristics :—

(i) Addition of a name finally, as Henry Cavendish changed to Henry Cavendish Percy.

(ii) Addition of a name medially, as W. S. Adams changed to W. S. Stanley Adams, by deed poll (*Times*, 31st Oct., 1888). James Macdonald changed to James Cumming Raff Macdonald, authorized by the Keepers of the Signet (*Scotsman*, 30th May, 1882).

(iii) Omission of the final name : In 1850 an attorney named Thomas James Moses applied to the Court of Queen's Bench to have the last name erased from the rolls, as he wished to be known as Thomas James ; and although no sanction of the change had been obtained by Royal Licence Mr. Justice Coleridge thought that the change ought to be permitted. Mr. Justice Earle (1849) granted a similar application in the case of William Duggett Ingledew, who, for a family reason, desired to abandon his third name.

(iv) Omission of a medial name : Edmund Jonathan Watkins Hornblower Clarke, an attorney, became Edmund Hornblower Clarke, upon an application before the Lord Chief Justice (*Herald and Genealogist*, vol. i, p. 355).

(v) Change of final name totally : Rump gives way to Ward (*Times*, 25th Dec., 1880) : Weatherhog becomes Travers (*Times*, 9th May, 1888).

(vi) Change of final name partially : Pigg is improved to Pegge (*Times*, 21st June, 1896) ; Vice is spelt Vyse (*Times*, 22nd Nov., 1876) ; Twaddle becomes Tweeddale (*Times*, 4th Jan., 1890) ; and a deed poll converts Uren into Wren (*Times*, 13th June, 1896).

(vii) Change of a medial name totally : J. W. Nicholl Carne became

[1] *Du Boulay* v. *Du Boulay* (1869), Law Reports, Privy Council, vol. ii, p. 430. Lord Dundonald, in an article in the *Nineteenth Century* (Jan., 1894), records that in the reign of Charles I a fine of £500 was imposed on a person for assuming the name of another family ; no source of the information is given, but the reference is evidently to an inn-keeper known as " Jack of the West ", who " assumed the name of West and the arms of the family of Lord Delaware. He was fined £500, ordered to be degraded and never more to write himself gentleman ". (M. Noble, *History of College of Arms*, p. 225.) There is nothing to show that the fine was for assuming the *name* of West, and had he rested content with so doing no notice would have been taken of his action.

[2] *The Laws of England*, by the Earl of Halsbury, 1912, vol. xxi, p. 349.

[3] *Barlow* v. *Bateman* (1730), Peere William's Reports, Chancery and King's Bench, vol. iii, p. 65.

[4] *Laws of England*, vol. xxi, p. 350.

J. W. Stradling-Carne by deed poll (*Times*, 4th Sept., 1877) ; George Jonathan Carley became George Leyburn Carley by deed poll, 4th Nov., 1879 (*Times*). This latter is a change of christian name.

(viii) Change in the sequence of the names : Maitland-Makgill-Crichton became Makgill-Crichton-Maitland (*Times*, 14th June, 1884).

Combination of the various methods of change may be found, as dropping one name and adding two : G. Troyte-Bullock, by royal licence, became G. Troyt Chafyn-Grove (*London Gazette*, 5th May, 1892, p. 2829). Changing one name partially and adding one : K. Turnour lost its identity in K. Turnur Fetherstonhaugh, by royal licence (*London Gazette*, 27th Dec., 1895, p. 969). By adding a name medially and finally, Swinnerton became a minor element of Milborne-Swinnerton-Pilkington (17 and 18 Vict., c. 1, l. e. 52). Reversal and medial addition converted Wellesley-Pole to Pole-Tylney-Long-Wellesley (*London Gazette*, 18th Jan., 1812, p. 129). Occasionally, by a reversal of the names, the forename becomes a surname, and vice versa : Lewin Joseph changed the order of his names, and was henceforth known as Joseph Lewin (*Times*, 13th Oct., 1898). In the cases of Thomas James Moses and William Duggett Ingledew, noticed above, it seems that for a time they must have lived without surnames, and until their second personal names had become so by repute. The incidence of the hyphen has been ignored in the above remarks, it appearing to be quite modern practice for which there is no authority, and is presumably to differentiate the surname from the christian name, and to show which names descend to the children by inheritance.

Although the law prescribes no rules limiting a man's liberty to change his name, yet " in order to preserve testimony and to obviate the doubt and confusion which a change of name is likely to involve, it is usual to adopt one of the three following courses, that is to obtain a private Act of Parliament, to obtain a Royal Licence, or to execute a deed poll ".[1]

" Recourse to Parliament for authority to adopt a new name is unusual " ; a recent instance is the private Act entitled " Clifton's Name ", 22 Vict. ch. 1 (1859) ; such an Act is not imperative in its terms ; it merely permits the assumption of a new name.[2]

" A Royal Licence has, like a private Act of Parliament, the advantage of giving a formal sanction to the change, and of securing, as far as possible, the recognition of the new name by the world in general. It has the further advantage that it secures a record of the reasons for the change and of all other matters relevant to the granting of the licence, inasmuch as

[1] *Laws of England*, vol. xxi, p. 349.
[2] Ibid., p. 352.

Royal Licences are recorded in the College of Arms pursuant to the terms of the licence." [1]

A petition for a Royal Licence for a change of surname has to be drawn up by an officer of the College of Arms, signed by the applicant and submitted through the Home Secretary to the Sovereign, when, if reasonable ground is stated, a grant will probably be made.

It should be particularly noticed that the Act of Parliament does not take away the former name, in fact, there is usually a special proviso to prevent its loss. The King's licence does not give the new name, but merely grants permission to take it, and it is accordingly voluntarily assumed.

By means of a deed poll, duly executed and attested, and enrolled in the Central Office of the Supreme Court, a person may evidence his assumption of a new surname in addition to or in substitution for his original name. [2]

During the last 150 years several thousands of families, principally in the upper and well-to-do classes of society, have formally changed their names. [3]

An exceptional case of change of surname is that of the foundling, which unfortunate mortal, not knowing his own family name, to prepare himself for a normal life, has perforce to acquire another by repute. The bastard, who also has to acquire a name by repute, is on a different footing, and in doing so he does not change his name, because he never had one.

Foreigners are now controlled by the Aliens' Restriction Act, 1919, which prohibits the assumption by an alien of any name other than that by which he was ordinarily known on 4th Aug., 1914. Exemption from this provision may be granted by a Secretary of State. The Act does not affect the assumption of a name by Royal Licence. [4]

Aliases. In medieval days, when a plurality of second names was not uncommon, two might be singled out for general use, and these might be connected by an *alias* or *dictus*, having apparently the same effect as the modern interposition of the hyphen in forming a "double-barrelled" surname :—

Herebertus filius Hereberti dicti Finch. 8 Edw. II (1315).
Vincentius Herbert *alias* Finch.
Harbard vocata vel Finch. Mon. in Brabourne Church, Kent. [5]

---

[1] *Laws of England*, p. 352, note t.
[2] Ibid., p. 354. For forms of deed poll, statutory declaration and notice of change, see *Encyclopædia of Forms and Precedents*, by Sir A. Underhill, 1925, vol. ii, pp. 2-6.
[3] Phillimore, ix.
[4] *Complete Statutes* (Butterworth, 1930), i, 205.
[5] *Miscellanea, Genealogica et Heraldica*, vol. ii, pp. 325-7.

The double name may point to marriage with an heiress, when it would be continued generation after generation until, as in this case, Finch survived. One such example may be cited:—Fisher Dilke of Shentoke, Warw., born in 1595, married Sybil Wentworth, a son of the marriage being called Fisher Dilke *alias* Wentworth. A grandson, born 1655, was called in pedigrees, Fisher Dilke Wentworth.[1] A third possibility is that bastardy is indicated, as in the case of the family of Lodge, illegitimately descended from the Lytteltons, who " at first wrote their surname Lyttelton *alias* Lodge ".[2] A fourth possibility is that the *alias* preserves the maiden name of a lady, but in that case the word " formerly " is generally used, as Margaret Eynesford formerly Swylyngton (1418), Elizabeth Lynch formerly Curthopp (1550),[3] or as in Scotland (see p. 393). Sometimes the *alias* introduces the nickname, such as the examples given on p. 80, in similar manner to the French *dit*-names, as Hervi le Breton dit Bon Repos.[4] In eighteenth-century parish registers may be found such entries as Jane Morgan *alias* Kettelbender, William Evans *alias* Tissy, Thomas Jones *alias* Tom Juggy.[5] Doubles which survived for a long time were Chapman *alias* Barker in Suffolk, and Richmond *alias* Webb in Wilts.

The use of the *alias*, as in the pardon noticed above (p. 402), more often corresponded to the modern application.

Joh'nes Rous de Barton super Humber *alias* dictus Johannes Tederych de Otteby in com. Suff. yeoman. 16 Hen. VI. (Gaol Delivery Roll 210, f. 15.)

Willelmus Elyot per nomen Will'i Baxtere de Sowthwold in com. Suff. bakere. Ibid., f. 16.

Christian Names. The control of the ancient ceremony of name-giving was appropriated by the Christian Church, and rules and laws relating to the bestowal of font-names are only to be found among the canons and ordinances made by ecclesiastical authority. The conferring of the personal name is now, in general, associated with the " entrance into the church ", through the sacrament of baptism, which rite may be administered at any time during life, the names so given being known as christian, baptismal, christened, or font-names. A child may, however, be baptized in a case of urgency by a lay person, but if the religious ceremony be dispensed with, there is no necessity for the infant to be given a name at all. The law does not demand a person to be named, but the resulting inconvenience would lead very soon to the child being dubbed with

---

[1] *Notes and Queries*, 3rd Oct., 1874, p. 271.
[2] *History of the College of Arms*, by Rev. Mark Noble, p. 439.
[3] Index to Wills (P.C.C.).   [4] Michaëlsson, p. 130.
[5] Radnor Parish Register. *Notes and Queries*, 30th Dec., 1882, p. 534.

an epithet or appellative, which would become the forename by repute, and serve all practical purposes as satisfactorily as the baptismal name.

An attempt was made by the ecclesiastical authorities to limit the choice of undesirable names which might be selected by parents ; the third constitution of Archbishop Peccham (A.D. 1281) has been translated as follows :—

" Let the priests also take heed that they suffer not nyse and wanton names to be given to the youngles when they be baptised specially of the women kind which names spoken sound to wantons, and if the contrary be done let it be redressed by the Bishops that confirm them." [1]

Dr. Blunt observes " this was anciently done by the bishop naming the child he was confirming by the new and not the old name, in the usual words of the confirmation office, ' Consigno te N signo crucis ✠ et confirmo te chrismate salutis,' etc." [2]

Bishop Scambler, of Peterborough, writing in 1567, said :—

" I may not change usuall or comen names at the confirmacion, but onlie strange and not comen : and further if the name be changed at confirmacion, it taketh effect but from the confirmacion." [3]

An addition to the baptismal name at confirmation is usual in the Roman Catholic church. [4]

In the sixteenth century, when the eminent lawyer Sir Edward Coke was compiling his Institutes, although a man could not have two names of baptism, yet his christian name could be changed at confirmation.

" If a man be baptized by the name of Thomas, and after at his confirmation by the bishop he is named John, he may purchase by the name of his confirmation. And this was the case of Sir Francis Gawdie, chief justice of the Court of Common Pleas, whose name of baptism was Thomas, and his name of confirmation Francis : and that name of Francis, by the advice of all the judges, in anno 36 Hen. VIII [1544–5] he did bear, and after used in all his purchases and grants." [5]

" And the court said that it may be that a woman was baptized by the name of Anable, and forty years after she was confirmed by the name of Douce, and then her name was changed, and after she was to be named Douce, and that all purchases, etc., made by her by the name of baptism before her confirmation remain good ; a matter not much in use, nor requisite to be put in ure, but yet necessary to be known." [6]

[1] 1534 Translation. Lyndwood's Provinciale (Bullard and Bell, 1929), p. 102.
[2] *The Book of Church Law*, by Rev. J. H. Blunt, 1921, p. 60.
[3] Lansd. MS. 50, f. 127.
[4] *Index to Changes of Name* (Phillimore and Fry), 1905, p. xxi. *Notes and Queries*, 10th July, 1926, p. 31.
[5] *Institutes*, 1823, vol. i, 3a.   [6] Ibid.

Dr. Blunt further states that Bishop Kennett has left on record in some MS. notes to the prayer book, which are now in the British Museum, an account of a case in which a bishop changed the name of a child. He records the fact as follows :—

" On Sunday, Dec. 21, 1707, the Lord Bishop of Lincoln confirmed a young lad in Henry VII's Chapel : who upon that ceremony was to change his christian name : and accordingly, the sponsor who presented him delivered to the bishop a certificate, which his lordship signed, to notify that he had confirmed a person by such a name, and did order the parish minister then present to register the person in the parish book under that name. This was done by the opinion under hand of Sir Edward Northey, and the like opinion of Lord Chief Justice Holt, founded on the authority of Sir Edward Coke, who says it was the common law of England." [1]

An instance of change of christian name also appears in a register of Cork Cathedral.

" 1761, Sept. 21. Robert St. George Caulfield, Lieutenant in His Majesties 93 Regiment of Foot, commanded by Col. Samuel Bagshaw, and eldest son of Robert Caulfield, minister of, and residing in the parish of Finglass, near Dublin, was by me presented to the Rt. Revd. Father in God, Jemmett, Lord Bishop of Corke and Ross, in the Cathedral and Parish Church of St. Finbarry, Corke, to be admitted to the holy rite of Confirmation and to be admitted to change his name of Robert St. George for that of William, and by the name of William I did then present him ; and the Bishop, consenting to the changing of his name to William did then confirm him William." [2]

An erroneous entry in the register has been corrected many years after the making of the mistake :—

1794, 23rd. Nov. Baptism. William, son of John and Elizabeth Ley, the " William " was an error for John and was corrected 29th June, 1843, by the Vicar in the presence of the father.[3] (Barnstaple Par. Reg.)

On 11th June, 1886, at St. John's Church, Tue Brook, near Liverpool, the Bishop of Liverpool confirmed a female candidate by her two baptismal names, with an additional christian name (being her mother's maiden surname), and signing a certificate to that effect which was afterwards noted in the candidate's baptismal register. It is said that the Bishop, nevertheless, expressed " an objection to the practice of changing a name once solemnly given in baptism ".[4]

Burn (1763) erroneously supposed that upon the review of the liturgy at the restoration of Charles II, and the alteration of the office of confirmation, whereby the bishop ceased to pronounce the name of the person confirmed, the possibility of

---

[1] *Church Law*, p. 60. [2] *Notes and Queries*, 2nd July, 1870, p. 17.
[3] Ed. by Thos. Wainwright, p. 212.
[4] *Notes and Queries*, 24th July, 1886, p. 77.

change of name likewise ended.[1] The above cases dispose of this view, and it is evident that the ecclesiastical law has not been altered, and that a change of font-name may take place at confirmation.[2]

The ecclesiastical authorities were not always consulted in the matter. A case of change of christian name by advertisement occurs in *The Times*, 13th May, 1878 :—

" Surgeon-Major James Spence, resident in Jersey, gives notice that his infant son, Edmund Lionel Warren ' Spence, having been baptized in these names without the paternal sanction, shall discontinue to use them, and shall be known as James Edwin Spence." [3]

In the following year George Jonathan Carley, by deed poll, 4th Nov., 1879, renounced and discontinued his christian name of Jonathan, and assumed and adopted the "christian name " of Leyburn.[4] A notice in *The Times* (1st Apr., 1880) announced that Henry Wyley intended to assume the christian name of James in addition to and before his name of Henry.[5]

Authority to take a new forename may also be given by Act of Parliament, as appears by a private Act, entitled " Baines Name, 1907 ", whereby the name of Henry Rodd was assumed in lieu of the original christian name Raymond Hill.

The view of Sir H. H. Shephard, LL.D. (1912), is that " a man may at any time assume another name in addition to or in place of his baptismal name, and that for all practical purposes the name so assumed may become his first christian name . . . The name which a man himself adopts, and which is adopted by his friends and other persons having dealings with him, becomes his name ". Abraham Langley, in 1814, had for three years been known, in the village where his banns of marriage had been published, by the name of George Smith ; it was held that the banns in which he was designated by that name were properly published, and that his original name would not have been the true name within the meaning of the statute, 26 Geo. II, c. 33.[6] Likewise " a person who, in executing an instrument, subscribes a first name which is not his christian name may be sued in that name, and is bound as he would be if he had signed his proper name ".[7]

Jews, Mahomedans, and unbaptized persons have no difficulty in effecting a change of first name, as is evidenced by

---

[1] *Ecclesiastical Law*, by Richard Burn, vol. i, p. 80.
[2] Sir R. Phillimore (*Eccl. Law of the Church of England*, 2nd ed., vol. i, p. 517).
[3] *Notes and Queries*, 6th July, 1878, p. 5.
[4] *Times*. See *Notes and Queries*, 15th July, 1882, p. 50.
[5] *Notes and Queries*, 15th May, 1880, p. 399.
[6] *Rex v. The Inhabitants of Billinghurst* ; Maule and Selwyn's Reports, K.B., vol. iii, p. 250.
[7] *Laws of England*, vol. xxi, p. 350. *Evans v. King* (1745), Willes, 554, and cases of later date.

the reversal of names announced by Lewin Joseph (p. 412 above), and the case of Abraham Solomon, who became Alfred Phillips.[1]

It seems perfectly clear that a forename may be bestowed at baptism or assumed at later date ; changed by the Church, by Act of Parliament, or at the will of the bearer ; added to or dropped entirely without formality. Provided that the modification is honestly made, and of common repute, the law would not uphold any objection. It will be seen from the notes which follow that the " registration " of a forename does not in any way improve its status.

Registration of Births, Deaths, and Marriages. Prior to the reign of Henry VIII, no authority had ordained that registration of births or deaths should be made, and it is clear from the nature of the evidence led at the proceedings known as " proofs of age ", that there was frequently no written record of a birth to which reference could be made. It appears, however, that in some instances entries relating to persons of social position were made in books, psalters, missals, calendars, etc., kept in both monasteries and parish churches, as the following extracts from inquisitions will evidence.

Births :—

1332, 5th May. At the proof of age of John son and heir of Thomas Mauduyt it was testified that said John was baptized in Wereminster church, Wilts. by the vicar, who wrote the day of birth in a certain psaltery. (Inq. p. m., vol. vii, p. 341.)

1332, 30th Mar. At the proof of age of John son and heir of Hugh de Lachedon it was testified that at his baptism in Maylond church, Essex, the day of his birth was entered in a certain missal. (Inq. p. m., vol. vii, p. 342.)

1333, 15th July. At the proof of age of Edmund son and heir of John de Benstede, it was testified that at his baptism in St. Margaret's church, Westminster, the chaplain noted the day of his birth in the missal of the said church. (Inq. p. m., vol. vii, p. 383.)

1350, 14th June. At the proof of age of William son and heir of William de Roos of Hamelak, John de Tilneye said that he was in the Abbey of Croyland when a letter came from the lord of Roos to announce to him the said William's birth, and the said abbot caused the day of the birth (*originis*) of the said William to be written in a certain book, which book and date the witness saw three days ago. William Bayard of Boston agreed, saying that he caused the day of the said William's birth to be inserted in certain memoranda, and in a kalendar, etc. Laurence de Leyk testified that he was in the priory of Freston on the day of the said William's birth, and he saw them write the day of his birth in a certain book in the priory. (Inq. p. m., vol. vii, p. 414.)

Deaths :—

1330, 26th Jan. At a proof of age a witness testified that on 1st Feb. 2 Edw. II (1309) he inserted the death of his sister in the

[1] *Times*, 18th Aug., 1862.

calendar of the church of St. Nicholas, Newcastle-upon-Tyne. (Inq. p. m., vol. ii, p. 235.)

1332, 6th Apr. At a proof of age a witness testified that twenty-two years previously he caused the death of his mother to be entered in the missal of the church of Hampstede, Essex. (Inq. p. m., vol. vii, p. 343.)

The advantages of a regular system of registration were not perhaps fully realized until the dissolution of monasteries in 1536, when so many records were dispersed ; at any rate, two years later, by an injunction of Thomas, Lord Cromwell, Vicar-General, it became compulsory to keep parish registers, wherein should be written the day and year of every wedding, christening, and burial and also " every person's name ". Similar injunctions were issued by Edw. VI (1547) and Elizabeth (1559).[1] An ecclesiastical mandate of 1603 is the first which provides for both " names and surnames " of the parents of those christened to be registered.[2]

In 1836 a General Register Office was established for registering births, deaths, and marriages (6 & 7 Wm. IV, c. 86). By this and subsequent Acts the birth of every child has to be registered, but it is not necessary to give it a name. By 37 & 38 Vict., c. 88, if a name has been registered and it is desired to change it, such may be done upon compliance with certain formalities (sect. 8). Doubtless many discrepancies remain uncorrected ; e.g. at a Lambeth inquest, 11th Feb., 1924, a witness stated that she was registered as Emily Sophia Jane, and christened Emily Charlotte Elizabeth[3] ; the latter would, of course, be the true name, no matter which was first given.

The Custom and Law of Scotland. What has been said regarding the bestowal of christian names and the assumption of surnames in England applies equally to the custom north of the border. For an early precedent as to change of forename reference may be made to history which records that John, earl of Carrick, eldest son of Robert II, when crowned on the death of his father in 1389, changed his name to Robert, John being supposed to be an unlucky name.[4] At what time it first became customary to obtain authority for change of name cannot now be determined. In A.D. 1489 James IV, at the supplication of his cousin Colin, earl of Argyle, changed the name of the castle and place " quhilk wes callit the gloume " pertaining to his said cousin ; and Parliament ordained that the castle should be called in time to come Campbele.[5] In like manner the royal approval, and consent of the three

[1] *The History of Parish Registers*, by J. S. Burn, 1829, p. 17, et seq.
[2] Ibid., p. 24.
[3] *Glasgow Bulletin*, 12th Feb., 1924.
[4] *History of Scotland*, by A. Lang, vol. i, p. 274.
[5] *Acts of the Parliaments of Scotland*, vol. ii, p. 222, c. 23.

estates of Parliament, was thought in some cases to be necessary to an effective change of surname. In 1528 it was ordained that Robert Bertoun of Overberntoun, upon his marriage with the daughter and heir of John Mowbray, " suld be callit mowbray & haue & beir þat surñem." [1] In the formal application it declares that the family (Mowbray) had been an old honourable house and done good service in the wars for the predecessors of James V, and the desire was that the said house should not pass from the surname. [2] A somewhat similar authority was given in 1581, upon the marriage of Edward Maxwell, son of John, lord Hereis, with Margaret, the daughter of William Baillie, laird of Lamingtoun, but it is of interest to note that the Act applied not to Edward Maxwell, but only to the first son born of the marriage, and his posterity. Other children of the union would presumably, in conformity with recognized custom, receive the name of Maxwell.

Thairfore oure said so,ane lord (James VI), etc., Hes statute and ordanit that the said williame baillie eldest lauchfull sone and apperand air (heir apparent) gottin betuix the saidis Eduarde and margaret hes willinglie past fra his surename of maxwell Ressauit (received) and acceptit in place thairof the said surename of baillie And armes of the said hous of lammingtoun. And thairfore decernis and Ordanis him now to be callit in all tymes cumming williame baillie And all his posteritie thaireftir to be callit baillies of thair surename. And newir to rewoke the samyn (same) nor to ressaue ony vther surename heireftir. And ordanes lettres of publicatioun to be direct heirvpoun gif neid beis in forme as efferis. [3]

A further instance of change of name is that of Harry, brother of the " noble and michtie lord Dauid erle of craufurde ", who, being the adopted son of John Charteris of Kynfawnis and likewise fiar of Kynfawnis, contracted 27th Sept., 1584, to accept the said surname of Charteris ; whereunto, in 1587, James VI and the lords of Parliament interposed their authority in the best and most sure form and likewise approved and confirmed the forenamed contract. [4]

The Gowrie (or Ruthven) Conspiracy of 1600, failing in its object to kidnap James VI, was the cause of an Act of Parliament abolishing the surname of Ruthven. In order that the infamy justly inflicted to the guilty shall not spot such as are innocent of treason, the King with the advice and consent of the estates of Parliament statutes and ordains " that the surname of Ruthven sall now and in all tyme cumming be extinguischit and aboleissit for euir ". The Act further ordains that those who bear the said surname and are innocent of the

[1] *Acts*, p. 321*a*. [2] Ibid., p. 320*a*.
[3] Ibid., vol. iii, p. 232*a*, *b*, c. 46. [4] Ibid., vol. iii, p. 516*b*, c. 122.

crime of treason shall renounce the surname of Ruthven and never use the same in time coming, but to take to themselves, their bairns and posterity any other honest and undefamed surname ; and to use the same in all contracts, bonds, etc.[1] On 30th Dec., 1602, all persons who had formerly borne the name of Ruthven were forbidden to approach within 10 miles of the royal residence.[2] By an Act of Charles I, in 1641, it was made lawful for the Ruthvens of Ballindean (Perthshire), their bairns and posterity, " to enjoy and assume to themselves the surname of Ruthven, and to use it as if the Act of 1600 had never been made against them." [3]

Early in the seventeenth century, Scotland was in a constant ferment with clan feuds and border raids, punctuated with massacres, burnings, robberies, and hangings. The MacGregors were among those who received blame for the disturbances, and on 3rd Apr., 1603, an Act passed whereby it was ordained that the name of M'Gregoure should be altogether abolished, and that the whole persons of that clan should renounce their name and take some other name, and that they nor none of their posterity should call themselves Gregor or McGregoure thereafter, under the pain of death.[4]

One entry only shows compliance with the Act. Various McGregors of Perth renounce their former " unhappie name " of McGregour, " and in all tyme heirefter tak to thame and call thameselffis the name of Johnnestoun " according to " thair grit and solemp aithis " given in the presence of the Lords of Secret Council, under pain of perjury and defamation, and further monetary pains.[5] In 1617 a further Act passed, ratifying, allowing, and approving the Act of 1603.[6] An entry on the Register of the Privy Council refers to one of the clan, Duncane McEane Duy in Rannache, who has neither renounced his name nor found caution as the rest had done. Duncan was committed to the Tolbooth in Edinburgh, there to remain at his own expense till he renounce his name and find the necessary caution.[7] Various other members of the clan who had taken the names of Douglas, Menzies, and Ramsey respectively, never having appeared to give proof that they intended to continue in their promised obedience, the Lords, in 1618, decreed a " sentence condempnitour " against the cautioners, and ordered forfeiture of the caution moneys, 5,000 merks in all.[8] The Clan Gregour having " brokene furth againe ", in 1633 a new and more severe Act was passed, by which they were deprived of all rights. No minister within

[1] *Acts*, vol. iv, p. 213, c. 2.
[2] *Register of the Privy Council of Scotland*, vol. vi, p. 511.
[3] *Acts*, vol. v, p. 460, c. 210.   [4] Ibid., vol. iv, p. 550, c. 26.
[5] *Reg. of P.C.*, vol. vi, p. 797.   [6] *Acts*, vol. iv, p. 550, c. 26.
[7] *Reg. of P.C.*, vol. xi, pp. 371–2.   [8] Ibid., p. 377.

the bounds of the Highlands or neighbouring " cuntries "
thereto was permitted to baptize and christen any male child
with the name of Gregour.[1] In 1661 the McGregors, having
carried themselves with loyalty and affection, his Majesty
King Charles II rescinded the Act of 1633 (c. 30),[2] but in 1693
(c. 62) it was revived, and the Act Rescissory of 1661 annulled
and made void.[3]

Various Acts of Parliament authorizing change of name
passed, and it may be of interest to give one such entry
verbatim.

1663, c. 26. Act for changeing the name of Souter of late used by
some of the name of Johnstoun.

The Estates of Parliament haveing heard a supplication presented
vnto them by Mr. David Johnstoun *alias* Souter Student in Divinity
for himselff and in name & behalff of his remanent kinsmen of that
name within the Shirreffdome of Pearth & fforfar Mentioning that the
petitioners predicessor & his brother of the sirname of Johnstoun in
the yeer 1460 (as they are informed) came from Annandale to Scone
in Perthshire, vpon some discontent, and ther attendit the ouner of
that place for a long time, and assumed to themselffs the Sirname of
Souter that therby they should not be noticed for the tyme ; One of
the breither dyeing without issue The other surviveing, for his good
deportment, wes maried to a Gentlewoman from which mariage
proceidit diverse honest men who are groun into considerable families
whairof the petitioners are descendit. And being desireous that they
may be restored to their true & antient sirname of Johnstoun Therfor
humbly craveing they may be impowered to alter their sirname and
that in all timecomeing they may be designed after the sirname of
Johnstoun. As the supplication bears ; Which being taken into consideration The Kings Maiestie with advice and consent of his Estates
of Parliament Doth heirby allow the supplicants to take the Sirname
of Johnstoun and that they and their posterity be designed and called
in all time comeing after the Sirname of Johnstoun Notwithstanding
of their former designation be the name of Souter And declares that
this change shall nowayes preiudge them nor their airs & successors
in any maner of way of the benefite of any writs or securitys wherin
any of them are designed by the name of Souter.[4]

In Scotland at the present day it is customary to refer
to a laird by the name of his estate, and it is probable that
formerly such titles were used by the landowner for signing
documents, for it is to be noticed that an Act of 1672 concerning the privileges of the office of Lyon King of Arms,
incidentally declares that it is only allowed for noblemen and
bishops to " subscrive by their titles ; And that all others
shall subscrive their Christned names, or the initiall letter

---

[1] *Acts*, vol. v. p. 44, c. 30.   [2] Ibid., vol. vii, p. 189, c. 195.
[3] Ibid., vol. ix, p. 324b, c. 62. Act for the Justiciary in the Highlands.
[4] Ibid., vol. vii, p. 467a, c. 26.

therof with there Sirnames, and may if they please abject the designations of their lands prefixing the word ' Of ' to the said designations ".[1]

In 1695 " Evan, formerly called M'Grigor " petitioned Parliament, craving liberty to assume the forbidden sirname of M'Grigor, he having been born about the time of the Act Rescissory in 1661, and having used the name in business, etc. The desire was granted, but only to himself during life, and upon condition that he gave his children another surname, for which purpose he chose Evanson, which was inserted in the minutes.[2]

In the nineteenth century it appears that authority for change of *christian* name could be obtained from the officials representing the Writers to H.M. Signet. The following advertisement appeared in the *Scotsman*, 30th May, 1882.

Notice of Change of Name. Notice is hereby given that I, James Cumming Raff Macdonald (heretofore named James Macdonald), have, by and with the authority of the Hon. the Keeper, the Deputy-Keeper, and the Commissioners of Her Majesty's Signet, taken and adopted the names " Cumming Raff " as additional Christian names, and that I, the said James Cumming Raff Macdonald, will at all times hereafter, and for all purposes, subscribe myself as under. Dated this 29th day of May, 1882. J. C. R. Macdonald.

A writer in *Notes and Queries* points out that whereas "it has been the practice of the Court of Session to recognize formally an assumption or change of surname by a member of one of the legal bodies in Scotland, viz. advocates, writers to the signet, and solicitors, who are members of the College of Justice, here we have a new departure altogether—new in three different ways. The names are christian names, not surnames ; the gentleman assuming them is not a member of the College of Justice ; and the officials recognizing the assumption only represent the Writers to H.M. Signet, who are not a judicial body at all ".[3] While " Cumming Raff " may not be correctly described as " christian names ", it is evident from the signature that they do not form part of the surname.

The modern view is that in Scotland, " unless in the case of an officer under the Crown, or the holder of a public office, it is not necessary for a person desiring to change his name to obtain the authority of the Court to do so, and a petition for such authority will be refused." (*Furlong*, 1880, 7 R. 910, per L. P. Inglis.) A Writer to the Signet having obtained the royal licence to assume an additional surname, presented a petition to the Court to sanction his using it in all legal acts

---

[1] *Acts*, vol. viii, p. 96a, c. 47.   [2] Ibid., vol. ix, p. 355, c. 2.
[3] 10th June, 1882, p. 445.

and deeds and judicial proceedings. Lord President Hope
said : " This petition should be withdrawn as unnecessary.
I do not remember to have ever seen an application of this
nature. In the case of a notary public I have seen such an
application, but not in any other. There is no need of the
authority of the Court to enable a man in Scotland to change
his name." (*Young*, 1835, 13 S. 262.) [1]

With regard to misnomer, great precision in naming a
panel was not called for, provided that there was no doubt
as to whom the indictment referred : e.g. James Bryce *alias*
Wight went *sine die*, because his real name was James Wight
(1619), and it was found to be a good exception in a prosecution
against certain thieves, that they were " not described by their
proper *surname* of Kennedy, but only by certain Highland
nicknames and *patronymics*, which had occasionally been
applied to them (1736) [2] ; on the other hand, it was held that
" no reasonable but a captious plea of misnomer could be
founded " on slight and immaterial modification of names such
as Fyshe Palmer, whose name was spelled Fische (1793).[3]

David Hume, an eighteenth-century professor of the
Scottish law, wrote : " It is indeed the genius of the English
practice, to observe an extreme and punctilious accuracy in
such matters ; but I cannot find, that in this respect we have
ever been disposed to follow their example, but rather, and I
think with as sound a judgment to disregard such criticisms as
unseemly niceties which serve only to disappoint the course
of justice, and to bring the law itself into contempt." [4] With
which opinion the layman will whole-heartedly agree. In the
case of witnesses, a citation was void, if the variation were
such as might possibly mislead or deceive the panel in his
inquiries concerning the individual who is summoned : thus
Farm for Fairholme (1737), Hubbart for Hibbut (1788), Law
for Low (1791), were successfully challenged.

Laws of Ireland. Outside the English pale (comprising
the present counties of Louth, Meath, Westmeath, Kildare,
Dublin, and Wicklow, the English law, introduced by Hen. II,
did not prevail ; the Brehons (native judges) administering
the ancient laws for the preservation of order amongst the
native Irish. As mentioned above (p. 37), an early monarch
is supposed to have enacted that surnames should be assumed,

[1] Green's *Encyclopædia of the Law of Scotland*, 1912. Finlayson says that
formerly in Scotland the false assumption of a name was equal to the false
assumption of coat armour, which was punished as forgery ; but he cites no
authority.

[2] The distinction between surname and patronymic is of interest.

[3] *Commentaries on the Laws of Scotland respecting Crimes*, 2nd ed., 1819,
vol. ii, p. 152–3.

[4] Ibid., p. 153.

but nothing of the law can now be traced, and no credence can be placed in the story. Nicknames are, however, mentioned, and seem to have been looked upon in some cases as slander. The third-century Book of Aicill, a code of ancient Irish " criminal " law, says :—

> Eitged mbriathar brath ocus air ocus lesainm.
> Eitgid [? offence] of words, i.e. spying and satirizing and nick-naming.[1]

According to the Heptads there are " seven kinds of satire of which the law makes mention for which honour-price is estimated according as is lawful. A nickname that clings, i.e. to say to him something which he thinks grievous or bad, so that it clings to him, such as, He is a *cell coire* " (a church in which milk-and-water only is drunk, a miserable place : Curry). The fine varied according to the length of life of the nickname, and also to its nature.[2] In the Senchus Mor (fifth century), a distress of five days' stay is fixed for a nickname (*imon lesanma*) ; " i.e. the thing that is for the name which is an annoyance (*ainm is len*) or which constantly sticks to a person (*is lista lenus*), i.e. when it is not known whether the name will stick at all ; the honor-price which is for it has a stay of three days, not having the wealth of his rank, extends it to five days." [3] Referring to " the sons of the Feini grades ", the penalty " for causing a blemish or giving a nickname is to be deducted as ' smacht '-fine from the price of the fosterage until it reaches two-thirds of it ".[4]

In view of the absence of statutory law concerning surnames in England, it is somewhat surprising to find regulations controlling their adoption in Ireland. By the preamble to the Statutes of Kilkenny, 40 Edw. III (1366), it appears that for a long time after the conquest of Ireland " the English of the said land used the English language ", etc., but many were now forsaking their language, laws, and usages, living and governing themselves " according to the manners, fashions, and language of the Irish enemies ". The lengthy statute ordained and established, among other matters, " that every Englishman use the English language, and be named by an English name, leaving off entirely the manner of naming by the Irish." [5] It became necessary for an Englishman desirous of retaining an Irish name to obtain the royal permission, and one such instance has been noticed above (p. 387), one Dyermyd

---

[1] *Ancient Laws of Ireland*, vol. iii, p. 93.   [2] Ibid., vol. v, pp. 229–233.
[3] Ibid., vol. i, pp. 185, 193.   [4] Ibid., vol. ii, 157.
[5] Q⁰ chescun Engleys vse la lang Englies et soit nome p' nome Engleys enterlessant oultermᵗ la manere de nom'e use p' Irroies. *Statutes of Ireland*, ed. by H. F. Berry, 1907, vol. i, p. 435.

Makmorghyth receiving a licence to have and bear the name of Makmorghyth.

In the following century a further step was taken, an attempt being made to stamp out the use of Irish names among the Irish themselves, and generally to anglicize the native Celt living within the pale.

1465. At the request of the Commons, it is ordained and established by authority of Parliament, that every Irish [man who dwells] among Englishmen, in the counties of Dublin, Meath, Uriell [Louth], and Kildare, go like unto an Englishman in apparel, and shaving off his beard above the mouth ; and that he be within one year sworn the liege man of the King . . . and take unto himself an English surname of a town, as Sutton, Chester, Trim, Skreen, Cork, Kinsale ; or a colour, as White, Black, Brown ; or an art, as Smith or Carpenter ; or an office, as Cook, Butler ; and that he and his issue use that name under pain of forfeiture of his goods yearly until the premises be done, to be levied twice a year to the King's wars, according to the discretion of the King's Lieutenant or his Deputy.[1]

Like that of McGregor, the surname of O'Neill suffered disgrace, being abolished by Act of Parliament, 11 Eliz., c. 1, the future taking of it to be adjudged high treason, the offenders suffering death and forfeiture.[2] Apparently this Act was never repealed, and it is evident that it continued to be essential to obtain authority to bear the name, because by licence (*London Gazette*, 13th Feb., 1808, p. 217) John Geoghegan, of Bunowan Castle (Galway) was permitted " to reject the surname which his ancestors had borne for about 800 years, from their progenitor, Eochagan, son of Cosgrach, chief of Cinel-Fiacha, in the tenth century, and to take a new name from his more remote and more illustrious ancestor Niall, of the Nine Hostages, monarch of Ireland, in the fourth century ".[3]

At the present day the Irish Free State does not enforce the use of either Irish or English names, but a general instruction has been issued by Oifig An Árd-Chlárathóra (General Register Office) to all Registrars of Births, Deaths, and Marriages in Saorstát Éireann, to the effect that they may make entries in their Register Books in the Irish language, if called upon to do so.

Reform and Reflections. It is manifest that in the British Isles there is a want of a uniform and clearly-defined system of naming, but even if a regularized arrangement were devised, its general introduction could not be enforced without the aid of the law. Moreover, if the necessary powers for

[1] *Statutes at Large*, Ireland, 1786, vol. i, p. 29 ; *Statute Rolls of Ireland*, 5 Edw. IV, c. xvi (vol. iii, p. 291.)
[2] *Statutes*, vol. i, p. 335.
[3] *Topographical Poems* (O'Donovan), p. 13.

compulsion were obtained, it seems hardly practicable to draft any satisfactory rules for orthographic representation. Should a name be spelled (i) according to its ancient form ; (ii) its modern corruption ; or (iii) a revised version, i.e. phonetically or according to the dictionary ? Few would agree to the first, even if the original spelling could be discovered ; most people would prefer to retain the present form, however corrupt ; a few of the more progressive or less interested would be willing to accept a new spelling.

In Turkey names are now spelled phonetically, but such practice does not make for uniformity, since people often disagree as to the correct pronunciation ; wherefore it appears that the only reforms in orthography which can be advocated are, first, that names which are dictionary words should be spelled as in the dictionary, Smythe becoming Smith, etc. ; and secondly absurd forms of names, which never existed, should be abandoned ; thus French should no longer be written " ffrench ".

In these days of equality of the sexes, what is to be done to preserve the married woman's surname ? It has been suggested that if John Smith marries Mary Brown, the male children of the union should be called Brown-Smith, and the female Smith-Brown.[1] But what is to happen whan a young Brown-Smith espouses a White-Taylor ? One or other name would have to be dropped, and the attempt to perpetuate the family appellatives of both parents fails. The only workable plan seems to be that when Mr. Brown weds Miss Smith, the parties should retain their own names, being further described in formal documents as husband or wife of so-and-so as the case might be, and colloquially as the Smith-Browns or Mr. and Mrs. Smith-Brown, or vice versa, if preferred. Sons of the marriage would be surnamed Brown, and daughters Smith, both names being perpetuated, the one in a line of males, the other in a line of females.

Although it may be held that the popular version of Mr. Bumble's considered opinion and emphatic summary of the law is perhaps a little too highly coloured, it cannot but be admitted that with regard to names and surnames legal procedure has not kept pace with the customs of the people. Now that so many of our most trivial daily requirements are ordered by authorities operating under powers conferred by Acts of Parliament, municipal bye-laws, and so forth, it is perhaps rather refreshing to find that forename or surname may be changed at will without state interference ; and yet so far as surnames are concerned, there is a crying need for control, and regulation by authority would be welcomed, in

[1] *Index to Change of Name,* by W. P. W. Phillimore, p. xvii.

both business and official circles. While every person should be perfectly free, without let or hindrance, to change his first name to any reasonable appellative, such being solely a personal matter, some check is undoubtedly called for to prevent a rogue from taking a surname of honourable antiquity, or one which has been made famous by modern efforts and ability.

On the Continent the law has for long held control, and has regulated the naming of the people with apparent success. In France the forename of a child must be registered within three days after birth, and only approved appellatives as found in the official list may be bestowed. Official authorization must be obtained for any change of name, and civil tribunals will restrain wrongful assumption, a year being given for objections to be lodged.

In Germany the choice of forename is limited, as in France. A person is not allowed to describe himself by any name other than that acquired at birth. The wife is bound to assume the husband's name, and upon divorce is only forced to resume her maiden name if she be the exclusively guilty party.

In addition to adopting the best features of the continental ordinances, the ideal regulations should limit the number of both forenames and surnames. In nomenclature as in other domains the best taste is displayed and the maximum practical value attained by distinctive simplicity.

A SHORT BIBLIOGRAPHY

General.

BACONNIERE-SALVERTE, A. J. E. History of the Names of Men, Nations, and Places in their connection with the Progress of Civilization. From the French of E. Salverte. Translated by L. H. Mordacque. 2 vols. *London*, 1862–64. 8°.

JEFFCOTT (WILLIAM THOMAS). A Dictionary of Classical Names for English Readers. pp. vi, 109. *Macmillan & Co., London*, 1913. 8°.

LE HÉRICHER (ÉDOUARD). Glossaire etymologique des noms propres de France et d'Angleterre, etc. *Paris, Caen* (printed), 1870. 4°.

—— Glossaire germanique, scandinave et hébraique des noms d'hommes, français et anglais, etc. pp. 38. *Avranches*, 1884. 8°.

LONG (HARRY ALFRED). The Names we bear ; a descriptive compendium of biblical, classical, and common names. With a preface by Rev. J. M'Cann. pp. 244. *W. Macrone, Glasgow* (1877). 8°.

—— Personal and Family Names. pp. 362. *Hamilton Adams & Co., London*, 1883. 8°.

SOLMSEN (FELIX). Indogermanische Eigennamen als Spiegel der Kulturgeschichte, etc. pp. xi, 261. *Heidelberg*, 1922. 8°. (*Indogermanische Bibliothek*. Abt. 4, Bd. 2.)

Anglo-Saxon (Old English).

CRECELIUS (WILHELM). Collectæ ad augendam nominum propriorum Saxonicorum et Frisiorum scientam spectantes. Edidit W. Crecelius, 4 pt. *Berolini, Eberfeldæ* (printed), 1864[–70]. 8°.

FORSSNER (THORVALD). Continental Germanic Personal Names in England in Old and Middle English times. pp. lxiii, 289. *Uppsala*, 1916. 8°.

KEMBLE (JOHN MITCHELL). The Names, Surnames, and Nicnames of the Anglo-Saxons. *Archæological Institute of Great Britain and Ireland*. 1846. 8°.

KLUMP (WILHELM). Die altenglischen Handwerkernamen sachlich und sprachlich erlautert. pp. viii, 129. 1908. *Anglistische Forschungen*, etc. Hft. 24. 8°.

REDIN (MATS). Studies on Uncompounded Personal Names in Old English. pp. xlv, 195. *Uppsala*, 1919. 8°.

SEARLE (WILLIAM GEORGE). Onomasticon Anglo-Saxonicum. A List of Anglo-Saxon proper names from the time of Beda to that of King John. pp. lvii, 601. *University Press, Cambridge*, 1897. 8°.

Asianic. *See* Lycian.

Assyrian, Babylonian, and Sumerian.

CHIERA (EDWARD). List of Personal Names from the Temple School of Nippur : a syllabary of personal names. pp. 88, pl. xxxvii. 1916. *University of Pennsylvania, Publications of the Babylonian section*, vol. ii, No. 1. 4°.

—— Lists of Personal Names from the Temple School of Nippur. Lists of Akkadian personal names. 1916. *University of Pennsylvania, Publications of the Babylonian section*, vol. ii, No. 2. 4°.

—— List of Personal Names from the Temple School of Nippur : Lists of Sumerian personal names. *Philadelphia*, 1919. 8°. *University of Pennsylvania, Publications of the Babylonian section*, vol. ii, No. 3.

CLAY (A. T.). Personal Names from Cuneifcrm inscriptions of the Cassite Period. pp. 208. 1912. (*Yale Oriental Series*, vol. i.) 4°.

HUBER (ENGELBERT). Die Personennahmen in den Keilschrifturkunden aus der Zeit der Könige von Ur und Nisin. pp. 208. 1907. *Assyriologische Bibliothek*, etc. Bd. 21. 4°.

RANKE (HERMANN). Die Personennamen in den Urkunden der Hammura-dynastie. Ein Beitrag zur Kenntnis der semitischen Namenbildung. pp. 52. *Munchen*, 1902. 8°.
—— Early Babylonian Personal Names from the published tablets of the so-called Hammurabi Dynasty (2000 B.C.). pp. xiii, 255. 1905. *University of Pennsylvania*. Series D, etc., vol. iii. 8°.
TALLQVIST (KNUT LEONARD). Assyrian Personal Names. pp. xxxii, 327. *Helsingfors*, 1914. 4°. (*Acta Societatis Scientiarum Fennicae*, tom. 43, No. 1.)

Austrian. *See* German.

Basque.
GRAY (JOHN). The Personal and Place Names in the Book of Deer. pp. 30. *D. Scott, Peterhead* (1894). 4°.
SCHUCHARDT (Hugo Ernestus Mario). Iberische Personennahmen. Extrait de la " Revue Internationale des Études Basques ". pp. 13. *Bayonne*, 1909. 8°.

Breton.
LOTH (JOSEPH). Les Noms des saints bretons. pp. 149. *Paris*, 1910. 8°.

Celtic.
ESSER (QUIRINUS). Beiträge zur gallo-keltischen Namenkunde. *Malmedy*, *St. Vith* (printed), 1884, etc. 8°.

Coptic. *See* Egyptian.

Cornish.
BANNISTER (JOHN). A Glossary of Cornish Names ancient and modern, local, family, personal, etc. . . . now or formerly in use in Cornwall . . . *London, Truro* (printed 1869–71). 8°.
CHARNOCK (RICHARD STEPHEN). Patronymica Cornu-Britannica, or the etymology of Cornish surnames, etc. *London*, 1870. 8°.
DEXTER (THOMAS FRANCIS GEORGE). Cornish Names. An attempt to explain over 1,600 Cornish names. pp. 89. *Longmans & Co., London*, 1926. 8°.

Danish.
NIELSEN (OLUF). Olddanske Navne samlede af O. Nielsen. pp. xvi, 118. 1883, etc. *Universitets Jubilæets Samfund*, No. 15, etc. 1881, etc. 8°.

Dutch and Frisian.
AC. GHENT. K. Vlaamsche Academie. Lijst der in Zuid-Nederland meest gebruikelijke voornamen. pp. 35. *Gent*, 1902. 8°.
WINKLER (JOHAN). De Nederlandsche Geslachtsnamen in oorsprung geschiedenis en beteekenis. 2 stk. *Haarlem*, 1885. 8°.
—— Friesche Naamlijst. *Leuuwarden*, 1898. pp. xviii, 459. 8°.
—— Studiën in Nederlandsche Namenkunde. pp. 328. *Haarlem* (1900). 8°.

Egyptian.
HEUSER (GUSTAV). Die Personennamen der Kopten. Leipzig, 1929–. 8°. (*Studien zur Epigraphie und Papyruskunde.*) Bd. i, Schrift 2, etc.

English and American. *See also* Scottish.
ARTHUR (WILLIAM). An Etymological Dictionary of Family and Christian Names, with an Essay on their derivation and import. *New York*, 1857. pp. iv, 300. 8°.
BARBER (HENRY). British Family Names. Their origin and meaning with lists of Scandinavian, Frisian, Anglo-Saxon, and Norman names. Second edition, enlarged. pp. xii, 286. *E. Stock, London*, 1894. 8°.
BARDSLEY (CHARLES WAREING). Curiosities of Puritan Nomenclature. pp. xii, 252. *Chatto & Windus, London*, 1880. 8°.
—— A Dictionary of English and Welsh surnames, with special American instances, etc. pp. xvi, 837. *Henry Frowde, London*, 1901. 8°.

BARDSLEY (CHARLES WAREING). English Surnames : their sources and significations . . . Fifth edition, with a new preface. pp. xxv, 612. *Chatto & Windus, London*, 1897. 8°.

—— The Romance of the London Directory. pp. 162. *" Hand and Heart " Publishing Office, London* (1879). 8°.

BATCHELOR (ALLEN). An Alphabetical List of over 2,200 curious Surnames. *A. Batchelor, Guildford* (1892). fol.

BJÖRKMAN (E.). Zur englischen Namenkunde. pp. x, 94. 1912. Studien zur englischen Philologie, etc. Hft. 47.

BLAGG (T. M.). Surnames. Their origin, meaning, and distribution. pp. 20. *S. Whiles, Newark*, 1900. 8°.

BOWDITCH (NATHANIEL INGERSOLL). Suffolk Surnames. *Boston (Mass.)*. 1857. 8°. *Privately printed*. Third edition. 1861.

BRADY (JOHN HENRY). A critical and analytical dissertation on the Names of Persons. *London*. 1822. 12°.

BROCKIE (WILLIAM). The family names of the folks of Shields traced to their origin, with brief notices of distinguished persons. To which is appended a dissertation on the origin of the Britannic race. pp. 113. *Brockie & Co., South Shields*, 1857. 8°.

CHARNOCK (RICHARD STEPHEN). Ludus Patronymicus : or, the etymology of curious surnames. *London*, 1868. 8°.

—— Prænomina : or, the etymology of the principal Christian names of Great Britain and Ireland. pp. xvi, 128. *Trübner & Co., London*, 1882. 8°.

DUDGEON (PATRICK). A short introduction to the study of Surnames. pp. viii, 104. *D. Douglas, Edinburgh*, 1890. 8°.

FALCONER (THOMAS). On Surnames, etc. 1862. 12°.

—— An Answer to Mr. Falconer on the assumption of Surnames without royal licence. *London*, 1863. 8°.

—— Supplement to an essay on Surnames. 1863. 8°.

FERGUSON (ROBERT), of Carlisle. English Surnames and their place in the Teutonic family. *London, Carlisle* (printed), 1858. 8°.

—— Surnames as a Science. pp. viii, 235. *Routledge & Sons, London*, 1883. 8°.

—— The Teutonic name-system applied to the family names of France, England, and Germany, etc. *London, Carlisle* (printed), 1864. 8°.

FINLAYSON (JAMES). Surnames and Sirenames. The origin and history of certain family and historical names ; with remarks on the ancient right of the Crown to sanction and veto the assumption of names, etc. *London, Manchester* (printed 1863). 8°.

GENTRY (THOMAS G.). Family Names from the Irish, Anglo-Saxon, Anglo-Norman, and Scotch considered in relation to their etymology. pp. 225. *Philadelphia*, 1892. 8°.

GOULD (SABINE BARING). Family Names and their Story. pp. 431. *Seeley and Co., London*, 1910. 8°.

GUPPY (HENRY BROUGHAM). Homes of Family Names in Great Britain. pp. lxv, 601. *Harrison & Sons, London*, 1890. 8°.

HARRISON (HENRY). Surnames of the United Kingdom : a concise etymological dictionary. 2 vol. *Eaton Press, London*, 1912.

HILL (GEOFFRY). Some Consequences of the Norman Conquest. (Christian names in England.) pp. ix, 251. *Elliot Stock, London*, 1904. 8°.

LOWER (MARK ANTONY). English Surnames. Essays on family nomenclature, historical, etymological, and humorous. With chapters of rebuses and canting arms, the Roll of Battel Abbey, a List of latinized surnames, etc. *London, Guildford*, 1875. 8°. 2 vol.

—— Patronymica Britannica. A dictionary of the family names of the United Kingdom. *London, Lewes* (printed), 1860. 4°.

NICHOLS (THOMAS). Christian Names of Men and Women popularly explained. pp. 128. *Routledge & Sons, London*, 1892. 8°.

NICHOLSON (EDWARD WILLIAM BYRON). The Pedigree of " Jack " and of various allied names. pp. 35. *Alexander and Shepheard, London*, 1892.

WEEKLEY (ERNEST). The Romance of Names. *Third edition, revised*. pp. xii, 250. *John Murray, London*, 1922. 8°.

—— Surnames. pp. xxii, 364. *John Murray, London*, 1916. 8°.

YONGE (CHARLOTTE MARY). History of Christian Names. New edition, revised. pp. cxliii, 476. *London*, 1884. 8°.

Flemish.

MANSION (JOSEPH). Oud-Gentsche Naamkunde. Bijdrage tot de kennis van het Oud-nederlandsch. pp. xiii, 323. *'s-Gravenhage*, 1924. 8°.

Frankish.

ARBOIS DE JUBAINVILLE (MARIE HENRI D'). Études sur la langue des Francs a l'époque mérovingienne. pp. xi, 232, 110. *Paris, Chalon-sur-Saône* (printed), 1900. 8°.

French and Norman-French.

COSTON (A. DE). Origine, étymologie et signification des noms propres et des armoiries. *Paris, Montelimar* (printed), 1867. 8°.
DAUZAT (A.). Les noms de personnes ; origine et évolution, etc. pp. vii, 211. *Paris*, 1925. 8°.
FERRIÈRE (ÉMILE). Étymologie de quatre cents Prénoms usités en France. pp. 165. *Paris*, 1898. 12°.
KALBOW (W.). Die germanischen Personennahmen des altfranzösischen Heldenepos und ihre lautliche Entwicklung. pp. 179. *Halle a. S.*, 1913.
LARCHEY (LORÉDON). Dictionnaire des noms contenant la recherche étymologique des formes anciennes de 20,200 noms relevés sur les Annuaires de Paris. pp. xxiv, 511. *Paris, Nancy* (printed), 1880. 12°.
LONGNON (AUGUSTE). Noms de Personne au Temps de Charlemagne. (Polyptyque de l'Abbaye de Saint-German des Prés, vol. i, pp. 254–404.) 1895. (*Société de l'Histoire de Paris.*)
MICHAËLSSON (KARL). Études sur les noms de personne français d'après les rôles de taille parisiens : Roles de 1292, 1296–1300, 1313, etc. *Uppsala*, 1927–. 8°. *Uppsala Universitets Årsskrift*, 1927. Bd. 1, Filosofi, No. 4, etc.
MOISY (HENRY). Noms de Famille Normands étudiés dans leurs rapports avec la vieille langue et spécialement avec le dialecte normand, etc. *Paris*, 1875. 8°.

Frisian. See Anglo-Saxon and Dutch.

Gaelic. See Scottish.

Gaulish.

ARBOIS DE JUBAINVILLE (MARIE HENRI D'). Les Noms gaulois chez César et Hirtius De Bello Gallico, etc. Ser. 1. Les composés dont *rix* est le dernier terme. pp. xv, 259. *Paris*, 1891. 12°.

German, Austrian, Prussian, and Swiss.

ADAMAK (E.). Die Räthsel unserer deutschen Schülernamen. pp. 143. *Wien*, 1894. 8°.
ANDRESEN (CARL GUSTAF). Die altdeutschen Personennamen in ihrer Entwickelung und Erscheinung als heutige Geschlechtsnamen . . . 2 Ausgabe. *Mains, Leipzig* (printed), 1876. 8°.
—— Konkurrenzen in der Erklärung der deutschen Geschlechtsnamen. pp. iv, 144. *Heilbronn, a/N., Bonn* (printed), 1883. 8°.
BASS (ALFRED). Beiträge zur Kenntnis deutscher Vornamen. Mit Stammwörterbuch. pp. 95. *Leipzig*, 1903. 8°.
FOERSTEMANN (E. W.). Altdeutsches Namenbuch . . . Zweite, völlig umgearbeitete Auflage. Bd. 1–2. *Bonn*, 1900–15. 4°.
FORSSNER (THORVALD). Continental-Germanic Personal Names in England in Old and Middle English times. pp. lxiii, 289. *Uppsala*, 1916. 8°.
HEINRICHS (C.). Studien über die Namengebung im Deutschen seit dem Anfang des xvi Jahrhunderts. pp. xiv, 510. 1908. Quellen und Forschungen zur Sprach- und Culturgeschichte der germanischen Völker. Hft. 102.
HEINTZE (ALBERT). Die deutschen Familiennamen geschichtlich geographisch sprachlich . . . Dritte, verbesserte und sehr vermehrte Auflage herausgegeben von Prof. Dr. P. Cascorbi. pp. viii, 280. *Halle a. S.*, 1908. 8°.
HEYNE (MORITZ). Altniederdeutsche Eigennamen aus dem neunten bis elften Jahrhundert, etc. [With an index by Weber.] *Halle*, 1867. 8°.

KAPFF (REINOLD). Deutsche Vornamen mit den von ihnen abstammenden Geschlechtsnamen sprachlich erläutert . . . Auszug aus dem " Deutschen Namenbuche ". pp. 94. *Nurtingen am Neckar*, 1889. 8°

KLEINPAUL (RUDOLF). Menschen- und Völkernamen, Etymologische Streifzüge auf dem Gebeite der Eigennamen. pp. xix, 419. *Leipzig*, 1885. 8°.

MICHAELIS (GUSTAV). Vergleichendes Wörterbuch der gebrauchlichsten Taufnamen, etc. *Berlin*, 1856. 8°.

POTT (AUGUST FRIEDRICH). Die Personennamen insbesondere die Familiennamen und ihre Entstehungsarten auch unter Berücksichtigung der Ortsnamen. Eine sprachliche Untersuchung. 2 vol. *Leipzig*, 1853–59. 8°.

SCHNACK (HENRY CHRISTIAN). Vollständige, alphabetisch geordnete Sammlung deutscher Vor- und Taufnamen, etc. pp. vii, 112. *Hamburg*, 1888. 8°.

SCHÖNFELD (MORITZ). Proeve eener kritische verzameling van germaansche volks- en persoonsnamen, etc. pp. xxv, 132. *Gronigen*, 1906. 8°.
—— Wörterbuch der altgermanischen Personen- und Völkernamen, etc. pp. xxxv, 309. 1911. (*Germanische Bibliothek*, Abt. 1, Reihe 4, Bd. 2.) 8°.

SOCIN (ADOLF). Mittelhochdeutsches Namenbuch. Nach oberheinischen Quellen des zwölften und dreizehnten Jahrhunderts. pp. xvi, 787. *Basel*, 1903. 4°.

STARK (FRANZ). Die Kosenamen der Germanen . . . Mit drei Excursen : 1. Über Zunamen. 2. Über den Ursprung der zusammengesetzten Namen. 3. Über besondere friesische Namensformen und Verkürzungen. *Wien*, 1868. 8°.

STEUB (LUDWIG). Die Oberdeutschen Familiennamen. *München*, 1870. 8°.

STRACKERJAN (CARL). Die jeverländischen Personennahmen mit Berücksichtigung der Ortsnamen. *Jever*, 1864. 4°.

TARNELLER (JOSEF). Tiroler Familiennamen. Viertausend Geschlechtsnamen die tirolischen und vorarlbergischen Hofnamen entsprossen sind, etc. Deutsche Stammwörter. Die zur bildung tirolischer hofnamen. pp. 201. 1923. 8°.

TOBLER-MAYER (WILHELM). Deutsche Familien-Namen nach ihrer Enstehung und Bedeutung : mit besonderer Rucksichtnahme auf Zürich und die Ostschweiz. pp. v, 234. *Zurich*, 1894. 8°.

TRAUTMANN (REINHOLD). Die altpreussischen Personennahmen. Ein Beitrag zur baltischen Philologie. pp. viii, 204. Gottingen, 1925. 8°. Ergänzungshefte zur Zeitschrift fur vergleichende Sprachforschung auf dem Gebiete der indogermanischen Sprachen. No. 3.

WELZ (JOSEPH). Die Eigennamen im Codex Laureshamensis. Aus dem Lobdengau und Württemberg. pp. 124. 1913. (Untersuchungen zur deutschen Sprachgesichte. Hft. 4.) 8°.

WERLE (GEORG). Die altesten germanischen Personennahmen. pp. 88. 1910. (*Zeitschrift für deutsche Wortforschung*, Bd. 12, Beiheft.) 8°.

WIARDA (TILEMAN DOTHIAS). Ueber Deutsche Vornamen und Geschlechtsnamen. *Berlin, Stettin*, 1800. 8°.

WITTE (HANS N.). Wendische Zu- und Familien-namen aus mecklenburgischen Urkunden und Akten, etc. 1906. Ac. Schwerin. Verein für mecklenburgische Geschichte. Jahrbücher, etc. Jahrg. 71. 8°.

Greek. *See also* Latin.

BECHTEL (FRIEDRICH). Die attischen Frauennamen nach ihrem Systeme dargestellt. pp. vii, 144. *Göttingen*, 1902. 8°.
—— Die einstämmigen mannlichen Personennamen des Griechischen, die aus Spitznamen hervorgegangen sind. pp. 86. 1898. Gottingen-Konigliche Gesellschaft der Wissenschaften. *Abhandlungen Philologisch-historische Klasse*. Neue Folge. Bd. 2. 4°.
—— Die historischen Personennahmen des Griechischen bis zur Kaiserzeit. pp. xvi, 637. *Halle*, 1917. 8°.

CURTIUS (GEORG). De nominum Graecorum formatione linguarum cognatarum ratione habita. *Berolini*, 1842. 4°.

FICK (FRIEDRICH CHRISTIAN AUGUST). Die Griechischen Personennamen nach ihrer Bildung erklärt, mit den Namen Systemen verwandter Sprachen verglichen und systematisch geordnet. *Göttingen*, 1874. 8°.

F f

HIRZEL (RUDOLF). Der Name. Ein Beitrag zu seiner Geschichte im Altertum und besonders bei den Griechen. pp. iv, 108. *Leipzig*, 1918. 8°. (*Abhandlungen der philologisch-historischen Klasse der sachsischen Gessellschaft der Wissenschaften*, Bd. 36, No. 2.)

SITTIG (ERNESTUS). De Graecorum nominibus theophoris. pp. xi, 167. 1911. *Academia Fridericiana*. Dissertationes Philologicae Halenses. Vol. xx, pars. 1. 1873, etc. 8°.

STONECIPHER (ALVIN HARRISON MORTON). Graeco-Persian Names. pp. viii, 86. *New York*, 1918. 8°. (*Vanderbilt Oriental Series*, vol. ix.)

Hebrew.

DREIFUSS (ERWIN MANUEL). Die Familiennamen der Juden, unter besonderer Berücksichtigung der Verhältnisse in Baden zu Anfang des 19 Jahrhunderts, etc. pp. xiv, 143. *Frankfurt*, 1927. 8°.

GRAY (GEORGE BUCHANAN). Studies in Hebrew Proper Names. pp. xiii, 338. *A. & C. Black, London*, 1896. 8°.

HYAMSON (A. M.). Jewish Surnames. pp. 26. *Edinburgh*, 1903. 8°.

MOWAT (WILLIAM). A Pronouncing Dictionary of Scripture Proper Names, with their meanings, etc. pp. 101. *Sunday School Union, London* (1903). 8°.

NOTH (MARTIN). Die israelitischen Personennamen in Rahmen der gemeinsemitischen Namengebung. pp. xix, 260. Stuttgart, 1928. 8°. (*Beiträge zur Wissenschaft vom alten und neuen Testament*. Folge 3. Heft 10.)

WUTZ (FRANZ). Onomastica Sacra. Untersuchungen zum Liber interpretationis nominum hebraicorum des hl. Hieronymus. pp. xxxii, 1200. 1914–15.

Icelandic. *See* Norwegian.

Irish.

IRELAND, REGISTRAR-GENERAL. Special Report on Surnames in Ireland. By Sir R. E. Matheson. pp. 78. *Dublin*, 1909. 8°.

—— Varieties and synonymes of Surnames and Christian names in Ireland, etc. pp. 76. *Dublin*, 1890. 8°.

WOULFE (PATRICK). Sloinnte Gaedheal is Gall . . . with explanatory and historical notes. pp. xlvi, 696. *M. H. Gill & Son, Dublin*, 1923. 8°.

Italian. *See also* Roman.

CHIAPPELLI (LUIGI). I Nomi di donna in Pistoria dall' alto medioevo al secolo xiii. pp. 35. *Pistoia*, 1920.

FUMAGALLI (G.). Piccolo Dizionario dei nomi propi italiani di persone, con le origini e i significati più probabili, etc. pp. viii, 277. *Genova*, 1901. 8°.

GAUDENZI (AUGUSTO). Sulla storia del Cognome a Bologna nel secolo xiii. 1898. 8°. Rome. *Istituto Storico*. Italiano Bullettino, etc. No. 19.

MIGLIORINI (BRUNO). Dal Nome proprio al nome comune. Studi semantici sul mutamento dei nomi propri di persona in nomi comuni negl' idiomi romanzi. pp. 357. *Genève*, 1927. 8°. (Biblioteca dell '' Archivum Romanicum '', ser. 2, vol. xiii.)

PIANIGIANI (O.). Che cosa significa il mio nome ? Saggio etimologico dei nomi propri, etc. pp. xii, 373. *Lucca*, 1911. 8°.

POMA (CESARE). Saggio di onomastica italiana . . . I cognomi longobardi in Italia. I cognomi in -olfo, -uino, -elmo. pp. 60. *Torino*, 1911. 8°.

SCHNELLEN (CHRISTIAN). Tirolische Namenforschungen. Orts- und Personen-Namen des Lagerthales in Sudtirol, etc. pp. xiv, 373. *Innsbruck*, 1890. 8°.

Japanese.

KOOP (A. J.) and INADA (H.). Meiji Benran. Japanese Names and how to read them. *Eastern Press, London*, 1920–23. 8°.

Latin and Roman.

FABIA (PHILIPPE). Onomasticon Taciteum, composuit P. Fabia, 1900. 8°. (Annales de l'Université de Lyon. Nouvelle série ii. Droit, etc.) ·Fasc. 4.

MEISTER (CARL). Lateinisch-Griechische Eigennahmen. Hft. 1. Altitalische und romische Eigennamen. *Leipzig. Berlin*, 1916. 8°.

NOGARA (B.). Il Nome personale nella Lombardia durante la dominazione romana. pp. xv, 272. *Milano*, 1895. 8°.

SCHULZE (WILHELM). Zur Geschichte lateinischer Eigennamen. pp. 647. 1904. 8°. Ac. Gottingen. *Königliche Gesellschaft der Wissenschaften.* Abhandlungen. Philol. hist. Klasse. N.F. Bd. 5, No. 5. 4°.

Luxemburg.

MUELLER (NIKOLAUS). Die Familien-Namen des Grossherzogthums Luxemburg zusammen gestellt. pp. 115. *Luxemburg*, 1886. 8°.

Lycian (Asianic).

SUNDWALL (JOHANNES). Die einheimischen Namen der Lykier nebst einem Verzeichnisse klein asiatischer Namenstämme. pp. vi, 309. 1913. *Leipzig* (*Klio. Beiheft* 11).

Manx.

MOORE (ARTHUR WILLIAM). Manx Names. Second edition, revised. pp. 261. *Elliot Stock, London,* 1903. 8°.
—— Surnames and Place Names of the Isle of Man. pp. xiv, 372. *Elliot Stock, London,* 1890. 8°.

Norman. *See* French.

Norwegian and Icelandic.

BJÖRKMAN (E.). Nordische Personennahmen in England in alt- und fruhmittel englisher Zeit. Ein Beitrag zur englishen Namenkunde. pp. xi, 217. 1910. Studien zur englischen Philologie, etc. Hft. 37. 8°.

HJELMQVIST (THEODOR). Förnamm ock familjenamn med sekundar användning i nysvenskan. Onomatologiska bidrag. pp. xxx, 411. *Lund,* 1903. 8°.

LIND (ERIK HENRIK). Norsk-isländska dopnamn ock fingerade namn från medeltiden samlade ock utgivna av E. H. Lind. 9 hft. *Uppsala, Leipzig,* 1905–15. 8°.
—— Norsk-isländska personbinamn från medeltiden, samlade ock utgivna med förklaringar. pp. viii, col. 416. *Uppsala,* 1921. 8°.

RYGH (OLUF). Gamle Personnavne i norske Stedsnavne Efterladt Arbeide. pp. xii, 357. *Kristiania,* 1901. 8°.

WESSÉN (ELIAS GUSTAV ADOLF). Nordiska namnstudier. pp. 118. *Uppsala,* 1927. 8°. *Uppsala Universitets Årsskrift,* 1927. Bd. 1. Filosofi, etc. No. 3.

Portuguese.

LEITE DE VASCONCELLOS (JOSÉ). Antroponimia portuguesa. Tratado comparativo, etc. pp. xix, 659. *Lisboa,* 1928. 8°.

Persian. *See* Greek.

Prussian. *See* German.

Roman. *See* Italian and Latin.

Sanskrit.

MACDONELL (ARTHUR ANTHONY) and KEITH (ARTHUR BERRIEDALE). Vedic Index of Names and Subjects. 2 vol., 1912. Indian Texts Series. 1907, etc. 8°.

Scottish.

BUCHANAN (WILLIAM). The History of the ancient surname of Buchanan : and of ancient Scottish surnames, more particularly the Clans. pp. 79. *A. Buchanan, Glasgow,* 1793. 8°.

JOHNSTON (JAMES B.). The Scottish Macs, their derivation and origin. pp. 56. *A. Gardner, Paisley,* 1922. 8°.

MACBAIN (A.). Etymology of the principal Gaelic national names, personal names and surnames. *Eneas Mackay, Stirling,* 1911. 8°.

MACBAIN (ALEXANDER). Personal and Surnames of the town of Inverness. pp. ix, 105. *Northern Counties Publishing Co., Inverness.* 1895. 8°.
SIMS (CLIFFORD STANLEY). The origin and signification of Scottish surnames. With a vocabulary of Christian Names. *Albany, N.Y.*, 1862. 8°.

Slavonic.
MIKLOSICH (FRANZ). Die Bildung der slavischen Personen und Ortsnamen Drei Abhandlungen, etc. pp. 354. *Heidelberg*, 1927. 4° *Sammlung slavischer Lehr- und Handbucher.* Reihe 3, No. 5.

Spanish.
CONTO (CESAR) and ISAZA (EMILIANO). Diccionario ortografico de apellidos y de nombres propios de persones, etc. pp. xxxviii, 118. *Londres*, 1885. 8°.
LETELIER (VALENTIN). Ensayo de onomatologia, ó estudio de los nombres proprios y hereditarios. pp. xxxi, 183. *Madrid, Santiago de Chile*, 1906. 8°.

Sumerian. *See* Assyrian.

Swedish.
KJÖLLERSTROM (P. A.). Svensk Namnbok. Dopnamn, ättenamn, ortnamn. pp. 175. *Ulricehamn*, 1895. 8°.

Swiss. *See also* German.
AEBISCHER (PAUL). Onomastica. Sur l'origine et la formation des noms de famille dans le canton de Fribourg. Dante Olivieri : I cognomi della Venezia Euganea, etc. pp. 271. *Geneve*, 1924. 8°. (*Biblioteca dell' Archivum Romanicum*, ser. 2, No. 6.)

Tyrolean. *See* German and Italian.

Walloon.
AEBISCHER (PAUL). L'Anthroponymie wallonne, d'apres quelques anciens cartulaires. pp. 96. *Liège*, 1924. 8°.

Welsh.
ROBERTS (ROBERT). Throup's Welsh Place and House Names. pp. 24. *T. Throup, Bradford* (1925). 32°.

Law of Names.
FOX-DAVIES (A. C.) and BRITTON (P. W. P. C.). A Treatise on the Law concerning Names and Changes of Name. pp. 118. *E. Stock, London*, 1906. 8°.
LEVI (SIGMUND). Vorname und Familienname im Recht. pp. 60. *Giessen*, 1888. 8°.
PHILLIMORE (W. P. W.) and FRY (E. A.). An index to Changes of Name under authority of Act of Parliament or Royal Licence, etc. 1760–1901. With an introduction on the Law of Change of Name. pp. xxxii, 357. *Phillimore and Co., London*, 1905. 8°.

INDEX OF NAMES AND ELEMENTS

This index is designed to be as helpful as possible generally, and includes in addition to surnames, all such forenames, descriptions, nicknames, elements, affixes, and words, which might possibly assist the determination of the origin of a modern surname, or the understanding of medieval descriptions, English and foreign. Space does not permit indexing all variants, and pp. 306–312 should be studied for possible equations. An asterisk indicates several occurrences on the same page.

INDEX OF MATTERS

An asterisk indicates several occurrences in different paragraphs on the same page.

A

ab, notes on Welsh, 122
Abatement of writs. *See* Misnomer
Abbreviations, list of, xx
Aberdeenshire local surnames, examples of, 242
Accusative case ending, example of obsolete, 289
Acquired surnames, 221, 264 ; classification of, 223
Acrostic names of Jews, 214
Actions, descriptions and surnames derived from, 32, 225
Act of Parliament to change name, 411, 412 ; to change name of castle, 492 ; examples of, 420, 422
Acts of Parliament cited :—
  Additions, Statute of, 1413, 402
  Aliens, 143–4, 198
  Aliens' Restriction Act, 1919, 267, 413
  Baines' Name, 1907, 417
  Births and Deaths Registration Acts, 401, 419
  Clifton's Name, 1859, 412
  De heretico comburendo, 198
  Ireland, 1465, 196, 210, 426
  Kilkenny, Statutes of, 1366, 128, 387, 425
  Labourers, Statute of, 1349, 151
  Lyon King of Arms, 1672, 422
  MacGregor Acts, 421–3
  Marriage Act, 26 Geo. II, 401 ; 4 Geo. IV, 401
  Marriage and Registration Act, 1856, 401
  Misprision, 14 Edw. III, 400
  Nantes, Edict of, 1598, 200
  O'Neill Act, 1568–9, 426
  Prærogitiva Regis, 407
  Ruthven Acts, 420, 421
  Theatrical Employers' Registration Act, 1925, 401.
  See also Laws.
Addition, derivation by, 271
Additions. *See* Descriptions
Additions, Statute of, 402
Addresses. *See* Descriptions
Agential Suffixes. *See* Suffixes
Agnomen, definition of, 44
Alet *v.* Nansladron, 394

Aliases, 80, 217, 413 ; an indication of bastardy, 414
Alien names, treatment of, 134
Aliens : settle in Britain, 48, 134, 198 ; encouragement given to, 198, 200 ; English names of, 158, 191, 192 ; fifteenth century, 190 ; map illustrating distribution of, 135 ; names of, in Britain, 23, 134, 189–93. *See also* Migration.
Aliens' Restriction Act, 1919, 267, 413
Alien Subsidy, 1439, 189
America discovered by Northmen, 20
Analyses of names. *See* Skeat ; Statistics
Ancestral name of Chinese, 8 n.
Anderida massacre, 16
Angevins in England, 142
Anglo-Norman : descriptions, 70–133 ; language, 114
Anglo-Saxon : animal names, 333 ; characteristic descriptions, 56, 67 ; classification of names, 50 ; conquest of Britain, 15 ; declension of names, 51 ; diminutives, 51 ; filial desinences, 58, 248 ; genealogical influence, 252 ; language prevails over Celtic, 18 ; language, nature of, 22 ; local descriptions, 57 ; nicknames, 53 ; occupational descriptions, 56, 57 ; orthography, decay of, 64, 85 ; personal names, 48 and *passim* ; personal names, a key to, 365 ; scarcity of descriptions, 64 ; descriptions among servile classes, 120 ; names, signification of, 49 ; names superseded, 108, 130, 166 ; suffixes, 51, 56, 57, 274 ; surnames denied, 59 ; names, survival of, 71, 109, 120, 121, 166
Animal language, 2
Animal names of Anglo-Saxons, 333 ; of Jews, 149
Animals, surnames approximating to names of, 231, 332, 333
Anthropologists aided by nomenclature, xiv, 159

law courts, 160 ; origin of, 3, 4 ; primitive, 5. *See also* Grammatical notes

Latinization of names, 130, 346, 394 ; erroneous, 394 ; examples of, 347 ; in legal process, 161, 394 ; letters used in, 346

Law, definitions of, 381

Laws relating to names, 381–428 ; French, 428 ; German, 428 ; Irish, 37 ; old Irish code, 424 ; Roman, 406 ; Scottish, 419–24

Legal records : enrolments in Latin, 160 ; extant, 382 ; pleas in English, 160

Leicestershire local surnames, examples of, 177, 239

Liber Niger Scaccarii, names in, 103

Liber Wintoniensis, names in, 83, 97, 99

Licence, royal, 412, 413 ; the earliest, 408

Licences to bear or change name :
1273, Motun, 407
1314, Deyncurt, 407
1367, Makmorghyth, 387, 426
1679, Cavendish to Percy, 408
1808, Geoghegan to O'Neill, 426
See also Change of name

Ligatures, confusion arising from, 297

Lincolnshire local surnames, examples of, 239

Linlithgowshire local surnames, examples of, 242

Lithuanians in Scotland, change of name by, 267

Local descriptions and surnames, 57, 84, 95, 97, 117, 173, 178, 187, 228, 238–44, 372–80 ; Anglo-Saxon, 55, 57 ; of Channel Islanders, 182 ; classification of, 222, 228 ; compounds, 234 ; Cornish, 181, 233, 235, 238, 377–9 ; derivation of, 372 ; in Domesday Book, 91 ; elements of, 373–80 ; with filial desinence, 252 ; Flemish, 56 n., 139 ; French, 80, 233, 243 ; Gaelic, 233, 380 ; Hebrew, 149 ; increase in, 133 ; Irish, 33, 243 ; Norman, 80, 91, 229 ; Norse, 68, 233, 276 ; in the North, reason for, 106 ; early proportion of, 108 ; large proportion of, 161, 228 ; Roman, 45 ; Scottish, 242 ; Welsh, 42, 125, 241, 377

Loegrians, 17 n.

Lombards : in England, 145 ; in Ireland, 145

de London *v.* Archbishop of Armagh, 391

Lorrainers in England, 145

Lotharingians in England, 145

Lunasting stone, names on, 24

Luscombe *v.* Yates, 410

Luxemburg derivatives, examples of, 293

Lyon King of Arms, an Act concerning, 422

M

mac dropped in Irish names, 129, 212 ; in Manx names, 184

MacGregor clan abolished, 421

Mac-names in Ireland : number of, 212 ; origin of, 37

Mahomedans, change of name by, 417

Man, antiquity of, 2

Manifold names and descriptions, 214

Man, Isle of : history of, 182 ; languages of, 183 ; Norse names in, 183 ; Scandinavians in, 22

Manorial Court Rolls, names from, 116

Marriage : Acts relating to, 401 ; customs, 268 ; not annulled by misnomer, 401 ; in United States of America, 391 ; change of name by women on, 390, 391 ; retention of name by women on, 390 ; retention of title by women on, 392

Marriage-name of Chinese, 8 n.

Mary as a male name, 247

Masters, surnames derived from, 192, 258–60

May crownings, surnames from, 258

Metathesis : definition of, 273 ; example of, 273

Metronymics, 245, 249 ; no indication of bastardy, 250

Middlesex local surnames, examples of, 239

Migration, influence of, 134–59

Military rank, surnames derived from, 259

Milk-name of Chinese, 8 n.

Miracle plays, surnames from, 258

Misnomer, 395, 424 ; in christian names, 395, 397 ; in descriptions, 395 ; examples of, 397 ; in marriage records, 401 ; in place-names, 399 ; in surnames, 398

Misprision, 395, 400

Mock office, surnames derived from, 258

Monastic records of names, 202, 418

Monmouthshire local surnames, examples of, 240

Monothematic names, definition of, 26

Mowbray, assumption of surname, 384